Historical and Sociolinguistic Approaches to French

Historical and Sociolinguistic Approaches to French

Edited by
JANICE CARRUTHERS
MAIRI McLAUGHLIN
AND
OLIVIA WALSH

OXFORD
UNIVERSITY PRESS

Great Clarendon Street, Oxford, OX2 6DP,
United Kingdom

Oxford University Press is a department of the University of Oxford.
It furthers the University's objective of excellence in research, scholarship,
and education by publishing worldwide. Oxford is a registered trade mark of
Oxford University Press in the UK and in certain other countries

© editorial matter and organization Janice Carruthers, Mairi McLaughlin,
and Olivia Walsh 2024
© the chapters their several contributors 2024

The moral rights of the authors have been asserted

All rights reserved. No part of this publication may be reproduced, stored in
a retrieval system, or transmitted, in any form or by any means, without the
prior permission in writing of Oxford University Press, or as expressly permitted
by law, by licence or under terms agreed with the appropriate reprographics
rights organization. Enquiries concerning reproduction outside the scope of the
above should be sent to the Rights Department, Oxford University Press, at the
address above

You must not circulate this work in any other form
and you must impose this same condition on any acquirer

Published in the United States of America by Oxford University Press
198 Madison Avenue, New York, NY 10016, United States of America

British Library Cataloguing in Publication Data

Data available

Library of Congress Control Number: 2023946230

ISBN 9780192894366

DOI: 10.1093/oso/9780192894366.001.0001

Printed and bound by
CPI Group (UK) Ltd, Croydon, CR0 4YY

Links to third party websites are provided by Oxford in good faith and
for information only. Oxford disclaims any responsibility for the materials
contained in any third party website referenced in this work.

Contents

Preface ... vii
Acknowledgements ... ix
List of figures ... x
List of tables ... xi
List of abbreviations ... xiii
The contributors ... xvi

1. New directions in the history and sociolinguistics of French
   Janice Carruthers, Mairi McLaughlin, and Olivia Walsh ... 1

2. Proclisis and enclisis in early Gallo-Romance: Evidence from sandhi phenomena
   Thomas Rainsford ... 25

3. The grammar(s) of reported discourse in medieval French literature
   Sophie Marnette ... 49

4. The evolution of the syntax of the subject in French and factors of variation
   Sophie Prévost ... 72

5. The evolution of 'background' from Middle to pre-Classical French
   Bernard Combettes ... 97

6. Women and language in the *Journal de la langue françoise* (1784–95)
   Mairi McLaughlin ... 121

7. The French language and eighteenth-century Italian women: Language of vanity or language of scholarship?
   Helena Sanson ... 144

8. The construction of authority and community in French official correspondence from Spanish Louisiana
   Jenelle Thomas ... 161

9. Language authority, language ideologies, and eighteenth-century bilingual lexicographers of French, German, and English. Comparing Abel Boyer, Christian Ludwig, and Lewis Chambaud
   Nicola McLelland ... 181

10. The history of terms for varieties of Gallo-Romance   198
    Douglas A. Kibbee

11. Elision, the neglected link in French phonology   216
    John N. Green and Marie-Anne Hintze

12. On the rise and fall of modern *français régional* in the rural Côte d'Or   238
    Rosalind A. M. Temple

13. Attitudes towards the French language: An analysis of the metalanguage used in twentieth-century French language columns   254
    Olivia Walsh

14. Comparing the prescriptivism of nineteenth- and twenty-first-century language experts in France   276
    Emma Humphries

15. Attitudes on Twitter towards French inclusive writing   297
    Anna Tristram

16. Breton dictionaries and contemporary corpus planning: Vocabulary and purism in the minoritized languages of France   322
    Merryn Davies-Deacon

17. France and its difficult relationship with foreign languages   344
    Philippe Caron

18. Minoritized languages in France and Ireland: Policy, practice, vitality   362
    Janice Carruthers and Mícheál B. Ó Mainnín

References   387
Index   452
Author Index   459

Preface

This volume is dedicated to our friend and colleague, Wendy Ayres-Bennett, Emerita Professor of French Philology and Linguistics and Emerita Fellow of Murray Edwards College at the University of Cambridge. Wendy is without doubt one of the most distinguished scholars of her generation. She has forged a global reputation for her work on the (socio-)linguistic history of French, the history of linguistic thought, multilingualism, and language policy and planning.

Wendy's research is notable for its breadth, depth, quality, and innovation. Her pioneering work on Vaugelas (Ayres-Bennett 1987, 2018) and on the genre of observations and remarks more generally (Ayres-Bennett and Caron 1996; Ayres-Bennett and Seijido 2011) emphasized the social dimension of language history long before the more recent societal turn in the language sciences. She has played a leading role in the development of historical sociolinguistics, with her research on variation in French from the seventeenth century onwards serving as an important bridge between scholars working in Anglophone and Francophone contexts (Ayres-Bennett 1996, 2004, 2011; and Seijido 2013). Her publications include books that have appeared on university reading lists for decades, especially her *History of the French Language through Texts* (Ayres-Bennett 1996) and *Problems and Perspectives: Studies in the Modern French Language* (Ayres-Bennett and Carruthers 2001). In recent years, Wendy has made significant contributions to a remarkable range of fields through some of the most wide-ranging and extensive handbooks documenting the current research landscape in Romance sociolinguistics (Ayres-Bennett and Carruthers 2018), language standardization (Ayres-Bennett and Bellamy 2021), and the French language (Ayres-Bennett and McLaughlin 2024). An important thread running through Wendy's publications is her determination to re-situate and visibilize the contribution of women to linguistics, from a special issue on the role of women in the history of linguistic ideas in Western Europe (Ayres-Bennett 1994a) to the trailblazing volume *Women in the History of Linguistics* (Ayres-Bennett and Sanson 2020).

Wendy has received a number of important awards and prizes over the course of her career, including two prizes from the Académie française (the *Prix d'Académie* in 1997, and the *Prix Georges Dumézil* in 2013) as well as the honour of her appointment as *Officier dans l'Ordre des Palmes Académiques* in 2004. Her global reputation is reflected in the seven periods that she spent as a visiting professor in France and the USA, including as the Pajus Distinguished Visiting Professor at the University of California, Berkeley in 2012. Her terms serving as President of the Society of French Studies, the *Société internationale de diachronie du français*, and the Philological Society all speak to the importance of her disciplinary service. Wendy's role as a field leader is also very clearly demonstrated by her role in several large collaborative projects. She is the main editor for the seventeenth- and eighteenth-century sections of Garnier's *Grand corpus des grammaires françaises, des remarques et des traités sur la langue (XIVe–XVIIIe s.)*. Wendy also served as Principal Investigator for the major AHRC-funded Open World Research Initiative project, 'Multilingualism: Empowering Individuals, Transforming Societies' (MEITS), and led a follow-on project on 'Promoting Language Policy'. Both of these projects included important policy work on the value of languages across a range of fields which has had a tangible influence on communities outside the academy.

The collaborative partnerships that underpin both her publications and her leadership of major projects are testament to Wendy's tireless championship of women and early-career scholars in academia. The extent of her intellectual influence on current research on the (socio-)linguistic history of French, and interconnected fields such as multilingualism and language policy, is reflected in the chapters in this volume, which include contributions from the next generation of scholars, many of whom have benefitted from Wendy's mentorship and support.

We dedicate this volume to Wendy as an expression of our gratitude for her unfailing support to us and to many other scholars, and in recognition of her immense contribution to the history and sociolinguistics of French.

Acknowledgements

The Editors would like to acknowledge the help of a number of people in the preparation of this volume. First, we would like to thank Emma Humphries and Merryn Davies-Deacon for translating the chapters originally written in French. We would also like to thank the anonymous peer reviewers who read chapters and gave invaluable feedback both to the contributors and to the editors. Thanks go also to Vicki Sunter at Oxford University Press for her clear and careful guidance through the publishing process. We are especially grateful to Jenelle Thomas who standardized the formatting of both the chapters and the references, and helped prepare the final manuscript for Oxford University Press. Sarah O'Neill also deserves special mention for the great care that she took preparing the index.

List of figures

11.1.	Contributors to rightward resyllabification	221
11.2.	Percentage realization rates of elision by site	232
13.1.	Position of French language columnists on the descriptive-prescriptive continuum	260
15.1.	Éditions Hatier tweet, September 2017	297
15.2.	Information sign at Université Paris Nanterre, September 2018	299
15.3.	Graffiti at Université Paris Nanterre, September 2018	299
15.4.	Selected concordance lines with bigram *langue française*, left-sorted	308
15.5.	Concordance lines with *massacre* + *langue française*	308
15.6.	Selected concordance lines with bigram *langue française*, right-sorted, examples with *est*	309
15.7.	Selected concordance lines with *français*, left-sorted, selected examples preceded by *le*	310
15.8.	Selected concordance lines with *français*, left-sorted, examples preceded by *les*	310
15.9.	Concordance lines with *genre* + *féminin*	312
15.10.	Concordance lines with *genre* + *masculin*	312
15.11.	Top hashtags	313
15.12.	Tweet sent by J.-M. Blanquer, 15 November 2017	319
18.1.	Linguistic map of France	363
18.2.	The official *Gaeltacht* and an estimation of the areas of Ulster Scots speech	365

List of tables

2.1.	Early GR texts included in the corpus	27
2.2.	Frequency of forms with linking [ð] by context in the northern GR texts, excluding following enclitic pronouns and articles	33
2.3.	Frequency of written double consonants for word-internal historical geminates and after function words claimed to trigger gemination in the early northern GR texts	36
2.4.	Pronominal paradigms in early northern GR	38
2.5.	Morphology of EAPs attested in the texts	39
2.6.	Synopsis of the properties of EAPs in the longer texts	42
2.7.	Phases in the development of three host plus clitic prosodic words in GR	43
4.1.	Rates of overt subjects (= all subjects: S) and overt pronominal subjects (= personal pronouns: Spp) in main declarative vs. subordinate clauses from the eleventh to the sixteenth century	83
4.2.	Rates of expression of first- and third-person pronouns	87
4.3.	Rates of expression of first- and third-person pronouns in direct speech and in narrative	88
4.4.	Rates of nominal and pronominal preverbal subjects in main declarative and subordinate clauses from the eleventh to the seventeenth century	90
6.1.	Gender of authors and authorities	128
8.1.	Official letters in French, 1770–91	166
9.1.	Metalinguistic markings, as listed in Chambaud (1761: xiv), with illustrative examples from his dictionary entries	194
11.1.	List of interviewees	218
11.2.	Raw occurrences of elision	222
11.3.	Raw occurrences of elidable particles	224
11.4.	Forms exhibiting minor variability or uncertain grammatical status	225
11.5.	Tokens of *que* and its compounds	228
11.6.	Distribution of unelided tokens	232
11.7.	Comparison of Katya's and Zoé's adult usage with earlier mean rates	234
12.1.	Selected function words from the *ALF* sample, preceded by their French equivalents	245
12.2.	The vowels of conservative French, with *ALF* transcriptions from point **19** and their assumed IPA equivalents	246

13.1.	Overview of French language columnists	256
14.1.	Summaries of corpora (*Le Courrier de Vaugelas* and *Courrier des internautes*)	286
14.2.	Use of *faute, erreur, correct(e)*, and *incorrect(e)* (*Le Courrier de Vaugelas* and *Courrier des internautes*)	288
15.1.	Tweet dataset: deleted tweets	306
15.2.	Corpus split between original tweets and retweets	306
15.3.	Top ten most frequent content words in the corpus	308
15.4.	Top collocates of *genre* (MI > 5.0)	311
15.5.	Top ten retweets	315
15.6.	Top ten favourited tweets	316
16.1.	Occurrence of lexemes in sources consulted	333
17.1.	Choice of first foreign language in France	349
17.2.	Choice of second foreign language in France	352

List of abbreviations

ACC	accusative
AHRC	Arts and Humanities Research Council
ALF	*Atlas linguistique de la France*
BBHA	*Brezhoneg… buan hag aes* (beginners' Breton textbook)
BFM	*Base de français médiéval*
C	consonant
CADS	corpus-assisted discourse studies
CBLP	community-based language planning
CE	cours élémentaire
CL	corpus linguistics
CMC	computer-mediated communication
CNESCO	Conseil national d'évaluation du système scolaire (now Centre national d'étude des systèmes scolaires)
Comp.	Complement
CP	cours préparatoire
CV	consonant–vowel
DA	discourse analysis
DAT	dative
DGLF	Délégation générale à la langue française
DGLFLF	Délégation générale à la langue française et aux langues de France
DIMA	Dispositif d'initiation aux métiers en alternance
DMF	*Dictionnaire du moyen français*
EAP	enclitic asyllabic article and pronoun
ESLC	European Survey on Language Competences
EU	European Union
F	feminine
GCSE	General Certificate of Secondary Education
GPS	Global Positioning System
GR	Gallo-Romance
GSS	glide, sonorant, or [s]
HoLLT	History of Language Learning and Teaching
IFTTT	If This Then That
IPA	International Phonetic Alphabet
INF	infinitive
IS	inverse subordination
ISO	International Organization for Standardization
JLF	*Journal de la langue françoise, soit exacte soit ornée*
JO	*Journal officiel*

LPP	language policy and planning
LR	language revitalization
L1	first language
L2	second language
M	masculine
MCVF	*Modéliser le changement: les voies du français* corpus
MEITS	Multilingualism: Empowering Individuals, Transforming Societies
MI	Mutual Information score
MS	manuscript
NCA	*Nouveau corpus d'Amsterdam*
NEG	negation
NSL	null-subject language
O	object
OBL	oblique
OGR	Old Gallo-Romance
OPLB	Office public de la langue bretonne
OR	oral représenté
OV	object–verb
OVS	object–verb–subject
PhP	phonological phrase
PL	plural
PRS	present
PSA	Peugeot société anonyme
PST	past
P1	first-person singular
P3	third-persons singular and plural
Q+A	question and answer
REFL	reflexive
RLS	reversing language shift
RML	regional and minority language
RT	retweet
S	subject
SBJV	subjunctive
SEGPA	Section d'enseignement général et professionnel adapté
SG	singular
SLI	standard language ideology
SPP	subject personal pronoun
S&TP	speech and thought presentation
SUBJ-V	subject-verb
SVO	subject–verb–object
SW	South West
TV	television
TVOF	The Values of French
UK	United Kingdom
ULIS	Unité localisée pour l'inclusion scolaire

USA	United States of America
V	vowel
VOL	volume
V2	verb second
VO	verb–object
VP	verb phrase
VSO	verb–subject–object
WH-	question words (*what, when, why*...)
XML	Extensible Markup Language

The contributors

Philippe Caron is Emeritus Professor of French Linguistics at the University of Poitiers. His current research focuses on the emergence of contemporary French around 1630, but he also has a major research programme devoted to the reconstruction of French pronunciation around 1700, in particular eloquence and verse. He has been hired for his expertise by actors and singers who wish to perform their repertoire in an historically authentic way. He has also published on the French Academy and Classical French dictionaries.

Janice Carruthers is Professor of French Linguistics at Queen's University Belfast. She has published widely on the temporal system of Modern French (tense, framing, connectives), the structure of oral narrative, French sociolinguistics, the syntax of Spoken French, corpus methodology, and language policy. She has also published two corpora of oral narrative, one in French and one, with Marianne Vergez-Couret (Poitiers), in Occitan. From 2017 to 2021 she was the Arts and Humanities Research Council's Priority Area Leadership Fellow for Modern Languages. Her research has been funded by the AHRC, Horizon 2020 (EU), and the British Academy.

Bernard Combettes is Emeritus Professor of French Linguistics at the University of Lorraine. He holds the 'agrégation de grammaire' and is the author of a thesis entitled 'Research on the order of elements in the phrase in Middle French'. His research focuses on two areas: the history of French (syntax and grammaticalization phenomena) and textual linguistics/discourse pragmatics (information structuring at phrase level and 'mots du discours'). He co-edited the *Grande grammaire historique du français* (De Gruyter, 2020).

Merryn Davies-Deacon is Lecturer in French Linguistics at Queen's University, Belfast, having taken up this position in 2020 after completing a PhD at the same institution as part of the major AHRC project 'Multilingualism: Empowering Individuals, Transforming Societies' (MEITS), led by Wendy Ayres-Bennett. Merryn is currently working on converting this PhD thesis into a monograph, to be published as part of De Gruyter's *Language and Social Life* series.

John N. Green *Chevalier dans l'Ordre des Palmes Académiques*, is Emeritus Professor of Romance Linguistics at the University of Bradford, where he was successively Head of Modern Languages, Dean of Social Sciences, Pro-Vice-Chancellor, and Founding Director of the Graduate School. He has published extensively on French phonology, Spanish morphosyntax and pragmatics, and on the history and historiography of Romance linguistics. He is a former Editor of the *Journal of French Language Studies* and currently a member of the Advisory Board of *Romance Philology*. He continues to collaborate with Marie-Anne Hintze on neglected aspects of linking in French discourse phonology and is engaged in further research into the history of Romance linguistics, including the lives and works of Romance scholars whose contribution has not been fully acknowledged.

Marie-Anne Hintze was successively Fellow in French in the Department of Language and Linguistics at the University of York and Senior Lecturer in the French Department at the University of Leeds. She co-authored *The French Language Today* with Adrian Battye (York) and Paul Rowlett (Salford) (Routledge, 1999). She is a former Editor of the *Journal of French Language Studies*. Her research interests and subsequent publications, pursued in collaboration with John N. Green (Bradford), have focused on French phonology, in particular the sociolinguistic and discourse aspects of linking phenomena.

Emma Humphries is currently a Lecturer in English Language and Linguistics at Cardiff University. Emma completed her PhD in French Sociolinguistics at the University of Nottingham and has previously held positions as the Research Project Manager of the AHRC-funded 'Promoting Language Policy' project (University of Cambridge) and as a Research Fellow on the AHRC-funded project 'Foreign, Indigenous, and Community Languages in the Devolved Regions of the UK: Policy and Practice for Growth' (Queen's University Belfast). Her research interests are in sociolinguistics, particularly language policy and language attitudes and ideologies.

Douglas A. Kibbee is Professor Emeritus at the University of Illinois at Urbana-Champaign. His book *For to Speke Frenche Trewely* (1991), explored grammatical works of medieval and Renaissance England. Subsequently he studied language policy issues and their intersection with grammar and linguistics in *Language Legislation and Linguistic Rights* (1998), *Language and the Law. Linguistic Inequality in America* (2016), and in a critical edition of Dupleix's *Liberté de la langue françoise dans sa pureté* (2018). He is preparing a critical edition of Jean de Wapy's *Remarques sur la langue françoise pour parler à la mode & selon l'air du temps* (1634).

Sophie Marnette is Professor of Medieval French Studies at the University of Oxford. Her research offers a linguistic and philological approach to literary issues such as the origins and evolution of medieval literary genres and the expression of narrative voice and point of view. Her first book (1996) focuses on storytelling in the French Middle Ages and her second book (2005) studies reported discourse in medieval literary texts as well as in contemporary oral narratives, press, and literature. Her current research project is entitled 'Quoting her: Discourse, Gender, and Genre in Medieval French Short Narratives'.

Mairi McLaughlin is Professor in the Department of French and an Affiliated Member of the Departments of Linguistics and Italian Studies at the University of California, Berkeley. She specializes in French/Romance Linguistics and in Translation Studies. She has published extensively on language contact in French and Romance, on the language of the media, and on journalistic and literary translation. She has held visiting positions at Balliol College, Oxford and at Paris VIII. Her research has been funded by the UC Humanities Research Institute, the France Berkeley Fund, the Hellman Foundation, and the Mellon Foundation.

Nicola McLelland is Professor of German and History of Linguistics at the University of Nottingham, with a particular interest in the history of grammar writing, history of language learning and teaching, and, most recently, the history of lexicography. In 2020 she was awarded the German Academic Exchange Service's Grimm Prize for her contribution to German Studies internationally. Her two most recent books are *German Through English Eyes. The History of Teaching and Learning German in England, 1500–2000* (Harrassowitz,

2015, open access) and *Teaching and Learning Foreign Languages. A History of Language Education, Assessment and Policy in Britain* (Routledge, 2017).

Mícheál B. Ó Mainnín is Professor of Irish and Celtic Studies at Queen's University Belfast and Director of the 'Northern Ireland Place-Name Project'. He has published on onomastics from a variety of perspectives (including place names in language policy and planning), dialectology, and early modern Gaelic language and literature in Ireland and Scotland.

Sophie Prévost is a Senior Researcher at Laboratoire Lattice in Paris (CNRS, French National Centre for Scientific Research). Her main research interest lies in the study of linguistic change, more especially in the syntactic and semantico-pragmatic domains. She has published several works devoted to the evolution of word order in French, as well as in the field of grammaticalization or constructionalization. She is the author of several chapters in the *Grande grammaire historique du français* (2020, Marchello-Nizia, Combettes, Prévost, and Scheer (eds)).

Thomas Rainsford is a Junior Lecturer at the Institut für Linguistik/Romanistik at the University of Stuttgart having previously worked in Cambridge, Lyon, and Oxford. His research focuses on the development of the phonology and syntax of medieval French, with special interests in prosodic changes such as the emergence of group stress and in changes in motion lexicalization such as the development of verb–particle constructions. He is the creator of the Old Gallo-Romance corpus (http://www.ogr-corpus.org) and a principal investigator in the DFG-funded SILPAC research group (https://silpac.uni-mannheim.de).

Helena Sanson is Professor of Italian, History of Linguistics, and Women's Studies at the University of Cambridge. Among her publications are *Donne, precettistica e lingua nell'Italia del Cinquecento* (Florence, 2007), *Women, Language and Grammar in Italy, 1500–1900* (Oxford, 2011), and the co-edited volumes *Conduct Literature for and about Women in Italy, 1470–1900: Describing and Prescribing Life* (Paris, 2016), and *Women in the History of Linguistics* (Oxford, 2020). She is the founder and editor-in-chief of the peer-reviewed journal *Women Language Literature in Italy/Donne Lingua Letteratura in Italia* (Fabrizio Serra editore) and of the book series *Women and Gender in Italy, 1500–1900* (Classiques Garnier).

Rosalind A. M. Temple is University Lecturer in French Linguistics in the Faculties of Medieval and Modern Languages, and Linguistics, Philology and Phonetics at the University of Oxford, and is a Fellow of New College. She has published on the phonetics and phonology of French and English from various perspectives, including experimental phonetics, language variation and change, and Firthian prosodic analysis. She is currently also researching aspects of the phonetics of Welsh.

Jenelle Thomas graduated with a PhD in Romance Languages and Literatures from the University of California, Berkeley in 2017 before working as a Departmental Lecturer in French Linguistics at Oxford University. Her research interests include the historical sociolinguistics of multilingualism, language variation and change, and language contact in the history of the Romance languages. She has published on genre and multilingualism in legal and epistolary documents from the sixteenth to the nineteenth centuries.

Anna Tristram was a Senior Lecturer in French Studies at Queen's University Belfast and is now a Teaching Associate in French Linguistics at the University of Cambridge. She is a sociolinguist who is interested in understanding the role that digital media play in the relationship between language and society—in particular, the expression of language attitudes and ideologies online. She also investigates language variation and change, specializing in morphosyntax. She has published a research monograph with Legenda (2014), entitled *Variation in French Morphosyntax*, and her research articles have appeared in the *Journal of French Language Studies*, *Transactions of the Philological Society*, and *Revue Romane*, amongst others.

Olivia Walsh is Associate Professor of French and Francophone Studies at the University of Nottingham. Her research interests include language ideologies and attitudes in the French language, with a particular interest in standardization and prescriptivism in France and the French-speaking world both in the past and in the current day, and, most recently, the French-speaking community in the UK and the USA. Her first book, *Linguistic Purism: Language Attitudes in France and Quebec*, was published by John Benjamins (2016). Her other work has appeared in publications such as the *Journal of Multilingual and Multicultural Development* and the *Journal of French Language Studies*.

1
New directions in the history and sociolinguistics of French

Janice Carruthers, Mairi McLaughlin, and Olivia Walsh

1.1 Overview

Historical and Sociolinguistic Approaches to French brings together two particularly dynamic areas of contemporary research on the French language through a series of chapters which showcase both diachronic and synchronic perspectives on a wide range of linguistic issues. Given the volume's central focus on historical and sociolinguistic approaches, a key aim is also to foreground current research in the interdiscipline of historical sociolinguistics which lies at their intersection and is an area which has undergone significant growth in recent years.

The unifying thread through the range of topics explored in this book is a data-driven approach. Corpora are central where linguistic data are analysed, including many new corpora containing both spoken data and written data from sources as diverse as correspondence, Twitter (known as X as of July 2023), and digitized texts from the Old French period through to the present day. Where the focus is metalinguistic, data are also crucial, taking the form of dictionaries, databases, language columns, periodicals, atlases, and legal texts. Theoretical and methodological approaches are consciously diverse; the chapters draw on a wide range of both well-established and innovative paradigms, with an emphasis on combining quantitative and qualitative tools. Indeed, many of these approaches have been facilitated by the wealth of corpora now available and include theories and methods which have strongly influenced scholarship on the French language in France and other Francophone contexts, in addition to those that are more closely aligned to developments in the Anglophone world, notably in the UK, Canada, and the USA. A distinctive feature of the volume is the incorporation of comparative and multilingual perspectives where these shed new light on important questions relating to French, including consideration of multilingualism within France, France's linguistic context in Europe, and the position of French in other multilingual settings around the world.

By bringing together the most recent and innovative scholarship, *Historical and Sociolinguistic Approaches to French* underscores not only the contribution of current research in these areas to shaping the research landscape in French linguistics but also the new directions in which the field is heading in the third decade of the twenty-first century.

1.2 Research context

1.2.1 Introduction

This section outlines the wider research context in which the volume was designed. It contains two sections: 1.2.2 on sociolinguistics and 1.2.3 on historical (socio-)linguistics. These sections chart the evolution of the two main areas of research but also explore in more depth some of the major preoccupations of the volume. As will become evident, the boundary between historical linguistics and sociolinguistics is far from sharp;[1] indeed the porosity between the two has facilitated the development of the interdiscipline of historical sociolinguistics. Amongst the many commonalities across historical and sociolinguistic approaches are the importance of corpus-based studies, the blending of quantitative and qualitative approaches, the foregrounding of multilingualism, and a growing diversification of the types of speakers, speech communities, and sources of linguistic data investigated.

1.2.2 Sociolinguistics

Research on the relationship between linguistic variables and social correlates has, at least until recently, been considered the dominant research domain within the field of sociolinguistics. Following Eckert (2012), scholars charting the evolution of the domain refer to three waves whose boundaries are admittedly not clear-cut. The first wave began in the 1960s with Labov's (1966) research on American English, in which quantitative corpus-based methodologies were deployed to uncover connections between linguistic variables and macro-social categories such as socioeconomic status, age, and gender. In so doing, this research shed new light on the relationship between language variation and change. For example, it helped to distinguish between 'change from below' and 'change from above': in the former, linguistic change is driven by mid- and lower socioeconomic groups whereas in the latter—which is much less frequent—it is higher socioeconomic groups which drive the change (Labov 1972a). Labov's (1972a) research also initiated an ongoing debate about how we might determine whether age-related variation in a given context should be interpreted as 'change in apparent time' (suggesting that usage in different age groups indicates that a change is taking place), or as 'age grading' (reflecting stable variation between groups of speakers of different ages).

---

[1] Labov (1994) is a clear example of this.

Since Labov's initial work, a large amount of research has been published in what came to be known as the variationist paradigm of sociolinguistics. Significant advances have taken place in the field, including the development of more sophisticated fieldwork methodologies, data analysis tools, and statistical modelling techniques.[2] The variationist research that has been undertaken on French concerns both metropolitan and non-metropolitan varieties (particularly Canadian French), with notable concentrations in the work of Canada-, UK-, and USA-based scholars. Despite its global influence, the relative lack of work in this paradigm by researchers in France has been attributed to a number of factors. Hornsby and Jones (2013), for example, argue that the design of French cities, and in particular, the marginalization of particular social groups in the *banlieue* (and away from the city centre) is methodologically problematic for the kind of social stratification that is pre-supposed by variationist models. In addition to a broader political climate that is less open to heterogeneity with regard to the official language, Gadet (2003a, 2004, 2017b) points also to particular research strengths in France which, through their prominence in work on linguistic variation, may have contributed to the relative marginalization of Labovian sociolinguistics. These strengths include the French philological tradition (including research on language change), dialectology, the analysis of spoken language (e.g. Blanche-Benveniste et al. 1990; Cappeau 2021), alongside the widespread use of the 'diasystem' framework (Flydal 1951; Weinreich 1954; Coșeriu 1981) which posits categories such as diatopic, diastratic, diamesic, and diaphasic variation (referring to variation related to place, social group, medium, and communicative context respectively).[3] To Gadet's list we could add the strength in France of early urban sociolinguistics and its emphasis on what is specific about urban speech as a factor in urban construction (Calvet 1994; Bulot 1999).

In terms of research on the French language in the variationist paradigm, phonological variables are the most common type studied, including much recent research on 'dialect levelling' within and across several regions of France and in other Francophone contexts.[4] In this volume, Green and Hintze (Chapter 11) offer an innovative exploration of variation in relation to elision in French which draws on important concepts in the variationist paradigm, notably the influence of linguistic factors (e.g. phonological factors) on the use of particular variables, the

---

[2] The extent of Labov's influence on sociolinguistic work across a range of languages is evident in standard works such as Tagliamonte (2012) and Chambers and Schilling (2013), in the vast range of articles published in variationist journals such as *Language Variation and Change* (Cambridge University Press) and in special issues such as the *Journal of Sociolinguistics* volume on Labov's influence in the last fifty years (Bell, Britain, and Sharma 2016).
[3] See also the discussion in Britain (2018).
[4] Examples include Hornsby (2006) on levelling in Northern France; Sankoff and Blondeau's (2007) work on /r/ in Montreal French; Armstrong and Low (2008) on /o/-fronting in central eastern France; Blainey's (2015) study of /ɛ/ lowering in Louisiana French; Boughton and Pipe's (2020) work on supralocalization and levelling; and Courdès-Murphy and Eychenne's (2021) research on levelling in nasal vowels in the French of Marseille.

importance of questions of style and register, and the implications of variation across different age groups in terms of 'change in apparent time' vs. 'age-grading'. Temple (Chapter 12) adds a diachronic dimension through a case study in Burgundy where she brings together variationist research on levelling, her own data from fieldwork, and data from the *Atlas linguistique de la France* (Gilliéron and Edmont 1902–10) to nuance widely held views about levelling in France, particularly in a rural context.

A particular feature of variationist research on French has been the focus on syntactic variables. A good example of this is work on variation between the long and short forms of negation in French involving, respectively, the realization and non-realization of the negative particle *ne*. The question at the heart of the matter has been the extent to which the data constitute evidence of a language change in progress towards increasing frequency of non-realization of *ne*. Panel studies involving some of the same speakers several decades later, taken alongside historical data, have revealed that while a change may well be in progress, it appears to be taking place over a longer time period than previously thought (Ashby 1981, 1991, 2001; Ayres-Bennett 1994c). Variationist research on other syntactic phenomena includes, to cite just a few examples, Ashby's (1982, 1988) work on detachment, Coveney's (1996) research on interrogation and negation, research on future forms by Wagner and Sankoff (2011), and by Abouda and Skrovec (2017), as well as Poplack et al.'s (2018) research on the subjunctive.[5]

The second wave of sociolinguistics is known as the 'ethnographic wave' (Eckert 2012) because its main innovation was the introduction of anthropological methods inspired by ethnographers including Hymes (1974) and Gumperz (1982, 2003). The use of methods such as long-term participant observation helped to minimize the effects of the observer's paradox to a much greater extent than was possible in first-wave sociolinguistic interviews.[6] Today, ethnographic interactional approaches continue to thrive with scholars such as Blackledge and Creese (2019) developing methodologies and frameworks to show what language use in everyday life 'can tell us about wider social constraints, structures and ideologies' (Copland and Creese 2015: 27). Macro-social categories such as age, gender, and socioeconomic status are still deployed in some second-wave studies but research in this paradigm tends to focus on speakers and their language use in more localized settings. Although French scholarship in anthropology and ethnography has had less of an influence on sociolinguistics in France (Greco 2020), some of the

---

[5] Gadet (2003a) argues that the notion of the 'syntactic variable' has been particularly problematic for researchers in the French tradition; this may also partially explain the predominance in the field of researchers based in Canada, the UK, and the USA.

[6] See for example studies by Milroy (1980); Cheshire (1982); and Eckert (1989). The 'observer's paradox' refers to the fact that speakers who are being observed by a researcher are likely to alter their speech, thereby undermining the validity of the data collected through observation (Labov 1972a: 209).

main second-wave methods have been adopted very successfully to investigate the use of French in various contexts. Participant observation has been productive for scholars working across a range of areas in French sociolinguistics such as phonology (Pooley 1994), language contact (McLaughlin 2011; Davidson and McLaughlin 2021a, b), and urban vernaculars (McAuley 2017).

Studies in the third wave of sociolinguistics are concerned with the way in which particular linguistic features index fluid social meanings (Eckert 2012: 94, 2016), hence the use of the term 'indexicality'. There is a clear contrast between first- and third-wave studies because scholars working in the third wave are not looking for links between linguistic variables and fixed social categories but aim instead to reveal how linguistic features create social meaning in context. There is also a contrast in the way in which style is conceptualized: in the first wave, speech styles are considered categories within the linguistic system (Labov 1972a), whereas in the third wave, style is a dynamic constructive process involving speakers creating social meaning through the conscious or subconscious selection of linguistic features in a particular context (Gadet 2017b). Indeed Gadet (2017b) notes the shift in the third wave to a speaker-oriented perspective (where variation is created by the speaker) and away from the more system-orientated first wave, where linguistic variation was viewed relative to an assumed norm. Third-wave studies of varieties of French in various contexts have begun to appear. For example, research currently being undertaken on urban ethnolects draws—implicitly or explicitly—on the notion of indexicality. Studies of the ways of speaking associated with the *banlieues* of major French cities such as Paris and Marseille have begun to reveal how salient features can carry social meanings in context, including associations with particular peer groups, regions, ethnic backgrounds, age groups, or social groups, while other features may be common across more than one region.[7] Indeed the description and analysis of urban ethnolects requires not a categorical but a nuanced approach which is sensitive to the idea of communities of practice and to the construction of complex social identities (Britain 2018; Carruthers and McAuley 2022).

From its beginnings in the analysis of linguistic variables and their social correlates, sociolinguistics has therefore expanded organically to include ethnographic, interactional, and indexical paradigms: socially meaningful variation is currently researched both at the macro- and micro-social levels.[8] As we have seen, non-metropolitan varieties have been an important focus for this research, notably in the case of Canada; there is also a growing body of sociolinguistic work on

---

[7] See for example Fagyal (2010); Gadet (2017a); Spini and Trimaille (2017); Carruthers and McAuley (2022); and the articles in two special issues of journals: the *Langage et société* issue devoted to Marseille (Géa and Gasquet-Cyrus 2017) and the *Journal of French Language Studies* issue on multicultural urban vernaculars (Cheshire and Gardner-Chloros 2018).

[8] See also the discussion in Bayley, Cameron, and Lucas (2013: 1) and in Eckert (2016).

French in Africa.[9] The increasing emphasis on a speaker-oriented perspective, social meaning, and questions of identity has, in turn, foregrounded the relationship between language use (by speakers, institutions, and communities) and language attitudes and ideologies. Both attitudes and ideologies play an important role in creating social meaning and are tightly linked to issues relating to language policy and planning, including 'questions of language maintenance/revitalization in which ideologies play a crucial role' (Calvet 1999: 17). The rest of this section concerns two foci of current research on the sociolinguistics of French which also represent important foci of this volume, namely language attitudes and ideologies, and language policy and planning.

Language ideologies consist of sets of beliefs that are shared throughout a community, whose ideological nature is often disguised because the beliefs become naturalized to the point that they are viewed as common sense (Silverstein 1979: 193; Milroy and Milroy 2012: 135; Fairclough 2013: 67). Attitudes, on the other hand, exist not only at the level of the community but also at the level of the individual, and they include feelings and behaviours as well as beliefs (Garrett 2010). However, because attitudes are often influenced by ideologies, the two phenomena tend to be studied in tandem using some of the same research methods (Walsh 2022).[10] The broadening of sociolinguistics and increased porosity of boundaries between different subfields has led to a notable increase in the number of studies of language attitudes and ideologies. Today, this work is being undertaken both within sociolinguistics and also in neighbouring fields such as applied linguistics, linguistic anthropology, and communication studies. Much of the research being carried out is interdisciplinary and the range of approaches used is increasingly diverse (Giles 2022). The broadening scope of language and cultural contexts across which scholars are now working is illustrated by the recently published volume *Research Methods in Language Attitudes* (Kircher and Zipp 2022a), which covers a range of analyses of language attitudes in different contexts. Two issues of the *Journal of Multilingual and Multicultural Development* (McLelland 2021a; Walsh 2021a) also demonstrate the broadening of studies of standardization to draw on language ideologies, especially the standard language ideology (SLI), and to include multilingual contexts, including non-standard and regional varieties from around the world.

Among the foundational studies of language attitudes are Lambert et al. (1960) and Hoenigswald's (1966) explorations of lay speakers' evaluative attitudes to language. Since then, a broad range of questions relating to speakers' attitudes to linguistic variation have been addressed. The various parameters of variation investigated include ethnic variation; social variation; foreign accents; regional

---

[9] See, for example, the journal *Le Français en Afrique* http://www.unice.fr/bcl/ofcaf/ (accessed 5 July 2022).
[10] With the exception of Chapter 18, throughout the volume 'Walsh' refers to Olivia Walsh. In Chapter 18 only, 'Walsh' refers to John Walsh.

variation; and gay and lesbian speech.[11] A second major focus of research on language attitudes across multiple language settings is their relation to social identity, with research showing how identity is related to group membership; how language is an important symbol of group membership and social identity; how language attitudes are linked to social attitudes and social status; and how language is central to the personal and social characteristics of individual speakers.[12] Finally, considerable attention has been paid to the implications of language attitudes for the languages which speakers decide to learn or use in particular contexts, and the languages which they pass on to their children.[13]

There is a growing body of attitudinal studies involving varieties of French. Many of the earliest publications focused on language attitudes in Quebec, often comparing attitudes of L1 speakers of French and English. This includes most notably Lambert et al.'s (1960) seminal paper on evaluative reactions to English and French speakers in Montreal using the matched-guise technique, as well as Preston's (1963) follow-up work on attitudes towards English, Canadian French, and European French speakers. Subsequent studies on language attitudes in Quebec have explored attitudes to speech styles (d'Anglejan and Tucker 1973), dialect perception (Giles and Bourhis 1976), and language-switching strategies used in cross-cultural encounters (Bourhis and Genesee 1980). As the number of publications has increased, the Canadian context has remained a strong focus of the research being undertaken on language attitudes and varieties of French. Later work takes social identity into account. For example, Genesee and Holobow's (1989) voice evaluation experiment shows evidence of more positive attitudes on the part of both Francophone and Anglophone Quebecers towards Quebec French. This increase in positive attitudes is related to social identity, since it 'can be interpreted as a consequence of the newly emerging perception of Quebec's distinctiveness as a society, as well as Quebecers' incipient sense of belonging to their province' (Kircher 2012: 348–9). Research has also been published on language attitudes and identity in Quebec, attitudes towards—and perceptions of—regional varieties of Quebec French, and attitudes towards contact with English.[14] Studies of language attitudes in France and Europe include attitudes towards urban vernaculars; language attitudes and identity in both France and Belgium; attitudes towards English in France; and issues related to spelling and writing, including attitudes

---

[11] On these topics, see Giles (1970); Lindemann (2003); Rodriguez, Cargile, and Rich (2004); Dewaele and McCloskey (2015); Hundt, Zipp, and Huber (2015); Hawkey (2018, 2020); Fasoli and Hegarty (2020).

[12] See, for example, Tajfel (1974); Giles and Johnson (1981); Grosjean (1982); Tajfel and Turner (1986); Cargile et al. (1994); Edwards (1994); Cargile and Giles (1997); Garrett, Coupland, and Williams (2003); Kircher (2016).

[13] Examples include Gardner (1982); Gardner and MacIntyre (1993); De Houwer (1999); Kircher (2022); Kircher and Zipp (2022b).

[14] For example, see Remysen (2012, 2016); Kircher (2014, 2015); Walsh (2014, 2016b); Remysen, Salita, and Barrière (2020).

towards spelling reform, the feminization of job titles,[15] and inclusive writing.[16] Tristram (Chapter 15) makes a new contribution to this body of work by analysing attitudes to inclusive writing in France using data from a recently created Twitter corpus which allows comparison of individual and official attitudes.

When it comes to language ideologies, a major focus of research is the SLI which holds that 'there is one particular form of a language which is the most "correct" or "best" form—spread via powerful institutions, including the education system, the mass media, and the employment sector—and that all other forms are incorrect' (Walsh 2021d: 870–1).[17] Until quite recently, most research on standardization and standard languages focused on nations in Western Europe which are largely perceived as monolingual such as the UK (Milroy and Milroy 2012) and France (Lodge 1993). It was widely assumed in this research that the speakers of the standard languages in question were monolingual, even if some studies tacitly acknowledged the existence of varieties related to the standard.[18] A shift is now perceptible and scholars have begun to consider the SLI from a multilingual perspective and in a wider range of contexts including multilingual regions, places outside Western Europe and the USA, and also settings in which minoritized and/or regional languages are used.[19] The diversification of the contexts studied, the sources used, and the methodological approaches adopted in this field have made it clear 'that language standardization has essentially to do with the transmission and perpetuation of ideology' (McLelland 2021c: 117). Much research has also centred on language ideologies relating to legitimacy, power, and political economy, examining the relationships between social groups, status, and languages (Gal 1989; Irvine 1989; Woolard 1998).

In the French context, much of the focus of language ideology research has been on the SLI and its perpetuation in France, most notably concerning the *remarques* genre, as we shall see in Section 1.2.3. Studies of later periods take the SLI more explicitly into account, often also dealing with language attitudes, exploring how language attitudes are informed by the SLI.[20] In this volume, Humphries (Chapter 14) examines the ideologies and attitudes revealed in two types of metalinguistic text, the nineteenth-century periodical *Le Courrier de Vaugelas* and the twenty-first-century website *Dire, ne pas Dire*,[21] with a novel comparison of the prescriptive advice offered in both. Similar research on other metalinguistic text

---

[15] For example, see Ager (1999); Oakes (2001); Boughton (2005, 2011); Flaitz (2007); Hambye and Francard (2008); Walsh (2015); Carruthers and McAuley (2022).
[16] See Dister and Moreau (2006); van Compernolle (2009); Abbou et al. (2018); Humphries (2019); Dister and Naets (2020); Dister (2023).
[17] See also Kroskrity (2000: 26); Lippi-Green (2012: 67).
[18] Examples include Joseph (1987); Linn and McLelland (2002). See also Walsh (2021b).
[19] See, for example, Hüning, Vogl, and Moliner (2012); Vogl (2012); McLelland (2021a); McLelland and Zhao (2021); Zhao and Liu (2021). See also Walsh (2021a).
[20] Examples include McLaughlin (2015); Humphries (2021); Walsh and Cotelli Kureth (2021).
[21] https://www.academie-francaise.fr/dire-ne-pas-dire (accessed 25 May 2022).

types such as language columns has been produced not only for the French of France but also the French used in Belgium, Switzerland, and Quebec.[22] Walsh (Chapter 13) builds on this work by offering a new analysis of the attitudes (re)produced in French language columns in France in the twentieth century and the role played by the SLI in their formation. Work on language attitudes and ideologies has further expanded to include regional and minority language (RML) contexts, with research carried out on numerous RMLs in France, frequently focusing on questions relating to legitimacy and authenticity, as we shall see in the discussion on language policy. An urgently necessary direction that has thus far yielded little research in French is work on race in relation to language attitudes and ideologies.[23]

Closely connected to language attitudes and ideologies is the area of language policy. Drawing on Fishman (1968, 1991) and Crowley (1990), Ricento (2006: 10–23) shows that as an academic field, language policy has developed and expanded considerably since its early role in language planning in the 1950s and 1960s, when Western-trained linguists were often involved in practical decisions about the role of colonial and indigenous languages in former colonies. He argues that the 1970s and 1980s were characterized by more critical approaches which, for example, exposed how notions such as stable diglossia reinforced racist linguistic hierarchies in the post-colonial context by devaluing indigenous languages relative to former colonial languages. The 1980s and 1990s saw a greater focus on linguistic human rights (Spolsky 2004: 113–32; Ricento 2006: 10–23; May 2011), most notably as regards the right to speak the language of one's choice and the right to protection of minoritized and endangered languages. Most of the scholarly literature on policy in this period focused on promotion-oriented rights such as those that support the use of minoritized languages in domains such as legislation, education, and administration; tolerance-oriented rights, which mainly concern private domains, were much less of a focus (May 2011). Since the 1990s, language policy has evolved into a greatly expanded field, with a number of different emphases such as language contact, language shift, revitalization, language planning, corpus building, as well as language rights (Ricento 2006: 10–23). It is also a firmly interdisciplinary field, not least because 'language policy debates are always about more than language' (Ricento 2006: 8).

According to one of the best-known accounts, language policy consists of three components (Spolsky 2004: 5): language practices (the everyday choices that

---

[22] See Remysen (2010, 2011, 2013a); Cotelli Kureth (2014); Ayres-Bennett (2015); Osthus (2015, 2016); Walsh (2016a, 2021d); Meier (2019).

[23] This question has been addressed in research on language attitudes and ideologies involving heritage speakers (Smith 2019) and on attitudes to urban vernaculars (Carruthers and McAuley 2022). On language and race in general and on the research field of raciolinguistics, see Alim, Rickford, and Ball (2016); Rosa (2019); Alim, Reyes, and Kroskrity (2020). For an early French approach, see Calvet (1979).

speakers make from the available repertoire); language beliefs or ideology (a set of beliefs held by the speech community); and language planning, management, or advocacy (direct efforts and interventions to influence language practice).[24] More recently, Spolsky (2019) has noted that even when a language policy has been articulated and promulgated, it can still be compromised or blocked by powerful non-linguistic forces such as war or famine. As the components and interdisciplinary basis of language policy suggest, it can concern a wide range of domains including family practice, education, the workplace, local government, the public space, and the media. The scope of language policy can also be quite diverse, from policy that is highly localized to a particular city, through regional, national, or even supranational policy such as the European Charter for Regional and Minority Languages.[25] In all instances, context is crucial, both in relation to the linguistic varieties attested in a given setting and to wider political, social, cultural, and economic factors, such that the issues at the heart of language policy can vary greatly between and within different nation states.

France has featured strongly in the global academic literature on language policy, often cited as an exemplar of a monolingual polity (see Spolsky 2004: 57–75) because Article 2 of the Constitution states that 'La langue de la République est le français'.[26] In terms of legislation, the two issues which have featured most prominently in the research space are the position of the regional languages of France (*Loi Deixonne* 1951; *Loi Molac* 2021)[27] and the question of linguistic borrowing, particularly from English (*Loi Bas-Lauriol* 1975; *Loi Toubon* 1994).[28] In the case of the latter, where the use of the French language (as opposed to English) and of French terminology (as opposed to borrowings) is made compulsory in certain contexts, the policy is clearly motivated by protectionism of French as the national language. Research on policy in this area suggests that there are difficulties policing implementation (see the discussion in Caron, Chapter 17) as well as tensions between state-level language legislation and company-level language management (Saulière 2014).

In the case of regional languages, the legislation (both in its development and its implementation) has encountered multiple challenges related to the tension between the desire to support minoritized languages (enshrined in the Constitution through the addition in 2008 of Article 75.1 which states that 'les langues régionales appartiennent au patrimoine de la France')[29] and the position of French

---

[24] Spolsky (2019) adds advocacy and advocates into the concept of language management.
[25] https://www.coe.int/en/web/compass/european-charter-for-regional-or-minority-languages (accessed 21 June 2022).
[26] https://www.legifrance.gouv.fr/loda/id/JORFTEXT000000571356/2019-07-01/ (accessed 21 June 2022).
[27] https://www.legifrance.gouv.fr/loda/id/JORFTEXT000000886638/ and https://www.legifrance.gouv.fr/dossierlegislatif/JORFDOLE000041575354/ (both accessed 21 July 2022).
[28] https://www.legifrance.gouv.fr/loda/id/JORFTEXT000000521788/ and https://www.legifrance.gouv.fr/loda/id/LEGITEXT000005616341/ (both accessed 21 July 2022).
[29] https://www.legifrance.gouv.fr/loda/id/JORFTEXT000000571356/2019-07-01/ (accessed 21 June 2022).

as the sole national language. Moreover, while it is possible to speak of an ideology of the standard in national language policy in France, a much more complex picture emerges when it comes to language practices and management on the ground; alongside national policy focusing on standard French, there is also regional language policy with varying levels of management, planning, advocacy, and community practice. Most research on language policy in France concerns the regional languages, considered both in their regional context and in relation to national-level policy, since the two are often interconnected, particularly in the educational and economic spheres. As noted in the discussion of attitudes and ideologies in this section, research on policy inevitably intersects with both of these. There is a very substantial body of research on policy in relation to regional and minoritized languages in France, including work on questions of vitality, revitalization, authenticity, standardization, legitimacy, language planning, online communities, economic investment, cultural identity, and educational policy and practice.[30] In this volume, Carruthers and Ó Mainnín (Chapter 18) discuss many of the challenges around revitalization, as well as other complex questions relating to authenticity, legitimacy, and different levels of ethnolinguistic, political, or community support in the French multilingual context. They offer a new comparison between policy, practice, and vitality in France and in the contrasting policy environment of Ireland. Elsewhere, Davies-Deacon (Chapter 16) explores the question of language planning in relation to dictionaries of Breton, including a discussion of attitudes to borrowings and neologisms; this chapter offers an innovative case study of lexical planning in the regional language with the most vibrant practice and the most developed management structures in France.

Legislation such as the Deixonne, Molac, Bas-Lauriol, and Toubon laws is considered to be overt language policy, but covert forms also exist. In France, these include policy relating to the rapid acquisition of French by newly arrived immigrant children (Escafré-Dublet 2014), policy concerning the language requirements for adult migrants seeking long-term residency in France (Adami 2012), and education policy relating to the languages taught in French schools, which is shown by research to be motivated strongly by instrumental factors (i.e. perceived utility) and dominated in practice by English (Garcia 2015; Caron, Chapter 17). Moreover, some researchers have explored different areas of policy alongside each other, underscoring inherent tensions and even contradictions: Garcia (2015) demonstrates the dominance of a very entrenched utilitarian education policy in relation to multilingualism, contrasting the position of foreign languages (especially English) with that of the regional languages in France, while Caron (Chapter 17) exposes the tension between the desire to suppress English

---

[30] See, for example, the series of chapters in Lieutard and Verny (2007); in Volume 223 of the *International Journal of the Sociology of Language* (Hornsby and Vigers 2013); in Kremnitz (2013); in Harrison and Joubert (2019); and the chapters relating to France in Jones (2015b) and Hinton, Huss, and Roche (2018). See also Adkins (2013); Hawkey and Kasstan (2015); Costa (2017); Oakes (2017); Hawkey (2018, 2020); Kasstan (2018); Lantto (2018); Davies-Deacon (2020); Hawkey and Mooney (2021).

borrowings in legislation on the one hand and the objective, on the other hand, of improving acquisition of the English language which is embedded in education policy.

The languages spoken by members of immigrant communities add another dimension to the policy question. However, despite the fact that a range of languages are spoken by French nationals within France (including dialectal Arabic, Berber, Yiddish, Romani, and Western Armenian),[31] they receive no official recognition or support through bilingual education which is reserved for regional languages (Kremnitz 2016). French also remains the official language in the Départements d'Outre Mer but creoles are the most widely spoken languages and have gained a certain level of recognition, at least within in the education system (Spolsky 2018). In former colonies, French is almost always in the (often complex) linguistic, cultural, and policy mix (Salhi 2002) and many are members of the Organisation internationale de la francophonie.[32] For example, French is retained as the sole official language in several African countries even if, as Spolsky points out (2018), political, economic, and social factors often mean that in some cases, it is not widely spoken in the population. In recent years there has been a perceptible shift in approach, at least at the surface level, where the robust strategy for the promotion of the French language now exists alongside an acknowledgement of the need to respect multilingualism and foster indigenous languages.[33] Finally, a very diverse set of language policies can be found in other Francophone countries including Francophone Europe and Canada; there is a substantial body of research on language policy in these contexts, touching on issues such as language and identity, the dynamics of multilingualism, geographic and demographic factors, and the relationship between regional and national policy, including a supranational dimension in the case of Europe.[34]

1.2.3 Historical (socio-)linguistics

Historical linguistics arguably has the longest history of any subdiscipline of the linguistic sciences. Founded in the nineteenth century, it has seen a number of important theoretical and methodological evolutions, and it remains a core subdiscipline of linguistics today. Partly because of the volume of historical texts

---

[31] For details on the languages in question, see the Cerquiglini report at https://www.vie-publique.fr/sites/default/files/rapport/pdf/994000719.pdf (accessed 18 June 2022).
[32] https://www.francophonie.org (accessed 19 May 2022).
[33] See https://www.diplomatie.gouv.fr/fr/politique-etrangere-de-la-france/francophonie-et-langue-francaise/engagement-de-la-france-pour-la-diversite-linguistique-et-la-langue-francaise/strategie-internationale-pour-la-langue-francaise-et-le-plurilinguisme/ (accessed 21 June 2022).
[34] See Conrick and Regan (2007); Heller (2008); Horner and Weber (2008); Horner (2009); Blommaert (2011); Vogl, Moliner, and Hüning (2013); Walsh (2016b); Oakes and Peled (2018); Hawkey and Horner (2022).

NEW DIRECTIONS IN THE HISTORY AND SOCIOLINGUISTICS OF FRENCH 13

available, there is a very strong tradition of research on the history of the Romance languages and on French in particular. The length and depth of interest in the history of French can be illustrated by general works on the history of the language from Brunot's (1905–53) thirteen-volume landmark publication to the recent *Grande grammaire historique du français* (Marchello-Nizia et al. 2020). The vitality of the field in recent years is illustrated by the website of the very lively Société internationale de diachronie du français which testifies to the number of events, publications, institutions, and individuals who are concerned in various ways with the history of French.[35] Also worth noting are two conference series (DIACHRO and SIDF), the section of the biannual *Congrès mondial de linguistique française* which is dedicated to the history of French, and Garnier's *Histoire et évolution du français* book series, founded and edited by Ayres-Bennett and Prévost.

A major strength of historical French linguistics has been the development of databases, corpora, and tools which allow historical texts to be analysed both quantitatively and qualitatively. A number of different threads in the development of these resources can be identified, the first of which is the production of large-scale electronic collections of texts. The largest database of historical French texts is *Frantext* which, as of December 2022, included 5,597 texts and a total of 266 million words.[36] Since *Frantext* originated as the source of examples used to compile the *Trésor de la langue française*,[37] the vast majority of the texts are literary. Its scale and accessibility nevertheless make it one of the most commonly used sources in research on the history of French. For example, in this volume, *Frantext* is the primary source of data for Combettes (Chapter 5), facilitating his diachronic analysis of the evolution of 'background' from Middle- to pre-Classical French. The quality and breadth of the corpus allows him to consider not only word-order developments and the evolving relationship between subordination, co-ordination, and parataxis, but also to view these in the context of changes in information structuring and textuality.

Building on a very strong tradition of philological scholarship on the medieval period, several important databases of Old French texts have been developed. One of the largest is the *Base de français médiéval* which contains a total of 170 texts written between the ninth and the end of the fifteenth century.[38] These large-scale collections of historical texts have led to major improvements in our understanding of the history of French and have challenged some of our assumptions about language variation and change. A good example of this is the *Grande grammaire historique du français* (Marchello-Nizia et al. 2020) where many of the contributors draw on these resources. In the current volume, Prévost (Chapter 4) shows

---

[35] https://diachronie.org (accessed 1 March 2022).
[36] https://www.frantext.fr (accessed 20 May 2022).
[37] http://atilf.atilf.fr (accessed 20 May 2022).
[38] http://bfm.ens-lyon.fr (accessed 20 May 2022). See also the *Nouveau Corpus d'Amsterdam* (https://sites.google.com/site/achimstein/research/resources/nca (accessed 20 May 2022)).

how new insights can be gained by using large-scale databases to analyse changes across a range of texts of various types in a very long timeframe, in her case a total of six centuries. Rainsford (Chapter 2) opts for a different approach in this volume, working instead on a shorter period of time, looking only at manuscripts copied before 1130. His contribution demonstrates the value of the newly developed *Old Gallo-Romance Corpus* which introduces two innovations into corpus-design for the Old French period: first, it contains multiple layers of annotation, and second, it unifies the treatment of Old French and Old Occitan manuscripts.[39]

A second thread in the development of electronic resources for studying the history of French involves the compilation of smaller research corpora which tend to broaden the range of genres and text types used in historical linguistic research. A central question of recent research on the history of French asks 'quelles sont les sources restées jusqu'ici peu exploitées dans les études diachroniques et dans quelle mesure permettent-elles d'étendre nos connaissances sur l'histoire du français?' (Ayres-Bennett et al. 2018b: 7). To illustrate how revealing studies of such corpora can be, we can cite Ayres-Bennett and Caron's (2016) study of five French translations of a single Latin text published at a crucial period in the evolution of the language between 1598 and 1659. With such a focused corpus, Ayres-Bennett and Caron were able to shed new light on the history of French by calling into question the validity of *français préclassique* as a period in the history of the language. In a similar vein, McLaughlin (2021) compiled a new corpus of historical newspapers and periodicals in order, not only to explore the history of journalistic writing in French, but also to show how data from an understudied text type can improve our understanding of the history of French and of language variation and change more generally.[40] In the current volume, Thomas (Chapter 8) makes a strong case for including data from another text type which is also characterized by relative communicative distance, namely official correspondence.

Across the case studies in her book-length study of linguistic variation in the seventeenth century, Ayres-Bennett (2004) shows how the two threads above can be combined such that the results of studies of more focused research corpora are informed by studies of large-scale databases, and vice versa. In general, as the available resources have increased both in number and type, comparison and triangulation between corpora has emerged as a key methodological approach which goes some way to make up for the impossibility of directly accessing speech from anything but the most recent past.[41] In her contribution to this volume (Chapter 3), Marnette undertakes a similar type of innovative triangulation, drawing together

---

[39] See http://www.ogr-corpus.org (accessed 20 May 2022).
[40] See also a number of the studies in Ayres-Bennett et al. (2018a).
[41] For example, see Ayres-Bennett (2004); Lodge (2004); Martineau (2009); King, Martineau, and Mougeon (2011); McLaughlin (2021).

two fruitful lines of enquiry on reported speech and combining these with newly digitized data. The first is research on the range of speech reporting strategies which are used in French and which vary according to factors such as text type (Marnette 2005, 2011). The second is comparative work which aims to identify the distinctive linguistic features of reported speech compared to the narrative voice, especially in Old French texts (Marchello-Nizia 2012, 2017; Glikman and Mazziotta 2013; Guillot et al. 2013).[42] Marnette combines the results of these large-scale quantitative studies with qualitative analyses of individual examples from newly digitized editions of one of the most important Old French texts which circulated outside France, the *Histoire ancienne jusqu'à César*.[43]

Speakers were not a primary focus of historical linguistic scholarship at the outset, and for a large part of the twentieth century, scholars focused mainly on the internal workings of linguistic systems with external factors being very much a secondary concern (Tuten and Tejedo-Herrero 2011: 283–5). This changed with the development of historical sociolinguistics as an interdisciplinary field which places the speaker at the heart of historical linguistic inquiry. Romaine's (1982) seminal study *Socio-historical Linguistics: Its Status and Methodology* is considered the founding text of the field which is now flourishing today. This is evidenced by the publication of the first handbook by Hernández-Campoy and Conde-Silvestre (2012a), the founding of the *Journal of Historical Sociolinguistics* in 2015, the development of at least two research networks,[44] and the establishment of three dedicated book series.[45] Hernández-Campoy and Conde-Silvestre (2012b: 1) define historical sociolinguistics as 'the reconstruction of the history of a given language in its socio-cultural context'. They highlight how the field broadened in parallel to the broadening of sociolinguistics described in Section 1.2.2: if historical sociolinguists originally aimed to explore language variation in the past and its relationship to change, today, their interests are much broader and cover 'other macrosociolinguistic facets, such as multilingualism, language contact, attitudes to language, and standardization' (Hernández-Campoy and Conde-Silvestre 2012b: 1).[46] In this third decade of the millennium, historical sociolinguistics is characterized by its breadth of scope, its inherent interdisciplinarity, and its complexity (Säily et al. 2017: 2).

---

[42] It is worth noting that a recent edition of *Langages* edited by Lefeuvre and Parussa (2020) reflects a new direction, as scholars—directly inspired by historical sociolinguistic research on English—turn to dialogue as a way of accessing speech in the past across a wider range of historical periods.

[43] See https://tvof.ac.uk (accessed 5 July 2022).

[44] See the *Historical Sociolinguistics Network* (https://hison.org) and the *North American Research Network in Historical Sociolinguistics* (https://narnihs.org/?page_id=6) (both accessed 20 April 2023).

[45] See the series *Advances in Historical Sociolinguistics* (https://benjamins.com/catalog/ahs), *Historical Sociolinguistics* (https://www.peterlang.com/series/6949), and *Languages and Culture in History* (https://www.aup.nl/en/series/languages-and-culture-in-history) (all accessed 5 July 2022).

[46] See also Auer et al.'s (2015: 9) definition of the scope of the field.

Accounts of the evolution of historical sociolinguistics emphasize the unequal treatment given to different languages and language families.[47] English was the focus of early works and as the field developed, attention started to be paid to other Germanic languages. French was the first Romance language explicitly to be investigated from an historical sociolinguistic perspective. Not unsurprisingly, the first studies were carried out by scholars working on French in Anglophone contexts and their work served as an important bridge between Anglophone and Francophone research traditions. This includes, most notably, Lodge's (1993) history of the standardization of French and Ayres-Bennett's (1996) history of the language through texts which foregrounds variation across different dimensions. Ayres-Bennett (2001) made an explicit call for historical sociolinguistic research on French before publishing the groundbreaking *Sociolinguistic Variation in Seventeenth-century French* (Ayres-Bennett 2004). There was growth in the number of historical sociolinguistic studies involving French and its varieties in the 2000s. Two important publications are Bouchard's (2002) sociolinguistic history of Quebec French as well as Lodge's (2004) sociolinguistic history of Parisian French. Other important publications from this period include Martineau's (2005, 2007, 2009) extensive work on Canadian varieties of French, much of which draws on the MCVF (*Modéliser le changement: les voies du français*) corpus which contains more than 2.5 million words, covers the history of the language from the Middle Ages until the eighteenth century, represents four large dialectal areas, and includes a range of genres and text types (Martineau 2008).

The publication of two edited volumes on historical sociolinguistics in Gallo-Romania by Aquino-Weber, Cotelli, and Kristol (2009) and Pooley and Lagorgette (2011) marks a crucial juncture, after which it becomes harder to survey and group all of the existing studies. The broadening of the scope of historical sociolinguistics around this time further complicates its history because a much wider range of studies can now be included.[48] One of the most obvious examples is the long and rich tradition of scholarship on language attitudes and ideologies in metalinguistic writing. The research has focused especially on two genres: first, books of remarks and observations on the language beginning with Vaugelas (1647), and second, language columns published in the press in Quebec, Belgium, France, and Switzerland.[49] Scholars interested in the tradition of the *remarques* inaugurated by Vaugelas's (1647) work are able to work in new ways and on a wider range of

---

[47] For example, see Russi (2016: 2); Säily et al. (2017: 2); Ayres-Bennett (2018b: 253). Of course, many of the world's languages and language families have no surviving textual record so they are *de facto* all but excluded from the field.

[48] This includes research not explicitly presented as historical sociolinguistic such as some of the earliest studies of the history of the language which placed the evolution of the linguistic system in its sociohistorical context (e.g. Brunot 1905–53).

[49] On books of observations and remarks see Ayres-Bennett (1987, 2018a); Caron (2004); and Ayres-Bennett and Seijido (2011). On language columns in the press, see Bochnakowa (2005, 2013); Remysen (2012, 2016–17a); Cotelli Kureth (2014, 2021); Walsh (2016a, 2021c, d); and Meier (2019).

texts thanks to the development and recent expansion of Garnier's *Grand corpus des grammaires et des remarques sur la langue française*.[50] Ayres-Bennett's (2015) exploration of the way that the language ideology of the *remarqueurs* persists in modern and contemporary language columns may come to represent a turning point whereby scholars will start increasingly to work on attitudes and ideologies in longer diachronic perspectives. McLaughlin's (Chapter 6) study in the current volume represents an attempt at creating this kind of bridge by drawing on scholarship on both the *remarqueurs* as well as language columns to analyse the presence and representation of women in the first periodical devoted to the French language (Domergue 1784–95).

The introduction of historical sociolinguistic approaches has had an important impact on historical French linguistics as a research field. At the highest level, as Ayres-Bennett et al. (2018b: 7) explain, the recentring of the speaker at the heart of language change has led to a new dynamism in historical French linguistics. In general terms, historical sociolinguistics has opened up the research field and changed perspectives on what can and should be done to further our understanding of the evolution of the language and related varieties. As in historical sociolinguistics in general, this has involved working against biases in traditional language history which are reflections of social biases (Auer et al. 2015: 6). The surviving textual documentation strongly favours white men belonging to the social elite, so historical sociolinguists are tasked with revealing the voices of those who are less frequently or directly represented in the textual tradition. For some time now, historical sociolinguistic studies have given more prominence to women, to younger speakers, to members of lower social classes, and to speakers from a wider range of geographic origins.[51] However, we are still far from seeing the balance completely redressed and therefore several studies in the current volume continue to move the field forward in this important direction. In her study, Thomas (Chapter 8) makes a fresh contribution to work on varieties of French used in North America by examining the use of French in a corpus of official letters from Louisiana during the Spanish colonial period. McLaughlin (Chapter 6) and Sanson (Chapter 7) both build on the work carried out especially by Ayres-Bennett (1994a, b, 2004, 2020b) to recentre women in the history of French both within France and elsewhere. As in the general field, the development of historical sociolinguistics has also opened the door to increased interaction between historical and contemporary, or between synchronic and diachronic, linguistic scholarship. This potential

---

[50] See https://classiques-garnier.com/grand-corpus-des-grammaires-et-des-remarques-sur-la-langue-francaise-xive-xviie-s.html (accessed 23 March 2022). On the expansion of the corpus, see Ayres-Bennett and Colombat (2016).

[51] See, for example, Branca-Rosoff and Schneider (1994); Ayres-Bennett (1994c, 2004); Lodge (2004); Martineau (2005, 2007); as well as many of the studies in edited volumes by Aquino-Weber, Cotelli, and Kristol (2009); Pooley and Lagorgette (2011); Rjéoutski, Argent, and Offord (2014); Ayres-Bennett et al. (2018a); Carles and Glessgen (2020); Remysen and Tailleur (2020).

was illustrated early on by Ayres-Bennett's (1994c) study of short-form negation in texts from the seventeenth century as well as by subsequent studies both by Ayres-Bennett (2004) and by others such as King, Martineau, and Mougeon (2011) and McLaughlin (2021: 131–90). In general, however, studies addressing the historical and contemporary together still remain in the minority. This is why Kibbee's (Chapter 10) study, in the current volume, of glossonyms in France is important because it shows the value of treating the historical and the contemporary together.

Recent general assessments of the state of historical sociolinguistics as a research field walk a thin line between highlighting the progress that has been made and drawing attention to the gaps in the field and the work that needs to be done. For example, in the conclusion to her chapter on historical sociolinguistics and the Romance languages, Ayres-Bennett (2018b: 273) celebrates this 'rich and promising field' but also underscores the lack of comparative work and the 'considerable refinement' that needs to be made to our analysis and interpretation of historical texts. The chapter therefore ends unambiguously, indicating that '[m]uch remains to be done'. One of the main current emphases to which a number of historical sociolinguistic studies in the current volume contributes is a focus on multilingualism and/or comparative methods of analysis. Multilingualism has for some time been identified as an area of growth in historical sociolinguistics (Nevalainen 2015: 245) and the value of comparative scholarship was clearly articulated by Säily et al. (2017: 15): 'A deeper understanding of such commonalities between patterns of use between languages and the different yet similar strategies of writers and speakers, provided by further cross-linguistic and typological studies, will certainly continue to advance the field of historical sociolinguistics.' A clear example of the value of comparative work involving French is Ayres-Bennett and Seijido's (2013a) edited volume on good usage which aimed, among other things, to determine to what extent ideas, terms, and models from the French tradition are found elsewhere (Ayres-Bennett and Seijido 2013b: 7). There is such a strong perception of the exceptionality of language attitudes and ideologies surrounding French that their volume added some nuance by placing French in a wider context.[52]

Historical sociolinguistic scholarship on French in multilingual contexts concerns for the most part either varieties of French spoken in Europe or varieties of French in North America.[53] There is a long tradition of interest in the use and status of French in European countries outside France. This work concerns two

---

[52] Estival and Pennycook's (2011) analysis of the image of the Académie française in English language ideologies illustrates the typical framing of French language ideologies as exceptional.
[53] For example, see Bouchard (2002); Klingler (2003); Aquino-Weber, Cotelli, and Kristol (2009); Spaëth (2010); DuBois, Leumas, and Richardson (2018); Skupien Dekens (2018); Thomas (2020). As noted in Section 1.2.2, there is a fast-growing body of sociolinguistic work on French in Africa and in other parts of the Global South but for the moment, this work remains for the most part focused on the contemporary period.

distinct situations: first, regions and countries such as Piedmont or Switzerland where Gallo-Romance varieties have always been used alongside other languages, and second, countries such as England and Russia where French came to play an important role as a prestige language. Interest in the historical sociolinguistics of French as a prestige language goes back at least as far as Kibbee's (1991) book on French in England during the Middle Ages. Rjéoutski, Argent, and Offord's (2014) *European Francophonie* illustrates the continuation of this interest today, showing how the geographical scope has broadened so that more is known about the use and status of French in countries further to the east, namely Romania, Russia, and Turkey. Three chapters in the current volume further our understanding of the historical sociolinguistics of French in multilingual contexts. Sanson (Chapter 7) and McLelland (Chapter 9) both shed light on French in Europe, examining respectively the value of French for Italian women in the eighteenth century, and bilingual French, German, and English dictionaries from the same period. Thomas (Chapter 8), for her part, sheds light on the use and status of French in a different and very specific kind of multilingual context, namely Louisiana after the end of French colonial rule and during the Spanish colonial period. Together, these chapters reflect two important facts that contemporary scholarship seeks to prioritize: first, that multilingualism is the norm rather than the exception, and second, the history of French in France constitutes just one part of the history of this language and its varieties around the world.

1.3 Chapters in the volume

Seventeen chapters follow this introduction, each showcasing new research on the history and/or sociolinguistics of French, including historical sociolinguistics. While the chapters dealing with earlier varieties of French come first and those discussing contemporary contexts appear later in the volume, the chapters are deliberately not structured into two discrete sections in order to better reflect historical linguistics and sociolinguistics as they stand today, characterized as they are by interdisciplinarity, multilingualism, and the porosity of boundaries. As noted in Section 1.1, the emphasis throughout is on innovative use of data (e.g. Chapters 4, 5, 11, 13), some of which have only recently become available (Chapters 2, 3, 6, 15), and on productive comparisons across time periods (Chapters 10, 12, 14, 16) and languages (Chapters 7, 8, 9, 17, 18) which allow us to shed new light on developments in the French language.

Thomas Rainsford (Chapter 2) examines the prosodic grouping of function words in Early Old French. Two methodological innovations allow him to arrive at an analysis of the morphophonology of clitic pronouns in this period. First, he uses the new open-access *Old Gallo-Romance Corpus* which contains the seven major Old French texts whose manuscripts were copied before 1130 (Rainsford

2021). The corpus design leverages the most recent technological developments to optimize historical linguistic scholarship at the interface of corpus linguistics and philology. Second, Rainsford uses data from Occitan to support his analysis, and the analysis itself is inspired by scholarship on another Old Romance variety, namely Italo-Romance. Together, the use of new corpus technology and the comparative approach allow Rainsford to offer a fresh insight on clitic pronouns in Early Old French.

Sophie Marnette (Chapter 3) brings together the two main threads of research on reported speech in Old French to propose a new grammar to account for the features of reported discourse at two different levels. At the macro level are the range of speech and thought reporting strategies that have been identified in Old French texts such as direct and indirect speech. Marnette uses textual data and previous research to show that variation should be built into the macro level because the strategies used vary according to such factors as medium, genre, and the status of the quoting and quoted locutors. The micro level concerns the linguistic features of the reported discourse itself which have been shown across a range of studies to differ from those of the narrative voice. This unifying proposal offers a promising way forward for research on the linguistic and discursive features of Old French texts especially as they relate to variation.

Variation is also at the heart of Sophie Prévost's Chapter 4 on two major changes affecting the syntax of the subject in French between the twelfth and the seventeenth centuries: the increase in the use of overt subjects, and the increase in the frequency of pre-verbal subjects. Drawing on the wealth of corpus resources available today for research on the history of French, Prévost compares both the chronology of the changes and also how they are affected by a range of variables. This language-internal comparative perspective proves very useful for understanding when and how these changes took place. At the most general level, the wealth of quantitative data leads to an intriguing finding which has the potential to shed new light on the relationship between variation and change: Prévost finds that in both cases, almost all of the internal and external factors involved in variation cease to have much of an effect once the new variant becomes dominant.

Bernard Combettes (Chapter 5) discusses the evolution of the distinction between foreground and background in narrative texts from Middle French through to the pre-Classical period. In a diachronic analysis that draws on a range of sources, Combettes considers developments in the discourse properties of foreground and background on the one hand, and the evolution of French syntax on the other, including phenomena such as subordination, inverse subordination, coordination, connectors, and tense agreement. The chapter sets these developments in the context of changes in the nature of textuality, particularly as regards the way in which narrative texts are constructed. Combettes shows how descriptive text emerges as an autonomous text type and how 'explicative' background, already attested in certain types of text in Middle French, develops in narrative texts.

Mairi McLaughlin (Chapter 6) explores where women are present and how they are represented in the first periodical devoted to the French language, namely the *Journal de la langue françoise* (Domergue 1784–95). This work builds on a tradition of scholarship pioneered by Ayres-Bennett (1994a, b; 2004, 2020b) that centres women in the history of French. Through quantitative and qualitative analyses of a full transcription of the periodical, McLaughlin uncovers the ways in which its discourse, both linguistic and metalinguistic, contributed to the reflection and construction of attitudes and ideologies surrounding women and language in late eighteenth-century France. The study also highlights the importance of the periodical medium which opened up a space for women to participate publicly in metalinguistic discourse.

Another chapter which contributes to diversification through a focus on women in language history is Helena Sanson's Chapter 7 on the French language in eighteenth-century Italy. Through careful close reading of a wide range of sources, Sanson draws attention to the value that knowledge of French represented for Italian women in this period. She shows how French allowed women access to intellectual developments taking place outside Italy and that some women went on to serve as cultural mediators by translating literary and scientific works from French into Italian. This interdisciplinary approach at the intersection of cultural, intellectual, and linguistic history allows Sanson to highlight the particularity of women's perspectives and relativizes the criticisms levelled at women at the time by men who associated their use of French with vanity and linguistic corruption.

Jenelle Thomas (Chapter 8) diversifies the field in a different way with her study of French letters from eighteenth-century Louisiana. Combining the tools of corpus linguistics with discourse analysis, Thomas analyses linguistic and discursive choices in a corpus of official letters written in French by officials, private citizens, and foreigners during the Spanish colonial period. This study underscores the value of expanding the scope of historical French linguistics to cover multilingual contexts where French was used alongside other languages. Thomas also makes an important contribution to historical sociolinguistics in general by demonstrating the interest of official correspondence. Despite the relatively formulaic nature of the text type, Thomas shows how the letter writers made choices which served to negotiate and construct their identity around centres of authority.

Nicola McLelland's study (Chapter 9) contributes to the field of language attitudes and ideologies in metalinguistic writing by taking an historical sociolinguistic approach to the analysis of a type of metalinguistic text that has been relatively neglected to date in this field, namely bilingual dictionaries. McLelland examines the construction of linguistic authority and adherence to language ideologies in three related eighteenth-century bilingual dictionaries involving French, German, and English. She presents evidence that the works of early modern bilingual dictionary compilers may serve as vehicles of the SLI, no less than monolingual codifications. Notably, this happens through their metalinguistic labelling, with some authors using a wide range of metalinguistic labels marking style, register, and social status, thereby clearly delineating what supposedly good language looks like for these authors.

Douglas Kibbee (Chapter 10) takes an historical sociolinguistic approach to examining and problematizing the various terms used to label and define the linguistic varieties spoken in France since the Middle Ages. He provides an overview of the relationship between the designation of linguistic varieties and political power, highlighting the many difficulties involved in clearly defining what the French language actually comprises. His research outlines how institutions and speakers have sought in the past, and continue to seek today, to distinguish languages from dialects,[54] idioms, *patois*,[55] etc., and further demonstrates how the labels used can themselves influence both which varieties are spoken and the ways in which such varieties are studied. Kibbee also shows how, from the Middle Ages to the present, the unity of the French state is seen to depend upon the unity of the language, despite the difficulties involved in actually defining what French is.

John N. Green and Marie-Anne Hintze (Chapter 11) return to the once well-studied phonological process of elision to present a comprehensive re-analysis of the process. Using data from a corpus of spoken standard northern French, the scholars challenge the assumption which prevails today that elision is easy to define, unitary, and categorical. The corpus data underscore the importance of this process in terms of its frequency, especially relative to liaison. The data also uncover new evidence about the contexts in which elision does not occur in contemporary French. This leads Green and Hintze to propose that elision should no longer be seen as a solely phonological process, since it is motivated by linguistic factors, discourse structure, and speaker variables. Their approach highlights the contribution of data-driven approaches to advances in linguistic theory.

Rosalind A. M. Temple (Chapter 12) offers a comparison of twenty-first-century linguistic data collected in the Côte d'Or, Burgundy, with a sample of data from the same region published in the *Atlas linguistique de la France* (Gilliéron and Edmont 1902–10). This approach allows Temple to explore a series of crucial contemporary questions about dialect levelling. First, she asks whether the levelling of regional linguistic differences in France is as widespread as is commonly thought,

---

[54] The term 'dialect' can be controversial in the context of Romance varieties in France. For many scholars, it is a neutral term when used historically, referring to certain varieties spoken prior to French emerging as the prestige form (see Chapters 2, 3, and 4 for example). It is much more problematic when used with reference to the twentieth and twenty-first centuries in France, where, with the exception of clearly identifiable regional languages (which may in turn have their own dialects, e.g. Occitan), a more neutral term (particularly in the Oïl region) is probably 'variety', which also suggests a greater sense of a continuum with current regional varieties of French. Several chapters in this volume engage with these issues (e.g. Chapters 10, 12, and 18) and the authors explain their choices and approach. 'Dialect' is used somewhat differently in the contemporary Italian context (Chapter 7) and less problematically in the discussion of different 'dialects' of Breton (Chapter 16) and Irish (Chapter 18), where in both cases, it refers to regional varieties of the language.

[55] See also Chapters 12 and 18 for discussion of the term *patois*.

or whether regional differentiation continues to exist to a greater extent than is generally acknowledged by recent scholarship. Second, she explores whether the dialects spoken in the Oïl region which are distinct from French and have their own names (e.g. *normand, bourguignon*) were replaced in the first half of the twentieth century by varieties of French (*français normand, français bourguignon*) which were then themselves subject to levelling. Finally, at the most general level, Temple considers whether the types of classification found in the research literature reflect language usage—and beliefs about language varieties—in practice.

Olivia Walsh (Chapter 13) examines a type of metalinguistic text that has been the focus of a considerable body of research in Quebec but remains underexamined in the context of France, namely language columns. Language columns consist of articles published regularly by a single author in the periodical press which discuss questions related to language, most frequently focusing on advising readers on supposedly correct and incorrect usages. Walsh analyses the metalanguage used to describe and make judgements about particular aspects of French language usage in order to determine, first, the attitudes towards the French language that are (re)produced in these columns during the twentieth century and, second, whether these attitudes change over time. Walsh also considers the role played by the SLI in forming these judgments.

Emma Humphries (Chapter 14) also contributes to scholarship on language attitudes and ideologies in metalinguistic texts. Her study compares two sources of language advice: the historical periodical *Le Courrier de Vaugelas* (1868–81) and the twenty-first century website *Dire, ne pas dire*.[56] Both sources have a question-and-answer format whereby readers' questions about the French language are published alongside responses from perceived experts. The chapter analyses the experts' responses, exploring, first, the metalanguage and imagery used to give language advice, and second, the extent to which it can be considered prescriptivist. Humphries's findings suggest that while there is considerable consistency over time in the use of prescriptive imagery, it is used to target different aspects of the language in each publication, and the perceived experts have different approaches to prescribing usage. Both approaches, however, have the potential to be interpreted as prescriptive by their readers.

In Chapter 15 which also deals with language attitudes and ideologies, Anna Tristram combines techniques from corpus linguistics and discourse analysis to examine attitudes to inclusive writing in France using a corpus collected from the social media microblogging site, Twitter. The study takes a dual approach to exploring the expression of attitudes in the corpus by investigating both the lexico-semantics of tweets and domain-specific expressive features such as retweets and favourites, thereby adding to the growing body of research into attitudes towards specific language features rather than to languages or varieties more globally.

[56] https://www.academie-francaise.fr/dire-ne-pas-dire (accessed 25 May 2022).

Tristram finds that there is a large degree of overlap between attitudes towards inclusive writing at the official and individual levels and argues that such attitudes are related to the strong SLI in France.

Merryn Davies-Deacon (Chapter 16) is also interested in language attitudes but in this case towards neologisms and borrowings, and towards corpus planning more generally, in the regional language of Breton. The chapter explores the validity of the common claim that language planners and language activists favour a purist, neo-Celtic lexicon over the French borrowings found in the Breton of traditional speakers. Davies-Deacon uses two methods of inquiry. First, she examines the lexicon included in dictionaries and terminology databases to track changes in attitudes towards neologisms and borrowings over time. Second, she analyses details from an interview with an employee of the state-sanctioned Breton language planning body to determine the official corpus planning process for Breton. This combination of approaches allows her to demonstrate that language planners in the twenty-first century may be taking different approaches from their predecessors.

In the penultimate chapter of the volume (Chapter 17), Philippe Caron examines attitudes and policy concerning modern language learning and the use of modern-language loanwords in France, arguing that there is not only a connection but also a tension between these two areas. Caron provides an overview of French educational policy towards modern languages from the 1980s onwards and also charts the official mechanisms for the creation of French neologisms to avoid English loanwords. He draws a parallel between, on the one hand, the negative French policy position towards loanwords, and on the other, pupils' (under)performance in modern-language learning, particularly when it comes to English.

Finally, Janice Carruthers and Mícheál B. Ó Mainnín (Chapter 18) offer a comparative exploration of language policy, practice, and vitality in relation to minoritized languages and varieties in France and Ireland. While there are a number of historical parallels, the twentieth- and twenty-first centuries demonstrate inverse policy positions in the case of the Republic of Ireland and France, with a complex political context in Northern Ireland. Drawing on wider theoretical debate in relation to language revitalization, the authors show that while contrasting policies have created major differences in terms of status and the number of L2 speakers of minoritized languages, there are many common challenges, including issues relating to authenticity and legitimacy, the complex dynamic between so-called 'new' and 'traditional' speakers, as well as the need for strong support for communities of speakers.

2
Proclisis and enclisis in early Gallo-Romance
Evidence from sandhi phenomena

Thomas Rainsford

2.1 Introduction

This chapter investigates the prosodic grouping of function words in early northern Gallo-Romance (GR) and the consequences of this grouping for the morphophonology of clitic pronouns.[1] I will draw together data from two linked phenomena: phonological sandhi, such as the elision of unstressed vowels before a vowel (1), and the morphophonology of object clitics (2) and (3):[2]

(1) **d**un   son   fils   uoil   parler   (*Alexis*, l. 15)
    of:one   his.M.SG   son   want.PRS.1SG   speak.INF
    'I want to tell of a son of his'

(2) si   grant   dolur   or   **m**est   aparude (*Alexis*, l. 409)
    so   great.F.SG   sadness   now   **me**:be.PRS.3SG   appear.PTCP.F.SG
    'such great sadness has now come upon me'

(3) si**m**   pais   pur   sue   amor (*Alexis*, l. 220)
    so:**me**   nourish.IMP.2SG   for   his.F.SG   love
    'please take care of me, for the love [of your son]'

In (2), the object pronoun *me* 'me' is proclitic, appearing in the onset of the first syllable of the following verb, while in (3) the pronoun is prosodically enclitic, appearing in the coda of the preceding adverb *si* 'thus'. In both (1) and (2) we can see the application of unstressed vowel deletion, reducing *de* to *d* and *me*

---

[1] The work presented here was begun during my time as a British Academy Post-Doctoral Fellow at the University of Oxford (2012–14). I am also grateful to the editors and two anonymous reviewers for OUP for their feedback on the initial version of this text. Any remaining errors and omissions are of course my own.

[2] The corpus texts are cited in diplomatic form with abbreviations resolved but word division unchanged.

Thomas Rainsford, *Proclisis and enclisis in early Gallo-Romance*. In: *Historical and Sociolinguistic Approaches to French*. Edited by: Janice Carruthers, Mairi McLaughlin, and Olivia Walsh, Oxford University Press. © Thomas Rainsford (2024). DOI: 10.1093/oso/9780192894366.003.0002

to *m*. However, enclitic asyllabic pronouns, such as *m* in (3), are an intensively discussed morphophonological puzzle, both with regard to their origins and their status within the synchronic grammar of early GR.[3]

In a departure from previous approaches, the present chapter re-examines pronoun morphophonology in the context of prosodic constituency in early GR more widely based on a survey of productive sandhi processes. In the framework of prosodic phonology, sandhi processes apply within a particular prosodic domain and as such they function as an important diagnostic for prosodic constituency. Following Selkirk (1996), two such constituents are essential for the study of the prosody of function words: the prosodic word (ω), typically aligned with the right or left edge of a lexical item (*lex*), and the phonological phrase (PhP). Clitic function words (*fnc*) can be integrated into this structure in three principal ways (Selkirk 1996: 188):

(4) a [*fnc* (*lex*)_ω]_PhP
    b [(*fnc lex*)_ω]_PhP
    c [(*fnc* (*lex*)_ω)_ω]_PhP

In (4a), free clitics are dominated directly by the phonological phrase, subject only to phrase-level phonological processes. In (4b), internal clitics are contained within the prosodic word itself, such that the clitic plus word as a whole is treated by the phonology as a single, indivisible prosodic word. In (4c), affixal clitics are included within a recursive prosodic word. In this case, word-level phonological processes such as stress assignment may apply to the inner prosodic word, the outer prosodic word, or both.[4] I argue in Section 2.3 that the correct configuration for early GR is the free clitic analysis shown in (4a), by showing that function words are primarily affected by sandhi processes operating at the level of the phonological phrase which are distinct from phonological processes found within the prosodic word. I also show that sandhi processes always involve a function word being prosodically attached to the following lexical item, and that patterns such as *[(*lex*)_ω *fnc*]_PhP, which would in theory be possible under the free clitic analysis, are not in fact attested in GR. In order to rule out these structures, I will assume that the phonological phrase must be aligned with the right edge of a prosodic word, i.e.:

(5) [… ω]_PhP

---

[3] See Kok (1985: 152–71); Horne (1990); Jacobs (1991, 1993); Burnett (2011).
[4] For example, Peperkamp (1997: 178–99) shows that stress shift onto enclitic pronouns in Neapolitan can be accounted for by a stress rule applying both to the inner and the outer prosodic word; Pescarini (2011) argues that Old Veronese vowel apocope applies cyclically to the inner and then to the outer prosodic word; Vigário (2003: 198–203) argues that the fact that word-initial stress in European Portuguese may fall either on a clitic or on the first syllable of a lexical item is evidence that the stress rule applies variably to the inner or the outer prosodic word.

Table 2.1 Early GR texts included in the corpus

Text	Title	Words	Language	Date MS [Text]	Provenance MS [Text]	MS
Eulalie	Sequence of St. Eulalia	193	Oïl	c900 [881/2]	Saint-Amand-les-Eaux	Valenciennes, Bibliothèque municipale, ms. 150
Alexis	Life of St. Alexis	4808	Oïl (Anglo-French)	c1120 [end 11th c.]	England [Normandy]	Hildesheim, Bibliothèque de l'église de Saint Godehard
Serments	Strasbourg Oaths	116	Oïl	c1000 [842]	Soissons [poss. Poitou]	Paris, BN lat. 9768
Passion	Clermont Passion	2875	Oïl (Oc features)	c1000 [c1000]	poss. Saint-Martial de Limoges [Poitou]	Clermont-Ferrand, Bibliothèque Municipale, ms. 240
SLéger	Life of St. Leger	1439	Oïl (Oc features)	c1000 [c1000]	poss. Saint-Martial de Limoges [Picardy/Wallonia]	Clermont-Ferrand, Bibliothèque Municipale, ms. 240
Boeci	Boeci fragment	2005	Oc (Limousin)	1100..1115 [c1100]	Fleury-sur-Loire [Saint-Martial de Limoges]	Orléans, Bibliothèque Municipale, no. 444
SFoi	Song of St. Foi	3702	Oc (extreme SW)	c1100 [c1060]	Fleury-sur-Loire [SW Oc]	Leiden, University Library, Vossiani lartini in-octavo 60

The chapter focuses on early northern GR, also known as Early Old French, which is a cover term for the varieties spoken in northern France from the ninth to the early twelfth centuries and documented in the earliest texts. The corpus (see Table 2.1) includes the most substantial and significant GR texts preserved in manuscripts copied before 1130.[5] Older texts in more recent manuscripts were excluded, since later scribes may update the written representation of sandhi and clitic morphology to reflect ongoing changes. Overall, the philological record is sparse and uneven. Critically, only two texts, *Eulalie* and *Alexis*, are uncontroversially written in a variety of northern GR. *Passion* and *SLéger* show marked southern GR influence, while *Serments* shows marked Latin influence and may originate from Poitou, on the border with southern GR. For this reason, the corpus also includes the two oldest southern GR texts, *Boeci* and *SFoi*. These are essential for the correct interpretation of the often confusing mixed data from *Passion* and *SLéger* and also provide extra comparative data for phenomena attested across all the GR varieties. Throughout the chapter, I will refer to 'early GR' if an observation is valid for both northern and southern dialect areas.[6]

The study is based on data from the Old Gallo-Romance (OGR) corpus (Rainsford 2021, 2022).[7] In addition to uniting the earliest Old French and Old Occitan texts in a single corpus, a number of layers of annotation unique to the OGR corpus enable philologically informed studies of early GR morphophonology. First, all texts are diplomatically transcribed using manuscript images or published transcriptions. Manuscript abbreviations are expanded and tokenization standardized across all texts to facilitate corpus searches; however, both expanded abbreviations and the original manuscript word division are recorded in the annotation. Second, in addition to manually verified lemmatization and part-of-speech tagging, inflectional morphology was manually annotated using information from the comprehensive glossaries included in print critical editions. Third, I have built on the methods developed for Rainsford (2020) to create a phonological layer of annotation, dividing each word into phonological segments and annotating the syllable structure, using a technique of automated transcription based on the spelling, and manual disambiguation and verification. The corpus was queried using both TXM (Heiden 2010) and ANNIS3 (Krause and Zeldes 2016) search engines in the preparation of this chapter.

The chapter is structured as follows. In Section 2.2, I compare the prosody and phonotactics of prosodic words and clitics in northern GR. Section 2.3 examines the sandhi phenomena found in the texts and they support a free clitic

---

[5] Some shorter texts are not included in the corpus, in part for reasons of feasibility and in part because there is often insufficient data in shorter texts to determine which phenomena are the result of productive rules and which are lexicalized.
[6] See Chapter 1, footnote 54, this volume.
[7] Available in open access at http://www.ogr-corpus.org (accessed 26 November 2021).

analysis of function words. Finally, Section 2.4 examines two puzzles of pronoun morphophonology.

2.2 Phonotactics of words and clitics in early northern GR

Excluding Latinate loanwords, the rhyme of an early northern GR word-internal syllable consists of a simple vowel and, optionally, a simple coda:

(6)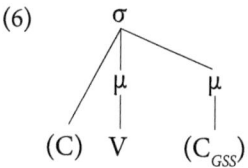

The only consonants permitted in the coda are the glides [j] or [w], sonorants, and [s] or [z],[8] and this is indicated in (6) by the abbreviation C_{GSS} ('glide, sonorant, or [s]'). Most function words in northern GR consist of single syllables which conform to the structure shown in (6) above. These include the definite article, possessive determiners, most subject and clitic object pronouns, complementizers, many relative pronouns, and the most grammaticalized prepositions (*a* 'to', *de* 'of', *en* 'in', *par* 'through', etc.).

Lexical items form prosodic words, and a number of cross-linguistic properties of the prosodic word may be used as diagnostics in GR.[9] First, the prosodic word is the domain of stress assignment. Stress in northern GR falls either on the penult, if the final vowel is [ə] (e.g. *mete* ['me.tə] 'put.SBJV.PRS.1SG'), or otherwise on the final syllable (e.g. *amer* [a.'mær] 'love.INF'). No prosodic word contains a syllable with only the reduced vowel [ə]. Second, the right edge of the prosodic word is not bound by phonotactic constraints on word-internal codas, supporting final consonants and consonant clusters beyond the set of C_{GSS} consonants found in the coda. Specifically, single obstruents (e.g. *nef* [næf] 'ship') and C_{GSS} plus obstruent clusters (e.g. *serf* [sɛrf] 'servant') are allowed in word-final position. All word-final obstruents are devoiced. Overall, although on the surface the word-final consonant is syllabified in the coda of the final syllable, underlyingly it has the characteristics of an onset (Scheer et al. 2020: 399).

Moreover, drawing on data from *Alexis* and the later *Song of Roland* text, Rainsford (2020) shows that the stressed vowel of a lexical item, and therefore of a

---

[8] See Morin (1986: 168); Jacobs (1992: 65); Rainsford (2020).
[9] On the properties of prosodic words, see Booij (1999) or the literature review in Revithiadou (2011).

prosodic word, is very rarely found in word-final position in northern GR. Instead, prosodic words end either in a final reduced syllable (7a) or a final consonant (7b):

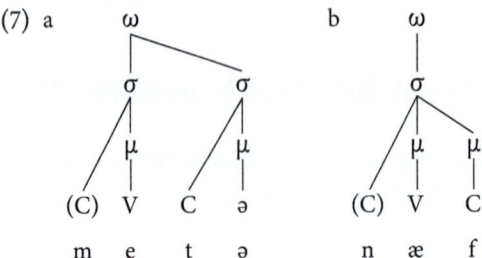

As can be seen from (7) above, while the stressed syllable itself may be light—i.e. an open syllable with a short vowel such as ['me] in (7a)—the prosodic word in northern GR must contain at least two moras, with an obligatory word-final consonant if stress is on the final syllable.

In summary, the distinction between unstressed clitics and stressed prosodic words is associated with important phonotactic differences in northern GR as illustrated by the difference between the structures in (6) and (7). These phonotactic differences can therefore be used as diagnostics when examining forms whose status is unclear, such as the combinations of hosts and enclitic pronouns discussed in Section 2.4.

2.3 Sandhi

2.3.1 Introduction

In this section, I examine three sandhi phenomena attested in the northern GR texts: the elision of unstressed vowels before a following vowel (Section 2.3.2); the presence of a linking [ð] before a vowel (Section 2.3.3); and the assimilation of final nasal consonants (Section 2.3.4), arguing that these processes are best explained by assuming the free clitic analysis of function words shown in (4a). In Section 2.3.5, I discuss apparent cases of gemination after a function word, which may present a challenge to the free clitic account.

There are two further sandhi processes attested in the texts which are not discussed further: the aphaeresis of word-initial [e] in a closed syllable, e.g. ⟨ma spuse⟩ 'my.F bride' (*Alexis*, l. 208),[10] and the loss of the final nasal consonant in NŌN > *ne* 'not'. Aphaeresis appears to be lexicalized rather than productive in northern GR: in *Alexis*, it is only found between a feminine possessive and the word *spuse*, with vowel elision preferred elsewhere. The development of *ne* is an idiosyncratic one and probably related to its role as a frequent host for enclitic pronouns (see Section 2.4.2).

---

[10] Note that [s] plus consonant onsets are not admissible in GR, and so [s] must be analysed as coda here.

2.3.2 Unstressed vowel elision

As in many Romance varieties,[11] final unstressed non-high vowels are deleted before a following vowel—e.g. ⟨legua⟩ 'the water' (*Alexis*, l. 267) shows the elision of the final [a] of *la*. Consonants preceding the deleted vowel, in this case [l], are then resyllabified into the empty onset of the following word-initial syllable.

The clearest evidence for vowel elision in the texts is the omission of the vowel in the written form, which is predominantly attested after monosyllabic function words. Graphical elision is systematic in all texts for forms of the definite article (*lo, la, le*), preverbal object clitics (*lo/le*, 'him.ACC', *la* 'her.ACC', *me* 'me', *te* 'you.2SG.OBL', *se* '3.REFL'), the preposition *de* 'of', and the possessive determiner *sa* 'his/her.F.SG'.[12] It is more sporadic in the northern GR texts (but systematic in southern GR) with forms of *que* 'that', *ne* 'nor', and *se* 'if' and, in *Alexis*, with *ne* 'not'. However, these forms also show variants with a linking [ð], which may be related to the lack of systematic vowel elision (see Section 2.3.3). After polysyllables, graphical elision is less common and is certainly not systematic in any of the northern GR texts. The most common types attested involve the final vowel of a determiner or adjective before a following noun, e.g. ⟨lung amfermetet⟩ 'long.F illness' (*Alexis*, l. 487), ⟨quatr omnes⟩ 'four men' (*SLéger*, l. 221), or the apocope of the final vowel of a preposition, e.g. ⟨entr els⟩ 'between them' (*Alexis*, l. 516). Only in *Passion* and *SLéger* are more varied examples found, such as between two verb forms (⟨fair estre⟩ 'make to be', *SLéger*, l. 60) or even across constituents:

(8) poblen   lo   rei   com muniet (*SLéger*, l. 83)
    people:in   the.M.SG.OBL   king.OBL   give.communion.PST.3SG
    'he made communion for the people to the king'

However, these sporadic attestations of vowel elision after polysyllables are complemented by the far more general rule of metrical synaeresis: final unstressed vowels do not count metrically when followed by a vowel within the same hemistich. While this could simply reflect poetic convention, evidence from the southern GR *SFoi* text suggests that there is indeed an underlying phonological basis. First, all cases of metrical vowel elision are represented in the spelling. Once diphthongs have been distinguished from vowels in hiatus, 591 of the 593 lines contain exactly eight written vowels up to and including the final tonic.[13] Second, synaeresis is not systematic, but appears to be sensitive to prosodic phrase boundaries. Overall, there are forty-seven contexts in the text where metrical synaeresis could be expected to apply after a paroxytone. Within these forty-seven contexts, aphaeresis of word-initial [e] in a closed syllable is systematic (ten occurrences), e.g. ⟨p[ro]feiran|cens⟩ 'offer.PRS.3SG incense' (l. 210). The remaining thirty-seven

---

[11] See, for example, Sampson (2016: 669).
[12] There are no tokens of *ma* 'my.F.SG' or *ta* 'your.F.SG' before a vowel.
[13] Line 553 *tuit a scrim en environ* 'all sword-fighting all around' is hypometrical with two vowels deleted in *escrima*; line 550 *Diuclicians es all pedrun* 'Diocletian is on a high rock' is hypermetrical if both hiatuses in *Diuclicians* are counted as in l. 113, 483.

contexts show twenty-two cases of elision and sixteen in which the vowel is retained. Eleven of the sixteen cases of vowel retention involve a non-elided vowel directly after the mid-line prominence (9):

(9) e   p[er]   la   terra   ep[er]   mar   (*SFoi*, l. 126)
and by   the.F.SG land and:by sea
'both by land and by sea'

The fact that synaeresis may be blocked, as in (9), in a position in the line that is often associated with a phonological phrase boundary in the early GR octosyllable (Rainsford 2011a), suggests that synaeresis reflects a phonological rule of vowel elision operating within the phonological phrase, but not across phonological phrase boundaries. However, it should be noted that elision can also be found in this context:

(10) diablad-|or   [et] homens uen   (*SFoi*, l. 136)
devil.OBL:worship.PRS.3SG and men.OBL sell.PRS.3SG
'[he] worships the devil and sells men'

In (10), the final [a] of *adora* 'worship.PRS.3SG' is elided despite being in the mid-line position.

Vowel elision does not apply within prosodic words. For example, forms of the imperfect subjunctive such as *ousse* [o.'y.sə] < °[aw.'wis.set] 'have.SBJV.IPF.1SG' (*Alexis*, l. 226) consistently show retention of a word-internal non-high vowel in hiatus, in this case [o], both in the spelling and in the metre. The loss of vowels in word-internal hiatus does not occur until the fourteenth century (Scheer et al. 2020: 477–8) and is unrelated to the sandhi phenomenon of vowel elision.

In summary, vowel elision is a phrase-level rule and applies equally to both function words and lexical items within the phonological phrase. Since the rule applies equally at the right edge of both clitics and prosodic words, but not word-internally, this suggests that clitics are, like prosodic words, directly dominated by the phonological phrase.[14]

2.3.3 Linking [ð]

The second major sandhi phenomenon found in the northern GR texts affects some monosyllabic function words, which show an alternation between a form ending in a final dental fricative [ð] (written ⟨d⟩ or ⟨t⟩) before a following vowel (__V), and a vowel-final form before a consonant (__C). This is shown in example (11) from *Eulalie*, which contains three tokens of *ne(d)* 'nor':

---

[14] For a comprehensive account of the development of vowel elision, see Premat (2023), which appeared while this chapter was in press.

Table 2.2 Frequency of forms with linking [ð] by context in the northern GR texts, excluding following enclitic pronouns and articles

Form	__V	__C
⟨ad⟩/⟨at⟩ 'to'	17/19	1/139
⟨et⟩/⟨ed⟩ 'and'	58/58	54/152
⟨od⟩ 'but'	0/0	0/3
⟨od⟩ 'with'	0/0	6/6
⟨net⟩/⟨ned⟩ 'nor'	3/11	0/30
⟨set⟩/⟨sed⟩ 'if'	3/12	0/8
⟨qued⟩/⟨quet⟩ 'that'	17/48	1/100

(11) **N e** por or **ned** argent **ne** paramenz (*Eulalie*, l. 7)
    nor for gold nor silver nor jewels
    'not for gold, nor silver, nor jewels'

For the northern GR texts, Table 2.2 shows the frequency of forms with final ⟨d⟩ or ⟨t⟩ by word in prevocalic (__V) and preconsonantal (__C) contexts. Before clitic pronouns and forms of the definite article, [ð] is never attested, and so these contexts are not included in the count of total __C contexts in the table.

The origins of linking [ð] can be traced to a small number of Latin monosyllabic function words with a final dental: AD 'to', APUD 'by, with', AUT 'but', ET 'and', QUID 'who.N.SG.NOM/ACC', and QUOD 'which.N.SG.NOM/ACC'. As shown in Table 2.2, the phenomenon is most frequently found with ⟨ad⟩/⟨a⟩ and ⟨ed⟩/⟨e⟩. The distribution of ⟨ad⟩ plus vowel vs. ⟨a⟩ plus consonant is systematic in all texts and the distribution of ⟨e⟩ plus consonant vs. ⟨ed⟩/⟨et⟩/⟨&⟩ plus vowel is also systematic in *Alexis* and *Eulalie*. In *Passion* and *SLéger*, the consonant-final form is dominant in both contexts; however, cases of ⟨e⟩ always appear before a consonant and agglutinated to the following word in the manuscript.

Linking [ð] is also etymological in tokens of ⟨qued⟩/⟨quet⟩, which are (with one exception) found only before a vowel. However, unlike *e(t)* and *a(d)*, the presence of an onset consonant means that vowel elision can apply instead of linking [ð] in __V contexts, and both forms are attested even in the earliest texts, e.g. in *Eulalie*, both ⟨Quelle⟩ (l. 6) and ⟨Qued elle⟩ 'that she' (l. 14) are found. Equally, there are some intermediate cases in which neither linking [ð] nor vowel elision are attested, resulting in a surface form in which an unstressed vowel is in hiatus with a following vowel, as shown, for example, by the fact that all five cases of ⟨que il⟩ in the corpus count as two separate syllables in the metre. In the case of ⟨sed⟩/⟨set⟩ < SĪ 'if' and ⟨ned⟩/⟨net⟩ < NĚC 'nor', linking [ð] is again attested alongside vowel elision and intermediate forms where no sandhi has applied. However, here linking [ð] cannot be etymological, but appears to have been extended on the model of *que(d)* and *e(d)* to other conjunctions with a final [e] vowel.

With regard to the structures sketched in (6) and (7) above, linking [ð] is anomalous in northern GR. It is distinct from the stable prosodic word-final consonant [θ] in words such as ⟨feit⟩ 'faith' (*Alexis*, l. 2), which is normally written ⟨t⟩ rather than ⟨d⟩, suggesting regular devoicing, and which is not subject to sandhi processes. However, it is also not a C_{GSS} consonant of the kind found in the coda of monosyllabic function words. Chasle (2008) argues convincingly that the status of linking [ð] is most similar to the latent consonants found in modern French liaison, which are underlyingly present but not associated with a slot in the underlying syllable structure. Function words with linking [ð] thus show the following variant of the structure in (6):

(12)
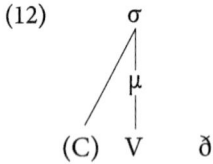

The unsyllabified latent consonant [ð] in (12) can only be realized if the onset of the following word is empty, providing a slot into which it can be syllabified. The fact that linking [ð] is not found after prosodic words follows simply from the fact that prosodic words, but not function words, have a slot in which a stable final consonant must be syllabified (see 7a).

In summary, linking [ð] is a latent consonant present in the underlying representation of some function words, usually for etymological reasons but also with limited analogical extension to phonologically and syntactically similar items. In terms of the analysis of prosodic constituency, the behaviour of linking [ð] is inconclusive, since the only phonological process in operation is resyllabification into an empty onset, a process found both at the level of the phonological phrase, as shown by the resyllabification of consonants following unstressed vowel deletion (Section 2.3.2) and within the word.

2.3.4 Nasal place assimilation

In addition to place assimilation within words, which is common in Romance,[15] the texts show clear evidence for the place assimilation of the final coda nasal of function words. With regard to the sandhi phenomena observed in the texts, few forms with final nasal consonants survive from Latin into GR and the only ones of interest for this study are NŌN > *ne(n)* 'no, not', IN > *en* 'in', and the possessive determiners *mon* 'my.M.SG', *ton* 'your.M.SG', and *son* 'his/her.M.SG'. Evidence for place assimilation is generally limited to the substitution of ⟨m⟩ for ⟨n⟩ before a following labial. This is particularly well attested in *Alexis*, both with possessive determiners,

---

[15] See Sampson (2016: 673); Schmid (2016: 483).

e.g. ⟨sum pedre⟩ 'his father' (l. 54, 74, 263, 337) and with the preposition *en*, e.g. ⟨ambailide⟩ 'as a grant' (l. 534), but is also found in *Passion*, e.g. ⟨som peccad⟩ 'his sin' (l. 508).

Nasal assimilation is extended to a limited number of other function words in which the nasal only becomes final after apocope and the deletion of a final consonant from the Latin etymon. This notably affects proclitic *en* < ĬNDE, e.g. ⟨ne tem perde⟩, '[that I'll] lose you because of it' (*Alexis*, l. 60). Indirect evidence that nasal assimilation has spread to *un* 'a.M.SG.OBL' is found in *Passion* and *SLéger*, in which the indefinite article is found five times before word-initial *m*. In four of these five cases, the article is simply written ⟨u⟩, e.g. ⟨en **u** monstier⟩ 'in a monastery' (*SLéger*, l. 95), which may represent a geminate [mm] (see also Section 2.3.5).

Like linking [ð], nasal assimilation does not appear to apply after prosodic words, except perhaps in the case of *tan* < TANTUM in *SLéger*, e.g. ⟨tam fud cruels⟩ '[he] was so cruel' (*SLéger*, l. 153). This could be taken as evidence that nasal place assimilation only occurs within prosodic words, and therefore that function words cannot be free clitics but must be parsed within the prosodic word, as in configurations (4b) and (4c) above. However, the evidence against a free clitic analysis is not decisive, since the lack of nasal place assimilation after prosodic words could equally well be explained by the onset-like properties of word-final consonants, which like nasal onsets are able to retain place distinctions.

2.3.5 Gemination? The case of double consonants

In particular in *Passion*, and sporadically in *SLéger*, we find cases of consonant doubling across word boundaries, for example:

(13) assos   fedels   (*Passion*, l. 92)
      to:his.M.PL.OBL   disciples.OBL
      'to his disciples'

The use of the geminate spelling ⟨ss⟩ is striking, and suggests that the etymological final [d] of Latin AD has undergone full regressive assimilation to the following consonant, creating a geminate, i.e. [asːos]. Given that final dentals are preserved in early GR as linking [ð], it is tempting to associate gemination with the presence of a latent consonant, as Chasle (2008) suggests.[16]

Historically, gemination is likely to have occurred in such contexts. Russo (2011, 2013a, b, 2014) presents a convincing philological analysis both of Late Latin charters from southern Italy and Pompeiian inscriptions showing regular regressive assimilation of final dentals, a phenomenon which persists in varieties of Italo-Romance as *raddoppiamento fonosintattico* ('phonosyntactic doubling').

---

[16] But not without reservations, noting in particular that the gemination attested after *de* 'of' cannot be explained by the presence of a latent consonant (Chasle 2008: 1653–4).

Moreover, Russo (2013a) shows that gemination is associated with a weak secondary stress on the function word, a claim supported by phonological and acoustic data from modern Italian.

If such an analysis holds true for early GR, it presents a challenge to the free clitic analysis, since free clitics are not parsed into a prosodic word and are not predicted to be stressable. However, a close examination of the texts casts doubt on the validity of assuming that a written double consonant represents a spoken geminate in early GR. In Table 2.3, I summarize the spelling conventions used in the northern GR texts: first, in contexts where phonological gemination is historically present word-internally and second, after monosyllabic function words which historically end in a consonant plus, following Chasle (2008: 1653) and Russo (2013a: 155), *de* 'of' and *se* 'if'.[17] To begin with, it can be observed that consonant doubling after function words is the exception rather than the rule in northern GR, as it is never found in more than 5% of contexts. Moreover, in constrast to the medieval Italo-Romace data studied by Russo (2013a), double consonants are not systematically used for etymological word-internal geminates either, except [rr] and [ss] (each doubled in over 75% of possible contexts) and, to a far lesser extent, nasals (doubled in 35.6% of contexts) and [l] (29.9% doubled). This would appear to support the view that word-internal geminates other than [rr] are lost in northern GR before the textual period (Scheer et al. 2020: 388). For example, in *Passion* we find forms such as ⟨appelled⟩ (l. 294) and ⟨apeled⟩ (l. 213) 'call.PST.3SG' in seemingly free variation. The frequency with which ⟨ss⟩ is retained does not necessarily reflect continued gemination, since degemination leads to the grapheme ⟨ss⟩ being repurposed to denote [s] as opposed to [z] in intervocalic

Table 2.3 Frequency of written double consonants for word-internal historical geminates and after function words claimed to trigger gemination in the early northern GR texts

Phoneme	Word-internal			After function word		
	Geminate	Simple	% Geminate	Geminate	Simple	% Geminate
p	1	22	4.4%	1	58	1.7%
t	3	69	4.2%	1	72	1.4%
k/tʃ	3	28	10.0%	0	49	0.0%
f	1	5	16.7%	0	13	0.0%
s	56	15	78.9%	4	80	4.8%
n/m	16	29	35.6%	1	68	1.5%
l	32	75	29.9%	6	132	4.4%
r	48	15	76.2%	0	23	0.0%

[17] These are *a(d)* 'to', *de* 'of', *e(t)* 'and', *ja* 'even', *ne* 'nor', *od* 'with', *o* 'where', *que(d)* 'that', *qui* 'who', *se* 'if', *si* 'thus'.

position. Moreover, in all four cases where ⟨ss⟩ is found at a word boundary, due to the agglutination of two words in the manuscript it actually occurs *visually* in word-medial position, as can be seen with ⟨assos⟩ in (13). In this case, the double consonant may simply have been used to unambiguously denote the sound [s]. The six cases of double ⟨ll⟩ in northern GR do not always involve manuscript agglutination; however, they always involve a pronoun or article derived from ĬLLE, e.g. ⟨el la⟩ 'and her.ACC' (*Passion*, l. 50), ⟨sillor⟩ 'thus them.DAT' (*SLéger*. l. 206). Rather than providing evidence for a generalized gemination rule, this may suggest that geminates are perhaps restricted to those contexts in which enclitic forms of ĬLLE develop. I return to this development of pronouns in such contexts in Section 2.4.2.

What remains? In northern GR, there are three slightly clearer cases after function words: ⟨a**nn**um⟩ 'to name' (*Alexis*, l. 16) after *a(d)*; ⟨a**p** petdres⟩ 'with stones' (*Passion*, l. 496), although this could be after *ab* 'with' rather than *a(d)*; and ⟨que**z** tasaldran⟩ 'that they will attack you' (*Passion*, l. 58) after *que(d)*, reading ⟨z t⟩ as a form of double *t*. Two further cases are found in *Passion*: ⟨sia**mm**espraes⟩ 'thus [I] have mistrusted' (*Passion*, l. 511) after *ai* 'have.PRS.1SG', and ⟨en m**&** trestoz⟩ 'in me completely' (*Passion*, l. 432) after disjunctive *me* 'me', if ⟨&⟩ is resolved as *et*. These final two cases in particular can perhaps be seen as evidence in support of the claim that gemination through assimilation was still marginally possible, in particular given the regressive assimilation of the final [j] glide in *ai*. On the other hand, both *ai* and disjunctive *me* are prosodic words rather than clitics. The southern GR texts also contain numerous cases of ⟨ss⟩ and ⟨ll⟩ of the type discussed above but no further clear cases of gemination.[18]

Given the limited evidence for retention of word-internal geminates in early GR and the fact that the most common cases of double consonants at word boundaries, ⟨ss⟩ and ⟨ll⟩, pose significant problems of interpretation, the philological evidence for the survival of a rule similar to Italo-Romance *raddoppiamento fonosintattico* in early GR is inconclusive at best.[19]

2.3.6 Interim summary

Although the sandhi phenomena discussed in this section do not all provide conclusive evidence in favour of considering function words as free clitics in early GR, I suggest that on balance the evidence favours this analysis. Unstressed vowel elision is a phrase-level rather than word-level process and applies equally to function words and prosodic words, which suggests that both are immediately

---

[18] In *SFoi*, frequent tokens of ⟨ll⟩ and ⟨nn⟩ are found both for etymological geminates, e.g. ⟨Bella⟩ 'beautiful.F.SG' (l. 45) and for palatals, e.g. ⟨vell⟩ 'old.M.SG' (l. 2). This may indicate a Catalan-like palatalization of the geminate sonorants [ll] and [nn] to [ʎ] and [ɲ] in this variety.

[19] See also Loporcaro (1997: 74–8) for a similarly sceptical view of the GR data.

dominated by the phonological phrase as in (4a). The behaviour of linking [ð] and the assimilation of coda nasals are compatible with this analysis, and I have argued that the philological evidence in favour of consonant gemination at word boundaries, which would indicate the presence of a weak secondary stress on the function word incompatible with a free clitic analysis, is not sufficiently strong when the wider context of the use of written double consonants is taken into account.

All sandhi processes discussed affect the right edge of function words, showing that they are grouped together with the following rather than the preceding lexical item, as predicted by the phrasing assumed in (5) above. Both unstressed vowel elision and linking [ð] involve the elimination of empty onsets, while nasal place assimilation involves coda weakening. Both tendencies are common from a pan-Romance perspective, and both continue to shape the prosodic development of later Old and Middle French, leading to the development of liaison and a regular CV syllable structure. Yet neither tendency is reflected in the puzzles of enclisis, and it is to this issue that I will now turn.

2.4 Pronouns and the definite article

2.4.1 Introduction

In this section, I reconsider two problems of pronominal morphophonology in the light of the prosodic analysis of early GR argued for in Section 2.3. In Section 2.4.2, I consider the status of enclitic asyllabic articles and pronouns (EAPs), i.e. forms of pronouns and articles consisting of a consonant or consonant cluster which attach to the end of the preceding word, e.g. *-m* 'me' in *sim* 'thus me' in (3) above. In Section 2.4.3, I examine the spread of strong forms of pronouns in post-verbal position.

Table 2.4 Pronominal paradigms in early northern GR

Pronoun	Strong m.	Strong f.	Clitic m.	Clitic f.
1SG		mei		me
2SG		tei		te
3SG.ACC	lui	li	le	la
3SG.DAT			li	
1PL		nos		nos
2PL		vos		vos
3PL.ACC	els	eles	los>les	las>les
3PL.DAT			lor	
3.REFL		sei		se

I assume that strong and clitic pronouns form two separate morphological paradigms in early GR as shown in Table 2.4.[20] The two paradigms have differing properties: for example, strong pronouns have the same distribution as NPs (e.g. they are used after prepositions or when the pronoun is not adjacent to the verb), while clitic pronouns are found only directly adjacent to the finite verb. Equally only third-person clitic pronouns retain the accusative–dative distinction.

2.4.2 Enclitic asyllabic articles and pronouns (EAPs)

The form of an EAP is related to that of the corresponding syllabic clitic by a process of non-low vowel deletion: the forms in Table 2.5 all show the deletion of [e] or [o] or more rarely [i]. The low vowel [a] is never deleted and thus the syllabic clitic *la* 'her.ACC' has no corresponding EAP. Table 2.5 also shows that although EAPs are found in all of the texts, their morphology and their distribution varies significantly. In general, the earlier the text and the further south its provenance, the greater the number of EAPs. Any analysis of the behaviour of EAPs must be able to account for this kind of intertextual variation. The key issue of interest for this chapter is determining whether the variation is fundamentally prosodic, i.e. caused by different sandhi processes and/or phrasal domains, or whether there is a morphological or lexical component giving rise to prosodically arbitrary differences.

As shown in Table 2.5, EAPs in all texts share the phonotactics of word-final consonant clusters. As at the end of a prosodic word, branching codas such as ⟨ls⟩ [ts] and ⟨nz⟩ [nts] and voiceless obstruent codas such as ⟨t⟩ are allowed. With

Table 2.5 Morphology of EAPs attested in the texts[a]

Syllabic	EAP by text						
	Eulalie	Alexis	Serments	Passion	SLéger	Boeci	SFoi
me	n/a	m, n	n/a	m	m	m	m
te	n/a	t	n/a	t	n/a	t	t
se	s	(s)	s	s	s	s	s
lo>le	l	l, (el)	n/a	l	l	l, (ll)	l, (ll)
los>les	n/a	s	n/a	ls	ls	lz, uz	ls, lz, (llz), (z)
li	–	–	n/a	(l)	–	l	l, ll, ill
nos	n/a	–	n/a	–	n/a	–	nz
vos	n/a	–	n/a	–	n/a	n/a	us
en	nt	n	n/a	n/a	n	n	n

[a] 'n/a': no contexts; '–': contexts but no EAPs; parentheses: minority form

---

[20] See Cardinaletti and Starke (1999) for a formal account of the distinction between strong and clitic pronouns. The third, weak pronoun category is not relevant for early GR.

regard to their hosts, they can in most cases only attach to words ending in a simple vowel.[21] Final glides block the use of asyllabic enclitics.[22]

However, beyond these common features, there are substantial differences between the texts. At one extreme, in the southern GR *SFoi*, there are no further constraints on the use of EAPs: they may attach to any kind of host, be it word or clitic, and even to the end of an XP, where a phonological phrase boundary would be expected, e.g.:

(14) co[n]   fal   venaire**ls**   cervs
     as   do.PRS.3SG:the.M.SG.NOM   hunter:**the.M.PL.OBL**   deer.PL.OBL
     matin (*SFoi*, l. 8)
     morning

'as the hunter does to the deer in the morning'

At the other extreme, the northern GR *Alexis* text shows significant restrictions on the occurrence of EAPs. First, there is a restriction on possible host words. Not only can EAPs not attach to full prosodic words (15)[23] but they are also blocked after function words such as *e* 'and' (16):

(15) Entre   **le**   dol   (*Alexis*, l. 466)
     between   **the.M.SG.OBL**   grief

'between the grief'

(16) e**le**   plus   (*Alexis*, l. 564)
     and:**the.M.SG.OBL**   most

'and mostly'

In both cases, a syllabic clitic is used instead. Second, syllables formed of a host plus EAP coda mostly have the phonotactics of a function word shown in (6), with the EAPs themselves generally limited to the C_{GSS} type. As a result, cases in which the non-C_{GSS} pronoun ⟨t⟩ would be expected show a great deal of variation: alongside one case in which it is used (17), there are cases where a syllabic pronoun is used, creating a hypermetrical hemistich (18), and in which no pronoun is used at all (19) (see Rainsford 2014: 31–2):

(17) si**t**   guardarai   (*Alexis*, l. 152)
     so:**you.2SG.OBL**   watch.over.FUT.1SG

'I will look after you'

---

[21] Consistent exceptions are found in *SFoi* and once in *Eulalie*, where asyllabic enclitics may attach to final ⟨n⟩, e.g. ⟨enl⟩ 'in the.M.SG.OBL' (*Eulalie*, l. 19), ⟨nons⟩ (*non* 'not' plus *se* '3.REFL', *SFoi*, l. 496).
[22] There are two exceptions in *SLéger*, both involving ⟨lui⟩: ⟨aluistramist⟩ '[he] send them to him' (*SLéger*, l. 86) and ⟨luil coman—dat⟩ '[he] entrusted him to him' (*SLéger*, l. 20).
[23] With the single exception of ⟨en terre el metent⟩ '[they] place him in the ground' (*Alexis*, l. 588). The form of the pronoun is unique and it does not occupy a metrical position, making it difficult to interpret phonologically with any certainty.

(18) Iate   portai   en men   uentre (*Alexis*, l. 456)
    once:**you.2SG.OBL** carry.PST.1SG in my.M.SG.OBL belly.OBL
    'once I carried you in my belly'

(19) pur quei   portai (*Alexis*, l. 444)
    for what carry.PST.1SG
    'Why did I bear [you]?'

Furthermore, the branching coda ⟨ls⟩ is reduced to ⟨s⟩ (see Table 2.5), which in turn leads to the EAP *s* '3.REFL' being replaced by a syllabic pronoun. Third, EAPs themselves become subject to active sandhi processes. Nasal place assimilation applies to the pronoun *m* 'me', which is written ⟨n⟩ except before labials:

(20) que tu**n**   reconfortasses (*Alexis*, l. 390)
    that you.2SG.NOM:**me** comfort.SBJV.IPFV.2SG
    'that you might comfort me'

The fact that the host plus EAP combination in (20) is subject to nasal place assimilation suggest that it is not a prosodic word with a stable final consonant as in (7) but a clitic as in (6). In *Alexis*, EAPs must be valid C_{GSS} codas and, as seen with *e* in example (16), not even all (C)V monosyllables are possible hosts, which suggests that the combination of host plus EAP is to some extent lexicalized.[24]

The remaining texts show intermediate systems. In *Boeci*, EAPs are regularly used, although there is no asyllabic form of *nos* (see Table 2.5) and enclisis is consistently blocked at the caesura, e.g.:

(21) anz   p[er] eueia **lo**   mesdren   e   preiso (*Boeci*, l. 27)
    instead for   envy   **him.ACC** put.PST.3PL in prison
    'instead, out of jealousy, they put him in prison.'

In (21), the caesura occurs after *eueia*, and no enclisis of the following object pronoun is found. We might infer that this restriction reflects a tendency for EAPs to attach only to hosts within the same phonological phrase. *Passion* and *SLéger* also show widespread use of EAPs, but as in *Alexis*, there is free variation even after monosyllabic function words, e.g.:

(22) ia**lo**   sot   bien (*SLéger*, l. 77)
    while:**it.ACC** know.PST.3SG well
    'while he knew it well'

(23) ia**l**   uedes   ela   si   morir (*Passion*, l. 335)
    while:**him.ACC** see.SBJV.IPF.3SG she   thus   die.INF
    'while she saw him die this way'

---

[24] See also Rainsford (2014) for the further development of these forms in later Old French texts.

A synopsis of the properties of texts for which there are a sufficient number of tokens to draw conclusions regarding the behaviour of EAPs is given in Table 2.6.

I now turn to the core question of the status of EAPs within the synchronic prosodic system of early GR. One possibility is that EAPs are generated in the phonological component of the grammar through an active rule of vowel deletion, and a number of analyses of this kind have been proposed.[25] A second possibility is that EAPs are allomorphs resulting from an historical rule of vowel deletion, and I suggest that this second view has a number of advantages. First, there is an obvious diachronic source of vowel deletion: non-low unstressed vowels are lost in GR through regular sound change (Scheer et al. 2020: 322–5), and this change is complete and no longer active by the textual period. It is therefore inconsistent to include the processes reducing *jo te* to *jot* or *de les* to *des* in the synchronic phonology of early GR if those reducing °*sotto* to *sot* 'foolish.M.SG' or °*filos* to *fis* 'thread.M.PL.OBL' are historical.[26] Second, a vowel deletion rule of this kind, which creates complex consonant clusters in the coda, does not fit with the other sandhi processes discussed in Section 2.3, which involve either resyllabification of consonants into empty onsets (vowel elision, linking [ð]) or the assimilation of codas (nasals). Third, while regular sandhi processes are consistent across the texts, possible host plus EAPs combinations vary greatly, suggesting instead that they are lexicalized allomorphs rather than generated by regular phonological processes. Finally, if function words in early GR are free clitics as defended here, there is no prosodic motivation for them to be grouped together into host plus EAP combinations unless such allomorphs have been lexicalized.

While an allomorphic analysis of EAPs is in my view to be preferred for early GR, their development clearly involves a stage in which they were enclitic on the host for purely prosodic reasons. Enclisis implies a stress on the host word; however, the most stable contexts in which EAPs are found is after Latin

Table 2.6 Synopsis of the properties of EAPs in the longer texts

Property	Alexis	Passion/SLéger	Boeci	SFoi
attach across PhP boundary	no	no	no	possibly
polysyllabic host	no	yes	yes	yes
monosyllabic hosts	some	all, variation	all	all
possible after ⟨n⟩	no	no	no	yes
non-C$_{GSS}$ forms	rare	yes	yes	yes
number of EAP types	5(–6)	6(–7)	7	9

[25] Beginning with work in the framework of generative phonology (Herslund 1976; Walker 1981), approaches in the late 1980s and 1990s (Horne 1990; Jacobs 1991, 1993) incorporate insights from prosodic and metrical phonology, while most recently Burnett (2011) adopts an optimality theory approach based on Selkirk's (1996) framework.

[26] In this regard, the early generative approach of Walker (1981) is consistent but at the cost of positing underlying representations far removed from the surface form.

Table 2.7 Phases in the development of three host plus clitic prosodic words in GR

Source	°non (ĭ)llu	°ad (ĭ)llos	°sīc me	°de (ĭ)llas
proto-GR	°['nonlo]	°['aːlos]	°['simːe]	°['delːas]
early GR	['nonl]>['nol]	['aɫs]	['sim]	['deləs]
Alexis	[nəɫ]	[as]/[az]	[sim]/[sin]/[siŋ]	[də ləs]

monosyllabic function words, e.g. *si* < sīc 'so', *no(n)* < nōn 'no', and *de* < dē 'of', which are (at best) minimal prosodic words and unlikely to have been consistently stressed.[27] It is possible that enclisis originates in Late Latin as a prosodic word-building process: function words are grouped into disyllabic prosodic words, which later develop into the monosyllabic host plus EAP forms found in early GR.

A hypothetical reconstruction of the historical development of three common host plus EAP forms based on the evidence of the earliest GR texts is given in Table 2.7. Working backwards, at the final stage of the development are the clitic host plus EAP forms found in *Alexis*, e.g. *as* [as] 'to the.M.PL'. These are descended from early GR host plus EAP clusters such as we find in all the other texts, which appear to have been prosodic words due to their word-final consonant phonotactics, e.g. *als* ['aɫs] 'to the.M.PL'. Crucially, before regular vowel apocope applied,[28] these forms are descended from proto-GR disyllabic paroxytones, e.g. °['aːlos] 'to the.M.PL'. Proto-GR stress was predominantly paroxytonic (Jacobs 1994: 53), and as in Latin, the number of monosyllabic lexical items was very limited. Thus, while the monosyllabic hosts alone are barely minimal words in proto-GR, grouping the host with a following enclitic pronoun or article would have had the effect of creating a stressable, disyllabic prosodic word.[29]

2.4.3 Post-verbal pronouns

The position of clitic pronouns with respect to the finite verb in early GR is determined by the Tobler–Mussafia law:[30] clitics are normally preverbal, but become post-verbal when the verb is clause-initial. In general, where a morphologically

---

[27] This observation is valid in other Romance varieties: Pescarini (2016: 750) and Vanelli (1998 [1992]: 179–85) make similar observations based on Italo-Romance data, i.e. that the initial context in which asyllabic enclitic forms of the definite article are found is after monosyllabic function words.

[28] The precise details of the development in cases of enclisis have been subject to debate for well over a century but detailed studies such as Melander (1928) are held back by the difficulty of applying sound laws to sequences larger than the word without an adequate theory of prosodic grouping. See Geisler (1982: 251–60) and Kok (1985: 152–71) for an excellent summary.

[29] Jacobs's (1993: 161) suggestion that enclisis has the function of making a light stressed monosyllable bimoraic in early Old French is based on a similar intuition; however, as discussed in Section 2.2, early northern GR did not require stressed syllables to be heavy.

[30] See, for example, Benincà (1995).

clitic pronoun is used post-verbally, it has the expected properties of a clitic: elision is found before a following vowel (24) and, in the texts in which EAPs are used after prosodic words, they also occur after verbs ending in a vowel (25), (26).

(24) mis   len   reclus   (SLéger, l. 155)
     put.PST.3SG **him.ACC**:in prison
     '[he] put him in prison'

(25) apellal   foll   (SFoi, l. 155)
     call.PRS.3SG:**him.ACC** mad.M.SG.OBL
     '[she] calls him mad'

(26) quedesamort   posches   neger (Passion, l. 238)
     that:of:his.FSG:death can.SBJV.PRS.3SG:**3.REFL** deny
     'that he may deny responsibility for his death.'

These configurations are compatible with the analysis of function words as free clitics: provided the finite verb itself does not occur at a phonological phrase boundary, the post-verbal clitic *le* is subject to unstressed vowel elision before the following preposition in (27), while the vowel-final verb is an appropriate host for the EAP *l* in (28):

(27) [(mis)_ω le en (reclus)_ω]_PhP

(28) [(apella)_ω l (foll)_ω]_PhP

However, in the *Alexis* manuscript, a strong form of the post-verbal pronoun is used in 1SG, 2SG and 3.REFL (29), while an unelidable clitic form is used in the third-person (30):[31]

(29) aidiez   **mei** aplaindra (Alexis, l. 462)
     help.IMP.2PL **me** to:mourn
     'help me to mourn'

(30) receit   **le**   Aleis   (Alexis, l. 283)
     receive.PRS.3SG **him.ACC** Alexis
     'Alexis receives him'

Although a strong form is used in (29), the syntactic status of the pronoun is unchanged: it is still syntactically enclitic on the verb.[32] What appears to have occurred here is a morphologically conditioned development of the free clitic system represented in the other texts. Strong pronouns are only substituted if they

---

[31] Note that evidence from later texts confirms that this only affects the final pronoun in a cluster.
[32] I assume with Klavans (1985) that syntactic cliticization and prosodic attachment are independent, contra Kok (1985: 203) and Dardel and Kok (1996: 174–6), who argue that stressed post-verbal pronouns cannot be considered clitics (Kok 1985: 171).

are exact morphological equivalents of the underlying clitic: the clitics *me*, *te*, and *se* do not encode the accusative/dative distinction and so can be replaced by an oblique strong form, while the accusative clitic *le* in (30) is not replaced by the oblique strong pronoun *lui*. The fact that it is a new development is shown not only by the fact that it only occurs in the latest northern GR text, but also by differences between the reading indicated by the metre, which is more likely to indicate an earlier form of the text, and the form used in the manuscript. In (29), the strong pronoun occurs before a vowel in a hypermetrical hemistich, and a similar example occurs in line 357. For this reason, critical editions typically reconstruct a clitic pronoun subject to vowel elision, i.e. *aidiez m'a plaindra* as the original form of the text, despite the fact that all surviving manuscripts show a unelided form.[33]

The substitution of a strong form for a clitic also indicates that the post-verbal pronoun is stressed. Moreover, there is some limited evidence in the early GR texts that this also holds for morphologically clitic post-verbal pronouns: note, for example, that the final vowel of *le* in (30) is not subject to unstressed vowel elision. More significantly, in *Boeci*, one case of post-verbal *en* 'of it' not only shows the final dental characteristic of tonic forms derived from ĪNDE, but is also marked in the manuscript with an acute accent:

(31) reluz **ént** lo palaz (*Boeci*, l. 162)
     glow.PST.3SG **of.it** the.M.SG palace
     'the palace glowed from it'

This diacritic is sporadically used throughout the text to denote tonic syllables.

Stress shift accompanied by the morphological substitution of a strong pronoun is a unique feature of GR within the Romance languages[34] but follows from the free clitic analysis of function words proposed in this chapter.[35] The starting point is the observation that post-verbal pronouns are unique as syntactic clitics by being able to occur in phrase-final position, particularly in imperatives, e.g.:

(32) O z **mei** pulcele (*Alexis*, l. 66)
     hear.IMP.2SG **me** girl
     'hear me, girl'

Now, if the right edge of the phonological phrase must be aligned with the right edge of a prosodic word (see (5) above), a clause ending with a free clitic is predicted to be ungrammatical:

---

[33] For example, line 442 of Zufferey's (2020: 477) edition.
[34] Stress shift is widely attested, for example, in Italo-Romance (e.g. Peperkamp 1997) and in dialects of Catalan, particularly in Balearic varieties (Torres-Tamarit and Pons-Moll 2019), but this appears to be a different kind of phenomenon, involving affixal enclitics integrated into the prosodic word and not showing GR-style morphological substitution.
[35] See the similar proposal in Rainsford (2011b: 204–7) based on Selkirk's (1996: 199–203) analysis of phrase-final function words in English.

(33) *[(Oz)ω me]PhP

Two possible repair strategies can be envisaged: either the pronoun is parsed as a prosodic word in its own right (34a), or it is affixed to the previous prosodic word (34b):

(34) a [(Oz)ω (me)ω]PhP
     b [((Oz)ω me)ω]PhP

However, solution (34b) does not necessarily entail stress shift—a stress pattern such as ['ɔts.mə] would be grammatical both at the level of the inner and the outer prosodic word—and certainly cannot account for the morphological substitution of a strong pronoun. This suggests that (34a) is in fact the correct analysis, and that the requirement for the clitic to be realized as a prosodic word triggers substitution of a morphologically equivalent strong pronoun. Where no strong pronoun can be substituted, the clitic pronoun itself is exceptionally footed and parsed as a prosodic word, e.g.:

(35) [(receit)ω (le)ω]PhP

A further piece of evidence that the presence of a phrase-final function word triggers the creation of a new prosodic word aligned with the right edge of the phonological phrase is provided by Foulet's (1924) observation on the morphology of object pronouns before post-verbal subjects. Where a post-verbal subject pronoun follows the object pronouns, it is the subject pronoun which is phrase-final and consequently the object pronouns remain morphologically clitic, i.e. *me*, *te*, and *se* are attested, e.g. *fet se il* 'says he' (Foulet 1924: 55ff.). However, vowel elision does not apply, and in verse texts, the final vowel of the post-verbal object pronoun is not subject to synaeresis, e.g.

(36) Estuet   **me**   il   que   plus   vous
     be.necessary.PRS.3SG **me** it   that   more   you.2PL.OBL
     die? (Gautier d'Arras, Éracle, l. 2356, ed. Raynaud de Lage 1976)
     say.SBJV.PRS.1SG

'Is it necessary for me to say more to you?'

This is unexpected if the clitics are free and dominated by the phonological phrase (37a). However, it is predicted if the requirement for a phrase-final prosodic word causes the subject pronoun and all preceding function words to be parsed together as a single prosodic word (37b), since vowel elision does not affect word-internal syllables:

(37) a *[(Estuet)ω me il]PhP
     b [(Estuet)ω (me il)ω]PhP

The reasons for which strong pronoun substitution and stress shift spread to phrase-internal contexts in *Alexis* (e.g. example (30)) and later Old French are less clear. Based on a corpus of later texts, Rainsford (2011b: 204–7) argues that this was due to a change in phrasing, with a phonological phrase boundary gradually becoming obligatory after all post-verbal clitic groups. However, it is also possible that the change was morphologically driven: put simply, although strong pronouns are initially introduced in post-verbal position to satisfy a prosodic requirement, they subsequently spread by analogy to other contexts where no such prosodic requirement exists. Indeed, the data discussed in Rainsford (2011b: 201) reveal lexically conditioned resistance to the spread of strong post-verbal pronouns, in particular in imperatives with *laisser* 'leave', to the extent that occurrences of *laissier m'ester* 'leave me be!' are found as late as the fourteenth century. This appears more typical of the diffusion of a new morphological variant rather than showing an underlying prosodic difference.

2.4.4 Summary

The preceding discussion has shown that two puzzles of early GR pronominal morphology can be accounted for by assuming a synchronic prosodic system in which all function words are free clitics. EAPs are created by regular sound change in the pre-textual period and are lexicalized by early GR, with developments in the later *Alexis* text suggesting that lexicalized host plus EAP combinations themselves develop into free clitics. Stress shift onto post-verbal pronouns, on the other hand, is a more recent development, which at least in its initial stage can be accounted for by assuming that post-verbal pronouns are free clitics which are exceptionally parsed as prosodic words due to their phonological phrase-final position.

2.5 Final remarks

By considering the status of the proclisis and enclisis of pronouns and articles (Section 2.4) in the light of the prosodic system and the productive sandhi processes attested in the earliest GR texts (Sections 2.2 and 2.3), I have been able to distinguish morphologized forms resulting from formerly active prosodic processes from the effects of synchronically active prosodic rules in early GR. While all GR varieties show similar developments, in particular the morphologization of enclitic forms and the prosodization of function words as free proclitics, there are nevertheless important and systematic differences between the earliest texts.

Methodologically, the present contribution has endeavoured to chart a middle way between the disciplines of linguistics and philology, bridging the gap between previous work with a strong descriptive focus and approaches which focus on developing a formal analysis based on selected examples. The richly annotated diplomatic transcriptions of the texts prepared for the OGR corpus were essential in achieving in this goal, as they exclude all forms 'corrected' by modern editors and retain a record of the manuscript word division, both of which are lost in other electronic corpora based only on critical editions. Yet this level of philological fidelity reveals a number of interesting details which pass unnoticed in previous studies, for example the fact that word-initial ⟨ss⟩ spellings are in fact found only where two words are agglutinated in the manuscript (Section 2.3.5), or that acute accents in the *Boeci* text mark stressed syllables, which in turn provides direct evidence that the post-verbal pronoun ⟨ént⟩ in (31) is stressed. With the approach adopted in the chapter, I hope to have confirmed 'the value of a strongly philological approach towards linguistics' (Adamson and Ayres-Bennett 2011: 205) in providing new insights into old puzzles, and through the continued development of the OGR corpus, I hope to make the data necessary for philologically informed work on early GR accessible in a form fit for the twenty-first century.

3
The grammar(s) of reported discourse in medieval French literature

Sophie Marnette

3.1 Introduction

The inscription of speech and thought presentation (S&TP) within medieval French narratives is a function of, amongst other things, the texts' medium (prose/verse), their literary genre, and the gender and status of the quoting and quoted locutors. Linguistically speaking, this affects the types and categories of S&TP used, as well as their length, their frequency, and the way they are introduced. The study of these factors investigates what can be thought of as the macro-grammar of reported discourse.

In addition, one can also study the micro-grammar of reported discourse by considering whether the morphology, the syntax, or the pragmatics of the quoted discourse (i.e. the characters' speech), differ from those of the quoting frame (i.e. the narrator's discourse). Without naively assuming that direct speech quoted in medieval literary narratives gives us direct access to the actual spoken vernacular(s) of the time, it is relevant to examine whether its grammar (e.g. word order, use of discourse markers, subject pronouns, tenses, etc.) varies significantly from the narrative part of the text. Similarly, it has been argued that these variations could be identified in the speech represented in the dialogues of theatre plays. This line of inquiry has been recently explored—mostly by French-speaking scholars—under the catch-all phrase of 'français oral représenté des textes littéraires médiévaux' following Christiane Marchello-Nizia's seminal article of 2012.[1] It has been facilitated by the development of databases that distinguish between the narrative part of literary text and the characters' direct speeches, and by new electronic corpora of medieval drama.

This chapter ties in narratological, stylistic, and linguistic insights from my own research and from recent developments in the study of *français oral représenté* to

---

[1] Marchello-Nizia (2012). See also Guillot et al. (2013); Rodríguez Somolinos (2013, 2016, 2018); Guillot, Prévost, and Lavrentiev (2014); Marchello-Nizia (2014a, b, 2017); Guillot et al. (2015); Guillot-Barbance, Pincemin, and Lavrentiev (2017); Glikman and Schneider (2018); Guillot-Barbance et al. (2018); Oppermann-Marsaux (2018); Parussa (2018); Sauwala (2018); Mazziotta and Glikman (2019); Vermander (2019, 2020); Lefeuvre and Parussa (2020); Marchello-Nizia et al. (2020).

Sophie Marnette, *The grammar(s) of reported discourse in medieval French literature*. In: *Historical and Sociolinguistic Approaches to French*. Edited by: Janice Carruthers, Mairi McLaughlin, and Olivia Walsh, Oxford University Press.
© Sophie Marnette (2024). DOI: 10.1093/oso/9780192894366.003.0003

offer an innovative global approach to the macro- and micro-grammar(s) of S&TP, highlighting in particular their intra- and intertextual variation, i.e. the fact that different grammars can compete within the same text (intratextual variation) and across textual genres (intertextual variation). The macro-grammar(s) of S&TP will be explored both in terms of the form and functions of reported discourses and of their framing (i.e. insertion) within the texts, while the micro-grammar(s) will be investigated both in terms of stable characteristics linked to the interactional quality of oral discourse and in terms of the spoken language's aptitude for linguistic innovation. The examples used here are mostly taken from a corpus of two digital editions of the *Histoire ancienne jusqu'à César*, an early thirteenth-century prose text, in a database recently developed by the European Research Council-funded project 'The Values of French' (TVOF).[2]

This study of S&TP at a macro- and micro-level thus ties together our understanding of medieval literary genres with that of the evolution of the French language while also bringing to the fore recent research on French language and literature that has so far mainly been available in French but not in English.[3]

3.2 S&TP categories

For the purpose of this chapter, the term 'reported discourse' will be used interchangeably with S&TP. The word 'discourse' will encompass both speech and thought (Marnette 2005: 49–63) and will be used both as a generic noun to refer to the process of reporting discourse and as a count noun to refer to particular occurrences. I will focus on the three main categories of S&TP while acknowledging that there also exist more hybrid categories on a continuum going from the narrator's discourse to the character's discourse.[4]

---

[2] See 'The Values of French Language and Literature in the European Middle Ages', https://tvof.ac.uk (accessed 4 July 2022). The project offers online searchable semi-diplomatic transcriptions and interpretive editions of the two most important manuscript witnesses of the text: Paris, Bibliothèque nationale de France, ms f. fr. 20125 (c. 1270) and London, British Library, Royal ms 20 D I (c. 1330).

[3] There are some publications in English on the representation in writing of early spoken Romance (including French), especially in the book *Historical Dialogue Analysis* edited by A. H. Jucker, G. Fritz, and F. Lebsanft in 1999 (see in particular contributions by Lebsanft, Koch, and Schrott). In their introduction, they offer a very helpful outline of the research traditions in the fields of Romance, German, and English linguistics that have been instrumental in the current interest in historical dialogue analysis, with an extensive bibliography. In addition, for recent research on the representation of oral language in late medieval and—mostly—early modern English texts, see amongst others: Kytö and Walker (2006, 2020); Walker (2007); Culpeper and Kytö (2010); Hernández-Campoy and Conde-Silvestre (2012a: 110–12, 158–9, 239–40). For an up-to-date discussion of speech representation in the history of English, see Grund and Walker (2021).

[4] I have shown that the study of unusual but overlooked phenomena such as 'indirect discourse without *que*' and 'direct discourse with *que*' (occurring both in medieval French and in Modern French) is essential for an in-depth comprehension of reported discourse categories in general (Marnette 2005: 182–8). This notably calls into question traditional definitions that distinguish indirect discourse from direct discourse purely based on the presence of subordination markers.

In direct discourse, the reporting speaker evokes the original speech/thought situation and conveys, or rather claims to convey, the exact words or ideas of the original locutor.[5] The pronouns, tenses, and deictic words of the original discourse are not transposed (1).

(1) Eneas sist jouste le roi et parla devant tous: 'Sire—dist il—**pour quoi doit on souffrir que cil nous die en present vilennie et outrage?...**' Dyomedés li respondi: 'Sire—dist il—**bien savés vostre raison conter et de ce devés estre liés;...**' Puis a dit Ulixés a Dyomedés: '**Sire, laissiés cel plait ester.**' (*Histoire ancienne* ms 20 D I §178.4–9; direct discourse in bold)

'Eneas was sitting next to the king and he spoke in front of all: "**Lord**—he said—**why must we suffer that this one should tell us in our presence obnoxious and outrageous words?...**" Dyomedés answered him: "**Lord**—he said—**you know well how to tell your tale and you must be happy about that...**" Then Ulixés said to Dyomedés: "**Lord, let this matter be.**"'

In indirect discourse, the reporting speaker transposes the original utterance into their own words. The reported discourse is subordinated to a reporting verb and is introduced by a subordinating conjunction (e.g. *que* 'that'). The pronouns, tenses, and deictics of the reported discourse are switched to the reporting situation of enunciation. Indirect discourse can also be expressed in an infinitival clause with or without a preposition. The conjunction of subordination is not always expressed, especially in verse (i.e. like English, Old French allowed for sentences such as 'he said he would come' as well as 'he said that he would come' while Modern French generally only accepts the latter).[6] Moreover, since in Old French literature, the story is often partly told in tenses linked to the present (indicative

---

[5] The term 'original' should not be interpreted as 'real' and 'anterior': reported discourse whether direct or indirect can refer to a future (and thus hypothetical discourse) and it can also summarize several discourses at once.

[6] See Marnette (1998: 115–16, 2001: 297–304, 2005: 180–8, 2013a: 301–4). In some cases, when the *verbum dicendi* can be used without a completive clause, one can hesitate and interpret a sequence either as indirect discourse without *que* or as an occurrence of narrated discourse followed by free indirect discourse:

S'il les trove, molt les MENACE
Ne laira pas ne lor mesface. (Béroul, *Le Roman de Tristan*, lines 1949–50)
'Were he to find them, he THREATENS them: *he will not fail to kill them.*'

There are also rare cases of what I call 'neutral discourse' where there is no difference between direct discourse and indirect discourse because the pronouns and tenses would be the same in both; for example, in *Mahomet jurent vengement en ert pris*, which could be edited as *Mahomet jurent: 'Vengemement en ert pris!'* ('By Mohammed they swear vengeance will be had', *La Prise d'Orange*, ms CE, line 1196).

present, present perfect, and future), indirect discourse can retain these tenses instead of using the past (Fleischman 1990), as it does in example (2):[7]

(2) Et li roys Edupus demena grant dolour, et se plaint et guemente et dist <u>que trop est mauvese sa vie</u>. (*Histoire ancienne* ms 20 D I §10.10; indirect discourse underlined)

'And king Edupus showed great sorrow, and he complains and laments and he said <u>that his life is too awful.</u>'

Free indirect discourse is characterized by the presence of features of direct discourse (direct questions, exclamations, deictics, colloquialisms, etc.) reported in the fashion of indirect discourse, i.e. with shifted pronouns and tenses but without being syntactically dependent on a reporting clause (i.e. without being directly subordinated to a *verbum dicendi* or *sentiendi* and without being co-ordinated to a previous reported clause).[8] Free indirect discourse does not always follow indirect discourse but can appear on its own and there are cases where the free indirect discourse does follow indirect discourse but is not semantically or syntactically subordinated to its *verbum dicendi* as in examples (3) and (4):

(3) Lors comencierent entr'aus a dire <u>c'or avoient il menti a Jacob lor pere cui il orent en convent qu'il sauf et en vie li ramenroient</u>; *mes ne feroient ja mes*, ce disoient, *quar il ne porroient.* (*Histoire ancienne* ms 20125 §327.4; free indirect discourse in italics)

'Then they started to say amongst themselves <u>that they had now lied to their father Jacob with whom they had agreed to bring him back unharmed</u>; *but they would never do that*, they were saying, *because they could not.*'

(4) Por ce manda li rois Anibal a Asdrubal son frere <u>qu'il deguerpist Espaigne, qu'il encontre Scipio le concele ne poroit tenir, et si s'en venist a lui en Itale.</u> *Et adonc quant lor gens seroit assamblee tote, il destruiroient Rome et sousmetroient tote la terre sans demorance a la poesté et a la segnorie de Cartage.* Quant li rois Asdrubal qui estoit en Espaigne oï ces comandamens de son frere le roi Anibal, il se mist sans atargier a la voie ... (*Histoire ancienne* ms 20125 §983.5–7; free indirect discourse in italics)

---

[7] This is of course also the case in Modern spoken French, as opposed to most written press or literary fiction. On tense and indirect discourse in French, see amongst others Bauer (1996) and Landeweerd and Vet (1996).

[8] As with indirect discourse, the tenses of medieval free indirect discourse are not necessarily in the past because the narration itself is partly told in the present tenses. See Marnette (1996, 1998: 116–17, 128–9, 144–51, 1999a: 390–2, 2005). Note also the now classic articles by Cerquiglini (1984); Rychner (1987, 1989, 1990); and Bruña-Cuevas (1988, 1989). For a discussion of the features characteristic of direct discourse but which can be found in free indirect discourse as well, see Tuomarla (1999: 85–95) and Rosier (2008: 78–82).

'For this reason, king Anibal sent for his brother Asdrubal <u>to leave Spain, which he could not hold against the Consul Scipio, and to come to him in Italy</u>. *And then when their people would be assembled, they would destroy Rome and submit all the land, without any delay, to the power and lordship of Carthago.* When king Asdrubal, who was in Spain, heard his brother king Anibal's orders, he set out without delay...'

3.3 The macro-grammar of reported discourse in medieval French

3.3.1 S&TP forms and functions

In previous research,[9] I have shown how what can be called the 'macro-grammar' of reported discourse can enable us to better grasp the elaboration and evolution of medieval literary genres. I examined how the range of functions associated with specific forms of reported discourse could be assembled into a system of particular strategies that determined distinct literary genres (notably *chansons de geste*, verse romances, prose romances, and chronicles) that were subject to change over time.[10] An exhaustive linguistic analysis showed that S&TP strategies affected aspects as diverse as the connection between the narrator and the audience or the apparent control of the narrator over their characters' discourses as well as the representation of notions such as truth or history. This approach thus highlighted the inherent variation of S&TP macro-grammar across textual genres, i.e. what one could call its intertextual variation.

The predominant use of direct discourse in *chansons de geste* is firmly linked to the staged orality of this type of text, in the same vein as the many narratorial addresses to the listeners–readers and the commentaries about the future fate of the characters (prolepses, wishes, questions, imprecations) and about the inherent good or evil of certain characters. The historical events told in the *chansons de geste* are thus re-lived by the community formed by *jongleurs* and their audiences, united behind the battles and the destiny of 'our emperor Charles' and 'our barons'.[11] Direct discourse participates in that feeling of authenticity.

---

[9] This section offers an overview of the main findings of Marnette (2005, 2011, 2013a, b, 2016, 2018) with regard to forms and functions of S&TP across medieval literary genres.

[10] Marnette (2005, 2013a) uses thirty-nine texts: eight *chansons de geste* (epics in decasyllabic verses), three *vies de saint* (hagiographical narratives in decasyllabic verses), nine verse romances (octosyllabic verses), nine prose romances, nine prose chronicles (historical narratives), and one *chantefable* (text alternating paragraphs in verse and in prose).

[11] The fact that these events are actually mostly fictional is irrelevant here because what makes them historical and true is that they are presented as such by the story and experienced as such by the audience. Similarly, I will not be discussing whether the events presented in the chronicles are historically true in the modern sense of the term. What is of interest is that they are presented as true by the narrative.

In chronicles, history is not re-lived but put at a distance, a difference which is clearly illustrated through their use of reported discourse. Not only do they generally employ fewer reported discourses than other genres, they also largely prefer indirect discourse to direct discourse lest the chroniclers give the impression that they could really remember everything that was said and how it was said, or that they could reconstruct some things they did not hear themselves. Interestingly, although some romances go to great lengths to present themselves as 'estoires' or 'chronicles', they easily betray that pretence through their use of reported discourse. Indeed, far from preferring indirect discourse as real chronicles do, they tend to employ direct discourse, thus giving the story psychological realism if not historical truth.

Verse and prose romances both use more indirect discourses than *chansons de geste* but fewer than chronicles do. This might be explained by the omnipotence and omnipresence of the narrative voice, be it the first-person narrator in verse romances or an impersonal narrative voice such as 'le conte' ('the tale') in prose romances, since the characters' words are thus transposed within the narrative discourse. Moreover, a substantial number of these indirect (and free indirect) discourses are reporting thoughts and not speech, which is also very different from *chansons de geste*. What is at stake is the personal development of the main characters, notably through the emergence and evolution of their love. Prose romances tend to propose a historical and/or religious truth that relies on clearly identifiable discourses and allows (in principle) for only one point of view, that of the narrative voice, to which the characters' discourses are clearly subordinated (hence the strong marking of reported discourses, the rarity of free direct discourse and free indirect discourse, etc.). Verse romances present truth as based on the verisimilitude of the events told and rely on the compositional skills of the author and on the way they describe feelings and situations that are coherent with the expectations of the genre. For example, the use of free indirect discourse allows the narrator to blur the boundaries between their discourse and that of the characters, also allowing for some ambiguity as to who is speaking (or thinking).

Further research carried out on a large corpus of lays and fabliaux ranging from the twelfth to the fourteenth century also allowed me to identify broad trends regarding the macro-grammar of reported discourse in these two literary genres.[12] In particular, I examined how female characters' discourse was framed and how it was expressed with the aim to assess whether female expression differed between the two genres and whether it was related to the specific ideologies that underlie each of them, therefore shedding new light on the inscription of lays and fabliaux in their respective literary horizons. This approach unearthed variation both

---

[12] The corpus includes thirty-two lays and sixty-two fabliaux. For a description of the corpus and the results of my research on S&TP in lays and fabliaux, see Marnette (2011, 2013b, 2016, 2018). It is important to note that the general trends identified can vary substantially from text to text (see Marnette 2022).

within texts (i.e. between male and female S&TP) and across textual genres (i.e. between S&TP presentation in lays and fabliaux). This meant that the variation in the macro-grammar(s) of S&TP was both intra- and intertextual.

Both fabliaux and lays are set in a hierarchical patriarchal world where male characters—and their social status—are usually introduced before female characters, whatever their relative importance in the narrative is. On average, the fabliaux devote more space to their characters' S&TP than the lays, and in particular more space to direct discourse, possibly because the core of their stories centres around witty characters (clever young men or sharp female adulteresses) tricking other unsuspecting characters (naïve young women or dim jealous husbands) through their lies and distortion of reality. In the fabliaux, the roles men and women play in the story (i.e. as trickster and/or tricked victim) tend to constrain reported discourse relatively more than their gender, so what appears to be marked is the content of reported discourse (lies, desire, crude words) rather than their length, frequency, or category. While the narrators' judgements (and especially their criticism of women) appear to retain a veneer of decency and morality for their stories, ultimately the characters' discourses, offered directly, would seem to probe the audience to call social hierarchies into question, including in some cases those of gender.

Lays tend to give less importance to their characters' speech and therefore more to the adventures happening to them (magical feats, love encounters, etc.), while also using on average more indirect discourse and free indirect discourse, therefore integrating the characters' discourse within the narrator's (especially in the *Lais de Marie*).[13] In the lays, as opposed to the fabliaux, women consistently speak less often and more briefly than men, but their speech is more likely to be reported in direct discourse, that is, non-transposed discourse (vs. indirect and free indirect discourse, i.e. transposed discourse, for men). In the lays, female discourse is thus rarer but more salient. It is therefore both directly staged and problematized, just as the very origin of the lays is both staged (often in the prologues and epilogues) and problematized, especially in the lays that are presented as originating from female protagonists and/or authors, such as Marie de France.

Furthermore, the study of individual texts that hover on the boundaries between lays and fabliaux has shed light on the possibility for authors to subtly mix reported discourse strategies linked to two or more genres in order to play with their readers' expectations. For example, this is the case for the *Lai d'Ignaure*, an early-thirteenth-century short verse narrative that calls itself a lay but contains features that strongly remind us of fabliaux, mainly the use of uncouth elements and/or the ridiculing of some characters, despite its courtly setting. A close linguistic and narratological analysis shows how the narrator's framing and reporting

---

[13] The title *Lais de Marie* refers to the twelve lays present in ms Harley 978. For a closer discussion of my views on Marie de France, see Marnette (2013b: 23–5, 2016: 100–1).

of their characters' gendered discourses can both help and hinder the listener–readers to adjust their expectations with regard to this rather atypical narrative, thereby interweaving the notions of gender and genre, and cautioning against modern attempts to classify medieval texts into distinct literary genres (Marnette 2022). This combination of two (or more) macro-grammar(s) thus illustrates instances of intratextual variation.

3.3.2 S&TP framing

Apart from Cerquiglini (1981) and Marnette (1998, 1999a, b, 2006a, b), relatively little was published on the grammar of the insertion of reported discourse in medieval texts until more recent work by Christiane Marchello-Nizia and her team on *oral représenté* (OR), which will be discussed in Section 3.4.[14] This grammar, or system, of insertion is indeed crucial to understand at a macro-level if we want to accurately identify reported discourses (and in the case of *oral représenté*, in particular, direct discourses) in order to scrutinize their morphology and syntax at a micro-level.

In Marnette (2006a, b), I argued that the signalling of reported discourse in medieval French reflected the specificity of literary texts during that period, i.e. that the macro-grammar of S&TP insertion varied intertextually.[15] Verse texts—especially the oldest ones—were connected to an oral tradition (in terms of composition and/or transmission and/or performance) but we now access them via manuscripts that combine markers of orality with markers of scripturality, in what were the first efforts to put the vernacular language, rather than Latin, into writing. The first prose texts which appeared in the thirteenth century were neither sung (like the epic *chansons de geste* or lyric poetry) nor recited aloud (like some lays, fabliaux, or possibly romances), but they were still most likely to be read aloud for an audience rather than read silently and individually (a practice that generalized from the fourteenth century onwards). Thus, in both cases, the transition between quoting discourse and quoted discourse had to be marked both for the listener(s) and for the person reading the text aloud. Morphological, syntactic, and lexical markers played on both levels as shown in the use of subordination markers (e.g. conjunctions *que*, *si*, etc. in indirect discourse), shifters (e.g. personal pronouns, verb endings, verb tenses, and spatio-temporal deictics are not transposed in the case of direct discourse), moods (e.g. use of subjunctive after verbs of opinion in indirect discourse), word order and modalization (e.g. interrogation, commands, wishes, exclamations, etc. in direct discourse), terms of address (titles and names often front segments in direct discourse), and *verba dicendi*

---

[14] The recently published *Grande grammaire historique du français* devotes a section to 'discours représenté' (Marchello-Nizia et al. 2020: 1702–28), which does refer to Marnette (1998).
[15] While Marnette (2006a, b) focused mostly on the insertion of direct discourse, attention was also paid to indirect discourse in Marnette (2001) and free indirect discourse in Marnette (1996).

and *sentiendi* (e.g. use of *inquit* formula in direct and free indirect discourse). There was also additional marking at the oral level via prosody and changes in the performer or the reader's voices and at the scriptural level via punctuation and typography. While quotation marks only appeared much later with the development of printing, direct discourse could be signalled through the use of capitals and/or the presence of commas, inverted commas, or full stops at the start or the end of the segment but this varied across time and across manuscripts. In some manuscripts, the name of the character speaking could also be mentioned in the left margin.[16]

Some literary genres such as *chansons de geste* and prose romances did tend to introduce direct discourse quite rigidly, often with *verba dicendi* or *sentiendi* preceding a segment in direct discourse (which Cerquiglini (1981) calls 'prolepse') and/or inserted within it or after it ('analepse' for Cerquiglini (1981)). Verse romances were more flexible and more likely than other genres not to use any *verba dicendi* (free direct discourse), especially within dialogues. Verse romances and lays also tended to allow for a smooth relaxation of the narrator's control where indirect discourse evolved into free indirect discourse and/or direct discourse.

To study the signalling of reported discourse, it is important not to limit oneself to the transitions between the quoting discourse of the narrator and the quoted discourse(s) of the characters but also to look at the transitions from one quoted discourse to another, i.e. within dialogues.[17] This was duly noted by Bernard Cerquiglini (1981: 22) in his seminal book, *La Parole médiévale*, which compared the insertion of reported discourse in verse and prose by focusing on the thirteenth-century prose transpositions of Robert de Boron's *Estoire du Graal*.[18] In romances, for example, indirect discourse often fronted dialogues (see example (5) below) contrary to *chansons de geste* where indirect discourse is relatively rare (Marnette 2006b: 36).[19]

(5) Herculés parla et dist <u>que bon consoil avoit donné li rois</u>: '**Faisons armer de nos gens une partie et s'en aille vers Troie, et l'autre demeure a la navie.**'
(*Histoire ancienne* ms Royal D I §180.1)

'Herculés spoke and said <u>that the king had given a good advice</u>. "**Let's arm one part of our people and let them go to Troy, and let the other part stay on the ship.**"'

As we have seen, the forms, functions, frequency, and the framing of S&TP, i.e. the macro-grammar(s) of reported discourse, can vary both intertextually across

---

[16] For example, in the *Roman de la Rose* (see Huot 1987: 90–5, 339–42) or in the *Roman de Jehan de Saintré* (see Marnette 2006b: 44–5).

[17] It is also possible to study how characters quote other characters or themselves (see Marnette 1999a).

[18] He showed amongst other things that the insertion of reported discourse within the narrative was much more constrained in the prose versions of the text than the verse one.

[19] For more on dialogues, see Denoyelle (2013, 2016).

texts[20] and across literary genres as well as intratextually within texts, for example in terms of the gender and status of the quoting and quoted locutors or in terms of the narratorial and/or gendered S&TP strategies within specific narratives. These types of variation will also be found at the level of micro-grammar.

3.4 Toward a micro-grammar of reported discourse in medieval French

3.4.1 Linguistic developments towards the notion of *français oral représenté*

The development of new technologies in the second half of the twentieth century allowed for substantial progress in linguistic research, notably in facilitating the study of the grammar of spoken languages, which could now be recorded, transcribed, and compared across time as computers made it easier to analyse much bigger corpora. This brought linguists such as Claire Blanche-Benveniste and her team in Aix-en-Provence to submit that there was a specific grammar of spoken French.[21] It also allowed linguists to better observe real change in progress versus apparent-time change (Labov 1994). For Modern spoken French for example, it was possible to confirm that the dropping of the particle 'ne' in negation (e.g. '(ne) . . . pas') was not only a difference occurring amongst generations (with young people dropping the particle more than older ones) but also a real change in progress as the comparison of corpora across time showed that the same speakers kept dropping the particle as they grew older, therefore showing a change in real time rather than change in apparent time (Ashby 1976, 1981, 1991, 2001; Marchello-Nizia et al. 2020: 1475). This helped strengthen the view that spoken language is the most fertile ground for change and innovations.[22]

In medieval French, too, the advent of computers allowed for the gathering of larger corpora of texts and permitted broader statistical analysis of linguistic features and their evolution across time, for example the evolution of word order from Old French to Middle French or the evolution of personal pronouns. The *Base de*

---

[20] In terms of variation across texts within the same literary genre, I mentioned differences across lays in Section 3.3.1. Cerquiglini (1981) and Marnette (1998) also showed that the study of S&TP strategies could show how genres evolved by pinpointing the differences in the use of reported discourses between earlier verse and later prose versions of Robert de Boron's *Estoire du Graal*. Similarly, Marnette (2005: 198–202) highlighted important evolutions in the use of reported discourse strategies in prose chronicles from the thirteenth to the fifteenth century.

[21] Blanche-Beveniste and Jeanjean (1987); Blanche-Beveniste (1997); Marchello-Nizia et al. (2020: 1466–79). It is important to note that what is suggested is not a pure dichotomy between spoken and written language but rather a continuum (Marchello-Nizia et al. 2020: 1466). See also Jucker, Fritz, and Lebsanft (1999); Carruthers (2006).

[22] It is also recognized, however, that some characteristics might have been oral for a long time (Marchello-Nizia et al. 2020: 1468–9).

français médiéval (BFM) corpus developed at the École normale supérieure in Lyon was seminal for these studies as were the databases developed for the *Dictionnaire du moyen français* (DMF) at the Université de Lorraine in Nancy and the Amsterdam corpus gathered in the 1980s by Anthonij Dees and his team (Vrije Universiteit Amsterdam), which led to the *Atlas des formes linguistiques des textes littéraires de l'ancien français* (Dees 1987).[23]

In parallel to these developments, there also developed new approaches to reported discourse that were firmly linked to discourse pragmatics and based on the French enunciation theory, which submits that the utterances (*énoncés*) of a discourse inevitably contain traces of the locutionary activity (*énonciation*) that produced them, the context in which they were produced, and the subjectivity of the producer.[24] Inspired by the theories of Bakhtin, Bally, Benveniste, and Ducrot, scholars now viewed the study of reported discourse both on a continuum allowing for the diversity of its forms and functions, and in context, i.e. not only through the study of nineteenth-century French novels but encompassing, for example, the study of medieval French, the modern press, or spoken French, through the use of electronic corpora. This has been particularly well-embedded in the research developed by the international interdisciplinary Ci-dit research group, founded in 2001 by Juan Manuel López-Muñoz, Sophie Marnette, and Laurence Rosier. A significant part of Ci-dit's research explores reported discourse in medieval French.[25]

The new spotlight on the grammar of spoken language, the advent of electronic databases and a better understanding of reported discourse helped bring about the notion of *français oral représenté* which is discussed in the next sections.[26]

---

[23] The BFM (http://bfm.ens-lyon.fr/spip.php?article 3390 (accessed 4 July 2022)) was started in 1989 by Christiane Marchello-Nizia and currently includes 170 texts which originally were mostly literary texts from the twelfth and thirteenth centuries but which now cover the earliest texts (ninth century) and also later ones (fourteenth and fifteenth centuries), including non-literary texts. The corpus mostly includes edited texts, not transcriptions, and does not refer to manuscript variants. It is lemmatized and tagged for parts of speech and morphosyntactic features. In March 2008, as part of the expansion of the corpus to include earlier texts, it was decided to tag it in a way that would differentiate between the narrative parts of the texts and the parts that are in direct discourse. The DMF (www.atilf.fr/dmf (accessed 4 July 2022)) is an electronic dictionary for fourteenth- and fifteenth-century French, which was developed in the 1980s and is now in its sixth version, being an evolutive dictionary. The *Corpus d'Amsterdam* has evolved into the *Nouveau Corpus d'Amsterdam* (NCA) which was edited (revised and lemmatized) by Pierre Kunstmann and Achim Stein (https://sites.google.com/site/achimstein/research/resources/nca (accessed 4 July 2022)).

[24] In the field of medieval French, this interest in enunciation theories was specifically developed by scholars such as Bernard Cerquiglini, Suzanne Fleischman, Christiane Marchello-Nizia, and Michèle Perret.

[25] López-Muñoz (1994–5, 1997, 1999, 2002); Marnette (1996, 1998, 1999a, b, 2005, 2006a, b, 2011, 2013a, b, 2016, 2018, 2022); Denoyelle (2013).

[26] For another introduction to the development of studies of *français oral représenté*, see the preface of the thematic issue of the journal *Langages* on 'L'Oral représenté en diachronie et en synchronie: une voie d'accès à l'oral spontané?' (Lefeuvre and Parussa 2020). Wendy Ayres-Bennett has shown interest in OR in seventeenth-century texts (Ayres-Bennett 2004) and is the author of the section on the syntax of spoken French in the *Grande grammaire historique du français* (Marchello-Nizia et al. 2020: 1466–79). See also Jucker, Fritz, and Lebsanft (1999).

3.4.2 The notion of *français oral représenté*

The language of medieval literary texts could not possibly be equated to the spoken vernacular dialects,[27] mostly because they were written in supralocal *scriptae* that were probably somewhat remote from actual speech but also because until the beginning of the thirteenth century, most texts were composed in verse.

This is not to say, however, that an oral dimension was absent from the texts. First, orality could play an important role in the composition, transmission, and performance of vernacular texts. This could be reflected in the storytellers' mixing of tenses typical of oral storytelling where the present is used to foreground events and past tenses are used for background elements, in addition to narratorial addresses to the audience or comments on the performance of the narrative in most verse texts.[28] Up until the fourteenth century, when individual silent reading developed, audiences were most likely to experience texts orally, even the prose ones, which would be read aloud.[29] Guillot-Barbance, Pincemin, and Lavrentiev (2017) have shown that the traits [+ orality] and [- orality] can be polarized in some genres—with short narratives, theatre plays, and lyric poems particularly showing oral traits—while other genres are more flexible. There is thus a certain amount of variation across textual genres, i.e. intertextual variation, to use Donaldson's (2014: 327) term.

Moreover, whether or not they were composed, transmitted, or performed orally, medieval texts did represent their characters' oral speech either via direct discourses in narratives or within dialogues in theatrical plays. Christiane Marchello-Nizia argues that in doing so, texts did more than simply signal these discourses via the use of reporting verbs, the non-transposition of pronouns and verb endings, the use of terms of address, etc.; these representations of orality, which she coined 'français oral représenté', exhibited an altogether different grammar from that of the narrative parts of the texts into which they were inserted.[30] This is what I have called the 'micro-grammar' of reported discourse, to distinguish it from the 'macro-grammar' of its forms and functions at the textual level. This variation is thus intratextual as different grammars compete within the same text (Donaldson 2014: 319).

Research on the micro-grammar of *oral représenté* (OR) has been made possible by the development of corpora such as the BFM, which allow for the parts

---

[27] See Chapter 1, footnote 54, this volume.

[28] Fleischman (1990: 10); Marnette (1998); Carruthers and Marnette (2007); Marchello-Nizia et al. (2020: 1466, 1489–91).

[29] Accordingly, while Old French syntax tended to be more thematically structured (i.e. Thematic referent—Verb second), which is typical of spoken language, Middle French syntax became more complex and argumentative, a change possibly due both to the switch to silent reading and to the heavier influence of Latin as an increasing number of religious and scientific texts were translated into the vernacular (Marchello-Nizia et al. 2020: 1739–44).

[30] Marchello-Nizia (2012, 2014a, b); Guillot-Barbance, Pincemin, and Lavrentiev (2017: 54–5).

in direct discourse to be linguistically tagged and then to be compared with the morphology and syntax of the narrative parts of the texts they are embedded in.[31] Another important corpus of OR is that of the *CoDiF* database, gathered by Gabriella Parussa and Florence Lefeuvre, which mainly includes theatre dialogues plus some didactic dialogues and legal documents like the transcripts of Joan of Arc's trial.[32] Similarly, Ingham (2016) compares two Anglo-Norman corpora: (i) year books, including much dialogic interaction in court hearings on the part of prosecution and defence attorneys and judges, thus illustrating features of spoken language, such as exchange pairs and turn-taking, as well as interpersonal language characteristics more generally; (ii) petitions to the English Crown (late thirteenth- to early fifteenth-century) clearly belonging to a written medium genre. In an unrelated article, Vermander (2019) highlights the relevance of legal documents such as charters, civil and criminal registers, letters of remission, trial transcripts, etc. for the study of OR because of the segments in direct discourse that they contain. Accordingly, Dourdy and Spacagno (2020) study a large corpus of trial transcripts, including Joan of Arc's trial (also included in *CoDiF*) and explain how the spoken words undergo a process of codification to be transcribed into official documents (for example through the use of indirect discourse instead of direct discourse) while still retaining traces of their original orality (especially when a witness quotes previous speech in direct discourse).

In addition, the development of exhaustive corpora of OR has influenced the way significant new editorial projects are being developed. This is the case for 'The Values of French Language and Literature in the European Middle Ages'

---

[31] See Guillot et al. (2013, 2015) for the description of how the BFM corpus was tagged for direct discourse in narrative texts and for dialogues in theatre plays and didactic dialogues. Guillot-Barbance et al. (2018), also working on the BFM corpus, explain how they identify sequences of OR, following Marchello-Nizia (2012: 248):

> 'L'épisode d'oral représenté (OR) se définit comme une séquence discursive se donnant comme une restitution à l'écrit de paroles prononcées oralement. Elle se compose d'une ou de plusieurs prises de parole (PP) qui s'enchaînent et qui constituent les unités internes de l'épisode. Dans la définition que nous adoptons ici, l'épisode d'oral représenté comprend également les éléments qui en précisent les limites externes et les articulations internes et que nous appellerons, à la suite de Marchello-Nizia, l'annonce, le rappel et l'incise'
> (Guillot-Barbance et al. 2018: 280)

Marchello-Nizia (2012: 260) notes that the morphosyntax of sequences introducing the direct discourse tends to present some similarities with that of OR, hence her decision to see OR 'épisodes' as integrating these sequences. For example, the *verba dicendi* tend to be in the present tense rather than in the past tense, a trend also noted within direct discourse. However, note that, in practice, it is unlikely that the sequence introducing the direct discourse (i.e. including a *verbum dicendi* or *sentiendi*), and the *inquit formulae*, are counted as part of OR in the actual corpus because the identification of segments in direct discourse is done via the tagging of quotation marks in the modern editions of the medieval texts. This would also not be the case for the element called 'rappel', i.e. the brief reference to the speech/thought event, which comes just after the direct discourse and signals the switch back to the narrator's discourse, with associated shift in persons and deictics.

[32] The corpus 'Oral représenté: Base de données CoDiF' currently includes 700,000 words. See Parussa (2018) for a description.

project co-led by Simon Gaunt and Simone Ventura which developed a rich corpus of two digital editions, and a further three fully aligned manuscripts of the *Histoire ancienne jusqu'à César*, an early thirteenth-century prose text.[33] This new database excitingly offers the unique possibility of comparing several versions of the same text while distinguishing between narrative segments, direct discourse segments, and indirect discourse segments, which allows researchers to take into account further fine-grained linguistic variation at the level of both macro- and micro-grammar. Since the versions were composed within a relatively short span of time (one or two centuries), it might therefore be possible to spot small linguistic changes that would otherwise not be spotted across different texts and across a longer time horizon.

Following Christiane Marchello-Nizia's seminal article of 2012, a number of studies relating to OR were gradually published in a series of significant collections of articles or special issues of journals, often as results of the yearly Diachro conferences and seminars, and of the biannual congresses organized by the Société internationale de diachronie du français, notably under the aegis of Wendy Ayres-Bennett.[34]

The next two sections (Sections 3.4.3 and 3.4.4) give an overview of recent research exploring the grammar(s) of OR. I will focus first on what can be seen as stable oral features linked to the interactional nature of direct discourse in narratives and dramatic dialogues, and second on what can be seen as innovations linked to spoken language. I will include studies on dramatic dialogues in this overview as many researchers do rightly see them as constituting OR, but it should be noted that they are not what would ordinarily be called reported discourse, even though they are—like reported discourse—formally framed within the text as speech presentation, with clear indications of the characters' names, and they are distinguished from the author's stage directions.

In short, studying variation at the micro-level of reported discourse (i.e. via the grammar(s) of OR) continues to develop our understanding of the variation of literary genres in synchrony and diachrony, while also opening a precious window on the variation and evolution of the French language in the short and long diachrony.

3.4.3 OR, stable oral features, and intertextual variation

This section concentrates on the stable oral features of OR, cross-referencing a series of publications between 2013 and now, which used different corpora but showed consistent variations across literary genres.

---

[33] https://tvof.ac.uk (accessed 4 July 2022).
[34] https://diachronie.org/ (accessed 4 July 2022). See Rodríguez Somolinos (2013, 2016); Ayres-Bennett and Rainsford (2014).

In a preliminary study of nine texts from the BFM, Guillot et al. (2013) have shown that the segments in direct discourse identified as OR in their corpus exhibited features different from non-direct discourse segments. Their study was expanded in a larger corpus of seventy-eight texts by Guillot et al. (2015) with the same methodology. Both studies found that the proportion of interrogative markers (pronouns, adjectives, and adverbs) and interjections was higher in OR and so was the proportion of first- and second-person personal pronouns and possessive adjectives with regard to the third person. OR sequences also used proportionally fewer noun phrases compared to the narrative parts of the texts. These findings by Guillot et al. (2013, 2015) can, of course, be linked to the conversational nature of direct discourse segments, which are more likely to refer to the speech participants (locutors and interlocutors) than to third-person referents; in addition, they tend to rely on the speech context more (using pronouns), which possibly explains their lower use of noun phrases. Similarly, Guillot et al. (2013, 2015) noted the high use of the conjunction *et* ('and') in the narrative parts of the text in contrast with the affinity of direct discourse for the conjunctions *car* ('because') and *mes* ('but') as well as for negative adverbs in general, traits that one could link to the more interactive and argumentative nature of dialogues as opposed to narration.

In a smaller-scale study, Mazziotta and Glikman (2019) selected a sample of three very different texts from the BFM to test the relative stability of OR characteristics vs. the narrative parts of these texts.[35] They were able to confirm previous studies, notably in highlighting OR's tendency to use pronominal rather than nominal subjects and to use infinitives with modal auxiliaries (Mazziotta and Glikman 2019: 14).

As Guillot et al. (2013, 2015) and Mazziotta and Glikman (2019) allude to, and as was confirmed by a study by Guillot-Barbance, Pincemin, and Lavrentiev (2017) on a much larger sample of 137 texts from the BFM corpus, the results can vary based on the textual genres under consideration, since some texts might exhibit characteristics close to OR even in their narrative parts, for example texts that make extensive use of comments by the narrator to the listeners–readers.[36] This is related to the complex links between medieval texts and orality already mentioned.

Gabriella Parussa, in a programmatic study of the large *CoDiF corpus*, also notes the ability of OR in theatrical plays to represent oral pronunciation, for example in eliding certain sounds, mimicking foreign accents, or in using the modal future

---

[35] The texts analysed are the *Chanson de Roland* (eleventh-century epic poem), the *Queste del Saint Graal* (thirteenth-century prose romance), and the *Prise de Constantinople* by Robert de Clari (thirteenth-century prose chronicle).

[36] This is confirmed by Glikman and Schneider (2018: 330–2) who studied the syntactic development of French parentheticals such as *je crois* 'I think' and their variation according to different text types. These parentheticals are more present in OR but also in genres privileging narrators' interventions, especially in verse texts. Their corpus included texts from the BFM and the DMF.

(Parussa 2018: 185–91). Similarly, Sauwala (2018: 202–6, 211–13) notes the use of elisions to represent oral speech in the Middle French play, the *Mystère des trois doms*, as well as its characteristic use of colloquial lexicon and insults in particular, some of which do not appear outside of dramatic texts.

Dourdy, Spacagno, and Sauwala (2019) compare the use of discourse markers in medieval trials, mystery plays, *chansons de geste*, and their prose versions (see Section 3.4.4). They too demonstrate that dialogic genres show more variety of discourse markers than epic stories and prose fiction. Moreover, some discourse markers which are closely related to the interactional context could only be found in theatre plays.

Vermander (2020) also relies on a corpus of plays (mainly the *CoDiF*) to explore the dialogic nature of OR, getting his inspiration from the field of conversation analysis. He pays particular attention to the role of discursive markers such as the interjection *Dea!* in indicating turn-taking between speakers, in signalling transitions, or functioning as fillers. The interjection *Dea!* is also studied by Parussa (2020) from a diachronic perspective (in the same thematic issue of *Langages*, see Section 3.4.4).

The above studies clearly show that OR displays some stable features linked to the interactional nature of direct discourse segments and theatrical dialogues while also allowing for intertextual variation, thereby pointing to the existence of several micro-grammars of reported discourse within and across texts.

3.4.4 OR and innovation

While being careful not to equate OR with real spoken language, Marchello-Nizia (2014a, b) suggests that just as actual spoken language is the place where most innovations take place, OR tends to exhibit more innovative features than the narrative parts of the texts:

> Oral has always been affirmed as a place of linguistic change. But for earlier ages the historian of languages is dependent on textual material and especially on written sources: to what extent do these documents reflect oral uses of native speakers? We assume that spoken language has left traces in written texts, and that linguists can have access to such data, by comparing intratextual usage and variations between narrative and 'represented speech' passages, i.e. passages that are designated by the author as delivered orally by the characters; the presence in the same text of narrative and 'speech' allows contrasting them. This approach has shown that a large number of changes could have developed first in the oral use of language.
>
> (Marchello-Nizia 2014a: 471)

Marchello-Nizia's view of OR as innovative is in keeping with findings by scholars in other languages (e.g. Romaine 1982: 152–7 on Middle Scots) or with intuitions from previous linguists working on Old French (e.g. Price 1971: 148). Recent studies have proven her right in showing that the parts where the characters' speeches were represented in direct discourse exhibited more innovative morphological and syntactic features than the rest of the text.[37]

Examples of such innovations at a morphosyntactic level include the use of the partitive article (e.g. *du pain* 'some bread', instead of just *pain*),[38] the use of *ce* as demonstrative modifier instead of *cest/cel* ('this/that'),[39] and the general loss of the nominal case system.[40] Marchello-Nizia (2014a: 481–4, 2014b: 169ff.) notes the creation of new morphological categories when exploring the progressive disappearance of the adverb of intensity *molt* (also spelled as *mout, mult, moult* 'a lot/very'), which could be used with nouns, adverbs, adjectives, and verbs, and its gradual replacement with the intensifier *très* ('very') used only with adjectives or adverbs, and the quantifier/intensifier *beaucoup* ('a lot') used only with nouns and verbs.[41] This evolution is borne out by a cursory look at the TVOF corpus where occurrences of *très* as an alternative to *molt* are more prevalent in the direct discourse segments, especially when modifying adjectives (6), (7).

(6) Dou quel m'esmerveillerai je premiers, o de la droiturete qui est en toi, o de la **tres** grande paine que tu pues soffrir de batailles? (*Histoire ancienne* ms 20125 §631.16)

'What should I first wonder about, either the rectitude that is in you, or the very great pain that you can endure from battles?'

(7) De ce ot Daires **molt** grant paine. (*Histoire ancienne* ms 20125 §730.2)

'Daires suffered very great pain from this.'

These changes entail restrictions on the place of the new intensifiers in the sentence while *molt* was very flexible. They are particularly noticeable in OR and Marchello-Nizia (2014b: 170) submits that the competition of *très* might have originated from its use in direct addresses at the start of direct discourse segments with the adjectives *chier* ('dear'), *doux* ('sweet'), or *bel* ('beautiful') with an affective meaning, a place where *molt* never appeared (8).

(8) Segnor et dames, ce plot **mout** a Tideus, si dist a lui meisme: 'E! Pollinicés, beaus **tres** dous amis, com liés je seroie si tu ravoies ton iretage et fusses sires de ceste grant segnorie!...' (*Histoire ancienne* ms Royal 20125 §433.3)

'Lords and ladies, this pleased Tideus a lot, so he said to himself: "Eh! Pollinicés, fair, sweetest friend, how happy I would be if you recovered your inheritance and were lord of this great land!..."'

---

[37] Marchello-Nizia (2012, 2014a, b, 2017); Marchello-Nizia et al. (2020: 25, 45, 1466–79).
[38] Marchello-Nizia et al. (2020: 986–7).
[39] Ingham (2016: 392–4).
[40] Schøsler (1984, 2001, 2013); Marchello-Nizia et al. (2020: 650).
[41] See also Ingham (2018: 252); Marchello-Nizia et al. (2020: 920–30).

At the syntactic level, one notes the reinforcement of negation, i.e. the addition of *pas, mie,* or *point* to the single negative particle *ne* which could be used on its own in medieval French (9), (10). Donaldson (2018: 222) observes that in the prose *Queste del Saint Graal* (composed *c.* 1225) and *Roman de Cassidorus* (1267), OR shows more reinforced negation in main clauses (64%) than the rest of the narrative (44.2%). In his view, these results bear witness to the presence of competing grammars within the same text (using Kroch 1989).[42]

(9) ... ne je **ne** sai Ø comment tant de rois et de princes seroient ici venu pour partir en tel maniere. (*Histoire ancienne* ms Royal DI §330.1)

'... and I do not know how so many kings and princes would have come here in order to leave in such a way.'

(10) Mes je **ne** sai **pas** comment tant roi et tant prince se honnissent pour lui ensint et perdent leur honneurs. (*Histoire ancienne* ms Royal DI §349.1)

'But I do not know how so many kings and so many princes shame themselves for him in this way and lose their honour.'

OR has also been identified as witnessing a rise in the use of subject pronouns whether personal or impersonal, instead of a null subject,[43] as well as the evolution from the verb second (V2) structure to an emerging Subject–Verb structure (SV) in main declarative clauses (11), (12). In his analysis of intratextual variation between OR and narrative in prose texts, Donaldson (2014) examines the rise of SV in OR and concomitant decline of non-SV orders in sequences of initial subordinate + main declarative, based on the assumption that this context is perhaps the first to reveal V2 loss in Old French.[44]

(11) Quant il bien nos ot ascoutés, il nos respondi mout paisiblement ... (*Histoire ancienne* ms 20125 § 632.8; il= subject, respondi = Verb)

'Once he had listened to us properly, he answered us very peacefully ...'

(12) Quant ce conseil fu donnez, maintenant s'armerent trestuit et deviserent leur gent. (*Histoire ancienne* ms Royal D I §81.1; s'armerent = verb second; trestuit = subject)

'Once this advice was given, immediately they all armed themselves (literally arm themselves they all did) and they allocated their people around.'

---

[42] See also Marchello-Nizia et al. (2020: 1256, 1471).
[43] Price (1971: 148); Vance (1981, cited in Vance 1997: 245); Ingham (2018); Marchello-Nizia et al. (2020: 1067–8).
[44] His corpus includes Villehardouin's *Conquête de Constantinople* (*c.* 1208), the *Queste del Saint Graal* (anonymous, *c.* 1225), the *Roman de Cassidorus* (anonymous, *c.* 1267), and Joinville's *Vie de Saint Louis* (*c.* 1306). The chapter takes into consideration previous studies by Vance (1997) and Steiner (2014).

Evolution in word order also includes the emergence in OR of topicalizing structures through dislocation. Härmä (1993: 721) and Marchello-Nizia (1998: 336) had already noted the presence of these structures in dialogues rather than in the narrative parts of the texts, especially in Middle French. Ingham (2016: 398–403) notes in particular a link between spoken language and the rise of pseudo-clefting (13) or ordinary left dislocation (14) with resumptive *ce* in his Year Books corpus. These are topicalizing structures where the dislocated constituent denotes entities evoked in the prior discourse:

(13) Pseudo-clefting:
Ceo qe chiet en nostre avantage nous le avons nomé.
'What works to our advantage we have specified'
(XXXIV Edw I p. 143 (1306) quoted by Ingham 2016: 401)

(14) Left dislocation:
Departisoun come entre estraunges purchaceours, ceo doune pas eide.
'A division as between strangers who were purchasers, that does not give aid'
(XVII Edw III 45 (1343) quoted by Ingham 2016: 401)

In the *CoDiF* corpus, which is composed mostly of theatrical plays, Parussa (2018: 194–5) also highlights the use of dislocated structures in order to thematize the subject or object as well as the use of structures in *quant à* + noun ('regarding X').[45] She notes that quite a few occurrences are in interrogative clauses.[46]

As already noticed by Zink (1997: 100–3) and Marchello-Nizia (1997 [1979]: 418–19), later studies of OR confirmed that it was more likely to offer innovative examples of direct interrogation without V–S inversion (Dourdy and Spacagno 2020: 129; Opperman-Marsaux 2018: 226–34; Sauwala 2018: 215–16).[47] This is the case even in non-rhetorical questions (contrary to what Zink (1997: 101) thought), and for both total and partial interrogations (i.e. yes–no questions and WH-questions).[48] These studies focus on Middle French and most of their examples of non-inversion are to be found in plays rather than in direct discourse segments inserted in narratives. A look at the TVOF corpus reveals a number of occurrences of non-inversions (15) including with the emerging locution 'est-ce que/qui' (16), (17), which resulted from the grammaticalization of an emphatic *ce* ('this/that'), for example from 'que est **ce** que je vois' ('what is **it** that I see') to 'qu'est-ce que je vois' ('what do I see?').

---

[45] On the emergence of *quant a*, see also Marchello-Nizia (2014b: 172–3).
[46] See also Vermander (2019: 61–2).
[47] See also Marchello-Nizia et al. (2020: 1221–3, 1227, 1476). Note that the normal word order for interrogation would be V–S but that there could also be occurrences with null subject.
[48] Opperman-Marsaux (2018: 226–34) focuses only on total interrogation.

(15) Ce sont [Subject Verb] li gré que je ai deservi que ore me rendés? (*Histoire ancienne* ms Royal D I §458.4)

'These are the good graces that I deserve which you are now giving me back?'

(16) Comment **est ce que** nous i deussons estre hounorez comme gent estrange, et se il fust venus en nostre païs nous l'eussions receu a grant honneur, et il nos congié de son païs si vilainement? (*Histoire ancienne* ms Royal D I §64.2)

'How [is it that] we should be honoured as foreign people, and if he had come to our land, we would have welcome him with great honour and he kicks us out of his land so horridly?'

(17) He! gens d'Itale, quele aventure **est ce qui** vous cours sus? (*Histoire ancienne* ms Royal D I §550.6)

'Eh! People from Italy, which adventure [is it that] comes upon you?'

The structure 'est-ce que' appeared first in partial interrogation, from the thirteenth century onwards, and later in total interrogation, from the fifteenth century (Marchello-Nizia et al. 2020: 742–3, 1228–33). Its use helps avoid V–S inversion in interrogatives, i.e. 'qui est-ce que je vois?' instead of 'que vois-je?' ('what do I see?').

Innovations in OR also occurred at the enunciative level via a process of pragmaticalization, i.e. when lexical items, in a given context, lost their propositional meaning in favour of an essentially metacommunicative, discourse-interactional meaning. Ingham (2016: 394–8) notes for example in his Year Books corpus the evolution of the temporal use of the discourse marker *or(e)* ('now') and of the connector *(de) puisque* ('since') to a causal use. Similar examples can be found in the TVOF corpus (18), (19).

(18) E **puis qu**'il est proudom et justes, ne seroit mie raisons ne droiture qu'il fust parsoniers de nos malice ne de nostre paine. (*Histoire ancienne* ms 20125 §333.3)

'And since he is a good and just man, it would not be reasonable nor right that he should be associated with our misdeed and our suffering.'

(19) **Or** voi je bien certainement que en vous n'a point de savoir et trop estes plaine de fol hardement quant vous tel chose m'osastes . . .) (*Histoire ancienne* ms Royal DI §292.5)

'Now I truly see that in you there is no wisdom and that you are full of foolish presumptuousness when you dared tell me such a thing . . .'

Through their studies of theatre plays, Sauwala (2018), Oppermann-Marsaux (2012), and Dourdy, Spacagno, and Sauwala (2019) observe the pragmaticalization in OR of adverbs and imperatives into discursive markers and expressive interjections. For example, Dourdy, Spacagno, and Sauwala (2019) show how locutions originally used as real invocations in prayers, oaths, etc. in religious/ritual contexts (e.g. *par ma foy* ('by my faith'), *par Sainte Marie* ('by Saint Marie')) evolved into the expressive foregrounding of a pragmatic meaning component in profane contexts (as the expression *Jesus!* did in English), especially in plays. Similarly, they show how the adverb *voire* ('truly, really') progressively lost its assertive function to gain a more expressive function, especially in interactional contexts such as plays where it can be used to answer a question, meaning 'assuredly' (see also Sauwala 2018: 211). Following Oppermann-Marsaux (2012: 11), Sauwala (2018: 201–11) and Dourdy, Spacagno, and Sauwala (2019) examine the evolution of initial imperative verbs such as *Va!* ('go!'), *Dictes!* ('Say!'), and *Tiens/Tenez!* ('Hold!') into discursive markers which we would translate as mere interjections in English ('Here you go!', 'Say!', 'Here you are!'), and which can sometimes be combined (20).

(20) *Dy va*, chartrenier, où vaiz tu? (*Le Mystère de Saint Vincent*, lines 11929–30)[49]

'Pray tell, jailor, where are you going?'

Parussa (2020), following Oppermann-Marsaux (2014), closely studies the discursive marker *dea* and its allomorphs *dia, dya, da*, from their emergence in OR in the fourteenth century, especially in plays, until their disappearance at the beginning of the twentieth century. The marker, which Parussa thinks could be an abbreviation of *dyable* ('devil'), expresses the locutor's disagreement or surprise regarding their interlocutor's previous utterance(s). It could be translated as 'Hell!' or 'Heck!' in English. She describes the pragmaticalization of *dea* which evolves in medieval French from expressing a strong emotion as an interjection (i.e. surprise), to expressing a strong assertion seeking to convince the locutor, as a discursive marker (21).

(21) Et comment, *dea*, n'esse autre chose? (*La Passion Notre Seigneur*, line 22341)[50]

'And how the heck is it not something else?'

As an aside, while OR corpora include various proportions of direct discourse segments taken from narrative texts and of dialogues from theatrical plays, this does not necessarily mean that linguistic innovations occur in similar ways in both types of OR. Oppermann-Marsaux (2018: 226–35) notes for example that there are proportionally slightly more occurrences of interrogation without inversion in theatre and that overall interrogative clauses in direct discourse segments inserted

---

[49] Example given by Dourdy, Spacagno, and Sauwala (2019: 20) and taken from *Le Mystère de Saint Vincent* (composed in 1471–6). The translation is mine.
[50] Example given by Parussa (2020: 92) and taken from *La Passion notre seigneur, d'Arnoul Gréban* (fifteenth century). The translation is mine.

in narrative texts tend to combine terms of address and/or interjections while they do not in theatre dialogues.[51] This latter trait, she submits, might be connected to the stronger need for narrative texts to combine markers to signal a change of locutor (i.e. from narrator to character or between characters) (Oppermann-Marsaux 2018: 235). This type of comparison which shows intertextual variation at the level of innovation could be fruitfully pursued in the future.

As shown here, research on the micro-grammar(s) of S&TP has undoubtedly yielded very rich insights so far but a huge part of its potential remains untapped to discover more about linguistic variation, both synchronic and diachronic. In many cases, linguistic hypotheses that could be checked manually through a few texts have now been confirmed through the use of new large databases. There is no doubt that in future cases, fresh insights will also be uncovered, especially with the advent of increasingly innovative electronic tools that can mine corpora in more systematic ways, possibly through the use of artificial intelligence and machine learning. The more layered corpora become the better: the TVOF is a good example as it uses lexical and syntactic tagging extensively; it not only distinguishes between the narrative part of the text and direct discourse like the BFM but also identifies indirect discourse; and it further allows for comparison of different versions of the same story composed within a relatively short span of time, which could give some insight about evolution in short diachrony rather than long diachrony. It would therefore be possible, for example, to compare the evolution of *molt/tres* and *beaucoup* or of word order both across types of discourse (narrative, indirect discourse, and direct discourse) and across shorter or longer periods of time.[52]

3.5 Conclusion

This chapter has offered an all-encompassing approach to reported discourse which embraces both macro- and micro-textual levels, and allows for a combination of narratological, stylistic, and linguistic insights into medieval texts and their ecosystems.

The study of the macro-grammar(s) of reported discourse, i.e. the forms, functions, and the framing of S&TP, reveals rich intertextual variation across literary genres as well as intratextual variation within texts, for example in terms of the

---

[51] Her corpus includes five Middle French prose narratives and ten Middle French theatre plays (mostly in verse) (Oppermann-Marsaux 2018: 227).

[52] For a description of how the TVOF's new functionalities can elicit fresh findings, notably in terms of linguistic variation across manuscripts within a relatively condensed timespan (short diachrony), see Morcos (2019); Ventura (2019); Ledgeway (2021); and Morcos, Noël, and Husar (2021). It would be interesting to refine their results further by checking whether there might be variation not only across manuscripts (intertextual) but within the same manuscript, between the discourse of the narrator and that of the characters (intratextual).

gender and status of the quoting and quoted locutors. Simply speaking, studying reported discourse helps us understand how literary genres differ from each other and why. Similarly, it can offer insights into narratorial and/or gendered strategies within specific texts.

The study of the micro-grammar(s) of reported discourse, under the guise of *oral représenté*, shows that several grammars compete intratextually since the syntax, morphosyntax, and the pragmatics of the quoted discourse are not the same as those of the quoting discourse, notably due to the inherent interactive nature of the characters' direct speech as opposed to the narration. However, there is substantial intertextual variation across literary genres in terms of micro-grammar, just as there was at the macro-level. In other words, stable oral traits can be detected both in narration and in direct discourse depending on the literary genre of the text under scrutiny, and the level of variation therefore fluctuates across genres. Variation can also be found when exploring the emergence of linguistic innovations in OR as different genres present different types and different rates of innovative features.

4
The evolution of the syntax of the subject in French and factors of variation

Sophie Prévost

4.1 Introduction

The notion of variation can be approached from various angles: diachronic, diatopic, diastratic, diaphasic, and diamesic. For the researcher who works on linguistic change, the diachronic dimension comes first. However, disregarding the other aspects would result in drawing an incomplete picture of the phenomenon under study: a change does not spread equally in linguistic structures, communicative situations, or groups of speakers. Considering these different aspects makes it possible to fully account for the modalities of change, as regards differentiated chronologies as well as modalities of propagation of new variants. Identifying the pioneering loci of change may also provide some answers to the thorny issue of the causes and motivations for the changes. However, studying language states prior to the seventeenth century makes access to diastratic, diaphasic, and diamesic dimensions very difficult due to the lack of relevant data. On the other hand, we can consider other criteria of variation such as the domain and/or the genre of the texts as well as their form (verse or prose), and the enunciative situation (direct speech vs. narrative), which highlight noticeable differences regarding the embedding of linguistic structures in language and their evolution. This study is devoted to two major changes that took place in French between the twelfth and the seventeenth centuries: the increase in overt subjects and their growing anteposition to the verb. Although these two changes are partly related from a linguistic point of view, a close examination of the data shows that they are not equally sensitive to the following criteria of variation: time, dialect,[1] domain, form, enunciative situation (direct speech/narrative), and verbal person. The study aims to account for both changes while attempting to highlight the specific influence of each of these different factors and to explain this contrasted situation.

---

[1] See Chapter 1, footnote 54, this volume.

Sophie Prévost, *The evolution of the syntax of the subject in French and factors of variation*. In: *Historical and Sociolinguistic Approaches to French*. Edited by: Janice Carruthers, Mairi McLaughlin, and Olivia Walsh, Oxford University Press. © Sophie Prévost (2024). DOI: 10.1093/oso/9780192894366.003.0004

4.2 The historical linguist faced with bad data

4.2.1 When? How? Why?

When studying any linguistic change, the historical linguist has to answer three fundamental, and partially related, questions: When? How? Why? The first question aims to identify not only the points of departure and of arrival, but also the intermediate stages of a change. Studying changes that took place in remote past states of the language offers at least one advantage: the passage of time allows us to determine with certainty the endpoint of a change, based on the stabilization of the variants (which does not preclude the possibility of a new change). Spotting the starting point of a change is less straightforward (regardless of the period under scrutiny), whether the change consists in the emergence of a new variant which gradually wins out over an already existing one, or in a change in the equilibrium between two (or more) existing variants. In both cases, one has to decide when the change really started, which does not equate with the mere advent of an innovation (whatever its form): it has to propagate through contexts (Andersen 2001). The quantitative aspect is certainly a key criterion (though it is not possible to give an absolute threshold), but it needs to be refined with a qualitative approach, especially as regards what exactly is meant by 'context'.

The 'how' question is actually a twofold one, as it concerns both the mechanisms involved in a change and the modalities of its propagation—an aspect that is related to the previous question. All studies based on corpora indeed show that a change does not spread evenly in the different loci of a language. Finally, the 'why' issue probably remains the most challenging one, as the identification of causes of and motivations for a change remains to a large extent speculative, all the more so the further back into the past we step. However, the answers to the preceding questions may provide some enlightening insights.

4.2.2 Variation and diachronic syntax

Sociolinguistic studies have enriched the ground of diachronic studies by emphasizing the social dimension of language and the fundamental role of variation.[2] These factors had in fact been already pointed out a few decades earlier, especially by Antoine Meillet (e.g. 1916). Jakobson also highlighted the prime role of variation in change: 'Pendant un certain temps, le point de départ et le point d'aboutissement de la mutation se trouvent coexister sous la forme de deux

---

[2] As underlined by Ayres-Bennett (1994c: 3), the interest in sociohistorical studies of French is relatively recent (starting in the 1990s: Lodge (1993, 2004); Ayres-Bennett (1996); Posner (1997), for instance) in comparison with studies of English (Romaine 1982). Ayres-Bennett was a remarkable pioneer in this domain, with landmark studies of seventeenth-century French language.

couches stylistiques différentes [. . .] Un changement est donc, à ses débuts, un fait synchronique' (Jakobson 1963: 37).

There is now a wide consensus that a change always results from variation,[3] although the inverse is not true because variation does not necessarily lead to change.[4] The first task consists in identifying the nature of the variation as well as the variants at stake. In the two cases under study here—the growing use of overt subjects and their increasing preverbal position—we are not dealing with the emergence of new variants. Null subjects and overt subjects on the one hand, and preverbal subjects and postverbal subjects on the other hand have always been attested and the change thus consisted in the evolution of their frequencies, namely a sharp decrease in null and postverbal subjects, and an increase in overt and preverbal subjects.

However, one may wonder how appropriate it is to consider that these are cases of variation. This question falls within the more general and long-debated issue regarding the relevance of addressing syntactic changes from a sociolinguistic perspective. The fact that Labovian sociolinguistic methodology was developed for phonology means that its application to syntax is far from self-evident. As Ayres-Bennett (2004: 10) recalls:

> the concept of the linguistic variable has been successfully applied to the phonological variation because of the arbitrariness of the linguistic sign [. . .] In the case of syntax the problem of determining identity of meaning for all variants of the variable is more acute. Gadet (1997: 11) suggests that this necessitates a looser interpretation of functional equivalence [. . .].

To identify the exact 'meaning' of two variants, and their equivalence or not, is all the more difficult when it comes to past language states, for which we do not have any native speaker's intuition. However, in the present case, a close examination of the contexts shows that, first, the variants were partially constrained by semantics (a null subject was used only if the referent was cognitively active), syntax (the verb-second constraint), and pragmatics (informational weight of the subject), and second—and this is in part correlated to the previous point—that there were semantic and/or pragmatic nuances opposing overt subjects to null subjects, and postverbal subjects to preverbal ones. For reasons given in Section 4.2.3, it can be claimed that the variation was not related to any social dimension. Nor was it associated with any stylistic effect, at least during the early stages: however, we do find such effects in certain uses of postverbal subjects in Modern French. In the light of what precedes, the notion of 'variant' may be questioned, if taken in a strict Labovian sense. However, following Gadet (1997: 11), I will adopt 'a looser

---

[3] This is not always true in the domain of the lexicon: a new term may appear as the result of the emergence of a new thing or concept, in which case it is not a variant of a term that already existed.

[4] See Prévost and Dufresne (2020: 23–7) for a discussion.

interpretation of functional equivalence', considering that null and overt subjects, be they preverbal or postverbal, when associated with a verb, are all variants of the same meta-function denoting the predicative relation between a verb and its subject.

4.2.3 Internal and external contexts; parameters of variation

Changes propagate through time but also through different types of contexts, whether internal (linguistic structures) or external (situations of communication and groups of speakers), and they do so at different paces; moreover, they do not necessarily spread in all contexts. To ignore the contexts of variation and of diffusion of a change gives a very impoverished picture of the phenomenon and it also prevents us from detecting some of the motivations for the changes, as the pioneering contexts may sometimes offer some clues as to why a change started out. The different contexts can be reinterpreted in terms of factors of variation, and from the point of view of the analyst, in terms of parameters of variation.

In contrast with the linguist studying present-day changes, the historical linguist has no direct knowledge of the way in which changes propagated through groups of speakers and through situations of communication. First, we do not have any recording of the spoken language before the late nineteenth century, and therefore we can only rely on written data. Second, there are no documents illustrating informal or semi-literate usages before the seventeenth century (and even at that time, there are few of them). Medieval documents all stem from literate writers, at a time when only a very small percentage of the population could read and write. Moreover, we do not have any reliable testimony of non-standard usages, as was the case from the seventeenth century on, thanks to the comments of the *remarqueurs* and grammarians. There might have existed low-literate documents in medieval French, but if this were the case, they have unfortunately not reached us. We are also mostly ignorant of the age and the gender of authors, and thus the influence that these parameters may have had on their writings. Until the seventeenth century, many documents were indeed anonymous, and even when the author's name is known, it is often difficult to establish the exact dating of the document and/or the date of birth of the author. In view of the expected methodology of a true sociolinguistic approach and of the above-mentioned limitations, the handling of past variations, and especially of medieval ones, is undoubtedly problematic since we are unable to take into account their diastratic, diaphasic, and diamesic dimensions.

However, we can consider other types of contexts. Although they do not have any social value, they allow us to observe how the changes progressively spread through written data according to external parameters. These are the domains of the texts (literary, historical, argumentative, juridical/legal, hagiographical/religious, didactic, and epistolary),[5] and their form (verse or prose), the hypothesis being that texts in prose were both less constrained and possibly more innovative, especially as prose developed later than verse. We can also consider, when relevant, some more specific features of the texts, such as the register. Although medieval texts pertain to formal and high-level registers, they may display some more spontaneous passages, in direct speech. This point leads us to address the critical question of spoken language. The fact that we do not have any access to spoken language of past language states deprives us of important information relating to the material dimension of the language (prosody, phonetics...) but also of access to informal registers. It is not a question of strictly equating spoken language with low-register usages, but spoken language may display less formal usages, which are not to be found in written data of this period, and it may, for this very reason, constitute a pioneering context for some changes, as can be observed in Modern French. In the absence of access to spoken language, we can consider direct speech, with, needless to say, due caution. I certainly do not claim that direct speech can be equated, whatever the period, with spoken language, since it may display over-corrected usages or, on the contrary, exaggerated and caricatural features. It may, however, be considered as a pale and/or imperfect reflection of spoken language and provide some interesting information, especially if it displays the first signs of some changes, in comparison with narrative passages.

Let us now turn to internal contexts. Just as changes do not spread at the same pace through external contexts, they do not propagate evenly through linguistic structures. As regards the evolution of the syntax of the subject, the following factors turn out to be relevant: the type of clause (main declarative vs. subordinate clauses), the presence of another argument, especially the object, and the verbal person (the latter factor being partially correlated to the opposition between direct speech and narrative, as we will see in Section 4.4.4).

4.2.4 Collecting the data

Collecting the data raises two difficulties, especially for past language states: the gathering of sufficient data illustrating the variables, and the composition of a balanced corpus. The first largely depends on the phenomenon under scrutiny. The evolution of the expression and of the position of the subject is not a rare phenomenon and therefore data is not lacking: all texts display an abundance of null and overt subjects, as well as preverbal and postverbal ones, albeit in varying proportions (which is precisely the change to be studied). The handling of

---

[5] These domains were identified by the *Base de français médiéval*'s team (http://corptef.ens-lyon.fr/spip.php?article62 (accessed 1 November 2020)) and stand as a reference among historical linguists working on medieval French.

internal parameters is not a problem either: all texts comprise main and subordinate clauses, transitive and intransitive structures, and, though less systematically, a diversity in verbal persons. Although all texts do not display stretches of direct speech, sufficient data can nonetheless be collected to allow us to compare direct speech and narrative passages.

Things are less straightforward when it comes to external parameters, namely the date, domain, and form of the texts. The further back into the past we go, the scarcer the texts are, and it is difficult to gather more than a few of them until the late eleventh century. They are so scarce, in fact, that we do not have to wonder which ones to select, but a balanced corpus cannot be built according to date, domain, and form. The situation improves from the twelfth century on, since many more texts from that period have reached us, but, until the thirteenth century, they are mainly religious, in verse, and Anglo-Norman, making it often impossible to separate out the different parameters. It is only from the thirteenth century onwards that the available texts are sufficiently diversified for the parameters to be handled separately, though certainly not as rigorously as for modern language states. The increase in texts over the centuries raises the question of how to build a corpus that is sufficiently representative from a quantitative and qualitative point of view, while remaining manageable as regards data collection and processing, especially when the changes studied are instantiated by a large amount of data.

Two last points deserve to be mentioned as regards the value of some parameters across centuries. First, as may have been noticed, I have not explicitly mentioned dialectal variation (which is acknowledged to have no longer operated, generally speaking, beyond the late fifteenth century; see Picoche and Marchello-Nizia 1991 [1989]: 25). Syntactic variation was indeed much less sensitive to the diatopic dimension than morphological variation, particularly as regards the evolution of the syntax of the subject (see Prévost and Marchello-Nizia 2020: 1059). A close examination of my data corroborates this statement, and this parameter will thus be alluded to only when relevant. Second, as regards the form of the texts, it must be pointed out that the opposition between prose and verse has evolved over the centuries. With a few exceptions, until the late twelfth century, all texts were written in verse: prose was an exception, and verse was the unmarked form. The thirteenth century offers a more balanced picture, with a growing use of prose, especially in didactic and historical texts. However, verse remained very much alive, especially in literary texts, even though the use of prose increased in this domain as well. From the fourteenth century on, the use of verse started to lose ground, and progressively became restricted to specific literary genres: poetry, songs, etc. In a word, while verse was the default form until the thirteenth century, it gradually became a stylistically marked form.

The paucity of documents, especially for the most remote past language states, the need to rely only on written data, the difficulty of separating out some parameters of variation—given these limitations, we may wonder how reliable and representative the sources are, and therefore how sound and valid the descriptions of changes and their interpretations are. Such a situation led Labov, a few decades ago, to label historical data as 'bad', in words which have become a sort of aphorism ('the great art of the historical linguist is to make the best of this bad data'). This remark deserves to be placed in a larger context, however, in order to clarify exactly what is meant by 'bad':

> The fundamental methodological fact that historical linguists have to face is that they have no control over their data. Texts are produced by a series of historical accidents; amateurs may complain about this predicament, but the sophisticated historian is grateful that anything has survived at all. The great art of the historical linguist is to make the best of this bad data—'bad' in the sense that it may be fragmentary, corrupted, or many times removed from the actual productions of native speakers.
>
> (Labov 1972b: 100)

As Romaine (1988: 1454) pointed out, historical data are 'bad' only if we try to put them on an equal footing with contemporary data and especially with spoken data. There are inherent limitations in studying them, and it must be admitted that they constitute a specific material, valid on their own, but quite different from modern states of the language. We therefore have, legitimately, to adapt our methodologies, and to accept that our claims about past linguistic structures, and their evolution, are only an interpretation of the available data. The more substantial and balanced the corpus under study is, the more our interpretation may come close to what past languages really looked like, and when and how evolutions proceeded.

It would certainly be exaggerated, and even false, to claim that the present study falls within a sociohistorical approach. More modestly, it aims to account for two major—and related—changes which have occurred in French, while taking into account certain parameters of variation that provide a more detailed picture of the evolution, as regards the 'when' and 'how' questions, and that even, to some extent and with due caution, make it possible to suggest some possible motivations for the changes.

4.3 A quick overview of the changes under study

Modern French is a fairly strict SVO language (at least in main declarative and subordinate clauses, on which I am focusing here), in which the expression of the subject is obligatory (with a few exceptions, among which contexts of close coordination or juxtaposition between verbs). These characteristics sharply distinguish Modern French from the earliest stages of the language.

Old French had inherited from Latin the possibility of not expressing the subject when its referent could be unambiguously identified. As a result, until the end of the twelfth century null subjects were very frequent and they even prevailed in main declaratives. A first major turning point took place at the beginning of the thirteenth century, and a second one occurred in the mid-sixteenth century, with frequencies of overt subject expression rising to more than 90%.[6] Old French was moreover characterized by the existence of a flexible word order (as regards the grammatical functions), allowing for preverbal objects, postverbal subjects, and for all six permutations of subject, verb, and object. The evolution towards an SVO (subject–verb–object) order spanned several centuries. The earliest change concerned nominal objects (the preverbal position of pronominal objects, inherited from Latin, was settled at the very beginning of French, with a few exceptions; see Marchello-Nizia 2020). While in Early Old French (until 1100) nominal objects prevailingly occupied a preverbal position, as was the case in Latin, OV order had fallen to 35% a century later (*Roland*, c.1100),[7] then to less than 10% in *Graal* and to only 5% in the early fifteenth century (Marchello-Nizia 2020).

In Modern French the position of the subject is more flexible than that of the object, at least in main declaratives and in subordinate clauses. However, postverbal subjects have receded considerably since Old French, along paths which differ according to their nature, nominal or pronominal. Postverbal nominal subjects did not decrease in a linear fashion, as will be seen in Section 4.5, but the mid-sixteenth century marks a turning point: preverbal subject rates have remained over 80% ever since (Prévost and Marchello-Nizia 2020: 1080). The evolution of preverbal pronominal subjects (personal pronouns) offers a quite different picture. As they already largely prevailed at the very beginning of French, they did not undergo a very significant increase over the centuries. From more than 80% in most texts, they had reached more than 90% by the early fourteenth century (Prévost and Marchello-Nizia 2020: 1080).

The reasons why null subjects were progressively lost in French (contrary to most other Romance languages) and why French evolved towards a strict word order is a long-debated, two-fold question. Traditional explanations relate the two changes to some other morphological and syntactic changes.[8] Old French possessed both a rich verbal morphology, which differentiated all the verbal persons, and a nominal declension, inherited from Latin (albeit reduced to nominative and oblique cases), which made it possible to discriminate the main grammatical functions. Old French was also characterized by the existence of a loose verb-second

---

[6] See Prévost and Marchello-Nizia (2020: 1055–74).

[7] Short forms such as *Roland* are used to refer to the texts in the corpus which are listed in Appendix I at the end of the chapter.

[8] See among others Foulet (1930 [1919]: 37–8, 446–61); Skårup (1975: ch. IV); Adams (1987); Vance (1997: 2, ch. 2, 3, 5).

constraint, resulting in the postverbal positioning of the subject when the preverbal position was occupied by another element. This constraint has also been put forth as an explanation for null subjects, based on the claim that null subjects were actually postverbal pronominal subjects (inverted because of the occupation of the preverbal position by another element), which had been omitted. Relying on the existence of some sort of inverse dependency between a rich morphology (verbal endings and nominal declension) and a relative syntactic freedom (null subjects and flexible position of the arguments), it has been claimed that the morphological erosion of inflectional endings expressing subject–verb agreement on the one hand, and the disappearance of the nominal declension on the other, entailed the generalization of overt subjects and the fixing of word order, especially the subject in preverbal position, henceforth compatible with the presence of another preverbal element, due to the loss of the verb-second constraint.

However, both the morphological and syntactic explanations have been called into question. As regards the relation between the loss of verbal morphology and the growing overt expression of subjects, the diachronic scenario was questioned by Schøsler (2002) and Roberts (2014) on the grounds of an apparent time lag between the two changes, though they make opposite claims about the temporal sequence of changes. Schøsler assumes that null subjects were largely lost at the beginning of the medieval French period, while verbal inflection continued to undergo phonological restructuring for several centuries more. Roberts also rejects a direct connection between the two phenomena because of an apparent time lag but, based on an extrapolation from written to oral data given in Foulet (1935), he dates the total loss of rich agreement to the twelfth century and the completion of the loss of null subjects only by the sixteenth century (for a detailed discussion, see Prévost 2018; Simonenko, Crabbé, and Prévost 2019).[9] As for the relation between declension and the identification of functions, first, even in a stage in which the decay of the case system was already advanced, there was still a flexible word order; and second, as Schøsler (1984) pointed out, there existed, from Latin onwards, other factors (among which valency and animate character) that enabled subjects and objects to be distinguished. Finally, the influence of the verb-second constraint and the consequences of its loss are challenged by the fact that it was not a strict rule in Old French (we find verbs in initial position, or, on the contrary, in third position, or even further on in the clause).

---

[9] It should be mentioned that there are some biases which make it difficult to assert the possible connections. There is indeed a methodological flaw in speculating on the pronunciation of morphological endings while relying on written data as concerns the frequency of overt subjects: it may be the case that subjects were more often expressed in spoken language. The time lag between verbal syncretization and the generalization of overt subjects may thus have been shorter than claimed by some linguists. Moreover, we may wonder what is meant exactly by 'loss', and whether it amounts to a mere quantitative approach, with the determination of a threshold.

Although none of these factors should be dismissed, they are not sufficient to fully account for the existence of null subjects and for the variation in word order in medieval French, nor for the loss of null subjects and the fixing of word order afterwards. This strictly morphosyntactic approach was supplemented by pragmatic and informational explanations. First, the increase in overt subjects, more specifically in personal pronouns, has been related to a need for expressiveness (or emphasis). This hypothesis was put forward early (Foulet 1930 [1919]), and taken up and further developed by Detges (2003) (see Prévost 2018 and Prévost and Marchello-Nizia 2020 for a detailed account). The increasing use of pronominal subjects for the sake of expressiveness allegedly brought about some sort of rhetorical devaluation, which in turn led to a more widespread—and thus pragmatically less marked—use of overt pronouns. We will see in the following sections that this hypothesis is supported by a close examination of the data. Second, the flexibility of word order has been accounted for by an informational principle, formulated either in terms of Topic–Comment (Lambrecht 1994) or in terms of Theme–Rheme (Firbas 1992). As the subject was a privileged topic or theme (especially the personal pronoun), it often appeared in preverbal position, and this position was therefore progressively reinterpreted as the position of the subject. French, it is argued, went from a word order based on an informational principle to a grammatical one, based on the ordering of the syntactic functions (Vennemann 1974; Combettes 1988).

As is often the case, it is most likely that different factors—morphological, syntactic, and pragmatic—jointly contributed to both changes.

4.4 The progressive obligatorification of overt subjects

As was recalled in Section 4.3, Old French had inherited from Latin the possibility of not expressing the subject when its referent could be unambiguously identified. However, it would be an exaggeration to consider that Old French was a true null-subject language (NSL). It is more appropriate to analyse it as a partial NSL. First, overt subjects prevailed in subordinate clauses right from the very beginning of French, and second, none of the supposed features of a NSL are observed: we find referential pronouns even in non-emphatic contexts and in the absence of any ambiguity, and expletive pronouns even in the earliest texts (ninth to eleventh centuries), albeit very rarely. While null subjects were very frequent and even prevailed in main declaratives until the end of the twelfth century, a first major turning point took place at the beginning of the thirteenth century: subject expression rose from 47% in *Passion* (c.1000) to 79% three centuries later (*Graal*, c.1225). A second turn occurred in the mid-sixteenth century: from this time on, subject expression overwhelmingly dominated, with frequencies rising up to those we find in Modern French (more than 90%), though there remained until the end of the seventeenth century some constructions that are no longer acceptable (see Prévost and Marchello-Nizia 2020: 1055–79).

This increase was in favour of pronominal subjects (personal pronouns). The data clearly show an inverse dependency between the decrease in null subjects and the rise of pronominal subjects, which is no surprise if one considers the proximity of null subjects and personal pronouns on accessibility hierarchies (Ariel 1988), both of them signalling a high degree of cognitive activation. The other types of subjects remained more or less constant over the centuries. Therefore, when dealing with the evolution of subject expression it would probably be more appropriate to consider only personal pronouns. However, as studies may noticeably vary on this point, both rates are indicated in Table 4.1, which provides a quantitative overview of the evolution of overt subjects (the data stem from the extensive study which was conducted in Prévost and Marchello-Nizia 2020).[10]

Table 4.1 highlights substantial discrepancies between frequencies, especially until the late thirteenth century, which are partly influenced by different factors or contexts, either external or internal, which are successively addressed in the following sections.

4.4.1 The form and domain of texts

The data in Table 4.1 clearly show that texts in prose are more advanced than texts in verse as regards subject expression. In the mid-twelfth century the frequency of overt subjects rose to 47% in *Eneas* (verse), but reached 81% in *Lapidaire* (prose), which is a highly untypical rate for the time. Similarly, at the beginning of the thirteenth century, *Graal*, in prose, displayed 79% of overt subjects whereas this rate was only 68% in *RenartDole*, in verse. The discrepancy becomes even clearer when different passages in the same text are compared, as is possible in *Aucassin*, a text in which passages in verse alternate with passages in prose. The prose sections exhibit higher rates of overt subjects than the sections in verse, with 67% vs. 48%, respectively.

The pioneering character of prose may well be a longstanding one. However, this criterion is difficult to verify, as we have only a few prose texts before the thirteenth century, and most of them are in fact translations from Latin (in which null subjects were frequent), which may have influenced the style of the translator. This is the case of the *Quatre livres des Rois*, which is a late twelfth-century prose translation of the Bible.[11] In this text, the frequency of overt subjects (58%) hardly exceeds that of contemporary texts in verse (*TroyesYvain* and *BeroulTristan*: respectively,

---

[10] Most rates are based on text samples containing 1,000 finite verbs. Only the following texts were analysed exhaustively: *Passion, SaintLégier, SaintAlexis, Lapidaire, Charters (CharteChièvres 1194 and/or CharteArras 1224), GersonSermon, ArchierBaignollet.*

[11] Translations were excluded from the data in Table 4.1.

Table 4.1 Rates of overt subjects (= all subjects: S) and overt pronominal subjects (= personal pronouns: Spp) in main declarative vs. subordinate clauses from the eleventh to the sixteenth century[a]

Texts	Domain	Rate of S	Rate of S in Declaratives	Rate of S in Subordinates	Rate of Spp in Declaratives	Rate of Spp in Subordinates
Passion (c. 1000)	relig.	47%	43% (162/362)	60% (71/119)	16% (37/237)	27% (18/66)
StLegier (c. 1000)	hagiog.	43%	42% (77/182)	48% (37/77)	15% (19/124)	33% (20/60)
StAlexis (c. 1050)	hagiog.	48%	41% (212/514)	65% (147/227)	11% (36/338)	42% (58/138)
Roland (c. 1100)	literary	51%	51% (345/675)	67% (136/205)	16% (63/393)	41% (48/117)
Lapidaire (mid-12th)	didact.	81%	74% (325/440)	92% (270/295)	55% (138/253)	74% (77/102)
Eneas1 (c. 1155)	literary	47%	38% (258/673)	69% (205/299)	13% (60/475)	47% (83/177)
BeroulTristan (late 12th)	literary	55%	44% (283/639)	74% (220/298)	16% (70/426)	54% (92/170)
TroyesYvain (1177–81)	literary	59%	44% (203/464)	78% (355/455)	19% (61/322)	64% (19/279)
ClariConstantinople (after 1205)	historic.	75%	52% (262/504)	96% (486/505)	24% (75/318)	92% (214/232)
Aucassin (late 12th–13th)	literary	65%	47% (281/593)	90% (295/329)	31% (141/453)	79% (130/164)
CharteChièvres (1194)	legal	90%	89% (42/47)	90% (82/91)	55% (6/11)	79% (34/43)
CharteArras (1224)	legal	95%	100% (4/4)	93% (14/15)	–	86% (6/7)
Graal (c. 1225)	literary	79%	60% (300/497)	96% (470/490)	37% (117/314)	93% (264/285)
RenartDole (early 13th)	literary	68%	61% (325/535)	86% (332/388)	36% (120/330)	74% (163/219)
Beaumanoir (1283)	didact.	88%	66% (183/278)	96% (693/720)	44% (75/170)	91% (258/285)
Joinville (1309)	historic.	82%	68% (286/419)	96% (510/533)	54% (157/290)	93% (300/323)
MachautFortune (1341)	literary	63%	57% (228/400)	69% (390/566)	40% (114/286)	48% (160/336)

Continued

Table 4.1 Continued

Texts	Domain	Rate of S	Rate of S in Declaratives	Rate of S in Subordinates	Rate of Spp in Declaratives	Rate of Spp in Subordinates
Mesnagier (1393)	didact.	65%	67% (225/334)	85% (398/470)	43% (78/183)	76% (224/296)
Griseldis (1395)	literary	56%	45% (193/428)	70% (315/448)	31% (106/341)	52% (147/280)
Manières (1396, 1399)	didact.	76%	85% (332/391)	85% (306/358)	81% (253/311)	78% (190/243)
QuinzeJoies (c. 1400)	literary	79%	66% (283/426)	90% (457/512)	55% (173/316)	82% (255/310)
GersonSermon (1402)	relig.	83%	72% (240/331)	95% (342/361)	57% (122/214)	88% (142/161)
PizanCité (1404–5)	didact.	70%	57% (190/336)	83% (497/599)	31% (65/211)	63% (177/279)
Pathelin (1456–69)	literary	85%	89% (402/453)	93% (242/260)	86% (309/360)	90% (163/181)
CentNouvelles (1456–67)	literary	78%	64% (234/365)	87% (508/581)	50% (133/264)	77% (240/313)
ArchierBaignollet (1468)	literary	81%	87% (162/186)	90% (87/97)	83% (118/142)	82% (46/56)
Commynes (1490–1505)	historic.	78%	64% (297/469)	91% (482/531)	32% (81/253)	79% (182/231)
JehanParis (1494)	literary	73%	59% (250/424)	87% (423/488)	42% (124/298)	74% (182/247)
Vigneulles (1515)	literary	75 %	57% (260/458)	92% (423/460)	42% (146/344)	87% (252/289)
CalvinLettres (1549)	epistol.	95 %	95% (318/336)	97% (617/638)	93% (240/258)	95% (404/425)
Rate of S: lower than 50%			Rate of S: between 50% and 80%		Rate of S: higher than 80%	

[a] The rates of overt S and of overt Spp are calculated out of: 'overt S + null S' and 'overt Spp + null S'.
Italics: texts in verse; roman: texts in prose.

54% and 59% of overt subjects). The situation after the thirteenth century is quite different, and, so to speak, opposite, since verse becomes more specialized from Middle French onwards. From this point of view, the thirteenth century offers the best picture, as this period is balanced between verse and prose, at least for literary texts.

The domain (cf. Section 4.2.3) also plays a major role but it largely overlaps with the previous criterion, and it is difficult to disentangle the two criteria. While literary texts were written both in verse and in prose (at least from the thirteenth century onwards), non-literary texts were on the other hand almost all written in prose. Therefore, we may wonder whether the modern and pioneering syntax of *Lapidaire*, in comparison with contemporary texts, results from its non-literary and didactic nature, or from the fact that it is written in prose, or from both, the two features (prose and non-literary/non-religious) still being infrequent at that time. The same question holds for *Beaumanoir* in the late thirteenth century. Similarly, the rate of overt subjects was higher in thirteenth- to fourteenth-century historical texts (*ClariConstantinople* and *Joinville*), but these texts were also written in prose. However, it is possible that in these texts the presence of multiple referents, which is inherent to historical writing, may have favoured the overt expression of subjects, for the sake of clarity. Likewise, the exceptionally high rates of overt subjects in legal charters probably result from the need to avoid any referential ambiguity. The domain and the form of texts seem to be still influential factors in the late fourteenth century. The frequency of overt subjects in *Griseldis*, a drama text in verse, rose to only 56%, vs. 65% and 76% in *Mesnagier* and *Manieres*, two contemporary non-literary texts in prose.[12]

It can be concluded from what precedes that both prose and the non-literary nature of the text favoured the propagation of overt subjects, though it is difficult to assess the exact contribution of each factor, as these two features are closely interrelated.

4.4.2 The dialectal parameter

The diatopic parameter does not seem to have been very influential in the expression of subjects. Admittedly, the data to support this statement are lacking: it is impossible to have a dialectal sampling before the thirteenth century, since Norman or Anglo-Norman texts largely prevailed until the late twelfth century.[13] Studies have been conducted on corpora of legal charters, which have the advantage of being reliably dated and located.[14] They have revealed only slight

---

[12] Note that the relatively low general rate of overt subjects in *Mesnagier* (65%) results from the fact that this rate takes all types of clause into account, and this text includes a high number of imperative clauses, with null subjects.
[13] On the other hand, the dialectal factor is no longer relevant after the fifteenth century.
[14] See Balon and Larrivée (2016) for a study on the increase of overt subjects in legal texts.

discrepancies, which, moreover, may differ from one study to another. Dees et al. (1980) thus pointed out that the rate of null subjects (at least in main declarative clauses) was higher in western dialects than in eastern ones. Schøsler (1984), on the other hand, showed that northern charters had the lowest rate of null subjects while Parisian ones had the highest.

4.4.3 Linguistic structures: Types of clauses and argument structure

From the earliest texts onwards, the overt expression of subjects, and more specifically of personal pronouns, was far more frequent in subordinate clauses than in main declaratives (with no significant disparities between the different types of subordinates).[15] Table 4.1 reveals a constant tendency during the whole period under scrutiny: the frequency of overt subjects in subordinates oscillated between 60% and 96% (except in *StLegier*: 48%) while in main declarative clauses it did not rise to 50% before the late twelfth century (with an exception in *Lapidaire*). The difference between the rates ranged from 20% to 30% if considering all the subjects, and exceeded 60 per cent, in some texts, if considering only personal pronouns. The discrepancies persisted beyond the late fourteenth century, although, from then on, the difference tended to decrease and was no longer systematic, some texts even displaying reverse tendencies (*Manières*). Interestingly, the greatest discrepancies are observed from the mid-twelfth century until the late thirteenth century, i.e. during the first significant rise in overt expression.

Subordinate clauses thus appear to be pioneering in comparison with main declarative clauses. This observation has been interpreted in a number of ways. According to one family of proposals, the main–subordinate asymmetry is related to the fact that subordinate clauses generally resist verb-second (V2) syntax (for two analyses along those lines, couched in a generative framework, see Adams 1987; Vance 1997). However, such an explanation does not account for all types of subordinate clauses, and the main–subordinate asymmetry remains so far largely unexplained (see Prévost and Marchello-Nizia 2020: 1063–4). It should be mentioned that in Latin it was, on the contrary, subordinate clauses which more readily allowed for subject omission. The change most likely took place during Late Latin, but there is a serious lack of data to fill the gap and provide an explanation for this noticeable change.

The argument structure also seems to have played a role in the expansion of overt subjects. Studies (Rouquier and Marchello-Nizia 2012) on the argument structure in the oldest texts (*Passion, StLegier, StAlexis, Roland*) indeed showed that subjects were far less often expressed when a direct object was present, the

---

[15] This is a long-established observation: see among others Franzén (1939: 14–34); Adams (1987); Hirschbühler (1989, 1990); Prévost and Marchello-Nizia (2020: 1062–4).

difference ranging from 20% to 30%. In *Roland*, for instance, the frequency of overt subjects is 40% with transitive verbs, but it rises to 67% with intransitive verbs. In *TroyesYvain*, the respective frequencies are 37% and 66%. However, the difference decreased sharply from the beginning of the thirteenth century on, especially in prose (*Graal*: 77% vs. 80%).

4.4.4 Direct speech vs. narrative; verbal persons

Lastly, two parameters need to be considered, which, though pertaining to different levels of analysis—the situation of communication as an external factor, and the verbal person as an internal factor—deserve to be handled together since they are closely related.

If we distinguish between the first-person singular (P1) and third-persons singular and plural (P3), the most frequent ones, we observe quite significant differences in the frequencies of overt expression of the personal pronoun, at least in main declarative clauses, as is evidenced by the data in Table 4.2. Without denying the existing disparities between texts, it can be seen that, from the oldest texts, the frequency of overt expression of P3 is always lower than that of P1 (except in *StAlexis*). As early as the beginning of the thirteenth century, the frequency of overt P1 oscillated between 80% and 94% (except in *RenartDole*), while the overt expression of P3 was not systematically dominant before the early fourteenth century.

These results imply that, from the early texts, in declarative clauses, 'I' (and in some texts 'we' and 'you') was expressed far more often than 'he/she/they'. In contrast, we do not observe any significant difference between persons in the

Table 4.2 Rates of expression of first- and third-person pronouns

Texts	Overt P1	Overt P3
StAlexis (*c.*1050)	17%	24%
Roland (*c.*1100)	34%	16%
Eneas1 (*c.*1155)	24%	22%
BeroulTristan (late 12th)	41%	25%
TroyesYvain (1177–81)	51%	39%
RenartDole (early 13th)	57%	52%
ClariConstantinople (after 1205)	82%	44%
Graal (*c.*1225)	80%	60%
Joinville (1309)	80%	70%
Manières (1396, 1399)	94%	62%
QuinzeJoies (*c.*1400)	83%	64%

Italics: texts in verse; roman: texts in prose.

subordinate clauses of these same texts, which may be due to the fact that, even in early texts, the rate of overt expression in these clauses was very high. These data bear out the idea that a turning point occurred in the early thirteenth century, when the expression of first-person pronouns became prevalent in all types of clauses, and almost systematic in subordinate clauses, in which the prevailing expression henceforth concerned all persons.

But this skewing in the distribution of overt first- and third-person pronouns also results from the fact that P1 prevailingly appears in direct speech. Focusing on the distribution of P3 pronouns in narrative and direct speech passages (in main declarative clauses), Table 4.3 shows that overt expression is always more frequent in direct speech.

However, it is not so straightforward to disentangle the effects of different person contexts and those of the opposition between narrative passages and direct speech. There are probably two converging factors at work here. First, as they refer to the speaker, person pronouns were a privileged place for expressiveness and emphasis, which resulted in a higher rate of overt expression. Second, first-person pronouns prevailingly occurred in direct speech, which may be considered as closer to the spoken language than narrative is. If we assume that spoken language may have been more advanced in its evolution, we may expect it to have displayed more overt pronouns, which may be reflected to a certain extent in direct speech.[16] The increasing use probably resulted in rhetorical devaluation, which led to a widespread use—and thus weakening—of pronouns. The change clearly

Table 4.3 Rates of expression of first- and third-person pronouns in direct speech and in narrative[a]

	Overt P1	Overt P3	
	Direct speech	Direct speech	Narrative
StAlexis (c. 1050)	17% (15/89)	40% (10/25)	23% (72/311)
Roland (c. 1100)	34% (45/132)	24% (29/120)	11% (19/175)
Eneas1 (c. 1155)	24% (13/54)	39% (24/62)	21% (95/448)
BeroulTristan (late 12th)	41% (47/115)	41% (41/100)	19% (48/255)
TroyesYvain (1177–81)	51% (39/77)	47% (41/88)	37% (135/362)
ClariConstantinople (after 1205)	82% (14/17)	60% (5/9)	44% (158/362)
RenartDole (early 13th)	57% (54/95)	53% (46/86)	51% (149/290)
Graal (c. 1225)	83% (74/89)	81% (48/59)	56% (185/330)
Manières (1396, 1399)	94% (148/158)	66% (63/80)	58% (38/66)
QuinzeJoies (c. 1400)	82% (103/124)	81% (57/70)	60% (177/297)

[a] I leave the introduction of statistical tests for a more extensive investigation.
Italics: texts in verse; roman: texts in prose.

[16] Moreover, as the first-person pronoun already existed in Latin, it was, in some ways, a few centuries ahead of third-person pronouns.

began with first-person pronouns, and then spread to the other persons (Detges 2003). The starting point was probably in (Late) Latin—though the precise date is debated.[17]

The preceding sections have highlighted that overt subjects initially increased more speedily in specific contexts: prose and non-literary texts, subordinate clauses, intransitive constructions, direct speech, and with first-person pronouns. These contexts thus appear to have been pioneering, and can be interpreted as factors in the propagation of overt subjects.[18] We will see in the following section that these contexts played a far less influential role as regards the evolution of the position of the subject.

4.5 The increase in preverbal subjects

The evolution of the position of subjects offers quite a different picture, as regards both the general chronology and the factors which were influential in the progression of overt subjects. As for the expression of subjects, I focus here also on main declarative and subordinate clauses, since they are the most frequent ones, and also because the position of subjects was highly constrained in the other types of clauses early in the period (interrogative, injunctive, exclamatory, and parenthetical clauses).

Although postverbal subjects, at least nominal ones, are not infrequent in Modern French, they have considerably receded since Old French, along paths which differ according to their nominal or pronominal nature,[19] as is evidenced by Table 4.4.

Table 4.4 clearly shows that nominal and pronominal preverbal subjects did not expand at the same pace. As they already largely prevailed at the very beginning of French, preverbal pronominal subjects did not undergo a very significant progression over the centuries. From more than 80% in most texts, they had reached more than 90% by the early fourteenth century, and their rate in subordinate clauses always oscillated between 94% and 100%, downgrading post-position to a very marginal phenomenon (1).

---

[17] See Ernout and Thomas (1951: 143); Väänänen (1981: 123); Pinkster (1987: 370); Touratier (1994: 23-5).

[18] I leave aside here syntactic, semantic, and pragmatic aspects, as it is not the purpose of this study (see Prévost and Marchello Nizia 2020: 1057-79 for a detailed account). Suffice it to say that null subjects first lost ground in non-coordinated structures, then in coordinated structures with different subjects and/or temporal orientation.

[19] Among pronominal subjects only personal pronouns, the most frequent, are taken into account here. The others have always behaved more or less like nominal subjects, with the exception of indefinite *on*, which was assimilated to personal pronouns from the seventeenth century on.

Table 4.4 Rates of nominal and pronominal preverbal subjects in main declarative and subordinate clauses from the eleventh to the seventeenth century[a]

Texts	Rate of preverbal nominal S in declaratives	Rate of preverbal pronominal S in declaratives	Rate of preverbal nominal S in subordinates	Rate of preverbal pronominal S in subordinates
Passion (c. 1000)	63% (73/116)	84% (31/37)	74% (20/27)	94% (17/18)
StLegier (c. 1000)	71% (30/42)	84% (16/19)	80% (4/5)	100% (20/20)
StAlexis (c. 1050)	38% (50/131)	78% (28/36)	67% (20/30)	100% (48/48)
Roland (1100)	53% (139/261)	81% (51/63)	53% (17/32)	100% (57/57)
Lapidaire (mid-12th)	87% (104/120)	94% (130/138)	91% (31/34)	100% (77/77)
Eneas1 (1155)	60% (105/176)	94% (44/47)	71% (39/55)	100% (85/85)
BeroulTristan (late 12th)	70% (122/173)	84% (58/69)	71% (34/48)	99% (91/92)
TroyesYvain (1177–81)	59% (64/109)	72% (44/61)	75% (43/57)	98% (176/179)
Aucassin (late 12th–13th)	72% (84/116)	83% (117/141)	87% (48/55)	99% (129/130)
ClariConstantinople (after 1205)	43% (52/122)	57% (39/68)	98% (128/131)	97% (211/217)
Graal (c. 1225)	49% (51/105)	80% (90/113)	94% (66/70)	98% (259/263)
RenartDole (early 13th)	57% (72/127)	78% (79/101)	87% (40/46)	99% (190/191)
Beaumanoir (1283)	76% (63/83)	71% (53/75)	98% (171/174)	99% (255/258)
Joinville (1305–9)	67% (65/97)	92% (144/156)	98% (78/80)	100% (299/299)
MachautFortune (1341)	83% (60/72)	90% (103/114)	88% (80/91)	100% (160/160)
Mesnagier (1393)	83% (59/71)	97% (65/77)	97% (66/68)	100% (218/218)
Griseldis (1395)	56% (31/55)	89% (92/103)	71% (41/58)	100% (147/147)
Manières (1396, 1399)	66% (42/64)	97% (244/251)	88% (46/52)	99% (191/192)

QuinzeJoies (c. 1400)	63% (46/73)	94% (163/173)	99% (252/255)
GersonSermon (1402)	55% (48/87)	93% (115/123)	99% (67/68)
Pathelin (1456–69)	100% (42/42)	90% (277/307)	71% (63/89)
CentNouvelles (1456–67)	82% (75/90)	90% (120/133)	100% (142/142)
ArchierBaignollet (1468)	71% (17/24)	95% (112/118)	80% (12/15)
Commynes (1490–1505)	46% (75/162)	89% (72/81)	100% (163/163)
JehanParis (1494)	67% (70/104)	92% (114/124)	92% (89/98)
Vigneulles (1515)	73% (64/88)	99% (143/144)	99% (238/239)
CalvinLettres (1549)	100% (36/36)	97% (255/262)	70% (7/10)
RonsardMisères (1563)	91% (85/93)	100% (80/80)	100% (42/42)
LéryBresil (1578)	93% (53/57)	93% (168/180)	81% (82/101)
Montaigne (1592)	90% (104/117)	96% (186/194)	100% (183/183)
BeroaldeParvenir (1616)	96% (79/82)	98% (202/207)	89% (88/99)
SorelBerger (1627)	98% (91/93)	98% (188/192)	100% (182/182)
Descartes (1637)	100% (19/19)	100% (110/110)	91% (51/56)
			99% (249/250)
			90% (87/97)
			99% (372/373)
			94% (84/89)
			100% (56/56)
			95% (106/112)
			99% (296/297)
			84% (84/100)
			100% (196/196)
			84% (60/71)
			99% (157/158)
			90% (96/107)
			99% (312/315)
			90% (138/153)
			100% (351/351)
Rate lower than 50%	Rate between 50 and 80%		Rate higher than 80%

[a] *Italics*: texts in verse; roman: texts in prose.

(1) Demi Espaigne   vus durat   il   en fiet *(Chanson de Roland)*
     O   V   S   adverbial
     Half of Spain   you will give   he   as fief

'He will give you half of Spain as yours'

This situation can be accounted for by the informational principle which governed word order: as typical topics, pronominal subjects tended to appear in preverbal position. From the fourteenth century onwards, the contexts allowing for postverbal pronouns began to narrow, especially as regards initial elements, which were progressively restricted to adverbs with an epistemic value (*peut-être, à peine,* ...), as is still the case in Modern French (for a more detailed account, see Prévost and Marchello-Nizia 2020: 1102–13).

The very high rate of preverbal pronouns from the earliest texts onwards may explain why almost none of the factors that proved to be influential in the growing use of overt pronouns are relevant here. First, neither the form (verse or prose) nor the domain of the texts seems to have had any influence, as is evidenced by the comparison of two mid-twelfth-century texts: *Eneas* (verse and literary) and *Lapidaire* (prose and didactic) which display similar rates of preverbal pronominal subjects (94%). Likewise, in the early thirteenth century, the rates in *Graal* (prose) and *RenartDole* (verse) are very close. Second, we do not observe any significant difference as concerns the direct speech/narrative opposition or the verbal person: depending on the texts, either first- or on the contrary third-person pronouns appeared more often in preverbal or in postverbal position. The only factor of variation is the type of clause, since subordinate clauses were slightly ahead of declarative clauses.

The post-position of nominal subjects has always been much more frequent:

(2) De Guenelun   atent   lireis   nuveles *(Chanson de Roland)*
    Comp.   V   S   O
    Of Guanelon   awaits   the king   news

'The king awaits news of Guanelon'

Moreover, postverbal subjects did not decrease in a linear fashion, as illustrated by Table 4.4. The rates of preverbal nominal subjects sometimes differed noticeably (at least in main declarative clauses) between contemporary texts, as is exemplified by *Aucassin* (72%) and *ClariConstantinople* (43%) in the early thirteenth century, or by *Commynes* (46%) and *JehanParis* (67%) in the late fifteenth century. It results from this that the rates were sometimes lower in some late fifteenth-century texts than in some late twelfth- or early thirteenth-century ones. The extension of preverbal nominal subjects during medieval French was indeed very slow and sporadic, and it was only in the mid-sixteenth century that a turning point occurred: since then, preverbal subject rates have always been over 80%.

The decrease in postverbal nominal subjects was accompanied by progressive restrictions on verbs, in favour of intransitive ones, and on the elements likely to precede the verb. While they were nearly unconstrained until the thirteenth century, whether from a formal or functional point of view, the possible range then progressively decreased: arguments started to lose ground early on, and the range of adverbial elements narrowed sharply during the seventeenth century, to the advantage of spatial and temporal adverbs. The post-position of nominal subjects is still well attested in Modern French, but it is restricted by the verb semantics and/or the weight of the subject and/or the presence of a locative element.

If we now turn to factors which proved to be influential in the growing use of overt subjects, we see that, as for pronominal subjects, only the type of clause seems to be relevant (albeit to a lesser extent than in the case of the expression of subjects). We observe in fact a constant difference in favour of subordinate clauses, which tended to increase from the early thirteenth century onwards, and declined sharply in the mid-sixteenth century, when both rates (declarative and subordinate clauses) of preverbal subjects reached over 90%. Apart from this factor, it is difficult to detect a clear tendency. There is no significant prevalence of preverbal subjects in direct speech, and the form of texts does not play a major part. For instance, in the early thirteenth century, *ClariConstantinople* and *Graal*, both in prose, displayed a lower frequency of preverbal subjects than *RenartDole*, in verse. The domain has, for its part, a variable influence during the whole period: non-literary texts (*Lapidaire*, *Beaumanoir*, and *Mesnagier*) systematically displayed high rates of preverbal subjects, but literary texts behaved in a quite irregular way, with contrasted frequencies. A final point to mention is that there is no systematic correlation between the more or less advanced stage of a text as regards expression, and its behaviour as regards the position of subjects: in comparison with contemporary texts, *Graal* displays a high rate of overt pronouns but a low rate of preverbal nominal subjects.

4.6 Conclusions and perspectives

The evolution of the syntax of subjects over the centuries has proceeded along differentiated chronologies and modalities, depending on whether one considers the expression or the position of subjects, and, in the latter case, the nature of the subjects.

We have seen that the two evolutions under scrutiny—increase in overt subjects and in preverbal subjects, either pronominal or nominal—display very different trajectories. Overt subjects, which were in a minority in declarative clauses at the beginning of French, went through a first rise in the early thirteenth century, then through a second one in the mid-sixteenth century. As for the position of subjects, pronominal ones had always prevailed in preverbal position, and therefore increased only slightly. The evolution of nominal subjects is the most complex one, as it was very irregular until the mid-sixteenth century, the Modern French situation being reached only in the seventeenth century.

Considering the question of expression as a starting point, I have identified a number of internal and external contexts which have proved to be factors conducive to the progression of overt subjects. On the other hand, most of these factors proved to have little—if any—influence as regards the evolution of the position of subjects.

The only factor common to all these changes is the pioneering nature of subordinate clauses, albeit with some nuances: there is a large discrepancy between the rates in declarative and subordinate clauses as regards overt subjects, while it is lower for preverbal pronominal subjects (due to the fact that, very early on, their frequency was very high in declarative clauses) and variable for preverbal nominal subjects. I do not have a truly satisfactory explanation for this observation, which moreover contradicts the idea that subordinate clauses are generally conservative (Vennemann 1975; Givón 1979), and which is all the more surprising since, in Latin, overt subjects were on the contrary less frequent in subordinate clauses. This question needs to be further investigated.

As to the other factors, two hypotheses may be formulated to account for their variable influence. The first is a quantitative one: it seems that, in general, the factors were no longer very influential once the change was advanced, that is, as soon as one of the variants had—consistently through the texts—overtaken the other one. This may explain why not all the factors had an effect, on the one hand, in subordinate clauses (as overt and preverbal subjects had always largely prevailed in them), and, on the other hand, on the increase in preverbal pronominal subjects, which prevailed in all contexts from the very beginning of French. This hypothesis is corroborated by the evolution of the position of nominal objects, which took place very early on (see Marchello-Nizia 1995): the reversal in frequencies of OV and VO occurred between the late ninth century and the early thirteenth century, which makes it difficult to analyse the change in detail since we can only rely on sparse data for the decisive period (and it is most likely that the change had already begun in Late Latin). If we look at the data in the twelfth to thirteenth centuries, it appears that only the opposition between direct speech and narrative was influential. VO order was more frequent in direct speech, although the difference was very slight (1–10%), and frequencies tended to level out from the end of twelfth century onwards.[20] It is not very likely that this factor played a major role, at least at that time. As regards the opposition between main declarative and subordinate clauses, no clear tendency can be discerned. VO order (vs. OV) was more frequent either in declarative or in subordinate clauses, depending on the texts, even in the

---

[20] Personal unpublished research.

most remote period. This factor, however, may have been influential earlier, in Late Latin, at the beginning of the change.

The question arises on the contrary as to the increase in preverbal nominal subjects. It is clear that prose did not offer a pioneering context, as it did for overt subjects. As for the domain, things are less straightforward: until the sixteenth century, non-literary texts (in particular didactic ones) displayed fairly high rates of preverbal subjects, but no clear tendency can be observed in literary texts. On the other hand, in Modern French, descriptive passages, whatever the textual domain, tend to favour postverbal subjects,[21] their usage pertaining most often to stylistic effects.[22]

The fact that the direct speech/narrative opposition strongly influenced the increase in overt subjects but had no effect on the increase in preverbal subjects may be accounted for by the fact that overt expression (especially first-person pronouns) was associated with expressivity and emphasis, which are more likely to appear in spoken language, and hence in direct speech (as it is a kind of reflection of it). No expressive effect has ever been associated with the preverbal position, and it is thus no surprise that direct speech was not a pioneering context for the propagation of preverbal contexts.

I am well aware that the preceding pages have sketched an incomplete picture of the role that different factors played in the increase in overt subjects on the one hand, and of preverbal subjects on the other. There still remain many aspects to investigate to provide a more thorough account. However, I hope to have shown that taking these different factors into account makes it possible both to refine the chronology of these changes and to (partly) suggest some motivations for the changes, while identifying the contexts (in the broad sense) conducive to these evolutions.

I would like to underscore the fact that this contribution does not claim in any way to provide a true sociohistorical study, but, more modestly, some kind of a variationist approach, which may, hopefully, bring new insights as regards two major and related changes which took place in the history of French.

Appendix 1   References of the texts of the corpus

[ArchierBaignollet] *Franc (Le) archier de Baignollet* (Frantext - Fr)
[Aucassin] *Aucassin et Nicolette* (Base de français médiéval - BFM)
[Beaumanoir] Philippe de Beaumanoir, *Coutumes de Beauvaisis* (BFM)
[BeroaldeParvenir] Béroalde de Verville, François, *Le Moyen de parvenir* (Fr)
[BeroulTristan] Beroul, *Tristan* (BFM)
[CalvinLettres] Calvin, Jean, *Lettres à Monsieur et Madame de Falais* (Fr)

---

[21] Though only in a relatively narrow set of contexts and the phenomenon quantitatively remains in the minority.
[22] See Carruthers (2018).

[CentNouvelles] *Cent nouvelles nouvelles* (Fr)
[ClariConstantinople] Robert de Clari, *Conquête de Constantinople* (BFM)
[Commynes] Philippe de Commynes, *Mémoires* (BFM)
[Descartes] Descartes, René, *Discours de la méthode* (Fr)
[Eneas] *Eneas 1 et 2* (BFM)
[GersonSermon] Gerson, Jean, *Sermon pour la fête de la Sainte Trinité* (Fr)
[Graal] *Queste del saint Graal* (BFM)
[Griseldis] *Estoire de Griseldis en rimes et par personnages* (BFM)
[JehanParis] *Roman de Jehan de Paris* (BFM)
[Joinville] Jean de Joinville, *Vie de saint Louis* (Fr)
[Lapidaire] *Lapidaire en prose* (BFM)
[LéryBrésil] Léry, Jean de, *Histoire d'un voyage fait en la terre du Bresil* (Bibliothèques virtuelles humanistes - BVH)
[MachautFortune] Guillaume de Machaut, *Remede de Fortune* (BFM)
[Manières] *Manières de langage* (BFM)
[Mesnagier] *Mesnagier de Paris* (BFM)
[Montaigne] Montaigne, Michel de, *Essais* (Fr)
[Passion] *Passion de Jésus-Christ ou Passion de Clermont* (BFM)
[Pathelin] *La Farce de maître Pierre Pathelin* (BFM)
[QuinzeJoies] *Quinze joies de mariage* (BFM)
[RenartDole] Jean Renart, *Roman de la Rose ou de Guillaume de Dole* (BFM)
[Roland] *Chanson de Roland* (BFM)
[RonsardMisères] Ronsard, Pierre de, *Discours des Miseres de ce temps* (BVH)
[SorelBerger] Sorel Charles, *Le Berger extravagant* (Fr)
[StAlexis] *Vie de saint Alexis* (BFM)
[StLegier] *Vie de saint Léger* (BFM)
[TroyesYvain] Chrétien de Troyes, *Chevalier au Lion ou Yvain* (BFM)
[Vigneulles] Vigneulles, Philippe de, *Les Cent Nouvelles nouvelles* (Fr)

5
The evolution of 'background' from Middle to pre-Classical French

Bernard Combettes

5.1 Introduction: Information structure and the complex sentence

In the field of information structure, the contrast between foreground and background is a topic that provides ample opportunity for exploration and has indeed already been the subject of a significant amount of research, especially contemporary synchronic studies. The commonly accepted definition of this contrast was developed from the 1980s onwards, most notably by Hopper (1979), Reinhart (1984), Tomlin (1985), and Thompson (1987), and essentially relies on the criterion of chronological order: the order of clauses in the foreground corresponds to the iconic sequence of events being narrated, while the clauses forming the background relate to states of affairs that are not part of the narrative line. This distinction is encoded by various markers, which are specific to particular linguistic systems. Generally, if information provided by the lexicon is excluded, markers of background sections come from two broad areas: verb forms and syntax. In the case of verbs, this takes the form of an opposition between bounded and unbounded aspectual properties, both in French and in many other languages: in Modern French, this corresponds to the opposition between the *passé simple* (or *passé composé*) and the imperfect.

The area of syntax can be divided into two subareas: positional syntax, insofar as the types of thematic progression that characterize the foreground and background tend to be realized in the form of specific syntactic patterns (Hopper 1979; Lambrecht 1987; Combettes 1993, 2011); and the system of subordination, in terms of the status of clauses according to a continuum that runs from parataxis to hypotaxis. The investigation of this second domain has resulted in much discussion (Thompson 1987) because of a lack of agreement: subordination is not necessarily reserved for the expression of background information alone. In the case of French, this can be illustrated by taking the case of inverse subordination, where the term itself is already a clear indicator that it consists of a reversal of the usual pattern; information in the foreground, i.e. the principal information, is expressed as a subordinate clause. Another case in point is the continuative relative

Bernard Combettes, *The evolution of 'background' from Middle to pre-Classical French*. In: *Historical and Sociolinguistic Approaches to French*. Edited by: Janice Carruthers, Mairi McLaughlin, and Olivia Walsh, Oxford University Press.
© Bernard Combettes (2024). DOI: 10.1093/oso/9780192894366.003.0005

subordinate, as in the example *il renversa le vase, qui se brisa*: here, the relative clause, which acts as a chronological extension of the matrix clause, again forms part of the foreground. One of the explanations proposed to account for this lack of consensus involves interpreting the decision to place foreground information in a subordinate clause as marking a particular discourse relation in addition to its usual temporal value (Thompson 1987: 450).

In this chapter, I offer a new approach to the question of the role of subordination in marking the opposition between foreground and background, particularly in terms of how it relates to paratactic constructions. I will focus on the diachronic dimension, since the development of these markers over time is particularly interesting. In fact, it is possible to identify variation on two axes, in terms of both the evolution of the linguistic system and the nature of the discourse in question: while the first may seem obvious, the second is less frequently taken into account. I shall examine this two-dimensional variation with a focus on the pre-Classical period, an interesting stage in the history of French because it is a transition period. The evolution of textual structures and of the way in which they are marked goes hand in hand with changes that affect textuality, which can relate, for example, to the way in which a text is created or to its narrative style. Thus, it seems appropriate at the outset to recall that descriptive text, such as it is, does not appear to have properly developed as an autonomous text type until around the middle of the fifteenth century. Finally, I will pay particular attention to a construction that relates to both verbal tense and subordination, namely inverse subordination. As its name suggests, it involves syntactic structure, but verb forms are also involved. In particular, I will attempt to show that it is useful to set this phenomenon in a more general context than the one in which it is normally framed.

Before tackling the period from the mid-sixteenth century to the first thirty years of the seventeenth, it is useful to summarize the situation in Old and Middle French texts.[1]

5.2 Old and Middle French

If we consider a long period that includes Old and Middle French, the general development of information structuring is characterized by background material becoming increasingly independent. It is, however, useful to distinguish two types of example which differ in terms of their length. The first consists of cases where there are sequences of background information which are relatively long and normally correspond to descriptions or to establishing context for a 'once

---

[1] Unless otherwise indicated, the examples in my corpus come from the *Frantext* database (www.frantext.fr (accessed 19 July 2022)), which is a particularly useful source of examples where the opposition between foreground and background is fully realized in narrative prose.

upon a time'-style narrative. The second type can involve shorter fragments, normally consisting of a single clause, which are woven into the narration and do not technically form an autonomous sequence or a separate background text that can be identified as such. Given that my interest is in the role of subordination, it is this second type that I shall examine here.

5.2.1 Old French

Examining Old French texts shows that the situation in this period can be characterized as one where background text is subordinated to foreground: this subordination is particularly evident in narrative prose texts. More broadly, we can relate this to the role of description, which is very much dependent on the main narration. One of the reasons for this asymmetric relationship is the importance granted to characters' actions and perceptions, which effectively act as channels through which descriptions are passed. From a syntactic perspective, this places the background information in a position of dependence on the clauses in the foreground. This dependence can be expressed by syntactic subordination, often with the use of a relative clause, as in example (1).

(1) si se regarde et voit un serpent qui portoit un petit lyon et le tenoit par le col as danz (*La Queste del Saint Graal*, Pauphilet 1949 [c.1225]: 94)

'thus he looks around and sees a snake which was carrying a small lion and was holding it by the neck with its teeth'[2]

It can also be marked by a conjunction such as *car*, as in example (2).

(2) et vit le plus bel lit qu'il onques veist. Car le liz ert granz et riches, et avoit au chevet une corone d'or mout riche [...] (*La Queste del Saint Graal*, Pauphilet 1949: 202)

'and he saw the most beautiful bed he had ever seen. For the bed was large and rich, and had at its head a very rich crown of gold ...'

Among the syntactic constructions that appear to favour this method of expressing the alternation between foreground and background, relative and circumstantial clauses are very common, as are certain correlative expressions that also permit the expression of specific relationships between two clauses. From the Old French period onwards, we find examples of a correlation involving *si* or *tant* ... *que* expressing a consequence: as a rule, this construction corresponds to the positioning of two clauses in the foreground, characterized by a sequence of two verbs in the *passé simple*, as in examples (3) and (4).

---

[2] Translations are literal rather than stylistic or natural, to illustrate the use of the specific linguistic forms of interest to the discussion.

(3) car il se deffendit si bien et tant fu vistes et preux qu'il les mist errannment a desconfiture, si qu'il leur fist guerpir le champ (*La Suite du Roman de Merlin*, Roussineau 2006 [1218]: 429)

'for he defended himself so well and was so agile and bold that he soon put them to flight, such that he made them abandon the battlefield'

(4) Mais tant fu sages [...] / Qu'au roi dou ciel se confessa (de Coincy 1966 [1218]: 129)

'But he was so wise ... / that he confessed to the king of the heaven'

In such sequences, it is very rare to find the sequence imperfect + *passé simple*, where the foreground information is dependent on a previously established situation. When the imperfect is used to express the cause element of a cause and effect relationship, this is normally done in a very frequent pattern (cf. example 2) where the foreground information uses the *passé simple* or the present, and the background information uses the imperfect, with the two linked by a conjunction such as *car*, as in example (5).

(5) Pas nel conut Guillelmes li guerriers, / Car de clarté aveit pou al mostier (*Le Couronnement de Louis*, Langlois 1920 [1130]: 54)

'Guillaume the warrior did not recognize him, / for there was little light in the church'

It is worth noting that the aspectual status of the *passé simple*, which can in certain contexts alternate with the imperfect, results in an ambiguity in example (4): in effect *tant fu sages* can be interpreted as foreground information with bounded scope, equivalent to *il fut (alors) si sage*, or as background information with unbounded scope, equivalent to *il était si sage*. Most interesting, however, is the near absence of the imperfect in the first clause of such constructions, suggesting that the status of this form hindered its use in independent clauses.

This type of information structuring, which favours hypotaxis for expressing background information, gradually came to be superseded and was no longer dominant after the Old French period. Instead, other discursive configurations began to enter into competition with it, with consequences for the types of syntactic construction used. As in a number of other respects, Middle French seems to have been a period of transition, which saw several important changes in the way in which background information was expressed.

5.2.2 Middle French

5.2.2.1 Developments in the preverbal zone

In Middle French, changes in the formation of the preverbal part of the sentence, which began to accept a greater number of constituents, brought about a more frequent use of relatives and secondary predicates such as appositive phrases and gerundives with an explanatory or descriptive value. As regards the distinction between foreground and background in complex sentences, the move away from V2 order was accompanied by the expansion of the initial part of the sentence to include constituents expressing background information, whether this involved circumstantial subordinate clauses, as in Old French (example 6), or secondary predicates, as in example (7).

(6) Et en tel estat que le Cueur regardoit les pucelles nagier, il eut pitié de la grant peine [...] (1457; d'Anjou 1980: 102)

'And as the Heart was watching the girls swim, he had pity on the great suffering...'

(7) Ainsi disant comme ilz parloient ensemble, et veue la mer qui estoit clere et necte ung bien petit doulcement undoyer d'un vent froiz [...], si cesserent les deux dames de nager (1457; d'Anjou 1980: 103)

'Saying such things as they were talking together, and with the sight of the sea which was clear and clean sweetly rippling a little with a cold wind..., the two ladies thus stopped swimming'

Example (7) illustrates the diversity of the syntactic structures that can open a statement and constitute background information: a form in -*ant* (*disant*), a circumstantial subordinate (*comme ils parloient*), and a participial subordinate (*vue la mer ondoyer*).

In addition, when background information has explanatory value, we often find that a relative is placed between the VP subject and the verb, as in example (8).

(8) Mais le Cueur, qui fain avoit de veoir le cymetiere de leans et aussi d'avoir acointance a dame Courtoisie l'enfermiere, pource qu'il la veoit si dame de bien, parla a elle [...] (1457; d'Anjou 1980: 119)

'But the Heart, which very much wanted to see the cemetery of that place and also to meet lady Courtesy the nurse, because he saw her as such a noble lady, spoke to her...'

This type of subordination where background information is followed by foreground information is sometimes only superficial, and it is not uncommon to find the construction disrupted. In example (9), the phrase *ainsi que* introduces a relatively long section of background information, which serves as context for the information in the foreground, *les firent coucher*: this second part of the passage is connected to the first by *dont*, which effectively serves to cancel the subordination. The clauses are thus in a paratactic relationship, although it is interesting that background in this case has come to be associated with a term that normally marks subordination.

(9) Ainsi doncques que Desir se lamentoit en tel point que cy dessus est dit pour la tormente de la mer qui le traveilloit sans repos, et non pas seulement lui, mais ses deux autres compaignons aussi, neantmoins qu'ilz n'en sonnoient mot et que nullement se plaignoient; mais c'estoit pource que de leur bouche n'eust peu yssir ung trestout seul mot, tant d'angoisse et de douleur sentoient, et moult tresbien apparoit a leurs visaiges. Dont quant les deux dames marinieres les apperceurent, si les firent couchier affin que [...] (1457; d'Anjou 1980: 104)[3]

'Thus when Desire was lamenting to the extent described above for the torment of the sea which was torturing him without rest, and not only him, but his two other companions as well, although they were not saying a word about it and were not complaining at all; but it was because not one sole word would have been able to come out of their mouths, they were experiencing so much anguish and pain, and it was very much apparent on their faces. So when the two sailor women saw them, they thus made them lie down so that . . .'

These observations about the development of these structures in Middle French appear to confirm the general trend, already very clear in Old French, of background information being associated with subordination. For reasons that will be discussed in the following sections, developments also occurred in the opposite direction, with the result that background information acquired greater syntactic autonomy. Perhaps as a result of the influence of the type of descriptive sequences found at the beginning of narratives to set the context (discussed at the start of Section 5.2), clauses containing background information appear more and more frequently as independent units, especially in a number of specific contexts.

5.2.2.2 Background and parataxis

The way in which paratactic phrases developed, both with and without linking words, created certain textual imbalances. As regards the order of clauses, it is more common for foreground information to precede background information. Expressing background information paratactically is thus essentially reserved for a comment after the fact, normally involving causality or opposition, hence the use of conjunctions such as *car* (example 10), *mais* (example 11), or *néanmoins* (example 12).

(10) [...] et pour un peu en perdit la parole. Car elle savoit par renommée qu'il estoit perilleux [...] (*Les cent nouvelles nouvelles*, Sweetser 1966 [c.1465]: 101)

'... and for a while she could not speak of it. For she knew by his reputation that he was dangerous ...'

---

[3] Note that *dont* in the original is the equivalent of modern French *donc*, translated as *so* below.

(11) Et quand elle vit qu'elle n'avoit puissance que de sa langue, Dieu scet s'elle la mist en œuvre, mais adressoit la plus part de ses motz venimeux sur la pouvre Jehannette [...] (*Les cent nouvelles nouvelles*, Sweetser 1966 [c.1465]: 272)

'And when she saw that she was able to use only her tongue, God knows if she put it to work, but she was addressing most of her poisonous words to poor Jeannette...'

(12) [...] mais pacience eurent; et neantmoins le travail de la mer dudit jour precedent leur faisoit leur repos trop plus savoureux ressembler [...] (1457; d'Anjou 1980: 107)

'...but they had patience; and nonetheless the work of the sea of the aforementioned preceding day was making their rest seem much sweeter...'

Even where there is no actual conjunction, a discourse organization element such as *d'autre côté* can make the oppositional relationship explicit in the same way as *mais*, as in example (13).

(13) il se doubta beaucop de point parvenir a son intencion, veu qu'il ne povoit obtenir d'elle ung seul baiser. Il se confortoit d'aultre costé des gracieuses paroles qu'il eut au dire adieu (*Les cent nouvelles nouvelles*, Sweetser 1966 [c.1465]: 316)

'he doubted very much that he would be able to do what he intended, given that he could not get one sole kiss from her. He was comforting himself on the other hand with the gracious words he received at their farewell'

All of this suggests that the association of background information with hypotaxis was historically strong enough, even in these cases of parataxis, to require the presence of an explicit marker of the asymmetry between foreground and background: coordination with *et* is the most basic way of doing this. This sometimes involves reinforcing a causal relationship (example 14), or an opposition (example 15) where the difference between two groups of characters is highlighted by *même*. In other cases, however, coordination is not accompanied by any particular semantic connection. The imperfect thus appears to alternate freely with the *passé simple*, as in example (16).

(14) son compaignon [...] se sentit tresmalade, et demandoit partout apres celui qui desja estoit mort (*Les cent nouvelles nouvelles*, Sweetser 1966 [c.1465]: 349)

'his companion... felt very ill, and was asking everywhere about the one who had already died'

(15) ilz se vouldrent prendre au marchant, et luy dirent autant de honte [...]; et mesmes les femmes luy vouloient courre sus (*Les cent nouvelles nouvelles*, Sweetser 1966 [*c*.1465]: 384)

'they wanted to attack the merchant, and said so many shameful things to him...; and even the women were wanting to attack him'

(16) Et les deux ouvriers [...] vindrent au dessus de la fosse saluer la compaignie, et leur disoient qu'ilz eussent bonne chere (*Les cent nouvelles nouvelles*, Sweetser 1966 [*c*.1465]: 355)

'And the two workers... came above the ditch to greet the company, and were wishing them good cheer'

This final type of sequence, where a background interpretation can be justified by the partial overlap of the two events (*vindrent*, *disoient*), is, however, found in a particular configuration: the clause containing the background information (*et leur disoient*) has no semantic relationship with the preceding clause (*vindrent au dessus de la fosse*), but rather with the clause that it governs (*qu'ilz eussent bonne chere*). In example (17), a chronological relationship—indicating the interruption of a state of affairs, which explains why the background information comes first—is established between the two final clauses, while the background clause is coordinated with the element to its left.

(17) Si se leverent et au ray de la lune regardoient le rochier et la marine aussi. Mais il ne tarda mye que Compaignie et Amictié prindrent leurs lignes [...] (1457; d'Anjou 1980: 107)

'Thus they got up and by the light of the moon were watching the rock and the shore as well. But there was no delay before Company and Friendship drew up their troops...'

The elements are arranged in the same way in example (18), where the clause in the imperfect is in a cause–effect relationship with the context to its right (with the sense 'as they thought he would return, they allowed him to pass').

(18) Ilz virent passer nostre cure, et leur jugeoit le cueur qu'il retourneroit la nuyt [...] Ilz le laisserent passer [...] et s'adviserent de faire un piege [...] (*Les cent nouvelles nouvelles*, Sweetser 1966 [*c*.1465]: 353)

'They came to pass by our priest, and were believing he would come back in the night... They let him pass... and decided to make a trap...'

Moreover, paratactic configurations start to appear at this time, precursors to the type of sequence that will emerge later on. The conjunction appears no longer to be obligatory; the use of specific tenses and the semantic value of the statements are enough to express the discourse relation, for example in cases where a causal link is established with the preceding context (example 19, 'it is in vain, because he was not as fast'), or with the following context (example 20, 'as he had a reply to give, he said'), or indeed, in examples of a concession relation, made explicit by *toutesfoyz* (example 21, 'even though he could no longer bear it, he swallowed').

(19) son père le suyt, mais c'est pour neant: il n'estoit pas si radde du pyé comme lui (*Les cent nouvelles nouvelles*, Sweetser 1966 [c.1465]: 325)

'his father follows him, but it is for nothing; he was not so fleet of foot as him'

(20) Si dist on au sire que [...] Il estoit fourny de sa response, et dist [...] (*Les cent nouvelles nouvelles*, Sweetser 1966 [c.1465]: 334)

'Thus they said to the lord that ... He was provided with his answer, and said ...'

(21) et ce fait, le serviteur se partit de leans. Le pouvre mary, qui tout avoit veu et oy, n'en povoit plus, s'il n'enrageoit tout vif. Toutesfoyz, [...] il avala ceste premiere (*Les cent nouvelles nouvelles*, Sweetser 1966 [c.1465]: 321)

'and with this done, the servant left that place. The poor husband, who had seen and heard everything, could bear it no longer without becoming very enraged. However, ... he swallowed the first one'

Whether we are dealing with this arrangement, in which the foreground information follows the background information, or its opposite (as in examples 10–16), there is an almost systematic use of markers highlighting the asymmetry that is characteristic of the opposition between foreground and background.

5.2.2.3 Correlative phrases

In correlative constructions, the trends described in Section 5.2.1 are still present in Middle French: the verb forms in the two clauses are normally identical. In example (22), the presence of the imperfect in the initial clause therefore continues in the background clause.

(22) Il avoit manierez tant modereez que ce qu'il faisoit plaisoit a Dieu et au monde (*Le Roman du comte d'Artois*, Seigneuret 1966 [1453]: 26)

'He had such polite manners that what he was doing was pleasing to God and to the world'

It should be noted that the *passé simple*, on the other hand, can be followed by the imperfect: in such cases, the consequence is thus presented as background information, as in example (23).

(23) Madame, qui de celle tres desiree nouvelle fut si joieusement reconfortee que son cuer ne savoit ou il estoit (de la Sale 1965 [1456]: 158)

'My lady, who was so happily comforted by this much desired news that her heart did not know where it was'

Nonetheless, during the fifteenth century, there are a few occurrences of the imperfect in independent clauses at the beginning of a sentence, where the event in the foreground is the second element in a correlation (examples 24 and 25).

(24) [...] dont tant se repentoit que, peu a peu, en celle grant douleur [...], le cuer lui failly (de la Sale 1965 [1456]: 154)

'... for which he was repenting so much that, little by little, in this great pain ..., his heart failed him'

(25) vouloit parfaire ses autres armes, mais tant estoit le sang qui en sailloit que force lui fut soy en desister (de la Sale 1965 [1456]: 165)

'he was wanting to repair his other weapons, but there was so much blood that was flowing from him that he was obliged to stop himself doing it'

In example (26), both of the possibilities just evoked appear in sequence: the background (*faisoit si mate chiere*) introduces a consequence that is foregrounded (*sa face se changa*), which, in turn, is followed by a consequence that is backgrounded (*elle sambloit*).

(26) le premier jour du partement son tres amé mary, pour lequel elle faisoit si mate chiere que sa face qui fu par avant blanche et tendre, coulouree comme ung ymage, se changa et degasta tellement que elle sambloit au regarder mieulx morte que vive (Seigneuret 1966 [1453]: 100)

'the first day of the separation from her much beloved husband, for whose sake she was so unhappy that her face which was formerly white and soft, pretty as a picture, changed and wasted away so much that she seemed to the sight better dead than alive'

This arrangement of clauses, in which background information precedes foreground information, can no doubt be considered a precursor to the move towards inverse subordination, which involves the same sequence of tenses and the same syntactic articulation. Another possible precursor to inverse subordination is a construction in which the first clause contains a negation expressing incompletion in relation to a temporal space, conveying a semantic value similar to counterfactual imminence (examples 27 and 28).

(27) Mais ne tarda pas l'espace de deux patenostres que les trois compaignons [...] arriverent au lieu ou [...] (1457; d'Anjou 1980: 109)

'But the delay was not even the time of two Lord's Prayers that the three companions arrived at the place where...'

(28) Mais n'eurent pas cheminé ung trait d'arc dedans ledit semetiere qu'entre les autres tombes apperceurent a part [...] (1457; d'Anjou 1980: 141)

'But they had not travelled one arrow's flight in the said cemetery that among the other graves they noticed elsewhere...'

However, structures of this type do not use the imperfect in the first clause, but instead the *passé simple* or *passé antérieur*: the imperfect and pluperfect do not seem to feature in this construction until later with the emergence of inverse subordination.

The main point to note about Middle French is that the status of background information differs depending on its position relative to the foreground information. While sequences of paratactic clauses are attested more and more frequently with foreground preceding background, cases where background comes at the beginning of the sentence seem almost always to result in hypotactic constructions.

5.3 The mid-sixteenth century

While the beginnings of change are perceptible in Middle French, as we have seen, the opposition between foreground and background in complex sentences changes more significantly in the sixteenth century. In this section, I will describe the developments affecting two aspects of this opposition—correlations and parataxis—using Marguerite de Navarre's *Heptaméron* (de Navarre 1960 [*c*.1545]) as the main source of examples.

5.3.1 Correlative phrases

First, it should be noted that correlative phrases presenting background information at the beginning of the sentence are becoming more routine and this leads to a distinct increase in the number of sequences where the imperfect is followed by the *passé simple*. As in the fifteenth century, correlation operates with the help of intensity markers (*si, tant, tel*). In background clauses, this often involves the description of a character's feelings or thoughts; if it is a causal relation, this can result in an action or a decision, or it can mark a new stage in the unfolding of the narrative (examples 29 and 30).

(29) Or, y avoit il long temps que ung varlet de son mary l'aymoit si desesperement, que ung jour il ne se peut[4] tenir de luy en parler (de Navarre 1960 [*c*.1545]: 19)[5]

(30) Amadour, qui regardoit la beaulté de sa dame, estoit si très ravy, que à peyne luy peut-il dire grand mercy (de Navarre 1960 [*c*.1545]: 58)

---

[4] Note in examples (29) and (30) that *peut* is the Old French form for *put* (and not the present form *peut*).

[5] In accordance with the style guide, translations are not provided for examples from the Renaissance onwards.

It is worth pointing out, however, that sequences of two *passés simples* in this same syntactic structure and with the same causal relation remain common; these cases involve two foreground clauses, as in example (31).

(31) Le paige [...] alla porter à sa maistresse la lectre contrefaicte, qui en eut telle joye que son mary s'apperceut bien qu'elle avoit changé son visaige (de Navarre 1960 [c.1545]: 256)

As expected, correlation can also be expressed in sequences where the foreground precedes the background: in these cases, the clause in the imperfect relates to a state of affairs that remains part of the description or serves as a comment but does not interrupt narrative continuity. In example (32), one correlation is followed by another, the first using *tant ... que,* with the sequence *passé simple* + imperfect, and the second using *tellement que,* with the sequence imperfect + imperfect: the clause in the *passé simple* refers to a phase in the character's life, while those in the imperfect, the second element of each correlation, describe the consequences that could serve as a contextual frame for the rest of the narrative.

(32) ung jeune et beau gentil homme [...] lequel creut en sa croissance tant en beaulté et vertu, qu'il gouvernoit son maistre tout paisiblement, tellement que, quant il mandoit quelque chose à sa seur, estoit toujours par cestuy-là (de Navarre 1960 [c.1545]: 275)

More generally, where there is no correlation *stricto sensu,* the sentence can contain the succession of verb forms that interest us here (i.e. the imperfect followed by the *passé simple*) with the first clause being independent. What this structure has in common with correlative expressions is that the causal relation is established between the two clauses, with the syntactic marking of correlation, replaced, in a sense, by the use of a subordinator such as *par quoi* or *en sorte que* (examples 33 and 34).

(33) y avoit entre eulx telle amytié que, horsmis la femme, n'avoient rien party ensemble.
Parquoy il declaira à son amy l'entreprinse qu'il avoit sur sa chamberiere (de Navarre 1960 [c.1545]: 43)

(34) Mais la racine de l'orgueil que le peché exterieur doibt guerir, croissoit tousjours, en sorte que, en evitant ung mal, elle en feit plusieurs aultres (de Navarre 1960 [c.1545]: 231)

It seems reasonable to suppose that this type of configuration also has influence on a construction that I have already mentioned in the discussion of the earlier periods, namely negation combined with *que*. In fact, the imperfect is increasingly found in these hypotactic structures and it is beginning at this point to take the place of the *passé simple* in the initial clause. Thus, as well as clauses that continue the former trend, in which the *passé simple* is generalized (example 35), we also find clauses using the imperfect, as in example (36).

(35) Il ne demora poinct ung mois en la compagnye après ses nopces, qu'il fust contrainct de retourner à la guerre, où il demoura plus de deux ans (de Navarre 1960 [*c*.1545]: 60)

(36) Et n'estoit pas encores à peine le mary hors la porte, qu'elle descendit en l'estable, où elle trouva que quelque chose defailloit (de Navarre 1960 [*c*.1545]: 211)

It is interesting that the influence from the more general pattern seems strong enough to expand beyond cases of negation: examples without negation may be rare but there are enough of them to show that the linearization of tenses is a sufficient marker of the relationship between foreground and background and these cases therefore foreshadow what will become the classic pattern of inverse subordination. The sense of imminence, formerly expressed using negation, can now be expressed using an adverb such as *déjà*, as in example (37).

(37) Desja estoit la my karesme, que la dame ne laissa, ne pour Passion ne pour Sepmaine saincte, sa manière accoustumée de mander par lectres sa furieuse fantaisye (de Navarre 1960 [*c*.1545]: 257)

On the other hand, in passages such as example (38), there is no element in the first clause that would establish a correlation with the conjunction *que* that begins the second part of the sentence, and this construction therefore no longer permits the expression of counterfactual imminence. The background corresponds to what would be rendered by a temporal clause (*alors que le comte était à Cognac...*), the relationship between the two clauses being what we would normally consider inverse subordination. At around the same time, inverse subordination also appears with the conjunction *quand* in example (39), an isolated example in the writing of Bonaventure des Périers.

(38) Le conte Charles d'Angoulesme [...] estoit à Coignac, que l'on luy racompta que [...] (de Navarre 1960 [*c*.1545]: 247)

(39) Il estoit desja à une lieue loing quand mes deux cordouanniers se trouverent à l'hostelerie (1558; des Périers 1980 [1558]: 112)

It is not until the beginning of the seventeenth century that this type of information structuring really becomes frequent.

5.3.2 The development of parataxis

At the beginning of the sentence, clauses expressing background information could appear in order merely to provide a contextual frame, without any particular logical relationship being expressed. In this case, the foreground clause is normally linked to the background clause using *et*, and the subject is not repeated, which gives a strong sense of continuity and creates a tight link between the two elements of the complex phrase. While there is no subordination in the strict sense, this arrangement of elements does express a highly dependent relationship between the two clauses, a relationship that can be likened to the one established by correlative expressions, as in examples (40) and (41).

(40) Mais, pour l'amour de sa femme, qu'elle aymoit plus que nulle autre, elle estoit si privée de luy, qu'elle ne luy dissimulloit chose qu'elle pensat; et eut cest heur qu'elle luy declaira toute l'amour [...] (de Navarre 1960 [*c.*1545]: 60)

(41) La contesse d'Arande s'estoit retirée en une maison de plaisance qu'elle avoit sur la frontiere d'Arragon et de Navarre; et fut fort aise, quand elle veit revenir Amadour (de Navarre 1960 [*c.*1545]: 61)

The semantic relationship is more precise when a contrast is expressed, as in example (42), where the connection is made by the conjunction *mais*.

(42) Et, congnoissant la fin de sa vye approcher, s'estoit le matin confessé et receu le sainct sacrement, pensant mourir sans plus veoir personne. Mais, luy, à deux doigtz de la mort, voyant entrer celle qui estoit sa vie et resurrection, se sentit si fortiffié, qu'il se gecta en sursault sur son lict (de Navarre 1960 [*c.*1545]: 51)

Example (43) is particularly interesting. The proposition *Bernaige avoit grande envie* shows no link with the preceding context: the use of *mais* assures some level of cohesion, which allows the phrase to function autonomously because the background is tightly integrated and requires no supplementary marking; the earlier tendency would have required the use of a subordinate clause to express the background, as is the case with *nonobstant que* in example (44).

(43) Le gentil homme tira ung rideau qui estoit devant une grande armoyre, où il veid penduz tous les oz d'un homme mort. Bernaige avoit grande envie de parler à la dame, mais, de paour du mary, il n'osa (de Navarre 1960 [*c.*1545]: 244)

(44) Le frere, nonobstant qu'il fust esmeu jusques à perdre la raison, si eut-il tant de pitié de sa seur, que, sans luy accorder ne nyer sa requeste, la laissa (de Navarre 1960 [*c.*1545]: 276)

It is nonetheless possible to identify some examples that do not make use of any specific marker, but are instead made up of a simple sequence of clauses. Example (45) presents a relatively long sequence of imperfects; the passage in the foreground, using the *passé simple* (*fut*), presents a change of topic, which corresponds to the alternation between characters.

(45) Floride, pour l'amitié qu'elle portoit à sa femme Avanturade et à luy, le chercheoit en tous lieux où elle le voioit; et ne se doubtoit en riens de son intention: parquoy elle ne se gardoit de nulle contenance, pour ce que son cueur ne souffroit nulle passion, sinon qu'elle sentoit ung très grand contentement, quant elle estoit auprès de luy, mais autre chose n'y pensoit. Amadour, pour eviter le jugement de ceulx qui ont experimenté la difference du regard des amans au pris des aultres, fut en grande peyne (de Navarre 1960 [c.1545]: 61)

Example (46) clearly shows how the background clause is gaining autonomy: unlike in example (45), the subject/topic remains identical in both clauses. However, this leads neither to the hypotactic construction that would be expected (*comme il voyait...*), nor to the use of a linking word such as *et* (cf. examples 40 and 41).

(46) Ung jour, il voyoit que sa femme ne dansoit poinct, commanda à Nicolas de la mener dancer (de Navarre 1960 [c.1545]: 263)

This development affecting background sections can result in fairly long sequences: while in example (45) the imperfects have an iterative value, this is not the case in example (47), where the background expresses a succession of individual processes. This extension of the imperfect is somewhat surprising, and difficult to explain: the causal value of the background ought to limit the use of this verb form to sequences like (*comme*) *elle allait au-devant de lui et lui portait [...], il lui dit*, etc. The phrases *faire son lit* and *attendre son retour*, which form part of the same narrative line as *fit le guet... se leva*, would seem to call instead for the *passé simple*.

(47) Et, ung jour, feit le guet, quant il se leveroit d'auprès d'elle, et se leva pareillement avec son manteau de nuyct; faisoit faire son lict, et, en disant ses Heures, attendoit le retour de son mary; et, quant il entroit, alloit au devant de luy le baiser, et luy portoit ung bassin et de l'eaue pour laver ses mains. Luy, estonné de ceste nouvelle façon, luy dist qu'il ne venoit que du retraict (de Navarre 1960 [c.1545]: 267)

Comparing this example to the previous examples shows how the status of background sections has evolved and, in tandem, how the aspectual opposition in which the *passé simple* was previously the unmarked form has been changed.

Despite some examples (e.g. example 45) that illustrate the emergence of autonomous background sections, occurrences of sequences in parataxis are relatively rare. There is, however, one important asymmetry: this autonomy can be seen in sequences where background precedes foreground, which, in many cases, indicates a relationship of causality. The opposite order, foreground followed by background, in which the second clause could indicate a cause or an effect, does not appear to be attested in an asyndetic construction: when this latter order is used, the relationship between foreground and background is marked by a conjunction or by subordination, as in examples (48) and (49).

(48) Toutesfois, elle languit encores une heure sans parler, faisant signe des oeilz et des mains; en quoi elle monstroit n'avoir perdu l'entendement (de Navarre 1960 [c.1545]: 20)

(49) Et après ces propos, s'en alla Amadour hanter le filz de l'Infant Fortuné, duquel il eut aisement la bonne grace, pource que tous les passetemps que le jeune prince aymoit, Amadour les sçavoit tous faire (de Navarre 1960 [c.1545]: 59)

What has changed from the preceding period is that the background in independent clauses is now more and more strongly associated with initial position, a characteristic that must be related to correlative expressions, which show the same division of labour for different verb forms.

It is thus possible to observe movement in two directions. First, descriptive passages are acquiring more autonomy, making use of a particular type of structure, and occurring more frequently in the texts. This increase in frequency is an issue that I do not explore here, since it is not related to the construction of complex sentences; it is nonetheless important to note that there is an increase in frequency because it relates to the evolution of paratactic expressions. Second, and we might say in parallel, background as a concept is also evolving in cases where it is reduced to one clause or to a short sequence of clauses. This development also occurs in two opposing directions: on the one hand, there is an increase in the autonomy of the background clause, which functions without any discourse relation marker, and on the other hand, this clause is grammaticalizing under the influence of correlative expressions that make use of the sequence background + conjunction + foreground, a structure in which the foreground seems to be syntactically subordinated to the background. It is this last emerging trend that will encourage the development of inverse subordination.

5.4 The early seventeenth century

The first thirty years of the seventeenth century, which correspond to the end of the pre-Classical French period, show an accentuation of the trends that I have described. The timing of these developments can undoubtedly be linked to concurrent changes affecting the status of the foreground/background opposition in discourse organization. More broadly, they are also connected to the way in which the literary text is created. I shall return to these points in Section 5.5.

5.4.1 The persistence of correlation

The evolution of the status of the background does not result in the disappearance of the system of correlations that characterized the preceding period. In terms of how background and foreground are distributed, there is a systematic use of sequences where the imperfect is found in initial position and a subordinator is used to mark the division between the foreground and the background. Correlations using *si . . . que* show this development clearly, as in examples (50) and (51).

(50) Il estoit si tard qu'il ne s'en put retourner (1627; Sorel 1972: 143)

(51) Il avoit si faim qu'il ne put refuser (1627; Sorel 1972: 148)

This subordination of the foreground also extends to phrases that are not correlative, whether they be subordinate clauses introduced by *de sorte que* (example 52), or, more rarely, relative clauses (example 53). However, expressions involving negation show systematic use of the *passé antérieur* in the first clause, with the pluperfect not yet being extended to this construction (examples 54 and 55).

(52) Elle avoit du vin [. . .] de sorte que [. . .] en fit apporter
    (1627; Sorel 1972: 137)

(53) Il y avoit cinq ou six petits enfants [. . .] qui accoururent
    (1627; Sorel 1972: 148)

(54) Il n'eut pas fait deux lieues qu'il se trouva [. . .] (1627; Sorel 1972: 150)

(55) Il n'eut pas si tost dit que [. . .] que chacun se douta [. . .]
    (1627; Sorel 1972: 156)

This resistance is likely to be the result of fossilization due to the lack of variety in the verbs used in this context—mostly *faire*, *dire*, and verbs derived from them—as well as the frequent presence of adverbs such as *sitôt*.

5.4.2 Parataxis

When examining paratactic expressions, it is useful to distinguish two types of construction which differ according to the content that is conveyed by the background clause. This clause sometimes has a merely descriptive value, where no particular logical link with the foreground is expressed; at other times, it can establish a link of cause, effect, or concession, and it is in such cases that a conjunction is often used to highlight the discourse relation. In general, the evolution of this structure seems to lead to this marker not being expressed, which suggests that the verb form—the imperfect or pluperfect—was enough to indicate the logical relation. This distinction between two types of parataxis was much less common in texts from earlier periods, given that the first category was rarely attested and that background clauses essentially functioned as explanatory commentaries.

5.4.2.1 Descriptive parataxis

A merely descriptive background establishes no logical link with the preceding context, but can be developed in the text that follows, in that it can act as a kind of frame for the events in the foreground. Sorel's *Le Berger extravagant* (1972, first edition 1627) offers a number of examples of this type of sequence, in which the use of *et* or a conjunction such as *mais* to introduce the foreground sometimes denotes a chronological relationship that is very similar to the one expressed by inverse subordination, where the foreground information serves to interrupt the situation described in the initial clause (examples 56–58).

(56) Charite [...] estoit fort importunée de cet entretien et Angelique l'obligea fort l'appelant [...] (1627; Sorel 1972: 136)

(57) Ce qui estoit de plaisant estoit que [...] il fondoit petit à petit, et enfin il chanta si bas que [...] (1627; Sorel 1972: 147)

(58) Ce parfait amant estoit en train de dire une infinité de choses [...] mais le maistre de la maison fit cesser tous ces discours (1627; Sorel 1972: 130)

Elsewhere, the clauses are juxtaposed without the link between them being marked in any way (examples 59 and 60).

(59) Il y avoit des gens en sa boutique qui venoient acheter des livres [...] Une vendeuse de salade [...] tira par le tablier une crieuse de poires cuites [...] (1627; Sorel 1972: 128)

(60) Ses ongles estoient desja rongez jusqu'à la racine, et il s'estoit mis en tant de diverses postures [...] qu'il en estoit tout lassé. Clarimond en eut quelque pitié (1627; Sorel 1972: 144)

This type of information structuring can clearly be very similar to that used in a descriptive text; passages conveying background information become longer and involve multiple clauses.

In other cases, the background sequence follows the foreground: this configuration is found in the same period in the work of authors such as de Rosset. This can involve, for example, description of characters, where we might have expected a relative subordinate clause introduced by *qui* or *lequel* (examples 61 and 62).

(61) A peine a-t-il achevé de proférer ces paroles qu'il aperçoit [...] une damoiselle bien vêtue [...]. Elle marchait à grande hâte, et semblait que [...] (1619; de Rosset 1997: 24)

(62) Comme il s'y entretient avec d'autres cavaliers, une jeune damoiselle y passe masquée. Elle était de belle taille et de fort bonne mine (1619; de Rosset 1997: 32)

However, it can also be used in descriptions of scenes, as in example (63), where earlier texts would have used verbs of perception or movement.

(63) Mais, le commissaire ayant menacé de l'enfoncer, on lui ouvrit. Elle était dans le lit, et lui à demi habillé (1619; de Rosset 1997: 19)

In example (64), the background involves a description of both the circumstances of the action and the character's personality.

(64) [...] une prochaine forêt, où elle marcha tout le reste de la nuit en pleurant, sans tenir ni chemin ni sentier. Les ronces et les épines l'arrêtaient souvent par ses blonds cheveux, dont elle en laissait des marques en plusieurs lieux. Toutefois elle ne s'en souciait guère [...] (1619; de Rosset 1997: 40)

In terms of the use of linguistic markers and the ordering of background and foreground, this increased independence of background clauses tends to reduce the differences that can exist between brief background passages and those that include entire sequences of text.

5.4.2.2 Parataxis with an explanatory function

Parataxis can also express a logical relationship, usually causal, where the background functions as a comment on the foreground information that it accompanies. This second configuration is especially interesting: while in the older system the discourse relation was normally made explicit by a conjunction such as *car* or a construction such as *c'est que*, the presence of such markers seems to be less and less necessary. In examples (65) and (66), the expression of background through parataxis is enough to permit the clause to be interpreted as a justificatory commentary, which could be rendered using *car* (*car il ne fallait plus qu'il vît*; *car il n'allait qu'à cloche-pied*).

(65) Ayant trouvé aussi dans son équipage le portraict metaphorique et toutes les choses qu'il gardoit [...], il les donna librement à Clarimond pour en faire ce qu'il luy plairoit. Il ne faloit plus qu'il vist des marques de ses anciennes erreurs [...] (1627; Sorel 1972: 545)

(66) Lysis [...] s'en retourna avec Anselme d'une fort plaisante façon. N'ayant qu'un soulier, il n'alloit qu'à cloche-pied, de peur de gaster sa chausse, et se soustenoit sur un baston [...] (1627; Sorel 1972: 90)

This type of commentary is found less frequently at the beginning of sentences, although we do see it in example (67), where explanatory parataxis appears to be a new development where we might otherwise find the use of a subordinate clause headed by *comme* (*comme il n'avait point de cheval...*).

(67) Il le pria de venir saigner son maistre. Le barbier n'avoit point de cheval, il s'en vint avec luy à pied [...] (1627; Sorel 1972: 248)

Finally, there is a specific context in which parataxis is accompanied by an opposition marker such as *mais*: in examples (68) and (69), the chronological value associated with interrupting a process produces a discourse relation that can be interpreted as expressing concession.

(68) Le mari [...] ne savait que dire ni que faire. Une fois, il voulait sans autre procédure se venger d'eux [...] Mais, puis après, venant à se représenter que [...], il dissimula sa juste douleur (1619; de Rosset 1997: 15)

(69) Le projet fut de s'en défaire [...] Une fois, Flaminie avait résolu d'y employer le poison. Mais Salluste, craignant que [...], prit sur lui la charge de le dépêcher (1619; de Rosset 1997: 56)

This pattern is very close to that found in inverse subordination: example (69) could for example be paraphrased as *Flaminie avait résolu... quand Salluste prit sur lui....*

It can therefore be surmised that the imbalances that I have pointed out in the sixteenth-century texts are by this point disappearing. Whatever the role of the background in parataxis, whether it has a descriptive or an explanatory function, the order of clauses no longer seems to be affected by constraints; moreover, in explanatory parataxis, the presence of a connector no longer seems necessary. Thus, we can see that background has become fully syntactically independent, and that it is additionally beginning to acquire what could be considered independence at a textual level, in terms of how descriptive passages are structured. These two consequences must surely be interpreted as the result of a general development that affects background in all its possible realizations. It must however be noted that in the specific case of a structure such as inverse subordination, the change appears to occur in the opposite direction, with the articulation of foreground and background resulting in the creation of a syntactic construction, as we will see in Section 5.5.

5.5 Emergence and extension of a construction: Inverse subordination

Although I have just described the change which led to a more systematic and frequent use of paratactic expressions, it should be remembered that circumstantial subordinate clauses expressing time, cause, and concession, along with relative clauses, remained the favoured structures for expressing background. It may seem surprising that at around the same time a type of syntactic organization developed that seems to go against the general trend, namely inverse subordination (IS), where the name itself reflects the abnormality of this type of phrase. Traditionally, this phenomenon is viewed as a sort of distortion of the usual link between the syntactic structure of a phrase and its semantic value: in this instance, background circumstances are given in the main clause, and the subordinate clause expresses the foregrounded event.

We will see here how this specific expression, which did not properly develop until the pre-Classical period, can be situated diachronically in the wider framework of the opposition between foreground and background. On a more theoretical level, the evolution of IS also seems to be interesting in that it is a good example of what might be considered the pragmaticalization of a construction.

Starting in the Old French period, we find examples of a type of clause linking which, through the use of *que*, marks 'la concomitance conditionnée' (Buridant 2019: 905), the combination of negation and *que* leading to the interpretation: P_1 *ne se produira pas sans que* P_2 *ne se produise*. This construction, which has sometimes been linked to IS, also seems to have developed with patterns such as *ne... pas plus tôt... que* or *à peine... que*. It should be noted that when this construction is used with a negative to indicate that the temporal interval is incomplete, and is thus close to counterfactual imminence, we do not find the imperfect in the initial clause, but rather the *passé simple* or *passé antérieur*, as in examples (70) and (71).[6] As these examples show, the value of this construction is essentially temporal, and the same can be said for expressions that use *à peine* (example 72).

(70) Mais ne tarda pas l'espace de deux patenostres que les trois compaignons ensemble leurs deux hostesses qui [...], arriverent au lieu ou [...] (1457; d'Anjou 1980: 109)

(71) Mais ilz n'eurent pas fait plus d'une mille, qui estoit la moictié du chemin, qu'il fut nuyt fermee, et commença la lune a luyre belle, clere et necte [...] (1457; d'Anjou 1980: 115)

(72) à peine eut achevé sa parole que le Comte luy respondit avecques une audace merveilleuse (Boaistuau 1977 [1559]: 219)

---

[6] The reader should note that example (70) is the same as example (27).

This sequence of two clauses initially expresses a chronological relationship but later evolves to have a more textual function and becomes a tool for structuring foreground and background. The fact that the construction expresses the interruption of a process, producing an effect of rupture, means that it lends itself to marking the progression of the narrative, signalling the transition to a new episode of the story. We thus find a large number of examples involving verbs such as *interrompre* or *empêcher*; these verbs often accompany a change in conversational turn (examples 73 and 74).

(73) Elle vouloit répliquer, lorsque le berger qui alloit chantant les interrompit (1612; d'Urfé 1966: 26)

(74) Il vouloit continuer, lorsque la survenue du roy l'en empescha (1612; d'Urfé 1966: 197)

Certain alternations clearly show the textual value attached to this construction. In the same text, IS is present, apparently in free variation, in contexts identical to those with the conjunction *mais* (examples 75 and 76).

(75) Il vouloit continuer, lors que la bergère, atteinte de trop de mal, l'interrompit: [...] (1612; d'Urfé 1966: 256)

(76) Il vouloit continuer, mais elle, toute impatiente, l'interrompit: [...] (1612; d'Urfé 1966: 302)

It is worth noting that the imperfect comes to be used in this construction, as the last few examples show; the *passé simple* and *passé antérieur* are however not completely eliminated from the first clause (examples 77 and 78).

(77) Il voulut continuer ses excuses, lorsque le père, ne pouvant supporter [...] l'interrompit par ses paroles (1619; de Rosset 1997: 37)

(78) Salluste n'eut guère demeuré dans ce lieu sacré qu'il vit entrer Flaminie, qui [...] (1619; de Rosset 1997: 53)

The variation here surely attests to the persistence of the older structure which, since Old French, has favoured the foregrounded forms in this construction, with the order of articulation of the phrases sufficing to express the chronology.

Uses that go beyond the mere description of a temporal sequence represent a new stage in the development of IS. Becoming in a sense more important, the background in this construction now begins to express a discourse relation of causality or opposition. It no longer simply marks a change in the continuity of the narrative, but instead points to the reasons or motivations behind a new state of affairs. Examples of this usage start to appear in significant number at the beginning of the seventeenth century. In examples (79–81), the content of the initial clause is in fact the trigger that brings about a new narrative sequence.

(79) Ce jeune seigneur n'eut pas plus tôt aperçu son beau visage qu'Amour [...] navra son cœur (1619; de Rosset 1997: 32)

(80) Et de faict Agis parvint heureusement à son dessein, car à peine estoit-il entierement party, que l'amour partit aussi de son ame, y logeant en sa place le mespris de ceste volage (1612; d'Urfé 1966: 337)

(81) mais à peine eut-il jetté les yeux sur l'endroit où il devoit donner le coup, qu'il fut saisy d'un estonnement extreme (1612; d'Urfé 1966: 522)

In these cases, the sentence-initial background clause is more than a temporal framing device: its presence is to some extent obligatory so that the foreground can emerge, with the background thus taking precedence over the narrative line.

Considered in terms of its textual role, this investigation of IS should be extended to other constructions that have the same arrangement of temporal forms and the same hypotactic structure (Le Draoulec 2014). This would mean that continuative relatives (Maurel 1992) should also be considered, as well as certain hypotheticals, which develop notably in Classical French; in certain contexts, when these belong to the irrealis category, they can express a relationship similar to counterfactual imminence (Combettes 2011). Example (82) could be paraphrased by *ils allaient le percer quand Consalve se jeta au milieu d'eux*. A study focusing on these phrases would be most welcome, since it would allow us to determine the various stages of their development and to situate them in the context of wider changes concerning foreground and background:

(82) [...] ils l'allaient percer si Consalve ne se fût jeté au milieu d'eux (de Lafayette 2006 [1671]: 167)

In the long term, we therefore see movement in two directions. One particular construction, the negative expression articulating 'la concomitance conditionnée' (Buridant 2019: 905), expands into other syntactic patterns, the common factor being the ordering of verb forms and, as a result, the structuring of foreground and background in complex sentences. Moreover, the meaning of this construction in its wider usage is affected by another type of change, whereby a logical relation is gradually favoured over a chronological relation and exploited in the way narration is structured. This change in the textual role of IS must be considered in relation to the changes in paratactic constructions examined here. The development of what can be considered a routine textual sequence consisting of background followed by foreground in juxtaposed clauses follows the same pattern. From a diachronic perspective, this example strengthens the hypothesis that certain constructions are the result of the grammaticalization of discourse regularities. According to this hypothesis, expanded IS would appear to be nothing more than a particular way of structuring information, its use encouraged by the recurrence of certain discursive configurations that already presented the opposition of verb forms in ways that characterized this type of phrasal structuring.

Whether it involves paratactic expressions or expressions that can be considered part of the broad category of IS, the evolution of information structuring to give greater textual importance and syntactic autonomy to background clauses must be considered alongside changes to discourse cohesion and, more generally, the creation of narrative text. In medieval prose, it is predominantly the narrative model that structures the coherence of the text in its entirety; background clauses appear to be highly dependent on the narrative line, at the level of syntax as much as at the discursive level. Descriptions and commentaries are subservient to the story, and have little influence over the way in which it unfolds. From the fifteenth century onwards, especially in the pre-Classical period, we can see signs that this trend is reversing. The greater independence given to background clauses runs in parallel with the importance accorded to explanation and to justifications for characters' behaviour and feelings: commentary, understood in its broadest sense, takes precedence over the narrative thread. Far from a mere accompaniment to the story, background clauses come to have a major role in providing impetus for events in the foreground. This new balance between foreground and background, which culminates in the aesthetic of the Classical period (Forestier and Bury 2007: 631–6), corresponds to changes in the way in which the fictional text is created, the principal aim of narrative no longer being so much to recount a succession of events in a way that emphasizes their chronology but to unveil the workings of the plot and reveal the wide range of factors that influence the unfolding of the story. As I have attempted to show here, this development over time has affected both the discourse status of the opposition between foreground and background and the syntactic patterns in which this opposition is embedded.

6

Women and language in the *Journal de la langue françoise* (1784–95)

Mairi McLaughlin

6.1 Introduction

This chapter explores the presence and representation of women in the first periodical devoted to the French language, namely the *Journal de la langue françoise, soit exacte soit ornée* (*JLF*) which was founded by François-Urbain Domergue and published in France between 1784 and 1795 (Domergue 1784–95).[1] The chapter begins with an introduction which outlines the research context and objectives. There then follow three sections which explore the presence and representation of women and gender in the *JLF* from three different perspectives: Section 6.2 concerns the principal figures who were involved and invoked in the *JLF*, Section 6.3 focuses on readers' letters, and Section 6.4 explores the thematics of women and gender. The chapter ends with a conclusion in Section 6.5.

This study of women and language in the *JLF* is situated at the intersection of three related research fields: research on French metalinguistic texts; research on language and the media; and research on language and gender. Historians of French have long drawn attention to the interest of texts written about the language. Of particular interest are the books of observations and remarks on French which developed into a genre in the wake of the publication of Vaugelas's (1647) *Remarques sur la langue françoise*. Scholarly interest in these texts culminated in the publication of the *Remarques* section of Garnier's *Grand corpus des grammaires françaises, des remarques et des traités sur la langue française*.[2] Some of the key lines of inquiry for scholars working on these books are what their intended functions were at the time, how they impacted the evolution of the language, and the role that they played in constructing language attitudes and ideologies.[3]

---

[1] Thank you to Jennifer Kaplan and to two anonymous readers for their feedback on earlier versions of this chapter. I am also grateful to many graduate students at UC Berkeley, especially those in my seminar on French metalinguistic texts, for sharing their ideas and being a constant source of inspiration.

[2] See https://classiques-garnier.com/grand-corpus-des-grammaires-francaises-des-remarques-et-des-traites-sur-la-langue-xive-xviiie-s.html (accessed 18 July 2022). See also Ayres-Bennett (2011a); Ayres-Bennett and Colombat (2016).

[3] See, for example, Caron (2004); Ayres-Bennett and Seijido (2011, 2013a).

Mairi McLaughlin, *Women and language in the* Journal de la langue françoise *(1784–95)*. In: *Historical and Sociolinguistic Approaches to French*. Edited by: Janice Carruthers, Mairi McLaughlin, and Olivia Walsh, Oxford University Press. © Mairi McLaughlin (2024). DOI: 10.1093/oso/9780192894366.003.0006

Linguists working on modern and contemporary French have also examined metalinguistic texts. Of particular interest are language columns published in the press in Quebec, France, Belgium, and Switzerland from the mid-nineteenth century onwards.[4] Some similar research questions have been addressed: scholars have traced the evolution and contours of the genre across place and time, they have explored the impact of language columns on variation and change, and they have examined their role in the construction of attitudes and ideologies. Remysen (2016–17b: 15) underscores the importance of debates about language in the media: 'en tant que "sites" ou "espaces discursifs" (Heller 2010), les médias ont en effet le pouvoir de conférer une forme de légitimité à certains discours sur la langue, les rendant ainsi dominants au sein de leur société'. This research can be seen as part of a wider interest in the relationship between language and the media with linguists increasingly recognizing the impact of the media on language variation and change (McLaughlin 2021: 262–3).

Today, significant societal changes have turned gender into a central theme of linguistic scholarship. Following Aikhenvald (2012: 33–4), a distinction is made between what was termed natural gender, i.e. sex; social gender; and linguistic, or grammatical, gender. Scholars are particularly interested in the interaction between linguistic and social gender. Traditionally, research on gender and language in France focused on the feminization of professional titles. Scholars examined the process of feminization and the ensuing debates at a series of key moments including the nineteenth century when social changes led to women taking on new roles, the mid-1980s when the Commission sur la féminisation des noms de métiers, grades et fonctions was founded and made its recommendations, and the late 1990s when the use of feminized forms was promoted, this time more successfully, by Lionel Jospin's government.[5] More recently, social change has led to both public debates and linguistic scholarship on inclusive language.[6] Inclusive language can be understood as an umbrella term referring to a range of strategies which aim to promote equality by ensuring the visibility and proper representation of groups that have traditionally been minoritized in society. When it comes to gender, this can involve avoiding the default masculine, by making the feminine visible (e.g. 'les étudiant·e·s'), and/or by widening the range of gender identities represented in language (e.g. 'iel' or 'øl').[7]

Given this interest in language and gender, it is not surprising that scholars have explored gender in French metalinguistic texts. A somewhat mixed picture emerges for the seventeenth century. On the one hand, the genre of the remarks is

---

[4] On France, see Bochnakowa (2005, 2013); Walsh (2021c); on Belgium, see Meier (2019); on Canada, see Walsh (2016a, 2021d); Remysen (2012, 2016–17a); on Switzerland, see Cotelli Kureth (2014, 2021).
[5] See, for example, Burnett and Bonami (2019); Christofides (2019).
[6] See Burnett and Pozniak (2021); Tristram (Chapter 15, this volume).
[7] For more information on gender-neutral pronouns in French, see Knisely (2020).

quite clearly dominated by men. Ayres-Bennett (1994b: 35) highlights the 'paucity and relative unimportance' of works on language written by or for women in the seventeenth century in general. This is reflected by the *Remarques* section of the *Grand corpus* (Ayres-Bennett 2011a) which contains only one volume by a woman and that work itself went unnoticed (Ayres-Bennett and Seijido 2011: 19). Similarly, men dominate the lists of authors of both literary and metalinguistic texts that are cited in books of remarks (Ayres-Bennett and Seijido 2011: 233–51). When women's language does get discussed, it can in some instances be portrayed very negatively; Ayres-Bennett (1994b: 48) cites Dupleix (1651) as the most extreme example. However, this tells only part of the story because an important thread running through metalinguistic thought in the seventeenth century is the association of women with good usage (Ayres-Bennett 1994b: 43). For example, Vaugelas (1647: 503–5) considered women to be reliable authorities on language because their speech was not corrupted by knowledge of other languages, especially Latin and Greek. Vaugelas is not just paying lip service to women here. Ayres-Bennett (1994b: 47) notes that 'Vaugelas se montre indulgent envers les femmes aussi bien dans les questions de principe que dans les détails'. It is also quite clear that women constituted an important part of Vaugelas's intended readership (Flutre 1954: 242–3; Ayres-Bennett 2020b: 102).

This focus on gender in research on books of remarks appears so far to be absent from work on language columns. This can in part be attributed to a difference in language attitudes and ideologies, since language columns appear in a period when women's language is less likely to represent either a model of good usage or a source of contamination; instead it is often the language of young people and journalists that are targeted by the more purist of the language columns.[8] Nevertheless, even a cursory glance at the primary texts and secondary literature indicates that this is a line of inquiry that will be worth pursuing in the future. It will be important to explore, among other questions, how the work of the few women authors of language columns relates to that of their male counterparts, and how topics relating to linguistic feminization and inclusive language are treated, especially in a comparative Francophone perspective.

The aim of this chapter is to examine women and language in the first periodical publication dedicated to the French language. The *Journal de la langue françoise, soit exacte soit ornée* was founded in September 1784 and a total of 166 editions were published, with some notable gaps, until August 1795 (Dougnac 1991). The title reflects the fact that most editions were divided into two sections: *Langue exacte* dealt with questions of language, whereas *Langue ornée* dealt with more literary or aesthetic questions. This chapter focuses on the *Langue exacte* section since this is the part of the periodical that centres on language. The bulk of the material published in *Langue exacte* consists of epistolary exchanges between

---

[8] For example, see Bochnakowa (2013); Cotelli Kureth (2021).

Domergue and readers of the periodical. Other materials include extracts and analyses of metalinguistic texts, as well as linguistic evaluations of a wide range of texts. The *JLF* shares the main features of form and content that Ayres-Bennett and Seijido (2011: 42–54) identify as characteristic of the genre of the remarks: the comments are relatively short, they are unordered, the readership is (generally) non-specialist, and the discussions tend to be motivated by a question or doubt about usage. The main difference between the *JLF* and seventeenth-century books of remarks is the periodical medium of publication. The most significant consequence of this difference is the interactivity that it permits: readers can exchange in a back and forth with Domergue that can at times span several editions, and the opinions of both parties can evolve through the correspondence. Along with later metalinguistic periodicals such as the *Courrier de Vaugelas* (Martin 1868–81), the *JLF* can be seen as part of the generic lineage from seventeenth-century books of remarks to modern and contemporary language columns.

As the first periodical dedicated to the French language, the *JLF* is often referenced in works on the history of French.[9] However, the body of scholarly research on the *JLF* remains relatively small. The most substantial work is found in the relevant sections of Busse and Dougnac's (1992) monograph on Domergue.[10] As well as offering detailed accounts of its contents and publication history, Busse and Dougnac emphasize the periodical's success. They link the success of the editions published in Lyon between 1784 and 1788 to the fact that 'Domergue saisit le moment précis d'une évolution socio-économique où la population provinciale veut se défaire des régionalismes pour avoir accès au bon usage du français' (Busse and Dougnac 1992: 56). The success of the editions published in Paris between 1791 and 1792, on the other hand, is attributed to 'l'actualité des questions de langage sous la Révolution'. Just a handful of other studies examine the *JLF*'s treatment of specific questions. This includes a dissertation and a related article on the treatment of neologisms by Dougnac (1981, 1982) as well as her article on the use of 'vous' and personal titles (Dougnac 1989). More recently, Choi (2006, 2007, 2008) wrote a dissertation and two book chapters on the *JLF*'s treatment of past participle agreement.

The question of women and language is not a major theme of any of this previous work. It only comes up in any substantial way in Dougnac's (1989) article on the use of 'vous' and personal titles in the *JLF*. As Dougnac (1989: 55–60) shows, the Revolutionary context prompted questions about the use of personal titles such as 'sire', 'seigneur', and 'monsieur'.[11] Most of the exchanges published in the *JLF* concern men's titles, but some thought is given to those used for women. Domergue is of the opinion that the terms 'madame' and 'mademoiselle' should

---

[9] See, for example, Siouffi (2007a: 864, 939). See also Dougnac, Hordé, and Auroux (1982: 117–22).
[10] See especially Busse and Dougnac (1992: 46–59, 93–103, 113–18).
[11] See also Siouffi (2007a: 934–5).

be abolished and favours the use of names without titles, or the feminized form 'citoyenne' (Dougnac 1989: 56–7). Dougnac does not offer much in the way of commentary; the main aim of her article being to share the contents of the *JLF*, but she does highlight the fact that women's titles received less attention than did men's. Although it goes unsaid, the reader has the impression that this asymmetry was important and presumably a reflection of inequality.

The current chapter draws inspiration from the research described above to present the first detailed study of women and language in the *JLF*. It is focused both on the presence of women and on their representation, especially as it relates to questions of language. The research blends qualitative and quantitative approaches, drawing on image copies of the original editions of the *JLF* as well as a full transcription of all of the *Langue exacte* sections. I have access to a full transcription because I am responsible for creating the digital and critical editions of the *JLF* as part of the expansion of the *Remarques* section of Garnier's *Grand corpus* to cover the eighteenth century (Ayres-Bennett and Colombat 2016). The chapter was initially inspired by the recurrence of gender as an important theme in the notes that I took during two general manual read-throughs of the *JLF*. The in-depth qualitative analyses that these notes led to are complemented by more systematic and quantitative analyses using the transcription. A plain-text version of the transcription was produced to enable full-text searches and more sophisticated text analysis by means of the AntConc concordancer.[12] By understanding where and why women are present in the *JLF* and how women and their language are depicted, we can consider how this important publication both reflected and constructed attitudes and ideologies relating to women and language in late eighteenth-century France.

6.2 The principal figures

This section examines the principal figures who are involved and invoked in the *JLF* in order to determine whether the same kind of male dominance seen in seventeenth-century books of remarks is also present here. It will be remembered that there were few metalinguistic texts written by and for women in that period, and that almost all authors and authorities cited in books of remarks are men (Ayres-Bennett 1994b: 35; Ayres-Bennett and Seijido 2011: 233–51). In what follows, I examine first the people responsible for the *JLF*, and second the main authors and authorities who are cited in its pages. The term 'authorities' is used for figures who are referenced or cited for their metalinguistic opinions; 'authors' refers to writers referenced or cited for any other reason.

---

[12] For more information on AntConc, see https://www.laurenceanthony.net/software/antconc/ (accessed 22 September 2021).

As indicated in Section 6.1, the *JLF* was founded and run by a man, François-Urbain Domergue. Domergue played a central role in the periodical which was aligned very closely with his own voice. Readers were clearly aware of this, since their letters were commonly published under the subtitle 'Lettres et questions adressées à l'auteur du journal'. As shown in (1), they also often invoke Domergue by name in their letters.[13]

(1) I.
De Lyon.
MONSIEUR,
UNE abonnée qui n'a pu persuader à une de ses amies qu'on doit dire *se promener* & non pas *promener*, prie M. Domergue d'éclaircir ce point.
(*JLF* 17 May 1786)[14]

Domergue is not the only linguistic authority to contribute to the *JLF* but the list of the main contributors provided by Dougnac (1991: 593) shows that none of them were women. Instead, the list includes groups such as 'membres d'une Société de gens de lettres, d'artistes et d'amis (?) [*sic*] établie à Lyon, à laquelle appartenait Domergue' and men such as 'Pierre Morel, dit Morel l'aîné, de Lyon, procureur et grammairien'. Things are slightly different when it comes to the publishers because two of the seven responsible for the *JLF* over the years were widow publishers, namely the 'imprimerie de la veuve Reguilliat' and the 'imprimerie de la veuve Belion' who published the periodical in Lyon between 1784 and 1785 (Dougnac 1991: 592). These two women certainly played a role in the publishing history of the periodical but it is hard to ascribe much significance to their presence when it comes to the question of attitudes and ideologies surrounding language and gender. The only thing that explains the presence of these women is the profession of their husbands via whom they are identified. In general, then, it is clear that the main figures involved in the founding, production, and publishing of the *JLF* are men.

Men also dominate the lists of authors and authorities who are referenced and/or cited in the *JLF* as illustrated by (2) and (3).

(2) Les grands écrivains morts, tels que J. Jacques, Voltaire, Buffon, Boileau, Racine, Lafontaine, &c. Les auteurs vivans qui ont de la célébrité seront soumis à une critique exacte & deviendront pour les amateurs de notre langue une source d'instruction & de plaisir. J'examinerai & les beautés dont ils ont enrichi notre idiome, & les fautes qui ont pu leur échapper. Nous commencerons, au n°. prochain, par l'examen grammatical de J. Jacques.
(*JLF* 22 January 1791)

---

[13] Domergue's responses tend not to be signed because any text not explicitly attributed to someone else is assumed to be his.
[14] Quotations from the *JLF* are accompanied by the date of publication of the edition in which they appear in parentheses.

(3) M. D. [sc. Monsieur Domergue] n'approuve pas trop que M. l'abbé Féraud ait pris l'abbé d'Olivet pour guide, & qu'il croit qu'il lui servira de garant. Quel guide est infaillible? s'écrie-t-il. J'avoue qu'il n'y en a point; pas même l'auteur du Journal de *la langue françoise, soit exacte, soit ornée*. Mais enfin il en faut un dans une route si difficile & si tortueuse; & jusqu'à présent il n'y en a point de plus sûr pour ce qui regarde la prosodie, ni qui ait une aussi grande autorité, que l'abbé d'Olivet. [...] Il est possible qu'il y ait quelques erreurs dans le traité de la prosodie de l'abbé d'Olivet; & je croirois avoir rendu un service essentiel au public, si mon dictionnaire donnoit occasion à mieux examiner cet ouvrage très-important, qu'on estime beaucoup sans le lire; & d'en discuter avec soin les principes. Ce travail seroit sur-tout digne de Mrs. de l'Académie françoise; & il occuperoit très-utilement les séances académiques. En attendant, je n'ai pu mieux faire, je crois, que de suivre les règles tracées par un si habile homme en cette partie.
(*JLF* 15 December 1787)

In (2), Domergue explains to the reader that he will start including detailed analyses of the works of great authors of the past and famous living authors so that readers can both learn and draw pleasure from them. Here, as in other similar cases, all of the examples of great authors are men.[15] Extract (3) comes from a letter published in the *JLF* where Jean-François Féraud, Domergue's famous rival (Seguin 1999: 260), responds to some severe criticisms that Domergue had made of his *Dictionnaire critique de la langue française* (Féraud 1787–8). Féraud justifies basing his work on Pierre-Joseph d'Olivet, referring to him as a 'grande autorité' and 'un si habile homme'. In passing he refers also to members of the Académie française. As in (2), all of the figures evoked in this extract are men. The absence of women at such moments does not come as a surprise. We saw in Section 6.1 that Ayres-Bennett (1994b: 35) already highlighted the 'paucity and relative unimportance' of works on language written by or for women in seventeenth-century France and Siouffi (2007a: 902) notes that there were even fewer 'femmes grammairiennes' in the eighteenth century. Nevertheless, the almost total exclusion of women authors and authorities merits our attention because of the role that it must have played in perpetuating the association between literary excellence and male penmanship on the one hand, and between linguistic authority and the male voice on the other.

Using the work that I carried out while preparing the edition of the *JLF*, it is possible to identify those rare cases in which women are invoked as authors

---

[15] One notable exception occurs when Domergue names a number of women writers to justify feminizing 'auteur' (*JLF* 1 March 1788).

and authorities. As part of the process, all individuals mentioned in the *JLF* were identified and then coded according to their status as authors of texts, authorities on the language, or neither of the above. For the purposes of the present chapter, I examined all authors and authorities in a random sample representing 10% of the total publication and coded them as women, men, or n/a.[16] Table 6.1 presents the frequency and relative frequency of authors and authorities in these three different classes.

Table 6.1 provides quantitative evidence to support the assertion above that men dominate both the authors of texts examined in the *JLF* and the linguistic authorities whose opinions are cited: women represent only 4.17% of authors and only 1.47% of authorities. The table also speaks to a gender disparity between authors and authorities: there are proportionally more women authors than women authorities. This can be attributed to the fact that women were accorded somewhat more space in the late eighteenth-century literary system than in the tradition of metalinguistic writing.[17]

It is worth pausing to examine from a qualitative perspective who the women are in Table 6.1. It is particularly revealing that of the four women authors in the sample, three appear because their poems were published in an edition of the *Almanach des Muses* which was analysed at length in an edition of the *JLF*.[18] The women are Henriette Bourdic-Viot, Adélaïde-Gillette Billet Dufrénoy, and the Marquise de La Ferrandière, three women of letters known for publishing their work in the *Almanach des Muses*. Extract (4) illustrates how their linguistic choices are analysed in the *JLF*.

Table 6.1 Gender of authors and authorities

	Women	Men	N/A	Total
Authors	4 (4.17%)	90 (93.75%)	2 (2.08%)	96 (100%)
Authorities	1 (1.47%)	62 (91.18%)	5 (7.35%)	68 (100%)
Total	5 (3.05%)	152 (92.68%)	7 (4.27%)	164 (100%)

---

[16] This essentializing classification was chosen to reflect the conventions of the time and it is unlikely to be appropriate for working on contemporary metalinguistic texts. The 10% sample equates to just under seventeen whole editions, or just under 50,000 words. The 'n/a' category includes, for example, institutional bodies and anonymous individuals whose gender could not be determined.

[17] Compare, for example, Siouffi's (2007a: 902) comment about the rarity of women grammarians in eighteenth-century France to the discussion of linguistic feminization in Section 6.4 which demonstrates the ground that had been gained by women authors.

[18] The fourth woman is the singer Antoinette Cécile Saint-Huberty whose pronunciation is referred to in a discussion of the oral vs. nasal articulation of the vowel in the prefixes 'im-' and 'in-' (*JLF* 30 July 1791).

(4) *Contemporain avec* l'éternité.

Contemporain est-il le mot propre? Il se dit des hommes qui ont vécu dans le même temps. Horace & Virgile étoient *contemporains*. Il se dit encore des auteurs qui ont écrit les choses qui se sont passées dans leur temps: les historiens *contemporains* ne disent pas toujours la vérité.

Dans ces deux acceptions *contemporain* est employé sans complément. Il en est une troisième qui en admet un, c'est lorsque *contemporain* se dit d'un homme avec qui on a vécu dans sa jeunesse; il est mon contemporain, il est le contemporain de mon père.

On voit que dans aucune de ces acceptions, on ne dit *contemporain avec*; je crois même qu'aucune ne rend l'idée de Mme. la baronne de Bourdic. Car, *contemporain* ne se dit que du passé, & il s'agit d'une chose toujours subsistante: *aussi vieux, aussi ancien* que l'éternité, auroit rendu l'idée d'une manière plus juste & plus correcte. (*JLF* 15 January 1787)

Extract (4) is typical of linguistic analyses of literary texts in the *JLF*: a line is singled out for a particular linguistic choice which is in doubt for some reason; the choice is then compared to proper usage which is illustrated by a range of examples; and finally, a judgement is reached and, if negative, a more correct alternative is proposed. It is tempting to read this as a gendered act whereby a woman's text is rewritten by a man but this does not seem viable since the works of men published in the *Almanach des Muses* are subject to the same treatment. Instead, this example speaks more generally to the role that periodicals played in providing a space where women of letters could be heard since it is not from printed books but from the *Almanach des Muses* that the examples of the writings of these three women are taken. The fact that works originally published in a periodical are then examined in another one only underscores the link between periodicals and women's writing.[19] These women also illustrate some general trends when it comes to women authors appearing in Domergue's periodical: they tend overwhelmingly to be living authors who write in French and who are members of the social elite. In this way, they represent a more restricted range than do male authors cited in the *JLF* who are known for writing in other languages (Latin, Italian, Portuguese etc.) and who might also be authors from the past (Corneille, Homer, Racine etc.). The traits that characterize women authors also characterize the only woman who is cited in the sample for her metalinguistic thought, namely Germaine de Staël-Holstein who published a short piece on the meaning of the close synonyms 'vérité' and 'franchise' (*JLF* 1 July 1786). Although de Staël's name is partially hidden—the piece is signed '*Par Mme. la baronne de S....*'—this is a rather exceptional case in which the *JLF* includes the work of a woman authority.

---

[19] See for example Van Dijk (1988) and McIlvanney (2019).

These analyses of the principal figures involved and invoked in the *JLF* have pointed to the absence rather than to the presence of women. This is not unexpected. Goodman (2002) offers a detailed analysis of gender and language in Revolutionary France. She explains that the link that was commonly made between women and purity of speech in the seventeenth century did not last (Goodman 2002: 199–200). In the eighteenth century, good usage came to be associated with written French which was under the control of men of letters. In consequence, women found themselves criticized for their poor command of written language. To cite just one example, the famous *salonnière* Madame Geoffrin had such poor mastery of spelling that her modern biographer draws attention to it in the very blurb of his book (Hamon 2010).[20] As Goodman (2002: 215–23) explains, various efforts were therefore made to improve women's spelling such as the publication of spelling guides for women.[21] What has been seen in this section therefore aligns with this general picture. However, in their recent edited volume on *Women in the History of Linguistics*, Ayres-Bennett and Sanson (2020: 2) adopt a different approach by widening the perspective beyond 'pioneers and exceptional women' to give space to 'the voices of non-exceptional women who nevertheless quietly moved forward our knowledge of languages, their description, analysis, codification and acquisition, *inter alia*'. Adopting a similar approach here means looking not at the main figures involved and invoked in the *JLF* but at the people who appear at the margins. The potential for this approach to deepen our understanding of women and language in the *JLF* is immediately illustrated by excerpt (5) which follows on directly from Féraud's defence of his choice to base his work on d'Olivet reproduced in (3).

(5) M. D. a pour oracles les dames de sa coterie, qu'il cite avec complaisance, sans les nommer. Mais je n'ai pas eu l'avantage d'être à portée de les consulter. (*JLF* 15 December 1787)

In (5), Féraud adopts a defensively mocking tone to dismiss Domergue and his coterie of anonymous women. In the *JLF*, it is primarily through letters from readers that a space was made for women to play a role in the evolution of French and its associated attitudes and ideologies, and so it is to readers' letters that we now turn.

6.3 Readers' letters

As indicated in Section 6.1, the most consistent type of content published in the *Langue exacte* section of the *JLF* are epistolary exchanges with readers. Within

---

[20] Thanks to an anonymous reviewer for pointing me to this telling example.
[21] For example, see de Wailly (1782) and Barthélemy (1788).

individual editions, the letters almost always appear together under a rubric entitled 'Lettres et questions adressées à l'auteur du journal' or some variation thereof. There can be up to six letters published in any one edition. The letter in (6) shows how they appeared on the page.

(6) III.
De Bastia en Corse.
DOIT-ON prononcer le *s* dans *as* & dans *Christophe*? Le *x* de *six* & de *dix* est-il nul ou sonore? (*JLF* 1 December 1786)

The letters are numbered within each edition and the sender's location is always indicated. The letter in (6) is particularly short; they can be much longer, and can include opening and/or closing formulae. In many cases, but not all, the letters are anonymous. In most cases, they are immediately followed by a response from Domergue or one of the other main contributors such as Morel. More rarely, a longer response is given elsewhere in the edition or in a subsequent edition.

Since letters can be anonymous, it is not always possible to know whether they come from a man or a woman. In some cases, however, the letter-writer's gender is revealed. The letter might be signed using a name and/or a title such as 'Isabelle R**' or 'Madame'. The morphosyntactic expression of grammatical gender in either the signature or the body of the letter might also indicate the writer's gender as in 'Une de vos Lectrices'. Finally, letters can contain information that identifies the writer as a woman either in passing or when they explicitly write from the position of a woman as happens in (7).

(7) De Saint Cyr au Mont d'Or.
MONSIEUR,
VOTRE journal renaît, & mes espérances avec lui. Je me suis retirée à la campagne, pour me livrer sans distraction à la première éducation de mes enfants. Persuadée que la routine déforme l'esprit & nuit aux progrès, j'ai adopté votre grammaire simplifiée, où la raison éclaire & accélère la marche; mais une grande difficulté m'arrête, & cette difficulté naît du vice de notre orthographe. Que de syllabes qui se prononcent d'une seule manière, & qui s'écrivent de plusieurs! Que de lettres qu'on écrit & qu'on ne prononce pas! Je ne doute pas, qu'un jour l'orthographe ne devienne l'image fidelle de la prononciation; mais en attendant, comment parer à l'inconvénient qui m'afflige! L'usage, me dit-on, supplée au silence des règles; mais cet usage est si long à acquérir; & une mère qui instruit ses enfants, ne jouit jamais assez-tôt du fruit de ses peines. Si cependant, Monsieur, il faut absolument recourir à l'usage, indiquez-moi, s'il est possible, le moyen le plus prompt pour le conquérir, car je ne veux pas attendre qu'il vienne à moi; je veux aller à lui par le chemin le plus court.
J'ai l'honneur d'être, &c. Une de vos abonnées. (*JLF* 22 January 1791)

In (7), the letter-writer explicitly identifies herself as 'une mère qui instruit ses enfants' and in asking for advice on learning orthography, she speaks to the same struggle with orthography that Goodman (2002) describes.[22] Most of the sources which Goodman cites, however, involve men underscoring the difficulties faced by women, often in order to promote the sale of their own works on spelling. In contrast, as a periodical built around interaction with its readers, the *JLF* offers women the possibility of speaking about language in a public forum from their own gendered positionality.

It is not just the publishing of letters from women but the way in which they are treated which turned the *JLF* into an important space for women publicly to share their metalinguistic thought. In his responses, Domergue gives differential treatment to letters from women. To begin with, he responds to women readers as women rather than just as readers. This is signalled by the various salutations used to open his responses where women are addressed as 'Madame', 'Mademoiselle', and, from July 1791, 'Citoyenne'. Domergue can also be seen to respond favourably not just to the questions from women, but to their metalinguistic opinions. This is illustrated by the response in (8) to a letter in which an anonymous woman reader identified two errors in the writings of Boileau.

(8) VOUS proposez des doutes comme on donne des démonstrations. Je n'ajouterai rien à vos remarques; la raison parle si victorieusement par votre bouche, que tout ce qu'on pourroit dire après vous, seroit foible & superflu. Vous avez la gloire d'avoir prouvé qu'un poète très-correct a fait deux fautes de langue que bien des grammairiens n'avoient pas apperçues.

Je vous prie, Madame, par l'intérêt que vous voulez bien prendre au Journal de la langue françoise, de l'enrichir souvent de vos observations. Leur justesse & leur clarté vous garantissent & ma reconnoissance & celle de mes lecteurs. (*JLF* 1 June 1786)

Domergue could not be more approving in his response: reason—the absolute authority—has spoken as if divinely through this woman's words and there is nothing more to add. Such a favourable response to a letter from a woman is far from unusual in the periodical and this must have sent the message to women that their presence was welcome and that their opinions were valued. This message is explicitly communicated in (8) by the invitation to contribute more observations. The legitimacy of the reader's metalinguistic thought is further reinforced by the link to the ideological values of 'clarté' and 'justesse' established in seventeenth-century metalinguistic discourse (Ayres-Bennett 2015).

There is also a hint, in the third sentence of the response in (8), that Domergue might be questioning the eighteenth-century hierarchy of the sexes whereby

---

[22] This example also reflects the common link between women and 'the transmission and acquisition of language' (Ayres-Bennett and Sanson 2020: 15–17).

authority over the language is held by men of letters (Goodman 2002). Domergue seems to be making a point when he accords glory to the woman reader for having spotted language errors that were made by a male poet known for his linguistic exactitude and that went unnoticed by male grammarians. If this is implied in (8), it is explicit in the opening and closing paragraphs of another of Domergue's responses to an anonymous woman reader (9).

(9) ON ne peut pas observer avec plus de sagacité, raisonner avec plus de justesse, ni critiquer d'un meilleur ton. Je vous félicite de réunir des dons aussi rares: je vous dois une explication, & je me la dois à moi-même. [...] Au reste, Madame, je ne suis point étonné d'avoir tort avec vous. Toutes les femmes qui ont bien voulu me faire des observations, m'ont prouvé qu'elles avoient raison; je ne puis pas en dire autant des hommes. (*JLF* 1 July 1786)

In the opening paragraph of the response in (9), Domergue adopts the same laudatory tone as in (8) and once again both reason (through the verb 'raisonner') and 'justesse' are evoked. In (9), however, the response is more personal because the question raised concerns Domergue's own use of a metalinguistic term. Even in this case where it is his own usage that is in question, Domergue approves the woman reader's linguistic sensibility and goes so far as to favourably compare the observations that women readers have made to those made by their male counterparts. This explicit comparison did not go unnoticed. In fact, just a few months later, another anonymous woman reader—or perhaps the same one—questions the linguistic form of this comparison because Domergue had elsewhere offered an analysis of the expression 'j'ai l'honneur d'observer à la cour' which would rule out the expression 'me faire des observations' in (9). This prompts the woman reader to wonder 'comment concilier vos principes & votre pratique' (*JLF* 15 November 1786). Domergue recognizes this 'grande incorrection' in his response, indicating that knowing that this woman is reading his periodical will lead him to be more attentive to his choices. However, it is the opening of the reader's letter, reproduced in (10), that really draws our attention.

(10) L'accueil favorable que reçoivent les questions qui vous sont adressées par les dames sur la langue, & la réponse obligeante que j'ai reçue, dans le N°.10 de votre Journal, aux doutes que je vous avois proposés, m'enhardissent à vous en proposer de nouveaux. (*JLF* 15 November 1786)

The reader in (10) explicitly testifies to the impact of the favourable treatment that was offered to letters from women in the *JLF*: the sharing and approval of women's letters about the French language led her to feel able to contribute more of them. The sentiment expressed here aligns with Siouffi's (2007a: 940) assessment of Domergue's main general contribution in the Revolutionary period which was to include everyone on an equal footing; in Siouffi's words '[c]ette ouverture de l'éventail humain associé à la langue constitue la vraie innovation de Domergue'.

Extract (10) testifies directly to the role that the sharing and positive treatment of letters from women readers played in creating a new space for women to share their metalinguistic thought in the public realm.

The final piece to be examined in this section shows what happens when the favourable, if not preferential, treatment offered to women was taken to its logical conclusion. A debate took place across a number of venues from late 1785 into 1786 about whether the title of Ovid's *Ars amatoria* should be translated as 'L'Art d'aimer'. In a piece published across two editions of the *JLF*, the semi-anonymous correspondent, L. V... reproduces and responds to a letter from an anonymous woman published in the *Journal général de France* (de Fontenay 1785–90). The position taken by L. V... is that 'L'Art d'aimer' is incorrect and that the proper title should be 'L'Art d'être aimé'. The woman reader had written to the author of the *Journal général de France*, the Abbé de Fontenay, in defence of the active version, 'L'Art d'aimer'. It is not so much the contents of the letter that interest us here but the representation of the gender of its author. The letter is signed 'Une de vos abonnées' and the author indirectly identifies herself as a woman when she explains 'je me suis fait expliquer mon Ovide'; it is only through instruction from a man that a woman could claim authority in this domain since women were not educated in Latin.[23] L. V... reproduces this letter in its entirety but he makes the claim in (11) that its author is not a woman.

(11) Vaincus, convaincus même, les partisans de l'expression condamnée n'ont pas voulu paroître avoir tort, & ils ont tâché d'obtenir par la ruse un triomphe constamment refusé par la raison. Le moyen dont ils se sont avisés n'est pas neuf; mais il fait encore des dupes, & en fera long-temps. (*JLF* 15 January 1786)

Quotation (11) shows that writing to the *JLF* as a woman was thought to offer an advantage.

In the next edition of the *JLF*, L. V... provides a response to the letter in which gender becomes even more salient. This is illustrated by the very title of the response (12).

(12) *RÉPONSE*
D'UNE ABONNÉE AU JOURNAL DE
LA LANGUE FRANÇOISE,
*A la DAME abonnée au Journal
général de France.* (*JLF* 1 February 1786)

The title attributes the response to a female reader—it is only at the end that the signatory 'L. V...' is given—and, significantly, the word 'DAME' appears in upper

---

[23] Beck-Busse (1994: 80) argues that such was the asymmetry in Latinacy between men and women that formulae such as 'à l'usage des dames et de ceux qui ne savent pas le latin' emerge.

case. This typographical choice simultaneously draws attention to and calls into question the letter-writer's gender. L. V... goes on to misgender the letter-writer by addressing her as 'Monsieur' and then explaining again why writing as a woman offered an advantage (13).

(13) MONSIEUR,
AH, pardon! votre secret m'échappe. Le Parnasse, je le vois, a aussi son carnaval, & vous vous êtes diverti à prendre un masque bien ridicule. C'est un moyen de fixer les regards, & vous avez réussi. (*JLF* 1 February 1786)

L. V... then claims with a transparent falseness to be a woman whose authority to judge the question stems both from their gender and from their knowledge of Latin (14).

(14) Pour moi, monsieur, je suis véritablement femme, & très-piquée que vous ayiez pris la livrée de mon sexe pour déraisonner plus à votre aise. [...] La question sur *l'art d'aimer* est doublement de mon ressort, & parce que je suis femme, & parce que je sais le latin. (*JLF* 1 February 1786)

The actual gender of L. V... matters little to us here, although it seems clear that L. V... is wearing only a mask of womanhood when they taunt the original letter-writer by saying 'vous êtes pris dans vos propres filets'. The end of the response is reproduced in (15).

(15) Avouez pourtant, monsieur, que vous avez triomphé, en lisant l'avis que vous avez extorqué à l'auteur du Journal de France, par une lettre obreptice & subreptice. Mais ici M. l'abbé de Fontenay a été plus galant que dialecticien; il n'a pas voulu condamner une femme; s'il avoit su de *quel sexe il retournoit*, la raison seule eût dirigé sa plume, & il n'auroit pas conclu de ce qu'il ne faut pas soumettre tous les mots à l'analyse, que l'expression dont il s'agit doive y être soustraite; il n'auroit pas affirmé, lorsque des grammairiens profonds donnent un sens passif à *ars amandi*, qu'Ovide lui donne un sens actif, sans l'établir par des preuves victorieuses. Aujourd'hui que j'ai fait tomber le masque, il ne verroit plus en vous, monsieur, que vous-même, & il ne seroit pas tenté de vous placer parmi nos logiciens & nos puristes. (*JLF* 1 February 1786)

The tone that L. V... adopts here is now harsh rather than mocking as they accuse the addressee of sending a letter both 'obreptice' and 'subreptice', discredit l'Abbé de Fontenay for being 'plus galant que dialecticien', and triumphantly claim victory for having 'fait tomber le masque'. Of course, L. V... is apparently wearing that very same mask and it seems well-chosen because Domergue expresses approval for both the contents and the pleasing form of this letter in his own response published in the same edition.

This example of epistolary transvestism is revealing because in accusing a male reader of identifying as a woman, L. V . . . must explicitly articulate why it is that women are seen to receive preferential treatment when writing in to periodical publications on matters linguistic. For L. V . . ., it is a combination of the conventions of the male code of gallantry coupled with the attention-grabbing, distracting, and/or seductive power of women's language. The fact that this example involves the *Journal général de France* underscores the fact that the *JLF* is not the only venue for such exchanges in eighteenth-century France. In fact, McLaughlin (2015: 19–20) showed that readers wrote to periodicals such as the *Mercure galant* (de Visé 1672–1710) with questions about language as early as the 1670s. There is currently a significant amount of interest in women and the history of the French press so it will be useful in future research to explore more generally how women's letters are treated.[24] It will be useful to determine, for example, whether this favourable treatment is widespread or whether it is particular to letters treating questions of language or to specific publications such as the *JLF*.

6.4 Thematizing women and gender

Through a combination of reading individual editions and carrying out full-text searches, I identified a range of metalinguistic topics addressed in the *JLF* which frequently led to the thematizing of women and gender. Some of those topics have already emerged in previous sections so we will not return to them here. They include the home and the education of children where women are seen to play a central role; orthography where women face gender-specific challenges; and Latin which remained broadly inaccessible to women. In other cases, such as pieces on grammatical gender or on a lexical item like 'accoucher', women and gender also come up. Such cases are not examined here since they involve only short mentions of women and gender which makes them less likely to play an important role in the reflection and construction of attitudes and ideologies. Instead, this section deepens our understanding of the role of the *JLF* by analysing items on personal titles and linguistic feminization. These items were chosen because of the depth and duration of the discussions and because of their general prominence in the *JLF*: the pieces tend to be longer than average; multiple individuals contribute to the discussions; and they span the publication history from 1784 to 1795.

The detailed and sustained interest in titles and linguistic feminization reflects the sociopolitical context of the end of the *Ancien Régime* and the early years of the Revolution. As Siouffi (2007a: 925) explains, there was a need for new terms, or a new use of existing terms, to describe the new social reality.[25] A key part of this

---

[24] See, for example, McIlvanney (2019).
[25] Domergue said as much when he famously proposed replacing 'royaume' by 'loyaume': 'Il faut un mot nouveau pour exprimer une chose nouvelle.' (*JLF* 1 August 1791).

were changes affecting the civil and social spheres: hereditary nobility and its titles were officially abolished in 1790; 'Monsieur' and 'Madame' were to be replaced by 'citoyen' and 'citoyenne' from 1793; and the use of 'vous' was outlawed in 1795 (Siouffi 2007a: 934–5). Women and equality of the sexes were central concerns in this period, as evidenced by, inter alia, De Gouges's (1791) composition of the *Déclaration des droits de la femme et de la citoyenne* in response to the famous *Déclaration des droits de l'homme et du citoyen* of 1789.[26] As the 'grammairien-patriote' (*JLF* 2 April 1791), Domergue's activities within and beyond the *JLF* were a key part of the Revolutionary movement for change and this included addressing the question of women and sexual equality. This section explores, first, items in the *JLF* on personal titles in general in which the question of feminization sometimes comes up, and second, items which focus specifically on the feminization of social titles.

As we saw in Section 6.1, Dougnac (1989: 55–60) drew attention to a collection of pieces on the use of titles and opening and closing epistolary formulae in the *JLF*. She identified the most detailed and lengthy series of exchanges which begins with a letter to Domergue from a semi-anonymous reader identified as 'François Leg. . .' asking a question about the meaning of the close synonyms 'tyran' and 'despote' (*JLF* 12 February 1791). Before Domergue responds to the content of the letter, he comments at length on its opening formula: 'A Urbain Domergue, Salut'. Domergue commends the reader for using what he calls 'la formule des âges de liberté' instead of 'monsieur' which was previously used in the *JLF* but is now condemned for encoding the social hierarchy which the Revolution has attempted to flatten. The comments made in passing about the opening formula become the most important part of Domergue's response because they are picked up on in a subsequent edition by the reader Pierre Lehardy (*JLF* 19 March 1791). This example illustrates the shift that took place when metalinguistic texts came to be published as periodicals: the interactivity introduced by the medium allowed readers to contribute to the selection of topics to be covered.

In his letter to Domergue, Lehardy agrees with his condemnation of 'monsieur' and he asks that a similar treatment be given to 'valet', 'serviteur', and 'servante' which are used at the end of a letter or to take one's leave in person (*JLF* 19 March 1791). Lehardy calls this an 'imbécille coutume' and Domergue agrees, referring to 'l'insignifiance, la bassesse & le danger de la formule qui termine nos lettres'. Domergue then prescribes new opening and closing formulae. The individual is to be addressed using their name, the title 'citoyen', and their profession so that, for example, the opening formula of his response to Lehardy would be 'à Pierre Lehardi, citoyen, médecin'.[27] As Domergue explains, '[v]otre nom indique ce que

---

[26] On De Gouges, see Mousset (2003).
[27] Note the orthographic variation in the name of this correspondent. He is known today as *Pierre Lehardy* but the name was spelled with a final -*i* in this extract from the *Journal de la langue françoise*.

vous êtes individuellement; le nom de citoyen ce que vous êtes politiquement, celui de médecin, ce que vous êtes dans l'ordre de la société'. An optional salutation can then be added. No closing formula is required at the end of the letter; '[o]n quittera la plume, quand on n'aura plus rien à exprimer'. These new guidelines respect two ideological principles articulated in Domergue's response, namely that all people are equal and '[l]a réalité seule peut plaire au françois régénéré'. These exchanges on titles and epistolary formulae attracted attention at the time and remain of interest today because they lay bare both the pressure that was put on language in this period and also the way in which linguistic problems were thought through. In addition, exchanges on titles and formulae are especially prominent in the *JLF* because it itself consists of published letters which makes both titles and epistolary formulae pervasive in its pages. This is a clear example of the periodical medium of publication impacting not just the form but also the contents of the metalinguistic discourse.

As Dougnac (1989: 56) points out, Domergue and his correspondents eventually turn their attention to women in this series of letters. Domergue's response to Lehardy ends with a short paragraph addressed to the '[s]exe aimable' whom he reassures he has not forgotten (16).

(16) Et comment ne saisirois-je pas avec empressement, cette occasion de vous rendre un hommage que vous méritez? Les femmes sont citoyennes, quel plus beau titre! Il leur sera donné dans les rapports civiques; les femmes règnèront toujours sur nous, elles seront toujours *dames* de nos pensées, & je laisse à l'amour, à la reconnoissance, le soin de les qualifier d'une manière digne du bonheur qu'elles nous dispensent. (*JLF* 19 March 1791)

Although Domergue addresses women in a typically florid style emphasizing themes of beauty and pleasure, the end of extract (16) shows that the linguistic prescriptions relating to women are parallel to those relating to men and that they are founded on the same ideological principles: the only political title to be used for women is 'citoyenne', the feminized form of 'citoyen'.

Knapen, the *JLF*'s printer, responds to Domergue's rejection of the term 'monsieur' in a subsequent edition where he appears to support the change but raises some practical questions (*JLF* 2 April 1791). For example, he asks whether the feminine titles 'madame' and 'mademoiselle' will meet the same fate as 'monsieur'. If so, he wonders '[c]omment désignera-t-on une femme d'un homme, une femme mariée de celle qui ne l'est pas?'.[28] Knapen is concerned that using only the first name will lead to confusion because of men such as 'Marie Voltaire' who adopt the names of female saints. Domergue is categorical in his response (17).

---

[28] Since Knapen appears to favour the changes, this is not an example of linguistic arguments being instrumentalized to support an ideological position against change as is often seen in modern and contemporary reactions to linguistic feminization and inclusive language.

(17) LES qualifications de madame, de mademoiselle, données d'abord aux femmes de la caste noble, exprimoient une idée de supériorité; prodiguées ensuite à toutes les femmes sans distinction, elles sont devenues insignifiantes. Sous ce double point de vue, elles doivent être proscrites; l'égalité décrétée par la nature & sanctionnée par la constitution, nous interdit toute expression de dépendance; & la justesse d'esprit qu'enfante la liberté, toute dénomination vide de sens. (*JLF* 2 April 1791)

He then explains that unmarried women will be known by their first name and their father's surname, whereas married women will be known by their first name and by the surnames of both their father and their husband. Domergue gives short shrift to Knapen's concerns about the ambiguity caused by men adopting female saints' names. He explains that those who adopt the name of a female saint also adopt the name of a male saint—in Voltaire's case 'François'—but he dismisses the whole practice as 'une bizarrerie, un manque de vérité' which should be done away with. This exchange illustrates the strong ideological motivations behind Domergue's engagement in the debate surrounding titles and we recognize the combination of utopian vision and pedagogical initiatives that characterize the metalinguistic discourse of the neological crisis of the early years of the Revolution (Siouffi 2007a: 932). Across this whole series of letters initially sparked by a reader's avoidance of 'monsieur' (*JLF* 12 February 1791), Domergue shows that he is prepared to dismiss practical concerns in order for linguistic usage to better reflect the new social reality.

The second group of exchanges examined in this section focuses on the feminization of what we saw Domergue refer to above as titles that indicate 'ce que vous êtes dans l'ordre de la société' (*JLF* 19 March 1791). Feminization clearly constitutes an important topic for the founder and readers of the *JLF*. This is indicated by the recurrence of letters on the question over time from some of the earliest issues published in 1784 to the last issues published in 1795. During two full read-throughs of the *JLF*, I identified a total of seven exchanges that treat the feminization of social titles in some detail; there is no space here to examine other brief mentions or indeed uses of feminized forms. The exchanges are all prompted by a reader's question about a specific feminized title. Most of the titles refer to roles that are either politico-administrative (e.g. 'ambassadrice', 'maréchale', and 'reine') or in the arts and letters (e.g. 'autrice', 'créatrice', and 'spectatrice'). The exchanges indicate that there are two distinct motivations for feminizing these different types of titles. The feminization of politico-administrative titles is not meant to indicate that women play those roles; instead, in Domergue's words, '[l]e besoin de plaire aux femmes, ou le besoin d'abréger, nous forcera toujours à transporter à l'épouse la qualification due à celui qui ne fait qu'un avec elle' (*JLF* 1 August 1791). In contrast, the feminization of titles in the arts and letters is motivated by the need to reflect new roles for women.

The feminized form that generates the most discourse within the *JLF* is 'amatrice' which is first discussed in the edition published on 15 November 1784 when 'une société d'*amateurs* de la langue françoise' provides Domergue with a range of opinions on the form and asks him for his view. Dougnac (1982: 7–8) highlights the importance of this exchange because excerpts from it were published five times in all: three times in the *JLF* and twice elsewhere. When the question re-emerges in the *JLF* in 1795, it is posed in such a way so as to further emphasize its importance: instead of reproducing the lengthy series of opinions shared by the language society in 1784, the reader simply asks '[a]matrice est-il françois, demande-t-on tous les jours?' (*JLF* 8 July 1795). This is a clear example of the double role of the *JLF* which at once reflects and constructs attitudes and ideologies. The question is treated in the periodical because it is on everyone's lips, but by stating that fact, its importance only grows. The fact that material from the *JLF* was also published elsewhere further underscores the role of the *JLF* because it illustrates one of the ways in which its metalinguistic discourse circulated beyond its own pages.

The initial exchange on 'amatrice' (*JLF* 15 November 1784) can be seen as representative of the positions generally adopted by readers and by Domergue and the other contributors. An asymmetry generally characterizes these positions because readers normally have a question or a doubt and thus tend to recognize a multiplicity of positions, whereas Domergue and the other contributors tend to take a specific stance. The exchange on 'amatrice' is no exception. In their letter, the language society quotes a range of opinions on the term 'amatrice' before asking Domergue for his 'avis'. The opinions quoted by the society include two outright rejections of 'amatrice' as a 'barbarisme' which cannot be French because it is not found in any dictionary. Slightly more space, however, is given to those contesting such proscriptions. A range of arguments are presented in favour of 'amatrice' including the fact that it was used by both Rousseau and the journalist Linguet, as well as the existence of analogous pairs such as 'acteur'/'actrice'. Both Linguet himself and a semi-anonymous 'allemand, versé dans notre langue' call into question the value of the dictionary in deciding such matters. Not only does a word such as 'créatrice' exist in French despite not being in the *Dictionnaire de l'Académie*, but the proposed alternative to 'amatrice', namely 'femme-amateur', is not included either.[29] Although different opinions are presented in the letter from the language society, the balance clearly tips in favour of the feminized form. The same can be said in general of questions from readers on the feminization of social titles.[30]

The 'auteurs du journal' provide a more categorical response to the language society (*JLF* 15 November 1784). They start by articulating the difference between

[29] Although Linguet does not specify which edition of the *Dictionnaire de l'Académie* he is referring to, it is most likely that it was the fourth edition (Académie française 1762).
[30] See, for example, a reader's question about feminizing politico-administrative titles such as 'maréchal', 'président', and 'prévot' (*JLF* 1 December 1786).

'néologie' ('l'art de former des mots nouveaux pour des idées nouvelles ou mal rendues') and 'néologisme' ('la manie d'employer des mots nouveaux sans besoin ou sans goût'). For the authors of the periodical, 'amatrice' falls into the first category and they provide various types of supporting evidence. The excerpt in (18) offers a concise summary of the criteria used to evaluate the case, namely a demonstrable need or lexical gap, aesthetic considerations, analogical support, historical models, and established usage.[31]

(18) Nous sommes donc d'avis que le mot *amatrice*, sollicité par le besoin, approuvé par le goût, parfaitement analogue, ayant des patrons recommandables, circulant déja dans la bonne compagnie, est frappé au coin des meilleurs mots françois. (*JLF* 15 November 1784)

For our purposes, it is the evidence that illustrates the need ('besoin') for the new form which is the most relevant. In (19) the authors can be seen explicitly evoking the social changes that have taken place which motivate the feminization.

(19) Depuis que les femmes cultivent leur esprit, depuis qu'à l'empire de leurs charmes, elles ajoutent celui des connoissances en tout genre, depuis qu'elles aiment les lettres & les arts, il nous faut un mot doué de l'inflexion féminine qui rende cette nouvelle idée, & ce mot est *amatrice*. (*JLF* 15 November 1784)

The fact that the expansion of women's sphere was evoked in such discussions is important because it communicated to readers the fact that women were occupying new roles in society and making inroads into learning,[32] even as Domergue and his readers continue to rely elsewhere on the tropes of women as the 'sexe aimable'. Here, as in other examples, Domergue and the contributors tend to come down clearly in favour of feminization.[33] It seems reasonable to conclude that at least a portion of the readership will have been persuaded by the wide range of arguments that Domergue and the contributors bring in support of linguistic feminization. At the very least, the length of the exchanges and the presence of different points of view will have communicated to readers the fact that using or avoiding feminized forms was not a neutral choice. In this way, the metalinguistic discourse on linguistic feminization in the *JLF* may have contributed to this type of inclusive language becoming a salient locus of variation and change at the end of the eighteenth century.

The final impact of these exchanges is linguistic rather than social. In sharing discussions of feminized titles, the *JLF* contributed to the diffusion of forms that

---

[31] See Dougnac's (1982) account of neological theory in the *JLF*.
[32] Another such example is found when a reader asks how to feminize 'apprenti' (*JLF* 15 March 1785).
[33] See the later exchange on 'amatrice' (*JLF* 8 July 1795) as well as comments on 'ambassadrice', 'maréchale', 'perruquière', and 'reine' (*JLF* 1 August 1791) or on 'autrice' and 'actrice' (1 March 1788).

were not (yet) in widespread use. The clearest example is found in the extract from the semi-anonymous 'allemand, versé dans notre langue' provided by the language society (*JLF* 15 November 1784). In advocating for the acceptance of 'amatrice', he claims that it is 'analogue au génie de la langue' and he supports this assertion with a list of thirteen pairs of masculine and feminine forms such as 'acteur/actrice', 'créateur/créatrice', and 'fondateur/fondatrice'. These examples are presented in two columns aligning masculine and feminine forms. This presentation underscores the potential for the *JLF* to contribute to the diffusion of feminized forms because it recalls the tabular layout of didactic materials which was meant to facilitate memorization. Revealingly, the quotation from a reader in (20) indicates that people were aware of the role that periodicals could play in the diffusion of linguistic innovations. The reader explains that having periodicals use the new orthographic reform supported by Voltaire will ensure that the innovations are diffused and adopted more widely.

(20) Il faudrait qu'on l'adoptât dans tous les écrits périodiques, les journaux, les gazettes. Ces sortes d'ouvrages, étant extrêmement répandus, accoutumeroient les lecteurs aux changements qu'elle offre. (*JLF* 1 March 1788)

When it comes to linguistic feminization, what makes the *JLF* especially likely to have played a role is the fact that it combines metalinguistic discourse promoting feminization with linguistic practice. In her study of sixteenth-century metalinguistic texts, Pagani-Naudet (2014: 188) highlights their form which tends to get overlooked: 'écrire une grammaire en français c'est livrer quelque chose en plus à l'imitation du lecteur'. There is something amplificatory about the effect in the *JLF* where Domergue supports the use of feminized titles while also using them very prominently in epistolary formulae. The most notable example is 'citoyenne' which appears in both opening and closing formulae from July 1791 onwards. Domergue may have been particularly attentive to aligning linguistic practice and metalinguistic discourse because of the interactivity of this epistolary periodical. As we saw in Section 6.3, readers of the *JLF* were quick to criticize Domergue when his own usage did not align with his metalinguistic discourse.

6.5 Conclusion

Through a tripartite investigation of the principal figures involved and invoked in the *JLF*, readers' letters, and the thematics of women and gender, I have endeavoured to show where women were present and how they were represented in the first periodical devoted to the French language. Since the *JLF* bridges *Ancien Régime* and Revolutionary France, it is probably not by chance that it is invariably those moments where readers and contributors must grapple with change that are the most revealing. In charting the presence and representation of women and language, I have identified some of the key ways in which both the linguistic practice and metalinguistic discourse of the *JLF* could have contributed to the reflection and construction of attitudes and ideologies surrounding women and language. Most importantly for language historians, we have seen that the shift to the periodical medium played a key role in opening up a new space in which women were able to share their metalinguistic thought in the public domain. The medium of publication was also crucial in allowing contributors and readers to engage in the process of language variation and change as they were able to comment directly on—and indeed enact—changes that were taking place at the time. This study opens up directions for future research on language, gender, and the *JLF*. Most obviously, a future study of the reception history of the *JLF* would let us measure the extent of its impact. Moving in a different direction, a comparison of letters written from men and women in the *JLF* would be a new way of exploring the workings of gender-based variation in the past.

7
The French language and eighteenth-century Italian women
Language of vanity or language of scholarship?

Helena Sanson

7.1 Introduction

Towards the end of the eighteenth century, in 1791, the Piedmontese polymath and historian Gianfrancesco Galeani Napione, count of Cocconato, deplored in his *Dell'uso, e dei pregj della lingua italiana* ('On the use and the merits of the Italian language') the habit of teaching French to well-to-do young girls at the expense of Italian: 'it is an excellent idea to teach them an educated and regulated language, and hence limit the use of coarse popular dialects: but why French?' (Galeani Napione 1791: II, 139–41).[1] The Italian language was codified at the beginning of the sixteenth century based on the fourteenth-century literary Tuscan used by the so-called Three Crowns, Dante, Petrarch, and Boccaccio (especially Petrarch for poetry and Boccaccio for prose). Especially outside of Tuscany and, to a certain extent, Rome,[2] competence in Italian needed to be acquired by means of grammars and dictionaries or by studying the 'good' authors of the past. For centuries, Italian remained therefore beyond the reach of the less learned, and women, given their restricted access to education, were often among them.

In the eighteenth century, Italian continued to be above all a literary language, conservative and archaic in nature, not commonly used in speaking, except on more formal occasions. This allowed for passive competence in the language, but it did not automatically imply active fluency. Everyday life was dominated rather by the local dialects.[3] Using Italian in speech instead of one's local dialect signalled affectation and could attract ridicule. As Stendhal (1817: 152) remarked in his

---

[1] I gratefully acknowledge the generous support of the Leverhulme Trust, which has allowed me to conduct research for this chapter.

[2] In Rome the local vernacular had undergone a strong process of Tuscanization in the sixteenth century, following the demographic setback caused by the Sack of Rome in 1527. This meant that it had lost its distinct southern traits in favour of a more Tuscanized variety. See on this point Trifone (2006: 61–94, 2008).

[3] It is well known that, in the context of Italy, the term 'dialect' refers to that rich range of Romance idioms, the so-called Italian dialects (e.g. Piedmontese, Friulian, Bolognese, Neapolitan, Venetian), that

Rome, Naples et Florence en 1817, 'La langue écrite de l'Italie n'est aussi la langue parlée qu'à Florence et à Rome. Partout ailleurs on se sert de l'ancien dialecte du pays et parler toscan dans la conversation est un ridicule'.

Alongside the expanding influence of literary Italian, in the eighteenth century the 'empire' of Latin (Waquet 2002) was still strong, especially in certain disciplines and fields of knowledge—among these scientific subjects, theology, and the law. As in previous centuries, learning the classical languages continued to be considered unsuitable for women by most moralists and educationalists (Sanson 2015). Nevertheless, the eighteenth century also saw a progressive overall decline of the Latin/Italian bilingualism that had existed until that point. In fact, a 'new bilingualism' (Devoto 1953: 101–14) between French and Italian took root in the peninsula. French became the language of elegant conversation—often, as we shall see, associated with women of a certain social rank or with social aspirations—but also of written communication, at times even used with a higher degree of competence than Italian.

The influence of French soon generated strong resistance. Moralists and men of letters claimed that it corrupted the Italian language and Italian customs and mores, turning what was once a virile and grave language into an effeminate and vain tool of expression. Women's interest in French language and culture was deemed particularly deplorable. It is well known that, across the centuries, women's use of language has been a recurrent object of discussion by thinkers and theorists. Their views, imbued with misogynistic stereotypes, often underlined women's tendency to linguistic affectation or to introduce deplorable innovations (Ayres-Bennett and Sanson 2020: 14–15).

This chapter explores the roles that knowledge of French played for eighteenth-century Italian women. After a general contextualization of the growing interest in foreign languages (French above all) across the Italian peninsula (Section 7.2), the chapter focuses specifically on women's interest in, and study of, French, which some theorists saw as an expression and an extension of female vanity that had to be blamed for the perceived decadence of Italian, and Italy's culture more broadly (Section 7.3). Yet French embodied a new cultural cosmopolitanism and allowed women access to the latest intellectual developments and trends that were taking place in France and Europe more broadly. Some women were also able to take on the role of cultural mediators and engage in current literary or scientific debates by means of their own translations from French into Italian: knowledge of French was for them an important tool of scholarship (Section 7.4). Rather than being a language of vanity that corrupted Italy's culture, French was for women a means to acquire and transmit knowledge (Section 7.5).

---

are still in use in the peninsula today. These are cognate languages, but they are not varieties of Italian as such. See also Chapter 1 (this volume), footnote 54.

7.2 Italy's Gallomania: French culture and language in everyday life

Already in the fifteenth century, with the spread of the printing press, we find in Italy (as in other countries in Europe) a production of conversation manuals in which two or more (even up to eight) vernacular languages are presented side-by-side in comparison. Half lexicons and half phrase books, these plurilingual works, which were 'clearly far removed from any scholarly intent, reflecting in themselves the needs, limitations, and characteristics of popular products' (Rossebastiano Bart 1984: 9–10), had a clear didactic aim. They intended to offer, in format and content, a quick and practical method to learn foreign languages to those who needed them in their travels or daily interactions, without resorting to interpreters. In sixteenth-century Italy, foreign languages were also seen as useful tools to be employed in courtly settings. The splendour and cosmopolitanism of the courts explain why Baldassar Castiglione had one of the speakers in his 1528 *Il Libro del Cortegiano* ('The book of the courtier') include knowledge of foreign languages—French and Spanish—among the accomplishments of the ideal courtier (Castiglione 2003 [1528]: Book II, Ch. 37). Not to mention the fact that the political situation of the peninsula was such that for decades it was the battleground of foreign political powers, namely France, indeed, and Spain.

But a clearer interest in foreign languages, including the production of grammars, really started to increase from the beginning of the seventeenth century. Compared to other European countries, this interest seems to have developed at a slower speed. The delay is doubtless partly due to the prestige Italian had enjoyed across Europe throughout the Renaissance, when it had been studied, together with its literature, by a refined elite of nobles and bourgeois, while being commonly used by merchants and adopted as a lingua franca in the Mediterranean.[4] Specifically—with reference to French—whereas the first grammar of Italian for the French, *La Grammaire italienne* by Jean-Claude de Mesmes, was published in Paris in 1549,[5] the first grammar of French written in Italian for Italians came much later. The *Grammatica italiana per imparare la lingua francese* ('Italian grammar to learn French') by Pierre Durand was published more than seventy years later, in 1625, by Francesco Corbelletti in Rome. As Ferdinand Brunot (1905–53: VIII, 85) pointed out: 'il est facile de comprendre pourquoi l'ascendant du français fut tardif en Italie. La langue italienne avait depuis un siècle et demi la primauté'.

In comparison, the first grammars of Spanish for Italians were published in the mid-sixteenth century, not far apart. Giovan Mario Alessandri's *Il paragone della*

---

[4] See on this respectively Richardson (2002) and Cremona (2002).
[5] For a modern edition, see Mesmes (2002[1549]). On the first grammars of Italian for the French, see Mattarucco (2003, 2018).

lingua toscana et castigliana ('Comparison between the Tuscan and the Castilian language') was printed in 1560 in Naples by Mattia Cancer (Alessandri 1560). It only had one edition.[6] The *Osservationi della lingua castigliana* ('Observations on the Castillian language') by Juan de Miranda was first printed in Venice in 1566 and went on to have another nine editions (the last one in 1595), all with the printer Gabriele Giolito.[7] But these were, in fact, isolated cases and the chronology is not coincidental: with the 1559 Treaty of Cateau-Cambrésis, between the Spanish and the French, a good part of the Italian peninsula found itself under direct Spanish rule, or in any case under Spanish influence, a situation that was to last for more than a century. We must wait until the seventeenth century to find other grammars of Spanish, for instance in the form of bilingual or trilingual works which presented their readers with the option of simultaneously learning Spanish and Italian, or Italian, French, and Spanish. Cases in point are Lorenzo Franciosini's (1624) *Gramatica spagnola, e italiana* ('Spanish and Italian grammar'),[8] or Antoine Fabre's (1626) *Grammatica per imparare le lingue italiana, francese e spagnola* ('Grammar to learn Italian, French, and Spanish').

After the 1659 Treaty of the Pyrenees that marked the end of the war between France and Spain, the influence of Spanish in the peninsula began to wane and then dissolved even more rapidly after 1680, when there started to be a clear increase in interest in everything French, resulting in what seemed to be a veritable Gallomania (Auzzas 1985). This was not a phenomenon limited to Italy: the eighteenth century saw the consecration of French as the universal language of educated and refined Europe, the language used to communicate internationally at high diplomatic levels, and the new language of science. In promoting his 1720 grammar *Nuovo metodo per insegnare il francese agl'italiani* ('New grammar to teach French to Italians') Charles Munier (1720: A3v) stressed that 'Je pourois dire néanmoins à [...] ceux qui l'ignorent [...] qu'elle [la langue française] est généralement préférée à toutes les autres de l'Europe, et que les étrangers de qualité, jusqu'aux Princes souverains mêmes, croiroient qu'il manqueroit quelque chose à leur éducation, s'ils ne la parloient.[9]

The ever-growing prestige of French eroded the importance Italian had enjoyed for centuries internationally and ended up impacting on its status and role within Italy. French could acquire such a hold across the peninsula because proper knowledge of Italian was limited even among the highest classes. The fact is that, for most of the eighteenth century, Italian was not taught in schools: school and education still remained very much in the hands of the Jesuit order, whose educational

---

[6] On Alessandri's grammar, see Polo (2017).
[7] On the first grammars of French in Europe, see De Clercq, Lioce, and Swiggers (2000). In Italy specifically, see Mormile (1989); Minerva (1996, 2002); Minerva and Pellandra (1997); Colombo Timelli (2000).
[8] For a modern edition, see Franciosini (2018 [1624]).
[9] The spelling in quotations from French primary sources has been preserved as in the original.

system privileged the study of Latin at the expense of Italian.[10] Across the peninsula there were in use intermediate registers between Italian—the literary language learnt, as we saw earlier, from books and grammars—and the dialect(s), that is to say, less localized varieties which speakers could switch to for the sake of exchange and communication, according to need and context. But there was no unitary Italian and in fact the local dialects continued to be people's mother tongues, irrespective of social rank.

In cosmopolitan eighteenth-century Italy, knowledge of foreign languages—and French above all, associated as it was with the refinement and cultural life of Parisian salons—progressively became an intrinsic part of the upbringing of well-to-do men as well as women. Towards the end of the eighteenth century, the Paduan Melchiorre Cesarotti, the most authoritative Italian linguist of the time, remarked in his *Saggio sopra la lingua italiana* ('Essay on the Italian language') (1785) that the French language had become 'very common throughout Italy: there isn't anyone without some degree of education to whom French is not familiar, if not even natural; the library of sophisticated women and men is only French' (Cesarotti 1785: 107). Some French travellers commented on the diffusion of French across the peninsula. Lalande (1769–70: VIII, 539), for instance, in his *Voyage d'un françois en Italie, fait dans les années 1765 & 1766*, observed that 'il y a dans toutes les villes des personnes qui parlent françois tant bien que mal'.[11] A number of renowned Italian authors, men of letters, and scientists even chose to compose their works in French and to use French in their correspondence: 'le français a servi aux savants, aux spécialistes les plus divers, pour l'exposé de leurs doctrines ou de leurs idées' (Bédarida and Hazard 1934: 33).[12]

In his *Colpo d'occhio su lo stato presente della letteratura italiana* ('A glance at the present state of Italian literature'), published between 1788 and 1789, anonymously, in the journal *Nuovo giornale letterario d'Italia* ('New literary journal of Italy'), and simultaneously in other periodicals, the Florentine lawyer and journalist Giovanni Ristori suggested that in 1788, across the peninsula, around 150,000 'educated people [were able to] read French', with the highest numbers in Lombardy (40,000) and the Veneto (30,000), two of the most culturally lively areas of Italy (Berengo 1962: 628). If the reliability of these figures cannot be entirely confirmed, what is interesting is the description Ristori offers of the range of interests of this 'numerous, immense class' of educated people: besides reading French, they composed verse, knew history, understood Latin, had good taste, a

---

[10] Italian was a subject of study only in some elite Jesuit institutions (Ballerini 1985: 232–3). The Jesuits, as is well known, ignored female education.

[11] On the linguistic experience of French travellers in Italy, see Cartago (1990); Serianni (1999) (also in Serianni 2002: 55–88). On the linguistic experience of travellers in early modern Europe, see Tosi (2020).

[12] On the use of French in Italy for everyday correspondence, personal diaries, and memoir writing, see also Brunot (1905–53: VIII, 92–4); Dardi (1984: 362–3); Mormile (1989: 113–14).

knowledge of music and painting, expressed their views on theatre, novels, and poetry, and even used a few Greek words and Latin sayings in their speech. Yet, Ristori commented, 'in the midst of so many scholars the book trade is in its last throes, since no buyers can be found' (Berengo 1962: 628), hence suggesting that this display of erudition was in fact 'muddled and uninteresting' and not based on sound studies (Cristiani 2003: 282). As for French books, they enjoyed good circulation across the peninsula. In the second half of the century, in Venice (one of the most important centres of book production and circulation in Italy), out of the 60,000 book titles that cleared customs between 1750 and 1790, at least 10,000 were in French (Dardi 1984: 369).[13] Not to mention those Italian printers who published works in French—such as the brothers Faure and Blanchon in Parma, Antonio Bulifon, Jacques Raillard, and Jean Gravier in Naples, Bouchard and, again, Gravier in Rome—as well as French/Italian bilingual editions, reprints of French works originally published in France, Italian translations of French works, and pseudo-translations from French.[14]

In some parts of the peninsula speakers might resort to French in everyday conversation to cover a gap in their linguistic repertoire, when their native dialect was inappropriate, or Italian too literary, and inadequate. In Piedmont, due to its geographical closeness to France and the bilingual structure of the state, French was used in everyday communication beyond the aristocracy and was necessary for the middle classes in liberal professions or in commerce.[15] In other urban centres of northern Italy too, such as Venice, French was used as a sign of distinction for the upper classes in elegant conversation (Zolli 1971).[16] It was also used in other areas of Italy for political and dynastic reasons, such as Parma, which saw the installation of Philip of Bourbon (married to the daughter of Louis XV) as Duke in 1749 (Bédarida 1928), and Florence, where the Lorraine dynasty established itself from 1737. A point worth mentioning, of course, is the fact that at the end of the century the influence of French became more overtly political when Italy fell under French control, following the Napoleonic Wars.[17] In the centre and south of the peninsula, French was also used, although less prominently. In his 1734 treatise *Dell'arte e del metodo delle lingue* ('On the art and method of languages') dedicated to Pope Clement XII, Giovanni Barba, the secretary of the Congregation for Studies in Rome, stressed how important it was to have people well-skilled in the living languages, such as French, in sovereign courts, given the day-to-day need to

---

[13] See Piva (1973), which is Dardi's source for this data.
[14] On this point see Brunot (1905–53: VIII, 90–1, 103–4, 118–19); Hazard (1910: 36–64); Dardi (1984: 353); Pasta (2014: 341–3).
[15] On the linguistic history of Piedmont, see Marazzini (1992). On the use of French in Piedmont, see Brunot (1905–53: VIII, 95–9).
[16] On this point, see also Brunot (1905–53: VIII, 100–8); Auzzas (1985).
[17] For an outline of the influence of French in the different states across Italy, see Brunot (1905–53: VIII, 85–137); Mormile (1989: 114–21); Dardi (1992: 18–29). See also Matarrese (1993) and Morgana (1994).

deal and interact with other nations (Barba 1734: 20). In Sicily, starting from the eighteenth century, the local elite also learnt French, whether studying it at home with private tutors or governesses, or at institutions such as the Collegio dei Nobili or in some *educandati* ('girls' boarding schools') that catered, as we shall see, for the daughters of well-off families (Lillo 2004).

The pervasiveness and spread of French were facilitated by the large influx of French people into the Italian peninsula, especially in certain professions (e.g. milliners, hairdressers, chefs, dancing instructors, artists).[18] There were also numerous teachers of French ready to satisfy the growing demand for the language. French language teachers found work at court, with aristocratic and rich bourgeois families, as well as in some educational institutions catering for the children of the upper classes. Many composed grammars, manuals, compilations of model letters, and dictionaries for their pupils, hoping to improve their own standing or make a profit in what was a very competitive field. The sheer number of such metalinguistic texts—grammars and dictionaries produced with an Italian audience in mind and preserved in libraries across the peninsula—is a clear sign of the penetration and success of French.[19] Existing French grammars by French authors were adapted for an Italian readership, other grammars were the work of Italian authors who at times did not hesitate to Frenchify their names to come across as more reliable. Authors, and publishers, responded to the incessant demand for tools to learn the language, striving to offer their readers innovative (at least in theory) methods to help them acquire it. As we saw earlier, some grammars were presented as bilingual, such as Michele Berti's (1692) *L'arte d'insegnare la lingua francese per mezzo dell'italiana o' vero la lingua italiana per mezzo della francese* ('The art of teaching the French language by means of Italian, or the Italian language by means of French'), which conveniently seemed to offer readers the possibility of simultaneously acquiring the grammar of French and of Italian, the study of which, as previously noted, was so often disregarded.

Among the most successful grammars of French at the time were, to name just a few, *La lingua franzese spiegata co' più celebri autori moderni* ('The French language explained by means of the most illustrious modern authors') by Michel Feri de la Salle, first published in Florence in 1697, and the *Nuova grammatica italiana e francese* ('New Italian and French grammar') by Louis Goudar, from Montpellier.[20] The first edition of Goudar's manual was brought out in Milan in 1744, followed by numerous subsequent editions and adaptations over a period that spans a century and a half. It was published about thirty times in the last decades of the eighteenth century alone, all across Italy: 'de tous

---

[18] On French travellers and professionals in Italy, see Bédarida (1928: 121–86, 217–303); Bédarida and Hazard (1934: 19–26); Brunot (1905–53: VIII, 123–4).

[19] To get a sense of their increase in number, see Table 5 in Minerva and Pellandra (1997: 373–85). On dictionaries of French, see Mormile (1993).

[20] For a bibliography of the many editions and reprints, see Minerva and Pellandra (1997: s.v.).

les auteurs qui ont publié en Italie aux XVIIIe et XIXe siècles, [Goudar] est celui qui a joui de la faveur du public de la façon la plus durable' (Lillo 1990: 10). Among the main dictionaries of French for Italians, the *Nuovo dizionario italiano-francese, estratto da' dizionari dell'Accademia di Francia e della Crusca* ('New Italian–French dictionary, based on the dictionaries of the French Academy and the Academy of the Crusca'), by the Abbé Francesco Alberti di Villanova (1772), went on to enjoy numerous editions well into the nineteenth century (Mormile 1993). The subtitle presented the dictionary as particularly 'useful, even necessary, for all those who would like to translate or read with profit books written in either of the two languages'. Among those who were interested in both reading and translating French books, as we shall see, there were also women.

7.3 French and Italian women: A language of vanity

The study of a living language was often encouraged for aristocratic and upper class ladies across Europe, as a sign of distinction: in his *Bibliothèque des dames*, Richard Steele observed that 'savoir plusieurs langues est une perfection sans laquelle il n'est presque pas possible qu'une dame soit bien élévée' (Steele 1724–7: I, 22). In Italy too, for women of a certain social standing, French became a suitable *art d'agrément* which contributed to their education and favoured sociability. It was seen as the language 'of noble people and specifically of the wittiest women and those who aspire to dazzle' (Galeani Napione 1791: I, 47–8). Lady Morgan (1821), in her travel diary *Italy*, commented that in Piedmont 'the women universally adopt the French toilet and language', adding in a footnote: 'The Piedmontese ladies told us, that not only conversation, but even the intercourse of notes, is carried out in French' (Lady Morgan 1821: I, 106). French similarly prevailed, she observed, among Milanese ladies: 'The *naïveté* of their Milanese idioms gives to their French (which is generally [spoken]) and to their Italian (which is occasionally spoken) a peculiar and spirited charm' (Lady Morgan 1821: I, 293–4). For those upper class women who welcomed foreign guests, artists, and men of letters into their salons, knowledge of French was a must.[21] In his 1739 collection of *Lettres familières*, Charles De Brosses recalled how in Bologna almost all ladies knew French and quoted Racine and Molière (De Brosses 1931: I, 269). Hesther Lynch Piozzi recalled a visit to Venice where the local countess, 'if she does not speak always in French to a foreigner, as she would willingly do, tries in vain to

---

[21] On Italian *salotti* ('salons') between the end of the seventeenth century and the early twentieth century, see, for instance, Musiani (2003); Betri and Brambilla (2004). On women's linguistic habits in the *salotti*, see Pellandra (2003).

talk Italian; and [...] laughs at herself for trying to *toscaneggiare* ['Tuscanize'], as she calls it' (Lynch Piozzi 1789: 221).

In eighteenth-century Italy, girls who were fortunate enough to receive an education would usually do so at home or in religious establishments and boarding schools (e.g. *educandati* or *conservatori*). Families who could afford it hired private teachers, male and female, to teach French to their daughters. Some authors of grammars of French for Italians were tutors who dedicated their works to Italian ladies, their own pupils (Sanson 2011: 227). Female tutors and mother-tongue governesses employed by bourgeois and noble families could make use of the numerous French *Abécédaires*, that is, primers, which became increasingly common (often with high print runs) starting from the nineteenth century (Pellandra 2003: 49–50). Rather than having their pupils learn and repeat grammatical rules by heart, as had been customary, they applied a maternal, natural method by means of conversation and readings. Some young women might learn French in educational establishments outside their home. At the Real Educandato Carolino in Palermo, for instance, created in 1779 for the daughters of the aristocracy, teaching of French was always imparted by native-speaker tutors, and from the beginning of the nineteenth century they specifically brought over the Visitandine nuns from a Savoy convent (Lillo 2000). The beginning of the nineteenth century also saw the creation of lay institutions—modelled on the Napoleonic *maisons impériales* of Écouen and Saint Denis, boarding schools for the education of daughters and sisters of members of the Legion of Honour—in which French played an important role. At the Collegio delle fanciulle in Milan, for instance, French was taught by a native tutor by means of the same texts used in France for learning the mother tongue (Colombini Mantovani 2000).

Teaching of French, as mentioned earlier, increased after the Napoleonic Wars (Colombo Timelli 2001). In Milan, for instance, between 1789 and 1821, twenty-three grammars of French were published for an Italian readership, either re-editions or reprints of Goudar, mentioned earlier, or completely new works (Conti 2001: 243).[22] Despite the presence of a number of French grammars dedicated to female figures, or conceived for female pupils, there does not seem to be in Italy a production of *grammatiche per le dame* ('grammars for ladies') of the kind that developed in France, Germany, or England in the eighteenth and nineteenth centuries.[23] This does not mean that authors ignored their female readers: ladies and what were deemed to be their specific learning needs (e.g. an approach to the study of grammar that was suitable even for those who, as was the case with women, did not have familiarity with Latin and its categories) are mentioned in their prefaces, catered for in their claims to have produced accessible and easy texts, or in

---

[22] See also Pazzi (2001) on the holdings of French manuals at the Biblioteca Ambrosiana between 1625 and 1860.
[23] On grammars for ladies in eighteenth- and nineteenth-century Europe, see Ayres-Bennett (1994a); Sanson (2011: 201–9, 2014, 2016); Beck-Busse (2014).

their providing dialogues, readings, and vocabulary lists that touch upon women's needs and tastes (Sanson 2011: 217–32). Addressing his readers in his *Metode pour apprendre aisément le françois* (1734), Guillaume Coutonnier advertised a future grammar-in-the-making which was going to be shorter for the use of ladies (Coutonnier 1734: unpaginated),[24] and Charles Munier, mentioned earlier, similarly claimed that he had simplified his grammar manual with the only objective of making the process of learning French easier for ladies by means of his new method (Munier 1720: a7v).

The appreciation of French by Italian ladies was at times explained by means of commonly held prejudices about women. Contrary to the gravity and literary nature of Italian, French was considered exotic and fashionable and, because of its perceived levity and superficiality, was believed to be more attractive to ladies, and more suitable for their presumed limited intellectual abilities.[25] In the discussions of contemporary authors across Europe on the subject of the *génie des langues* we find ample use of gender-related commonplaces in their defences of the superiority of their own tongue. It is well known that Italian was at times branded by French thinkers as weak and effeminate, as the language of love. In *Les Entretiens d'Ariste et d'Eugène*, for instance, Bouhours (1671) had described Italian as 'molle & effeminé, selon le temperament & les moeurs de leur païs', a 'coquette toujours parée & toujours fardée' (Bouhours 1671: 62, 70).[26] Italian intellectuals, such as Lodovico Antonio Muratori (1706) in his *Della perfetta poesia italiana* ('On perfect Italian poetry'), objected to these views, by stressing how, on the contrary, Italian had been forged by the wars and barbarities of Italy's history and was therefore grave, majestic, and 'virile' in nature (Muratori 1706: II, 157). As such, the reasoning went, it was of course less apt to be suitably acquired by the female sex: 'even though Italian women at times speak with great propriety, they still cannot embody the ideal of good speech, and have to leave this glory to men' (Muratori 1706: II, 154).

Interestingly, the same kind of misogynistic prejudices were used by Italian men of letters to challenge the spread of French across the peninsula. Indeed, the influence of French soon came to be perceived as ubiquitous and unstoppable. It became, as Cesarotti (1785: 106) defined it, 'the rock of scandal, the bone of contention, the Helen of our Iliads'. The opposition of those who deemed French language and culture damaging to the Italian language, customs, and mores stemmed from the belief that a pervasive French influence would inevitably cause linguistic and moral decadence in Italy, obliterating centuries of cultural greatness

---

[24] On Coutonnier's grammar, see Guarnieri (2001).
[25] On women learning languages in eighteenth- and nineteenth-century Italy, see Pellandra (1989, 2003).
[26] On ideas about the Italian language by French theorists and men of letters, see Stammerjohann (2013: 178–207).

and rendering Italy a servile country.[27] The scientist Antonio Vallisnieri (1733: 257) branded the French tastes and manners that had spread to the fields of comportment, clothing, food, home decoration, garden planning, and building villas as 'French scabies' that attacked the simplicity of Italian customs. Towards the end of the century, the Mantuan polygraph and physician Matteo Borsa (1785), in his *Del gusto presente in letteratura italiana* ('On the present taste in Italian literature'), pondered: 'What more shameful sign of servitude is there than losing that distinctive imprint which makes us stand aside from other nations, which makes us a nation, also in the eyes of the rest of the world?' (Borsa 1785: 16). The widespread influence of French destroyed 'the national spirit', and reduced Italians to 'superstitious worshippers of all things foreign' (Borsa 1785: 18).

Admiration for France, its language, and its culture was expressed by both men and women, but this trend was perceived as being particularly marked and considered especially deplorable in women, who, it was believed, were by nature more easily influenced and swayed by pernicious trends and fashions (Sanson 2011: 143–9). It was women who came to be held responsible for the seemingly unrelenting interest in the French language and culture and the consequent corruption of the linguistic and moral status of Italy and its people. Women were accused of unashamedly and blatantly promoting a foreign culture and language, and by so doing betraying Italy's own language and culture and condemning it to servitude. There are several such comments and observations in the writings of theorists and men of letters whose views on linguistic purity were intertwined with clear misogyny. Already at the end of the seventeenth century the poet Francesco Fulvio Frugoni (1689; posthumous) had mocked in his *Il cane di Diogene* ('Diogenes' dog') the widespread parroting of French manners, customs, and language in Italy, directing his attacks also against the vanity of women who insisted on speaking French even though they knew it poorly, inappropriately mixing Italian and French, exposing themselves to ridicule (Frugoni 1689: V, 397–400). Another case in point is the Brescian priest, playwright, and novelist Pietro Chiari, who, in his *Lettere scelte* ('Selected Letters') (Chiari 1751–65: II, 144), ridiculed women's widespread habit of randomly and inappropriately using French terms in their speech, which he saw as a deplorable sign of affectation and a clear display of their ignorance.

Not surprisingly, then, in the course of the century, a growing number of educationalists felt that Italian women needed to be Italianized and freed from an excessively Frenchifying education (Sanson 2011: 159–66). Attitudes towards female education in eighteenth-century Italy were still ambivalent,[28] but various

---

[27] On reactions and oppositions to the influence of French in Italy, see Brunot (1905–53: VIII, 125–31). On the dichotomy between Gallophilia and Gallophobia in eighteenth-century Europe (focusing on Germany and with two essays also on Italy), see Heitz et al. (2011).

[28] According to some moralists, more access to study would distract women from their roles as wives and mothers, whereas others believed that better education would help women preserve their morality

moralists now turned to express their support in favour of women gaining proper knowledge of Italian, urging them to assiduously study its grammar and the great authors of the past.[29] They strongly deplored the fact that Italian was not among the subjects young women were taught.[30] The Sienese Giovanni Niccolò Bandiera (1740), for instance, in his *Trattato degli studj delle donne* ('Treatise of Studies for Women'), encouraged women's access to study—within limits, of course, and provided they were of a certain rank.[31] He believed it could act as an antidote to female vanity, therefore benefitting the institutions of marriage and the family, as well as society as a whole. He also believed that knowledge of foreign languages, French and English in particular, was a valuable opportunity for upper class women to engage socially and to learn, he wrote, 'many things which have either not been translated yet into Italian or which preserve all their beauty in full [. . .] in the language in which they were conceived' (Bandiera 1740: II, 39–48). In essence, Bandiera pragmatically accepted French as a suitable discipline for upper class women to study, while acknowledging the importance of Italian: 'I would want them [women] to know first of all our beautiful Italian language' (Bandiera 1740: II, 48).

Some Italian women indeed followed Bandiera's suggestion whereby studying French provided access to knowledge not yet available in Italian.

7.4 French and Italian women: A language of scholarship

The strong interest in France and its culture means that the eighteenth century saw a lively production of translations into Italian from French.[32] Works of all kinds, in verse and prose, from novels and plays to scientific works, literary journals, and periodicals were rendered into Italian, often reworked and freely adapted, sometimes also at the expense of quality and content. Knowledge of French offered the possibility of being up to date with literary and scientific news, as well as current and political affairs, and was often the means of accessing works originally

---

and in turn allow them to be better educators of their offspring. See on this Sanson (2011: 149–72), with a specific focus on language and linguistic education. For a more general discussion, see Guerci (1987).

[29] On grammars of Italian and women in eighteenth-century Italy, see Sanson (2011: 209–17).

[30] It is only after political unification (in 1861) that we have the establishment of a state schooling system in Italy, open to both boys and girls, in which the study of its grammar was included as a necessary means to acquire Italian, which by then had become the national language of the newly formed state. The outcomes of this approach were inevitably limited, also in light of the fact that pupils—and teachers—were native speakers of dialect. See on this De Mauro (1963).

[31] Bandiera intentionally ignored lower class women in his treatise because he considered them unworthy of attention.

[32] See on this, for instance, Brunot (1905–53: VIII, 88–120); Hazard (1910: 42–5, and *passim*); *Il Genio delle lingue* (1989); Dardi (1992: 23–9); Matarrese (1993: 52–60); Cantarutti and Ferrari (2013). Specifically on translations of French works of theatre into Italian, see Ferrari (1925); Santangelo and Vinti (1981).

composed in other languages, initially less studied, such as English and German, for which French acted as intermediary:[33] 'La langue française jouait en Italie comme ailleurs son rôle d'intermédiaire' (Brunot 1905–53: VIII, 93).

This means that French was not necessarily only a language of vanity, synonymous with decadence and corruption. For those women who could study and learn the language, it meant in fact having direct access to a whole world of new knowledge and the latest intellectual developments and novelties in Europe. They could explore new ideas which they could then make their own. For lack of other intellectual opportunities, study of French offered alternative routes to learning and scholarship. Some women also decided to disseminate the knowledge they had acquired, by means of their own activity as translators, making this same knowledge accessible to others and adopting the role of cultural mediators between Italy and other countries in Europe. In eighteenth- and early nineteenth-century Italy, women translated into Italian from Latin and Greek, but above all from French, English, or German. Their translations included fictional and non-fictional works, poems, novels, theatre, literary criticism, geography, historiography, devotional texts, children's literature, works of conduct, politics, art criticism, philosophy, and science (Sanson 2020: 72–5, Sanson 2022b). Most of their translations were in fact from French (Sanson 2022b, Sanson forthcoming).

The names of these women translators appear on the title pages of their works, or elsewhere in other paratextual material. Sometimes, they signed their works only with their initials, or published them anonymously, attribution being nevertheless possible thanks to other contemporary sources.[34] Inevitably, as is often the case when investigating women's lives, finding information about their studies, including their language studies, is often complicated by a lack of sources and evidence. Only piecemeal information remains about their linguistic training, if any.[35] We therefore know very little of the exact circumstances in which they managed to acquire their education outside institutional settings. The same applies to their study of French. In this respect, some women were still able to learn French despite their lower status and fewer educational opportunities, often as a result of occasional access to books and by means of self-teaching. In the Veneto area, one case in point is the journalist Elisabetta Caminer Turra (1751–96) who taught herself French by reading French novels from the library of her father, Domenico Caminer, also a journalist and playwright, and the founder of the periodical *L'Europa letteraria* ('Literary Europe') in 1768. In a letter to the scientist Lazzaro Spallanzani, dated 4 February 1769, the then eighteen-year-old Elisabetta

---

[33] On the bridging role played by France and French between Italy and England and Germany, see Hazard (1910: 349–427, 1921); Graf (1911).

[34] On this point, see, Sanson (2022b, forthcoming).

[35] See on this Pellandra (2003).

Caminer Turra (cited by Unfer Lukoschik 2000: 249) expressed her regret at the intellectual limitations imposed on her as a woman. She wrote:

> Monsieur, [. . .] je suis bien fachée de ce que ma situation ne me permettra pas de devenir quelque chose de raisonnable. Il faudra que je me borne à traduire, ou tout au plus à faire quelque morceau de poësie. Les sciences pour les quelles j'aurais peut-être quelque disposition me seront interdites à jamais.

Knowledge of French, in fact, offered Caminer Turra a remarkable way to turn her situation around and she became one of the protagonists of Enlightened Venice and Veneto despite her humbler origins, making a name for herself as a journalist, periodical editor, translator, and theatre director. Early on she collaborated with her father on *L'Europa Letteraria* (1768–73)—eventually replacing him as editor—for instance by writing reviews or publishing excerpts of her own translations once she became a prolific translator.[36] She went on to render into Italian a whole range of original French works, as well as English, German, Danish, and Russian works by means of intermediary French translations. Among others, between 1772 and 1776 she produced ten volumes of theatre plays in translation, with two more coming out in 1794.[37] Most of these plays belong to the genre of the *comédie larmoyante*,[38] the new bourgeois drama, popular with the Venetian public. Caminer played an important role in the history of Italian theatre, 'almost single-handedly launch[ing] the fashion of the *drame* in Italy' (Castelvecchi 2013: 103). Other authors she translated into Italian are Diderot, Sedaine, Beaumarchais, and Mercier, but she also devoted her efforts to rendering into Italian French pedagogical texts by Madame Le Prince de Beaumont and François Marmontel. More broadly, she was successful in the dissemination of knowledge and foreign trends in eighteenth-century culture. Her close intellectual ties with France are also clearly reflected in her journalistic activity, in her reviews, in her selecting and amending articles when editing her *Giornale enciclopedico* ('Encyclopaedic journal', 1774–82),[39] which played an important role in the diffusion of the European Enlightenment across Italy, as well as a means to promote women's education (Unfer-Lukoschik 2000: 250–1).

Geographically speaking, there seems to be a higher concentration of women translators in the centre-north of Italy, particularly in Lombardy, the Veneto region, Piedmont, Tuscany, and Rome. But this does not mean that the southern part of Italy lacks significant examples of such figures. In fact, eighteenth-century Italy could boast some internationally renowned women scientists—such as the

---

[36] Caminer Turra has been the object of a number of scholarly works, but specifically on her role as translator, see De Paolis (2006).

[37] See Caminer Turra (1772, 1774–6, 1794).

[38] *Comédie larmoyante* refers to the French sentimental comedy inclining to melodrama that flourished in the mid-eighteenth century.

[39] Later *Nuovo giornale enciclopedico* (1782–9) and then *Nuovo giornale enciclopedico d'Italia* (1790–7).

Milanese Maria Gaetana Agnesi (1718–99) and the Bolognese Laura Bassi (1711–88)—despite the fact that science was an overall less welcoming field to women. In Naples, a well-known centre for scientific studies, we find a cluster of women translators, including Giuseppa Eleonora Barbapiccola (1702–c.1740), who rendered into Italian the *Principia* by Descartes as *Principj della Filosofia* ('Principles of Philosophy'), in 1722. Rather than the 1644 original Latin, she availed herself of the 1647 French translation by Claude Pico. She undertook her translation, as she explained in the preface, in particular for the benefit of other women who, she believes, were 'better suited for the study of philosophy than men' (Barbapiccola 1722: fol. ††2v). In 1789, also in Naples, the learned Marianna Vigilante brought out her translation of *The First Principles of Astronomy and Geography* by Isaac Watts (1726), basing her work on the seventh edition (1765) of the text. Vigilante had studied classical and modern languages, as well as natural sciences, physics, and astronomy. As she wrote in her dedication and her Note to the reader (Vigilante 1789: vii–x), she had translated Watts's work hoping to be helpful to 'society [...] despite the imbecility of my sex' (Vigilante 1789: vii). She also explained that she had added her own observations and corrections to the original text: in this specific case, Vigilante's translation was directly from the original English but what is interesting here is the fact that she revised and corrected certain aspects of the original text based on her own expertise and scholarship.

The same approach was indeed adopted by another Neapolitan learned woman of the time, Maria Angela Ardinghelli (1730–1825), who translated into Italian the work of the English naturalist Stephen Hales on the physiology of plants. Ardinghelli's translation of Hales's works came out in Naples in three volumes in 1750, 1752, and 1756, with a further edition in 1776. In Ardinghelli's case, as we read in her preface to the 1756 *Statica de' vegetabili* (originally *Vegetable Staticks* (1727)), the Italian version was produced by comparing the French translation—made a few years earlier by the naturalist Georges-Louis Leclerc, Comte de Buffon (Hales 1735)—with the original English (Ardinghelli 1756: unpaginated). But Ardinghelli had done more than producing an Italian translation of Hales's text: when she noticed that data in the tract were inaccurate, she intervened and corrected them, recalculating the original figures and results, and adding footnotes for this purpose. In her Note to the reader, she explains: 'various calculations are wrong, which are also wrong in the English text. I have taken the liberty of correcting them all. I have also added various annotations, in which I have either clarified some opinions of the author or I have more validly proved them' (Ardinghelli 1756: unpaginated).[40]

Ardinghelli's standing in the domain of natural knowledge in fact extended beyond her translation, and beyond Italy. She was the only woman whose letters were regularly read at the meetings of the Académie des Sciences in Paris over the course of two decades, having been recruited by Abbé Jean-Antoine de Nollet,

---

[40] Ardinghelli's name does not appear on the title page of the 1756 edition, but rather at the end of the dedication. It features on the title page of the 1776 edition.

well known in the field of experimental physics, during his journey through Italy in 1749 (Bertucci 2013: 227). Ardinghelli would use French when conversing with foreign scientists who were visiting Naples, as well as English. She is said to have been taught by the best tutors in Naples, but her contemporary Mazzuchelli, who wrote when Ardinghelli was still alive, pointed out that she had a natural gift for languages: 'she learnt French and English mostly on her own, rather than with the assistance of teachers' (Mazzuchelli 1753: 980). Her translation of Hales no doubt played an important role in allowing her to become a mediator between the Neapolitan and French communities of naturalists, thus creating a network of exchange between the two cities of Naples and Paris (Bertucci 2013: 228–9).

In their translations, the scholarship of women translators comes to the fore in several ways. By means of translations, they could express their voices and the expertise they had acquired in fields and disciplines from which they might otherwise have been excluded and in which they might have encountered more direct opposition, had they composed their own original works. By making French and European culture available to a wider range of readers, they also contributed to modernizing Italian, freeing it from its conservative and literary nature, making it a more subtle and adaptable means of expression, more versatile and more broadly understood, across social ranks, and hence allowing for wider access to knowledge.[41] The literary Italian used by women translators in their works, as we saw earlier, was a language they had had to study and make their own, therefore having to overcome a double linguistic hurdle: they had to adequately learn both their source and target language, French and Italian.

While rendering the original texts into Italian, women translators were also able to make their own voice heard and show their expertise in the liminal spaces of the translations' paratexts. At times, their studies and knowledge become evident in the prefaces, translator's notes, or footnotes of their works: this is where they present and discuss their translation strategies or contextualize, historically and literarily, the works and authors they are translating, at times intervening in current debates (Sanson 2022b).[42] Under the shield of their translations, women could display their scholarship in a less direct and disguised manner, protecting themselves from censorship and gender-related prejudices.[43] Their agency in terms of translation, cultural mediation, and scholarship was made possible first and foremost by their study of French.

---

[41] See on this point Giuliano (2019). More generally, on the influence of French on Italian from the point of view of language (lexicon, morphology, and syntax), see Dardi (1992); Matarrese (1993: 53–70); Morgana (1994).
[42] On the role of paratexts in translations by women, see Hosington (2017).
[43] On women's use of paratextual material in their translation to express their voice and knowledge, and more broadly on the role of translation for women in Italy, between the sixteenth century and the present time, see Sanson (2022b) and the various chapters in Sanson (2022a).

7.5 Conclusions

Tracing the history of the French language (or any language, for that matter) means of course exploring its fortune also beyond the geographical and political borders of France. This is especially useful in the eighteenth century when French became across Europe a 'langue [...] universelle', as Rivarol (1784) wrote in his *De l'universalité de la langue française*, acknowledging a phenomenon that had naturally developed over time. But investigating the fortunes of French among eighteenth-century Italian women is much more than a mere anecdotal episode in the varied history of 'Le Français hors de France au XVIIIe siècle' (Brunot 1905–53: VIII). It means unravelling those social, cultural, and political events and trends, as well as widespread prejudices and beliefs, that are inextricably linked with the life and evolution of languages. It also means, in this specific case, acknowledging another moment in the often ignored path towards access to study and knowledge in the history of women—a path which was rarely straightforward or without obstacles—and in the history of language learning more broadly.

Starting from the eighteenth century, French and foreign languages became a desirable skill for Italian women, across social ranks. But there was always a fine line, which could easily and quickly shift, between what was acceptable and what was reproachable in terms of women's learning and use of language. The study of foreign languages—and French specifically—could be for some women far from an expression of vanity. It could be instead a tool for acquiring knowledge and then exchanging it and discussing it with other learned figures. It also allowed women, and women translators in particular, to further communicate this knowledge, making it available to a wider readership, contributing to the renewal of the Italian language, and incorporating in their translations their own scholarship and expertise in less direct and more disguised manners.

In eighteenth-century Italy, and in Europe more broadly, the gap left by the decline and reduced use of Latin in some fields of knowledge was filled in by the national languages. French, in particular, 'embodied for everyone [...] the spirit of the new cultural cosmopolitanism, allowing for an effective circulation of knowledge' (Dardi 1984: 348). Learning French allowed Italian women to take on an active role in acquiring and circulating this knowledge. Rather than subtracting from the greatness of Italy's language and culture, Italian women used French to contribute to it.

8
The construction of authority and community in French official correspondence from Spanish Louisiana

Jenelle Thomas

8.1 Historical sociolinguistics and official correspondence

Numerous studies have highlighted the importance of a variety of document types for expanding and diversifying our knowledge of historical language practices, from metalinguistic texts and parodies to official texts and ego-documents (Ayres-Bennett 1990, 2004, 2018b; Schneider 2013; van der Wal and Rutten 2013). Many studies have focused on informal or private rather than formal or public texts based on the idea that they might allow access to historical orality or features common to spoken language (Oesterreicher 1997). However, this raises two issues. First, spoken language and informal language should not be conflated; as Koch and Oesterreicher (2001) argue, it makes sense to think of both spoken and written language as existing on a continuum between the language of immediacy and the language of distance—that is, between informal, spontaneous exchanges between close interlocutors on one end and more formal, prepared speech between multiple or unknown interlocutors on the other. Second, informal, spoken language is not the only type of communication that should draw our interest. Texts showcasing the language of distance also play a vital role in illuminating the broad range and variability of historical language use. Genres such as diplomatic letters, sermons, treaties, legal texts, or the press can provide evidence for features used in formal, planned, and genre-specific discourses in French (Balon and Larrivée 2016; Ayres-Bennett et al. 2018a; McLaughlin 2021).

Official letters, which differ from personal correspondence in their focus on the professional roles and goals of the interlocutors, have an important place in historical sociolinguistic analysis.[1] In particular, official letters are characterized

---

[1] Private and official letters are also better understood as existing on a continuum rather than as discrete categories, given that letters might contain elements of both personal and professional relevance, and that the concept of privacy was understood differently historically than it is today (Del Lungo Camiciotti 2006a: 156, 2010: 6).

by more defined power imbalances between author and recipient, allowing us to explore the interactions between writers at different places on the social hierarchy. Commercial and official letters are more frequently employed to issue orders and requests than personal correspondence; however, like personal letters, they may also contain descriptive or phatic elements (Bergs 2004; Dossena 2006: 190). Therefore, despite characterizations of commercial and official correspondence as more formulaic than private ego-documents, these types of text also provide a site for identity negotiation and persona management which affect the choice of linguistic features (Del Lungo Camiciotti 2006a, b; Dossena 2006).[2]

In communication and interaction, both written and spoken, historical and contemporary, speaker/writer identities are understood to be both emergent and dynamic (Bucholtz and Hall 2005; Hernández-Campoy and García-Vidal 2018), in that speakers make certain characteristics and features relevant when they 'orient to particular identities from a portfolio of possible identities' (Clifton and Van De Mieroop 2010: 2450). This orientation of speaker identity is performed in relation to both the immediate addressee and the larger set of 'centres of authority' whose presence we project into every interaction (Blommaert 2007). As Dossena (2006: 191) notes, 'the purpose for which the message is sent [...] is bound to influence the encoder's linguistic choices, in relation to the social role(s) that he or she is expected to perform in that context. Such roles are linked, in turn, to the cultural framework in which the epistolary exchange is found to occur'.

This chapter will show that official correspondence, like private correspondence, is a site for the negotiation and construction of the writer's identity, specifically in relation to centres of authority. Using official letters written in French during the Spanish colonial period in Louisiana at the end of the eighteenth century, writers are shown to use request and reporting strategies according to their level of seniority in the governing hierarchy of the colony, but also as a way of claiming a particular role within that structure and the larger community. This orienting of identity around centres of authority is clearly visible in expressive and descriptive portions of the official letters. Section 8.2 introduces the corpus and situates it in its sociohistorical context, Section 8.3 discusses the construction of authority in official correspondence through the choice of request and information-sharing formulae, and Section 8.4 explores writer positioning in reference to the governmental hierarchies, religious authorities, and national powers and identities at play in the colonized territory. Discussion and some conclusions are presented in Section 8.5.

---

[2] In fact, more educated writers with mastery of genre-specific practices may have a larger repertoire of features from which to choose (Auer 2015).

8.2 French official communication in Spanish Louisiana

8.2.1 France, Spain, territory, and language

The period of Spanish control of the Louisiana territory officially lasted from 1763 to 1800. France had ceded control of the territory to Spain in the secret Treaty of Fontainebleau in 1762, but the 1763 Treaty of Paris divided the western section of the territory, which remained under Spanish control, from the eastern portion ceded to Britain, with the new border running down the centre of the Mississippi river. As the borders were redrawn, the inhabitants of these lands suddenly found themselves the subjects of different imperial powers. A formerly French citizen living in Ste. Genevieve (located in modern-day Missouri), for example, was now a Spanish subject, while their counterpart in St. Vincennes, across the river (modern-day Indiana), was living in British—and eventually American—territory. Thus the daily reality of this hypothetical French speaker did not match up neatly with the idea of national or linguistic borders. On the one hand, this person likely continued speaking French as part of daily life; as Dubois, Leumas, and Richardson (2018) have shown, the vitality of the French language in Louisiana continued long after the French officially ceded the territory to Spain, especially in daily interactions outside New Orleans. On the other hand, daily life continued to include contacts with non-Francophones, especially in border regions, given the presence of traders and militias, new immigrants,[3] and the Native American tribes whose land the Europeans were colonizing. Finally, the language of administration had changed, meaning that official business conducted in New Orleans and affecting life in the territory would be in Spanish.

However, even for officials, the choice of language was not straightforward. While the most senior Spanish officials did communicate with the crown and each other in Spanish, surveys of official correspondence show that the colonial governors penned and received letters in French and English as well as Spanish (Thomas 2020). The practicalities and attitudes related to this situation are illustrated in (1). In the letter in (1a), written in Spanish, the governor directs the commandant of Natchitoches to convey an attached order, written in French, to the residents of his post. In (1b) the commandant of Plaquemines writes to the French envoy to the United States regarding the residents' feelings about France:[4]

---

[3] Crucially, newcomers to Spanish Louisiana were not required to be Spanish subjects, only Catholics from non-enemy nations (Din 2014).

[4] Letters from the Bancroft Louisiana papers (1767–1816) (BANC MSS M-M 508 f. 256) and the Louisiana Research Collection at Tulane (https://louisianadigitallibrary.org/islandora/object/tahil-lpc%3A200 (accessed 19 April 2021)). Neither is included in the corpus analysed in this chapter.

(1a) executara Vm al pie de la letra quanto contiene la orden que acompaña, haziendo la ostensible a los habitantes de Natchitoches, (motivo por el qual esta escrita en frances)[5] (Carondelet to Trudeau, 15 March 1796)
'You will execute the accompanying order to the letter, conveying it clearly to the residents of Natchitoches (for which reason it is written in French)'[6]

(1b) vous réunirès Les esprits que la Politique Español á cru devoir diviser, Et Si quelqu'un de nos Compatriotes, à pu oublier un moment qu'il Etoit français, Le remord (Favrot to Genêt, 1794)

Both letters were written in the last decade of Spanish rule; they showcase the national loyalties and linguistic preferences of the inhabitants of the territory thirty years after the Spanish takeover. Those who had considered themselves French citizens before the redrawing of borders had largely retained their allegiance. Likewise, they continued to use the French language, a circumstance acknowledged by the Spanish administration, as seen by the practical choice in (1a) to write in French.

However, the use of French for administrative purposes appears to have been merely tolerated as a practical necessity. Official communication between the governors and high-ranking officials was almost exclusively in Spanish, even though many of the commanders of regional posts had been recruited from the French military and administrative ranks when the Spanish took control. This is evident in the patterns of letters and responses exchanged between citizens, regional commanders, and the upper echelons of government. Take, for example, a 1781 letter from the commissioner to the Choctaws to the governor of West Florida. This letter is in French, whereas the governor's response, drafted in the margin on the same piece of paper, is in Spanish.[7] This suggests at least passive bilingualism amongst the highest ranks, but equally that writers were unlikely to accommodate to interlocutors in their choice of language in official communication; a situation which stands in contrast to personal communication (Thomas 2020). This non-accommodation may be partly attributable to the inherent power imbalance of official communication, as superiors are less likely to accommodate to a recipient of an inferior status, but even letters from authors with similar status, such as foreign dignitaries, seem to presume that any necessary translation will be done at the recipient's end.

For authors writing upwards in the hierarchy, the calculus of language choice is more complex. It seems logical to assume that official letters would not generally have been regarded as private, since information or requests for aid might be passed along to other officials. The presence of this 'auditor' or 'overhearer' also affects linguistic choices, including the choice of code in multidialectal or

---

[5] All examples directly reproduce the spelling, punctuation, and typography of the originals.
[6] Throughout the chapter, glosses are included for examples in Spanish and for those that pose particular challenges of comprehension.
[7] BANC MSS M-M 508 f. 73.

multilingual contexts (Bell 1984, 2001). Secondly, letters sent from citizens to officials acknowledge, and explicitly appeal to, the authority of the addressee as a representative of the Spanish crown, and so, in orienting themselves toward this centre, letter-writers might be expected to find Spanish a more appropriate code for communication. While this choice may be constrained by language competence—many would not have been able to write in multiple languages—at least a few of the writers in the corpus did have the ability to compose letters in Spanish. Regardless, there is tension between the use of the French code—and its associations with France—and the identity assumed by addressing a letter to representatives of the Spanish crown, claiming a subject's right to aid or protection, or even to attention when reporting news. French-language official communication thus holds a particular place within the Spanish administrative apparatus and, specifically, in the negotiation of authority and community as writers orient themselves towards sometimes conflicting centres.

8.2.2 The corpus

The corpus is drawn from the Bancroft Louisiana Papers, a collection of incoming and outgoing gubernatorial correspondence in Spanish, English, and French from the colonial period.[8] The letters were transcribed as part of a larger project on official communication (cf. Thomas 2020), but the focus of this chapter is the thirty-six official letters written in French between 1770 and 1791, totalling approximately 16,700 words. This period, which covers the administrations of Governors Luis de Unzaga y Amezaga (1770–77), Bernardo de Gálvez (1777–85), and Esteban Rodríguez Miró y Sabater (acting governor 1782–5; governor 1785–91), captures a point of stability during the middle of the Spanish period, when the Spanish crown had assumed full control of the territory and before the secret treaty ceding it back to France. The letters have been divided into three groups according to their authors' relationship to the Spanish government:

> Group A (Officials): high-ranking officials in the Spanish administrative and military apparatus, including commandants and lieutenant governors (14 letters; 7,300 words);
> Group B (Citizens): those living in Spanish-controlled territory but not part of the leadership, including inhabitants, priests, traders, merchants, and interpreters (12 letters; 4,800 words);
> Group C (Foreigners): those not under Spanish control, including priests and inhabitants east of the Mississippi; Native American leaders; Americans; and foreign governors (10 letters; 4,600 words).

---

[8] BANC MSS M-M 508. See Kinnaird (1946) for discussion and translations. Transcriptions are as diplomatic as possible. Any emphasis is present in the original text. The symbol ^ indicates an insertion, and square brackets [] an unclear letter or word.

Table 8.1 Official letters in French, 1770–91

Number of letters	AUTHOR	AUTHOR POSITION	RECIPIENT	RECIPIENT POSITION
Group A				
1	Cruzat	lieutenant governor, Illinois (upper Louisiana)	People of Vincennes	community
1	Cruzat	lieutenant governor, Illinois	Officials of Kaskaskia and Cahokia	foreign leaders (American judicial bodies)
1	Cruzat	lieutenant governor, Illinois	Rogers	foreign leader (commander of eastern Illinois)
1	Cruzat	lieutenant governor, Illinois	Dodge	foreign citizen/trader/Native American agent (Virginia)
1	De Blanc	commandant, Natchitoches	Miró	governor
1	Favrot	commandant, Plaquemines	Miró	governor
1	Filhiol	commandant, Ouachita	De Blanc	commandant, Natchitoches
1	Filhiol	commandant, Ouachita	Miró	governor
1	Forstall	commandant, Opelousas	Miró	governor
2	Peyroux	commandant, Ste. Genevieve	Miró	governor
3	Villiers	commandant, Arkansas post	Gálvez	governor
Group B				
1	Bernard[o]	priest	Miró?	governor
1	Favre	interpreter	Bouligny	commandant, Natchez
1	Favre	interpreter	Juzan	commissioner to Choctaws
1	Judice	citizen	Unzaga y Amezaga	governor
1	Juzan	commissioner to Choctaws	Gálvez	governor
1	Juzan	commissioner to Choctaws	Ezpeleta	governor, Mobile (West Florida)
1	Le Dru	priest	Dunegant	commandant, St. Fernand
1	Linder	priest	Favrot	commandant, Plaquemines

Number of letters	AUTHOR	AUTHOR POSITION	RECIPIENT	RECIPIENT POSITION
1	Malliet	citizen	Cruzat	lieutenant governor, Illinois
1	Menard	merchant	Villiers	commandant, Arkansas post
1	People of Ste. Geneviève	community	Leyba	lieutenant governor, Illinois
1	Rouquière	citizen (trader)	Piernas, Pedro	lieutenant governor, Illinois
Group C				
1	Clermond	foreign leader (Osages)	Piernas	lieutenant governor, Illinois
1	Damas	foreign leader (governor of Martinique)	Miró	governor
2	Dodge	foreign citizen/trader/ Native American agent (Virginia)	Cruzat	lieutenant governor, Illinois
1	Gibault	priest	Miró	governor (acting)
1	People of Vincennes	community	Cruzat	lieutenant governor, Illinois
1	Qui te Sain	foreign leader (Taovayas)	Gálvez	governor
2	Vallinière	priest	Miró	governor
1	Vallinière	priest	Peyroux	commandant, Ste. Genevieve

As can be seen in Table 8.1, the letters in the corpus are mostly directed upward in the military and administrative hierarchy: citizens might write to commandants, while commandants write mostly to the governor. This is consistent with the assertion that letters addressed downward in the social scale, especially from the highest ranks, would be written in Spanish rather than French. The authors represent a range of backgrounds and professions ranging from low to upper class: traders, merchants, priests, and career military men who, while they hold high status in the military, generally do not belong to the nobility or planter elite. Groups B and C are more heterogeneous as regards social status and relationship to the colonial government than group A.

8.3 Power and authority

This section focuses on the power relationship constructed between interlocutors in official correspondence through an examination of two of the 'sociopragmatic functions' of letters (Bergs 2004): requests and reports. While both are frequently found in official letters and are the primary functions of letters sent from officials to the governor in Spanish Louisiana (King 2011: 265), they arguably differ with regard to the power relationship. Letters with a reporting function can be directed toward social inferiors, superiors, or peers, whereas requests or orders are conventionally directed upwards or downwards in the hierarchy, respectively. Bergs (2004: 213) argues that because reports are descriptive, they are less concerned with marking social relationships. However, it will be shown that in fact the form chosen for reports—like requests—is affected by the power relationship between the interlocutors. Both can be analysed as reflecting the role that letter-writers assume in relation to the administrative structure of the colony.

8.3.1 Requesting

The preferred strategies for requests vary from language to language, but the following broad classes of request strategies have been shown to hold cross-linguistically: requests which are direct (mood derivables, where the illocutionary force is indicated by the mood of the verb; performatives; statements of obligation and desire); conventionally indirect (e.g. suggestions); and non-conventionally indirect (e.g. hints) (Blum-Kulka, House, and Kasper 1989: 18). In a study of Spanish-language official letters from colonial Louisiana, King (2011) found that the direction of correspondence—upwards or downwards in the official hierarchy—was a significant factor in the choice of request strategies, and superiors used more direct strategies. Subordinates used a greater number of indirect strategies; however, they also used a large proportion of direct requests, specifically with the formulaic *suplicar* ('request, ask, beg').

In the French-language correspondence in this corpus, direct requests are the most common strategy for commandants and lieutenant governors (Group A). Direct requests are sent upwards in the hierarchy to both the governor and other correspondents. There are no examples of mood derivable requests (e.g. use of the imperative or future tense) among this group—in contrast with what might be seen in communication downwards in the hierarchy, for example in the Spanish letter in (1a). Instead, the preference is for performatives, including those using the verb *demander*, as in (2a). The examples in this section show that *demander*, like its Spanish counterpart *suplicar*, is a frequent formula for direct requests. Direct requests may be further softened through hedging, as in example (2b), where the author adds 'dare' in the conditional to the *demander* formulation. Statements of desire, the least direct of the requests in the direct category, also appear in letters from this group, for example using 'j'espère'.

(2a) je vous demande M au nom du Roy D'Espagne mon maître les Six colliers[9] que Les nations hoyatanons et Kikapous m'envoyoient par le nommé chapeau et que vous avez contraint celui ci de vous donner ce qu'il a fait Sans résistence vû L'autorité que vous prites avec Lui Les Intentions du gouvernement Espagnol étant de ne rien alterer de l'aliance qu'il a contracté avec les susdits états unis de L'amerique (Cruzat to Dodge, 15 December 1780)

(2b) j'oserais vous demander que la traitte S[u]t devolüe á tous les habitans de ce Poste Sans distinction (Filhiol to Miró, 16 March 1790)

Despite the prevalence of direct request strategies among the Group A authors, there are also instances of indirect requests of the type shown in (3). They are all directed to the governor, that is, upward in the hierarchy. In this example the request is also downgraded by a conditional statement using *si*, as well as the use of *permettre*, highlighting the results and the benefit to the troops and colony. Example (3) also explicitly refers to the constraints imposed by the administrative hierarchy, namely that actions cannot be taken unless ordered by the governor.

(3) S'il plaisoit a V. S. ^{rie} de me permettre d'y établir ma résidence et d'y transporter la troupe et les effets du Roi, elle feroit je crois le bien de ce district et celui de la troupe, laquelle y vivroit a meilleur compte le lieu est sain et fertile, on peut y bâtir en pierre maisons forts, moulins, &c. J'en ai parlé a M. Dn M. Perez, lequel m'a dit ne pouvoir rien faire sur ce sujet a moins que V.S. ne l'ordonne (Peyroux to Miró, 8 March 1788)

In contrast, the citizens in Group B show a wider range of request strategies in their letters. A few mood derivable requests are exchanged between citizens of generally equal social standing, as in the use of the future in (4a). Other examples of mood derivables come from letters authored by priests, as in (4b) ('prevenez les'). This use in a letter to a commandant can be explained by the fact that priests, while subject to the governing authorities like other citizens, also exist within the parallel hierarchical structure of the church. In using a mood derivable in conjunction with the performative element, 'je vous prie', a priest constructs himself as an authority on par with a civil official, one who is interested in the welfare of the town's inhabitants but who also acknowledges the other's authority through formulations like 'your citizens'.

(4a) Vous aurez la bonté de m'envoyer la Medaille de Mingomastabè (Favre to Juzan, 25 November 1783)

---

[9] While Cruzat uses the word 'colliers' rather than 'courriers' multiple times in the text, the objects in question are letters or reports, referred to by Dodge as 'paroles'.

(4b) en communiquant ma lettre a Mrs vos habitans prevenez les, je vous prie, de ma part (Le Dru to Dunegant, 1 August 1791)

Like the requests of officials, most requests from citizens directed upward in the hierarchy are direct, as in (5), but there is one case of an indirect (suggestatory) formula, given in (6)

(5a) jaimplore votre justice Et Demande que langlais Zabulon Soit punit (Menard to Villiers, 29 May 1780)

(5b) les Suplians ont recours avous Monsieur, pour quil vous plaise interposer votre autorité, et prendre les moyens necessaires pour arretter le brigandage de ces nations (People of Ste. Genevieve to Leyba, 28 March 1779)

(6) Si cétoit un effet devotre bonté de m'envoyer quelques livres depoudre Ce Seroit dun grand Secours pour Ceux que jelaisse icÿ (Malliet to Cruzat, 9 January 1781)

While this distribution between direct and indirect requests is similar to that of requests penned by officials, the authors in (5) and (6) downgrade their requests to a greater extent than officials do. The appeals to 'justice', 'authority', and 'goodness' highlight the superior status of the recipient, and the noun 'suplians' in (5b) and doubling of verbs in (5a) to include not just the formulaic *demander* but also the stronger *implorer* underscore the author's role as a petitioner. Finally, there is syntactic downgrading in the use of subjunctive and conditional verb forms. Unsurprisingly, the lower social status of citizens is reflected and constructed in the way they formulate their requests, which also are requests for intervention on the part of the governor rather than for permission to carry out some action, as was the case for officials (2b).

The identity of the writer and the power differential are also important variables conditioning the use and form of requests for the group of foreign authors (C), since there is more variety of social status than in Group A. For example, direct requests from Group C come from foreign leaders, such as a chief of the Taovaya nation (7a) and the governor of Martinique (7b), or from priests (8).

(7a) mon perre Le peux De fusi De ache est De pioche que nous avon trouve tous En Ruine a ne pas pouvoir [Servir] je te prie De macorde un forgeron (Qui te Sain to Gálvez, 4 November 1780)

'My father the few guns hatchets and pickaxes that we have found all ruined unable to [Serve] I ask you to grant me a blacksmith'

(7b) Je serai infiniment reconnoiSsant des bons traitemens que vous voudrez bien leur faire à ma recommandation & desbons office[r] que Je prie Votre Excellence de leur rendre dans les circonstances où ils pourront en avoir beSoin (Damas to Miró, 4 July 1783)

(8a) Je Demande humblement Votre approbation pour me mettre moy Et mes Biens Sous La protection DeSa majesté Catholique a S.ᵗᵉ Genevieve, Et ferai tout mon possible pour Remplir Les Devoirs D'un Bon Citoyen Et D'un prêtre Zelé (Gibault to Miró, 29 July 1782)

(8b) J'insiste donc a ce qu'il Soit condamné au moins a mil ecus d'amande (Valinière to Miró, 14 March 1788)

Although these can all be classified as direct requests, they differ in their forcefulness, ranging from (8b), the most direct, to (7b) which combines more ('je prie') and less ('je serai infiniment reconnoiSsant') direct requests in a single sentence. In the letter in (8b) the priest Valinière, full of righteous anger at the behaviour of the commandant of the town across the river, calls upon the authority of the Spanish government in his capacity as a religious and moral authority. On the other hand, in (7b), the governor of Martinique shows a gentlemanly deference when asking a favour of a fellow governor. The priest Gibault—who asks 'humbly' (8a)—and Chief Qui te Sain of the Taovayas, who prefaces his request with a description of a state of affairs which prevents them from defending themselves (7a), construct requests which must be 'granted' or 'approved' by the governor, whom they position as the ultimate authority responsible for safety and peace in the region.[10] Here, the amount of downgrading is not directly correlated with an externally defined social status or rank, but rather is used to construct the identities of the interlocutors inside a particular relationship. Priests—when submitting to civil authority—display deference, but are more direct when claiming the authority given to them by their ecclesiastical position.

The people of St. Vincennes also belong in the foreigner group (C) because of the town's location on the eastern side of the Mississippi river. In (9), they use an indirect request which is a variation of the formula used by the people of Ste. Genevieve across the river (5b), including the lexical items *recourir* and *qu'il vous plaise*. The repetition of the latter, along with the formal *octroyer*, formalizes the request as one appealing to the goodwill of the powerful addressee.

(9) Les Suppliants recourent á Vous Monsieur a ce qu'Il vous plaise leur procurér tel Secour quil Vous plaira Leur octroyér (People of St. Vincennes to Cruzat, 1780)

The similarity between the two petitions shows the formulaic nature of this type of request and a similarity in positioning of the two communities despite St. Vincennes being outside Spanish-controlled territory. The letters written by

---

[10] This is also seen in Qui te Sain's use of 'my father'. The use of kinship terms, often combined with the informal *tu*, and frequently seen in communication between indigenous groups and Spanish colonial officials, should not be read literally as a parent–child relationship but as a part of the complex negotiation of diplomacy, as Turner (2006: 51–2) and Cook (2015) have argued for the Iroquois, Mohawk, and Onondaga.

foreigners (Group C), regardless of their rank, show similar request strategies to those within the territory (Group B), although they vary depending on the perceived and constructed power differential between the author and addressee. In Section 8.4, we see that these appeals from foreign individuals are enabled through a construction of community which relies on shared national belonging, the existence of shared allies and enemies, and the construction of a shared project of peace and prosperity.

8.3.2 Reporting

The form of requests can be used to index both codified and emergent power relationships between interlocutors, but descriptive texts such as reports are not inherently appellative and are thus more neutral. However, there is still variability in the way reports are presented. In this corpus, some report sections begin simply with declarative statements relaying information, but many include specific formulae introducing the reporting function, often as a way of opening the letter. These information-sharing formulae function as a means of justifying the communication and signalling the topic at hand, but also construct the relationship between interlocutors.

For the officials (Group A), the most frequent information-sharing formulae are simple declarations, as in (10). These mark the speech act of reporting in a neutral way, in a parallel to the direct requests with little downgrading seen in Section 8.3.1. This type of locution, as well as one which entirely foregoes the use of information-sharing formulae, presents reporting as an expected part of communication between a commandant and his superior officer, the governor.

(10) je vous en feres part ainsy que de tous ce quil aura de nouveau (Forstall to Miró, 10 June 1787)

Also well-represented are verbs or phrases of reporting such as *informer* or *faire part* coupled with formulations expressing the honour of doing so, as in (11). Less frequent are constructions which emphasize a feeling of responsibility to share information, as in (12). These references to honour and responsibility mark the asymmetrical power relationship between the interlocutors more explicitly than neutral formulae and position the act of reporting as a service to be rendered and as one of the duties associated with the role of a subordinate officer.

(11) j'ay l'honneur de vous dire (Villiers to Gálvez, 25 June 1780)

(12) je ne veux pas vous l'aiSser ignorer la craint qu'on a icy (Forstall to Miró, 10 June 1787)

A final category, very infrequent among letters from Group A, is one where writers note that they are imposing on the addressee by providing information, as in (13). This is more deferential than the previous methods and, in contrast, implies that the communication of information might be unwelcome or not part of the writer's expected role. This effect is further compounded in example (13) by the explicit communication of the source and trustworthiness of the information, showing that the writer takes care to send only important information.

(13) quelqu'avis indirects qui me Sont parvenus me font croire aujourd'huy que ces Nations pourront venir et que je puis prendre la liberté de vous en entretenir (Filhiol to Miró, 16 March 1790)

In contrast to the majority of letters from high-ranking officials, letters from citizens (Group B) are much less likely to use the first strategy of presenting information, instead preferring to include justification or apologies. Even when the neutral or 'honour' formulae are used, as in (14), they frequently appear in conjunction with a clause justifying the act of writing or apologizing for the imposition. For example, in (14b), 'honour' is mentioned twice and combined with assurances of truth and apologies and excuses for the mode of presentation. In (15), the author is more deferential still in requesting permission to share important information and emphasizing the potential imposition upon the recipient with the words 'dare' and 'liberty'. In this way, the lines between report and request are blurred as the addressee must consent to the presentation of information.

(14a) je vous fais part de toutes Ces Nouvelles parceque je pense quelles meritent quelque Consideration (Linder to Favrot, 13 November 1786)

(14b) voila monsieur ce quilat l'honneur devous informer il vous prie delexcuser sil névas pas luÿ même vous les dire de bouche la fatique quil at eu dans un Si penible voyage l'en empêche pour le présent il vous prie de Croire que ce Sont des nouvelles certaines et justes quil at l'honneur de vous faire Sçavoir (Mailliet to Cruzat, 9 January 1781)

'Here sir is the information he has the honour to give you he asks you to excuse him if he does not come himself to tell you in person the exhaustion that he has had from such a difficult trip prevents it for the present he asks you to believe that this news which he has the honour of making known to you is certain and just'

(15) jé né pas hose prendre Laliberté de vous marquer La conduitte de Lanation de ce village jespere Monsieur que vous voudrois Bien mepermaitre vous En faire un petit détail (Rouquière to Piernas, 14 June 1772)

The differences between the writing of citizens and officials highlight the projected role of the author within the colonial power structure. Both are writing to someone in a position of authority over them: citizens to commandants and commandants to the governor. However, this difference in usage is not attributable solely to the power differential between interlocutors, but rather to the role assumed or adopted by the writer as a reporter of information. While reporting is presented as an ordinary activity for officials, it is an explicit act of loyalty for citizens, who potentially overstep their authority in undertaking a responsibility which is nevertheless necessitated by circumstance.

Foreigners (Group C) pattern more closely to the officials in Group A in their reporting of information. Specifically, reports make almost exclusive use of the honour formula, although there also is one case where the writer, the priest Valinière, expresses a sense of obligation ('obligé') in reporting (16). He presents himself here, as in his requests in (8b), almost as a peer, compelled by his responsibilities and conscience to report misconduct, although he is careful to also refer to the proper division of the civil and religious spheres. He makes the distinction between 'ici' and Ste. Genevieve, clearly delineating the two geographical areas of which only the latter is under Spanish command, and implicitly claiming some authority over the former.

(16) je Suis obligé quoi qu'avec peine de vous en informer Le Sr Peyroux Commandant de Ste Genevieve dit autrement [Misere] ne ceSse depuis Son arrivée de Se mêler de tout ce qui Se paSse ici (Valinière to Miró, 23 February 1788)

These examples show that there are differences in the ways authors present information. High-ranking officials in the government (Group A) generally prefer neutral formulae which take for granted their right and responsibility to write to other officials, even superiors. They also prefer direct request strategies. Although there is a hierarchical relationship between interlocutors, writers in this group tend to use unmarked formulae without downgrading. Similarly, authors living outside the official control of the Spanish government (Group C) do not present themselves as having a need, nor any responsibility, to report information to the representatives of the Spanish government. They use the honour formula in presenting it as a favour rendered, for example framing the transmission of information about the movements of Native American groups as a diplomatic courtesy.

Letters from citizens (Group B), however, more frequently present the act of informing as an intrusive one which imposes on the addressee's limited and valuable time and energy, a face-saving act (Brown and Levinson 1987). In so doing, they construct, confirm, and highlight the power differential between author and recipient in a way that officials do not, and they foreground an identity of the responsible and loyal citizen who, while having no formal role in the governance of the territory, is driven by a sense of responsibility toward the common good. This contrasts with the officials, who perform their professional role of moving information up the chain of command and then enact the resulting policy.

8.4 Community

Up to this point we have seen that reporting and request strategies correlate to some extent with the power relationship between interlocutors. Broadly, the degree of attenuation and justification in the formulation of report or request formulae increases as the social status of the writer decreases. However, this analysis of linguistic forms as tied to social status and relative power between interlocutors relies heavily on an interpretation of this interaction as only involving the writer and addressee. As seen in Section 8.3, the way letter-writers attenuate the force of requests or justify reports can in fact be tied to the role they claim within the hierarchy and governance of the region, that is, the way they orient themselves towards both their interlocutor and the larger sociohistorical context. This becomes even more evident in the phatic, expressive, and descriptive parts of official letters, particularly in the ways writers refer to themselves and the larger context and community, including both their interlocutor and more abstract entities such as the nation.

Officials in the Spanish army (Group A) present themselves as productive, zealous, hard-working, and responsible, even in difficult conditions; in short, as model officers working both for their own advancement and the good of the colony. Compare the three different officers represented in (17). In all three examples, the desire to earn the approval of a superior officer—the addressee—specifically by successfully carrying out orders, is clearly expressed. The use of the participial forms 'en remplissant mes devoirs' and 'en me conformant a ses intentions' present these actions as conditions for earning favour or advancement. In contrast to requests and reports, phatic sections highlight the power asymmetry between writer and addressee in a way that clearly links the interlocutor with the larger hierarchy of command and government, and the larger context of family, king, and country, as explicitly mentioned in (17a).

(17a) Je mepresente En Officier d'honneur et Remply de Zèl Pour mon Souverain, En remplissant mes devoirs, Jefais mon avancement et le bonheur demafamille Et vous Toujours Rempli de bontés pour moy, Pouvez me favoriser dans Cette affaire, et me mettre à meme Enpeu de Temps d'avoir un sort plus heureux, C'est ce que Jattends Des biens faits de Votre Seig.[rie] meprescrivant dela maniere don Jedois vous proposer cette expedition (De Blanc to Miró, 20 January 1790)

(17b) Je ferai toujours mon possible pour meriter l'estime de V. S. [rie] en me conformant a ses intentions. Pour commencer a donner une forme stable aux Etablissemens qu'elle ma Confié, J'ai réformé plusieurs anciens abus sur les clotures qui nuisoient beaucoup a l'agriculture et à la population (Peyroux to Miró, 8 March 1788)

(17c) La crainte que J'avois monsieur de passer dans Votre Esprit pour un homme Vain et qui Veut faire son appollogie m'a toujours empeché de Vous mettre sous les yeux les peines ^et^ les soins que je me suis donné pour l'Etablissement de ce Poste ajouté aux depenses que J'ay fait, mais je m'y trouve Engagé par les circonstances. Et pourquoy rougirois-je de Vous dire? que J'ay Encouragé l'agriculture, J'ay attiré des cultivateurs et J'En attends encore. Je leur ay fait des avances J'ay pourvu a leur Subsistance Je nouris Encore actuellement les familles des malhureux chasseurs qui ayant eté pillé par les osages ne peuvent aller en chasse ne peuvent pas payer et n'ont pas le moyen de vivre, tandis que je devrois Etre aidé dans une action si Conforme a l'humanité Je me trouve Contrairé par l'homme dont je me plains (Villiers to Gálvez, 25 June 1780)

To this end, the commanders present a series of achievements made for the good of those under their command, and the larger goals of the Spanish crown. In (17c), this takes the form of two parallel lists each structured with two verbs in the past and a final one in the present tense, emphasized with 'encore'. These concrete proofs of his ability as a leader, past and present, and the efforts and sacrifices needed to produce success, are placed in contrast to a potential interpretation of him as a weak, vain man. This claim to strength and accomplishment is oriented towards the hearer in the use of the rhetorical question 'why should I blush to tell you?' but relies on a constructed position as a person useful to the colonial project, and framing the statements not as boasts but as confidences made to a commanding officer. This personal responsibility as an agent of the crown entrusted with resources is further seen in the extensive use of the first person and the possessives peppering these letters: 'ma troupe', 'ma garnison'. In (17c), this discourse of responsibility and orientation towards the goal of colonial peace and progress—also present in example (3)—is combined with the framing of the commandant's work as 'humanitarian', encouraging a reading of him as a kind man interested in the overall health of the community. He, and by extension his work on behalf of the crown, is placed in opposition to other forces at play in the colonial landscape, specifically the Osages and a bad apple in the community. In this way, officials orient themselves towards not just their specific interlocutors, but to the people under their command, as well as the Spanish king, the empire, the colonial project, and the other powers in the region.

This positioning is also clear when officials communicate with external interlocutors, as in the exchange between the People of St. Vincennes and the lieutenant governor, Cruzat, in (18).

(18a) Les habitants du poste du S.ᵗ vincennes et des [ouyas] et ont L'honneur de Vous représentér trés respectueusement que Comme Estants tous citoyens françois Les alliés de la Cour d'espagne et de L'amerique septentrionalle, quils Seroient Expozés á touttes Sorte de dangers par rapport aux nations des Miamis (People of St. Vincennes to Cruzat, 1780)

(18b) aussitot que Jai réçû Votre requête je me Suis Senti Le coeur navré de la plus vive douleur voyant la triste et critique Situation ou Vous vous trouvez [...] ne desirant rien tant que de Secourir par toutes Sortes de Voyes equitables ceux qui Sont dans Láffliction, mais vous considerant dependents comme je Vous crois des Etats Unis de L'amerique par droit de conquête je ne puis rien faire [sans] La participation et Consentement des Superieurs de ces dits etats comme alliéz qu'ils sont de L'Espagne et de la France en concequence Vous devez Messieurs vous adresser a ceux qui Sont aux Illinois pour qu'iceux agissant d'accord et unanimement avec moi nous puission Vous Secourir (Cruzat to the People of St. Vincennes, 15 December 1780)

Firstly, let us take Cruzat's response (18b). Like the commandant in (17c), he presents himself as a humanitarian, dwelling on the emotions he felt upon receipt of the petition. Words referring to pain or affliction are used alongside several adjectives, sometimes doubled for maximum effect ('triste et critique'). In this exchange, there is also a negotiation of both personal and national power and jurisdiction. Via the act of petitioning, the People of St. Vincennes position Cruzat as a person of authority, and specifically one with the power to affect their situation. In contrast, Cruzat at first explicitly rejects the idea of having control over the situation, divorcing his personal desire to help from his professional role. In the final line, however, he reclaims his authority in declaring his intention to act 'd'accord et unanimement' with the Americans, followed by the first person plural *nous*. As in his letter in (2a), Cruzat takes on a role as the representative of the Spanish king, and as such one who both acknowledges the rights of foreign powers and confirms and upholds the alliances between France, Spain, and the United States.

While the officials in Group A, whatever their birthplace, focus on their role as Spanish officers, the citizens in Spanish-controlled territory (Group B) still claim a French identity, as seen in a trader's description of the conduct of the Grand Osages (19).

(19) jé appris qu'ils avoit tués & pillie trois français épris deux prisonniers (Rouquière to Piernas, 14 June 1772)

The citizens of St. Vincennes (18a), too, claim French citizenship, using it to justify their right to request protection from the Spanish crown. This seems at first contradictory, since the French no longer have any official authority in the area. However, it shows both the enduring sense of French allegiance and the importance of European identity in Spanish Louisiana, where a claim to French identity does not appear to be in conflict with being a Spanish subject. Authors may write in French and describe themselves and their peers as Frenchmen while at the same time insisting on their loyalty to the Spanish crown or petitioning the Spanish for the help they feel is due to them as residents of the territory. While questions of national sovereignty and jurisdiction are highlighted in diplomatic communications between officials and foreign entities, as in lieutenant governor Cruzat's reluctance to act in American territory (18b) and his indignation at Dodge's overreach in intercepting his mail (2a), for the citizens petitioning for aid, this distinction between European countries is not foregrounded. In fact, several missives, when they mention the Spanish at all, mention them together with the French without a coordinating conjunction, almost as though they were synonyms or a blended identity, as in (20).

(20) quil etté bon englais quil ne voulé pas fairre comme Les treteur espagnolle frensais (Favre to Bouligny, 8 November 1785)

This French/Spanish identity is sometimes contrasted with the English, but also with various of the Native American groups, both allies and enemies, either named or referred to as 'les nations' or with the pejorative terms *sauvage* or *barbare*. Thus, although writers in the citizen category (Group B) do not claim Spanish identity in the way officials (Group A) do—notably as representatives of the crown, not Spanish citizens—the act of mentioning France and Spain together or highlighting existing alliances positions them as Europeans permitted to claim the protections of the Spanish colonial apparatus. Allied foreign leaders (7a) also rely on these alliances and a shared defence against invasion as providing a shared identity, rather than orienting towards divergent aspects.

As seen in their use of requests and reports, priests inside and outside the Spanish territory (Groups B and C) claim a special place within the network of authority and community of the colonial ecosystem. In (21), a priest in the Spanish territory writes to the civil authorities to complain about a lack of action from the ecclesiastical authorities. In this letter, which begins by referring to the orders of 'Sa majesté Catholique' that missionaries should no longer receive a tithe, he negotiates his position between the church structure and the governmental one. He uses a religious reference to upgrade his reported request, while also adding the—albeit common in this context—adjective 'Catholic' to refer to the king. This places his orientation to the two centres in alignment rather than in conflict.

(21) Je lui écris donc encor par Cette occasion et le Conjure par les entrailes de jesus Christ de mettre fin à mes ^peines et^ de mes infirmités (Bernard to Miró, 27 April 1787)

8.5 Conclusion

Official communication is frequently presented as a rigid genre, full of formulaic discourse dictated by the topic and the power relationship between interlocutors. However, official letters are far from homogeneous in their sociopragmatic functions, their addressees, and the context in which they are written. Even the frequent grouping and interchangeability of the terms 'official' and 'business' in referring to non-private communication may disguise internal differences, just as the terms 'public' or 'non-private' disguise the reality that in fact public communication also 'constitutes a form of social intercourse' (Del Lungo Camiciotti 2006a: 158).

I have shown that the expression of writer identity is performed through public letters in French from eighteenth-century Spanish Louisiana. Through report and request formulae, as well as more descriptive or phatic sections of their letters, writers use official communication to orient their identities both in relation to their specific interlocutors and the centres of authority relevant in the sociohistorical context. There is little variation in the use of forms of address and closing formulae across the corpus, but other interlocutor-oriented structures such as requests and reports are more variable, indexing both the writer's social status and their assumed role in the colonial project. Foreign officials present reporting as a somewhat neutral service, while for officials in the Spanish administration, information-sharing is presented as part of the job, and thus the power imbalance between interlocutors is not foregrounded. However, for ordinary citizens under Spanish control, the responsibility for reporting is claimed through apologies for potentially overstepping their authority. In requests, citizens, whether residing in the Spanish territory or not, present themselves as needing protection, while officials request permission to carry out actions on behalf of the government. While both groups make use of direct, and to some extent indirect, request strategies, citizens use downgraders more frequently.

Public communication is a particularly relevant source for examining how writers orient their identity towards larger social structures in their texts. In eighteenth-century Louisiana, writers were navigating both the governmental chain of command and the evolving landscape of nationality and language. On the one hand, letter-writers in the corpus claim a French identity for themselves and others and show little inclination to shift to using Spanish in either private or official communication even thirty years after the Treaty of Paris. On the other, equating writer identity with national origin, the nation controlling the territory one inhabits, or even language choice, is clearly a simplistic or even anachronistic view of identity. In communicating—in French—citizens of the Spanish territory and foreigners appeal to alliances and a broader European identity, while officials focus on their professional role as representatives of the Spanish government rather than their personal identity. Priests and missionaries, meanwhile, alternately claim the authority of the religious power granted to them and downplay that identity when appealing to authorities as a resident of the territory.

Official letter corpora, and formal public communication more broadly, are valuable sources for the study of historical uses of French, inside and outside of France. Future research on this corpus and other official communication should take into account the context of production—in this case, a multilingual environment—and genre factors in addition to speaker-conditioned variables, but given the range of authors represented, this text type is a rich source for the study of sociopragmatic as well as other variables (e.g. orthography). As such, it takes its place in the ever-increasing range of document types essential for illuminating the dynamics of historical French language use, be it informal or formal, private or public.

9
Language authority, language ideologies, and eighteenth-century bilingual lexicographers of French, German, and English

Comparing Abel Boyer, Christian Ludwig, and Lewis Chambaud

Nicola McLelland

9.1 Introduction

This chapter presents a case study exploring language authority and language ideologies in the complex history of vernacular bilingual lexicography in eighteenth-century Europe, a period which saw the emergence of an established genre of bilingual dictionaries (i.e. specifically between two vernacular languages).[1] Many of these works are comparatively neglected, as scholarship has, certainly in the case of German and English, devoted attention instead to the century's landmarks in monolingual lexicography, not least Johnson's (1755) *Dictionary of the English Language* a 'towering achievement of lexicography and letters' (Reddick 2009:

---

[1] Most sixteenth- and seventeenth-century European lexicography was at least bilingual (often trilingual or polyglot), commonly with Latin as one of the languages, and most studies of European lexicography in these centuries are therefore necessarily wholly or partly concerned with bilingual dictionaries (see for example Jones 2000; Considine 2008; Cowie 2009). Bilingual lexicography was, in that sense, nothing new. In fact, the first monolingual dictionaries commonly emerged from bilingual (or multilingual) ones. For example, Estienne's (1538) *Dictionarium latinogallicum* ('Latin–French Dictionary') and *Dictionaire francois-latin* (Estienne 1539; second edition, 1972 [1549]) and their revised editions formed the basis of Nicot's (1606) first French language dictionary. Bilingual dictionaries also drew on monolingual dictionaries once they became available—in French, Abel Boyer (1699) took the Académie française's (1694) dictionary as the starting point for his French–English dictionary, and Chambaud (1761) used the Académie française's (1740) dictionary. However, eighteenth-century bilingual lexicography was not, as modern dictionary users today might assume, solely derivative of existing monolingual works. For example, Ludwig's (1716) German–English dictionary has no direct link to either monolingual lexicographical tradition, and some of its German entries seem to be the earliest lexicographical attestations of the words (e.g. from the semantic fields of marriage and prostitution: *Eheband, Eheschänder, Ehefeind; Hurenblick, Hurenhengst, hurentzen* 'marriage bond, adulterer, enemy of marriage, whore's glance, whoremonger, to call a whore').

155), and Adelung's (1774–86) *Versuch eines vollständigen grammatisch-kritischen Wörterbuches Der Hochdeutschen Mundart* ('Attempt at a complete grammatical-critical dictionary of the High German dialect'), and *Grammatisch-kritisches Wörterbuch der hochdeutschen Mundart* ('Grammatical-critical dictionary of the High German dialect') (Adelung 1793–1801), which 'set a lexicographical standard' (Considine 2014: 141; see also Schrader 2012). It is that comparative neglect which this study seeks to help address, on the premise that such bilingual dictionaries merit attention on their own terms (Boisson, Kirtchuk, and Béjoint 1991; Fontenelle 2015), and that questions that have been previously applied to eighteenth-century monolingual codifications are relevant to these bilingual works too. Prescriptivism and standard language ideologies have been prominent themes in studies of monolingual grammars and dictionaries of the eighteenth century,[2] so offer a useful starting point for comparison with bilingual works. Here, therefore, I examine the language ideologies, explicit and implicit, of Christian Ludwig (1660–1728), whose English–German dictionary appeared in 1706; of Lewis Chambaud (d. 1776), whose French–English dictionary was published in 1761; and of their shared basis, the French/English dictionaries (1699, 1700) of Abel Boyer (1667?–1729).[3] I also took into account John Bartholomew Rogler's (1763) revision of Ludwig's dictionary, as it is nearly contemporary with Chambaud's (1761) work, but in practice this added relatively little to the analysis. As we shall see, comparing these lexicographers' ideologies—in their own words and in their lexicographic practice—reveals more differences than similarities, but the differences are illuminating, both for the history of bilingual lexicography and when viewed alongside what is known of monolingual lexicography of the period.[4]

Dictionaries, whether or not their metalanguage is explicitly prescriptive or descriptive, are likely to be read as authoritative: authoritative information about how to use or understand language is what lay users want from them. Making the reasonable assumption that dictionaries are more often consulted than grammars, we can expect the authority of dictionaries to have greater reach, including on points of grammar (e.g. verb valency, conjugation, preposition government of case), which may well be specified in dictionaries, either explicitly or implicitly

---

[2] E.g. Beal, Nocera, and Sturiale (2008); Auer (2009); Wild (2009); Havinga (2018); Caron and Ayres-Bennett (2019); Tieken Boon van Ostade (2019).

[3] I use labels of the form L1–L2 (e.g. 'English–German') to refer to dictionaries that are unidirectional L1 to L2, while L1/L2 (e.g. 'English/German') refers to bidirectional dictionaries, or to the wider bilingual lexicographical tradition (unidirectional and bidirectional).

[4] On French and German lexicographical history, see especially Quemada (1967); Matoré (1968); Jones (2000); Henne (2001); Considine (2008, 2014). Other kinds of comparison within and across English, French, and German bilingual lexicography would also reward study. It would be illuminating to compare the two Leipzig-based competitors Christian Ludwig and Theodor Arnold's lexicographical output (see note 6 below) with their grammatical works, for example, and to compare the works of the near-contemporaries Chambaud and Arnold from the perspective of the history of language learning and teaching (HoLLT), since they, like Ludwig, were very active as language teachers, and likewise published other language learning materials beside their dictionaries. Another *desideratum* is to triangulate the French/English and English/German dimensions explored here with French/German lexicography, which begins already in the sixteenth century (see Hausmann 1988, 1991; Rettig 1991).

in examples given (McLelland 2021b: 282–3). Rutten and Vosters (2021) note only the role of monolingual, national dictionary projects in their discussion of 'language standardization from above', but in theory at least, bilingual codifications could certainly play a role as 'standard-creating' texts (in the sense of Zgusta 2006; see McLelland 2021b: 265), i.e. contributing towards the establishment of a standard language. Ayres-Bennett (2020a) identifies three elements of codification texts as relevant to evaluating a text's prescriptive status: first, their metalinguistic labelling and description; second, their coverage of varying or changing usage; and third, their effect on actual usage. The third of these determining factors—to what extent dictionaries in general, and bilingual dictionaries in particular, may have had an effect on language usage—is methodologically not straightforward and is beyond the scope of this article (attempts to determine such impacts of monolingual codifications—but not dictionaries—include McLelland 2014, Havinga 2018, and Ayres-Bennett 2020a). Equally, the second of Ayres-Bennett's areas of focus remains a desideratum, i.e. to consider to what extent the nomenclature, equivalences, and examples in bilingual dictionaries acknowledge current usage, variation and variability, and changing usage. Here, I am concerned only with the first of Ayres-Bennett's elements: metalinguistic reflection on language, and its potential contribution to the promulgation of a standard language ideology, with its assumption that there are such things as distinct, bounded languages, with boundaries that must be patrolled to ensure the integrity of correct language (Gal 2006: 14). Specifically, I examine the dictionaries of Boyer, Ludwig, and Chambaud to address the following questions:

(i) To what extent do these bilingual lexicographers create and claim for themselves an authority on language, going beyond mere documentation of language?

For non-native speakers and learners, the authority of bilingual dictionaries is potentially even greater than for monolingual dictionaries, as users often have reduced access to their target language, and are unable to, or less willing to, rely on their intuition about at least one of the two languages. Do the lexicographers reinforce this presumption of authority, in their construction and legitimation of their own authority on language, and if so, how?

(ii) To what extent do the metalinguistic labelling and other metalinguistic description of language express particular language ideologies, such as a standard language ideology?

What do these bilingual dictionaries tell their users about language, and about their object languages in particular, through how they define and delineate correct or acceptable language (including pronunciation) and through their metalinguistic labelling? Might they differ from, and perhaps even run ahead of, their monolingual counterparts, as we know can be the case for foreign language grammars, whose users seek certainty about a language they may not know well (McLelland 2015: 50, 222–47)?

Before addressing these questions, I begin by setting the three lexicographers' works in context. Abel Boyer's (1699) bidirectional *Royal Dictionary* of French and English, his abridged 1700 version, and several later editions are part of a lively tradition of French/English lexicography since Palsgrave (1530) (Hausmann 1991). Boyer (1699), first published in London, draws heavily on the Académie française's (1694) French dictionary (Cormier 2004) and was presumably chiefly intended for English speakers wishing to improve their French—it was not until 1756 that his *Royal Dictionary* (Boyer 1756) was published in France, in Lyon (Cormier 2008: 157). However, Boyer's (1700) abridged version explicitly also targeted a French-speaking market learning English: the preface is bilingual rather than only in English, and the title page trumpets the marking of 'accenting of all English words, to facilitate the Pronunciation of the English Tongue to foreigners'. Boyer influenced later bilingual lexicography: up to 20% of the additions made by Stevens (1705) to his English–Spanish dictionary may come from Boyer (Cormier and Fernandez 2005: 302); Boyer was also used in the compilation of the English–Irish Dictionary of Begley and McCurtin (1732) (Mac Coinnigh 2012), and, I have discovered, a later edition of Sewel's English–Dutch dictionary revised by Egbert Buys (1766; the first ed. of 1691 has a Dutch–French source, according to Hall 2004).

Boyer also very directly influenced the two lexicographers with whom I compare him here, Christian Ludwig and Lewis Chambaud. Ludwig (1706) used Boyer's work as a basis for his English–German dictionary, which was the very first German/English dictionary and thus a relative latecomer in European bilingual lexicography, a fact which Hausmann and Cop (1985: 184) attribute to the weak status of German and English in early modern Europe, compared to the relatively stronger languages of French, Italian, and Spanish. The market for English/German dictionaries developed much later than the French/English one, and began in Germany, where interest in English was somewhat ahead of English speakers' interest in German. Ludwig's (1706) dictionary was responding to a change in Anglo–German relations from previous 'entfremdung und widerwillen' ('alienation and antipathy') to 'eine erwünschte vereinigung' ('a desired unification') through the anticipated royal dynastic connection (Ludwig 1706: b1^v). Ludwig's later German-to-English dictionary (Ludwig 1716) was also the first of its kind. Ten further editions of Ludwig's two dictionaries appeared between 1706 and 1821. Ludwig's main competitor was Theodor Arnold (1683–1761), whose German–English and English–German dictionaries appeared in twenty-five editions between 1736 and 1822. The first bidirectional work did not appear until Prager (1757/60, 1768).[5] Ludwig's (1706) dictionary, while intended for Germans seeking to increase their knowledge of English (Ludwig 1706: preface b2), is in fact

---

[5] On the early history of German-English lexicography, see Hausmann and Cop (1985); Stein (1985).

trilingual, a *Dictionary English, German, and French*, since it is a version of Boyer (1699) with the addition of German. Ludwig's work is thus an instance of Lillo's (2016: 6–7) 'multilinguisme bilingue', a label Lillo applies to nineteenth-century lexicography with its 'chassé-croisé' of translations and adaptions of bilingual works for new language pairings, but which is certainly characteristic of earlier periods too.[6]

Lewis Chambaud's (1761) dictionary is, like Ludwig (1706), a direct successor to Boyer, but in the French/English tradition. Pirated and/or revised versions of Boyer's dictionaries had appeared in the first half of the eighteenth century and into the 1850s (notably by Reformed Minister and Fellow of the Royal Society David Durand; see Cormier 2010: 175–6), but a new departure was marked by Chambaud, a London-based French teacher and author of language manuals, whose 1761 French–English dictionary (with two further editions in 1771 and 1776; see Cormier 2010: 177; 185) seems to have threatened the 'hegemony' of Boyer for the first time (Cormier 2010: 177). Chambaud had reportedly spent twenty years compiling his dictionary, and a long preface set out how the work was an improvement on Boyer's many shortcomings (Cormier 2010: 179), referring to Boyer (1753) by an unknown reviser (Cormier 2010: 184). Chambaud's dictionary was followed by one other French/English dictionary in the eighteenth century, whose author Thomas Deletanville (1771) explicitly intended it for use in schools (Cormier 2005: 185), and which has received no scholarly attention to date.

A key difference between the French–English and English–German traditions is their relationship to monolingual lexicography. Boyer's (1699) dictionary was based on the Académie française's (1694) dictionary, and we shall see that Chambaud (1761) referred to the Académie's (1740) dictionary and others. In Germany, however, despite Stieler (1691) (see Jones 2000: 661–5), it was not until the 1770s that there were fully-fledged German monolingual dictionaries which could inform the bilingual German–English tradition, most notably Adelung's epoch-making German dictionaries (Adelung 1774–86, 1793–1801). Monolingual English dictionaries were available earlier in the century: Arnold (1736) drew on Bailey's English dictionary (Arnold and Bailey 1721), and Rogler's (1763) revision of Ludwig drew on Johnson (1755) and Dyche and Pardon (1744 [first ed. 1735]). However, these were not yet available to Ludwig (1706), who in any case simply followed Boyer's nomenclature—he did not, for

---

[6] Some authors, like Ludwig, adapted an existing dictionary for a new language (likewise Arnold 1736, whose English–German dictionary also includes French; his 1752 edition adds Latin too). Others produced bilingual dictionaries for more than one pairing of languages (e.g. Matthias Kramer, who produced bilingual dictionaries of French, Italian, German, and Dutch in the eighteenth century; Bray 2000; Glück 2019). There is also a much longer tradition of polyglot dictionaries. See e.g. Considine (2008: 288–313) and note 1 above.

instance, make use of Kersey (1969 [1702]), the first 'general dictionary of English' (Cormier 2003: 39).

9.2 The dictionaries, their authority, and the legitimation of their authority

Having set the broader context for the three lexicographers' work, I turn to the first of my two research questions: how, and to what extent, do these bilingual lexicographers create and claim for themselves an authority to pronounce on language and its use?

'A Dictionary ought not to be a bare Collection of Words, but must serve likewise to firm young People's Judgement in the right Use of a Language, and teach them the different Signification of Terms' (Boyer 1699: A3r, also cited by Cormier 2008: 154). Boyer's (1699) explicit assertion that a dictionary should help shape people's 'Judgement in the right Use of a Language' attests to the fact that early modern bilingual lexicographers could be just as conscious of their role in guiding usage as their contemporary monolingual counterparts, perhaps even more so, as language learners might well be more vulnerable to error. We shall see that Boyer, Ludwig, and Chambaud indeed all claim authority over the language they codify, though to differing degrees.

For his 1699 dictionary, Boyer's French authorities were, the title page announces, Richelet's (1680) *Dictionnaire françois*, Furetière's (1690) *Dictionnaire universel*, and the Académie française's (1694) dictionary—the first three monolingual dictionaries of French (Cormier 2004: 21)[7]—as well as Guy Tachard's (1692) French–Latin dictionary, and the remarks of Vaugelas (1647), Ménage (1672, 1676), and Bouhours (1674, 1675). As for English, Boyer's title page alludes to 'the Best Dictionaries', but Boyer bemoans the 'Lame and Imperfect Pieces' available to him for English (Boyer 1699: A2v preface). In the absence of suitable dictionaries as authorities, Boyer seems to have resorted to personal authorities, 'learned English Gentlemen' (Boyer 1699: preface), a category notably not quite comparable with Vaugelas's (1647) benchmark of 'la plus saine partie de la Cour' (Vaugelas 1647, cited from Vaugelas 1984 [1647]: 40–1). At least one such gentleman may have had concrete influence: Boyer was seemingly more ready to include dubious terms—i.e. neologisms not yet widely used—in his English nomenclature than in his French nomenclature, a difference that Cormier (2008) attributes to the influence of Boyer's friend John Savage, who, in a 1696 letter to Boyer cited by Cormier (2008: 165), expressed his inclusive approach to neologisms: 'As for the Authority

---

[7] Nicot's (1606) *Thresor de la language françoyse* is often considered the first dictionary of French, and is certainly a landmark, but many of its entries have only Latin equivalents or explanations. See Wooldridge (1977: 17–36).

of making new Words, I have not assumed it, tho I think it but proper, to have a word to express every particular meaning; and where a Language is defective, 'tis allowable to supply it'. Boyer notes that 'Luxuriant and Eloquent Writers' may step 'out of the common Road', but Boyer has sought to include only phrases 'consecrated' by 'Use, the sovereign Umpire of Languages' (Boyer 1699: A3v), assuring his readers that he has marked as dubious any 'Words which I have found in any Writer of unsufficient Authority' (Boyer 1699: A3r).

As for which writers constitute a sufficient authority, Boyer's title page mentions 'the Works of the Greatest Masters of the English Tongue; such as Archbishop Tillotson, Bishop Sprat, Sir Roger l'Estrange, Mr. Dryden, Sir William Temple, &c.' from whom, according to the preface, he 'collected a great many new Words and Expressions'. As well as the poet John Dryden (1631–1700), still well known today, Boyer's other authorities, all contemporary or nearly contemporary with Boyer, were well regarded in their day for their style. John Tillotson (1630–94), Archbishop of Canterbury, was a renowned preacher, whose sermons were much cited and much re-used by other clerics, and whose style was much praised in the eighteenth century, including by John Locke, for example. Boyer's citation of him is noteworthy, since it pre-dates any of Rivers's (2004) evidence for Tillotson's reputation, despite the fact that Rivers mentions Tillotson's influence on (later) eighteenth-century lexicography. The same is true of Boyer's mention of Bishop Thomas Sprat (bap. 1635–1713), a writer, poet, and member of the Royal Society, who published a history of the Society in 1667. Sprat supported the idea of establishing an English language academy, and in the eighteenth century Pope (1688–1744) listed Sprat among English prose authors from whom an authoritative dictionary for writers might be drawn (Morgan 2008), but again, Boyer's mention of Sprat pre-dates Pope's endorsement of him. Roger L'Estrange (1616–1704), prolific author, journalist, and press censor, was admired for his 'vigorous, colloquial prose and mastery of dialogue' (Love 2007). Finally, Sir William Temple (1628–99) was a diplomat whose biographer Davies (2009) notes his 'lively and perceptive observations', and whose reputation owed much to Swift's publication in 1700–09 of many of his writings—but again, Boyer's (1699) inclusion of Temple in his list of great writers interestingly pre-dates Swift's popularization of Temple. Although Gibbs (2004) credits the publication of Boyer's dictionaries with having given him 'entrance into English intellectual and social circles', Boyer—resident in England since 1689—seems already to have been impressively *au fait* with English literary circles when he published his dictionaries.

Ludwig (1706) makes no explicit statement about authority or sources in his preface; his title page merely assures us that his dictionary is based on 'the best new English dictionaries', without elaboration. Presumably he had no desire to draw attention to his very close debt to Boyer, though the debt was clearly no secret once the work was published: in his revised edition, Rogler (1763: first page of preface) noted that Ludwig had made 'eine getreue Uebersetzung' ('a faithful translation') of Boyer, and 'noch das teutsche darzu gesetzt hat' ('added the German to it'). As noted above, Rogler himself was able to draw on the English dictionaries that had been published in the meantime, telling us that most of his additions are taken from Samuel Johnson's (1755) dictionary and William Pardon's (1744) dictionary published in Dublin (i.e. Dyche and Pardon 1744, first ed. 1735) to add some 12,000 words, as well as 'unentbehrliche Redensarten und *Idiotismi*' ('indispensable sayings and idioms; Rogler 1763: first page of preface), drawing especially for technical terms on Dyche and Pardon's work, 'peculiarly calculated for the use and improvement of such as are unacquainted with the learned languages especially' and so containing 'difficult Words' (Dyche and Pardon 1744: title).

Chambaud seems to have agreed with Boyer about the responsibility of the dictionary compiler to guide the 'right Use of a Language' (Boyer 1699: A3r). In his earlier *Treasure of the French and English Languages*, Chambaud (1750) had already buttressed his own authority by drawing on that of the Académie française, which he had consulted (though what that consultation might have meant in practice is unclear): 'In compiling this vocabulary I have consulted *Méssieurs de l'académie Françoise*, concerning such words as might be doubtful; and the learner may depend upon the propriety of all the words therein contained' (Chambaud 1750b: preface, p. 3). In his 1761 dictionary, Chambaud's two-page catalogue of sources consulted (Chambaud 1761: xv–xvi) includes some twenty French dictionaries of various kinds, as well as several grammars including the *Grammaire Générale et Raisonnée* (Arnauld and Lancelot 1968 [1660]), and the *Remarques sur la langue françoise* of Vaugelas (1647) not, however, Bouhours (1674) and Ménage (1672, 1676), mentioned by Boyer.[8] But as in his 1750 *Treasure*, it is again the Académie française that takes precedence in Chambaud's (1761) preface, where he offers a similar assurance: when uncertain how to pronounce unfamiliar words, he claims (without further detail) that he 'applied to the French Academy to be informed of their pronunciation' (Chambaud 1761: x). Correct pronunciation was, as we shall see below, evidently as important to Chambaud as correct written language.

The Académie française's (1740) dictionary is indeed the source of many of Chambaud's examples, including, under *Langue*, the proverbial: 'L'usage èst le tiran des langues (en matière de langue, l'usage l'emporte sur les règles) *Use or custom is the standard of languages*'.[9] It is evident that Chambaud is fully aware of the theoretical discussion about (good) usage and analogy that informs the proverb. Compared to both Boyer and Ludwig, he takes by far the most explicitly theoretically founded approach to his work, articulating his position in regard to the three traditionally competing arbiters of correctness for any grammarian or

---

[8] However, Chambaud (1750a: 126–7) refers to Ménage, as well as Vaugelas, in his discussion of whether the number twenty-one should be followed by a singular or plural.

[9] Compare the Académie française's (1740) dictionary: 'On dit prov. que L'usage est le tyran des langues, pour dire, qu'En matiére de Langue, l'usage emporte sur les règles'.

lexicographer: custom, analogy, and the usage of 'good writers'. Since 'Custom has not yet authorised our affixing the acute accent to the e of articles and pronouns, or to the last syllable of the infinitive and nouns ending in *er*', Chambaud does not do so either (Chambaud 1761: xi), and he assures us that when in doubt, he has relied on 'Analogy, and the constant practice of the best writers' (Chambaud 1761: x). 'Good writers' are arguably Chambaud's ultimate authority, however, since even where they differ, he resorts neither to wider custom, nor to analogy to adjudicate, but tolerates both variants: 'When a word is written diversely, and each way of writing is supported by the authority of good writers, I set down both ways' (Chambaud 1761: xiii).

As for whom Chambaud (1761: xv–vi) considers to be 'good writers', his list of sources encompasses a wide assortment of histories and other reference and literary works. Predictable inclusions are, for example, a French edition of Terence's comedies, and Fénelon's (1699) *Les Aventures de Télémaque, fils d'Ulysse*, both widely used teaching texts, as well as works by Rabelais, Molière, and Voltaire, including his *Candide*, first published in 1758, only three years before Chambaud's dictionary appeared. With admirable foresight, Chambaud remarks that he has drawn on some authors still living 'whose works may probably be read when the French monarchy is no more' (Chambaud 1761: vii). The wide chronological range of authors is deliberate: Chambaud tells us that he has included some obsolete terms because they are used by 'some antiquated French writers', such as Brantôme, Montaigne, and Rabelais, 'who are nevertheless still read', while some humorous expressions of La Fontaine have been revived by Voltaire, but are thus far found in no French dictionary, 'not even in the voluminous Trévoux' (Chambaud 1761: vi–ii; referring to the anonymous 1721 French–Latin dictionary that he lists third among his sources, Chambaud 1761: xv).

Not only is Chambaud's list of sources extensive, so is his use of them. Chambaud (1761: vii) asserts that his dictionary contains no example 'that is not necessary to illustrate either the signification of the word, or its grammatical construction', but he certainly gives more examples than Boyer, and the examples are often longer than in Boyer and even than in the Académie française dictionary.[10]

---

[10] For example, amongst several passages cited under ĒSPRIT, Chambaud cites the French philosopher and satirist Jean de La Bruyère's *Les Caractères*. He offers—without naming it—Nicholas Rowe's published English translation (La Bruyère 1723) in which, ironically, *beaux esprits* remains untranslated:

> Les sôts lîsent un livre & ne l'entendent point; les ēsprits médiocres croient l'entendre parfaitement; les grands ēsprits ne l'entendent quēlquefoîs pâs tout entier: ils trouvent obscur ce qui èst obscur, comme ils trouvent claîr ce qui est claîr; les beaûx ēsprits veulent trouver obscur ce qui ne l'èst point, & ne pâs entendre ce qui èst fort intēlligible.
>
> *A fool reads a book, and understands nothing in it; a witling reads it, he fancies he is presently master of it all without exception; a man of discernment sometimes does not comprehend it entirely, he distinguishes what is clear from what is obscure: whilst the beaux esprits will have those passages dark which are not, and affect not to understand what is really intelligible.*

Godard (2020: 237) has noted that in Chambaud's (1750a) essay on the teaching of languages (published as a preface to his French grammar), the 'genius of the language' and 'idiom of the language' are key terms, occurring seventeen and fifteen times respectively, and 'almost always next to each other'; they encompass for Chambaud both grammatical specificities and other idiomatic (e.g. lexical) peculiarities. Chambaud's use of longer examples reflects this preoccupation, being, he says, 'designed to exhibit the genius and manner of writing of the language, as well as its expressions' (Chambaud 1761: vii). However, Chambaud's use of literary authorities also has an additional purpose. A dictionary should, he suggests, be a work that can be 'read through with pleasure, like any other book of Literature. In that view I have introduced whatever is most interesting and entertaining in the best French writers' (Chambaud 1761: vii). This approach—while partly a consequence of Chambaud's personal commitment to the promotion of good French among the English (as we shall see in the following section)—no doubt also reflects the maturity of this language learning market compared to the more modest expectations that Ludwig (1706), and, contemporary with Chambaud, Rogler (1763) had of German learners of English.

9.3 Language ideologies in theory and practice

We have seen that all our lexicographers explicitly assert the role of dictionaries as authorities on language, although to differing degrees. It is therefore illuminating to consider how they apply language ideologies to their object languages, first, in the paratexts of their dictionaries and their other publications, and second, in their lexicographical practice.

Boyer (1699) observes in his dedication that French has become 'Universal, not only in all the Courts of Europe, but also in the Armies, and amongst Men of Business' (Boyer 1699: second page of dedication). Boyer ascribes the French language's success both to its expressiveness and beauty (a criterion of quality), and to the 'Fame of their [French] King' (a link between language and nation). As for English, the monarch is 'eminent over all the Princes of the Universe [...] at this Time no Nation makes a greater Figure, nor is more fam'd for Martial Valour, Learning or Trade than the English'. However, English scores lower for Boyer on the quality criterion: English would have greater sway if its 'Richness, Delicacies and Expressiveness [...] were sufficient to spread it abroad', the implication being that they are not (Boyer 1699: second page of dedication). Ludwig's (1706) pitch for English to a nascent German-speaking readership similarly makes no claims for the qualities of English as a language, but rather for the status of its speakers. Acknowledging the strongly growing German interest in English, Ludwig notes 'die regung, welche ietzto mehrere als sonst iemahls zu erlernung der Englischen sprache treibet' ('the excitement which now drives more people than ever before to learn the English language'), since 'macht und ansehen berühmter völcker mit der ausbreitung ihrer sprachen in gleichen schritten gehen' ('power and esteem of famed peoples go in step with the spread of their languages') (Ludwig 1706: b2). Whereas Boyer had implied that his own language, French, was superior to English, for Ludwig there is no hint of competition between his own German language and English, the language he is promoting. On the contrary: in Ludwig's (1716) German–English dictionary, published a decade after his English–German dictionary, he instead emphasizes the affinity between those two languages, and their shared superiority to French. An example under the headword *Sprache* reads, 'So wol die teutsche als die Englische sprache sind weit wort-reicher als die Frantzösische, both the German and the English tongues are more copious behalf [sic, in the sense of *by half*] than the French'. The same point about copiousness is made for German in Ludwig's (1716) preface to justify the omission of French for reasons of space, by contrast with his 1706 work: 'weil die teutsche sprache überaus wort-reich ist' ('because the German language is exceptionally rich in words'; Ludwig 1716:)(2). Ludwig here perpetuates a long-running trope from language patriots of the seventeenth century, the exceptional richness of the Germanic languages, thanks to their capacity for derivation and compounding (see McLelland 2011: 46–50).

As for good language use, and especially how to guide foreign language learners to use the language well, Ludwig (1716) implicitly reflects controversy over how best to learn a language, in his entry under *Sprache* in his German—English dictionary: 'Eine sprache ohne *grammatic* und aus der blossen übung lernen, to learn a language by rote, by practice only or without a grammar'. The importance of grammar to inform the proper, rational study of a language was already being advocated in the mid-seventeenth century by the German grammarian Schottelius, who argued that mere practice was insufficient to ensure mastery, but Schottelius was primarily thinking of the need for Germans to study the rules of their *own* language (McLelland 2011: 60–2). Ludwig now implicitly applies the importance of studying grammar to foreign language learning too. A year later, in the preface to Ludwig's (1717) grammar of English for German learners, he distinguishes between learning through 'die *fundamenta* und *rationes* [...] *a priori scientificè*' ('the foundations and rational bases, scientifically, *a priori*') and learning 'wie ein *empiricus*, ohne alle regeln und *observationes*', 'durch die blosse *praxin à posteriori* ohne regeln' (Ludwig 1717: Vorbericht, p.)(5ᵛ: 'like an empiricist, with no rules or observations', 'through practice, *a posteriori*, without rules').[11] The latter method is, Ludwig considers, all the more difficult when not in the country where the language is spoken; such learners will 'fast immer' ('almost always') have doubts; far

---

[11] It may seem odd to equate empiricism with the absence of 'observations', but '*observationes*' is to be understood here in the sense of 'remarks' or 'statements of information'; early modern grammars often contain such 'observations' which might, for example, state an exception to a general rule just given.

better to learn '*à priori* gründlich und glücklich [...], was im schreiben und reden nach einer regel gehe, und was zu einer *exception* gehöre' ('*a priori*, thoroughly and successfully [...] what goes according to a rule in writing and speaking, and what is an exception'). Teachers, then, have an important role to play; in his 1716 German–English dictionary, Ludwig, himself a teacher of language, notably includes *Sprachmeister* under his entry for *Sprache* ('a teacher of some foreign language; a master that teaches it'), found neither in Boyer's entries under *langue, langage*, nor in Boyer's or Ludwig's (1706) entry for *language*, though *language-master* is added by Rogler under *language* in his 1763 revision of Ludwig (1706).

Chambaud held similar views to Ludwig about the importance of grammar-based teaching, and expressed them even more forcefully. His 'Essay on the Proper Method' for teaching and learning French that precedes his 1750 French grammar accords with Ludwig's view of the necessity of teaching grammar rather than relying simply on parroting by memory (see McLelland 2017: 95–7). Chambaud makes the same point in the preface of his 1750 *Treasure*: '*If it was possible to learn a language otherwise than grammatically,* [...] this book would serve the purpose' (Chambaud 1750b: A2, my emphasis). Unsurprisingly, then, where Boyer, following the Académie française's (1694) dictionary, had equated a 'dead' language with a 'grammatical' language (under *language*: 'Language morte *ou* Grammaticale, *A Dead or Grammatical Language*'), Chambaud (1761) removes the equation, for in his view it is evidently not only dead languages that are, or should be, grammatical. Chambaud instead glosses: 'Langue morte (cĕlle qu'un peuple a parlé, maîs qui n'èst plus que dans les livres) *A dead language*'.

Beside a language's qualities and its grammaticality, as language teachers, both Ludwig and Chambaud were explicitly concerned with the practical question of what language variety to present as the target. Ludwig (1717: 4), in his grammar of English, would draw attention to regional variation in English and to sociolinguistic differences that resulted from education, making clear that his grammar dealt only with the London-centred variety of educated people:

'Die *Englische pronunciation* ist entweder die Londonische, die man um London herum findet, und welche die gelehrten insgemein durch gantz England gebrauchen; Oder, die besondere des gemeinen volckes in gewissen provintzen./Wir werden eigentlich nur von der ersten handeln: [...]' ('The English pronunciation is either the London one, which one finds in and around London, and which the learnèd in general use through the whole of England; Or, the particular, of the common people in certain provinces./We will in fact deal only with the first:...').

Ludwig's grammar contains 139 pages of detailed explanation of English pronunciation, recognized as a significant challenge in Germany,[12] but he gives no

---

[12] Ludwig's account of English pronunciation is thus almost exactly double Chambaud's sixty-eight pages (Chambaud 1750a: 5–73) on French pronunciation in his admittedly much shorter grammar

further details about regional and/or social variation. There is no evidence to suggest that Ludwig's (1706) dictionary favours a London-based, educated language or that it stigmatized certain variants and varieties; after all, he simply adopted Boyer's word list.

Indeed, Ludwig scaled back the metalinguistic marking of words compared to Boyer, reducing Boyer's six different labels (whose application has been analysed by Cormier 2008) to just three, covering only proverbs, obsolete words, and 'figurative & jocose' usage (Ludwig 1706: *Advertisement to the Reader* [b3v]), and also using those labels noticeably less. An anonymous review of Boyer's (1699) dictionary had criticized the 'Swarm of *Distinction*; *Hands* and *Daggers* of all sizes, blazing *Stars* [. . .]' which made Boyer's work '*Puzzling* and *Troublesom*' (Anon. 1699?, also cited by Cormier 2008: 155–6), and it is likely that Ludwig's pared-down metalinguistic marking reflects a desire to cater to a still immature market of German learners of English, a market largely interested in receptive knowledge of English, so not needing to be warned of possible *faux pas* in their own use of English. Ludwig thus omitted Boyer's indications of 'vulgar' and 'mean' usages, for example, leaving unmarked *He won't bate an Inch on't*, which Boyer labelled 'mean' under BATE. Ludwig also avoids the various subject labels used by Boyer ('a Term of Grammar', 'a Term of Physick', etc.), though often instead finding ways to integrate the information into the German equivalences (e.g. compare Boyer 1700 and Ludwig 1706 under *patronymical, peccant, peck*).

Chambaud (1761) takes the reverse approach to Ludwig, and also goes beyond Boyer in the amount and kind of metalinguistic information he includes on the object language.[13] Chambaud had alerted learners to the social stratification of French in his earlier *Treasure* (Chambaud 1750b: 4), promising to give 'the ordinary, natural, and familiar ways of expressing one's self [sic] among the polite sort of people, upon the most useful subjects', and warning that 'In *France* we avoid nothing so much as to speak as the common people do. There are really, as it were, two languages in the French tongue; the one spoken by well bred people, the other by the vulgar; and people's education is presently known by their speaking'. Chambaud (1750b: 4) therefore considers it necessary for his dictionary users to know both the common forms of language 'to understand the people speak', and also 'the polite ones to express themselves by', an approach that was far from the norm in contemporary monolingual French dictionaries (and a nice teacherly distinction between receptive and productive skills too). This desire to reflect sociolinguistic and register nuances is also reflected in Chambaud's metalinguistic marking. He

---

(172 pages, compared to Ludwig's 997 pages). Between 1770 and 1840, some thirty-three English pronunciation guides were published in Germany, which, averaging at about one every two years, indicates strong demand for help with English pronunciation (Klippel 1994: 109, citing Schröder 1975).

[13] Unlike Boyer in his two-way dictionary, Chambaud does, however, like Ludwig, restrict his labels to the object language only, in his case French. Both Ludwig and Chambaud presumably assumed that metalinguistic guidance about the equivalences given would be superfluous to the users of their one-way dictionaries, who were already competent in their own language.

uses a total of ten metalinguistic labels (see Table 9.1) compared to Boyer's six.[14] Only two of Chambaud's categories—proverbial and figurative usage—coincide exactly with Boyer's. Chambaud's markings include, for example, a symbol to mark 'a common, familiar expression, or form of speech, which is confined to usual conversation only' (used e.g. under LIPÉE for 'Il a eu là une franche lipée (un bon repàs qui ne lui a rien couté). *He has had an excellent meal at free-cost*') and one for 'Poetical, Oratorial, High or Sublime style' (used e.g. under LIEU for 'Ces bâs lieûx (la terre) *This lower world*'), as well as making wider use than Boyer had of subject labels (such as specifying terms of grammar, anatomy, and geometry under PANICULE, PANCREAS, PARALLÈLE).

Table 9.1 Metalinguistic markings, as listed in Chambaud (1761: xiv), with illustrative examples from his dictionary entries

Metalinguistic label and definition	Example
1. *'Denotes that the word, or sentence, is used in the figurative sense.'	[under LÎE, *s. f.*] *la lîe du people (la plus vile & la plus bâsse populace) *The riff-raff or dregs of the people.*
2. ‖ 'Is the mark of a common, familiar expression, or form of speech, which is confined to usual conversation only.'	[under LIPÉE] ‖ Il a eu là une franche lipée (un bon repâs qui ne lui a riēn couté). *He has had an excellent meal at free-cost.* Other examples include LONGUET, ĒTTE, *adj.*, LOQUE, *s.f.*, LOURDERÎE *s.f.*, LUTINER *v.n.*
3. ⚜ 'Poetical, Oratorial, High or Sublime style.'	⚜ LONGANIMITÉ, *s.f.* [la clémence qui porte à soufrir les injûres dont on pouroit se venger. *Longanimity, forbearance, long-suffering.* Other examples include: MATINIÈRE, *adj.*; [under MOISSON, *s.f.*] *Une moisson de lauriérs*; [under MONT, *s.m.*] *le double mont*; [under MORDRE] *Mordre la poussière*; [under SE MUTINER] *Les flôts, les vents mutinés*
4. † 'A Proverb, or proverbial form of speech.'	[under A] † Il ne fait ni A ni B, (il ne sait pâs lîre, se dit aussi aû figuré d'un homme ēxtrêmement ignorant) *He knows not A from B; He is a mere Ignoramus* [identical to Boyer (1699)]
5. ǂ 'A Vulgar, low, mean expression, or form of speech.'	[under ABLATIF, *s.m.*] ǂ Il a mis cela ablativo tout en un tâs (tout ensemble, avēc, confusion & désordre) *He has put it higgledy piggledy* Other examples include: LONGIS, *s.m.*; LOQUÈTTE, *s.f.*; POILOUX, *s.m.*; RABONIR

---

[14] In his 'Explanation of Marks and Abbreviations made use of in this Work' immediately following the preface, Boyer (1699: [A4r]) also includes ☞ for 'The different Significations of a word' and 'R. A Remark', as well as various abbreviations to indicate parts of speech.

Metalinguistic label and definition	Example
6. ‡ 'Obsolete words, and expressions growing old; as also ludicrous words and terms of humour, and of the Hudibrastic[a] or burlesque style.'	‡ LIĒSSE [joïe, gaieté : vieûx mot qui n'a plus usage que dans cette phrâse] Vîvre en joîe & en liësse, *To live jovially, to make merry.* Other examples: LÔS, *s.m.*; LOURDÎSE, *s.f.*; LOUVAT, *s.m.*
7. § 'Irony and joke.'	[under MUSEAU, EAÛX, *s.m.*] ☞ § Il èst biēn nécēssaîre, vraiment, de faîre tant de dépense pour vous graîsser le museau, *Truly, there's great occasion to be at such expence to grease your snouts.* [The source, not given by Chambaud, is Molière, *Les Précieuses ridicules*, Scene IV]
The last three symbols used by Chambaud are combinations of those above:	
8. *† 'Denotes a Proverb, or proverbial form of speech. in the metaphorical or figurative sense.' [punctuation sic]	[under ABOYER] *† Tous les chiēns qui aboyent ne mordent pâs; tout chien qui aboye ne mord pâs (tous ceûx qui menacent ne font pâs toujours du mal) *Barking dogs seldom bite.*
9. †⊥ 'A vulgar, low, or mean proverb in the metaphorical or figurative sense.'	[under AIGUÏSER, *v. a.*] *†⊥ Aiguïser ses couteaûx (se préparer aû combat) *To prepare one's self for fighting.* *†⊥ Aiguïser ses dents, *To prepare one's self to eat heartily.* [Another example, under LOUER] Il a des chambres à louer, *He is out of business.*
10. ☞ 'Points at Phrases, Idioms, and other remarkable modes of expression.'	[under MOURIR] ☞ Ah! que voilà un aîr qui èst pâssioné; èst-ce qu'on n'en meurt point? *Ah! How passionate a tune is that! Don't it kill one with delight?*

[a] I.e. in the verse style of *Hudibras*, a mock-heroic satirical poem by Samuel Butler, published 1663–78.

Besides Chambaud's concern for sociolinguistic acceptability, his adherence to a standard language ideology is also evident in what he has to say about acceptable French pronunciation, though not in the dictionary itself, but in his earlier *Treasure* and grammar (Chambaud 1750a, b). In his *Treasure*, Chambaud warned against native speakers from many regions whose language would make them poor teachers, reserving his strongest ridicule for the Swiss. In one of the dialogues, the slow progress made by a learner over six years is ascribed to having a Swiss master: 'Oh, I ask no more questions [. . .] It would make the French split their sides with laughing, if they were to hear that French is taught in any of the world by Swisses [sic]' (Chambaud 1750b: 196). In his grammar of the same year, Chambaud (1750a: xxii–iii) similarly urged care in the choice of teacher, warning against Normans, Gascons, Picards, and Provençals, whose 'accents, beside the idiom peculiar to the people of those Provinces, are so vastly different from the true *French* accent'.[15] He notes that 'Schools in *England* are stocked with people of those Provinces of France for Teachers, without mentioning Suisses (another old sort of *French* Masters); the generality of which, besides their bad accent, know not the first principles either of the *French* Tongue or of Grammar' (Chambaud 1750a: xxiii). This is a relatively rare attestation from the pre-modern period of the standard language ideology being applied to the spoken language; it certainly pre-dates English pronouncing dictionaries (Beal 2008).

9.4 Conclusion

This chapter set out to explore to what extent three related bilingual dictionaries act as authorities promulgating a standard language ideology which we know is a feature of monolingual language codifications of the period in Europe. It was hypothesized that with an intended audience of non-native speakers of the object languages—even more in want of clear guidance than users consulting a work about their own language—the lexicographers might bolster their authority at least as explicitly and strongly as in monolingual codifications, and perhaps even more so. As noted earlier, we know that foreign language grammars may make prescriptions—or embrace emerging variations—earlier than their monolingual counterparts (McLelland 2015: 50, 222–47). This study offers tentative evidence that some bilingual lexicographers do the same, though to varying degrees depending on the context, and though much more remains to be done to analyse their lexicographical practice. Boyer's early sanctioning of certain contemporary English writers as exemplars of good language stands out, as does both Boyer's and Ludwig's early attention to showing correct pronunciation. However, beyond a reference in the title to 'the best new English dictionaries', Ludwig— who after all in reality simply adopted Boyer's nomenclature—does little to assert his authority, though his reviser Rogler does signal his own use of recently published English dictionaries. Boyer and Chambaud, by contrast, both explicitly claim a strong linguistic authority for their dictionaries, an authority rooted both in their sources and in their criteria for deciding what words, phrases, and examples qualify for inclusion. Both allude to the authority of the Académie française, to good writers, and to established usage as criteria; both also explicitly allow established usage to trump the first two criteria. There is nothing particularly innovative in this, but it is notable how closely and explicitly these bilingual dictionaries accord with what we know of monolingual codifications of the seventeenth and eighteenth centuries.

All three lexicographers also variously comment on questions of the qualities of language. Ludwig's reference in his 1716 preface to Schottelius's (1663)

---

[15] Chambaud thus appears to be no more forgiving of *norman* and *picard* speakers, whose varieties are at least *langues d'oïl*, than of speakers of the *occitan* varieties, *gascon* and *provençal*.

and Bödiker's (1690) grammars suggests he was well aware of seventeenth-century German linguistic patriotic language work, and Ludwig draws on a well-established topos about the exceptionality of the Germanic languages when he notes the copiousness of both German and English. Ludwig also takes Schottelius's (1663) emphasis on the importance of grammar not just for learning Latin but also for native speakers mastering their own vernacular language, and applies it to learning a foreign language, English. Half a century later, Chambaud (1750a, b) is of the same opinion; both Ludwig and Chambaud were practising language teachers, and besides ideological conviction, Chambaud certainly also considered expertise in French grammar a differentiator in his crowded London market of French teachers (McLelland 2017: 124).

In his 1717 grammar, Ludwig shows some awareness of sociolinguistic and regional variation. He devotes considerable attention there to the problem of English pronunciation, and his 1706 dictionary, like Boyer (1700), indicates the pronunciation of all English words. There is no evidence, however, that Ludwig considered English pronunciation anything more than a practical difficulty for learners. How other German/English lexicography in the eighteenth century developed in this regard remains to be investigated. By contrast with Ludwig's lack of attention to English regional varieties, for Chambaud (1750a), many native speakers of French seemingly fall short of an acceptable standard of French pronunciation (as well as idiom and grammar). Yet in terms of lexicographical coverage, Chambaud (1761) is tolerant in theory at least, allowing explicitly for the inclusion of words and expressions that learners should not use, but which they might need to recognize. To what extent that approach is in fact reflected in Chambaud's dictionary entries requires further investigation, but Chambaud's elaborate metalinguistic labels certainly suggest a nuanced awareness of a language with fixed bounds of acceptability, both diachronically (with the 'obsolete' category) and synchronically with respect to style, register, and social status (not, however, with explicit mention of regional variation, by contrast with his opinions on regional pronunciation). Chambaud's detailed metalinguistic labels may, like his extensive use of authentic sources to make his dictionary a work to 'read through with pleasure', reflect the greater maturity of the French-learning market in England, compared to the only emerging market of English-learners in Germany, which was largely made up of beginners, as Rogler still recognized in his revision, considering that dictionaries were 'hauptsächlich für Anfänger' ('chiefly for beginners'; Rogler 1763: [2] of preface). Significantly, though, Chambaud's apparent openness to including non-standard language arguably goes beyond equivalent French monolingual dictionaries of the time (Walsh and Kibbee 2024), and this, together with his sophistication and independence in exemplification of usage, particularly invites closer examination.

10
The history of terms for varieties of Gallo-Romance

Douglas A. Kibbee

10.1 Introduction

'A language is a dialect with an army and a navy', a quip variously ascribed to the Maréchal de Lyautey and to Max Weinreich, captures the relationship between the designation of linguistic varieties and political power.[1] How should we define the terms that denote the object of our research? What, for example, is French? The question turns out to be very complicated. How can we delimit the boundaries of a language without excluding the variation that is natural in all languages? Which variation is captured by which name? Throughout history and still today the French (and other French speakers around the world) argue about the terms that denote their forms of expression.

How do we get from sixteenth- and seventeenth-century remarks on what is or is not French, to Gaston Paris's (1888) 'parlers de France' to the *Loi Deixonne*'s (1951) 'langues régionales' to Cerquiglini's (2003) 'langues de France' and Éloy's (2004) 'langues collatérales'? Along this path, how are the various terms—*langue, dialecte, idiome, parler, patois*—used—and why?

The most recent of dictionaries, the *Trésor de la langue française informatisé*, offers the following definitions:

> **Langue** Système de signes vocaux et/ou graphiques, conventionnels, utilisé par un groupe d'individus pour l'expression du mental et la communication.
>
> **Dialecte** Forme particulière d'une langue, intermédiaire entre cette langue et le patois, parlée et écrite dans une région d'étendue variable et parfois instable ou confuse, sans le statut culturel ni le plus souvent social de cette langue, à l'intérieur ou en marge de laquelle elle s'est développée sous l'influence de divers facteurs sociaux, politiques, religieux, etc.[2]

---

[1] Given the breadth of the chronology and the space limits of this contribution, I ask the readers' forbearance for what may seem a superficial treatment of a complex topic. More detailed studies are listed in the bibliography. Van Rooy (2020) is an excellent starting point. Note that I consider these terms only within the context of the history of France; an extension to other Francophone countries would be useful but falls outside the limits of this contribution.

[2] See Chapter 1 (this volume), footnote 54.

Douglas A. Kibbee, *The history of terms for varieties of Gallo-Romance*. In: *Historical and Sociolinguistic Approaches to French*. Edited by: Janice Carruthers, Mairi McLaughlin, and Olivia Walsh, Oxford University Press.
© Douglas A. Kibbee (2024). DOI: 10.1093/oso/9780192894366.003.0010

Idiome (a) langue propre à une nation ou un peuple; (b) usage linguistique propre à une communauté considérée dans sa spécificité; (c) manière de parler propre à une profession ou un autre groupe.

Parler (a) Ensemble des moyens d'expression utilisés par un groupe social, dans un cadre géographique restreint, par un groupe, à l'intérieur d'un domaine linguistique donné; (b) variété d'une langue utilisée par un groupe social déterminé.

Patois (a) Parler essentiellement oral, pratiqué dans une localité ou un groupe de localités, principalement rurales. (b) Système linguistique restreint fonctionnant en un point déterminé ou dans un espace géographique réduit, sans statut culturel et social stable, qui se distingue du dialecte dont il relève par de nombreux traits phonologiques, morphosyntaxiques, et lexicaux. (c) Langage obscur et inintelligible. (d) Langue spéciale à un groupe, à un domaine d'étude.

This definition of *langue*, contrary to the quip cited above, makes no mention of territory or political status, but embraces the Saussurean notion of system, without problematizing how variation might affect that system. The definition of *dialecte* assumes that there is some form of the language that is not a dialect, a standard form that is stable. *Idiome*, in this formulation, acknowledges the political nature of such a designation, attaching the form to a nation. The ensemble of these definitions lays out the challenges of defining any of the terms—the relationship between linguistic boundaries and political, territorial, and social divisions, standardization (stability)—but fails to mention other factors often cited in such definitions, such as mutual intelligibility and speakers' awareness/consciousness of linguistic divisions. In Section 10.2 I shall briefly recapitulate current thinking about the object of the science and the ideological assumptions that underpin such approaches. Then in Section 10.3 I trace the history of this terminology in the French context.

10.2 Linguistic and non-linguistic factors in linguistic terminology

If a language is a system, at some point variation will lead to a breakdown of that system. This is the point pursued by structural linguists who focus on reception— the ability of the listener to understand. Understanding depends to a certain extent on the effort a listener is willing to make (Rubin 1992) and how much exposure the listener has had to the other linguistic variety. Wolff (1959), studying Nigerian 'linguistic media' (his fashion of avoiding other terms), also noted attitudes based on social prestige—the relatively prosperous Kalabari find the impoverished Nembe unintelligible, while the Nembe claim to understand perfectly the Kalabari.

Various empirical tests of mutual intelligibility have been proposed:[3]

- comparing terms in a basic vocabulary to determine the number of cognates (Swadesh 1950)
- predicting an appropriate word in a simple paragraph (Gooskens et al. 2018)
- assessing informants' ability to translate accurately a text from a neighbouring variety (Voegelin and Harris 1951 (combined with informants' perception of dialectal boundaries))
- assessing the ability to answer questions about a story heard in another variety (Casad 1974)
- assessing how many changes/adjustments are necessary to translate basic terms from one language variety to another (the Levenshtein Distance Normalized technique used by Wichmann 2019).

Wichmann specifically applies this method to establish a cut-off point, at which two varieties can be said to be mutually unintelligible and therefore distinct languages.

Others have been less optimistic about the criterion of mutual intelligibility. Agard (1971: 6; elaborated upon pp. 19–20) stated flatly that 'mutual intelligibility does not furnish a relevant criterion for differentiating dialect from language', preferring regular phonological, morphological, and syntactic correspondences at a deep structure level. However, Wolff (1959: 35) found that 'there is a very low correlation between lexico-structural comparability on the one hand and intelligibility, claimed or proven, on the other'.

An alternative is offered by Chomsky (cited in Joseph 2020: 21 from Hill 1962: 29), emphasizing production: anything he can say as a native speaker of English is automatically English. However, there are certainly sentences that some native English speakers can produce that Chomsky himself would not imagine saying and sentences he might produce that would be unimaginable for many English speakers (without considering content). Production is no more reliable than reception in providing empirical limits of linguistic terms.

Dialectometry, most notably applied by Goebl (2004, 2008, 2018) to Gilliéron and Edmont's (1902–10) *Atlas Linguistique de la France* (*ALF*) from the early twentieth century, attempts to impose methodological rigour and terminological precision to the distinction between terms. In his study of linguistic variation in the northern and eastern regions of European *francophonie*, comparing Dees's work on thirteenth-century charters and the *ALF*, he finds that 'l'individualité diatopique de certains paysages linguistiques traditionnels, telles la Picardie, la

---

[3] Casad (1974: 52–66) describes a number of intelligibility tests used by linguists between 1950 and 1974; van Rooy (2020: 207–11) brings this survey up to 2018.

Wallonie, la Lorraine ... ressort fort bien par le biais d'une CAH [classification ascendante hiérarchique]' (Goebl 2008: 22).[4]

These problems have led other linguists to emphasize the awareness of a group of speakers that they speak differently from another group of speakers, the point at which, to use Kloss's (1967) terminology, an *ausbau* language, a 'language by development' or 'elaboration', separates from another language. The consciousness of difference, and the evaluation of difference, is a crucial part of the formation of a linguistic community.[5] Speakers' consciousness of difference is hard to pin down, often, perhaps usually, inconsistent from one speaker to another, and likely influenced by non-linguistic factors (conflating political boundaries with linguistic boundaries, or religious difference with linguistic difference).[6]

Whatever the method, the choice and number of informants is crucial. The responses to the Abbé Grégoire's (1790) questionnaire were generally written by dignitaries, representing the local chapters of the Amis de la Constitution. Coquebert de Montbret (early nineteenth century) sent his requests for translations of the parable of the Prodigal Son to prefects, who often delegated the task to a subprefect or local clergyman.[7] Gilliéron and Edmont (at the turn of the twentieth century) favoured older, uneducated speakers from rural locations, distinguishing those informants whose language was 'mixed with French' (often schoolteachers) and frequently commenting that younger residents no longer spoke the *patois* that was recorded in their atlas.[8] Bourciez's (1895) collection of translations of the same parable, in southwestern France, has one person's version (or at most two) from any given locale. The researchers preparing the regional atlases of Gallo-Romance, inspired by Dauzat's (1939) appeal and produced from the 1940s through the 1970s, typically searched for the *petits paysans* (as noted by Aurembou 1973: 395), during a period when the isolation of rural communities was rapidly diminishing and the mobility of the population increasing. The goals of these surveys were to emphasize difference, not to reflect the full sociolinguistic range of any community.

---

[4] Further refinements of dialectometry, applied to Basque translations in Bourciez's collection, are found in Aurrekoetxea et al. (2020).

[5] Labov (1972a: 158) saw the shared evaluation of variation within a group as constitutive of a linguistic community: 'A speech community cannot be conceived as a group of speakers who all use the same forms; it is best defined as a group who share the same norms in regard to language'.

[6] Sériot (2019 [1997]) presents a most extreme version of such confusion in the conflict, often bloody, over the categorization of the people of Macedonia—Slavs who speak Greek, Slavs who speak a Slavic language but write it with a Greek alphabet, Christianized Turks, Bulgarian Catholics, Slavs converted to Islam... (2019 [1997]: 265)—and offers five interpretations of the linguistic situation (2019 [1997]: 270-3), concluding with Meillet's (1928: 133) assessment that 'il est puéril de faire intervenir la linguistique dans des questions de frontières de cet ordre'.

[7] For a detailed look at how the Napoleonic survey was conducted in one newly formed *département* (Tarn-et-Garonne) see Bourdoncle (2009: especially pp. 44-52).

[8] Even within the limits of the number and the nature of the informants, experts argue over the approach taken, Gilliéron and Edmont preferring the *instantané* (first, immediate response), Séguy (1973: 34) a more reflective response.

Any territorial representation of linguistic difference depends on the density of speakers of a particular form. What percentage of the residents of a particular region use the forms that are used to establish a particular language or dialect? Given mobility of populations and universal education in the national language, how many residents of Picardy (for example) actively use the forms that distinguish that region according to dialectologists? The definition of the terms under study may inform our understanding of the politics and ideology of identity and *terroir*, and their influence on the science of language.

10.3 Evolving terms and attitudes in France

10.3.1 The many varieties of Gallo-Romance (to 1300)

Consciousness of difference in France was first expressed in the partition of Charlemagne's Holy Roman Empire by his three grandsons, in the Treaty of Verdun recorded by the *Serments de Strasbourg* (842)—Louis taking the Germanic eastern part of the empire, Charles the Romance western part, and Lothair the polyglot intermediate region, stretching to Italy. Recognition of further linguistic subdivision within the Romance-speaking section was unimportant as all official activity was conducted in Latin. The feudal system facilitated further differentiation, which the very gradual extension of royal power would render more and more problematic. Already in 1180, Conon de Béthune (1921: 5) contrasted *français* and his native *artésien*, which, he claimed, was intelligible to the royal court but ridiculed.

The terms referenced the regions (*picard, normand, poitevin*, etc.): it was only in the thirteenth century that the first use of *patois* appeared, and *dialecte* not until the sixteenth century. Courouau (2005) traced the early use of *patois*, in 1285 an object of mockery in Jacques Bretel's *Le Tournoi de Chauvency* (Bretel 1932 [1285]: 37), described as 'faus' and contrasted with 'françois bel et joli'. The meaning of *patois* in the medieval documents is ambiguous, though usually pejorative, as it sometimes refers to non-Romance languages or even to animal languages.

10.3.2 Centralization of power and attitudes towards variation (1300–1539)

The gradual centralization of power in the royal court, through royal officials (*baillis* and *sénéchaux*) throughout the kingdom from the mid-thirteenth century, and in the royal chanceries, further accentuated the difference between the speech of urban centres and rural communities. Language was associated with nation, as the idea of a nation took hold. Philippe VI (reigned 1328–50), who had no training in Latin, demanded that notaries prove their ability to write in French as well as in Latin as a condition for employment (1342) and similar requirements were imposed for the notaries assigned to the international trade fairs of Champagne and Brie (1349). These measures started the path towards a national language unifying the people of all the king's territory.

The edict of Moulin-lès-Tours (1454) required that oral customary laws of the regions be recorded in writing, under the supervision of the Parlement de Paris, a process that confronted regional difference with an ever more standardized form of a national language. Bovelles (1973 [1533]: 77), noting different forms of Gallo-Romance without preferring one over the other, explicitly connects these differences to the many versions of customary law that the Valois kings were trying to bring under their control. Commynes (2007 [1479]: 458–9) noted Louis XI's belief that national unity depended on a single law, a single system of weights and measures, and a single language. And the oft-cited *Ordonnance de Villers-Cotterêts* (1539) required that all legal documents be written in 'langage maternel françois' (article 111), an ambiguous phrase later clearly interpreted as the language of the royal court.

10.3.3 Equality and inequality of varieties in the sixteenth century (1530–1600)

In the first half of the sixteenth century the point of reference for classical humanists was ancient Greece, where five varieties were considered co-equal. Was Greek one language with five dialects, or were there just five dialects/languages? That is, was 'dialect' merely a synonym for 'language' or did it represent something different?[9]

In mid-sixteenth-century France, opinions about how this related to the French situation were mixed. The French Hellenist Antesignanus (Pierre Davantès) used the terms *lingua*, *dialectus*, and *idioma* more or less interchangeably to describe differences in *loquelae varietas* ('a variety of manners of speaking'), while also contrasting good speech (the royal court in Paris) from the speech of 'foolish women' (*sermo muliercularum* in Paris).[10] The poet Ronsard (1550) introduced the term *dialecte* into French, when he spoke of using his 'naïf dialecte de Vandamois', directly comparing linguistic variety in France to the Greek context. When Auger Ferrier objected to Jean Bodin spelling his name Oger, Bodin, writing as 'René Herpin', defended the spelling as representing a praiseworthy (*louable*) manner of

---

[9] See van Rooy (2020: 62–72) for a thorough review of the Humanist reaction to the varieties of Greek.

[10] All of this information about Antesignanus is drawn from van Rooy (2016).

speaking, a 'François naturel', contrary to the regional form which required 'twisting one's mouth as if one were cracking nuts'. Nonetheless Bodin (1583: 11 v°) concluded 'je trouverai bon le dialecte de chacun'.

However already that equality was challenged, as Palsgrave (1530: I, xiii v°) noted that the 'most perfect' French was found in the region between the Seine and the Loire, and '...there is no man, of what parte of Fraunce so ever he be borne, if he desire that his writynges shulde be had in any estymacion, but he writeth in suche language as they speke within [these] boundes...'. Similarly Étienne Pasquier (1607: 950–1) observed that whereas previously people addressed the court of their region in the local variety (he specifies Picard, Champenois, Provençal, and Toulousain), by the second half of the sixteenth century 'tous ces grands Duchez et Comtez estant unis à nostre Couronne, nous n'escrivons plus qu'en un langage, qui est celuy de la Cour du Roy, que nous appellons langage Francois'.

As for *patois*, Palsgrave (1530) used the term simply to designate the 'recordyng of byrdes', continuing the 'animal language' sense that dominated medieval usage. The lawyer Abel Mathieu (1559: Adresse à la reine, f. 2 r°) considered *patois* an outdated language, contrasting the 'antique patois de mes grans meres' to 'nostre parler commun' (f. 25 v°). Later in the century the jurist François Hotman applied the term to Breton,[11] but I have not found, in the sixteenth century, any use of *patois* to designate a contemporary form of French.

10.3.4 *Le bon usage* and the characterization of variation (1600–1700)

The confrontation of linguistic difference occasioned by the centralization of power led to an increased attention to commonality, a shared language of all the (elite) people, as suggested already by Mathieu. Vaugelas sought out the 'most common opinion' (of courtiers, e.g. 1647: 356); Chiflet (1659: 29) provided a list of nouns 'commonly condemned by everyone' and described 'common rules of syntax' (Chifflet 1659: 130 ff.). This common language was contrasted with many forms that, though clearly used by French speakers, were considered by grammarians and *remarqueurs* as 'not French'.[12] Bouhours (1692: 38–9), for example, declared that 'qui diroit, *l'éclaircissement de l'air, l'éclaircissement des brouillards, ou des nüages*, comme le dit un de nos plus célébres Ecrivains, ne parleroit pas François'. The fact that it was used by a well-reputed author did not grant this phrase acceptance as French (contrary to what Chomsky would claim (see Section 10.2)). The distinction of French/not French could apply to word choice, syntax (Ménage 1675: 516–18, placement of the adjective *redouté*), archaisms (Buffet 1668: 33: *horsmis*), neologisms (Macé 1651?: 188: *fratricide*), social class

---

[11] 'Patois vulgaire de ceux que nous appellons Bretons Bretonnans' (Hotman 1573: 29).
[12] For the emergence of the concept of 'not French' in seventeenth-century French metalinguistic works, see Mazière (2010).

(Buffet 1668: 60: 'ne démarés point de la'), as well as to regional variation (Buffet 1668: 82: *moy itout* spoken by *les provinciaux*).

While the term *patois* is rarely used by grammarians[13] or the *remarqueurs*, in literary usage it has negative connotations of archaism, crudity, social class, and regionalism, but also positive connotations of expressivity and unpretentiousness. A thriving literary production in various regional varieties of Gallo-Romance was reduced, in the seventeenth century, to comic effect (Gondret 1989). On the positive side, Guy Patin, a medical doctor mocked in Molière's *Le Malade imaginaire*, apologized in false modesty for not writing his correspondent in 'belles paroles' and 'fleurs de rethorique', instead settling for his 'patois de Picardie' (Molière 1907 [1643]: 278). The *patois* could be a sign of provincial ignorance, or of popular wisdom.

10.3.5 Territorial expansion and the reconsideration of language (1700–70)

The seventeenth and eighteenth centuries were marked by territorial expansion that forced the monarchs and then the governments of the Revolutionary period to confront linguistic difference.[14] Alsace and Lorraine, Flanders, Roussillon, and Corsica brought new non-Francophones under the royal domain. The linguistic varieties spoken in these regions were variously referred to as *langues* or *idiomes*, terms often used interchangeably, though *idiome* was frequently used for a less prestigious variety of Gallo-Romance or a clearly foreign language such as German or Italian. In a monarchy, subjects are not required to learn the king's variety; indeed, as the leaders of the Revolution recognized, linguistic difference over a small distance served the nobility well as it could be used to catch runaway serfs.[15]

As the eighteenth century progressed, reason and scientific method dominated intellectual thought. Biblical sources for linguistic diversity, such as the Tower of Babel (Genesis 11: 1–9), were challenged by historical/political explanations. Nicolas Fréret used what Droixhe (2007: 205) has termed *paléo-comparatisme* to contest the notion of a common 'Japhetic' European language, which had been

---

[13] Oudin (1640: 173) is the exception, and he only used the term once, to refer to future-tense forms of the verb *boire* in the *patois de Paris*, that is, lower class usage in the capital, stating categorically that 'a man who speaks clearly will never use those forms'.

[14] Thus the ever-growing interest in counting the number of languages, as in Gessner (*Mithridate sive de differentiis linguarum* ('Mithridate or concerning the differences of languages') 1555), Megiser (*Specimen quadraginta diversarum et inter se differentium linguarum et dialectorum* ('a sample of forty diverse languages and dialects') 1593; later editions expanded the coverage to fifty), Duret (*Thrésor de l'histoire des langues de cest univers* 1613, which included animal languages and bird songs), Müller (*Oratio orationum* ('prayer of prayers') 1680), a passion continuing to the present-day work of the Ethnologue and the Glottolog.

[15] Noted in the Abbé Grégoire's report recommending the elimination of linguistic variety (1794): 'La féodalité conserva...cette disparité d'idiomes comme un moyen de reconnaître, de ressaisir les serfs fugitifs et de river leurs chaînes'.

used to trace a genealogy back to Babel. Rousseau (1781 [1755]) saw the origin of language in the passions—love, hate, pity, and anger—first within family units, and then spread through groups by mutual agreement on the meaning of signs. The diversity of languages would then reflect the 'climate' and the 'nature of the soil': *terroir*, the natural world, would drive the diversification of language in humans, each language representing the 'complete history of a people' (Volney 1826 [1795], cited in Hafid-Martin 1995: 134).

Diversity did not necessarily mean domination. In the middle of the eighteenth century, the Abbé Girard (1982 [1747]: 20-1) contrasted the equality of dialects among the Greeks, 'les manieres particulieres reconnues pour polies', with the unique model for good French, the language of the royal court and the capital. He recognized two degrees of corruption in the French of his day, the one based on a lack of education and inattention to good usage (the language of the lower classes in Paris and of *honnêtes gens* from the provinces) and the other from a mixture of archaic and modern varieties, the *patois* spoken by peasants from provinces far away from the capital.[16] Among the *patois* he groups Breton, Auvergnat, and Provençal, which today, of course, we would consider to have quite different relationships to French.

The *Encyclopédie* reserved the term *dialecte* for describing Greek variation, but added that if the term could be applied to French, one might say 'dialecte champenois' (Diderot and d'Alembert 1751-72: IV, 933-4). Under *idiome*, defined as a variety of language spoken in some regions and synonymous with *dialecte*, it gives the example 'idiome champenois' (Diderot and d'Alembert 1751-72: VIII, 496).

10.3.6 The Enlightenment and the Revolution (1750-1800)

In the article on *langue* the *Encyclopédie* contrasted, in the increasingly democratic spirit of the second half of the eighteenth century, the conception of usage as a legislator rather than, as in Vaugelas (1647), as a tyrant. Any given language is composed of 'usages propres à une nation pour exprimer les pensées par la voix' (Diderot and d'Alembert 1751-72: IX, 249)—a definition that combined uniformity (propriety), politics (within a nation), purpose (the expression of thought), and means (the voice). France, unlike Italy and Germany (according to this opinion), was not composed of a collection of equal peoples, but rather a single nation. As such, France was compared to Rome, a nation in which only one form of the language was legitimate. Any variation from that norm, in pronunciation,

---

[16] This conception of the *patois* would be repeated in Féraud's dictionary. Féraud (1787-8: III) foreshadows the interest in *patois* for reconstructing the history of the language: 'le mélange de l'anciène avec la nouvelle façon de parler, qui a formé divers langages particuliers, qu'on nomme patois dont la connoissance peut servir à pénétrer dans l'origine des langues et des Peuples'.

morphology, or syntax, was a provincial *patois*. *Territoire*, a political notion, is more important than *terroir*.

The critical attitude towards variation was emphasized by Charles Rollin (1730), who presented a plan to teach French in the schools. He encouraged all teachers in the provinces to note the defects of language and pronunciation heard on the streets in order to anticipate correcting these errors among their students. Jean Desgrouais (1766: Préface, v) took up the challenge, proposing 'not to teach how to speak well, but rather how not to speak poorly'. His *Gasconismes corrigés* was reprinted frequently through the early nineteenth century, and much imitated for other regions.

The politics of uniformity and equality would arise again during the French Revolution. Would equality be achieved by translating the decrees of the Revolution into all the linguistic varieties of the country? After a brief and costly flirtation with this policy (Schlieben-Lange 1996), diversity was abandoned in favour of uniformity. The survey sent by the Abbé Grégoire (August 1790) asked forty-three questions about the *patois*, contrasting local variation with the *idiome national*. Though he never defined *patois*, the nature of his questions provides some indication of how he differentiated *patois* from *langue*.[17] Some questions connected his investigation with the concerns of the Enlightenment, the sources and types of variation and interactions between *patois*, the national language, and other European languages. He also sought to localize variation, in towns and in the countryside, and between neighbouring regions. Were *patois* standardized through dictionaries, grammars, literary works? Could they express the full range of ideas necessary for the new citizen? And perhaps most important, for his purposes, did language influence behaviour, that is, did *patois* detract from the formation of the ideal citizen of the new nation? Regional variation was 'grossier', 'laid', 'barbare'—a jargon (Madonia 2006).

Grégoire's conclusions with regard to the moral effects of speaking *patois* led to the institution of universal and uniform schooling throughout the country, with the focus on instruction of the national language: French would be the language of the school grammars. Other forms of Gallo-Romance and other languages (German, Italian, etc.) were threats to national unity, and had to be eradicated.

10.3.7 Romantic and scientific approaches to variation in the nineteenth century (1800–70)

The opposition between the national language and *patois* or *dialecte* was pursued through the ever more bureaucratic French state. The department of the Hautes-Alpes offered a prize for a dictionary that would help eliminate non-standard

---

[17] He did not define *dialecte* either; in question 27 he seemed to equate *patois* with *dialecte*.

language among its youth, and many such volumes were written.[18] In education, national exams (*brevet, baccalauréat, agrégation*), a national inspection system (from 1833), and finally mandatory education (1880s), all reinforced these distinctions. At best, the patois might be used to teach the national language, as indicated by Comman (1806) and the Abbé Pétin (1842), though that remained a controversial approach. A series of periodicals assisted teachers and the general public in defining what was French, from Domergue's *Journal de la langue françoise* (1784–95, continued under various names until 1840), through Prodhomme's *Revue grammaticale et littéraire* (1867–9), the *Courrier de Vaugelas* (1868–81) (Glatigny 2001) and newspaper columns devoted to language questions. *Langue* was the speech of the educated, guided by reason towards the best interests of the nation; *patois* was the speech of the *paysan abruti*, still in the grips of tradition, superstition, and religion.

At the same time, scientific interest in comparative linguistics, historical interest in linguistic variety as a reflection of the history of peoples, and the Romantics' vision of the wisdom of the common people inspired positive attention to the *patois*. Was the *patois* of the *terroir* the authentic speech uncorrupted by the artificial interference of schools and grammar books, thus the image of an original form of the *langue*?

The goal of Coquebert de Montbret's[19] survey of linguistic variety in France, conducted from 1807 to 1812, was thus quite different from the Abbé Grégoire's. He made no value judgements about the purported relationship between linguistic variety and the moral character of the speakers. As director of Napoleon's Bureau de Statistique, he worked entirely through official channels, addressing his request to the prefect of each department. And he used, most frequently, the term *dialecte*, which, as we have seen, referred historically, in the Greek context and among the French intelligentsia of the eighteenth century, to a situation of equality. The collection of translations of the parable of the prodigal son would, he explained to one prefect, allow him to know 'en quoi les divers dialectes de la langue française se ressemblent et en quoi ils diffèrent' (cited in Merle 2010: 36). This comparison would allow him to map difference, even between inhabitants of the mountains and the plains within a single department, or between different *arrondissements* of a single city (as in Marseille).

One of his informants was Joseph-Jacques Champollion-Figeac, who launched French dialectological writing with his *Nouvelles recherches. . .* (1809). Champollion-Figeac (1809: preface, viii–ix) complained that previous writers writing about linguistic diversity in France had not consulted original

---

[18] The challenge in the Hautes-Alpes is presented in McCain (2018: 4) and was met by Jean-Michel Rolland (1810). Such works were also produced for Lorraine, Lyon, Nantes, Périgord, Basses-Pyrénées, and other regions through the first half of the nineteenth century.

[19] Charles-Étienne Coquebert de Montbret conducted the survey from 1807 to 1812. His son Eugène published the results in 1831 (Coquebert de Montbret and de Labouderie 1831).

documents, did not know even one of the *idiomes vulgaires*, and had never travelled from one part of France to another to make accurate comparisons. For Champollion-Figeac, the French language had been formed from the popular speech of the provinces.

The roots of that popular speech were believed to be Celtic. The same year as Coquebert de Montbret's questionnaire, another was launched by the Académie Celtique under the direction of Jacques-Antoine Dulaure, focused on folk traditions in France as vestiges of Celtic culture (Senn 1981). Napoléon's Celtomania gave official approval to another vision of the history of the nation, one that would reach back further than Rome and valorize the regional varieties of Gallo-Romance, with emphasis on the 'Gallo-' (Dousset-Seiden 2005). Champollion-Figeac (1809: 23) emphasized the division between urban and rural Gaul after Caesar's conquest; the varieties of modern Gallo-Romance that survived in the *patois* were the key to understanding the history of the French language: 'Pour caractériser une langue dans tout ce qui lui est propre, c'est dans l'intérieur du pays où elle est parlée qu'il faut l'étudier'. Charles Nodier (1834: 82-3) described the *patois* as 'la partie la plus franche et la moins altérée des langues' and Schnakenberg (1840: Avant-propos, v) found in the 'patois les racines innombrables par lesquelles la langue nationale tient au sol natal et par lesquelles elle reçoit sa force, sa vie, sa couleur, sa poésie'. Numerous regional societies promoted the collection of local literature, though the Parisian elite remained ambivalent.[20] For Schnakenberg (1840: 1, 3), the French language lost its native grace when it imposed on itself the restrictions of seventeenth-century mannerisms. He contrasted cultivated language, academic French—the work of humans—with the spoken language, the 'natural idioms of the Gaulish soil'—the work of God.

As the natural, authentic form of the language, the *patois* and the medieval texts were the worthy subject of scientific research. Schnakenberg (1840: 36) compared the regional varieties of Gallo-Romance, north and south, focusing on pronunciation and verbal morphology rather than the lexicon. While he used the terms *patois*, *idiome*, and *dialecte* interchangeably, he distinguished degrees of difference, and several times insisted on the gradual change from one dialect to another by 'almost undetectable nuances' (e.g. Picard to Parisian). Schnakenberg combined the study of contemporary regional variation with historical studies of medieval texts. Paulin Paris, conservator of manuscripts at the Bibliothèque Nationale and the first professor to hold the chair of Medieval French Literature at the Collège de France (1853–72), pursued this research in preparing many critical editions of medieval works. He sent his son, Gaston Paris, to Germany

---

[20] Gerson (2003: 211–15) describes both sides of the intellectual discussion. Particularly interesting is Émile Egger's (1843: 249) extended critique of Pierquin de Gembloux's *Des Patois et de l'utilité de leur étude* (1841), essentially a critique of identity politics: 'Il ne suffit plus d'être Français, on doit se souvenir que l'on est avant tout Gascon, Picard ou Normand'; Egger wondered if he should be sorry to be born Parisian.

to study with the founders of comparative and historical linguistics. Gaston Paris then entered the École des Chartes, where he met Paul Meyer. Together they would dominate the study of language in France into the early twentieth century.

10.3.8 Science and the nation in the second half of the nineteenth century (1860–1900)

Two new surveys at the end of the Second Empire, one by Victor Duruy in the schools (1864; Chervel 1992: 252) and another by Charles Robert in the military (1865; Furet and Ozouf 1977: 324–5), revealed that many young subjects of the emperor did not speak standard French, or even any French at all. As the Third Republic sought to re-establish the idea of the nation after the disastrous Franco-Prussian War (1870–1), Paris and Meyer rejected the notion of dialect, preferring to see a geography of individual traits:

> La science…nous apprend qu'il n'y a pas deux Frances, qu'aucune limite réelle ne sépare les Français du nord de ceux du midi, et que d'un bout à l'autre du sol national nos parlers populaires étendent une vaste tapisserie dont les couleurs variées se fondent sur tous les points en nuances insensiblement dégradées.
> (Paris 1888: 435–6)

The notion of *parlers populaires* allowed Paris to incorporate a certain amount of variation within a single French language *une et indivisible*. Paris began his teaching career at the newly founded École pratique des hautes études in 1869; his students would change the conception of *patois*, placing them within a scientific framework, as 'the most reliable data for general philology' (Rousselot 1887: 2). Paris founded in 1889 the Société des parlers de France, which began publication of a scientific journal, *Le Bulletin des parlers de France*, in 1893, alongside his students' publication, Gilliéron and Rousselot's *Revue des patois gallo-romans* and Clédat's *Revue des patois* (1887–8), which would be renamed the *Revue de philologie française et provençale* (1889–96).

To every social movement there is a counter-movement. The conceptions of *langue*, *patois*, and *dialecte* promoted by Paris and Meyer were not universally accepted. Several societies formed in the 1850s to promote the revival of regional languages as literary languages. A petition in 1870 asked, 'ne pouvons-nous pas demander qu'ils [*parlers locaux*] restent les idiomes de la poésie et de la conversation, qu'ils soient, conjointement avec lui [*le français*], la langue de l'école primaire?' This petition for *langues provinciales* reflected the split between northern and southern perceptions of linguistic variation in France. The *méridionaux* considered the northern variations 'scarcely different from French that we all speak', and thus not really languages, but rather *patois* that were unworthy of protection (de Gaulle 2001 [1870]: 13).

In the 1870s the divisive issue was the demarcation of a boundary between *Oïl* and *Oc* varieties of Gallo-Romance.[21] In 1872, Paris and Meyer launched their scholarly journal, *Romania*; that same year, young linguists based in Montpellier started their own, the *Revue de linguistique romane*. In the summer of 1873 Octavien Bringuier and Charles de Tourtoulon headed east from the Gironde (on the Atlantic) to trace a line separating northern and southern varieties. Their work was published in 1876, and rejected by Paris,[22] who sent his student, Antoine Thomas, to conduct his own study of the Creuse in order to disprove the findings of the Montpellier scholars. The mixing of traits in the 'Croissant'[23] challenged this notion of separate languages (Brun-Tringaud 1992). The Italian dialectologist Graziadio Ascoli further complicated the question with his delimitation of a *francoprovençal* region, today seeking recognition as a language (as *l'arpitan*; see Bichurina 2016; Meune 2018).

10.3.9 Regionalism, identity, and human rights (1900–2021)

After a quarter century of the Third Republic's intense centralization, the provinces grew ever more restless, creating literary journals, demanding schooling in their regional language, even pushing for separatism (Thiesse 1992). In 1900 the *Groupe régionaliste* was founded to unite the provinces in opposition to Parisian domination.

The definition of linguistic terms inserted itself into the political realm at the end of World War I. The victors imposed minority treaties on the states newly formed from the Austro-Hungarian and Ottoman empires. Among the conditions guaranteed minorities were the free use of the mother tongue and, if the demographics of a region justified it, instruction in the minority language in state schools. The Marquis d'Estourbeillon submitted a petition to Woodrow Wilson and the Peace Conference demanding that France abide by the same terms of minority recognition required of Poland and the other new countries. The French government dismissed the request with the claim that France had no minorities, the standard response to regional movements.

Nonetheless, teaching with regional languages and even schools in regional languages began late in the nineteenth century, such as the efforts for Provençal by

---

[21] In the 1750s the Abbé Claude Carlier proposed a third division, the *langues d'ouen*, for the northeastern varieties. See, for example, Jochnowitz (1973) and Baggioni and Martel (1997).
[22] 'Il ne faut pas excepter de ce jugement [that there are no dialects in France] la division fondamentale qu'on a cru, dès le moyen âge, reconnaître entre le "français" et le "provençal" ou la langue d'oui et la langue d'oc' (Paris 1888: 4).
[23] A term invented by Jules Ronjat in 1913, describing the shape of the region stretching across central France from Angoulême to Vichy (Brun-Tringaud 1992: 24).

Frère Savinien (from 1876) and Picard by Daniel Haigneré. Haigneré sought to establish, in his dictionary and grammar of *le patois boulonnais*, the 'only rational, grammatical and etymological' orthography for the entire Picard region (Fournet 2012: 71). Defining a variety in an official context constrains variation.[24]

After several generations of the *école républicaine*, the French government began to feel less threatened by the acknowledgment of difference. Dauzat (1927) proclaimed that virtually everyone in France knew the national language, though an ever-diminishing number were bilingual in (relatively) standard French and some local variety, whether it be closely related to the standard (e.g. Norman) or completely unrelated (Basque). He defined dialects as 'variétés d'un type linguistique qui s'est morcelé sur un vaste territoire' (Dauzat 1927: 30), and *patois* as the dialect that has forever lost all social value, and now is only oral and only spoken by rural people (Dauzat 1927: 30). The *patois*, even for its speakers, is a mark of shame and ignorance (Dauzat 1927: 31).

The social definition was subject to reversal, to a regeneration of social value, pursued as a right to identity over the course of the twentieth and twenty-first centuries. Regional rural identity became fashionable again under the Vichy régime. The decision of Minister of Public Instruction Jérôme Carcopino to allow the teaching of certain regional languages was part of Maréchal Pétain's celebration of regional cultures and languages (Faure 1989: 200–13). Carcopino foresaw a limited programme, allowing the *dialecte occitan* (not *langue*) to be taught outside of school hours as an optional course, no longer than ninety minutes per week, which would serve 'as a brother to the French language'; militant Félibres imagined a full undergraduate degree programme.

Even in this favourable political climate, fierce opposition came from the national union of schoolteachers. The director of elementary instruction, Adolphe Terracher, himself a dialectologist, wrote to the regional school inspectors expressing his scepticism about whether these *parlers populaires* have the dignity of a literary language ('exception infiniment rare', according to Terracher), or are rather 'le mélange des formes et des vocables de plusieurs localités d'une région ou d'une province géographiquement mal définies et des formes et mots du français commun plus ou moins assimilés' (letter of 13 March 1942).

Under quite different political circumstances, a similar bill, popularly known as the *Loi Deixonne* (1951), allowed the teaching of Basque, Breton, Catalan, and Occitan.[25] The official title of the law describes these as 'langues et dialectes locaux',

---

[24] Michel Bréal was sceptical about teaching local languages, believing that the differences meant that the students were required to learn the *parler local* at the same time as the national language. For the debates between Bréal and Savinien see Boutan (2003). Current efforts for the promotion of Picard take a different approach to standardization (Martin, Rey, and Reynès 2020).

[25] The initial version of the bill (1947) targeted only Breton. A subsequent version (6 February 1949) extended coverage to *provençal*, and in June to *catalan* and *languedocien*. *Provençal* and *languedocien* were then joined under the term *langue d'oc*, at the request of the *député* André Monteil (Finistère), in order to exclude the *patois limousin* (Martel 2016: 131–46; see also Gardin 1975).

thus avoiding the thorny question of status, while the parliamentary discussion also used the term *langues régionales*. At the same time Alsatian, Flemish, and Corsican were excluded as being simply *patois* of national languages (German, Dutch, Italian) taught in their proper form as a school subject.

A circular of 29 March 1976 took into account the diversity of southern Gallo-Romance by referring to *langues d'oc* (plural) and allowing the spelling used in instruction to vary according to local *dialectes*, seemingly referring to the same linguistic variety by two different terms. Groups representing those local variations—*auvergnat, limousin, gascon, provençal*, etc.—have challenged the composite construction of *occitan* (Lafitte and Féraud 2006; Costa 2012), and *Occitanistes* have challenged the plural of *langues d'oïl* (Engelaere 1994).

The protection of regional and minority languages, limited in the minority treaties to newly formed states, was universalized in international human rights through the United Nations Charter (1945), Universal Declaration of Human Rights (1948), and subsequent international covenants. From the Declaration of Galway (1975) these rights were considered in various European contexts, notably by the Council of Europe and the European Parliament (European Union), leading to the European Charter for Regional[26] or Minority Languages (Council of Europe, 1992). While France has never ratified the Charter, the text has inspired much discussion of the terms used to describe varieties of Gallo-Romance, with the major challenge being the status of varieties of the *langue d'oïl* (northern French; McCrea 2019). The Charter explicitly denies protection to 'dialects of the national language', encouraging the reclassification of varieties previously described as 'dialects of French' as 'langues de France'.

Accordingly, the linguist Bernard Cerquiglini (2003) prepared a report recognizing seventy-five *langues de France*. He distinguished carefully the *français régionaux* ('l'infini variété des façons de parler cette langue [le français national et standard]') from the varieties of the *langue d'oïl*—*franc-comtois, wallon, picard, normand, gallo, poitevin-saintongeais, bourguignon-morvandiau*, and *lorrain*. He contrasted the diversity of the *langues d'oïl* from *occitan*, the latter being the sum of all its parts. The *langues d'oïl*, *occitan*, and *francoprovençal-arpitan* were qualified as languages distinct from the national language because their history is as old, or older, than the national standard (Viaut 2020: 52). This history is the *patrimoine*, the heritage of the French nation, consistently invoked as a reason to protect and to teach them in legislation from the Vichy régime through the *Loi Molac* (April 2021).

The political drive to recognize difference is countered by limited consciousness of that difference. Several studies over the past fifty years have evaluated speakers' attachment to, or even awareness of, difference. Châtenet (2000) found

---

[26] Viaut and Pascaud (2017) describe the variety of interpretations for 'regional language' in the European context.

that even in a small village of *la France profonde* (Saône-et-Loire), young people have no knowledge of the morphology and syntax of the regional *patois*, and can identify only a few words from this variety. Natural transmission of local varieties (between generations) is very low (Héran, Filhon, and Deprez 2002). Revitalization efforts have resulted in a situation where there are more 'new speakers' than traditional speakers, sometimes leading to conflict (Bichurina 2016: 234–6).[27] The role of local associations in revitalization has led Léonard and Jaguenneau (2013: 288) to propose another sociolinguistic model to capture their resilience as an archipelago of 'micro-aires' where the vernacular survives as a kind of cultural practice.

At the same time, political considerations both broadened and constricted the definition of that national language, the *langue française*. It was broadened to allow for more variation in spelling and grammatical agreement, through *tolérances officielles*, first in 1901 and then again in 1976: students would not be penalized for using previously proscribed forms. However, it was constricted by the proscription of borrowed terms, almost all from English. The *Loi Bas-Lauriol* (1975) and the *Loi Toubon* (1994) determined that such terms were not French, even if most French speakers used them regularly. In the parliamentary debates over the *Loi Toubon*, an amendment was proposed to define French as 'usage... dans le strict respect de l'orthographe, de la syntaxe et de la grammaire telles qu'elles sont définies par l'Académie Française' (cited in Éloy 1997: 94).

10.4 Conclusions

Linguistic science (before that, grammar) and politics have been interacting through the centuries to define how we should consider variation in language. The scientific definition, however empirical it may attempt to be, inevitably conceals relationships of power and thus has political implications.

Tillinger (2013: 16–17), after reviewing the scientific uses of the terms considered here—*langue, dialecte, idiome, parler, patois*—makes a valiant effort to assign them specific meanings. He would designate three divisions in Gallo-Romance: *les langues d'oïl, les langues d'oc,* and *francoprovençal*. The first two are divided into individual *idiomes*, standard French being one among a number of *idiomes* of the *langues d'oïl*, just as *gascon* is one among a number of *idiomes* of the *langues d'oc*; *francoprovençal-arpitan* would then be a *langue*, with multiple *dialectes*. *Dialectes* would be defined strictly geographically, and could be divided infinitely into sub-dialects, down to the level of the idiolect. However, we have seen the problems in tracing geographic boundaries.

Éloy (2004) has proposed the notion of *langues collatérales*, varieties that are close to the national standard and share much of its history. The problem, as we

---

[27] See also Chapters 16 and 18 (this volume).

saw in the opening paragraphs, is defining when close is too close, or not so close. Quantifying difference in language, and the perception of difference, has its own problems.

The history of the use of the terms to describe varieties of Gallo-Romance speech in France illustrates how completely intertwined the two scientific and political approaches are. The development of orthographic standards in the later Middle Ages, in conjunction with a growing legal and administrative bureaucracy, encouraged recognition of difference. Territorial expansion and the centralization of power replaced the Greek tradition of co-equal dialects with the Roman tradition of a single unifying form, and the subsequent devalorization of difference. The methods of scientific dialectology magnify difference through the choice of informants and localities. The science accompanied the politics: dictionaries, grammars, and commentaries on language defined the standard, and the lack of such scientific production for other varieties consigned them to the class of *dialectes* or *patois*. The creation of those scientific texts for regional varieties required standardization and artificial versions, in which authentic speakers might have trouble recognizing their own speech. Competing visions of what is natural and what is artificial, and the relative value of the two, have led to different scientific perceptions of difference, and different political interpretations of difference. Linguistic difference could mean ignorance and separatism or the authenticity of the *terroir*. Uniformity could mean artificiality or national fervour. Or all of the above. The scientific and political definitions are illusions, and delusions, and reflect the fundamental challenge of conventional language.

11
Elision, the neglected link in French phonology

John N. Green and Marie-Anne Hintze

11.1 Introduction

Among the linking processes in French phonology that promote, and occasionally block, the creation of new CV onsets in continuous speech, elision is the least well investigated (Klausenburger *passim*, reprised 2014). It was not always so. A mere glance at its historiography shows that earlier generations of grammarians were acutely aware of elision as a powerful and constraining force, especially, but not exclusively, in poetics. We claim the continuing relevance of the grammaticological tradition, while challenging the prevalent assumption in modern phonological theory that elision is easily definable, unitary, and categorical in application. Drawing on a corpus of interviews with middle class speakers of standard northern French, we first establish that final-vowel elision remains the most productive driver of rightward resyllabification, and then provide evidence of non-compliance with normative expectations. Analysis of the sites where elision is most likely to fail, and where avoidance seems to be increasing, shows that the intralinguistic conditions on elision are more complex than hitherto acknowledged. We argue that the impetus for its avoidance does not originate in phonology, but rather in discourse structure and conversational management.

11.2 Historical context

Remarqueurs, their successors, and some of their forerunners, have recognized for centuries that there is something odd about French elision. Unlike their modern counterparts, who associate elision with liaison, they perceive an unwanted interaction between elision and *h aspiré*. Their usual aim is to warn foreign learners or speakers of non-standard French (especially those living south of the Loire) against eliding vowels that used to be separated by an audible [h-] but are now shielded only by its ghost. The term '*h aspiré*', to which we return briefly in Section 11.5, is a poor choice—the likely consequence of starting out from spelling rather than pronunciation.

One of the first to observe a specific link between elision of a final vowel, and *enchaînement* leading to a new CV syllable, is Robert Estienne (1972 [1557]: 10), whose section 'De l'apostrophe' notes: 'A, E, & I, souuent ne sescriuent point, principalement E ... Et cela [emploi de l'apostrophe] ce faict a fin qu'on ne pronõce la lettre ostee, & que tellemẽt les deux mots soyent ioincts en vng, qu'il n'y ait qu'vne pronontiation de deux'. De Bèze (1584: 82) is keen to stress that the process is obligatory: 'Omne *e* fœmininum sequente quacunque vocali, eliditur in pronuntiatione, ut *l'auaricieux, l'espee, l'ingrat, l'ouvrier*, & sequente *h* quiescente *l'homme: l'huis*: ... Magnum igitur vitium est istam elisionem non observare ...'.[1] Not to do so would result in hiatus, the vowel-to-vowel link to which classical poetics was so averse.[2] The notorious prohibition attributed to Malherbe and echoed by Boileau (1961 [1674]: 162): 'Gardez qu'une voyelle à courir trop hâtée/Ne soit d'une voyelle en son chemin heurtée' in fact has long antecedents. Over a century earlier, Ronsard's (1585) *Art poétique* had expressed the same caution: 'Tu euiteras autant que la contraincte de ton vers le permettra, les rencontres des voyelles & diftongues, qui ne ſe mangent point'.[3] More than one literary critic has been embarrassed to note that Boileau's couplet fails to obey its own maxim, though the authors of the *Grand Larousse* article on 'Hiatus' (Guilbert, Lagane, and Niobey 1972: 2424) believe that his choice was deliberate and playful, and that the real prohibition was against identical vowels in sequence—a tenet that continues to be invoked today.[4] Whatever the motivation in the classical period, its consequence was to press into service any intervening consonant that would break up the hiatus, including those not always articulated in pre-consonantal environments, or to suppress one of the vowels by means of elision. Of these, elision was seen as the more important.

Even so, the term itself is seldom defined and its exact reference seems to vary from author to author. In both traditional and theoretical accounts, a bewildering array of terms is used to describe the process: aphaeresis, (vowel) loss, schwa-deletion, (vowel) suppression, synalepha, truncation, *amuïssement, effacement*, and even *écrasement* (Bruneau 1931: 67). More picturesquely, Ronsard had said that the vowel 'ſe mange' (1585: 36). These terms cannot all be exact synonyms. We return to their overlaps in Section 11.5. In the meantime, we need a working

---

[1] 'Any *e* followed by a feminine word [starting with] any vowel, is elided in pronunciation, as in *l'auaricieux, l'espee, l'ingrat, l'ouvrier*, & when followed by a silent *h l'homme: l'huis*: ... It is a great mistake not to observe this elision.'

[2] We return below (Section 11.5) to the definition and use of this term.

[3] Originally published 1565; cited from the reprint. Ronsard's injunction is endorsed by Vaugelas, who describes hiatus as 'cacophonie' (1647: 351–3; see also Ayres-Bennett 2018a: 132–3, *Remarque* 190). Nearly a century later attitudes to hiatus in prose have softened, but not in poetry: Dangeau (1754: 25) condemns the juxtaposition as dysphonic, and De Choisy emphasizes its total prohibition: 'La Poësie ne souffre point la rencontre des voyelles, quand elles font ce qu'on appelle un *hiatus*. On ne peut mettre en Vers, *il a été*' (1754: 261).

[4] An anonymous referee points out that the 'forbidden' sequences are carefully placed at the hemistitch, which attenuates their impact.

definition for our data analysis. For this purpose, we distil the essence of the grammaticological tradition and focus on the loss of a single final vowel that would have been pronounced in the citation form of the word, as in *puisqu'elle* /pɥi.sk+ɛl/ vs. the dictionary lemma *puisque* /pɥi.skə/.

11.3 Corpus design and methodological decisions

The data presented here derive from a corpus that we assembled in the 1980s based on interviews conducted by Marie-Anne Hintze with educated speakers of standard northern French, mostly from the Lille region, including a group from a single extended family. To achieve a better balance of age and gender, three further texts were added from broadcast interviews with prominent public figures. Two of the family members, who were schoolchildren at the time of the first interview, consented to a follow-up over eleven years later, so allowing us to build in a small longitudinal dimension. Our subjects are briefly profiled in Table 11.1, with their ages and occupations at the time of the interview. All may be described as middle class. The family members are given fictitious names and all other interviewees have been anonymized, including the public figures, so as not to give them undue prominence.

Table 11.1 List of interviewees

Sub-corpus and interviewee	Code	Age	Occupation		
1 Family group				**Generation**	**Relationship**
Albert	A	63	Appeals judge	First	Parents/ grandparents
Jeanne	J	58	Mother, charity worker		
Luc	L	35	Magistrate	Intermediate	Son
Sara	S	38	Teacher		Daughter
Urbain	U	22	Student	Second	Son
Xavière	X	29	Osteopath, movement therapist		Daughter
Zoé (first interview)	Z1	11	Schoolchild		
Katya (first interview)	K1	10	Schoolchild	Third	Daughters of Sara
Zoé (second interview)	Z2	23	Teacher		
Katya (second interview)	K2	22	Research student		
2 General corpus				**Interview type**	
Monsieur C	C	≈ 45	Civil servant	Personal	
Monsieur D	D	60	City mayor	Personal	

Sub-corpus and interviewee	Code	Age	Occupation	
2 General corpus				**Interview type**
Monsieur G	G	40	Manager, French national rail service	Personal
Monsieur H	H	38	Workplace doctor	Personal
Madame M	M	35	Geriatrician	Personal
Monsieur V	V	≈ 45	Journalist, newspaper manager	Personal
Monsieur Y	Y	≈ 33	Manager, French national rail service	Personal
Madame Q	Q	57	Politician	Public television broadcast
Monsieur R	R	65	Physician, president of the national council	Public radio broadcast
Madame W	W	58	Politician	Public television broadcast

Note: For the speakers not known personally to the interviewer, age was estimated on appearance and seniority.

Our transcriptions are impressionistic, the outcome of numerous listenings by the authors, separately and together. The methodology is predicated on recording features of authentic connected discourse that are often edited out, notably intakes of breath, pauses, hesitations, fillers, and glottal onsets. Our basic unit of transcription is the rhythm group, which we define as a perceptible disturbance to the contour of delivery.[5] It is not necessarily coterminous with the breath group, and certainly not equivalent to the syntactic constituent. Taken together, these methodological decisions alter very significantly the sites in which linking can take place and the relative frequency of the links actually performed.

The primary transcriptions are based on traditional orthography, supplemented by our notational conventions but not modified for non-normative pronunciations. We can therefore take the apostrophe as a rough guide to the location and prevalence of elision. Doing so entails a decision on compound forms that once had a regular internal elision but now seem to function as unanalysed wholes. Basing our judgements on distributional and semantic criteria, we exclude from the statistics eleven forms that we believe have been lexicalized. Those incorporating a bound morph that no longer has independent meaning can

---

[5] Our method is described in more detail in Green and Hintze (2001), together with sample transcriptions. We use the following notational conventions: | rhythm boundary; ˃ intake of breath; (.) short silent pause; ... lengthening of an existing sound; _ consonantal link, with the realization specified if ambiguous.

be safely excluded: *aujourd'hui* (21 tokens), *d'emblée* (1), and *prud'homme* (1). Distributional criteria can be invoked for: *d'abord* (20), *d'ailleurs* (51), *d'après* (1), *d'autant* (6), *d'habitude* (1), and *n'importe* (8), since their second elements have quite different meanings when used independently. For *d'accord*, we differentiate between the full predicate *être d'accord (avec)* of which we retain three tokens as elisions, and the lexicalized filler, which is used only sparingly by our speakers. The final exclusion is the set phrase *n'est-ce pas* (6), perhaps more controversial because of its transparent compositionality in traditional orthography. In all, these decisions remove 119 tokens from the data set, 14 of /n/ and 105 of /d/.

Though most of the excluded forms are sparsely attested in the corpus, *d'ailleurs* and *aujourd'hui* are much more frequent, and together account for 60.5% of the total. Rather surprisingly, the instances of *aujourd'hui* are confined to the general corpus; no family member seems to need the word.[6] By contrast, *d'ailleurs* is widely distributed: only Monsieur H and Madame M from the general corpus and Sara from the family fail to use it. We emphasize that the exclusion is on semantic grounds: the meaning of the locative adverb *ailleurs* is quite different from that of the discourse marker. The exclusion of *n'est-ce pas* also merits a further comment. Once common as a discourse marker for seeking assent or signalling a conversational turn, it declined sharply in popularity in the later twentieth century. In our corpus, it has very low frequency and range, uttered by only three speakers (Messieurs D, R, and Luc), all male and two elderly.[7] There is an alternative readily available in *hein*, which garners 277 tokens and is used by all but three speakers (R, V, and W), none of them in the younger cohort.

Our conventions treat initial glides as consonantal, so that *oui* is transcribed /wi/ and therefore does not constitute a potential site for linking. We are fortunate to have no tokens of the controversial *ouate*, but if we had, we should expect *la ouate* without elision (see Sten 1952). Likewise, the few instances of initial <y> are treated as consonantal /j-/, as in *le yaourt, de York*—*pacē* Grevisse and Goosse (1986: 69), who explicitly commend *d'York*.

11.4 Analysis

11.4.1 Sources of links and their orthographic representations

That French speakers prefer open CV syllables and maximize their occurrence in continuous speech has become a commonplace.[8] It leads to an easy assumption

---

[6] It is worth noting that speakers in the general corpus use *aujourd'hui* to refer generally to the modern era, so that it would translate as 'nowadays' rather than literally 'today'.

[7] It is likely that Luc intended to produce one more token, since there is a faint, breathy [spa] at the end of one speech, but there is nothing audible before it in the rhythm group, so no elision. The low usage of *n'est-ce pas* is corroborated by Coveney (1996: 242–3). We hypothesize that lexicalization did not help it compete with *hein*.

[8] Fouché (1959: xliv–v); Delattre (1966); Encrevé (1988: 23–8); Carton (2001: 12).

within phonology that elision, liaison, and *enchaînement* work together to increase the frequency of consonantal onsets. Though links from all three sources could justifiably be called *enchaînements*, the conventional labels limit classic *enchaînements* to those made with fixed final consonants onto lexemes starting with a vowel or purely orthographic <h>, as in *usine à gaz* [y.zi.na.gaz] and *la même heure* [la.mɛ.mœʁ]. The relative contributions of these processes are seldom made explicit.

Our transcription system and methodological principles systematically record fillers and intrusive hesitations that have vocalic onsets and provide new sites for linking. Accordingly, we have an additional source to supplement the time-honoured trio. The new category includes numerous tokens of fixed final <-r> resyllabified onto an intrusive hesitation, as in *pour__euh(...)* [pu.ʁø(ː) ~ pu.ʁœ(ː)] and some less common instances like the extra link with /ʒ/ made by Urbain in | avec la notion de mariage__hein? | [ma.↓ʁʲa.↑ʒɛ̃]. The sources for all the rightward consonantal links identified in the corpus are quantified in Figure 11.1. As can be readily seen from the bar chart, elision, at just over 40%, is the greatest contributor to forward resyllabification, outdoing liaison by more than ten percentage points. Our new category of fillers provides almost 9% across the full corpus, so this source is far from negligible. We have found no clear recognition in the literature of the predominance of elision and no acknowledgement whatsoever of the contribution of *pauses sonores* or fillers.[9]

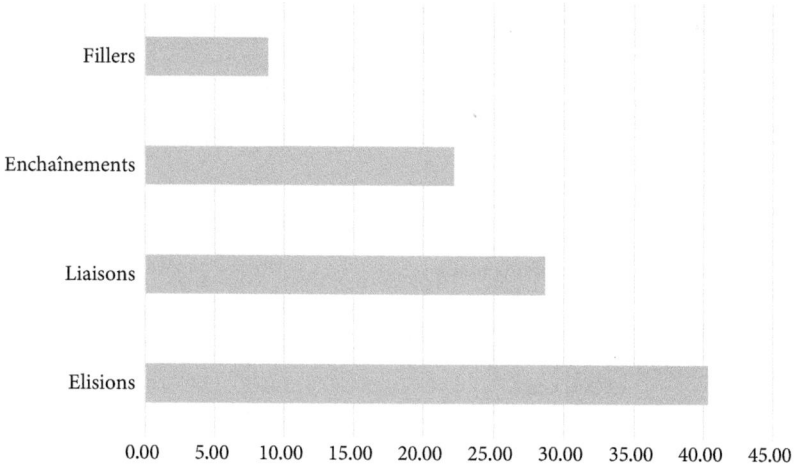

Figure 11.1 Contributors to rightward resyllabification

---

[9] We recognize the different grammatical status of intrusive hesitations like *euh*, which have discourse functions but no meaning, and *hein*, which has both discourse functions and meaning as a question tag. For present purposes, we aggregate them as fillers because they both create new sites and are both liable to be edited out of transcribed speech.

By contrast, there is widespread recognition and discussion of the role of so-called '*h aspiré*' in blocking consonantal links (see, among many, Encrevé 1988: 196–203). This is fully corroborated in our data and can be illustrated by utterances of family member Sara and her two daughters:

(1) S: | parce que | le hasard | fait bien les choses |
    K2: | j'ai envie d'étudier | le rôle de | la Hongrie | dans les relations internationales |
    Z1: | avait | (.) un haut | blanc | avec des | des ronds rouges |

While we have no exceptions to the norm, it is important to keep a sense of proportion. Tokens of *h aspiré* are not frequent in our corpus. Six speakers manage an interview of up to an hour without producing any (Messieurs G, H, V, Y, Albert, Urbain, all male). Overall, expectation is around one occurrence every eleven minutes.[10] It contrasts starkly with expectations for liaison at roughly one per seven seconds, elision at one per five, and any kind of consonantal link, at one per two seconds.

Turning now to elisions, the raw occurrences per consonantal link for the general and family corpora are given in Table 11.2.

Table 11.2 Raw occurrences of elision

	General	Family
Raw data by phonology		
/s/ from total of <ç, c', s'>	543	456
/l/ from <l'> (sum of *le* and *la*)	487	254
/d/ from <d'>	331	217
/k/ from <qu'>	254	216
/ʒ/ from <j'>	83	204
/n/ from <n'>	116	55
/m/ from <m'>	20	34
/t/ from <t'>	0	2
Total elisions made	**1834**	**1438**
Raw data by orthography		
<ç'> = <ça>	2	1
<c'> = <ce>	443	402
<s'> = <si>	20	7
<s'> = <se>	78	46
<l'> = <la>	226	140
<l'> = <le>	261	114
<t'> = <tu>	0	0
<t'> = <te>	0	2

[10] There are more tokens in the extraneous parts of the interviews, slightly reducing the interval between expected occurrences. For a detailed account of the distribution and operation of *h aspiré* in this corpus, see Green and Hintze (2004).

The lower section illustrates the extent of syncretism within standard orthography: there is no one-to-one match between sound and representation. While the apostrophe remains quite a good guide to the location of links, spelling acts to obscure the contribution of /s/ and /l/ to the total. The most frequent links in both groups are made with /s, l, d, k/, contributing 88.06% and 79.49% to the respective totals. The salient differences are in the relative frequencies of /ʒ/ and /n/, most probably caused by topic of conversation and informality of register, since family members made great use of *je* when discussing their professions and opinions, and were more inclined to omit preverbal negative markers. The high frequency of /s/ and /l/ is due to a very small number of types: determiners and pronouns for /l/ and, for /s/, the phrases *c'est* and *c'était*. Of these, present-tense *c'est* bears responsibility for 413 tokens in the general corpus and 492 in the family, far outnumbering tokens of the imperfect, with thirty-one and seventy-two respectively.[11]

11.4.2 Categorical elision

For convenience of exposition, we begin with the forms for which elision before an adjacent vowel onset is generally believed to be categorical and for which our corpus offers no contradictory evidence. They comprise the monosyllabic pronouns and determiners ending in schwa (*je, me, te, se, ce, le*), the feminine determiner and object pronoun *la*, the partitive and preposition *de*, and the negative particle *ne*. A similar statement can be found in many traditional and more modern atheoretic descriptions (for instance Grevisse and Goosse 1986: 53; Valdman 1993: 191) and is not regarded as controversial. It does, however, mix phonological and grammatical criteria and this could blur the determining factors when elision is less predictable. Table 11.3 summarizes the distribution of these particles across all interviews, together with the ratio of full and elided shapes.

For all nine morphemes, elision can be regarded as categorical: we find neither failures to elide in valid sites nor false elisions. A few further comments are needed. *Te* is infrequent and, unsurprisingly, only attested within the family group; its elided allomorph overlaps with that of *tu*, to which we return later in the section. As a graphy, <s'> has a small area of overlap with <s'> from *si* but can usually be identified without difficulty. *Ce* is the only item in the table to have more elided than full tokens, a predictable consequence of the prevalence of *c'est*. The graphy <l'> represents a large category with 813 tokens, deemed to split almost equally into 409 feminine and 404 masculine, though with wide variations among speakers depending on the topic of conversation (for instance, *l'instruction* is used ten times by Albert and *l'école* fifteen times by Sara); for each gender, the determiner is far more frequent than the object pronoun. We do not attempt to draw distinctions within *de*, though it is clearly polysemous. There is one instance of unelided *de*

---

[11] The total of seventy-two includes two false starts. With a single token in the entire corpus, the plural *c'étaient* is vanishingly rare.

Table 11.3 Raw occurrences of elidable particles

	General	Family	Total	Ratio
je	314	410	724	
j'	83	301	384	
All {je}	397	711	1108	1.89 : 1
me	25	101	126	
m'	20	58	78	
All {me}	45	159	204	1.62 : 1
te		16	16	
t' = <te>		4	4	
All {te}	0	20	20	4.00 : 1
se	120	106	226	
s' = <se>	78	60	138	
All {se}	198	166	364	1.64 : 1
ce	279	241	520	
c' = <ce>	443	566	1009	
All {ce}	722	807	1529	0.52 : 1
le	562	508	1070	
l' = <le>	261	143	404	
All {le}	823	651	1474	2.65 : 1
de	1204	963	2167	
d'	331	271	602	
All {de}	1535	1234	2769	3.60 : 1
ne	150	95	245	
n'	116	87	203	
All {ne}	266	182	448	1.21 : 1
la	590	540	1130	
l' = <la>	226	183	409	
All {la}	816	723	1539	2.76 : 1

before *h aspiré* (Monsieur C: *de Hainault* [də͡ɛ.no]), and one before a glide (Zoé2: *de York* [də.jɔʁk]). Otherwise, the single token of *de* not eliding before a vowel (Monsieur Y: | de a | d'avoir |) can be dismissed as a false start.[12] Nor is there anything unusual in the phonological behaviour of *ne*, though its use is notably lower among family members, almost certainly attributable to the informality of the discourse.

Among the occurrences of *l'* is a subset of thirty-five tokens of *l'on*, spread over ten speakers (Madame Q, Messieurs C, D, H, R, V, and Albert, Luc, Urbain, and

---

[12] In the statistics, no special status is accorded to proper names or toponyms. The total for *de* includes eight tokens of *(Nord-)Pas-de-Calais*, four each in Messieurs C and V.

Xavière in the family group). This is not a rare form nor—perhaps surprisingly—one confined to older speakers or higher registers. Of the total, twenty-seven are in the sequence *que l'on*. At 77.14% of potential sites, this is much higher than random expectation, raising the intriguing question of whether some speakers may be avoiding a taboo form, or at least using a set phrase that might once have been an avoidance strategy for /kɔ̃/. Yet, with 161 tokens across the corpus, *qu'on* is by no means rare, and every speaker has at least one instance, so the choice of *que l'on* is not even categorical for any one individual, though Monsieur R (an older male) has a heavy preponderance. We have been unable to find any clear pattern in the data: the distribution appears to be unconditioned.

11.4.3 Minor exceptions

The next set of forms to be considered shows evidence of minor variability, or of uncertain grammatical status, or both. Table 11.4 records the raw data for both subcorpora. Unfortunately, the critical tokens are too few to support any secondary calculations.

Table 11.4 Forms exhibiting minor variability or uncertain grammatical status

	General	Family	Total
tu	2	61	63
t' = \<tu\>	0	5	5
All {tu}	2	66	68
si	114	109	223
s' = \<si\>	20	7	27
All {si}	134	116	250
cela	17	3	20
ça	170	323	493
ç'	2	1	3
All {cela}	189	327	516
c'est-à-dire	12	10	22
c'est__un(e)	4	4	8
All /st/ + *c'est_*	16	14	30

As noted under *te* (Table 11.3; see also Section 11.5), second person singular pronouns are much less frequent in the corpus than first person and confined to family interactions. Of the sixty-eight tokens of *tu*, thirty-three occur in Katya's first interview. Only three of these are deemed to be direct address forms; the others are rather fillers or reassurance markers, with twenty-two instances of *tu vois*, eight of *tu sais*. The elision of *tu* to *t'* is rare, commanding only five tokens. Its interest lies in the grammatical syncretism between second person subject and object clitics in prevocalic position. The categories themselves are not merging, but share an allomorph and allograph, just as *le* and *la* share <l'>. The elision of *tu* to *t'* is only attested in the informal second interview with Zoé. The occurrences fall within two connected passages that are worth quoting in full:

(2) Z2: | (.) euh si t'avais envie d'y aller... | eh bien t'y allais | et là c'était | ça te servait à quelque chose | mais si t'avais pas envie d'y aller |
Z2: | en France__euh | t'as... | un__élève__euh... | (.) euh insolent | (.) euh... | bon ben euh | il prend ses__affaires | et il sort | (.) et puis | tu | tu t'arranges | pour le faire conduire par le délégué euh | jusqu'en permanence | où t'as un surveillant ou | (.) bon. |

These are not address forms but generalizations. She is contrasting the mechanisms available in French and British schools for dealing with unruly pupils and is using *tu* in the same way as a generic *vous* or *on*. Among the other tokens of *tu*, only three offer comparable prevocalic sites, none of which shows elision:

(3) U: | Non bien sûr | mais tu as raison | (.)
U: | tu imagines des... | (.) des gens |
Z2: | autant que tu ailles__en permanence | [aĩ.jã]

Only the first of Urbain's statements is a direct address; both the other attestations are generic. All three seem to be potential sites, as they are phonologically identical to those used by Zoé in the earlier examples. It is clearly rash to draw inferences from such tiny numbers, especially when the only four tokens of *t'* from object pronoun *te* come from the same two family members. Even so, our data imply that the elision of *tu* in prevocalic position is variable, possibly determined by register.

The elision of *si* to *s'* before an identical /i/ vowel (hence, effectively limited to *si* followed by *il*, *ils*, and possibly *y*) is accepted as categorical by most traditional grammars and orthoepic texts (see, among many, Gaiffe et al. 1936: 45; Grevisse 1980: 78). There are twenty-seven tokens of normative elision scattered through the corpus, most of them entirely humdrum, like *s'il s'agit*, *s'il y a*, *s'il y avait* (a dozen instances in all, including near equivalents). Conversely, no elision is made in five <si il> sites, or in a further one represented as <si y> in the orthography but phonologically identical, as in:

(4) G: | (.) et si il y a | des__intempéries |
H: | pour dire si il__est apte | ou non |
H: | et si il__y avait un__accident | s'il__était tué |
A: | Si il le fait pas | si il passe__outre |
U: | savoir si y avait des possibilités |

Some of these sites may be mildly contrastive, but none has been marked out as specially emphatic, and none shows lengthening of /si/. The four speakers involved are all male, but otherwise cut across ages, professions, and family ties. On this evidence, elision in /si+i/ cannot be considered categorical. If treated (with all due caution) as a variable, its realization rate would be 27/33, or 81.82%. The definition of a valid site, however, is grammatical rather than purely phonological. Phonological adjacency is essential, but the *si* can only be the conjunction that introduces the protasis of a conditional utterance. The *si* used as a strong affirmative probably excludes elision because the context implies contrastive emphasis. Elision is absolutely impossible when *si* is an intensifying adverb: **il est s'inédit que*, **il est s'hypocrite que*. Dauzat (1950: 55) and Grevisse (1980: 78) both notice this constraint (choosing the bizarre example **s'adroit*, with non-identical vowels), but their observation has fallen by the wayside.

Ça is a frequent item in our corpus, attested for every speaker. Its full form *cela* is comparatively uncommon, and the elided version *ç'*, vanishingly rare. No robust conclusions can be based on a mere three tokens, all somewhat problematic, reproduced as (5):

(5) W: | eh bien | ç'aurait été | très difficile de la faire maintenant |
    W: | car je crois | que ç'aurait été | (.) une campagne | extrêmement dure |
    S: | (.) Bon | ç'a été fait. |

The <ç'> in these tokens could represent either *ce* or *ça*. Though the two forms often overlap, they are not identical in distribution or meaning. In formal registers, *ce* (or *ç'*) can be used with all tense-forms of the verb *être*, including those conjugated with the auxiliary *avoir* (as in *c'est, c'était, ce sera, ce serait, ce fut, ç'avait été*, even *c'eut été*). In less formal contexts, *ça* can be substituted, though generally not in the present or imperfect. So, Sara could have said *ça a été fait* or *cela a été fait*, whereas Madame W could not have said **ça aurait été très difficile de la faire maintenant* (or **cela...*) because the reprise clitic *la* in the dependent clause is not compatible with either *ça* or *cela* as its antecedent.

Despite the tiny numbers, the precise status of <ç'> matters because grammarians and theoretical linguists have taken diametrically opposing positions on the elidability of /a/ (see Section 11.5). For the moment, the phonological implications of treating <ç'> as a potential reflex of *ça* are unclear. Elision is certainly not categorical, or even normal: we find thirty-five tokens of unelided *ça* + vowel, the most frequent being *ça a* /saa̯/, *ça allait* /saa̯/, and *ça (y) est* /saɛ̯ ~ saʲɛ/ (with respectively fifteen, four, and three occurrences). We deem most of the tokens (25/35) to be sentential subjects, which might indicate a grammatical motivation, but the others (including two more tokens of /saa̯/ that are not subjects) occur in sundry contexts, with no obvious phonological constraints or grammatical correlates.

A different issue of grammatical status is raised by the normative elision of *ce* combined with another adjustment, the loss of the [e ~ ɛ] vowel of *est* (which we symbolize by <`>). This reduction is only attested in the phrases *c'est-à-dire* and *c'est un ~ c'est une*, those with *c'est-à-dire* being almost three times as common. Typical examples are given in set (6):

(6) C: | C'est__une__assemblée | [sty.na]
   D: | et c'est__un suffrage__au second degré | [e.stœ̃]
   M: | (.) c'est__à-dire sont... | (.) ce sont des studios | [sta.diʁ]
   Y: | [...] l'infrastructure | c'est__à-dire que nous | nous payons | [sta.diʁ]
   K2: | c'est__à-dire que l'histoire | en soi | (.) m'intéresse | [sta.diʁ]
   L: | un délit | c'est__une__atteinte__à... | l'intégrité physique. | [sty.na.tɛ̃t]
   S: | c'est__à-dire | le catéchisme | (.) [sta.diʁ]
   U: | (.) c'est__un défaut de concentration que j'ai | [stɛ̃.de.fo]

In all, there are thirty tokens in the corpus, spread over ten speakers, divided fairly evenly between family and non-family. Whether this vowel loss should be treated as elision is a moot point. It fits better with what Valdman (1993: 191–2) terms *effacement*, an optional reduction in colloquial speech that is not enshrined in standard orthography. That would be consistent with other tokens produced at rapid tempo when *c'est-à-dire* is further reduced to [saˈdiʁ] and *est* is wholly eliminated. If, contrariwise, the instances were accepted as double elisions, the constraints would be complex. Note that all the tokens involve a /t/ liaison, regarded by all normative accounts as obligatory—albeit, in the case of *c'est-à-dire*, embedded in a set phrase, which most analysts treat as a separate subcategory.[13]

11.4.4 *que* and its compounds

We now come to sites involving *que* and its compounds *alors que, bien que, jusque, lorsque, parce que, puisque, quelque, quoique*. The aggregate of 1,666 tokens makes this series the single most frequent in the corpus, used by all speakers and spread fairly evenly between the general and family groups. *Parce que* takes a comfortable lead, followed by *puisque, quelque*, and *jusque*; the only apparent rarity, with a single token, is *quoique*. The incidences of full and regularly elided forms for all the relevant lexemes are summarized in Table 11.5.

Table 11.5 Tokens of *que* and its compounds

	General	Family	Total
alors que	3	13	16
alors qu'	3	1	4
bien que	5	3	8
bien qu'	3	2	5
jusque	4	1	5
jusqu'	9	21	30

---

[13] The term *forme figée*, exemplified by *tout à coup* [tu.ta.ku] is due to Delattre (1966: 43), and later adopted by Encrevé (1988: 47). Fouché's much more detailed analysis (1959: 469–77) unpacks these

	General	Family	Total
lorsque	10	0	10
lorsqu'	7	2	9
parce que	83	95	178
parce qu'	15	17	32
puisque	19	17	36
puisqu'	7	8	15
quelque	18	18	36
quelqu'	4	6	10
quoique	0	1	1
quoiqu'	0	0	0
Other *que*	473	378	851
Other *qu'*	206	214	420
All *que*	615	526	1141
All *qu'*	254	271	525
Total {que}	869	797	1666
Of which:			
qu'il(s)	104	66	170
qu'elle(s)	24	25	49
qu'on	69	92	161
qu'un(e)	10	19	29
qu' + otherV	47	67	114

The lower part of the table gives a breakdown of the most frequent environments for normative elision, showing that 409 of the 525 tokens, or 77.90%, are attributable to just four types and their minor variants, namely: *(-)qu'il(s)*, *(-)qu'elle(s)*, *(-)qu'on*, *(-)qu'un(e)*. Of these, we have already discussed *qu'on* in a different context. In order to form an impression of the wider productivity of elision, other sites were examined for potential patterns. A representative sample is reproduced as set (7):

(7) G: | parce qu'en général | il fait appel |
M: | de travailler à l'hôpital__euh | (.) en tant qu'étudiante |
Q: | (.) c'est ce le terme | qu'emploient les techniciens |
V: | (..) par__un | pourcentage | presqu'aussi léger |
A: | C'est__un peu | le même principe qu'en__Angleterre |
S: | c'est maintenant | (.) et qu'après | ça ne sera plus possible. |
U: | (..) qui vont jusqu'à ne pas se donner la main |
Z2: | je me suis rendu compte | qu'effectivement euh... |

Although, in principle, elision can operate in any phonological environment, it seems to cluster before /a, o, ã/ from *à*, *au*, and *en*, respectively. Zoé's

---

tokens into their component parts; he refers to *locutions*, but does not group instances into a discrete category.

qu'effectivement and the inverted *que*+Verb+Subject relative clause uttered by Madame Q constitute rarer types.

Against these, our methodology identifies up to 184 instances where a potential elision is not made. We qualify the statement because the total will vary according to the strictness of the definition of legitimate sites. In other words, we need a more nuanced view of sites than has hitherto been necessary. Incontrovertible sites are those in which the elidable vowel occurs adjacent to a vocalic onset within the same rhythm group. These are not very frequent, but thirty-six indisputable tokens are scattered throughout the corpus, predominantly in the family group. They are also well attested in otherwise unused portions of the interviews.[14] We cite set (8) in illustration:

(8) C: | parce que autrefois il__existait | euh | des__instances régionales | [paʁ.skə̃o.tʁə]
    D: | c'est__à-dire | que il__y a un gouvernement | [kə̃i.li.jɑ̃œ̃]
    G: | parce que alors | si j'ai une gare TGV | (.) [pa.skə̃a.lɔʁ]
    Q: | aux postes les plus__importants | que elles__auraient certainement remplis | [kə̃ɛ.lɔ.ʁɛ]
    Q: | euh | parce que elle se positionne | en vue des échéances électorales | [pa.skə̃ɛl]
    Q: | je considérais | que il y aurait un changement | [kə̃iʲɔ.ʁɛ]
    A: | c'est très__important | parce que un__avocat au conseil | [kə̃œ̃.na]
    A: | (.) euh | que on peut | euh mettre__à | rendre la justice | [kə̃ɔ̃.pø̞ː][15]
    K1: | il faut que on | on__ait de la patience | [i.fo.kə̃ɔ̃]
    K2: | bon | encore que en… | (.) si on__est prof d'histoire__en prépa euh | [kə̃ɑ̰̃ː]
    L: | puisque il s'agit de fermetures | d'entreprises par__exemple | [pɥi.skə̃il.sa.ʒi]
    L: | puisque il__est bien connu | que la justice ne peut résider en France | [pɥi.skə̃i.lɛ]
    S: | il s'est__avéré | que il__y avait des clivages | [kø̃iʲa.vɛ]
    S: | et il__est_ | incontestable | que on faisait attention | à mes enfants | [kø̃ɔ̃.fə.zɛ̃a]

The largest group of sites, with a total of 106 tokens and a clear preponderance in the general corpus, is made up of those that cross a rhythm boundary. For these, our impressionistic transcriptions (which were completed before the analysis of elisions began) quite often indicate a vowel-to-vowel link (*enchaînement vocalique*) over the boundary symbol. The instances in set (9) are representative:

---

[14] We draw on this source for illustrative purposes only. They are not included in the statistics.
[15] Some of our speakers make frequent use of creaky voice (transcribed with subscript tilde) before a pause, to signal their wish to retain the conversational turn. It seldom interacts with elision.

(9) D: | eh bien que | elles__arrêtent de se plaindre |
    D: | (.) parce que | il ne pensait plus |
    G: | (.) qui font que | à un moment donné |
    G: | ont fait que | aujourd'hui | le camion est capable de |
    H: | c'est__à-dire que | il__existe | je suppose__en__Angleterre |
    H: | parce que | encore__une fois |
    Q: | (.) Euh je crois que | on__a tort | de s'attarder |
    Q: | je crois que | effectivement il faut revenir là-dessus |
    Q: | parce que | ils__ont été marginalisés par le chômage |
    R: | euh lorsque | il__y a eu au départ |
    R: | parce que | une__action | est | techniquement possible |
    W: | écoutez | je crois que il y a | euh | un consensus | (.) euh |
    Y: | c'est que | on__a un certain nombre de | tarifs |
    A: | vous voyez que | un pourvoi en cassation |
    J: | parce que | au début | on disait | oui |
    J: | (.) alors que | on se rend compte | que statis | statis |
    S: | et que | attendre l'aide de la municipalité |
    Z2: | c'est que | on s'en rend absolument pas compte_ | _euh |
    Z2: | c'est que | on__était tous | un petit peu dispersés euh |

The corpus also attests sites where there is a greater separation between the elidable vowel and its trigger, usually caused by a silent pause after the rhythm boundary, as in set (10):

(10) Q: vous__observez que | (.) en France
    W: | (.) je trouve que | (.) on comprend très bien |
    A: | Il__est certain que | (.) à partir du moment...
    J: | (.) parce que | (.) y avait une petite__opposition...
    S: | que | (.) elle__a fini par se tailler |
    U: | étant donné que | (.) on__a souvent l'occasion...
    Z2: | qui fait que | (.) on parle de cette façon-là |
    Z2: | et c'est vrai que... | (.) en bonne Française je |

In a further subgroup (11), there is also an intrusive hestitation:

(11) G: | (.) euh | parce que | (.) euh... | on__observe vraiment... |
    Q: | (.) il ne faut pas que | (.) euh y ait une surenchère là-dessus |
    W: | parce que | (.) euh... | il__y a eu | beaucoup de recherches |

Table 11.6 summarizes the raw data for the unelided tokens, grouped according to their discoursal context. Comparison with Table 11.5 shows a substantial overlap of sites: those where elision is most likely to be performed are the same as those where it is most likely to fail. In all of them, the trigger vowel belongs to a personal pronoun or determiner.

Table 11.6 Distribution of unelided tokens

	General	Family	Total
que il(s)	3	3	6
que elle(s)	0	1	1
que on	0	3	3
que un(e)	0	1	1
que + otherV	2	8	10
que euh	2	13	15
All *que* +V	7	29	36
que	*il(s)*	17	6	23
que	*elle(s)*	2	2	4
que	*on*	9	12	21
que	*un(e)*	3	1	4
que	otherV	14	14	28
que	*euh*	21	5	26
All *que*	V	66	40	106
que	(.) V	15	11	26
que	(.) *euh*	11	5	16
All *que*	(.) V	26	16	42

The percentage realization rates are given in Figure 11.2. Though the overall realization rate for elision remains high, and compliance obviously improves in line with the strictest definition of a site, it nevertheless falls short of 100% in every subgroup. This is not categorical. Moreover, non-elision is barely skewed across the subcorpora: family members are more willing to avoid elision where the vowels are immediately adjacent (which could be an effect of informality and register), but the overall scores are very similar.

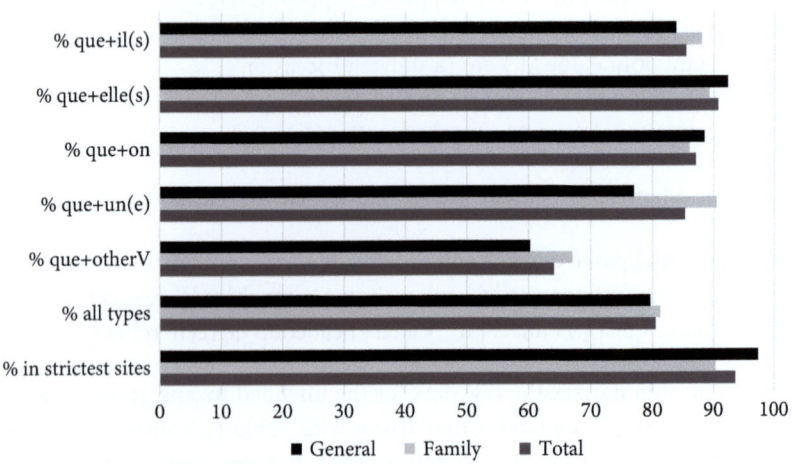

Figure 11.2 Percentage realization rates of elision by site

The hierarchy of sites presented so far does not exhaust the possibilities. In a few of the instances already cited and in others by no means uncommon both within and outside the corpus, the speaker launches the first lexeme of the new rhythm group with a glottal onset. Despite the pioneering work of Malécot (1975), the presence of glottals in French speech is not widely acknowledged, even less integrated into phonological accounts. The northern French version of a glottal onset may be less prominent than its German counterpart, but it certainly exists. There are hundreds of tokens in our transcriptions, in similar distributions to those reported by Malécot. What is surprising is that speakers are using a non-vocalic element as a further block to elision in what would otherwise be a valid site. Set (12) reproduces a few examples from many:

(12) D: | (.) C'est__ainsi que… | [ʔ]un certain nombre de lois |
G: c'est__à-dire que | (.) [ʔ]une ville |
G: | (.) euh | parce que | (.) euh… | [ʔ]on__observe vraiment… |
H: | parce que | euh | [ʔ]un bon médecin traitant |
R: | Est-ce que l'on__a réfléchi | que | [ʔ]actuellement peut__être |
Y: | (.) alors que | [ʔ]en ce qui concerne les__aéroports |
A: | d'autant plus | que | euh | [ʔ]à la chambre sociale |
K2: | parce que | [ʔ]ils n'ont pas les | (.) enfin ils n'ont pas le | les réflexes de |
K2: | c'est__à-dire que | [ʔ]on peut avoir__envie | de travailler |
S: | à un point tel | que euh | [ʔ]à certains | moments |
S: | (.) mais il__est bien__évident | (.) que | [ʔ]en réunion | (.)
U: je sais pertinemment que | (.) [ʔ]à vouloir trop prévoir |
Z2: | qui fait que | (.) [ʔ]on parle de cette façon-là |
Z2: | et c'est vrai que… | (.) [ʔ]en bonne Française je |

From a phonological standpoint, the most salient consequence of non-elision of *que* and its compounds is the creation of numerous vowel+vowel sequences that are not conventional diphthongs. Since orthoepists regard these as dysphonic and even un-French, one has to ask why native speakers are producing them in sites where there was no need to do so. We have numerous tokens of [əi͡] and [əa͡] and fewer but still multiple instances of [əo͡, əɛ͡, əɛ͡, əɔ͡]. In principle, it seems that any combination is possible. The fact that [əu͡] is unattested probably only reflects the scant incidence of /u-/ words in the lexicon. A sequence like *l'idée est plutôt respectée qu'oubliée*, which would give a site for elision or non-elision, does not seem outlandish.[16]

---

[16] Further examples of each of the above token sets can be found in Green and Hintze (2021).

11.4.5 Developmental trends

We conclude this section with a brief comparison of the two interviews with Katya and Zoé, which may offer an insight into developmental trends. The first interviews, at ages ten and eleven respectively, produced strong evidence of compliance with normative elision, liaison, and *h aspiré*. Katya had only a single exception: *qu'est-ce que il__y a eu encore?* [kəˀ.lʲãỹã.kɔʁ], and Zoé had none. A direct statistical comparison between their two performances is not viable.[17] Instead, we compare their later behaviour with that of the adults in the general and family corpora, where an interval of eleven years is less likely to have wrought significant change. The results in Table 11.7 are striking.

Table 11.7 Comparison of Katya's and Zoé's adult usage with earlier mean rates

	Total 1980s General	Family	1990s K2	Z2
% *que* + *il(s)*	83.87	90.32	66.67	—
% *que* + *elle(s)*	92.31	87.50	—	—
% *que* + *on*	88.46	89.61	80.95	66.67
% *que* + *un(e)*	76.92	88.89	—	—
% *que* + otherV	60.26	69.33	50.00	63.16
% all types	79.62	83.59	73.68	72.97
% in strictest sites only	97.32	93.86	70.00	90.00

Despite a few categorical realizations in sites with very few tokens (marked —), overall Katya and Zoé have far lower rates of compliance with elision norms than their adult counterparts. As we noted, the most compliant sites are before determiners, or personal pronouns other than *on*. The most vulnerable are *que + on*, and those where the onset vowel belongs to some other part of speech. In the case of these two young women, Katya even more than her sister, the trend has accelerated. This is clearly not a case of conventional age-grading: neither speaker is approximating to the adult norm. We cannot exclude the possibility of a fashion within the peer group, or even gender group, that will eventually die out. Even so, the clear grammatical differentiation, and the emergence of *on* as a lead form, point towards an incipient change.

---

[17] We had insufficient usable material from the 1980s interviews for a full sample comparable to that of the adults. It is not legitimate to scale up from such sparse tokens.

11.5 Discussion

There are few empirical studies of elision against which to calibrate our findings. Casali's (1997) cross-linguistic survey confirms that elision is a very widespread means of avoiding undesirable vowel+vowel sequences; its directionality cannot be predicted from adjacency alone, but the second of the two vowels cannot be deleted across lexical word boundaries. His data set does not include any Romance language, but his main finding holds good for French. The major international research programme *Phonologie du français contemporain* (Durand, Laks, and Lyche 2014; Detey et al. 2016), which has shed invaluable new light on the worldwide diversity of French and on many structural features of the contemporary language, most notably liaison and the distribution of schwa, is almost silent on elision. Detey et al. (2010), for instance, flag tokens in the transcribed interviews but there are only two passing mentions in the book itself.

In relation to the minor sites with few tokens (*t'*, *s'*, *ç'*) and the double vowel loss from *c'est-à-dire* [sta.diʁ], we find few echos in the wider literature. The reduction of *tu as* to *t'a*, usually regarded as modern colloquial, has remote avatars: it is attested sporadically in Ronsard (Grevisse 1980: 76–7), where it is dubbed 'literary', and in the diary of an eighteenth-century Parisian glazier (Lodge 2004: 168), where it cannot be. On the variability of [sil ~ siil], we have found no headline challenge to the orthodox view that elision is categorical, though Encrevé (1988: 214) acknowledges minor variation in the same contexts as we do. There was, however, a challenge over a century ago from Passy (1917: 116), whose observations were presumably rooted in late nineteenth-century usage, to the effect that normative elision is characteristic of reading and high registers only, and is avoided in everyday speech. On reduction in *c'est*, which had been noticed by Martinon (1913: 182–3), one promising path peters out. According to Torreira and Ernestus (2011), a parallel reduction of *c'était* to [ste] in the Nijmegen Corpus of Casual French is nearing categorical in some contexts. We have no cause to dispute this finding, but it is not replicated in our corpus, where 103 tokens of the imperfect offer no comparable instance.

On <ç'> there is no consensus. For Encrevé (1988: 252, n. 38), 'En principe, *ça se n'élide pas*', so <ç'> can only betoken *ce* with an orthographic adjustment. For Dauzat (1950: 117) too, *ça* is invariable but he adds the stronger claim that it is spreading precisely because it serves as a satisfactory replacement for awkward reductions of *ce* as in *ç'avait été*. Neither Tranel (1996) nor Garrapa (2012) specifically mentions *ça* but it would be swept up by their contradictory treatments of *la*. In Tranel's analysis, /a/ never elides; what appears like elision in *la* is ascribed to an allomorphic substitution. Garrapa counterclaims that elision of /a/ is categorical and fully parallel to that of schwa. Our data support categorical elision of /a/ in *la*, but not in *ça*. These /saa/ sequences culled from the general corpus—D: *ça a toujours__été*; H: *ça a été une très grande__évolution*; W: *comment ça allait*; Y: *ça a des__inconvénients*—prove that elision is far from categorical and that links of identical vowels (*pacē* Boileau) are not prohibited.

We note that Garrapa (2012: 145) defines elision as 'the deletion of the first of two adjacent vowels across word boundaries', a formulation very similar to our own working definition and consistent with that of Casali (1997), and of the *remarqueurs* and their predecessors. Other linguists apply the label 'elision' more widely: to the loss of consonants (Passy 1917: 115; Ashby 1984; Lodge 1996, 2004) or of whole syllables (Pustka 2011). We see little advantage in a wider definition, particularly not that assumed by Pustka, whose interesting study of *par exemple*, *peut-être*, and *par contre* attributes pronunciations like [pa.ʁɛg.zɑ̃ᵖ] not to word frequency but to the whole prosodic context and collocational frame. For us, this is not elision but final-syllable truncation. There is scope for a taxonomic realignment of elision and schwa deletion, including Valdman's *effacement*, which clearly overlap. It would leave awkward residues (as adumbrated by Tranel) and further erode the claimed categorical status of elision.

The definition of 'hiatus', notwithstanding its hallowed usage in poetics and orthoepics, is likewise problematic. In relation to modern French, it seems to us almost as unsatisfactory as '*h aspiré*'. Both terms mark the locus of an event in historical phonology, but misrepresent its reflex in the contemporary language. In the tokens that we adduce of non-elision of adjacent vowels or of those crossing a rhythm boundary with no other intervention (token sets (8) and (9)), there is certainly no gap and the transition is perfectly smooth in both perception and spectral trace. At conversational tempo or slightly faster, the instances sound like binucleic monosyllables.[18]

Elision has always been the *parent pauvre* of generative phonology, duly listed among the linking phenomena that have been subject to such intensive, and occasionally acrimonious, debate over the past five and a half decades, but presumed to be invariable and hence barely investigated in its own right.[19] What has not been queried is the proposition that elision is a purely phonological process. We have reason to doubt this. Many of the tokens we have examined demonstrate constraints or lesser influences from other linguistic levels. Our data on *que* and its compounds suggest a very different analysis. The location of rhythm boundaries, hesitative fillers, silent pauses, and above all glottal onsets, are all conspiring to separate *que* from its dependent clause. The standard generative analysis sees *que* as a complementizer head of an embedded sentence, so that the constituent

---

[18] Whether some of them should be treated as a new generation of diphthongs is another moot question that we cannot explore here.

[19] An honourable exception, Montreuil (1987), focuses on the consequences of elision rather than the process itself. Encrevé (1988: 24–5), makes a similar complaint about the neglect of *enchaînement*. We cannot expatiate here on the history of generative phonology and the reasons for its concentration on liaison, schwa, and *h aspiré*. Klausenburger (1994, reprised in 2014) is a reliable guide.

boundary comes before *que*. This does not accord with the behaviour of our speakers. Instead, they use *que* as a discourse marker. It functions either as a floor-holder while they formulate their thoughts, or as a signal of the imminence of a subordinate clause whose truth-conditional status or pragmatic implicature could vary from its co-text. As such, non-elision of *que* has very little to do with phonology.

11.6 Concluding remarks

Beyond any doubt, rightward resyllabification creating new CV onsets remains an active and very productive process in French discourse. We have shown that normative elision is the chief contributor, significantly ahead of liaison, and that some 9% of the total derives from a source hitherto disregarded: links onto *euh* and *hein*. Despite its productivity, elision is not wholly categorical: minor inroads are made by *si*, *tu*, and probably *ça*, major ones by *que* and its compounds. Non-elision is variable according to register and personal style. We have shown reason to believe that elision is susceptible to influences from grammar, lexis, and discourse coherence, so that its treatment cannot be confined within phonology. It follows that elision in modern French, even limiting its definition to the loss of a single vowel, cannot be regarded as a unitary process. We have to leave for further research at least three questions. Was elision ever the unitary counterpart to liaison? Is non-elision spreading and becoming sociolinguistically marked? If so, what are the intralinguistic consequences? As Carton (2001: 13) observed some years ago, using his own term for hiatus: 'La disjonction, qui participe au fonctionnement de la liaison et de l'élision, continue à gagner du terrain'.

12
On the rise and fall of modern *français régional* in the rural Côte d'Or

Rosalind A. M. Temple

12.1 Introduction

Much has been made by sociolinguists in the twenty-first century of the levelling out[1] of regional linguistic differences across France, which is presented as a recent development. For example, Gadet's (2003b: 105) textbook states as fact that 'la variation diatopique va s'atténuant' and Hornsby and Pooley (2001: 306) assert that 'on assiste indéniablement à des phénomènes de nivellement ou d'uniformisation phonologique qui touchent d'abord les zones non-méridionales de France'. Pooley (2006: 386) goes so far as to claim that, '[n]owhere else in western Europe are phonological regiolectal features levelled to such a degree over a large area'. Detey et al. (2016: 58), however, claim that, '[e]ven in northern France there seems to be much more variation, geographical and social, than [Armstrong and Pooley (2010, 2013)] recognize'.

Blanchet and Armstrong (2006) tell us how the revolutionary *desideratum*—that the language of the Republic should be 'une et la même pour tous'—only began to impact the majority of citizens towards the end of the nineteenth and into the twentieth centuries. By around three quarters of the way into the twentieth century, the received wisdom was, as Walter (1982: 52) puts it,

> que les différences entre un lettré parisien et un lettré toulousain sont beaucoup plus considérables que les différences entre un lettré toulousain et un ouvrier de la même ville, ou entre un lettré parisien et un ouvrier parisien. Ce qu'il faut reconnaître, c'est que les différences sur le plan géographique l'emportent pour le moment, dans nos régions, sur les différences sociales.

That high point of diatopic variation in the French language seems to have lasted just a couple of decades. On the other hand, there have been recent efforts to revive (and renew) the tradition of producing linguistic atlases, suggesting, sometimes explicitly, that local varieties are alive and (sometimes) well (e.g. Hall 2013; Boula

---

[1] Or more strictly, the widespread diffusion of the supralocal norm, following Kerswill (2003).

Rosalind A. M. Temple, *On the rise and fall of modern* français régional *in the rural Côte d'Or.* In: *Historical and Sociolinguistic Approaches to French.* Edited by: Janice Carruthers, Mairi McLaughlin, and Olivia Walsh, Oxford University Press. © Rosalind A. M. Temple (2024). DOI: 10.1093/oso/9780192894366.003.0012

de Mareuil, Vernier, and Rillard 2017). Moreover, debates about regional varieties are certainly alive and well beyond the world of academe, in the press and social media, most recently in the legislation currently working its way through the French parliament to outlaw discrimination on the grounds of accent.[2]

These conflicting perceptions of the nature and vitality of regional variation in French may in part be a function of different traditions, for example large-scale variationist vs. dialectological approaches: most of the studies cited in support of the claim of widespread levelling are first-wave variationist-inspired urban studies, where Trudgill's (1974) gravity model of the diffusion of change would predict that spreading supralocal norms would arrive first, whereas dialectological studies tend still to focus mainly on selected rural informants.[3] Alternatively, perhaps some linguists have underestimated the extent to which regional variation remains in some areas, as argued by Hall and Hornsby (2015) among others. A further possibility is that successive generations of linguists have simply been discovering something that has in fact been present for a while: might it be a matter of the timing of the rise and fall of *français régionaux* not being what it seems? The standard narrative is that the *dialectes d'oc, d'oïl*, and *francoprovençaux* emerged out of a long process of dialectalization following the decline of the Roman empire. The majority of the non-elite inhabitants of the expanding kingdom and subsequent republic of France spoke one of these *dialectes* or a regional language until the nineteenth century.[4] During that century and particularly the early twentieth century the *français régionaux* emerged through the intensification of contact between French and the *dialectes*, to the high point where Walter (1982: 52) reports them as the main vector of variation in France, but they in turn have been in decline since the late 1980s. In the *Oc* domain and the so-called peripheral regions of *Oïl* (cf. for example Boughton and Pipe 2020, on Alsace), there is a clear-cut case to be made for *français régionaux* emerging out of contact with French in this time frame and subsequently being influenced by changes spreading from the political centre, as demonstrated clearly in work by Mooney (e.g. 2016a, b). However, the picture may be less clear-cut in at least some parts of the northern Gallo-Romance area, where the substrata are most closely related to French. Here evidence for a two-stage process is harder to come by, leading one to wonder whether the levelling of *français régionaux* that is currently being observed might actually be the continuation of a single, centuries-old process of

---

[2] *Proposition de loi [#2473] visant à promouvoir la France des accents*. https://www.assemblee-nationale.fr/dyn/15/textes/l15b2473_proposition-loi (accessed 5 July 2022). The aim of the bill is of course to improve social equality, but it is telling that the majority of examples in media reports and in the preamble to the *proposition* itself concern regional variation.
[3] With the exception of the 'Towards A New Linguistic Atlas of France' (TANLAF) project (Hall 2013).
[4] See Chapter 1 (this volume), footnote 54.

rise and fall in dialectalization, rather than the completion of a lifecycle which took off in earnest only just over one hundred years ago.

This chapter was originally intended to bring an empirical case study from rural Burgundy to bear on some of these apparent paradoxes, but the COVID-19 pandemic intervened to make that impossible, so my aim now is to present some thoughts relating to these questions, drawing on a preliminary analysis of a sample of speech collected in 2016 as part of my original pilot study and a consideration of some data from the *Atlas linguistique de la France* (*ALF*, Gilliéron and Edmont 1902–10) at the closest point to the location where that sample was recorded.[5] The *ALF* set out to map geographical variation in Gallo-Romance at the end of the nineteenth century as scientifically as possible, recording (in detailed phonetic transcription) over 600 samples of speech at *points d'enquête* which were distributed primarily on geographical grounds rather than being driven by specific philological points of interest.[6] Just under 200 maps, one for each lexical item or short phrase of interest, were published in successive *fascicules* during the first decade or so of the twentieth century, thus shortly before the putative rise in *français régionaux* began to gain pace. According to the two-stage narrative, we should thus expect the speech of rural Burgundy in the *ALF* to reflect a particular *dialecte d'oïl* and to be substantially different from both the speech of other regions at the time and from the speech of this location a century later, at the beginning of the twenty-first century.

12.2 Background

The contemporary location of interest is a village in the Montbard *arrondissement* of the Côte d'Or, and the *canton* of Venarey-Les Laumes. The location was chosen because I had observed striking cross-generational continuities in the branch of a particular family which had stayed in or near the village, which contrasted sharply with other members of the same generations who had moved away. According to the archives of the École des hautes études en sciences sociales and the Institut nationale de la statistique et des études économiques,[7] the population of the village declined from over 1,000 in 1793 to 303 in 1968, and 162 in 2018, just after the pilot data were collected. The family concerned have farmed nearby for at least three generations.[8] Members taking part in the pilot conversation were a couple in

---

[5] I should like to record my debt of gratitude to the late Robert and Paulette, who welcomed me into their homes and family over almost four decades and took an active interest in my interest in their speech and the matters discussed here.

[6] A brief summary of the *ALF* methodology may be found in Temple (2000).

[7] *Des villages de Cassini aux communes d'aujourd'hui* http://cassini.ehess.fr/fr/html/6_index.htm (accessed 5 July 2022); https://www.insee.fr/fr/statistiques (accessed 5 July 2022).

[8] A broader sample of inhabitants of the village from the older generations was also recorded, but the present chapter focuses on a few members of the family in order to permit intergenerational comparisons.

their early nineties (pseudonyms Jean and Jeanne), their youngest son (mid-fifties, 'Paul'), who now runs the family farm and his eldest son (early thirties, 'Philippe'), together with myself and their daughter-in-law, who was born and partly raised roughly 30 km away (and is not included in the analysis). I have known the family intimately for many years, and past experience led me to expect no accommodation effect on their speech from my presence. The conversation analysed here lasted roughly one and a half hours. It was unstructured and largely concerned naturally arising topics which the different generations disagree on strongly, leading to some rather heated (though good-humoured) exchanges which were perfect for mitigating any Observer's Paradox effects (e.g. Labov 1972a: 209).

For comparison with the contemporary speakers, I selected the closest location to the village in the *ALF*, point **19**, Gissey-sous-Flavigny, which is in the same *arrondissement* and *canton*, and is 3.5 km away as the crow flies[9] and 6 km by road.[10] The informant is an *employé de chemin de fer* in his forties, living in Darcey, 7 km from our village and 6 km from Gissey. No comments are given in the *Nomenclature des localités* (Gilliéron and Edmont 1902: 29) about his speech. Forms from the next closest point, **16** (Martrois and Pouilly en Auxois), were also noted for comparison from time to time, although this is much further from the village (43 km by road) and is in the *arrondissement* of Beaune, as well as being near the junction of two major roads, and as close to Dijon as it is to Beaune. The maps were consulted on the excellent CartoDialect 5.4.6 site,[11] which allows the researcher to zoom in around the same part of successive maps and has a very useful search function.

As discussed by Hornsby (2006), a variety is identified by a combination of features, an insight taken for granted in early sociolinguistics but one which has subsequently often been ignored in practice, in favour of quantitative studies of one or two variables in a given variety, so a range of lexical, phonetic, and morphosyntactic features are listed and/or discussed briefly in the samples presented in this qualitative pilot analysis. For the *ALF* I examined all the maps with headwords beginning with the letter *A* (1 ABEILLE to 104 AVRIL), in addition to selected others relating to features of interest thrown up by these maps and by the contemporary conversations, as well as features mentioned by Taverdet (2012) in his brief discussion of historical sources of the speech of Burgundy. For the recent data, this allows me to examine which combinations of features are present in the speech of given individuals, rather than generalizing over a population. The phonetic transcriptions given are from auditory analyses, with visual inspection of spectrograms using Praat (Boersma and Weenink 1992–2021): no instrumental analysis has yet

---

[9] http://www.cartesfrance.fr/carte-france-ville/21299_Gissey-sous-Flavigny.html (accessed 5 July 2022).
[10] https://www.viamichelin.fr (accessed 5 July 2022).
[11] http://lig-tdcge.imag.fr/cartodialect5/#/ (accessed 5 July 2022).

been undertaken. Generalizations to be drawn from both sources are thus limited, but there are nevertheless some interesting observations to be made.[12] Since issues of nomenclature and categorization are central to this chapter, before I turn to the linguistic data I consider metalinguistic evidence from the introductory material to the *ALF*, in order to examine how Gilliéron characterizes his object of study.[13]

12.3 Metalinguistic evidence from the *ALF*

There has been much discussion in the literature of the distinction between *français régional* and *dialecte*, the latter referring to the outcome of pre-medieval dialectalization in the Gallo-Romance domain. As noted in Section 12.1, it is probably not the case that parallel distinctions can be made across Gallo-Romance; in fact, it may be that such categorizations are actually unhelpful in general. Nevertheless it is interesting to see how the *ALF* presents the variation at hand. Certainly Gilliéron's (1880) introduction to his earlier *mémoire* on the *patois* of Torgon,[14] an isolated hamlet in the Valais *commune* of Vionnez, talks of the *patois* (pl) of the Canton, of the invasion of French, particularly into urban communities,[15] and of the influence of each on the other, suggesting potential dialect obsolescence effects on the *patois*, and the emergence of a *français régional*. In this case, there is a clear division between *patois* (= *dialecte*?), *français regional*, and *français d'Île de France*.

In the *Atlas* the use of the term *patois* seems more fluid in practice, if not in theory. The terms *patois* and *parler* are used almost interchangeably in the *Notice servant à l'intelligence des cartes* (Gilliéron and Edmont 1902) and the first page presents the *ALF* as a response to Gaston Paris's call for the conservation (through what would now be called documentation) of endangered varieties of Gallo-Romance, which suggests that they are sub-varieties of the historical *dialectes* in the sense just discussed. However, after pointing out in no uncertain terms how unrealistic would be the task of producing a monograph on the *patois* of each *commune*, the *Notice* goes on to reset the agenda to be one of establishing 'sur une base sérieuse l'*histoire linguistique* de la France' (Gilliéron and Edmont 1902: 3) by providing data with which to identify *aires* based on various levels of linguistic analysis, without reference to pre-existing philological expectations, as is well

---

[12] Unfortunately pandemic constraints meant that it was not possible to access a copy of Taverdet's (1975–88) *Atlas linguistique et ethnographique de Bourgogne* as a further, chronologically intermediate, point of comparison.
[13] Gilliéron was the initiator of the *ALF* project; he was a linguist and dialectologist. His co-editor, Edmond Edmont, was his fieldworker and had been selected for his acute listening skills combined deliberately with his linguistic naivety, so as not to prejudice the data as a result of any preconceived conceptions about what the characteristics of any given *parler* ought to be.
[14] See the discussion of the term *patois* in Chapter 10. See also Chapter 18, Section 18.3.2.
[15] He estimates that about half the inhabitants of the Valais speak French.

known. This would indicate, rather, that a dialectal pedigree is not a prerequisite for the inclusion of a term as part of a genuine *patois*.

There is explicit reference in the *Notice* to contact between the 'langage littéraire' or the 'langage de Paris' and local 'parlers populaires':

> De ce choix n'étaient point exclus des mots d'origine récente, pas plus que ceux que les patois ne peuvent posséder de leur propre fonds et qu'ils doivent au langage littéraire. Il nous importait, en effet, de mettre en lumière la façon dont les parlers populaires se comportent vis-à-vis de cette phalange de mots importés, dans quelle mesure ils se les assimilent à leur fonds ancien, à quel degré ils sont en communion avec le langage de Paris et accessibles à toute invasion. Ce sont des témoignages intéressants de leur état vital.
>
> (Gilliéron and Edmont 1902: 4–5)

Moreover, the *Nomenclature des localités* (Gilliéron and Edmont 1902: 29 ff.), which gives details on each, includes comments like 'les jeunes ne parlent plus guère patois.' (Location **1**, Marcigny, Nièvre) or 'parler de la partie rurale; dans le bourg le patois est fortement mélangé de français.' (**4**, Luzy, Nièvre) or 'c'est le parler des vieillards. Les jeunes gens et les personnes d'un âge moyen parlent français', all of which suggests a clear sense of what is *français* and what is other. In contrast, the term *patois* is used with reference to location **16** (see Section 12.2) without a comparative note, despite the fact that many of the entries in the latter location appear nevertheless to be more similar to French, than the same item in Luzy, for example CARTE 20 AIRE has ***ér*** for **16**, but ***tǫ́ŕé*** for **4**, (although the reverse is very frequently the case: CARTE 55 ARÊTE (*de poisson*) gives ***èŕód*** for **16** but ***àŕét*** for **4**).[16] *Patois* is also ascribed to the speaker at the closest point to Paris, **226** (le Plessis-Piquet, Seaux, Seine). Now part of the Paris conurbation, this community had almost doubled in size over the nineteenth century, to 475 inhabitants, yet was still a rural location. However, it had also become a popular leisure destination for Parisians, so it is unsurprising that the *patois* is spoken only by 'quelques rares vieillards' (Gilliéron and Edmont 1902: 36). Yet in the first 100 maps there are very few forms elicited from those *patois* speakers which are notably different from casual French, for example ***j*** [ʒ] for *nous* (91 NOUS AVONS) or ***vŭ*** [vy] for *eu* (102 J'AI EU; 103 IL Y A EU).

This brief overview suggests that there is very often no clear dividing line to be drawn[17] between what constitutes *dialecte* and *français régional* in the *ALF*, nor is it wholly clear how these relate to the term *patois* as used by Gilliéron and Edmont.

---

[16] The following typographical conventions will be used here: transcriptions copied from the *ALF* will appear in ***bold italics***; transcriptions giving the closest IPA equivalent will be within square or slashed brackets; headwords from the maps will be in CAPITALS; other orthographical representations in standard/supralocal French will be in *italics*.

[17] With hindsight, of course.

Although their metalinguistic use of the term seems to correspond to traditional *dialecte*, what it refers to in practice is not so clear-cut. This raises questions concerning the timeline of the supposed rise and fall of the *français régionaux* in the *Oïl* domain across the twentieth century: might it be the case that what has taken place is a rise and fall in the nomenclature we ascribe to these varieties, partly due to the enormous amount of dialectological work that was able to be done when the data from the *ALF* became available, while on the ground there has been a gradual evolution towards more uniformity across the domain which actually goes back at least to the turn of that century, when the *ALF* was compiled? Demonstrating this would require a large-scale examination of the *ALF* data, and discussion of cases of recent and historical bidialectalism. The rest of this chapter aims to provide a modest springboard for such an examination, firstly by asking of this small sample of *ALF* data at a single location whether it already looks to modern eyes like something one might call *français régional* and secondly by using it as a point of comparison with some twenty-first-century data from a location situated very close by.

12.4 Linguistic evidence from the *ALF*

Of the 100 or so lexical items sampled at point **19** only two, *gǣl* [gœ:l] for FIGURE and *gǣlé* ['gø:le] for ABOYER, are almost unique to Gissey-sous-Flavigny in the Côte d'Or and surrounding *départements* (with one other instance in the Yonne). Five other non-standard words were shared with some or all of the surrounding *départements*: *jặsõ* ['ʒɑ:sɔ̃] (AIGUILLON), the only one noted by Taverdet (2012: 68) as specifically Burgundian; *mŏ€ ĕ myĕ*[18] [muʃ ɛ mje] (ABEILLE), which is very widespread including at point **226**, discussed in Section 12.3; *rĕgŭzĕ* [regyze] (AIGUISER); *krĭ* [kri] (CHERCHER); *s ę́sté, ĕsté* ['se:ste, ɛste] (S'ASSEOIR, ASSIS); *vĕrn* [vɛ:rn] (AUNE). A handful of other items obviously cognate with the French word had markedly different pronunciations: *ĕlmĕ, ĕlmĕt* [ɛlme, ɛlmɛt] alternating with *y ặlǣm* [j ɑlœm] (ALLUMER, ALLUMETTE, J'ALLUME); *ĕrŏd* [ero:d] (ARÊTE (*de poisson*)); *ĕpǣn* [epœn] (AUBÉPINE); *ọ̆jdǣ* ['o:ʒdø] (AUJOURD'HUI). All these were shared with numerous surrounding points, except for *ặyŏ* [ɑ:jo] (AIL), which is only noted in Gissey. Thus in over 85% of this sample the lexicon of Gissey is essentially shared with French, and most of it is shared over a fairly wide geographical area.

Comparison of morphosyntactic and phonological characteristics across varieties will be restricted to comparison with French. The prepositions which appear in Table 12.1 are obviously cognate with French, with most pronunciation

---

[18] *Faute de mieux*, the symbol '*ʋ*' is used in place of the *ALF* symbol for [u] (*u* represents the *ALF* symbol for [y]).

Table 12.1 Selected function words from the *ALF* sample, preceded by their French equivalents*

Prepositions	*à* - *ė̃* [ɛ], *ă̊* [ɑ], *d(ė)* [d(ə)]; *de* - *d, dė* [d, də]; *où* -*ŏ*; *pour* - *pő, pǎr* [po, pɑr], *ė̃* [ɛ] {= *à*}; *sous* - *dzǽ* [dzø]; *sur* - *sŭ* [sy].
Negation	*ne* - *n, nė* [n, nə], {zero}; *pas* - *på̃, på̩* [pɑ, 'pɑ:], *pwẽ* [pwɛ̃] (in *il n'y a pas de*); *plus* - *pŭ* [py].
Conjunctions	*et* - *ė́* [e]; *ou* - *ŏ* [u].
Articles	*un* - *ĭ, ĩn* [i, in]; *une*- *ŭᵒᵉn, ĩn* [yᵒᵉn, in]; *le* - *lė́, l* [lə, l]; *la* - *lè̩* [lɛ]; *les* - *lė́, lė́z* [le, lez]; *du* - *dŭ* [dy]; *de la* - *d lè̩* [dlɛ]; *des* - *dė́, dė́z* [de, dez].
Demonstratives	*ce* - *s* [s]; *cet, cette* - *st, ė̀st* [st, ɛst], *stė* [stə] {f}; *celui-ci* - *stŭ̩sė́* ['styse]; *celle-là* - *stė́lė̩* [ste'lɛ].
Interrogatives	*où* - *lè̩vŏ* [lɛvu].
Subject pronouns	*je* - *ĭ, y** [i, j]; *tu* - *tŭ, t* [ty, t]; *elle* - *ė̀, ė̀l** [ɛl, œ:l]; *il* - *ė̀l, ǎ̀l, ė̀* [ɛl, œl, ɛ]; *on* - *ã̊* [ɑ̃]; *nous* - *ĭ, y* [i, j]; *vous* - *vŏz* [vuz]; *elles* - *ė̀l*, ė̀l, ė̀* [œ:l, ɛl, ɛ]; *ils* - *ė́, ė̀* [e, ɛ].
Object/reflexive pronouns	*me* - *m* [m]; *te* - *t* [t]; *lui* - *lŏ, lĭ* [lu, li]; *se* - *sė, s* [sə, s]; *nous* - *nŏ* [nu]; *vous* - *vŏ, vŏz* [vu, vuz]; *les* - *lė́, lė́z* [le, lez].
Strong pronouns	*moi* - *mwè̃* [mwɛ̃]; *toi* - *twè̩* [twɛ]; *lui* - *lŏ* [lu]; *nous* - *nŏ* [nu]; *eux* - *ǽ* [œ].

* indicates forms mentioned by Taverdet (2012) as Burgundian.

differences consistent with more general local phonological characteristics rather than being specific to these prepositions. Two points of difference are evident: the use of a cognate of *dessous* for *sous* and the occasional use of a cognate of *à* where French would have *pour*. *Pour* is also notable for its variable local ([po]) and French ([pɑr]) pronunciations, consistent with a non-French variety in the process of being invaded by French, as mentioned in the quote given in Section 12.3. A similar pattern is observed with the other function words in Table 12.1: most are close cognates with French, whose pronunciations are ascribable to broader local phonetic patterns, with a few exceptions such as the use of negative *point* (in a '*de* phrase', as observed more widely across the *ALF* by Burnett 2019: 197), the demonstrative pronouns, and the first- and third-person subject pronouns *ĭ, y* [i, j] and *ǎ̀l, ė̀l, ė̀(l)* [œl, œ:l, ɛ(l)] (masc.). There are three questions in the maps sampled. At point **19** the two WH-questions have *que* followed by SUBJ-V word order: *lè̩vŏ k tu vè̩* [lɛvu k ty 'vɛ:] (OÙ VAS-TU?); *kė t ė̀* [kə t ɛ] ((*quel âge*) AS-TU?). The Yes–No question uses *est-ce que* as is frequent in contemporary French.

Table 12.2 shows the vowels observed in the sample with their equivalents in conservative Standard French citation forms.[19] Distributions of the variants were

---

[19] Potentially phonemic length distinctions are not noted here.

Table 12.2 The vowels of conservative French, with *ALF* transcriptions from point 19 and their assumed IPA equivalents

/i/	ĭ, ĭ [i, ɪː]	/y/	ŭ, ŭ̀, œ̆ [y, yː, œ]	/u/	ŏ, ŏ̀, ŏ̀ [u, ʊ, ʊː]
/e/	ĭ, é̀ⁱ, é, è [i, ẹ, e, ɛ]	/ø/	ǽ, ǿ [ø, øː]	/o/	ó, ó̀, ò [o, oː, ɔ]
/ɛ/	é, é̀, è, è̀, ò̀ [e, eː, ɛ, ɛː, ɔː]	/œ/	ŭ́, œ̆, œ̆́, œ̆ [yː, ø, øː, œː]	/ɔ/	ó, ò̀, ò, œ́ [oː, ɔ, ɔː, øː]
/a/	è̀, è̀, á̀, à̀, à̀, ằº [ɛ, ɛː, aː, ɑ, ɑː, ɑ]	/ɑ/	è̀, á̀, á̀, à̀, à [ɛ, a, aː, ɑ, ɑː]		
/ɛ̃/	ẽ́, ẽ̀ [ẽ, ɛ̃]	/œ̃/	œ̃ [œ̃](?)	/ɑ̃/	õ̀, aº, ã̀ [õ, ɑ̃, ã]	/ɔ̃/	õ [ɔ̃](?)

noted, but since the sample is small they are not analysed here. One distributional point is worth noting, however: many vowels with following heterosyllabic nasals still show historical regressive nasalization, as in **brã̀kõɲé** [brɑːkõɲe] (168 BRACONNIER). A four-term system of nasalized vowels seems to have been preserved, although the absence of quality marking makes it difficult to be sure what the degree of openness is in /œ̃/ and /ɔ̃/. The close vowels are also similar to French but with [œ] for /y/ in a few cases, and laxed variants of /i, y, u/. The mid and open vowels are very variable, but it would be premature to conclude that all oppositions have been neutralized. /e/ has a striking number of raised variants, often as close as [i]. In combinations with semi-vowels, whereas /j/ is mostly pronounced as in French, /ɥi/ sequences are pronounced variably as [œː] in **é́gœ̀y** (14 AIGUILLE), [ɥɪː] in **wɪ̆y** (702 HUILE), and [y] in **jŭ̀yè** (734 JUILLET). /wa/ sequences are still pronounced [wɛ], except in *-oir(e)*, when they are pronounced [ɛː] or [u].

Very few articulatory characteristics are particularly noteworthy for consonants, except that /r/ is still apical, as it seems to be in the whole area, and /l/ is sometimes palatalized to [j] both in codas (see *huile*) and in /gl/ clusters (e.g. **ằvœ̀gy** [avœːgj] (80 AVEUGLE)). Word-final singleton liquids are also frequently elided, as in **è̀vrĭ** (104 AVRIL) and **pœ̆́** [pøː] (101 N'AIE PAS PEUR), the latter possibly akin to what Sankoff and Blondeau (2007: 580) call a 'vocalized variant' in their study of variable (r) in Montréal French. Final clusters are variably reduced, but sometimes this is reduction to the liquid: *cidre* and *coudre*, for example, end in [dr], whereas *cendre* and *moudre* end in [r] and *descendre* and *perdre* in [d]. Liquid–consonant sequences are noted by Taverdet (2012: 6) as also having elided liquids in some locations, but again this is variable at point **19**; for example /rn/ is realized as [rn] in *journal*, [r] in *dernier* and [n] in *journée*.

Finally, the *ALF* is not the best source for prosodic information, and although **19** is one of the points where accented syllables are marked in the transcriptions, the marking is not wholly systematic. However, there are many instances where it is marked, and it often falls on the penultimate—rather than the final—syllable of a word or sequence, as in *juillet* and *avril*. These examples also illustrate how accentuation does not necessarily correspond with vowel length: there the accented vowels are marked as short, whereas the words *gǣlə́* ['gœːle] and *(s) ę́stę́* ['seːste] mentioned in the earlier discussion of lexis have long vowels in their penultimate accented syllables. In final syllables marked as accented, all the vowels examined are long, except in the verbal forms *irę̀* [iˈrɛ] (29 (QUELQU'UN) QUI VOUS IRA) and *(kė̀ t) ė̀* [kəˈtɛ] (86 (QUEL ÂGE) AS-TU?). Vowels are long and short in both open and closed syllables, both finally and non-finally.

What may we conclude from this small sample? There are some clear differences between many of the forms here and standard French, but it is less clear that they are different enough to be classified as a separate *dialecte* on synchronic grounds: many are shared to a greater or lesser extent with other *points d'enquête* often extending over a pretty wide area, sometimes including the Île de France. I shall return to the implications of this after examining the data from 100 years on.

12.5 Local speech in the twenty-first century

In the one and a half hours of contemporary conversation analysed, only one vocabulary item occurred that was related to those noted in the *ALF* sample discussed in the previous section: *gueuler* for 'protest'. Other non-standard vocabulary items noted included *homme* for 'husband', which is almost universal across Oïl and Oc on *ALF* map 814 (MON MARI) and was used by both Jeanne and her son.[20] The nouns *petiot* and *petiote* were used by all generations to refer to children and to sons and daughters of people mentioned, whatever their age. *ALF* (623 MON PETIT GARÇON) has *mõ ptĭ gȧrsǫ̃* at point **19** although point **16** and many points to the south and southeast have *ptyǫ́* for the adjective. Jeanne also uses *gars* for 'son' (not her own), which is one of the forms given for **19** on map 572B (MON GARÇON > *gȧ̀, gȧ̀rsõ*), and Philippe used *fille* for 'daughter' but less frequently than *petiot(e)*. Jean also used the word *filles*, but only to refer collectively to myself and his daughter-in-law when he was serving *apéritifs*. A salient characteristic not represented in the *ALF*, but noted by Taverdet (2012: 87) as typical of Burgundy, is the use of the definite article with male and female proper names, both first names of friends and acquaintances (including the local *curé*!) and the surnames of politicians such as *le Macron* and *le Trump*. All members of the family do this, and no individual was referred to by name without a definite article. The only lexical item of those whose pronunciation was commented on in the *ALF* sample was *aujourd'hui* and the only pronunciation here was as in contemporary French, but with an apical /r/ by Jean and Jeanne, i.e. [oʒurdɥi].

Of the marked function words noted in Section 12.4, most were pronounced as in standard French, albeit with general reduction phenomena. No equivalent of *dzǽ* was used for *sous*, but Jeanne did use [dsy] as well as [syr] for *sur*. Neither

---

[20] The word *mari* was not used by any of the speakers.

of the younger men did so. Jeanne also used [syr] instead of *dans* (e.g. in *sur le journal*) and *à* (*sur Semur*).[21] *Ne* was mostly absent in negation but all speakers used it at least once; none, however, used *point* as a *forclusif*. Demonstrative pronouns were pronounced as in French; the reduced forms [st] and [stè] reported in the *ALF* were frequent, including in initial position, but an equivalent of metathesized **èst** did not occur. The only local pronominal form was Jean's use of [œl] (as well as [ɛl]) for *elle*. Philippe, however, does use [i] for *l(e)* in *elle l'est* [ɛl.i.ɛ] *sûrement moins que lui*. Yes–no questions were formed with declarative word order and with *est-ce que* by all speakers, and Jean, Jeanne, and Philippe all use *qu'est-ce que*. The only other WH-questions are posed by Jeanne, who most frequently uses the structures with *que* observed in the *ALF*, for example *où qu'il habitait? comment qu'elle s'appelle? Que* also occurs with relative *où* and *comment* in her speech.

As far as pronunciation is concerned, the close vowels /i, y, u/ are pronounced by all as in supralocal French. The mid-vowels are pronounced variably, as indicated in the *ALF*, but there is no systematic *loi de position* and phonemic distinctions appear to be partly maintained. All four speakers frequently produce close [e̞] for /e/, again as indicated in the *ALF*, and the younger two also use [i, i̞], particularly Paul (which led to difficulties in understanding the acronym VTH [vi̞tiaʃ] until the meaning[22] was given in full). However, all but Paul, the youngest, also have occasional [ɛ] for non-final /e/. All speakers use [ɛ] in final open syllables, such as *mais, -ait, (à-peu-)près, paquet*, although Paul also uses [e] (*fais*). All four frequently use a closer vowel in closed syllables, such as *bêtes, arrête, peut-être, quand-même*, as well as [ɛ] elsewhere. Only *bête* occurs in the *ALF*, with the same pronunciation at point **19** but also in many other Oïl locations in maps 129A and B. /o/ is generally pronounced [o] by all, but /ɔ/ is often also closer for the three older speakers than in standard/supralocal French (e.g. *encore, rapport*), again a pattern observed at **19** and more widely in the *ALF*. Similarly, /ø/ is pronounced consistently as [ø] but /œ/ is sometimes pronounced as a closer vowel by the two younger speakers. Thus, Paul produces *gueule* (Vb) as both [gœ:l] and [gø:l]. The open vowels show the most variable pattern across all the speakers: /a/ is frequently pronounced as [ɑ], both long and short (e.g. *occasion* [okɑ:zjɔ̃], *explication* [eksplikɑsjɔ̃], *passé* [pɑsɛ], *va* [vɑ], *assez* [ɑse]); /ɑ/ is most often pronounced as a back vowel by all speakers, very retracted in the case of Philippe, but occasionally a fronter variant is used (e.g. *pas* > [pɑ, pa] (neg.), *là* > [lɑ, la], *déjà* > [deʒɑ]). /wa/ is never pronounced [wɛ], as recorded in the *ALF*, but the vocalic nucleus is almost always an open back vowel, sometimes raised to [ɑ̝] or [ɔ] by all but the youngest speaker. He is the only one to produce a more fronted [wa],

---

[21] The headword *dans* does not appear in these contexts in the *ALF*: it always occurs with common nouns denoting physical locations (e.g. 226 DANS LES CHAMPS).
[22] 'Variétés tolérantes aux herbicides'.

for example in *varois* > [vaʁwa], which is a quasi-technical term for him, since he works for an agrochemical company.

Consonant articulations are for the most part unremarkable, except that there is a clear generational split between the older couple, who use categorical [r] and the younger father and son, who always produce uvular articulations, mostly fricatives and approximants, but also occasionally a uvular trill. Word-final clusters are regularly reduced in all contexts by all speakers, but there is no evidence of elision of singleton coda liquids either word-finally or in heterosyllabic C.C sequences, except in third-person pronouns as is the widespread pattern in supralocal French.

Finally, there are striking prosodic patterns which I have long come to associate with the local area, consistent with the non-final accent marking in the *ALF*. Impressionistically these were more consistent in the older speakers, but even the youngest produced them at various points in the conversation. Generally vowels in canonically stressed syllables were lengthened, but occasionally the vowel in the preceding syllable was also long, with the stress marked by intensity and/or a rise in intonation (as in *faucheurs* > ['fo:ʃœ:r] (Jean)). Mostly this could not be construed as an *accent d'insistance*, as illustrated by (1):

(1) on s'est [ɛ:] dit 'il est pas pa[ɑ·]se' (Jeanne).

Open long vowels were always back, suggesting that there is some interaction between the vowel distributions previously described and suprasegmental effects. That said, /e/ was also occasionally lengthened, as in les [le:z] hommes (Jean, offering drinks). Perhaps paradoxically, the rhythm is also often very regular, with word-internal schwa apparently being pronounced more frequently than in supralocal French, and frequent epenthetic schwa word-finally. These are very sweeping generalizations which will need to be developed with acoustic analysis of the patterns of variation in timing, intensity, and pitch, so I refrain from commenting further here.

The picture in this sample is, then, a mixed one: all speakers produce some non-standard features which are noted at point **19** in the *ALF* and for all but the youngest there are lexical and morphosyntactic examples as well as features of pronunciation. We come to the discussion of whether these are sufficient to suggest a continuum of change through the twentieth century or not in Section 12.6.

12.6 Discussion

In Brunot's (1911) discourse on the foundation of the *Archives de la parole* at the Sorbonne in 1911, as the final *fascicules* of the *ALF* were being prepared for publication, he sets out the paradoxical aims of using the new technology supplied by Pathé on the one hand to improve the teaching of correct pronunciation from the banks of the Garonne to the Conservatoire de Paris, which would hasten the uniformization of the nation's speech (Brunot 1911: 12),[23] and on the other to conserve its moribund *patois*:

> Nous avons autour de nous de grands vieillards qui se meurent, ce sont nos patois. Un à un nos villages [...] abandonnent leur vieux parlers séculaires. Dans quelques années il sera déformé ou aura vécu. Le français, qui n'a même pas sur eux le droit d'aînesse, aura pris pour lui toute la France du Nord.
> (Brunot 1911: 13)[24]

The debates about the rapid levelling out of regional variation referred to in Section 12.1 focus on what has happened in the hundred years since, with the development of *français régionaux* and their subsequent demise, or maintenance (e.g. Hall and Hornsby 2015). I would argue that the selective observations presented in this chapter suggest that it might be instructive to revisit the starting point of this narrative, at least so far as the *français régional* of this small corner of Burgundy is concerned.

Some *ALF* forms are more restricted in distribution than others—this is no great insight—but there is little evidence in my small sample for a clearly defined *parler* belonging to Gissey-sous-Flavigny (**19**), or even the Côte d'Or. It appears that most forms and patterns in the sample are far more widespread than might be expected if it were the case that the *patois* referred to in the *Atlas* represented the last of the clearly identifiable historical *dialectes* of the rural *Oïl* domain, or the even the beginnings of contact-induced *français régionaux*. This is, of course, consistent with the long-standing received wisdom that dialects form continua and are rarely definitively circumscribable, which none of the authors I have cited would deny. Nevertheless, the discourse surrounding regional variation in France, with its frequent classificatory emphasis, tends to lose sight of this, leading to a historical narrative that does not fit the snapshot we have seen of these two rural locations roughly 270 km southeast of Paris.

Comparing the two samples shows how there are some features which have apparently disappeared over the past century, such as the first-person plural subject pronouns *ĭ* and *y* (now replaced by *on* for all these speakers), and some which appear to be moribund, such as third-person *ĕl* or the apical [r], now only used by the two older speakers. Others are still very much present but with some variation, like the prosodic features and the lengthening of non-final vowels. The local use of definite articles with proper names is categorically present across the generations.[25] The *ALF* shows how some of these characteristics are more local (e.g. the

---

[23] Presumably an enterprise of which his hero the Abbé Grégoire would have approved.
[24] Brunot explains the paradox himself: while this is desirable from a sociopolitical perspective, it is less so for scholars and fans of the 'pittoresque'.
[25] This is not attested in the *ALF*, presumably because the proper names elicited (e.g. JEAN, JACQUES, MARIE, PIERRE) were generic rather than referring to particular individuals.

pronouns) than others (e.g. variable (r)). Again, this would not be denied in any of the discussions cited, and yet the classificatory discourse implicitly invites us to determine what is local (and whether *dialecte* or *français régional*) and non-local. Sometimes this is made explicit and a key part of an argument. For example, a recent paper investigating the distribution of /e/ and /ɛ/ in Normandy (which is not dissimilar to the distributions mentioned here) explains the apparent discrepancies between studies of Norman French as due to the fact that, '[The authors] all say that they are describing the French of their area, but it seems likely that in some instances the speakers were actually speaking Norman' (Hall 2019: 6), and goes on to discuss the difficulty speakers themselves have in distinguishing between 'Norman' and the informal French of Normandy (Hall 2019: 9–10). This begs the question of what constitutes 'Norman': if the speakers themselves have difficulty identifying it, does that not suggest that categories are being imposed which are not necessarily meaningful to them? Moreover, the categorization is potentially unhelpful to linguists in that it allows the dismissal of data deemed to be other in order to maintain the account of the *français régional*[26] of a given region as a 'single variety' (Hall 2019: 6). This is but one example that arises out of what I have referred to as a classificatory approach that has informed the discussion of diatopic variation in France for a long time and which arises from the dominant chronological narrative.

Evidently a preliminary analysis of a very small sample of data is an insufficient basis on which to overturn an august tradition and enormous amounts of meticulous data collection and analysis, but it does give pause for thought. My original intention when I began to collect the contemporary data was to find evidence for the persistence of a local *parler* down the generations, *contra* the stronger claims of exceptional regional dialect levelling in France. As a result of seeking to find a baseline for that *parler* in the *ALF*, I have come to a more cautious view of what might be local in a variety with which I have been familiar for many years. Furthermore it has led me to question my own longstanding teaching practices of explaining to students at the beginning of courses on variation the importance of differentiating between *dialectes* and *français régionaux*, as though the difference between these terms was of the same order across France, or at least across the *domaine d'oïl*, together with the accompanying narrative that the mass decline of the *dialectes* only really set in after the 1914–18 war. This was accompanied by a concomitant rise in *français régionaux*, until they too underwent rapid decline towards the end of the twentieth century, victims of supra-local French. In the present sample at least, the extent of shared forms and structures is often far broader than that narrative would suggest, which leads back to the questions posed in my introduction: despite the evidence of widespread bidialectalism, it is clear that the demise of local *patois* was already well underway when the *ALF* was produced and even

---

[26] By implication, this would also apply to the *dialecte* concerned.

where explicit reference is made by Gilliéron and Edmont to *patois* and *non-patois* speakers the data, limited as they are, indicate that it would be hard to determine whether many forms should count as *dialecte* or *français régional*. I would suggest, then, that at least in some of the non-peripheral rural parts of the *Oïl* domain, what we have observed in recent decades may not have been the supposed rapid decline in the *français régionaux* which had emerged during the twentieth century, but rather the continuation of a process which was probably well underway in the century before. Again this is not a new insight, as evidenced by Gauchat's (1905) famous study of the *parler* of the Swiss village of Charmey, which was the first study to demonstrate how variation within a variety might indicate that a pattern of gradual diachronic change was underway. Whether or not it is an accurate insight, setting aside the vexed question of what counts as *dialecte* and what counts as *français régional* might allow fresh insights by twenty-first-century linguists into both the history of *Oïl* varieties and their contemporary status.

Having invoked the understanding of speakers in Normandy, it would be remiss to ignore speakers' own attitudes to local varieties. What of the many dialect societies and local associations[27] who take an interest in their local *patois*, which they see as different from French, but which I appear to be dismissing out of hand? Or of recent projects like the *Atlas sonore des langues régionales de France*,[28] wherein even the sample of the *patois* of Tours is well-nigh incomprehensible on first listening, despite the persistent belief of the inhabitants of that city (confirmed in regular anecdotes from students on their years abroad) that they speak the best French of the Republic? Do these not suggest that the dominant narrative is correct, and provide evidence of the persistence of features from locally distinctive historical *dialectes*? In the first case, it is unsurprising that local language is an important element of local identity, as is evident on a blog site devoted to the village where my recordings were made.[29] Sometimes the associated varieties are enregistered, with speaker-generated labels (most famously, perhaps, the *Chtimi* of the far northeast), but in this particular blog the list of local words surviving into the second half of the twentieth century are simply referred to as belonging to 'le parler local'. Interestingly, while several of the words are familiar to me (e.g. *souper* for *manger*) and one or two (*dépialer* for *enlever la peau*; *petiot(s)* for *enfants*) occur in the pilot recordings, some are not, and although many correspond to non-French *ALF* entries for point **19** (e.g. *cra* for *corbeau*, *ALF* **krȁ** [krɑ:] (CARTE 324), and *pieuvre* for *pleuvoir*, *ALF* **pyȅvr** [pjœ:vr] (CARTE 1034)), the corresponding *ALF* entry for others is actually more like the French (e.g. *enfant* > *ȁfã* [ɑ̃fɑ̃]). This tells us that features

---

[27] Not to mention the numerous social media sites, for example https://www.facebook.com/francaisdenosregions (accessed 5 July 2022) which is linked to the late and much lamented Alain Rey's last coffee table book on regional variation in the lexicon (Avanzi, Rey, and Vicenti 2020).

[28] https://atlas.limsi.fr/ (accessed 5 July 2022).

[29] Not referenced, in order to preserve the anonymity of my speakers. The relevant page of the blog is dated 2007.

perceived as local were alive and well towards the end of the twentieth century, when the blog author was being brought up in the village, but also that there must have been variation present at the time the *ALF* data were collected. Similarly, in the *Atlas sonore* many of the forms in the version of Aesop's *La Bise et le soleil* fable recorded in Tours do not correspond to the *ALF* entries for the four points in the *Indre et Loire*, the closest of which is about 27 km from the city, although some do. Thus the transcription gives *eul soulet* (pronounced [øl sulɛt]) for *le soleil*, but the *ALF* has the more French **sŏlèy/sŏléy/sŏlé**$_y$ [sɔlɛːj, sɔleːj, suleːʲ] (CARTE 1241), and I was only able to find one instance of metathesis in the masculine definite article in this *département*, which is otherwise given as *l* or *lé* [l, lə]. However, *la bise* is transcribed in the *Atlas sonore* as *la galarne*, which does partially correspond to the *ALF* entry for point **408**, Saint-Antoine-du-Rocher, **vã̄ d gàlèrn** [vã̄ d gɑlɛrn], although the other three points in the *département* have **bíz** [biz] (CARTE 133). Again, then, there is evidence of variation at the turn of the twentieth century. What the twenty-first-century transcriptions represent in day-to-day reality is an open question. The aim of the atlas, like Brunot's, is to conserve disappearing *langues de France*. Participants were generally well educated and were recruited through public appeals (cf. Boula de Mareuil, Vernier, and Rillard 2017) so it is possible that their renderings err on the side of Brunot's 'pittoresque' rather than reflecting a living reality, but it would seem that there is a reality in living memory. Whether that reality constitutes a *dialecte* which has persisted alongside a *français régional* since the time of the *ALF* is the kind of categorizational question I have already suggested is best set aside.

Even the small snapshot from the *ALF* presented in this chapter gives a mixed picture of the *parler* of Gissey-sous-Flavigny at the turn of the twentieth century: the majority of the maps show forms at least partially shared with other *Oïl* varieties, sometimes over a very wide area, and we see evidence of forms which we know were the same in earlier periods of the history of French (e.g. *point* or contemporary /wa/ > [wɛ]). No historical dialectologist (or modern sociolinguist) would be surprised at this, and the contemporary evidence, again a very small snapshot, which crucially excludes morphological and systematic phonological detail, shows that developments in a neighbouring village have followed, or are still following, the historical trajectory of French (e.g. /wa/ > [wa, wɑ], /r/ > [r, ʁ]). Maybe the time has come to look back to the pre-isogloss days of the production of the *ALF* and revisit the history of *Oïl* dialects and *français régionaux* in the twentieth and twenty-first centuries following Gilliéron and Edmont's principle of coming to the data on the ground as they are without reference to philology or categories of analysis to see what that might tell us. Maybe that would also bring us closer to the reality of the speakers who evidently sometimes have difficulty relating to the categories imposed on them by linguists.

13
Attitudes towards the French language
An analysis of the metalanguage used in twentieth-century French language columns

Olivia Walsh

13.1 Introduction

Chroniques de langage, articles discussing questions related to language which are produced by a single author and published regularly in the periodical press (Remysen 2005: 270–1), have been regularly produced in France since the early twentieth century. Authors of these columns are generally language professionals, such as journalists, literary authors, or educators, and, more rarely, professional linguists. The content of the columns can be very varied, both across different authors and also within a single column. However, all deal with questions of language, and most authors focus on advising readers on the correct and incorrect use of the French language. As such, language columns can be viewed as successors to the tradition of texts of observations and remarks on the French language, initiated by Vaugelas's (1647) *Remarques sur la langue françoise utiles à ceux qui veulent bien parler et bien escrire*; both types of text are aimed at non-specialist audiences and discuss not just grammatical errors but more specifically points of doubtful usage and areas of hesitation (see Ayres-Bennett 2015).

This chapter examines a sample of language columns produced by six French authors during three key periods of the twentieth century to determine, first, the attitudes towards the French language that are (re)produced in these columns and second, whether these attitudes change over time. To do so, the study examines the metalanguage used by the authors to describe and make judgements about particular language uses to determine their attitudes towards what they consider to be correct and incorrect French. The role played by the standard language ideology (SLI) in forming these judgements is then considered. It is of particular interest to carry out this research now, to determine whether recent research findings that there has been a general tendency over time towards a more open approach to variation in French, that is, towards a less prescriptive, more descriptive view of language usage (see Kibbee and Craig 2019: 77) also hold true for this genre of metalinguistic discourse in the twentieth century. Language columns are particularly interesting to examine in this regard, because their epilinguistic nature means that they offer particularly revealing insights into the application of the SLI (see Remysen 2005: 272). They are also more widely distributed and read than other normative works such as grammars (see McLelland 2021b: 283) which may possibly mean that they have more influence on French speakers' ideas about, and attitudes towards, standard French than other normative works such as grammars or dictionaries (see also Walsh 2021c: 870). The current study is part of a larger project examining the language ideology displayed in French and Québécois language columns from 1865 to 2000.[1] The language columns used in the study have been taken from the *FranCHRO* corpus of language columns, which was developed as part of this project.[2] The study is one of relatively few to provide any detailed analysis of the work of French language columnists in France.[3]

Section 13.2 introduces the texts used in the study and their authors, and discusses the reasoning behind the time period that was chosen for analysis. Section 13.3 introduces the concept of SLI. Section 13.4 examines the metalanguage used by authors to discuss the French language, concentrating in particular on the kinds of terms they use to talk about usages that they judge to be correct/incorrect and the terms they use to describe, advise, or prescribe certain usages. Section 13.5 provides a discussion of this analysis, determining first, whether there are particular types of metalanguage used by those authors who take a more prescriptive or descriptive approach; second, whether particular types of metalanguage reflect a stronger influence from the SLI; and third, whether there are any changes in the kinds of metalanguage used over time.

13.2 Sources

The sample of texts taken from the *FranCHRO* corpus for the present study includes texts from the language columns produced by six authors across three different time periods, the 1920s–30s, 1940s–60s, and 1970s–80s.[4] Fifty articles from each author forms a corpus of 300 articles and roughly 290,000 words. This corpus size allows for a very detailed discourse analysis of each article, in particular, a detailed qualitative analysis of the metalanguage used by each author. The articles

---

[1] This project, 'A History of Language Purism in France and Quebec (1865–2000)' was funded by the Leverhulme Trust (2015–18).

[2] This corpus began to be collated from various archival sources between 2015 and 2018, and work to extend the corpus is ongoing. The language columns that make up the corpus are in the process of being digitized to form the first online searchable database of language columns from the French press in France in the twentieth century.

[3] See Cellard (1983); Osthus (2006, 2016); Munro-Hill (2017, 2018); Walsh (2021c); Walsh and Cotelli Kureth (2021).

[4] Note that the articles for Cohen's 1940s column and for Cellard and Bourgeade's columns have been taken from printed collections of their language columns (Cohen 1950; Cellard 1979; Bourgeade 1991). All other articles are taken directly from the relevant newspaper. It was necessary to use this mix of original and reprinted sources, because collating the corpus is ongoing, involving a time-consuming process of consulting microfilm *in situ* at libraries in London and Paris. At the time the study was carried out, it had not yet been possible to collect enough articles from the actual newspapers to complete the corpus, therefore articles from printed collections were used. Articles in such collections may occasionally have minor edits or corrections, and so, where possible, the original articles are used.

produced by each columnist are not of equal length—they vary between, at their shortest, 400 words on average per article (Bourgeade) and, at their longest, 1700 words (Lancelot).[5] However, each of the three time periods has a balance between authors who produce longer and shorter articles (see Table 13.1).

The language columns were published in a variety of newspapers, all of which were intended to reach a serious audience, rather than being of a purely entertaining nature. Political alignment of these papers varies from the centre-right (*Le Figaro magazine, Carrefour*), through the centre (*Le Temps*), and centre-left (*Le Monde, L'Œuvre*) to the strongly left (*L'Humanité, Les Étoiles*). In each period, the two columns appear in papers that are of different alignment, as shown in Table 13.1. The political alignment of the paper, however, does not appear to play a clear-cut role in the attitudes displayed by the column's author. For example, both Cohen (1940s/60s) and Cellard (1970s) publish in left-leaning newspapers (Cohen strongly left, Cellard centre-left) and display quite strongly descriptive views. However, Snell (1920s), who is far more prescriptive in his attitudes, also publishes in a centre-left-leaning newspaper.

Table 13.1 Overview of French language columnists

Columnist	Sample dates	Column	Newspaper	Political leaning of newspaper	Average words per article (rounded)
Victor SNELL (1874–1931)	1929–30	*La Grammaire en zig-zag*	*L'Œuvre*	Centre-left	500
LANCELOT [Abel HERMANT] (1862–1950)	1933–5	*Défense de la langue française*	*Le Temps*	Centre	1700
Marcel COHEN (1884–1974)	1945–6 1961–4	*Regards sur la langue française*	*Les Etoiles, L'Humanité*	Strongly left	1400
André THÉRIVE (1891–1967)	1953–5	*Clinique du langage*	*Carrefour*	Centre-right	500
Jacques CELLARD (1920–2004)	1972–4	*La Vie du langage*	*Le Monde*	Centre-left	1300
Pierre BOURGEADE (1927–2009)	1987–9	*La Vie des mots*	*Le Figaro Magazine*	Centre-right	400

[5] The majority of articles used in the sample have not yet been digitized and exist only in .jpeg form. The average word count was therefore calculated by counting the number of words in twenty articles for each author, averaging the total, and rounding this up to the nearest fifty, for ease of comparison.

The three time periods were chosen as being representative of three periods of change in the status of the French language at home and abroad. They include the interwar period (1920s–30s) when the French language continued to enjoy its privileged status as a prestigious international language of diplomacy that had endured for several centuries; the post-war period (1940s–60s) when the political and economic power of France decreased and it saw its role shift from that of a relatively dominant global power to a much more minor one; and a period towards the end of the twentieth century (1970s–80s), where this minor role was confirmed, as the political, economic, and cultural power and influence of the USA continued to increase. Across the period from the 1940s–80s, the position of the French language as a prestigious, international language of diplomacy saw a corresponding decline (Rickard 1989: 153–4; Lodge 1993: 236; Oakes 2001: 154).

The authors in the sample have different backgrounds, training, and professions. They can all be seen to have some sort of language 'expertise' (see Remysen 2005), although only two, Marcel Cohen and Jacques Cellard, could be said to be professional linguists: Cohen was a university professor who worked on Semitic and Ethiopian languages as well as on French (Leslau 1988: 1) and was also, incidentally, a member of the communist party; Cellard's work as a linguist focused mainly on lexicography, and he was also a journalist and author. The other columnists use language as part of their professional craft but cannot be classed as linguists. Victor Snell was a Swiss lawyer who later became a journalist writing for mainly left-wing publications in France (Douglas 2002: 14). Lancelot (Abel Hermant) was a French author who was one of the few members of the Académie française ever to be ejected, in his case for collaboration during the war (Académie française no date). André Thérive (Roger Puthoste) was an author and journalist (Larousse 2002: 1225), as was Pierre Bourgeade (Larousse 2002: 175).[6]

13.3 Language columns, prescriptivism, and SLI

Prescriptivism generally involves recommending or condemning certain language usages. It often arises during the process of standardization, in particular during codification (see Haugen 1966), where the structure of the language is decided upon and explicit rules about its usage are laid out. Codification is generally accompanied by prescriptivism, which labels certain usages as correct or otherwise acceptable in some way, thereby implying the rejection of others. Indeed, Milroy and Milroy (2012: 22) state that 'prescription becomes more intense after the language undergoes codification [...] because speakers then have access to dictionaries and grammar books which they regard as authorities'. Language columnists are a further form of authority to whom speakers may turn when they experience a hesitation in usage; indeed, language columns can also arguably be viewed as

---

[6] For more detail on the careers of the individual columnists, see Walsh (2021c: 73–4).

codifying texts themselves (see McLelland 2021b: 263), even if this is not their explicit aim. They can thereby help to maintain the SLI.

The SLI is the belief that 'there is one particular form of a language which is the most "correct" or "best" form—spread via powerful institutions, including the education system, the mass media and the employment sector—and that all other forms are incorrect' (Walsh 2021d: 870–1; see also Kroskrity 2000: 26; Lippi-Green 2012: 67). The SLI contributes to a resistance to change in language (in fact, Milroy and Milroy (2012) view what they call the language 'complaint tradition'[7] as resistance to change) and a negative view of variation. This often leads to an increased fixation on prescriptive rules, to keep the language in an unchanged, unvarying form (or, at least, to attempt to do so, given the inevitability of language change). The SLI is also linked to ideologies of power and legitimacy—the belief that one language variety is the best gives that particular variety (and its speakers) more prestige than the other varieties that are spoken in a given culture, and also more legitimacy (given, for example, that the standard variety is the variety used in education, administration etc.) (see Joseph 1987; Bourdieu 1991). Much of the material in language columns is in response to reader questions about the legitimacy of particular usages, which demonstrates the fact that language columns are an important site of SLI (re)creation (see Kroskrity 2010 on sites of ideologies), although of course the choice of which questions to respond to remains with the language columnist.

The genre of language columns is often believed to be a bastion of lay SLI and prescriptivism and, indeed, the articles in many language columns do display strongly prescriptive tendencies. However, a recent analysis of the means by which language columnists construct the authority necessary to make pronouncements about French language usage and impose particular language ideologies has shown that, in fact, the authors of language columns are not uniformly prescriptive but can be seen to be display approaches that vary from prescriptive to descriptive (Walsh 2021c: 86–7). According to Ayres-Bennett (2020a: 187):

> descriptive texts are based on the descriptive norm; starting from the 'facts' or with usage, they describe what is 'normal', 'regular', or 'frequent' in language usage, without making a value judgment about it. The prescriptive 'norm' on the other hand is more subjective: here one thinks of an ideal model; the norm prescribes what should be said, or more usually written, based on value judgments. The prescriptive norm is typically based on the descriptive norm, that is, it often begins with the observation of usage, but then a notion of what is right and wrong, correct and incorrect, is added.

---

[7] The 'complaint tradition' (Milroy and Milroy 2012: viii) 'involves complaint by speakers about so-called misuse of language and linguistic decline' and, according to Milroy and Milroy, has altered little since the eighteenth century (see also Milroy and Milroy 2012: 24–46).

These concepts are not always easy to separate in practice, as Ayres-Bennett (2020a: 201–2) acknowledges. A reader may interpret a descriptive passage as prescriptive, especially if they are reading with the expectation of receiving language advice, for example, in a grammar or, indeed, in a language column. It is also not always the case that individual authors are wholly prescriptive or descriptive; they may show both prescriptive and descriptive tendencies, depending on what they are discussing. For instance, Vaugelas, the best-known seventeenth-century *remarqueur*, is famous for his prescriptive approach to the French language. However, much of his work in fact had a relatively open approach to variation. The explicit statements that he made about language included 'expressions of both a descriptive and a prescriptive stance' (Ayres-Bennett 2016: 111) and the use of metalanguage in his observations equally showed 'a mix of prescriptive and descriptive language' (Ayres-Bennett 2016: 112). It may therefore be more accurate to view description and prescription as the endpoints of a continuum or cline rather than as binary categories, with the approach of individual authors tending more towards the prescriptive or descriptive end (see Ayres-Bennett 2016: 104).

A recent study carried out using the same sample of articles from the *FranCHRO* corpus (Walsh 2021c) consolidates this view that individual authors do not always display a clearly prescriptive or descriptive view. The study examined the use of references (to dictionaries and grammars and to literary works) made in the sample and showed that the authors vary in their levels of prescriptivism. While Lancelot (1930s) displays an almost uniformly prescriptive approach and Cohen (1940s/60s) a very strongly descriptive approach, the other four authors fall somewhere between the two approaches, with Snell (1920s) and Thérive (1950s) tending more towards a prescriptive approach on the whole, although both can be more descriptive at times (in particular Thérive), and Cellard (1970s) and Bourgeade (1980s) being more likely to take a descriptive approach, although both also display prescriptive tendencies at times (Bourgeade is far more likely to do so than Cellard). While some studies have suggested that—in the French tradition at least—there has been a general tendency over time towards more tolerance of variation (i.e. towards a more descriptive view, see Kibbee and Craig 2019: 77), this is not unequivocally the case here. As can be seen in Figure 13.1, while it is certainly the case that the earlier columnists tend towards the prescriptive end of the continuum, and that no columnists after 1940 are found to be very highly prescriptive, it is not the case that all later columnists are strongly descriptive and that they become more descriptive over time.[8] Cohen—who falls in the middle of the period examined (1940s/60s)—is very much at the descriptive end and Bourgeade, the most recent columnist (1980s) can be found somewhere in the middle. It is

---

[8] This continuum is a graphical representation of the qualitative results of Walsh (2021b), which showed that language columnists in the twentieth century in France cannot be seen as a unified group reflecting a single language ideology. Rather, they reflect a range of positions on the prescriptive-descriptive continuum.

of note that it is the two professional linguists, Cohen (1940s/60s) and Cellard (1970s), who are the most descriptive. This is of course not unsurprising, given the concerted move in the twentieth century towards a descriptive approach to the study of language, following Saussure's (1916) *Course in General Linguistics* (see Hodson 2006). As Trask (1999: 47–8) notes, 'modern linguists utterly reject prescriptivism, and their investigations are instead based on descriptivism'.

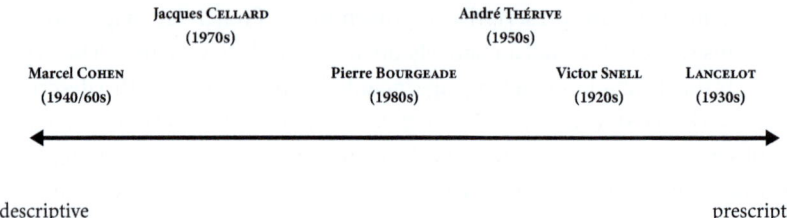

Figure 13.1 Position of French language columnists on the descriptive-prescriptive continuum

These general tendencies were reinforced by a further recent study on the type of metaphor used by French (and Swiss) language columnists (Walsh and Cotelli Kureth 2021). Common language metaphors (e.g. of illness, colonization, war, gardening) were used by Snell (1920s), Lancelot (1930s), Thérive (1950s), and, occasionally, Bourgeade (1980s) to encourage the use of a particular, correct usage and to reinforce a prescriptive point of view, whereas Cohen (1940s/60s) and Cellard (1970s) never used metaphors for these purposes, instead using them to promote a descriptive view, or a view that was tolerant of variation, to help explain a point, or to add humour (Bourgeade also occasionally used metaphor for the latter purpose) (see Walsh and Cotelli Kureth 2021: 484). It seems therefore that the chronological development from a more prescriptive to a more descriptive approach noted by Kibbee and Craig (2019: 77) is not unambiguously evident here either. Although the two earliest columnists, Snell (1920s) and Lancelot (1930s) certainly display the most prescriptive view, the most recent columnist, Bourgeade (1980s) displays both prescriptive and descriptive tendencies. These two recent studies (Walsh 2021c; Walsh and Cotelli Kureth 2021) examined the use of references to create authority and the use of metaphor in language columns. By examining a further site where language attitudes are explicitly and implicitly evident—metalanguage—the current study will allow us to further clarify whether or not language columns reflect the general trend towards descriptivism and whether the suggestion that this is a linear progression can be supported.

In the case of authors with prescriptive tendencies, both studies (Walsh 2021c; Walsh and Cotelli Kureth 2021) show very clearly that they were influenced by a strong SLI. The most prescriptive authors made far more reference to the Littré (1863–78) and Académie française dictionaries, to the *remarqueurs*, and to literary works from the early modern period (Walsh 2021c: 77–8). That is, they referred more often to institutions, grammarians, and literary texts that hold particular cultural weight in France and that evoke a period when the French language was considered to be at its best which calls on ideologies of prestige and legitimacy that are linked to the SLI. Indeed, seventeenth-century French literature, in particular, is often linked to a golden age of the French language (see Paveau and Rosier 2008: 21).[9] Although all authors in the study—prescriptive and descriptive—used a range of metaphors for varying purposes, the most prescriptive authors made more frequent use of metaphors and images that are typically found in purist language discourse, for example, metaphors of war and battle (see e.g. Thomas 1991; Jones 1999), and used them to very clearly promote one particular usage as correct or to reinforce a prescriptive point of view that views one form of the language as the best or most correct (Walsh and Cotelli Kureth 2021).

Both of these recent studies demonstrated, first, that the prescriptive and descriptive stances taken by the different authors vary in a way that is more complex than a straightforward chronological development from more prescriptive to more descriptive and, second, that there is a much higher use of references that invoke a prestige form of language and metaphors that reflect a purist attitude by those authors who display a more prescriptive stance. The current chapter builds upon these two earlier studies by examining the types of language used to describe and also to recommend or condemn particular usages, to see whether there are particular types of metalanguage used by authors who take a more prescriptive or descriptive approach, whether particular types of metalanguage reflect a stronger influence from, or adherence to, the SLI, and also whether there are any changes in the kinds of metalanguage used over time. This will also allow us to determine whether the somewhat unclear chronological patterns in authors' prescriptive or descriptive tendencies are maintained here or whether there is a clearer trend towards descriptivism, and whether there are any particular types of metalanguage that can be associated with one or the other tendency, or whether it is more a question of degree, with more prescriptive authors using certain metalanguage more frequently, for example, as was the case with metaphor. Section 13.4 presents the metalanguage used by the six language columnists broadly in chronological order (although note that Cohen and Thérive overlap), which will allow any trends over time to be clearly apparent.

13.4 Metalanguage in language columns

13.4.1 Introduction

Given that the authors of language columns provide their readers with expert language advice, a close analysis of the metalanguage used by these authors can reveal

---

[9] See Watts (2000) for more on the golden age topos.

what kinds of language judgements they are passing on to their readers; even where an author may claim to be more descriptive than prescriptive, the type of language they use to describe certain usages may be more revealing of their actual stance towards language and this in turn may determine the kind of ideology that they communicate to their readers. Rhetorical devices, including categories of classification (barbarisms, errors, good usage, etc.) and deontic 'X is to be avoided' statements, declaratives, and imperatives can be viewed as genre-typical features of grammars, dictionaries, and other kinds of codification texts that denote either explicit or implicit prescriptivism (see McLelland 2021b: 270–1). A close reading of each of the 300 articles in the sample examined was therefore carried out to determine, first, what kinds of terms they use to talk about usages that they judge to be incorrect (e.g. 'faute', 'erreur', 'incorrect(e)') and, second, the terms they use to describe, advise, or prescribe certain usages (e.g. 'il faut dire X, il ne faut pas dire Y'; 'dites X, ne dites pas Y'; 'on dit, on ne dit pas', etc.).

13.4.2 Language and correctness

Terms associated with language and correctness, for example, terms labelling usages as 'incorrect(e)' or 'correct(e)', and terms such as 'erreur', 'faute', 'fauti(f)(ve)', 'impropre', 'défectueu(x)(se)', etc., while relatively common in the texts of certain authors examined, are less common across the sample as a whole than might be expected in a genre that is viewed as essentially prescriptive. They are used most frequently by Snell (1920s), somewhat less frequently by Lancelot (1930s) and Thérive (1950s), infrequently by Bourgeade (1980s) and Cellard (1970s), and barely at all by Cohen (1940s/60s). This is surprising, given that earlier studies (Walsh 2021c; Walsh and Cotelli Kureth 2021) have shown that Lancelot, for example, is highly prescriptive and might be expected to make more use of such terms. However, he simply has a different strategy for marking usages as (un)acceptable, as shall become apparent.

Snell (1920s) often makes reference to the acceptability (or not) of certain usages, using terms such as 'incorrect(e)', 'faute', or 'erreur'. To note just a small selection of examples from the sample of texts examined, he states that a particular use of the verb 'controuver' is an 'erreur' and an 'impropriété' (12 March 1929); that '"[c]ombien en avez-vous tués" est une faute' (02 April 1929); that '[c]'est une faute' to use 'formidable' to mean 'énorme, étonnant, incroyable' (09 April 1929); and that '"[c]e que c'est beau!"' is an 'incorrection certaine' (30 April 1939). He occasionally uses the term 'barbarisme', as, for example, when he states that '*ne pas . . . que* est une grosse faute, un barbarisme' (in spite of the fact that 'l'usage [. . .] tend nettement à le faire admettre') (21 May 1929); and that using '[c]elui, celle, ceux, celles' before an adjective or participle is a '[b]arbarisme détestable qui tend malheureusement à se généraliser' (11 June 1929). It appears that the term 'barbarisme' is broadly equated with 'faute' here.[10] He also sometimes refers to a 'faute grossière' or 'une grosse faute' (as in 21 May 1929 above, see also e.g. 28 May 1929, 4 June 1929, 23 July 1929) or adds other negative judgements, stating, for example, that an incorrect use of the term 'ingambe' is 'un contresens grossier' and a '[f]aute trop répandue' (29 October 1929); and that the use of '[i]ls, masculin pour remplacer deux mots féminins constitue une faute flagrante' (05 November 1929).

Snell occasionally uses even more strongly negative terms including, on separate occasions, 'détestable', 'disgracieux', 'inexcusable', and 'injurieuse'. For example, he states that the term 'imbrisé' forms part of a series of 'adjectifs disgracieux' (26 February 1929); that using the form 'ne pas... que' is 'inexcusable' (28 May 1929); that the usage 'en faveur et contre le projet' is a '[t]ournure détestable, injurieuse', because it should be 'en faveur du' and 'contre le' and 'il est impossible de substituer un complément à l'autre' (16 July 1929). He uses these relatively infrequently, however, and certainly far less frequently than more neutral terms such as 'faute'. In many instances, therefore, Snell very clearly takes a strongly prescriptive stance, not only viewing one usage as correct and others as incorrect but clearly seeing it as his role to highlight such correct usages and encourage speakers to avoid the others.

Snell does, however, sometimes accept that usage can play a more important role than grammatical correctness in certain cases, and that usage can in fact lead to changes in what is viewed as grammatically acceptable, which may suggest a partly descriptive approach, allowing for variation and change in language. In particular, this seems to be the case when a usage has become especially widespread or frequently used. For example, when discussing the use of 'ne pas... que' (21 May 1929), he states that there is no doubt that this is grammatically incorrect but that 'la pratique' ignores this. As he says, 'La doctrine est formelle: *ne pas... que* est une grosse faute, un barbarisme. L'usage, au contraire, tend nettement à le faire admettre.' Later in the article he discusses at what point a 'faute de construction' that is very frequently used stops being an error. This would appear to show him to be open to some variation or change, at least where it is sanctioned by 'common usage' and frequently used. However, his very next sentence as he moves onto a new topic would appear to negate this approach: 'Chaque fois que nous le pouvons, évitons les fautes' (28 May 1929).

Lancelot (1930s) does not use 'faute' or 'erreur' very frequently (nearly all of the examples in the sample are noted here), in the sense of marking particular usages as errors (in fact these terms are more often used by readers asking him whether a particular usage is correct/is an error). Lancelot instead tends to use a

---

[10] See Ayres-Bennett and Seijido (2011: 77) on the use of the term 'barbarisme' by the *remarqueurs*; Ayres-Bennett (2015: 57–8) on the use of the term by language columnists; see also Humphries (2021: 175–8).

more negative language, employing terms such as 'barbarisme' (employed thirteen times in the sample), 'barbare' (eighteen times), 'monstre' (seven times), 'vulgaire' (twenty-four times), 'affreu(x)(se)' (fourteen times). Where he does use 'faute', it is generally alongside reinforcing terms to demonstrate a highly prescriptive approach.[11] Lancelot was the author of several very prescriptive volumes on the French language[12] and a member of the Académie française (before his expulsion for collaboration during the war), and his approach is therefore perhaps unsurprising. For example, he notes that: 'Cette faute, très fréquente, est l'une des plus grossières que l'on puisse commettre' (27 September 1934); 'je n'écris pas [. . .] *La manière de traiter les belles-mères comme elles méritent de l'être*, parce que cela, c'est une faute énorme' (2–3 January 1935); 'Ils disent *réussir une entreprise*, *réussir un ouvrage*; c'est une très grosse faute, on réussit *dans* une entreprise, on réussit à faire ceci ou cela' (19 April 1934); and that using 'donné' invariably in a particular situation is 'une faute incontestable, évidente' (8 March 1934). In the latter article, Lancelot goes on to say '[é]pargnez-moi, je vous prie, l'objection qu'elle est courante: ce n'est pas ce qui l'empêche d'être une faute', demonstrating that an expression being in common usage is not a factor in his appraisal,[13] and thereby highlighting a very prescriptive approach that adheres strongly to the SLI.

He also frequently refers to 'fautes' marking some kind of social judgement; indeed, he is often the one making the judgement. For example, in response to a reader arguing that 'les fautes' are not an issue if they do not create confusion, he states that '[l]es fautes d'orthographe n'ont pas le seul inconvénient de "créer des confusions": elles peuvent aussi témoigner le défaut d'éducation de ceux qui les font' (27 September 1934). He also sometimes marks certain errors as 'faute de concierge' or 'faute de cuisinère'. For example, he states that '*s'en rappeler* est toujours une faute de concierge' (9 February 1933). This serves to reinforce a clearly prescriptive view that sees only one very particular form of socially elite usage as acceptable. He makes this explicit more than once. For example, he states (9 August 1934) 'j'ai répété sur tous les tons que le bon usage que nous devons suivre en parlant ou en écrivant est le bon usage d'aujourd'hui'. He alludes to what he means by 'le bon usage', by referring, for instance, to the 'vocabulaire des gens bien élevés' (9 March 1933); 'le français des honnêtes gens' (29 March 1934); or 'les personnes comme il faut' (11 April 1935). He makes this even more explicit

---

[11] The other frequent use of 'faute' in this sample is in response to readers who have dared to suggest that Lancelot himself has made an error; suggestions that are always quickly and strongly rebuffed (see e.g. 23 February 1933).

[12] For example, *Xavier ou Les entretiens sur la grammaire française* (1923), *Lettres à Xavier sur l'art d'écrire* (1925), and *Savoir parler* (1936), see Abel Hermant, BnF: https://data.bnf.fr/fr/12090487/abel_hermant/fr.pdf (accessed 22 December 2021).

[13] In fact, the linguistic authorities relied upon by Lancelot are very reflective of a strong SLI. As outlined in Walsh (2021c), he assigns clear authority to the Littré and Académie dictionaries, to the *remarqueurs* and to the French early modern authors. For him, 'usage' means the usage laid out in these guides and not that of ordinary speakers.

on occasion, for example, when he says '[s]eul compte l'usage de ceux que l'on appelait au grand siècle les honnêtes gens, et que décidément je préfère appeler, comme sous Louis-Philippe, les gens comme il faut' (11 April 1935). His marking of errors as 'de concièrge' or 'de cuisinière' work to reinforce this prescriptive view that only the usage of 'les gens comme il faut', or the social elite, can be viewed as acceptable.

Thérive (1950s), like Lancelot, does not in fact use terms such as 'correct(e)'/'incorrect(e)', 'faute', or 'erreur' very frequently. It is interesting that, on the few occasions in the sample where he does, he refers to the error being unimportant, for example, 'des fautes vénielles' (14 January 1953); 'un peu incorrect' (6 January 1954); 'un peu barbare' (24 December 1952). However, in spite of this, he can be negative about the error. For example, he describes one of the 'fautes vénielles' as a 'tour bizarre' and states '[n]ous ne parviendrons pas à le justifier'. When discussing nominalization which he sees as 'un peu incorrect', he states that '[e]lle marque la tendance de la langue contemporaine à créer des mots composés dans le genre d'*aveugle-de-guerre, assurés-sociaux, timbre-postes*, qui eussent faire hurler nos aïeux'. Similarly to Lancelot, the lack of these terms in the sample does not reflect a lack of prescriptivism. Rather, Thérive prefers to use more judgemental language when discussing usages he views as incorrect. For example, in the sample examined, he uses expressions such as 'ces vilaines formules' (29 October 1952); 'impropriété' and 'monstre orthographique' (26 November 1952); 'épouvantable' (3 December 1952); 'sauvage' (17 December 1952); 'prose d'illettrés' (21 January 1953); 'ridicule [...] pédant et maladroit' (4 February 1953); 'pédant et artificiel', 'des monstres inviables', 'ridicule', and again 'monstre' (3 March 1954); 'ces bizarres périphrases' (17 March 1954); 'mal fait, inutile et prétentieux' (24 March 1954); 'pas bien louable', 'trop laide, quasi parodique, et grossier' (31 March 1954). Unlike Lancelot, however, Thérive does not comment very often on the usage of particular speakers. He refers to 'les bons gens' and their usage on only two occasions in the sample of fifty articles (19 November 1952 in a discussion of the possessive; 17 December 1952 with regard to the usage of the term 'Nord-Africain').

Cohen (1940s/60s)[14] rarely uses the terms 'faute', 'erreur', or 'correct(e)'/ 'incorrect(e)' and there are very few examples in the sample of fifty articles examined. In general, Cohen uses his articles to simply discuss various terms/expressions/grammatical constructions and their usage and, in particular, their development or history, but he rarely refers to them being correct or acceptable. Rare examples include the following (Cohen 1950: 26): 'On trouve maintenant écrit quelquefois au passé simple indicatif des expressions comme: il

---

[14] As noted in Section 13.2, at the time of the study it had not yet been possible to collect enough of Cohen's articles from *L'Humanité* to form an adequate corpus and articles from printed collections were used. This is the reason for which the sample of Cohen's articles spans the 1940s and 1960s.

poussa la porte jusqu'à ce qu'elle se ferma; mais cette tournure ne peut pas jusqu'à présent être considérée comme correcte'. A further example takes a forgiving tone towards the error in question (Cohen 1950: 39): 'La nuance est parfois fragile entre *emmener* et *amener*, et il n'est pas étonnant que certaines personnes la comprennent mal'. This lack of negative language is in line with the overwhelmingly descriptive approach displayed by him at nearly all times. This is possibly related to his status as an academic linguist. Walsh (2021c: 82–3) found, for example, that his column takes a very explanatory approach towards language, with few value judgements about correctness, but instead involves discussions informed by relevant academic literature about how and why language is used in a particular way or changes over time. Cohen also explicitly views 'usage' as the usage of the common people rather than of an elite social group (Walsh 2021c: 87). This may well be related not only to his work as a descriptive linguist but also his political adherence to communism.

Cellard (1970s) makes very little use of the terms 'erreur', 'faute', 'correct(e)', etc. and even less of strongly negative terms. In the sample examined, only one example of highly negative terminology and two examples of 'faute'/'correct(e)' were found. The former is in relation to using company names formed from acronyms without an article (e.g. 'SOCOMMAR' rather than 'la SOCOMMAR'), and here Cellard uses a style of language that is quite unusual for him. He starts by saying (13 March 1972) '[g]las, alarme, alerte! C'est sans délibérer ni désemparer que l'arrêt sera rendu: il s'agit de *la* société, de *la* compagnie, *l'*union, *le* groupe, *les* postes, etc.' and goes on to state that 'il y a là une dégradation parfaitement gratuite non seulement de la langue des affaires et de l'économie mais de la langue tout court'. Of course, this is not in fact very strong language, compared to that of some other columnists, but it is unusually so for Cellard. As noted, this only occurs once in the whole sample, and it appears to be a reaction to the increased use of acronyms for company names, which Cellard views negatively. As he says, '[v]ivre dans un univers d'initiales n'est déjà pas si attrayant qu'il faille de surcroît mutiler ce qui ne l'est que trop'. It is in this context of the use of acronyms that he comments negatively on the lack of article used. Cellard also states (3 July 1972) that using the terms 'technologie' and 'technologique' for 'technique' is 'une deviation particulièrement inacceptable' and that using 'technologie' outside of its 'acception correcte et unique' is 'prétentieux'. He states in an article later that month (31 July 1972) that: 'Grammairiens et spécialistes tiennent pour: "Il demande *qu'on* lui explique", et non: "à ce que . . .". Ce dernier tour reste une faute, mais vénielle, et explicable sinon excusable.' Here he rationalizes the 'faute' by noting that it is minor and easily explained. On the whole, he avoids referring to usages as 'errors' or 'faults' to be corrected, and in the vast majority of his articles, he simply describes usages—and changes in language—without making any particular value judgements about their acceptability, demonstrating a generally descriptive approach, similar to that displayed by Cohen (1940s/60s), also an academic linguist. It is difficult to tell whether Cellard's generally descriptive approach has a different effect on readers than the more prescriptive approaches displayed by authors such as Snell and Lancelot. As noted by McLelland (2021b: 267), 'even seemingly descriptive statements may be interpreted prescriptively' and '[a]ny description can become, to its readers, normative' (on this point, see also Hodson 2006; Cameron 2012: 7–8; Ayres-Bennett 2016: 105–6).

Bourgeade (1980s) does not make extensive use of terms such as 'faute', but where he does, it is generally in a clearly prescriptive manner. For example, he refers to the expression 'débuter une conférence' as a 'solécisme grossier' (Bourgeade 1991: 28). In a discussion of the term 'débuter' being used transitively, he states 'De toutes ces fautes, il en est une qui a le don de m'exaspérer et qui, chacun l'a remarqué, se répand, ces temps-ci, sur les divers médias, à une vitesse extrême: c'est l'emploi des deux verbes *débuter* et *démarrer* de manière transitive, et non intransitive, comme il le faudrait'(Bourgeade 1991: 17).

Bourgeade (1991: 28) returns to this in a later article, stating that, 'Ce qui est faute est devenu licence. Demain, sans doute, les trois petites lettres, *Fam.* (*familier*), qui accompagnent l'énoncé de cette licence disparaîtront, la faute sera devenue la règle, le français s'affaiblira encore, et il s'affaiblira dans la laideur'. In a discussion of Hanse's (1987) *Nouveau dictionnaire des difficultés du français*, Bourgeade (1991: 66) states that:

> M. Hanse, ayant tout lu, m'a paru excessivement porté à l'indulgence. Il est peu de fautes avérées, en effet, qu'on ne puisse trouver sous la plume de nos contemporains, et le fait que des écrivains de plus ou moins grand renom les aient commises ne change rien au fait qu'elles sont des fautes. Un exemple entre vingt: M. Hanse relève que Sartre et de Gaulle emploient *avatar* dans le sens de mésaventure, et il incline à le leur pardonner. Pas de pardon, bien sûr, pour un tel crime.

In a discussion of media language, Bourgeade (1991: 17) states that:

> Notre malheureuse langue est maltraitée sur les divers médias (pas seulement sur TF 1), et les courriers des lecteurs des magazines spécialisés sont submergés par les doléances des téléspectateurs, ou des auditeurs, relevant les innombrables fautes commises par les privilégiés du monde cathodique dont nous parla un jour Le Canard enchaîné.

Although his use of these terms is relatively rare in the sample examined, they are often reinforced by other, more negative terms, such as 'grossier' and 'laideur', by verbs such as 'maltraiter', or by equating such fauts to a 'crime' (also through use of the verb 'commettre'). He also very occasionally uses terms such as 'monstre', for example, 'le trinôme *mieux-disant culturel*, de quelque côté qu'on le prenne, est un monstre' (Bourgeade 1991: 18) (see also 'monstrueux', Bourgeade 1991: 77). He therefore clearly presents a prescriptive view at times in his articles. This is arguably balanced by a more descriptive approach on the whole, but it shows that Bourgeade does at least partly adhere to a view that sees one form of language as the best or the most correct form. This is in spite of the fact that he explicitly claims to take a descriptive approach. For example, in a discussion of Hagège's *Le Français et les siècles*, Bourgeade (1991: 11) states that 'Hagège ne s'est pas contenté de *décrire*, il a fallu qu'il se mêle de *prescrire*, ou d'ouvrir la voix aux prescripteurs. Or l'usage ne peut se prescrire [...] L'usage reste le seul maitre de l'usage'. However, Bourgeade (1991: 28) does go on to acknowledge later on that his approach is not always clear-cut:

> Je reconnais que je suis en pleine contradiction. Il y a un mois, je demandais que l'on abandonnât l'imparfait du subjonctif en raison de l'usage; aujourd'hui, je demande qu'on continue à ne pas dire débuter une conférence malgré l'usage, et malgré le Petit Larousse dont je supplie respectueusement les rédacteurs de revenir, ne fût-ce que pour un temps, sur la consécration accordée (par erreur, peut-être?) à ce solécisme grossier. Mais cette contradiction, n'est-elle pas au cœur même du travail de ceux qui ont en charge la rédaction des dictionnaires, qu'il s'agisse du Dictionnaire de l'Académie ou des dictionnaires privés? Tantôt ils doivent se prononcer pour l'usage, tantôt ils doivent se prononcer contre l'usage, si celui-ci est par trop fautif. Question d'intuition.

It appears, therefore, that his choice to take a prescriptive or descriptive approach is a purely personal one. Some deviations from the norm appear to annoy him more than others and, in these cases, his desire to describe is apparently overruled by an impulse to prescribe, based on his own 'intuition'.

13.4.3 Prescribing and advising

An author's stance towards a particular usage can also be revealed through the kinds of verbs and other terms that they use to advise speakers to either use or avoid particular usages. These include the impersonal verb 'falloir', the modals 'devoir' and 'pouvoir', imperatives such as 'dites' and 'ne dites pas', and simple statements such as 'on dit/écrit' and 'on ne dit/écrit pas'. It is clear that these formulae do not all have the same strength; for example, 'il faut dire' is arguably stronger than 'on dit'. However, even where authors present usages as statements of fact, the use of the phrase 'on dit X' implies that 'on ne dit pas Y', and it is likely that readers will read this as a prescription. In this way, such expressions can be interpreted as covertly prescriptive (see Ayres-Bennett 2020a: 190–1; Humphries 2021: 182–3). The sample of articles was analysed closely for the presence/absence of forms such as: 'on (ne) dit/écrit (pas)'; 'il (ne) faut (pas) (dire/écrire)'; 'on (ne) doit (pas) dire/écrire'; 'on (ne) peut (pas) dire/écrire'; and 'il vaut mieux dire/écrire'. This was a highly qualitative manual analysis of printed texts (no in-text searches could be carried out due to the fact that much of the corpus was not in text-searchable format), which gathered and analysed all instances of forms using verbs such as 'doit', 'peut' etc., as well as forms with similar meaning such as 'on met obligatoirement' or 'on est bien obligé de' (see discussion of Thérive later in this section, for example).

Snell (1920s) makes regular use of 'falloir', and always in a strictly prescriptive manner, very definitely presenting the usage which 'il ne faut pas dire' as incorrect. This is perhaps not unexpected, given his highly prescriptive use of terms such as 'faute' and 'erreur' and negative terms such as 'détestable', 'disgracieux' outlined in Section 13.4.2. For example, when he says 'Il ne faut pas dire "sélectionner" qui entraînerait "sélectionnement" (je ne sais trop si quelque barbare ne l'a pas déjà osé); il faut dire *sélecter*.' (19 March 1929), the use of 'il ne faut pas' is supported by a negative appraisal of anyone who does not follow this advice as a 'barbare'. Similarly, he criticizes Paul Claudet for the title of one of his books, *Conversations dans le Loir-et-Cher*: 'C'est mauvais, surtout de la part de quelqu'un qui prétend à l'Académie. Il faut dire, pour bien dire: "En Loir-et-Cher". Et cela, non par simple usage, mais parce que c'est la règle de grammaire' (12 March 1929). Here, he expresses astonishment that someone aiming to become a member of the Académie française would employ this usage, and also notes that this is not simply a question of usage but also a rule of grammar, thereby reinforcing his prescriptive stance. He also sometimes uses further expressions to cement his prescriptive stance, as for example, when he says (26 March 1929): 'Sans le moindre doute la négation était obligatoire, et il fallait: l'on *n*'aurait, victoire *ne* fut ...'.

Snell also makes use of 'on doit/ne doit pas dire', 'on peut dire', 'il vaut mieux dire', and 'on dit/on ne dit pas'. Although he very occasionally uses these formulae in a way that allows for a hierarchy of acceptability, in most cases, they are used to highlight the one correct way of saying something. For example, he states (5 March 1929) that '[f]ortuné ne doit pas être employé pour riche' and goes on to reinforce this by adding that 'Littré, citant Nodier, dit que c'est une faute'. He reinforces his statement (2 April 1929) that 'il vaut mieux dire "chacun son auto"' by adding that this is 'seul vraiment correct'. Even where he acknowledges that a certain usage might be allowed, he often still advises the reader against it. For example, in a discussion (14 May 1929) of the usage 'autrement plus vaste', he concedes that 'on pourrait employer cette forme' in certain circumstances but that 'ce n'est pas à recommander', and in the same article in a discussion of the expletive 'ne', he states that 'on peut donc le supprimer, mais il est plus correct de le mettre'. There are only two occasions in the sample where these terms are used, and more than one usage is accepted. In a discussion (30 July 1929) of the sentence '[u]ne lettre confidentielle dont la divulgation peut causer tant et de si graves dommages', Snell states that '[m]ieux eût valu dire, en supprimant le et malencontreux: ... *Dont la divulgation peut causer tant* de si *graves dommages*. (Et mieux encore: *tant de graves dommages*, car "tant de si" n'est pas très heureux)'. In a later discussion (31 December 1929) of the sentence '[c]'est de ce bulletin DONT parle irrévérencieusement Jules Renard', Snell notes that '[i]l faudrait: "C'est de ce bulletin *que* parle ..."' but that '[o]n pourrait dire aussi: "C'est ce bulletin dont parle ..."'. In the majority of cases, then, such terms are used by Snell to unequivocally present a prescriptive view. Also, the terms 'on peut' or 'on dit'—while they may appear weaker than 'il faut' or 'on doit'—are used by Snell in a manner which makes very clear that one usage, and one usage only, is being recommended as correct.

Rather unexpectedly, given his highly prescriptive use of very negative terms such as 'monstre' and 'affreux' outlined in Section 13.4.2, Lancelot (1930s) makes very little use of 'il faut dire', 'on doit dire', 'on peut dire', etc. in this sample. Where he does use such terms, it is generally to present one usage as the only correct one, and he often reinforces 'il faut dire' or 'on doit dire' with an intensifier, e.g. 'hors de doute', as in the following examples: 'Pour revenir à *cariatide*, étant convenu que l'υ est représenté en français par l'*y*, il est hors de doute qu'il faut écrire *caryatide*' (27 June 1935); 'Il est hors de doute que l'on doit dire *entrer* et non *rentrer* quand il s'agit d'un lieu où l'on pénètre pour la première fois' (11 April 1935). In an article discussing agreement, he again refers to a lack of doubt about a usage (3 May 1934): 'il faut donc écrire *la joie que m'a causée*. Il n'y a pas ombre de doute ni de difficulté. Ce n'est pas même un cas particulier. C'est l'application la plus élémentaire de la règle des participes, qui est elle-même l'une des plus simples de la grammaire française'. Here he not only stresses the lack of possible discussion but passes a judgement on the reader for not knowing this 'simple' rule. Indeed, he notes that 'les enfants de huit ans' would know the rule. In fact, rather than using phrases such as 'il faut dire' or 'on doit dire' he very often makes his attitude towards particular usages clear by passing judgement on the authors of such usages. Further examples include him noting that 'il faut vraiment être possédé par le démon de la perversité pour écrire *rester à court*, comme ce traducteur, alors que le dernier cancre de la maternelle n'ignore pas que l'on dit *rester court*' (22 February 1934); and that speakers who use certain terms 'ne sentent aucunement le génie de leur langue maternelle' (23 February 1934). Such scathing judgements are indeed common in the sample of fifty articles examined; Lancelot frequently criticizes speakers of French, and he also sometimes uses irony or sarcasm to put speakers down. This is often in response to a reader questioning his judgement and may well be a deliberate ploy by Lancelot to cement his authority as language arbiter.[15] By questioning or mocking the usage of others, he is presenting himself as the ultimate authority on questions of language usage.

---

[15] For example, Lancelot (23 February 1933) responds to a correspondent who has claimed he made a mistake (on which point Lancelot does not agree), by asking sarcastically 'Aurai-je cependant le courage et la patience de lui remontrer à mon tour qu'il a tort de confondre *se rappeler DE fautes* et *se rappeler DES fautes*, que, dans ce dernier cas, *des fautes* est complément direct et *des* est pour certains ? Non, je n'aurai pas cette patience [...]'.

Thérive (1950s) makes relatively little use of phrases such as 'il faut' or 'on doit dire'. Where he does, it is often in a fairly straightforward way. For example, he simply notes (18 February 1953) that '[d]égingandé doit se prononcer comme il s'écrit: *déjinghandé* pour être plus clair'; that (20 January 1954) '[o]n met obligatoirement après le nom l'épithète qui désigne et spécifie la classe ou l'espèce: *une loi pénale*' and that (19 Novembre 1952):

> on emploie le possessif pour rappeler des objets impersonnels: *'l'approche d'une petite ville, une rivière baigne ses murs'*, écrit La Bruyère. Ajoutons que, lorsque ce nom de chose est sujet de la phrase on est bien obligé d'user du possessif *son, sa, leur* etc. 'La Seine prend sa source près de Langres.'

He only very occasionally uses an imperative, e.g. in a discussion of the terms 'commando' and 'détachement', he says '[é]crivez donc: détachement' (25 February 1952); and on the use of 'on' for 'nous', he says 'ne l'employons qu'avec cette nuance-là pour éviter ces vilaines formules: Nous, on aime le sport' (29 October 1952). Where he does use imperatives or modals, it is with clearly prescriptive purposes, he is laying out the correct answer. It is interesting that he does not make more use of these, however, particularly given the fact that the frequently negative language he uses (examples in Section 13.4.2) makes it very clear that he has strong opinions about what usages are—and are not—acceptable. This highlights the usefulness of examining more than one aspect of metalanguage to determine an author's approach.

In line with his highly descriptive approach discussed in Section 13.4.2, Cohen (1940s/60s) rarely uses phrases such as 'il faut' or 'on doit dire/écrire' and there are very few examples in the sample examined. On one occasion, he says (Cohen 1950: 26): 'Si on veut employer le subjonctif, il faut introduire *ce*, et il en résulte une tournure plutôt disgracieuse: *ne reste pas planté là jusqu'à ce que je me mette en rogne*; *ce n'est pas la peine d'attendre jusqu'à ce que je sorte*.' However, on the whole he simply describes usages rather than prescribing, as in the following example (Cohen 1950: 41): 'On met l'indicatif quand il s'agit d'une declaration ferme [...] On met le subjonctif avec des verbes de volonté [...] Pour les verbes qui indiquent une opinion, on emploie en général l'indicatif'. He also acknowledges variation, as for example, when he says (18 March 1963): 'On dit normalement [...] Mais on dit aussi [...]'. The use of 'normalement' could perhaps be viewed as an acknowledgement of prescriptive rules, although it could also very well be purely descriptive. The fact that he uses so few deontics or imperatives telling readers how to use language reflects his descriptive approach, and this is furthermore not supplemented/replaced by highly judgemental or negative language anywhere in the sample of articles examined (as is the case for Lancelot and Thérive, for example).

In accordance with the descriptive approach displayed by Cellard (1970s) outlined in Section 13.4.2, he rarely uses forms such as 'il faut dire' or 'on dit' and only very occasionally uses verbs such as 'devoir'. Where he does, he includes himself with his readers by using the 'nous' form of the verb. For example, he says (17 July 1972) '[n]ous devrions dire et écrire constamment: "je souhaitais qu'il pût", et non "qu'il puisse"; "j'avais ordonné qu'il chantât", et non "qu'il chante". Il est notoire que nous n'en faisons rien . . .'. He is using the verb 'devoir' here in an ironic manner, noting what 'we should do', were 'we' to follow prescriptive rules and comparing this with what 'we actually do'. It is quite clear from his articles that this is a deliberate choice, as he is openly critical towards approaches to language that are too prescriptive/purist and frequently notes that a language is in constant evolution and undergoing variation in usage, and that it is common usage that determines what is/is not acceptable in a language (rather than the usage of a particular, elite group). For example, he states that '[l]'usage engendre la règle, non l'invers' (29 December 1971); 'ce n'est pas la règle qui fait la langue mais la langue qui fait les règles' (13 March 1972); and 'la langue décidera—la langue parlée l'a déjà fait—dans le sens de cette logique' (8 May 1972). He also refers on other occasions to 'le peuple' actually deciding on usage (see e.g. 19 June 1972).

Although Section 13.4.2 showed that Bourgeade (1980s) displayed a level of prescriptivism, with some use of terms such as 'faute' and negative qualifiers, he did not make extensive use of such terms. A descriptive approach is more apparent here. He makes very little use of phrases such as 'il faut/on doit dire/écrire'. One of the few examples is in a discussion of the transitive use of 'débuter' (Bourgeade 1991: 17, see Section 13.4.2 for full example) where he notes that it is not being used intransitively 'comme il le faudrait'. However, he does not otherwise tell readers what to say or write, and his view, discussed in Section 13.4.2, that it is current usage which is the most important factor in determining acceptability, appears to be to the fore here. For example, in a discussion of the imperfect subjunctive he asks '[l]'Académie ne pourrait-elle, une fois pour toutes, donner raison à l'usage et constater la mort de l'imparfait du subjonctif?' (Bourgeade 1991: 22). Although he can move between two opposing views—descriptive and prescriptive—in his articles, the prescriptive stance is less evident here when looking at his use of verbs such as 'falloir' and 'devoir'. This reinforces the prior observation made about Thérive noting the benefits of analysing more than one aspect of metalanguage to determine an author's approach.

13.5 Discussion

This chapter aimed to determine the answer to three questions: (i) Are particular types of metalanguage used by those authors who take a more prescriptive or descriptive approach?; (ii) Do particular types of metalanguage reflect a stronger influence from the SLI?; and (iii) Are there any changes in the kinds of metalanguage used over time?

In answer to question (i), it appears from the sample examined here that the most prescriptive authors—Snell (1920s), Lancelot (1930s), Thérive (1950s)—either make very frequent use of terms such as 'faute' and 'erreur' (Snell), or instead use much more strongly negative terms, such as 'monstre' (Lancelot and Thérive). The more descriptive authors—Cohen (1940s/60s) and Cellard (1970s)—make very infrequent use of terms such as 'faute'/'incorrect(e)' and little to no use of any strongly negative terms. Bourgeade (1980s) falls somewhere between the two, making some use of 'faute' and frequently reinforcing this with some negative terms, but only very occasionally using more strongly negative terms. It would appear, then, that—as one would expect—there is a fairly clear type of metalanguage associated with more prescriptive authors. It is unexpected, however, that there is not a broader use of 'faute', 'erreur', and 'correct(e)'/'incorrect(e)' in the articles of Lancelot and Thérive. In terms of prescribing and advising, one might similarly have expected to see a heavy use of phrases such as 'il faut/il ne faut pas dire', 'dites/ne dites pas', 'on doit dire', etc. in this sample of texts from what is commonly viewed as a highly prescriptive genre. In fact, this is not the case, on the whole. While Snell (1920s) makes frequent use of such forms, the other two more prescriptive authors—Lancelot (1930s) and Thérive (1950s)—do not. Where they do, this is generally in a clearly prescriptive manner making it very clear that only one usage is being recommended, but it is certainly unexpected to find such little use of these forms in the sample examined. Cohen (1940s/60s), Cellard (1970s), and Bourgeade (1980s) also rarely use such forms. Where Cellard does so, it is using the inclusive 'we' form of the verb, aligning himself with his readers. It would appear from the sample of texts examined, that the clearest marker of prescriptivism is in fact the use of strongly negative terms ('monstre', 'affreux', 'grossier').

In answer to question (ii), the use of terms such as 'faute', negative terms such as 'monstre', and forms such as 'il faut dire' or 'dites' clearly reflect a strong influence from the SLI, displaying a view that only one form of language is the correct form and that other forms are unacceptable. We know that language ideologies go beyond language itself, taking linguistic features to index non-linguistic ones (such as a speaker's social background for example) (on indexicality, see Irvine and Gal 2000). The use of highly negative metalinguistic terms such as 'affreux' or 'grossier' by Snell (1920s), Lancelot (1930s), Thérive (1950s), and—very occasionally—Bourgeade (1980s) explicitly enacts this indexicality—they work to link certain forms of French with a lack of legitimacy (see Bourdieu 1991 on legitimacy in language) and a reduction in prestige value, which can then be assumed to be passed on to the speaker who uses these forms. The metalanguage being used by these prescriptive authors is manifestly reinforcing the SLI by making these links. Discussions of usage in the articles make it very clear that the correct forms are associated with social prestige (or legitimacy). This is evidenced most clearly by Lancelot (1930s) with his social judgements about the language of 'des honnêtes gens' and 'des gens bien élevés' and his concerns that certain usages will mark speakers for their lack of education. Cohen (1940s/60s) and Cellard (1970s), on the other hand, are more forgiving towards errors and generally describe usages and language changes without any comment on their acceptability. For these authors, particular usages do not index any kind of social value, and they clearly show less adherence to the SLI. Bourgeade moves between these two approaches—he clearly adheres more strongly to the SLI than either Cohen or Cellard, but he nevertheless remains open to variation, which suggests some weakening of this ideology.

In answer to question (iii), there does appear to be a trend towards a less prescriptive view—and less frequent use of the types of metalanguage described here—across time, and this trend appears to be more robust than that found in my earlier studies of the columnists (Walsh 2021c; Walsh and Cotelli Kureth 2021). In this case, Bourgeade (1980s) quite clearly falls more on the descriptive end of the continuum, and there appears therefore to be a fairly clear trajectory from the 1960s onwards towards a more descriptive approach. Both authors from the first period (1920s–30s) are highly prescriptive, although Snell (1920s) occasionally gives a nod to variation, and both show quite a high use of negative metalanguage. The authors from the second period (1940s–60s) appear to show a shifting scene, with Thérive (1950s) using similar metalanguage to the earlier columnists whereas Cohen (1940s/60s) is resolutely descriptive. This may of course be more a reflection of the individual authors; amongst language columnists in general, there is no doubt that Cohen is something of an outlier. The authors from the third period (1970s–80s) are, however, on the whole quite descriptive and open to variation in general, and the metalanguage that they use reflects this. Although Bourgeade is not purely descriptive—the metalanguage he uses occasionally reflects what must be considered as a relatively prescriptive point of view—he only rarely uses language associated with prescribing and describing. The use of the metalanguage in these columns does, therefore, appear to show more robust evidence for Kibbee and Craig's (2019: 77) view that there is a general move towards more tolerance of variation in the French tradition. It has also, of course, been shown that both descriptive and prescriptive approaches are frequently found within a single work (see, for example, Hodson 2006 on eighteenth-century grammars of English). This is certainly the case here and it reinforces the argument that there is not always a clear-cut distinction to be made between descriptivism and prescriptivism, or that such a distinction can even be made in practice (see Hodson (2006); Cameron (2012); Oaks (2021)).

Indeed, it may make little difference to the reader whether a given author takes a deliberately prescriptive or descriptive stance, or uses particularly prescriptive or negative language, as it is highly possible that they read even descriptive pronouncements as prescriptive. As Joseph (1987: 18) states, 'unfortunately, even if one takes great pains to write a descriptive grammar, readers may impose a prescriptive interpretation on it' (see also Ayres-Bennett 2020a: 190; McLelland 2021b: 267). This is likely to be equally true for language columns. The question of how readers interpret metalinguistic texts is one that could fruitfully be examined, not only for language columns but also more broadly, to determine whether our insistence, as linguists, on the distinction between prescriptivism and descriptivism is in fact perceived by readers and whether it plays a role in their reaction to such texts.

14
Comparing the prescriptivism of nineteenth- and twenty-first-century language experts in France

Emma Humphries

14.1 Introduction

France has often been described as a country with a highly standardized language and a long history and tradition of prescriptivism (Ayres-Bennett 2016: 100). This chapter presents a diachronic analysis of two dialogic sources of language advice from two time periods, the late nineteenth century and the twenty-first century. Both periods saw significant change for the French language, but the language commentary of these periods has been—thus far—less studied than that of the seventeenth and eighteenth centuries. The advent of free, compulsory education in the 1880s introduced more French citizens than ever before to the standard language. In the twenty-first century, the internet has increased the potential for global interaction, connecting greater numbers of people and providing a new platform for metalinguistic discussions. Through an analysis of the metalanguage and imagery used by perceived language authorities in their recommending and condemning of usages, this chapter seeks to answer three main questions. First, how does the metalanguage and imagery show engagement in the activity of prescriptivism? Second, to what extent is the metalanguage and imagery indicative of a prescriptivist ideology? And third, does the metalanguage and imagery across the two prescriptivist texts suggest change or stability over time? In responding to these questions, the chapter will discuss the issues underpinning significant change in the two periods in question.

Le Courrier de Vaugelas (1868–81), was a bimonthly print publication which published questions sent in by readers in France and abroad and responses to these questions written by the publication's editor, Éman Martin, a former French language teacher. Martin published and answered 1,837 questions from his readers across 240 issues. The *Courrier des internautes* (2011–present) is an online language advice service, hosted on the *Dire, Ne pas dire* section of the Académie française website.[1] Responses are written by the Service du dictionnaire (Service), a group affiliated to the Académie française (but separate from the *académicien·ne·s*), comprising approximately thirteen professors and language professionals. The use of the same question and answer (Q+A) structure in both resources facilitates the diachronic comparison.

An extensive body of research into French language commentary already exists. Language commentary of the seventeenth and eighteenth centuries has been well studied, particularly the expert discourses of the *remarqueurs*.[2] The language commentary of *chroniqueurs* ('language columnists'), most popular during the twentieth century, has also received scholarly attention,[3] including the extent to which they are a continuation of the genre which began with the publication of Vaugelas's (1647) *Remarques sur la langue françoise utiles à ceux qui veulent bien parler et bien escrire* (Ayres-Bennett 2015).

Through analysis of these metalinguistic texts across time, a stable tradition of metaphors and metalanguage has been observed. This chapter's comparison of sources from two comparatively less-studied time periods can further this discussion, showing ongoing use of the same imagery and metalanguage in the nineteenth and twenty-first centuries. What is more, whereas the aforementioned texts are primarily monologic, giving insight into just one perspective (the language authority), the two sources studied here are dialogic. *Le Courrier de Vaugelas* and the *Courrier des internautes* publish language advice in a Q+A format. Readers send in language questions to a perceived expert and these are published alongside a response. This gives access to two approaches (expert and lay) and sheds a different light on the study of historical and modern prescriptivist texts.

Until the advent of the internet, when possibilities for global interaction became both simple and readily available to huge numbers of people, dialogic texts were more infrequent and consequently less studied than monologic texts. Glatigny analysed samples of responses from *Le Courrier de Vaugelas*, considering whether its editor could be considered a *remarqueur* (Glatigny 2004), and the extent to which his recommendations align with the linguistic codex (Glatigny 2001). Besides these two studies, *Le Courrier de Vaugelas* has received little scholarly attention. Online metalinguistic texts are also thus far little studied in the French context. Two recent studies, however, include Tarnarutckaia and Ensslin (2020), who find evidence of the myth of the inherent clarity of French in video game

---

[1] http://www.academie-francaise.fr/dire-ne-pas-dire (accessed 14 April 2021). This section, added to the website in 2011, primarily consists of short pieces of language advice and opinion pieces.

[2] Ayres-Bennett has made significant contributions to this area of study, including Ayres-Bennett (1993, 2020a); Ayres-Bennett and Seijido (2011) to name just three, and Caron's (2004) edited volume traces the genre from the sixteenth to the twentieth century.

[3] For example, Bochnakowa (2005); Remysen (2012); Walsh (2016a); Walsh and Cotelli Kureth (2021). See also Walsh (Chapter 13, this volume).

discussions on Reddit, and Paveau and Rosier (2008), who use online metalinguistic texts to analyse French purism.

Section 14.2 introduces the concept of prescriptivism, presented as both an ideology and an activity. Section 14.3 gives a brief overview of the types of metalinguistic texts which have been produced and studied in France. This discussion is limited to publications which are relevant to the two sources analysed in this chapter, beginning with the *remarqueurs* in the seventeenth century, through to online metalinguistic discussions in the twenty-first century. Section 14.4 introduces the two language advice resources analysed in this chapter, *Le Courrier de Vaugelas*, and the *Courrier des internautes*, in greater detail. The chapter then turns to the analysis of responses to readers' questions in these two resources, starting in Section 14.5 with the metalanguage used and continuing in Section 14.6 with a discussion of metaphors. The two sources—whose audiences consist of language enthusiasts with an interest in the correct use of the French language, in France and abroad—align in their language and imagery with each other and the longer history of French metalinguistic texts. However, they also differ in important ways, notably in their use of external authorities.

14.2 Defining prescriptivism

Prescriptivism relies on a belief that there are correct and incorrect ways to use language. For the most part, definitions of prescriptivism agree that it involves making a distinction between how a language should or should not be used. This is illustrated in Langer and Davies's (2006: 46) definition: 'Prescriptivists believe it is acceptable to prescribe certain usages and to stigmatize others as incorrect or bad, even when these are commonly used by all sectors of the population'. Prescriptivism is part of the standardization process in that it is one way in which the standard is maintained (see Milroy and Milroy 2012), alongside other mechanisms, such as the spread of literacy and the hierarchization of varieties (Milroy and Milroy 2012: 22). As such, prescriptivism can be conceived of as both an activity and an ideology; the activity of recommending and condemning uses as a form of language maintenance, and the ideology that usages can be correct or incorrect, good or bad.

One of the earliest definitions of the concept of ideology as applied to language was provided by Silverstein (1979: 193) who defined language ideologies as: 'any sets of beliefs about language articulated by users as a rationalization or justification of perceived language structure and use'. This definition suggests that we are consciously aware of the language ideologies which we hold and are able to articulate them. However, the question of awareness has been a point of discussion in the study of language ideologies (Kroskrity 2004: 497), with suggestions that they in fact work on both a conscious and an unconscious level (Paffey

2012: 16). Awareness, specifically the fact that ideologies can be both conscious and unconscious, is one of three central 'planks' to language ideologies as conceived by Kroskrity (2016: 98–102). The second plank is positionality, the idea that we each approach language from our own specific social, economic, and political position, and that language ideologies are affected by this position. Kroskrity's third plank, multiplicity, centres around the fact that we all hold multiple positions in society based on numerous social factors (e.g. gender, education, age) and consequently hold multiple positionalities. These can be—and are—shared across groups of speakers in society, as highlighted in Irvine's (1989: 255) definition of language ideologies as: 'the cultural system of ideas about social and linguistic relationships, together with their loading of moral and political interests'.

The framing of prescriptivism as a language ideology allows us to make the following three features of prescriptivism explicit (as per Kroskrity 2016):

(i) Prescriptivism can function at both a conscious and an unconscious level. Speakers may not, therefore, be able necessarily to articulate their prescriptivism.
(ii) Prescriptivism can be about more than just language, ideas about correct/incorrect language are ideologically motivated and tied to other ideologies, e.g. nationalism.
(iii) Prescriptivism, as an ideology, is shared amongst groups of speakers.

Furthermore, it allows for the comparison of prescriptivism with other ideologies (Costa-Carreras 2018: 310), e.g. purism. As a behaviour, prescriptivism is the effort to impose 'correct'[4] ways of using the language through the recommending and condemning of certain usages and/or varieties. This can be on an individual level, e.g. correcting a friend's language use, and on an institutional level, e.g. through the education system. In this chapter, the ways in which the experts from both sources recommend and condemn uses is examined through, firstly, their use of metalanguage, to directly recommend and condemn usages; and secondly, their use of metaphors, to more implicitly stigmatize or promote usages. This sheds light on the extent to which the advice given to their readers can be considered prescriptivist.

When considering the extent to which a text is prescriptivist, Ayres-Bennett (2020a: 190–1) suggests that analysis must consider both the intention and effect of an author's work, as well as the way in which it is interpreted by its audience. Taking this approach shows that categorizing Vaugelas, for instance, as purely prescriptivist is to oversimplify his position; some acceptance of variation can also be found in his *Remarques*. An author's intention and a reader's reception of a text may not always align (Joseph 1987: 18). After all, those consulting metalinguistic

---

[4] That is, ways of using the language that are perceived by the prescriptivist as correct.

and codifying texts are not usually doing so to find different usage options, but rather to find one correct answer (McLelland 2013: 220).

Standard language ideology and purism are two additional language ideologies which overlap, in some ways, with prescriptivism, and the three ideologies (prescriptivism, standard language ideology, and purism) often manifest side by side in metalinguistic texts. In this chapter, Vogl's (2012: 13) conception of standard language ideology is followed, which conceives of the ideology as built around two core aspects: a belief in correctness and a belief in the 'one best variety', i.e. the standard variety. Purism overlaps with prescriptivism in its desire to control the language and how it is used.[5] However, purism goes further than prescriptivism in two key ways (Walsh 2016b: 9). Firstly, purism entails a belief that a language currently exists in a pure form; changes to the language are therefore corruptions or declines. Secondly, these impure forms must be removed to protect the language. These three ideologies will guide the analysis in Sections 14.5 and 14.6.

14.3 Metalinguistic texts

The two language advice publications analysed in this chapter, *Le Courrier de Vaugelas* and the *Courrier des internautes*, are both dialogic metalinguistic texts. The discourses published in both are interactions between an audience of interested readers and perceived language experts. In the French context, monologic texts have been far more numerous, however. These include collections of *remarques* and observations on the French language, grammars, dictionaries, and *chroniques de langage* (newspaper columns which deal with questions of language).[6] This section briefly introduces examples of some such monologic and dialogic texts before turning in Section 14.4 to examine *Le Courrier de Vaugelas* and the *Courrier des internautes* in greater detail. Following Milroy and Milroy's (2012: 22–3) framework of standardization, prescriptivism is a form of maintenance of the standard—a discussion of prescriptivist texts is thus linked to the history of standardization in France. This is a history which has been well-documented and, consequently, will not be discussed here.[7]

No discussion of metalinguistic texts in France is complete without a discussion of Vaugelas, his 1647 *Remarques sur la langue françoise*, and the *remarqueur* genre of which it marked the start (Rickard 1992: 40). Defined by Ayres-Bennett

---

[5] See the discussion of purism in Chapter 16, this volume.
[6] *Chroniques de langage* are not always exclusively monologic—the topic of columns is sometimes influenced by readers' letters. However, these letters are not frequently published and the extent to which a column is influenced by its readers is usually unclear.
[7] See Brunot's thirteen volumes (1905–53); Rickard (1989); Trudeau (1992); and Ayres-Bennett (1996).

(2006: 263) as 'volumes of generally short observations or remarks on points of doubtful usage', *remarques* were metalinguistic texts aimed at perfecting the French of first-language French speakers, a move away from previous texts which were aimed primarily at foreign language learners. Whilst the work of Vaugelas, and the *remarqueurs* who followed, went some way to consolidating a prescriptive norm in France (whether intentionally or not), the publication of Vaugelas's *Remarques* also sparked introspection amongst its readers who began to consider their individual language use and the role of 'l'oreille', or instinct, in matters of correct language use (Siouffi 2007b: 16). Ayres-Bennett's study of the *remarqueurs* has yielded useful approaches to texts to address questions including what is said and how in the *remarqueur* genre (Ayres-Bennett 2004, 2006; Ayres-Bennett and Seijido 2011); the use of metaphors (Ayres-Bennett 2009, 2011b); and normativity in the genre (Ayres-Bennett 2016, 2020a).

The role, and even simply the existence of, the Académie française has been the basis of much commentary on the French language within and outside of France (Estival and Pennycook 2011: 325–6). The founding of the Académie française in 1635 certainly established the importance of the language as a concern of the French state (Ayres-Bennett and Tieken-Boon van Ostade 2016: 106). Yet, the publication output of the Académie has been far from prolific; the Académie's last dictionary was published in 1935, with its ninth edition still in progress.[8] In its publications, a prescriptivist and purist approach to the French language is frequently made explicit. For instance, the Académie's opening text states that it aims to 'donner des règles certaines à notre langue et à la rendre pure, éloquente et capable de traiter les arts et les sciences' (Académie française 1635: Art. 24)[9] and the Académie's first dictionary consolidated a hierarchization of varieties by distinguishing between the usage of the *peuple* and *le bon usage*.

Although the ideological position of the Académie is well known, its influence and status in the twenty-first century are not as powerful as is often believed (Ayres-Bennett and Tieken-Boon van Ostade 2016: 106). Whilst for some, the Académie 'is a national icon, a proud symbol of a long tradition, of the love and respect the French have for their language' (Adamson 2007: 51), Robitaille (2002: 51) asserts that almost no one in France knows 'ni ce qu'elle fait, ni à quoi elle sert' (Estival and Pennycook (2011: 329) express a similar sentiment). The continued existence of the Académie française does, however, suggest some desire on the part of the state to maintain a standard French language and highlights the value placed on its protection; the importance of even only symbolic authority cannot be dismissed (Edwards 2012: 15).

Chroniques de langage, which first appeared in French newspapers in the nineteenth century (Osthus 2015: 163), are in many ways a continuation of

---

[8] Available here: http://www.dictionnaire-academie.fr/ (accessed 14 April 2021).
[9] See Wolf (1983) for a summary of this text and an overview of the Académie's role during this period.

the *remarqueur* genre (Ayres-Bennett 2015). The columns are usually written by a single author, who discusses specific points of the French language, often in a context of correct/incorrect usages (Remysen 2005: 271). Although some *chroniqueurs* base their columns around questions from readers, for the most part readers' questions are not published, and the discourses are primarily monologic. Turning to studies of the *chroniqueurs*, Walsh (2021c) analyses how authority is constructed in *chroniques de langage* from France, and Walsh and Cotelli Kureth (2021) examine the use of metaphors in French and Swiss columns. The linguistic features discussed in columns from the newspaper *Le Figaro* have been analysed by Bochnakowa (2005, 2013), and the normativity of discourses in Quebecois columns, a tradition dating from the late nineteenth century, has been the focus of Remysen's (2011, 2012, 2013b) works.

Dialogic texts, although less frequent, have been a significant metalinguistic resource in France. In the late seventeenth century, Callières, a member of the Académie française, published records of conversation, the first of which recounted *bon mots* and witty anecdotes (Callières 1692), and the second of which was a comparison of the *bon usage* of the Court with the language of the middle class (language to avoid) (Callières 1698). A diplomat, Callières also wrote influential texts on the art of negotiation. In his analysis of dialogues, Callières's observations offer an insight into the spoken language of the time, alongside his metalinguistic commentary. Given that audio recordings of speech would not be possible until the early twentieth century (Nevalainen 2015: 245), this is a rich source for the analysis of oral language of the period.

The *Journal de la langue françoise soit exacte, soit ornée*, published on and off between 1784 and 1795 by François-Urbain Domergue, was a predecessor to *Le Courrier de Vaugelas*. The *Journal* comprised two main sections. The first contained readers' questions about the language published alongside Domergue's responses, in a format later also seen in the *Courrier*. The second section (dealing with the *langue ornée* promised in the title) discussed style and elegance in language. A desire to aid the diffusion of the language and of ideas of correctness permeate this publication. The *Journal* saw considerable popularity due to the timeliness of Domergue's venture: 'Domergue saisit le moment précis d'une évolution socio-économique où la population provinciale veut se défaire des régionalismes pour avoir accès au bon usage du français' (Busse and Dougnac 1992: 56). Comprehensive biographies of Domergue and discussions of his publications, including the *Journal*, are found in Dougnac (1982) and Busse and Dougnac (1992); analyses of Domergue's responses to readers' questions and his approach to language advice are found in Choi (2007), with a focus on agreements, and Dougnac (1982), with a focus on neologisms.[10]

The audience for prescriptive texts has evolved greatly since the days of Vaugelas and his seventeenth- and eighteenth-century successors, who were writing for

---

[10] See also McLaughlin (Chapter 6, this volume).

a specific and limited audience from elite French society.[11] In the late eighteenth century, a report by Abbé Grégoire (1794: 3–4) on the use of the French language in France found that six million of the country's twenty-five million inhabitants spoke no French at all, and a further six million struggled to hold a conversation in French. The audience for prescriptivist and metalinguistic publications began to increase—and would continue to increase—in the late nineteenth century. Following the introduction of free and compulsory education, teachers and concerned parents began to seek guidance on using the standard language in guidebooks and language advice publications, e.g. *Le Courrier de Vaugelas* (Kibbee 2021: 213).

In the twenty-first century, almost all adults who have received an education in France have been exposed to the standard French language. Not only are questions about the language potentially more relevant to a much larger audience of literate adults, but the internet has made access to, creation of, and interaction with metalinguistic texts easier than ever before. Blogs are one form in which we find online metalinguistic discussion. For instance, *Langue sauce piquante* is a blog run by proofreaders from *Le Monde* which discusses correct language and current affairs,[12] and *Bescherelle ta mère*[13] is an example of what Heyd (2014: 497) terms 'grassroot prescriptivist photo blogs'. These are blogs run by laypeople, rather than institutional authorities, which aim to entertain, and which engage in metalinguistic commentary which can 'range from benevolent and amused interest to harsh, normative critique'. *Bescherelle ta mère*, which is hosted as a website, a Facebook page (liked by approximately 733,000 users), and a Twitter (known as X as of July 2023) account (175,500 followers),[14] publishes photos of language 'fails' with humorous, at times harsh, captions.[15] The form and style of metalinguistic texts online is now much broader; it is no longer limited to texts which have been published professionally, in fact, anyone can start their own online venture. What is more, interacting with such websites is simple and often instantaneous. As Osthus (2003: 139) affirms: 'En fait il ne faut ni être linguiste ni académicien pour juger sur le bon usage et les normes. Il suffit de se brancher sur Internet'.

14.4 *Le Courrier de Vaugelas* and the *Courrier des internautes*

Le Courrier de Vaugelas (*Courrier*) was a fortnightly publication, which ran from 1868 to 1881 (ten print runs of twenty-four issues each), under the editorship of

---

[11] Despite a low potential audience, Vaugelas saw much popularity within the circles which could access his texts (Osthus 2016: 334).
[12] https://www.lemonde.fr/blog/correcteurs/ (accessed 14 April 2021).
[13] https://bescherelletamere.fr/ (accessed 14 April 2021).
[14] Number of likes and followers correct as of 8 May 2021.
[15] See, for instance, the following example: https://bescherelletamere.fr/meme-un-enfant-aurait-pu-corriger-ce-pull (accessed 14 April 2021).

former French teacher Éman Martin.[16] From 1886–7, the *Courrier* had two additional print runs (twenty issues), under the editorship of author Edmond Johanet. This chapter looks only at the first, larger run of the publication under the original editor, Martin (in part due to issues of space and accessibility of documents, but this also serves as a control—only one person's approach). The subscription-based *Courrier* was distributed in France (for ten francs per year) and abroad (fourteen francs per year), with readers from across France, Europe, and as far-flung as Canada, Mauritius, and Japan.

The publication's front page states that it is 'consacré à la propagation universelle de la langue française', and that it will answer the grammatical and philological questions of its readers in France and abroad. A desire to spread the language outside of France was shared more generally in France at the end of the nineteenth century (Adamson 2007: 11), as evidenced, for instance, by the establishment of the Alliance française in 1883, an organization which aims to promote and diffuse French globally (Alliance française no date). The *Courrier*'s aim thus reflects the broader top-down desires observed in late nineteenth-century France. The use of Vaugelas's name in the publication's title instantly links the *Courrier* to the *remarqueur* tradition.

What follows is an examination of the Q+A section of the *Courrier*, the largest section of the publication. In total, over Martin's 240 issues, the *Courrier* printed 1,837 questions and responses, with the number of questions varying between issue from four to sixteen questions (7.7 questions per issue on average). Within the publication, questions are split into two sections by reader location: 'France' for questions sent from readers within France; and 'Étranger' for questions which were sent from outside of France. Reader location is not considered in the analysis here. The total publication length was always eight pages, the only exception being the final issue of each print run which was longer as it contained summaries of all questions from the twenty-four issues in the run. In addition to the Q+A section, each issue contained a biography of a grammarian, e.g. Henri Estienne (over six issues from 1 July 1870 to 15 September 1870), a list of new grammatical and literary publications, and a smaller section listing past publications. From the third print run onwards (1 October 1871), the *Courrier* included a 'Passe-temps grammatical' which consisted of phrases containing language errors found in the periodical press that the reader was challenged to find and correct. Martin thus attempted to provide content which was educational and entertaining.

In 2011, the Académie française website was extended to include a new section, *Dire, Ne pas dire* which aimed to help its visitors 'approfondir [leur] connaissance de la langue française'. Users are also invited to send in their questions 'sur un

---

[16] Martin was taken ill during the final run of the *Courrier* and died a few months later in 1882.

point précis de français'[17] and some of these are responded to publicly on the *Courrier des internautes* (*Internautes*) section of the site.[18] Other content includes short pieces of advice about language use, under headings such as 'Emplois fautifs' and 'Néologismes et anglicismes', alongside longer blog-style pieces in the 'Bloc-notes' section and discussions of language history and evolution in the 'Bonheurs et surprises' section. Although a new addition to the website, the original prescriptivist aims of the Académie are still present, as is made clear by *académicien* Pouliquen (2013) who expressed his hope that this interactive aspect of the website would lead to a more open relationship 'avec ceux des internautes qui se disaient sensibles au bon usage de notre langue et qui semblaient douter de notre réactivité face aux agressions dont elle était victime'.

Analysis in this chapter focuses on the *Courrier des internautes* section of the website (readers' questions and responses from the Service). When the data were collected in April 2017, this section of the website contained a total of 300 questions and 278 responses (twenty-two questions—amongst the earliest to be put online—were published without response or were comments rather than questions which did not necessitate a response). In this way, the data available are directly comparable in form to the Q+A section of the nineteenth-century *Le Courrier de Vaugelas*. The *Internautes* webpage does not separate questions by the geographic location of the question senders but in most cases (281 questions), the reader has provided their location, and this is published alongside their name. Again, reader location is not considered in this analysis.

Courrier des internautes' responses are written by members of the Service du Dictionnaire. However, given that the advice service is hosted on the Académie's website and each published response brandishes the tagline 'L'Académie répond', the published advice benefits from the Académie's institutional authority (see Walsh 2021c for a discussion of types of authority in language advice) and, in many cases, users are likely unaware of the Service and its role on the website. Since the first question went online in October 2011, questions and responses have been published sporadically, usually appearing a few at a time around once a month. However, with approximately 5,000–7,000 questions sent to the platform every year (personal correspondence with the Service, July 2019), the number of published questions is by no means representative.

Data from *Le Courrier de Vaugelas* and the *Courrier des internautes* were collected and collated using a 'web for corpus', as opposed to a 'web as corpus', approach (see de Schryver 2002); all data used are stored offline, creating static and stable corpora for analysis. PDF versions of the 240 issues of *Le Courrier de Vaugelas* are available through the Gallica archive,[19] and were downloaded into an

---

[17] http://www.academie-francaise.fr/questions-de-langue (accessed 14 April 2021).
[18] It is unclear whether questions which are not published still receive a response.
[19] https://gallica.bnf.fr/ (accessed 14 April 2021).

offline corpus. This offline corpus amounts to: 240 issues; 1,837 questions from readers and the same number of responses; and approximately 830,400 words.[20] The corpus (formed as it is of PDFs) is not searchable and consequently samples of questions were created for qualitative analysis.[21] Data from the *Courrier des internautes* webpage were collected manually and inserted into an offline, searchable corpus. These data total 300 questions, 278 responses, and 40,909 words. An initial scoping of the data showed that eight questions and responses were duplicates; these were deleted from the corpus and replaced with the subsequent eight published questions and responses. See summaries of the two corpora in Table 14.1.[22] The following sections will discuss these data, specifically the expert responses, focusing, firstly, on the metalanguage used to advise readers on their language queries and, secondly, the metaphors and imagery used. Discussions of both the metalanguage and metaphors give insight into whether the approaches to language advice taken by the experts of the two publications can be considered prescriptivist and the extent to which each publication reflects the period of change in which it was created.

Table 14.1 Summaries of corpora (*Le Courrier de Vaugelas* and *Courrier des internautes*)

Source	Date	Corpus size	Sample size
Le Courrier de Vaugelas	1868–81	1,837 questions and responses from 240 issues (approx. 830,400 words)[a]	140 responses sampled[b] (48,598 words)
Courrier des internautes	October 2011–April 2017	300 questions and 278 responses (40,909 words)	278 responses (23,990 words)

[a] As the *Courrier* corpus is not searchable, the total word count is based on an average word count, calculated using the data of ten issues.
[b] The sampling method is described in detail in Humphries (2021).

14.5 Metalanguage

Le Courrier de Vaugelas and the *Courrier des internautes* are both language advice services. Perceived language experts offer their advice to a readership which is anxious to use the language correctly. As Service du Dictionnaire member, Patrick Vannier explains: 'Nous écrire, c'est déjà s'intéresser à la langue [...]. Cela écarte tous ceux qui ne font pas de fautes et tous ceux qui ne savent pas qu'ils font des

---

[20] One issue of the *Courrier* (published 1 December 1870) was not available via Gallica and has therefore not been included in this sample.
[21] Attempts were made to convert the PDF files into searchable text files but the number of inaccuracies which this process created made it unfeasible.
[22] The use of these data was approved by the University of Nottingham ethics committee.

fautes ou à qui cela ne pose aucun problème' (Vannier cited by Ratouis (2018) in the newspaper *Le Point*). The experts in both publications are in positions of authority in the eyes of their readers.[23] The term 'expert' is used throughout to refer to those giving the language advice to reflect both their own self-positioning—as able to recommend and condemn language usages—and how they are perceived by their audience. Looking at specific elements in the language used in responses shows that the experts use metalanguage to enforce prescriptions in two different ways: first, the metalanguage can reinforce prescriptions by emphasizing the authority of the author; and second, the language itself can be prescriptive. Prescriptivist language and authority creation in the responses is analysed here through a discussion of lexis related to correction (e.g. the use of 'fautif' and 'correct') and the expressions used to give advice, which includes deontic modals, e.g. 'il faut dire', and expressions related to opinion or preference, e.g. 'je crois que'.

The experts from each publication take different approaches to advising their readers. This is evident even from initial quantitative analysis which shows a stark difference in the average word count of responses from the two publications: *Courrier* = 305 words; *Internautes* = 80 words. In the *Courrier*, Martin shows a tendency to present his linguistic prescriptions implicitly, for instance by stating a preference for one usage over another. Following the tradition of the *remarqueurs*, Martin also relies heavily on external linguistic authorities (90% of Martin's responses contain at least one reference to literature or to a reference text).[24] Martin's approach to responses is methodical, presenting and assessing the evidence (in the form of etymological discussions and analysis of external authorities) before reaching and presenting a final conclusion. The Service du Dictionnaire, on the other hand, provides brief responses and, perhaps unsurprisingly, rarely draws on external authorities, relying more heavily on the Académie's own publications when references are made. The Service's frequent use of deontics and lexis associated with correction similarly firmly positions the Académie as a confident authority, and as willing and able to make rulings on how the language must be used.

Prescriptions are presented and enforced in responses from both sources using lexis associated with correctness (e.g. *erreur, correct(e), incorrect(e), faute*).[25] Use of metalanguage of correction often presents the clearest examples of recommending or condemning usages. See, for instance, the following two examples, each containing variants of 'correct':

---

[23] This is true to differing extents amongst readers. Whilst some openly praise the authorities and thank them for their advice, others critique specific responses and/or the more general approaches to the language of each expert.
[24] Based on a sample of 140 responses which contained 506 total references.
[25] As the *Courrier* corpus was not searchable, only a selection of terms was analysed quantitatively.

(1) Et voilà pourquoi, à l'heure présente, il y a comme cent ans que, pour parler **correctement** notre langue, il faut qu'on dise: c'est un des plus belles orgues qu'il y ait en France. (*Courrier*, 1 June 1870: 130)[26]

(2) Je nettoie est la seule forme **correcte**. (*Internautes*, 12 January 2013)[27]

As shown in Table 14.2, this type of metalanguage is drawn on less frequently by Martin than by the Service.

Table 14.2 Use of *faute, erreur, correct(e)*, and *incorrect(e)* (*Le Courrier de Vaugelas* and *Courrier des internautes*)

	Courrier No. of uses in responses (n=140)	*Internautes* No. of uses in responses (n=278)
erreur	6	7
faute	11	7
correct(e), incorrect(e)	5	49

Qualitative analysis of how lexis associated with correction is used shows that linguistic correctness is presented as a continuum in the two publications from the two time periods. That is, variations are presented to readers as more or less correct, rather than as a binary of correct vs. incorrect. See, for instance, the following examples:

(3) j'en conclus que cette phrase est fautive. Il fallait que l'auteur dît seulement: *il mit du linge sécher*, et **mieux encore**: *il mit sécher du linge*. (*Courrier*, 15 December 1869: 41)

(4) **Toutes les formes que vous proposez sont correctes**. *Il en est de même de/pour* se rencontre plus que *Il en va de même de/pour*, mais **cette dernière forme est de meilleure langue**. D'autre part, il faut une espace insécable avant et après le point d'interrogation. (*Internautes*, 2 December 2012)[28]

In both responses, the experts distinguish between usages which belong to best usage and others which, although not incorrect, are not as correct as the alternatives, thus creating a hierarchy of acceptability in language use. This is not unique to these publications, of course, with a similar approach (referred to as a sociolinguistic model) observed in the work of Vaugelas, for instance (Ayres-Bennett 2004: 68–9). In some cases, this is linked explicitly to styles and/or register, for example:

---

[26] Emphasis my own in this and all subsequent examples from the two sources.
[27] http://www.academie-francaise.fr/erwin-g-france (accessed 14 April 2021).
[28] http://www.academie-francaise.fr/elliott-c-fontenay-sous-bois (accessed 14 April 2021).

(5) On considère *partir pour* comme **plus élégant et plus soutenu**, mais *partir à*, plus familier, est **également correct.** (*Internautes*, 13 April 2013)[29]

In others, however, e.g. example (3), the ruling is simply framed in terms of correctness.

In examples (3) and (4), neither expert makes an explicit ruling for or against one specific form, although the contrasting of 'correct' with 'best' usage can be considered an implicit ruling. To understand whether a metalinguistic text is prescriptivist, both author intention and audience interpretation should be considered (Ayres-Bennett 2020a: 190–1); the two positions do not always align (Joseph 1987: 18). The nature of the publications, i.e. language advice, is relevant here. First, readers (not necessarily all readers) consider those responding to their questions to be in a position of authority. They are contacting the experts because they believe that they have the knowledge to answer their question. Second, the readers are seeking guidance and advice which, presumably, they intend to adopt. Readers consulting metalinguistic texts, such as these, are not often looking for different usage options, but rather to find one correct answer (McLelland 2013: 220). This is evident in the framing of questions:

(6) J'entends ici, à Paris même, des personnes qui prononcent *désir, désirer*, sans accent sur *de*; d'autres qui prononcent ce *de* en y mettant un accent. **Lequel, selon vous, vaut le mieux?** (*Courrier*, 15 June 1870: 141)

(7) J'aimerais savoir **s'il faut dire** 'prendre une voiture, un bus...' **ou** 'emprunter une voiture, un bus...'. (*Internautes*, 6 June 2013)[30]

Whilst it is not possible to know how readers have interpreted the experts' responses, those who seek a categorical response, as in examples (6) and (7), may well interpret even an implicit ruling prescriptively.

The analysis reveals a second means by which metalanguage enforces prescriptions. See, for instance, the use of deontic modals in the following two examples:

(8) **il faut dire** *san dessus dessous*, et pas autrement. (*Courrier*, 1 March 1879: 3)

(9) **On doit dire** *ksilophone*. (*xylophone*, *Internautes*, 6 April 2017)[31]

Martin uses expressions with the deontic modals *falloir* and *devoir* in 41 of 140 responses—this is more frequently than the Service and in a smaller sample of responses. Whilst Martin's use of deontics does occasionally present explicit prescriptions (example 8), in others the modals describe the process required to find the correct answer, as in the following:

---

[29] http://www.academie-francaise.fr/nathalie-r-sceau (accessed 14 April 2021).
[30] http://www.academie-francaise.fr/bangaly-k-cote-divoire (accessed 14 April 2021).
[31] http://www.academie-francaise.fr/camille-t-france (accessed: 14 April 2021).

(10) Pour décider si un mot est bien ou mal fait, **il faut le comparer** avec ses similaires, et, selon qu'on lui trouve avec eux de l'analogie de formation ou qu'on ne lui en trouve pas, **on doit le déclarer bon ou mauvais**. (*Courrier*, 1 June 1869: 130)

Other deontics are hedged by Martin, e.g. 'il **me semble** qu'il faut' (*Courrier*, 15 March 1875: 187). Despite this seeming formulation as mere impression or opinion in the early section of the response, Martin's final ruling is nevertheless more assertive and direct:

(11) l'expression *langue d'oil* [sic] **doit naturellement** se prononcer *langue d'oui*.

Martin's argumentation and use of opinion are arguably rhetorical tools, a form of authority creation, of endearing himself to the audience and guiding them through his process. Through improving and emphasizing his authoritative position, he strengthens the potential impact of his prescription on his audience.

Martin rarely presents categorical rulings but rather couches his prescriptions in opinion, using constructions to express preference and opinion, e.g. 'mon avis' and 'je trouve', eighty-two times in 140 responses. In comparison, there are only nine uses of such constructions in the 278 *Internautes* responses. See, for instance, the following example from the *Courrier*:

(12) **Je crois que** *bougrement* (qui ne se trouve ni dans le dictionnaire de l'Académie ni dans celui de M. Littré, sans qu'on puisse toutefois lui contester sa qualité de mot français), vient de l'adverbe latin *pulchrè*, et, pour essayer de vous faire partager **mon avis**, je vais montrer qu'il peut en venir, et qu'il est peu probable qu'il n'en vienne pas. (*Courrier*, 15 November 1868: 26)

Glatigny's (2004: 187) analysis of a sample of Martin's responses similarly noted the expert's inclination towards personal preference when prescribing usages. Further support is found in Martin's frequent use of the first-person pronoun *je* (512 uses in 140 responses); only twenty-four uses of *je* are found in the 278 *Internautes* responses. These opinion and preference-based statements are accompanied by reasoned and methodical explanations which draw support from linguistic knowledge and external authorities. For instance, in response to a question about the word *bougrement* (example 12),[32] Martin presents a five-point argumentation in support of his opinion, using arguments related to derivational morphology, comparisons with Latin, and citing the *Dictionnaire de la langue verte* and the *dictionnaire de Quicherat*. Martin's concluding lines then express a hope that he has managed to convince his readers of the validity of his opinion. However, what Martin has presented could be more accurately described as a researched and supported explanation, rather than a simple opinion. By walking the reader

---

[32] The question is as follows: 'Pourriez-vous m'expliquer comment un aussi vilain mot que *bougrement* a pu être employé dans le discours familier à la formation des superlatifs?'.

through his explanation, Martin bolsters his own authority, lending greater conviction to his prescriptions. Furthermore, readers who position the editor as an authority may, consequently, interpret his opinions and preferences as facts and prescriptions.

Martin's approach stands in stark contrast to the assertive style of *Internautes* responses. The Service du Dictionnaire positions itself firmly as an authority (as also seen through its reliance on Académie resources) and presents its advice as linguistic fact. Rather than discussing and explaining why a usage is correct or incorrect, the Service du Dictionnaire simply presents its ruling, with little to no discussion. Advice is presented using deontic modals (as in example 9) or simply as fact, e.g.:

(13) **On construit** le verbe *rêver* avec la préposition *de* quand on l'emploie au sens propre de 'faire un rêve, des rêves': *cette nuit, j'ai rêvé de vous*. En revanche, au sens classique de 'penser profondément à quelque chose, méditer', **on dit** *rêver à*: 'elle rêve à ce prodigieux destin'. (*Internautes*, 8 November 2012)[33]

Backed by the authority of the Académie française, the Service rarely explains why or how it has reached its solution, but rather the solutions are presented as indisputable facts or explicit prescriptions.

There are nine expressions of preference and seventeen constructions related to recommendations in the 278 *Internautes* responses. These expressions are also most frequently used with third-person rather than first-person pronouns, e.g.:

(14) **il est préférable** d'employer un véritable impératif car l'infinitif impératif ne s'adresse pas à une personne en particulier. (*Internautes*, 12 July 2016)[34]

The Service is not presenting its own personal preference but rather what it is framing as universal preference. The effect is similar to those constructions which present prescriptions as simple facts. Given the authoritative position of the Académie—at least in the eyes of *Internautes* users, if not further afield—the likelihood of such expressions being interpreted as prescriptivist rulings is high.

This brief qualitative analysis of responses shows that prescriptions are presented differently in the two resources. In the *Courrier*, Martin recommends and condemns usages more implicitly. He hedges his deontics and less frequently uses lexis associated with correction. Instead, he draws on external authorities and argumentation to present his prescriptions as opinions based on rational and logical facts. The Service, on the other hand, draws infrequently on authorities and rarely provides explanation or context in its responses. It either presents its rulings as linguistic fact or uses deontic modals to make clear that there is one correct

---

[33] http://www.academie-francaise.fr/jacquine-j (accessed 14 April 2021).
[34] http://www.academie-francaise.fr/emilie-t-france (accessed 14 April 2021).

answer to the reader's query. This may reflect the difference in readers' access to texts between the two time periods. Martin summarizes the positions stated in other texts to which his audience may not have access. *Internautes* users, on the other hand, have access to the internet and therefore to a far greater amount of information; to contact the Service, rather than an alternative advice platform, is a choice. The extent to which the advice given is read by readers as prescriptivist is not measurable with the available data. In this analysis, the presumed authoritative positions of the experts from the two publications are tentatively relied on to suggest that even implicit prescriptions and statements hedged with opinion have the potential to be interpreted as prescriptions by readers whose purpose for accessing the publications is to seek language advice.

14.6 Imagery

The use of imagery in metalinguistic texts has a long history, in France and elsewhere in Europe, which can be traced back at least as far as Horace and Quintilian (Ayres-Bennett 2011b: 239).[35] The metaphors found in metalinguistic texts often (but not always) rely on the personification of a language, highlighting notions of a living and/or pure language. This is clear, for instance, in images which present languages as healthy/diseased (Langer and Nesse 2012: 617) or of the body of language as under attack (Hohenhaus 2002: 170–2). Such metaphors are highly emotive and draw on shared knowledge and assumption between the author and their readership (Cowling 2007: 168–9).

The use of metaphors in metalinguistic texts is often associated more specifically with purist discourses. Thomas's (1991: 19–24) study of linguistic purism proposes that there are seven 'self-images' of the purist used in metalinguistic texts: 'the miller'; 'the gardener'; 'the metallurgist'; 'the grinder' (found almost exclusively in Czech purism); 'the physician'; 'the genealogist and geneticist'; and 'the priest'. In all seven images, the purist is positioned as willing and able to protect the language, e.g. the gardener has the knowledge to identify what is harmful to their garden (the weeds), and the skills to remove the weeds to maintain the garden in a healthy state. Paveau and Rosier (2008: 57) analyse purism and purist discourses in French metalinguistic texts primarily from the twentieth and twenty-first centuries. They suggest that the imagery found in such texts falls in to four main categories: aesthetic arguments (*beau/laid*); political arguments (*langue de la liberté*); pseudo-linguistic arguments (*clarté de la langue*); and metaphorical arguments (*langue en bonne santé*).

---

[35] See Ayres-Bennett (2011b) for a succinct but detailed discussion of the history of metaphors in French, Jones (1999) for analysis of their use in a German context, and Bermel (2007) for Czech.

The Académie française has often been viewed as 'the prescriptive body par excellence' (Linn 2013: 372) and the institution's own articulations of its aims and role, e.g. through its dictionary prefaces, have firmly positioned it as purist. Consequently, we might expect that the responses published on the *Courrier des internautes* website, brandishing the Académie's name, would make use of such metaphors. However, the following analysis will show that responses from the Service use relatively few metaphors. Its readers, on the other hand, both use metaphors more frequently and use a much more varied selection of imagery (see Humphries 2021). In *Le Courrier de Vaugelas*, editor Martin uses metaphors more frequently than the Service and on a number of occasions opts for extended metaphors which lend structure to his response. This may again be a strategy to make his responses more entertaining and/or a result of his responses being longer than those published by the Service.

Imagery relating to war and invasion has a long history in European purist discourses (Jones 1999: 66) and is found in the two corpora analysed here.[36] As such, the two sources can be considered to be building upon, and engaging with, a longer tradition of metalinguistic commentary in the French context. Nationalism can play a significant role in the development of linguistic purism (Thomas 1991: 43) and such metaphors strengthen the association between the protection of a language and the protection of a nation and/or a cultural identity, exploiting the established ideological link between language and nation (Gordon 1978). The notion of the 'defence' of French dates back at least to du Bellay's (2001 [1549]) *La deffence, et illustration de la langue françoyse* and imagery related to defence and battle is found in the responses of both *Le Courrier de Vaugelas* and the *Courrier des internautes*.

In the sample of 140 *Courrier* questions, Martin uses two images related to invasion. Perhaps surprisingly, in both cases the 'invasion' in question is an internal threat, rather than an external or foreign target. For instance, in response to a question about the use of *argot*, Martin writes:

(15) Tel est, esquissé à grands traits, l'ensemble des causes qui ont amené **l'invasion de l'argot** dans la langue française. (*Courrier*, 15 October 1874: 106)

Argot is positioned as other, as outside of the boundaries of the standard French language, and therefore its usage represents an unwanted addition to the language. Martin's response continues to explicitly mention purity and taste, taking his condemning of *argot* beyond a simple question of appropriate register:

---

[36] A wider range of metaphors was observed in the two corpora, including health, law, and danger (see Humphries 2021). See also the discussion in 18.2.2 of Chapter 18, this volume.

(16) Que l'argot soit l'unique langage employé par les voleurs entre eux, [...] je n'y trouve rien à redire; mais quand je vois ceux qui vivent dans **la société honnête** prendre plaisir, en quelque sorte, à émailler leurs discours de vocables **d'une source aussi impure,** je ne puis que m'en attrister profondément avec **les gens de goût.**

Looking at the responses to *Internautes* users, imagery of defence and threat is used by the Service du Dictionnaire. See, for instance, examples (17) and (18):

(17) Dans un document ou texte professionnel, il convient donc de respecter cette 'règle': hélas la sobriété de **l'orthotypographie française est menacée** par d'autres manières d'écrire, principalement anglo-saxonnes, où l'emploi de la majuscule est très fréquent, et parfois quelque peu anarchique. (*Internautes*, 3 March 2016)[37]

(18) Nous nous efforçons de **combattre ces travers**. (*Internautes*, 5 February 2016)[38]

Whereas the threats identified by Martin in the *Courrier* were internal to the French language, in example (17) the Service du Dictionnaire positions the influence of the English language as an external threat, in concordance with what Thomas (1991: 79–80) labels 'xenophobic purism'. The response from which example (18) is taken continues to explain the Service's approach to protecting the language from what the reader describes as the disrespectful use of the language by journalists: 'plutôt que de faire une injonction ad hominem, nous préférons traiter la question de manière générale'. The use of 'nous' in this example, referring to either the Service specifically or the Académie more generally, firmly positions the institution as able to 'protect' the language from threat. In this way, the image is similar to those seven self-images of the purist identified by Thomas (1991: 19–24).

In both language advice resources, imagery related to war and defence is used to reinforce an aspect of the ideology of prescriptivism: the belief that usages can be good or bad. This can be persuasive in the context of a prescriptivist response; the prescription recommends or condemns a usage, and the imagery provides an evocative and emotive explanation as to why adherence to the prescriptions is important, e.g. the language is in danger. Though the imagery used doesn't necessarily condemn or recommend usages itself, it does go some way to implicitly reinforcing the prescription.

Whilst images of war and defence have endured across the two time periods, the enemy has changed—from internal to the language in the nineteenth century, to external in the twenty-first century. This is further reflected in the wider samples of questions from the two sources: only three of 1,837 *Courrier* questions concern

---

[37] http://www.academie-francaise.fr/murielle-v-france (accessed 14 April 2021).
[38] http://www.academie-francaise.fr/pierre-i-france (accessed 14 April 2021).

borrowings, in comparison to twenty-six of 300 *Internautes* questions (of which twenty-three are about Anglicisms). Borrowings are not limited to the twenty-first century—industrial and commercial growth in nineteenth-century France brought with it an influx of lexical borrowings (Rickard 1989: 131)—but, with mass media and globalization, borrowings are more visible now than previously and attitudes towards borrowings into French, particularly from English, have changed (see Wise 1997). The observed change from metaphors targeting internal threats to external threats and the greater frequency of concerns surrounding borrowings in the twenty-first century source reflect this broader shift in attitudes across the two time periods.

14.7 Conclusion

Analysis of the metalanguage and imagery used in responses from two language advice services, *Le Courrier de Vaugelas* and the *Courrier des internautes*, sought to show the extent to which the discourses could be considered as engaging in the activity and the ideology of linguistic prescriptivism. The comparative approach allowed not only the comparison of sources from two periods of linguistic change in France, the late nineteenth century and the twenty-first century, and two mediums, print and online, but also the wider and longer tradition of language commentary in France.

Similarities across the two resources were observed, particularly in the use of war and defence metaphors. This imagery, which presents the language as under attack, has a much longer history in European language commentary; its presence in these two resources shows its continued presence in prescriptivist discourses. However, the target of the imagery changed, from internal threats in the nineteenth-century *Courrier*, to external in the twenty-first-century *Internautes*, reflecting a broader shift in concerns about borrowings across the two time periods. The experts' approaches to prescribing usages also differed in significant ways. Whereas Martin draws significantly on external sources to support his prescriptions, which are often phrased as opinions, the Service presents its prescriptions as simple linguistic facts, which do not need to be supported or evidenced. This difference perhaps reflects the experts' awareness of readers' access to texts in each time period. For Martin's readers, access to metalinguistic texts and information was limited (small number of texts and printed only). In comparison, internet users engaging with the Service have a wealth of easy-to-access sources and can therefore conduct their own research on the positions of other authorities. The outcome of both approaches, however, is—at least implicit—prescriptions which have the potential to be interpreted as such by each readership.

Whilst only the responses from perceived language authorities are analysed here, the use of dialogic texts, including language advice services, can offer new perspectives to the study of prescriptivism. Using the readers' questions for instance can give insight into how lay language enthusiasts discuss language and the areas of the language which cause them difficulty or interest. The number and accessibility of such texts has grown immensely with the internet and offers new perspectives for the study of both lay and expert approaches to the language and prescriptivism.

15
Attitudes on Twitter towards French inclusive writing

Anna Tristram

15.1 Introduction

In September 2017, Éditions Hatier published a school textbook which employed *écriture inclusive* on its pages.[1] In this form of writing, masculine and feminine grammatical genders are shown at the same time on items taking agreement, separated by graphical means, such as a full stop, dash, slash, or *point médian*. For example: *les étudiant.e.s*; *les étudiant-e-s*; *les étudiant/e/s*; *les étudiant·e·s*. When the publisher announced this with the tweet shown in Figure 15.1, it unleashed 'un tapage médiatique' (Abbou et al. 2018: 140) which lasted several weeks. Inclusive writing was widely discussed in newspapers and magazines, and on television and radio programmes at the time. Several years after this initial flurry of interest, searching online demonstrates that popular blogs, podcasts, and radio and television programmes devoted to the topic still regularly appear, and academic interest in the topic continues.[2]

Figure 15.1 Éditions Hatier tweet, September 2017

In a country with a long history of language planning, and official and unofficial bodies devoted to the policing of the language, it is unsurprising that the

---

[1] My thanks are due to the editors of this volume, to the anonymous reviewers, and to Jane Lugea and Rachelle Vessey for feedback on earlier versions of this chapter. Any remaining errors or omissions are my own.

[2] See, for example, an open letter published by academics on the weekly current affairs site Marianne.net (Tribune Collective, 18 September 2020) and a reply published one week later on the investigative journalism site Mediapart.fr (Les Invités de Médiapart, 25 September 2020). See also, amongst many others, Manesse and Siouffi 2019; Tibblin 2020; Bosworth 2021; Burnett and Pozniak 2021; Kamblé-Bagal and Tatossian 2022; Pingeot 2022; Simon and Vanhal 2022.

Anna Tristram, *Attitudes on Twitter towards French inclusive writing*. In: *Historical and Sociolinguistic Approaches to French*. Edited by: Janice Carruthers, Mairi McLaughlin, and Olivia Walsh, Oxford University Press.
© Anna Tristram (2024). DOI: 10.1093/oso/9780192894366.003.0015

Académie française soon joined the discussion. In October 2017, the Académie issued a *déclaration* against inclusive writing, warning that 'devant cette aberration "inclusive", la langue française se trouve désormais en péril mortel' (Académie française 2017). This *déclaration*, and others which have come before, gives a clear picture of the Académie's attitude towards inclusive writing, even if a subsequent report (Académie française 2019) indicates acceptance of some limited aspects of feminization of the language, as discussed in Section 15.2.2. What is less clear is the extent to which attitudes at the official level—that is, where the French state and its institutions are concerned (cf. Walsh 2014, 2016b)—are shared by individuals. To explore the attitudes of individuals, this study combines techniques from corpus linguistics (CL) and discourse analysis (DA) to analyse a corpus of tweets which mention inclusive writing.

The study proceeds as follows: Section 15.2 sets out the context of the study, with a definition of *écriture inclusive* discussed in Section 15.2.1, and the history of linguistic equality in France explored in Section 15.2.2. Section 15.3 looks at how language attitudes can be understood and measured. The methodology and approach to data analysis are discussed in Section 15.4, with results presented in Section 15.5. Section 15.6 brings together the findings of the study, and in Section 15.7 some conclusions and suggestions for future research are discussed.

15.2 Context and definitions

15.2.1 What is meant by *écriture inclusive*?

The debate which took place in late 2017 seems to have 'fait entrer l'expression "l'écriture inclusive" dans le vocabulaire commun' (Klinkenberg 2019: 16), but what is encompassed by the term can vary significantly. There are also other terms in circulation which are sometimes (but not always) used interchangeably (e.g. *langage non sexiste, langage/rédaction épicène, langage dégenré*; Gardelle 2019: 153). Rabatel and Rosier (2019: 9) note that, grouped under the term *écriture inclusive*, 'on retrouve aussi, plus classique, la féminisation des noms de métiers et de fonctions [...] ainsi que des questions d'accord (en nombre: le masculin pluriel comme générique, l'accord de proximité, le *elle* universel, etc.'. Thus, while in some discussions, *écriture inclusive* is the superordinate term, encompassing a variety of techniques for non-sexist language, in other accounts, it is the reverse, with *écriture inclusive* being just one among various 'techniques de visibilisation' (Klinkenberg 2019: 19). Haddad's definition (2017: 4), for example, falls into the former camp:

> L'écriture inclusive désigne l'ensemble des attentions graphiques et syntaxiques qui permettent d'assurer une égalité de représentations des deux sexes. Concrètement, cela signifie notamment: renoncer au masculin générique ('des acteurs du développement durable'), à la primauté du masculin sur le féminin

dans les accords en genre ('des hommes et des femmes sont allés'), ainsi qu'à un ensemble d'autres conventions largement intériorisées par chacun et chacune d'entre nous.

In this study, the terms *écriture inclusive/inclusive writing* are used to designate graphical techniques for making both genders visible on items taking agreement (e.g. *les candidat·e·s*), and *non-sexist language* is used to denote the full range of techniques, including graphical alternations, doubling of forms (e.g. *les candidats et les candidates*), feminization of job titles, use of epicene terms (e.g. *élève*), etc. Where necessary, it is specified whether a term is being used in a broad or narrow sense. Some examples of inclusive writing are shown in Figure 15.2 (featuring the *point médian*) and Figure 15.3 (full stop).[3]

Figure 15.2 Information sign at Université Paris Nanterre, September 2018

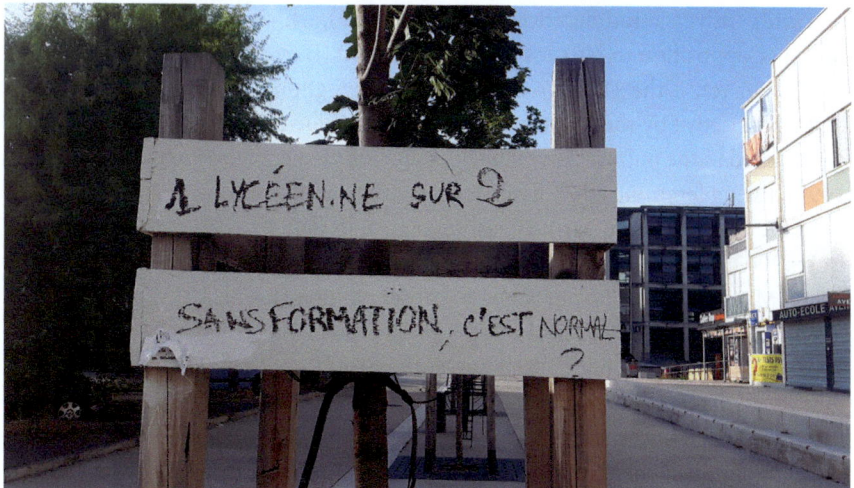

Figure 15.3 Graffiti at Université Paris Nanterre, September 2018

[3] Photographs by the author.

15.2.2 Linguistic equality in French: Developments at the official level

The state and its official bodies play an active part in legislating and policing the French language, and matters of linguistic equality have been no exception. The history of political and legislative developments around linguistic equality is largely the history of the feminization of the language, since the majority of government *circulaires*, commissions, reports, and guides in this area have been concerned with surveying, creating, and approving (or not) feminized job titles. In this section, official developments and reactions to these job titles are briefly reviewed with reference to what they reveal about attitudes at the official level towards non-sexist language.[4]

France was the first European country to introduce political reforms to tackle linguistic (in)equality (Burr 2003: 120). However, the pace of change in France has been slow, and attempts at reform have typically met with strong resistance. For example, when a Commission de terminologie relative au vocabulaire concernant les activités des femmes was established in 1984, the Académie was swift to issue a *déclaration* in which it stated its view that the masculine should be used as a supposedly neutral gender, and opposed all attempts at feminization, since this '[risque] de mettre la confusion et le désordre dans un équilibre subtil né de l'usage' (Académie, 14 June 1984). While the establishment of the commission in 1984 caused 'a massive sexist and political outcry' (Burr 2003: 123), its proposal (published in the *Circulaire du 11 mars 1986* (Fabius 1986))—that feminized job titles were to be used in all government documents, including school textbooks—was met with 'universal indifference' (Burr 2003: 123), which was taken as an indication that opposition to reforms had been quelled (Burr 2003: 124; cf. Houdebine 1987: 13). Yet, if the 1986 *circulaire* was largely ignored, it nonetheless led to a further initiative by the Institut national de la langue française, which eventually culminated in the publication of the booklet *Femme, j'écris ton nom* (Becquer et al. 1999), listing feminine equivalents for hundreds of professions.

In the late 1980s and early 1990s, resistance to feminization continued, which Burr (2003: 124) argues was ideological in nature (cf. Muller 1994). In early 1998, Prime Minister Lionel Jospin issued a further circular (Jospin 1998) and asked the Commission générale de terminologie et de néologie to undertake another study. While the circular was not in itself 'revolutionary' (Burr 2003: 124), since it merely reinforced that of 1986, Burr (2003: 124) argues that there was a shift in attitudes at this time—even in the face of fierce opposition from the Académie. Later research seems to confirm this: for example, in their quantitative study of forms used to refer to women in the Assemblée nationale, Burnett and Bonami (2019) report a

---

[4] See Burr (2003); Viennot et al. (2016); Viennot (2017); Omer (2020), among others, for more detailed discussion of the history of linguistic equality in France.

significant increase in the use of feminized terms after 1998. They argue that these changes and 'differences in the effectiveness of Fabius/Jospin's language policy are (indirectly) the result of changes in gender ideologies in France between the mid 1980s and mid 1990s' (Burnett and Bonami 2019: 5). Specifically, Burnett and Bonami (2019: 5) hypothesize that:

> Jospin's reinforcement of Fabius' policy in 1998 was successful because it strengthened an existing association between feminine g-gender [sc. grammatical gender] and a female political persona; whereas, Fabius' original policy was unsuccessful because it tried to build on ideological structure that was not shared by a large portion of the Assemblée Nationale.

The Académie issued a further *déclaration* in 2002 which aimed to reinforce that of 1984, and made further efforts to suppress and proscribe feminization via the press and by lobbying politicians (Cerquiglini 2019; see Viennot et al. 2016 for detailed discussion). However, with the force of the wider movement towards the feminization of the language beginning to prove irresistible, Viennot et al. (2016) note that a further statement on the subject (published as a *mise au point*; Académie 2014) had lost some of the intransigence of the preceding two, and the Académie largely accepted the feminization of job titles (e.g. *pharmacienne*), though generally not that of official functions and their associated titles, e.g. *ministre*; Omer 2020: 5).[5]

In 2017, inclusive writing burst into public consciousness and the spotlight was once again thrown on matters of linguistic equality. In a circular of 21 November 2017, Prime Minister Edouard Philippe reminded officials that feminization practices as recommended in the government guide *Femme, j'écris ton nom* (Becquer et al. 1999) must be followed. A final point, however, is explicit in discouraging the use of inclusive writing:

> En revanche, je vous invite, en particulier pour les textes destinés à être publiés au Journal officiel de la République française, à ne pas faire usage de l'écriture dite inclusive, qui désigne les pratiques rédactionnelles et typographiques visant à substituer à l'emploi du masculin, lorsqu'il est utilisé dans un sens générique, une graphie faisant ressortir l'existence d'une forme féminine. Outre le respect du formalisme propre aux actes de nature juridique, les administrations relevant de l'Etat doivent se conformer aux règles grammaticales et syntaxiques, notamment pour des raisons d'intelligibilité et de clarté de la norme.
>
> (Philippe 2017)

---

[5] The Academie argues (Academie française 2014, §4–5) that official functions and grades and their associated titles should remain 'neutral', i.e. masculine, since 'les particularités de la personne ne doivent pas empiéter sur le caractère abstrait de la fonction dont elle est investie, mais au contraire s'effacer derrière lui'.

Thus, though supportive of non-sexist language more generally, Philippe explicitly bans *écriture inclusive*, appealing to notions such as clarity and intelligibility, though, notably, this ban covers only texts published in the *Journal officiel* (JO). A circular issued in May 2021 by Jean-Michel Blanquer, Minister for Education, Youth and Sport, effectively bans inclusive writing in the whole domain of education, and specifically the use of the *point médian* (Blanquer 2021). A number of proposed laws relating to inclusive writing have also been put forward since the renewed interest in non-sexist language, all essentially seeking to ensure that inclusive writing is banished from as many contexts as possible, whether public or private.[6]

Continuing a trend towards greater acceptance of feminization, the Académie's next move was to publish a report on *La Féminisation des noms de métiers et de fonctions* (Académie 2019), in which it adopted the feminization of job titles and functions. The report does not mention *écriture inclusive*, and ends by cautioning that 'dans bon nombre de cas, l'usage est encore loin d'être fixé et qu'il continuera d'évoluer', and furthermore, that '[les évolutions linguistiques] ne peuvent être envisagées que dans le respect des règles fondamentales de la langue et selon l'esprit du droit français' (Académie française 2019: 20). Omer (2020: 5) notes that it is significant that this report was not accepted unanimously, unlike the *déclarations* of 1984 and 2002, but rather by a large majority; thus, if the Académie's attitude towards feminization is changing, it is by increments only.

In the government's response, we can see some willingness to respond to demands for greater linguistic equality, even if the pace of change has been slow. The attitude of the Académie française has evolved from a refusal of any kind of feminization to a gradual acceptance of limited aspects of it, though inclusive writing (in its narrow sense) is not accepted by either the government or the Académie (cf. Omer 2020: 6).

15.3 Understanding and measuring language attitudes

When debates about language take place online, those taking part may reveal their attitude towards language features and practices, such as non-sexist language, or users of these. Language attitudes have traditionally been defined as 'any affective, cognitive or behavioural (i.e. conative) index of evaluative reactions towards different varieties and their speakers' (Ryan, Giles, and Sebastian 1982: 7). As Kutlu and Kircher (2021: 3, n.1) note, this definition refers only to attitudes to language varieties (language, dialects, accents, etc.) and their speakers, but there is a

---

[6] Amongst these are Chenu et al. (2020); Masson (2021); Teissier et al. (2021); Gruny et al. (2022); Blanc (2022). At the time of final revisions to this chapter (May 2023), searching in the *Journal Officiel* suggests that none of these laws has yet been passed.

growing body of literature that considers attitudes to particular language features; for example, quotatives (e.g. English 'I was like ...'), vocal fry (speaking with a croaky or rough sound), and phonetic variables (see Kutlu and Kircher 2021), to which this study aims to contribute. According to this definition, there are three aspects to consider: feelings (affect) about the language/linguistic feature or about its speakers/users; beliefs about it (cognition); and behaviours towards it/its users (actions or intention to act; Kutlu and Kircher 2021: 3; see also Cargile et al. 1994).

Attitudes may, in turn, give an insight into underlying language ideologies, which are defined as sets of morally and politically loaded beliefs about language structure and use in a social world (Woolard 2020: 1, citing Irvine 1989). France is often regarded as a country in which standard language ideology is particularly strong, and where prescriptivist and purist ideas about language permeate society (Lodge 1993: 3, 234). Standard language ideology is defined by Lippi-Green (1997: 64) as 'a bias toward an abstract, idealized homogeneous language, which is imposed and maintained by dominant institutions and which has as its model the written language'. Its relationship to prescriptivism and purism is complex: prescriptivism involves the idea that there is only one correct form of language, i.e. the standard form, and therefore that any deviation from this is unacceptable. Purism is characterized by a desire to rid a language of some undesirable element(s), and to maintain the language in its current perfect (standardized) form (Walsh 2016b: 9).[7]

With the Académie française holding a particularly prominent place in public discourse about language, and with a long history of language laws and interventions, it is easy to assume that standard language ideology, prescriptivist, and purist viewpoints are shared by the French population at large. However, studies which investigate this empirically are few (exceptions include Paveau and Rosier 2008; Walsh 2016b; Humphries 2021). This study therefore seeks to investigate the extent to which language attitudes towards inclusive writing (and more broadly, non-sexist language) manifested at the official level are shared by individuals.

There are various possibilities available to researchers wanting to know how different polemical linguistic issues are perceived by ordinary speakers. Survey data can provide insights: Walsh (2014, 2016b), for example, deploys online questionnaires and interviews to discover attitudes to linguistic purism in France and Quebec; Humphries (2014) uses similar techniques to investigate acceptance of feminized titles in France and Quebec. The rise of computer-mediated communication (CMC) means that large-scale textual data are readily available which can give an insight into what ordinary people are thinking about a particular

---

[7] See Walsh (2016b) for more detailed discussion of the complex relationship between standardization, prescriptivism, and purism. See also the discussion in Walsh (Chapter 13, this volume) and Humphries (Chapter 14, this volume).

issue—though with some caveats, which may differ according to the different platforms in focus. For example, users of social media tend to be young to middle-aged: while 94% of those aged 18–24 used social media in France in 2019, this falls to 35% for those aged 60–69 and just 19% for those aged 70–79 (Statista no date). People tend to engage online in discussions they feel strongly about—meaning extreme views may be more prominent. Online debates can be heated and potentially distorted—many people express views online which they would hesitate to articulate person-to-person; misogyny is also rife (cf. Bartlett et al. 2014; Jane 2017; Ging and Siapera 2018). As Rosier (2019: 42) observes, questions of language in particular may elicit 'des échanges extrêmement vifs, voir haineux et violents, violence amplifiée par la configuration technologique et la viralité numérique'—i.e. it is precisely because these debates are taking place in the online world that they become so vitriolic. Thus, viewpoints expressed online cannot necessarily be taken as representative. Nevertheless, studying discourse online can provide a window into public views and attitudes, and Twitter in particular has become a key venue for public discussion in recent years (see e.g. Russell 2013).

Twitter (known as X as of July 2023) is a social media platform on which users send short (<280 characters) messages, known as tweets, to their followers—people who have chosen to receive updates from them on their timeline (a homepage for the individual user). Users can engage in mutual or non-mutual following relationships, and (unless a user's account is private), tweets can reach a wide audience by means of Twitter's in-built features such as re-tweeting (forwarding a tweet to one's own followers) and the use of hashtags, which allows users to search for and link their content to that of other users by prefacing a word or phrase with the '#' sign (see further discussion in Section 15.5.2.1). Users can also favourite a tweet, indicating that they like its content. Twitter has become an important source of data for a wide variety of disciplines (see e.g. Sloan and Quan-Haase 2017), since it provides a ready source of linguistic and social data, which can be collected relatively easily.[8] With certain caveats in mind (regarding how representative data from social media, and Twitter in particular, may be), this study uses data from Twitter to address the following research questions:

- What kinds of arguments are used for and against French inclusive writing in the corpus of tweets?
- What kinds of language attitudes do these reveal?
- To what extent do these correspond to attitudes at the official level?
- How does this debate fit into the wider context of the feminization of the French language/*langage non sexiste*?

---

[8] There are a number of ethical issues which arise when using CMC data for academic research. Lack of space precludes full discussion of these (see e.g. Ess 2019). This project received full ethical approval from Queen's University Belfast.

15.4 Methodology and data analysis

This study combines techniques from corpus linguistics and discourse analysis. In corpus linguistics, bodies of machine-readable texts are analysed to study patterns of word use, while in discourse analysis, instances of language use (whether written, oral, or sign) are analysed in their wider context to explore the relations between discourse and social and cultural developments in different social domains (see e.g. Jørgensen and Phillips 2002). Studies which draw on both CL and DA have sometimes been termed *corpus-assisted discourse studies* (CADS); others prefer the term *corpus-informed discourse analysis* (e.g. Kircher and Fox 2019; see also Hyland 2009; Breeze and Olza 2017), since the latter implies no hierarchical relationship (cf. Baker et al. 2008). CL and DA techniques complement each other: CL analyses, which tend to be quantitative, can reveal systematic discursive patterns; DA, with a largely qualitative approach, enables the researcher to better understand and explain such patterns, because it takes into account the broader social, political, historical, and cultural context (Baker 2010: 141). The combination of CL and DA for the analysis of attitudes and ideologies is particularly useful, as it can uncover less explicit beliefs about language which other research instruments (such as questionnaires) are less attuned to.

CL analyses vary in their approach, depending on the research aims, but tend to be focused around word frequencies (highly frequent or infrequent words), collocations (words which repeatedly co-occur with words of interest to the study), and concordances (studying words of interest in their discourse context). CL studies may also look at n-grams, repeated sequences of words of different lengths (e.g. bigrams such as *langue française*).[9] This study uses CL and DA techniques to examine attitudes from two angles: their expression through lexicosemantic means (i.e. through the words and collocations in the corpus; for example, the adjectives which collocate with *écriture inclusive*), and through domain-specific expressive features (i.e. Twitter approbation measures such as retweets and favourites, as well as hashtags).

To create a corpus, an application called If This Then That (IFTTT no date) was used to collect tweets. This application allows a user to set up a search for particular words or hashtags on Twitter. Every time the search terms are used (i.e. a tweet is sent containing one of them), the application collects the tweets containing the search terms, plus some associated metadata. The search terms for this study were 'écriture inclusive', the hashtag '#écritureinclusive', and orthographic variants of these. The collection ran from 2 May 2018 to 12 September 2018.[10] One limitation

---

[9] Keywords—words of high and low frequency as compared to a relevant reference corpus—are also important in CL. For reasons of space, keyword analysis is not undertaken here.

[10] While the collection does not cover the period immediately after the publication of the school textbook, there was still considerable discussion online about the topic. As Vessey (2017: 282) notes,

of IFTTT is that each time it is triggered (i.e. one of the search terms is used), it only collects the first fifteen tweets containing the search terms; however, for a topic of relatively modest magnitude, this should not be a critical limitation.[11] The corpus of tweets was checked for deleted tweets at the time of analysis.[12] Of 15,258 tweets, 6,474 (42%) had been deleted, leaving a corpus of 8,784 tweets for the analysis (Table 15.1). The remaining tweet corpus was made up of 48% original tweets (i.e. tweets composed by the user) and 52% retweets (i.e. a tweet forwarded by a different user to their own followers) (Table 15.2).[13] There were 6,924 unique users in the dataset; the vast majority of these (99%; n=6,850) sent four tweets or fewer, 0.1% (n=68) sent five to nine tweets, and only 0.01% (n=6) sent ten or more tweets. This indicates that there are very few people in the corpus who engage with the topic repeatedly and with any longevity.

Table 15.1 Tweet dataset: deleted tweets

	Number of tweets
Original corpus	15,258
Deleted Tweets	6,474 (42%)
Remaining corpus after deleted tweets removed	**8,784 (58%)**

Table 15.2 Corpus split between original tweets and retweets

Type of tweet	Number of tweets
Original tweets	4,233 (48%)
Retweets	4,551 (52%)
Total	**8,784**

it can sometimes be useful to collect data during times of relative 'linguistic peace' (Cardinal 2008), to avoid the most 'inflamed and exaggerated' viewpoints.

[11] For non-pro users of IFTTT (i.e. free accounts), the applet performs a 'trigger check' once an hour (a trigger check is when IFTTT checks for new trigger events, i.e. for any uses of the search terms that have been entered into the applet). Thus, if the number of tweets per hour is vastly superior to fifteen (including retweets), only a sample of these is collected. See note 13 regarding retweets.

[12] This was a condition of ethics approval for this study, since participants (i.e. Twitter users) may be considered to have withdrawn from the study if they have deleted their tweets. The Hydrator app (no date) was used to check for deleted tweets. Due to circumstances beyond the author's control, there was a significant hiatus between data collection (2018) and analysis (2020).

[13] Retweets appear in the corpus multiple times if they were among the first fifteen tweets captured by IFTTT each time it was triggered. Thus, the same tweet may appear multiple times in the corpus (since retweets can also themselves be retweeted). Retweets can therefore skew the overall figures for word frequencies, and are analysed separately, as explained in Section 15.5.1. In newer versions of IFTTT applets, it is possible to exclude retweets from the collection.

15.5 Results

Section 15.5.1 presents corpus linguistic analyses of the most frequent content words in the data, further investigating their use through collocation and concordance lines, to look at how words are being used and associated with others in the debate. Together, these analyses can reveal patterns in what people are discussing when they debate *écriture inclusive*, as well as the associations underpinning their attitudes. Section 15.5.2 explores domain-specific semiotic means afforded by Twitter (beyond the lexicosemantic) for indexing attitude, including retweets, favourites, and hashtags.

15.5.1 Corpus linguistic analysis

Generating a list of the most frequent words in the raw corpus results in a relatively uninteresting list, as the search terms and grammatical (i.e. function) words are frequent, and retweets skew the overall figures. Some studies taking a CADS approach retain retweets, URLs, and other such strings (e.g. Vessey 2016), while others eliminate them at the point of collection (e.g. Kutlu and Kircher 2021). Here, retweets were removed for the CL analyses and examined separately (see Section 15.5.2.2). The corpus was manipulated in R using the rtweet package (Kearney 2019; R Core Team 2013) and other standard packages to remove user handles, URLs, 'RT' (a string indicating a retweet), search terms, and other strings which are not relevant for revealing the content of what people say when they discuss inclusive writing.[14] A French stop-word list was also applied, to remove grammatical/function words (e.g. *je*, *le*). A list of the ten most frequent non-function words was then generated (Table 15.3). Collocations and concordances were explored in #LancsBox, free corpus analysis software developed by corpus linguists at the University of Lancaster (Brezina, Weill-Tessier, and McEnery 2020) for all ten of the most frequent terms. For reasons of space, the top four terms only are reported on in detail, with some brief comments on other words in the top ten.

Perhaps unsurprisingly, given the topic of interest, the top two content words in the corpus are *langue* (absolute frequency 269) and *française* (188). These occur together as the bigram *langue française* 121 times. Analysis of concordance lines shows that in four (different) tweets, the exact phrase *notre belle langue française* occurs (Figure 15.4). In these tweets, which all express sentiments against inclusive writing, emotive verbs such as *massacrer*, *dénaturer*, and *déformer* are used to describe the effect of inclusive writing on the French language. In fact, *massacre* (as a verb/noun) appears six times in the corpus; five of these are with *langue française* (Figure 15.5).

[14] The frequency of search terms is uninteresting as by definition they are highly frequent, since they were used to identify and collect tweets.

Table 15.3 Top ten most frequent content words in the corpus

Position	Word	Absolute frequency	Relative frequency (per 10,000 words)
1	langue	269	27.9
2	française	188	19.5
3	genre	155	16.1
4	lire	142	14.8
5	femmes	139	14.4
6	masculin	133	13.8
7	utiliser	121	12.6
8	vraiment	119	12.4
9	français	117	12.2
10	féminin	110	11.4

Left	Node	Right
connaissant bien la grammaire de notre belle	langue française	conversait comme il écrivait et pointillait ainsi
inclusive Cest stupide et déforme notre belle	langue Française	L'écriture inclusive celle des cancres qui ont
qui ne fait que dénaturer notre belle	langue française	Il reste toujours la possibilité de faire
on se rend compte que notre belle	langue française	est de nouveau massacrée par le biais
dutilisateur on utilise pas l'écriture inclusive dans	langue française	C'est vrai que l'écriture inclusive peut gêner
tu parles bafoue les milliers données de	langue française	autant que lécriture inclusiveEnsuite si tu penses
de France2 le mot chef est en	langue française	un mot exclusivement masculin Écrire cheffe est
inclusive Pourriez vous écrire le français en	langue française	Stop à l'écriture soidisant inclusive Merci Arrêtez
évoluer n'importe comment Le masculin l'emporte en	langue française	C'est plus simple que de se prendre
créé comme lécriture inclusive par ailleurs la	langue française	étant évolutiv... Les gens ils découvrent lécriture
nest pas un mot incompatible avec la	langue française	contrairement à lécriture inclusive par exemple xD

Figure 15.4 Selected concordance lines with bigram *langue française*, left-sorted

Left	Node	Right
que lutilisation de lécritureinclusive qui massacre la	langue française	ContentMarketing Vitve l'écriture inclusive pour le web
Surtout venant de quelquun qui massacre la	langue française	à chaque tweet Grâce à lécriture inclusive
agresse mes yeux ce massacre de la	langue française	Et non les Africains ne seraient pas
et tolérer un tel massacre de la	langue française	qui plus est de la part de
saigne des Arrêtez le massacre de la	langue française	A l'écriture inclusive Ecritureinclusive Je sais même

Figure 15.5 Concordance lines with *massacre + langue française*

Figure 15.6 shows the concordance lines where the right-sorted context begins with *est* (8/121 occurrences of the bigram *langue française*), to allow exploration of some of the qualities that are ascribed to the language. Several examples comment that the French language is already *riche*, *complexe*, or *compliquée*. Not all tweets evaluate complexity in the same way: for some, this is a positive trait; for others, it is a burden. Nevertheless, this argument tends to be used to insist that inclusive writing should not be adopted—either because it is unnecessary, since the French language already has other resources to deal with the issue of sexism in language (see example 1), or because it adds to the already heavy burden of French orthography (example 2). Example (2) also features the argument that there are more important issues to address than inclusive writing—a frequent theme, which is discussed further in Section 15.5.2.1.

Left	Node	Right
dans le service Cela prouve que la	langue française	est bien vivante perso je fais un
lAcadémie Mexicaine de la langue hein La	langue française	est cette belle langue qui me permet
même sans les bails lgbt si la	langue française	est comme ça prq tu te plains
on se rend compte que notre belle	langue française	est de nouveau massacrée par le biais
plus grande majorité de personne lemploie La	langue française	est déjà assez compliqué pour quon l'alourdisse
extensions de mots Je pense que la	langue française	est déjà bien assez riche pour la
un peu le niveau du débat La	langue française	est suffisamment riche et complexe pour se
compris ce sujet de lécriture inclusive La	langue Française	est trop suffisamment riche pour chercher un

Figure 15.6 Selected concordance lines with bigram *langue française*, right-sorted, examples with *est*

(1) @user La langue française est suffisamment riche et complexe pour renoncer à lécriture inclusive. Par exemple suite à un commentaire dun ami américain je nécris plus les hommes politiques mais les personnes politiques (user_6125)[15]

(2) @users j'ai jamais compris pourquoi on nécessite l'écriture inclusive. La langue Française est trop suffisamment riche pour chercher un prob inutile de genre sur les mots. Y'a plus important a régler et ce sera génant pour la francophonie aussi ailleurs (user_5057)

The word *français* also appears in the top ten most frequent words (Table 15.3; n=117). In most cases, it is used nominally, referring either to the language or (less frequently) to French people. Figure 15.7 shows selected concordance lines where *français* is preceded by 'le' (and refers to the language). The beauty of French is also a theme here: for example, two tweets (lines 13 and 14 in Figure 15.7) use the phrase *cette belle langue quest le français*, one featuring the verb *dénaturer* and the other *détruire*. Another tweet (line 15 in Figure 15.7, expanded in example 3) argues that inclusive writing cannot be part of the French language, and that since the masculine form has always been given priority, changing this would be disastrous for education, because this relies on literary works (in which *le masculin l'emporte sur le féminin*).

(3) @users À aucun moment l'écriture inclusive ne fait partie de la langue française, c'est vous qui l'avez inventée. Depuis la nuit du temps le français donne la priorité au masculin, et changer cette règle serait un désastre pour l'éducation du français qui s'appuie sur des œuvres écrites (user_6224)

In example (4) (line 7, Figure 15.7), the tweeter poses the rhetorical question 'for or against inclusive writing'; their answer, that they are 'bleeding from their eyes', indicates clearly they feel it is abhorrent (cf. Humphries 2021). The tweeter mentions one of the proposed gender-neutral third-person singular pronouns, *iel*.

---

[15] Tweets often feature non-standard orthography and grammar and idiosyncrasies in punctuation; features such as *ne* deletion and use of emojis are widespread. All tweets and examples from tweets are transcribed exactly as they appear, with the original spelling and punctuation. Parts are reworded to ensure anonymity.

▲ Left	Node	Right
est écrit sur les 4 continents Le	français	en écriture inclusive ne l'est que par
On ne peut pas maîtriser correctement le	français	langue millénaire et empreint de nombreuses subtilités
République Française une et indivisible c'est le	français	pas l'espérantoL'écriture inclusive elle est une variation
contraire à l'idée d'écriture inclusive ellemême Le	français	standard qui n'utilise pas l'écriture inclusive est
même un truc pour les feignasses Le	français	permet d'écrire les étudiants et les étudiantes
ont déjà du mal à lire le	français	Mais ça répondait à quelquun qui trouvai
Genre IEL REALLY Arrêtez de niquer le	français	svp niklefrenC pour oucontre— Je sais pas
linguistique mais défend bec et ongles le	français	sans connaître son histoire et à quel
CE1 Vous ne maîtrisez déjà pas le	français	comment voulezvous maîtriser lécriture inclusive Il y
l'écriture inclusive en ne maîtrisant pas le	français	correct Sur ton simple thread il y
écrire Lécriture inclusive cest que pour le	français	Ou les autres pays à langues latines
shabitue vite Navrée de tapprendre que le	français	est une langue vivante et que par
Elle dénature cette belle langue questle	français	Une prise en otage injuste et injustifiée
qui détruit cette belle langue questle	français	mon cerveau FOND Jai mangé avec mon
inventée Depuis la nuit de temps le	français	donne la priorité au masculin et changer
lécriture inclusive Questce quune langue totalitaire Le	français	dit petit nègre Lire de lécriture inclusive
inclusive implique de savoir aussi écrire le	français	Lécriture inclusive Platon a dit que la
accepter lecriture inclusive Pourriez vous écrire le	français	en langue française Stop à l'écriture soidisant

Figure 15.7 Selected concordance lines with *français*, left-sorted, selected examples preceded by *le*

Crying-laughing emojis and the vocabulary used (*niquer*, 'to screw/fuck something up') indicate that the author of this tweet also believes inclusive writing to be damaging to the French language.

(4) Pour ou contre l'écriture inclusive? Personnellement je saigne des yeux. Genre 'IEL' REALLY??? 😭😭Arrêtez de niquer le français svp 🙏 #niklefrenC [URL] (user_1526)

There are fewer examples where *français* means 'French people'. Figure 15.8 shows selected concordance lines with *les français*. In example (5) (line 4 of Figure 15.8), several themes are evident. The tweeter calls on French people to defend their language—which has already suffered the 'amputation' of various diacritics—from the 'capricious' demands of inclusive writing, which threatens to 'deform' the language. In another tweet, shown in (6) (line 5 of Figure 15.8), the author appears to be favourable to inclusive writing, but only if it is properly used, since otherwise, it would reinforce the stereotype that the French are not good at spelling, a theme which is taken up again in Section 15.6.

▲ Left	Node	Right
professionnel•le•s Quand on voit quen 2018 les	français	se battent pour lécriture inclusive je sais
constitution un outil d'exclusion en différenciant les	français	sur leur sexe il fallait oser Que
cette personne Omg mais je déteste les	français	putainOnEu Y a PaS bEsOiN dE IEcRiTuRe
Que Dieu maudisse lécriture inclusive Que les	Français	laissent les Belges avec leur nouvelle langue
critiques du genre ça prouve que les	Français	sont nuls en orthographe T'as pas tout

Figure 15.8 Selected concordance lines with *français*, left-sorted, examples preceded by *les*

(5) Que les Français laissent les Belges avec leur nouvelle langue belge, et qu'ils gardent leur énergie pour défendre la langue française 'phonétisée', amputée (en France) d'accents et de tirets, et déformée par les revendications capricieuses qui donnent l'écriture inclusive. [*link to another tweet*] (user_5211)

(6) Svp l'écriture inclusive c'est cool, mais apprenez à l'utiliser sinon vous alimentez les critiques du genre 'ça prouve que les Français sont nuls en orthographe' (user_4759)

The third most frequent content word in the corpus, *genre*, appears 155 times. Since inclusive writing concerns gender, one might well expect this term to be frequent. While in many examples, it appears with the meaning 'grammatical/real-world gender', it also appears with a range of other meanings, including 'type of' (e.g. in the tweet corpus we find: 'ce genre d'idées'; 'ce genre de connerie quest l'écriture inclusive'), and as a discourse marker, loosely translated as 'like' (see example 4). Thus, its polysemy seems to lie behind its statistical preponderance, giving it somewhat less interpretive significance.

Among the top collocates of *genre* (Table 15.4; ranked by Mutual Information Score)[16] are *neutre*, *féminin*, and *masculin* (along with *théorie* and *personne*).[17] Many of the tweets containing these terms discuss the issue of the generic masculine. For example, one tweet (line 1 and 2, Figure 15.9) remarks that since there are two genders in French, it was a 50/50 chance which would be used as a 'neutral' gender, which ignores the sociocultural factors influencing the choice of masculine as neutral. The author continues that they would settle for a generic feminine as a preferred option to inclusive writing, stating that: 'Moi ça me dérange pas. Je préfère ça à l'écriture inclusive qui est du grand n'importe quoi' (user_1349). Another (line 2, Figure 15.10) argues that there is a misconception around the rule of *le masculin l'emporte sur le féminin*, noting: '[c']est un raccourci pratique mais faux. Le masculin est le genre de base parce que c'est le genre non marqué (neutre et masculin ont fusionnés)' (user_1370) (cf. Charaudeau 2019). Another tweet (line 6, Figure 15.10) puts forward similar arguments: 'Mais dans

Table 15.4 Top collocates of *genre* (MI > 5.0)

Index	Position	Collocate	Mutual Information Score	Frequency (as collocate)	Frequency (in corpus)
1	Left	théorie	8.54	9	15
2	Right	neutre	6.30	7	55
3	Right	personne	5.36	7	106
4	Right	féminin	5.08	6	110
5	Left	masculin	5.03	7	133

[16] The Mutual Information Score indicates the strength of the co-occurrence relationship between a node (here, *genre*) and its collocates. There is no upper limit to the score; the higher the number, the stronger the relationship; here, collocates with a score of 5 or more are shown.

[17] *Masculin* and *féminin* are themselves among the top ten most frequent content words. The analysis of these as they appear with *genre* gives a sense of the usage of these words; lack of space prevents inclusion of a more detailed analysis of these terms as top content words.

la langue française le masculin est un genre non marqué, si je dis: il y a eu 25000 coureurs, je désigne indifféremment et les hommes et les femmes ... Ce qui veut dire que l'écriture inclusive est complétement inutile ...' (user_5724). Similar arguments are found among the tweets featuring both *genre* and *neutre*, indicating that the position historically supported by the Académie—*le masculin l'emporte sur le féminin*—has been internalized by individuals engaging in this debate online.

Left	Node	Right
si tu veux on peut mettre le	genre	féminin colle le genre neutre Moi ça
peut mettre le genre féminin colle le	genre	neutre Moi ça me dérange pas Je
de la néoConstitution afin de visibiliser le	genre	humain féminin car chacun constate jour après
de bras en bleu Obsolescence programmée du	genre	féminin Elle utilise lécriture inclusive Il y
darrêter linjonction à lécriture inclusive quand on	genre	au féminin à propos de métiers dévalorisés
neutre et lécriture inclusive tu peux me	genre	au féminin oLa Buse— Okok Yvette Horner

Figure 15.9 Concordance lines with *genre + féminin*

Left	Node	Right
pratique mais faux Le masculin est le	genre	de base parce que cest le-genre
2 que ça soit le masculin le	genre	neutreMais tu sais si tu veux on
mot est désigné pour une personne de	genre	masculin le féminiser nenlève rien á sa
manque nest pas lécriture inclusive mais un	genre	masculin Ah ça je te jure on
te concernent pas quelles nexistent pasConcernant le	genre	masculin les militants de lécriture inclusive considère
la langue française le masculin est un	genre	non marqué si je dis il y
neutre mais que le masculin est un	genre	non marqué Si jen crois lactualité récente

Figure 15.10 Concordance lines with *genre + masculin*

The fourth most frequent content word is the verb *lire*. Left sorting the concordance lines for this term shows that *lire* appears in twenty-eight tweets in the formulation '[ADJECTIVE] à lire'. Most adjectives in this construction are negative (listed here with spelling as it occurs in the corpus): 'chiant' (and variants) occurs six times; 'pénible' four times; 'desagréable' three times; 'relou' (2), 'dégeulasse' (1), 'long' (1), 'fatiguante' (1). However, 'facile' also occurs three times, as well as 'agréables' (1) and 'drole' (1). Closer examination of examples with *facile* reveals that only one displays a positive attitude towards *écriture inclusive*, highlighting the importance of qualitative analysis of discourse context to understand the attitudes in the corpus.

In this exploratory CL analysis, some themes have emerged: notably, the idea that *écriture inclusive* is damaging to the French language. Tweets often praise the beauty of the French language, and lament the perceived harm done to it by inclusive writing, with language ranging from the mild (e.g. *désagréable*) to the more extreme (e.g. *massacre, chiant, niquer*). Examining highly frequent words also shows that the aphorism *le masculin l'emporte sur le féminin* is well known to individuals engaging in this debate online—and that it is used to justify the use of the generic masculine, as well as to deny any need for inclusive writing.

15.5.2 Twitter-specific features

Like other social media platforms, Twitter has several 'in-built popularity measurements' (Shifman 2011: 190) which provide a ready means of investigating user approbation online; these include the favourite and retweet buttons. Hashtags (strings of text prefaced by the '#' symbol, e.g. *#metoo*) function on Twitter as a way of grouping together tweets on a given topic: clicking on, or searching by, a hashtag brings up all tweets which feature that hashtag. Zappavigna (2011: 800) argues that hashtags are used as a means of ambient affiliation, in that users 'affiliate with a copresent (Goffman 1963), impermanent, community by bonding around evolving topics of interest'. The following sections report on hashtags (15.5.2.1), retweets (15.5.2.2), and favourites (15.5.2.3) in the corpus.

15.5.2.1 Hashtags

Perhaps the most surprising aspect of the use of hashtags in the corpus is that they are rare (Figure 15.11). Even the most frequent, *#écritureinclusive*, occurs only twenty-five times in total, and only when all associated orthographic variants (e.g. *#EcritureInclusive*) are included. Alongside the fact that most Twitter users engaging in this debate send only one or two tweets in the corpus, this indicates that the discussion around *écriture inclusive* is relatively diffuse, and that it lacks a cohesive set of hashtags to pull people together in 'ambient affiliation' (Zappavigna 2011, 2015).

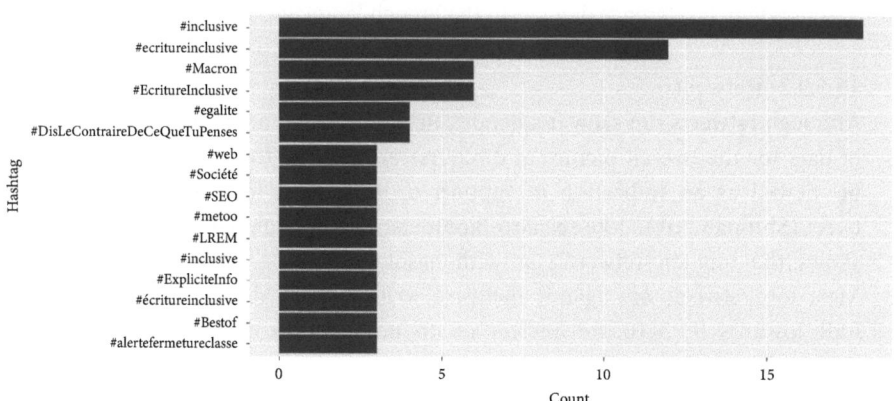

Figure 15.11 Top hashtags

Other hashtags used in the corpus include *#égalité* (and its variants, e.g. *#EgaliteFH*). Tweets featuring *#égalité* or a variant thereof were generally more favourable towards inclusive writing, seeing it as part of a general drive towards equality. For example:

(7) Bravo @user d'avoir adopté l'écriture inclusive dans votre campagne de recrutement! #ecritureinclusive #Recherche #EgaliteFH [URL to recruitment page of government research service]

314   TRISTRAM

This attitude is far from universal, however, and there are other instances (not necessarily involving this hashtag) where self-described feminists/proponents of equality reject inclusive writing. The English-language hashtag *#metoo*, associated with a social movement to talk openly about sexual abuse and sexual harassment, which went viral on Twitter during October 2017, also appears (n=3). In France, the associated hashtag was *#balancetonporc*, which also features in the corpus, albeit only twice. Perhaps unexpectedly, the tweets in the corpus featuring *#metoo* and/or *#balancetonporc* are critical of inclusive writing; for example, the tweet in (8) implies that social media campaigns will not solve the real problems associated with sexism, such as sexual harassment (cf. Van Compernolle 2009).

(8) Du coup #balancetonporc et #metoo n ont pas résolu le problème? Peut etre parce que la solution n est pas l ecriture inclusive et autres conneries de salon mais dans l action et la sanction (user_4877)

This brief examination of hashtags reveals that, at least in this corpus, they are not being used to create ambient affiliation (Zappavigna 2011). The topic lacks a single hashtag around which Twitter users can co-construct their discourse and come together as a community. The main themes which emerge amongst the hashtags are that inclusive writing is a distraction from real issues; there are fewer hashtags which reference damage to the French language.

15.5.2.2 Retweets

Although retweets can skew frequency calculations, they are an important source of data for the overall picture of discourse around the topic, as retweeting can be viewed as an indication of support or agreement for the content of the tweet (Shifman 2011: 190; see also Blommaert 2015; Highfield 2015). Table 15.5 shows the top ten retweets; as with hashtags, numbers are quite modest.[18] Most top retweets are against inclusive writing: 6/10 display a negative attitude towards it; 3/10 are unclear or do not take an overt position; one is positive.[19]

Some themes emerge: notably, once again, that *écriture inclusive* is a threat to the French language. Tweet 1 in Table 15.5, for example, features several adjectives ending in *-age*, all of which imply the French language has been 'tinkered' or 'tampered with' by those unqualified in matters of language. Tweet 3 implies that

---

[18] The figure in column three of Table 15.5 indicates the number of times the tweet was retweeted in total (as indicated by metadata collected with the tweets). Not all of these retweets are present in the corpus, because of the rate limitations of IFTTT, as described in Section 15.4.

[19] The attitude in the one positive tweet (number 2) is ambiguous, but closer examination of the wider context and consultation with a native speaker clarify that the user is in favour of inclusive writing: the sense is 'even those who might be thought to be against inclusive writing, such as homophobes, are using it'. For other unclear tweets, even after further investigation, it was not possible to categorize them with confidence.

ATTITUDES ON TWITTER TOWARDS FRENCH INCLUSIVE WRITING   315

Table 15.5 Top ten retweets

Position (attitude)	Tweet text	Number of retweets
1 (negative)	Au revoir à l'écriture inclusive, ce bricolage, ce bidouillage, ce scribouillage, ce tripatouillage de la langue.	2462
2 (positive)	N'empêche les homophobes aussi utilisent maintenant l'écriture inclusive et ça c'est beau. [*link to a tweet, now deleted*]	1947
3 (negative)	Une majorité des Français sont POUR l'écriture inclusive, selon un sondage. Sauf que ... Selon la même étude, seuls 12% des sondés sont capables d'expliquer ce que c'est. #BullshitDetector	690
4 (unclear)	En tout cas, je suis content que le gouvernement actuel ait adopté l'écriture inclusive ! L'Etat de droit.e.	669
5 (negative)	Comment l'écriture inclusive veut dire qu'on fait des fautes d'orthographe. [*image of a rainbow flag with inclusive writing on it*]	662
6 (negative)	Il faut le redire: l'écriture inclusive exclut. Quand on veut vraiment etre inclusif, on dit l'Homme et pas l'homme, la femme, l'hermaphrodite, le transsexuel ... Et quand on connaît le Français, on sait que l'Homme ne renvoie pas au masculin, pas plus que Sa majesté au féminin.	626
7 (unclear)	Parce qu'en réalité, ce n'est pas l'écriture inclusive ou l'éducation sexuelle qui menacent l'école aujourd'hui, mais les conditions d'enseignement: fil sur la situation des écoles: des bâtiments sans chauffage ou toilettes.	602
8 (negative)	L'écriture inclusive, pourquoi pas. S'il faut ça pour rentrer dans le.a. moule.	530
9 (negative)	Qu'est ce que ça m'agace de lire des trucs en écriture inclusive ... Dès que j'aperçois des tirets je sais déjà que ça va parler d'un truc à la con (parce que faut voir QUI utilise l'écriture inclusive ...) et qu'en plus ce truc à la con sera illisible. C'est juste ridicule 😂😂😂	501
10 (unclear)	Les gens: OUAIS LES FEMINISTES VOS COMBATS CA SE RESUME A L'ECRITURE INCLUSIVE ET LE MANSPREADING CA SERT A RIEN QUAND FAUT PARLER DE VIOLENCES Y'A PERSONNE Féministes: dénoncent les violences gynéco Gens: MAIS A CAUSE DE VOUS LES GENS N'AURONT PLUS CONFIANCE DES SOIGNANTS	492

écriture inclusive is confusing, since many people do not actually understand what it is. Tweet 8 implies that *écriture inclusive* is ridiculous, as demonstrated by its erroneous use, *le.a.*, on the article with *moule*, and faddy, since those who use it are just following the crowd to fit in. Tweet 9 is more explicitly negative, using informal, pejorative language (*con*, 'stupid'), crying-laughing emojis, and arguing that use of *écriture inclusive* renders French illegible. Orthographic errors also come up in the retweet top ten: tweet 5 argues that anyone using *écriture inclusive* is also likely to make spelling mistakes.

15.5.2.3 Favourites

The option to favourite a tweet also allows users to indicate their approbation for the content of a tweet. Attitudes towards inclusive writing in the favourites are exclusively negative; Table 15.6 shows the top ten. Two of these (tweets 2 and 6) indicate approval for a member of the Real Academia Española, who announced he would quit if the academy adopted Spanish inclusive writing. Tweet 5 links *écriture inclusive* to paedophilia and to the Arabic language, in a sarcastic comment

Table 15.6 Top ten favourited tweets

Position (attitude)	Tweet text	Number of favourites
1 (negative)	Comment l'écriture inclusive veut dire qu'on fait des fautes d'orthographe. [*image of a rainbow flag with inclusive writing on it*]	1758
2 (negative)	Bravo à Arturo Perez Reverte qui menace de quitter l'Académie royale espagnole, si l'écriture inclusive était adoptée. Il a été soutenu par Javier Marias et Mario Vargas Llosa. La littérature contre les précieuses ridicules.	932
3 (negative)	'L'écriture inclusive abolit le lien originel du vocable et du chant. Elle rend impossible la poésie, dont elle signe l'arrêt de mort dans l'espace public. Elle ajoute la lourdeur graphique à l'aberration nominale.' Citation de J.-M. Delacomptée	876
4 (negative)	Je suis scandalisé qu'un inspecteur de l'éducation nationale utilise l'écriture inclusive quand il écrit aux professeurs. Ce militantisme est déplacé de la part d'un fonctionnaire ayant autorité sur d'autres. Il convient que @jmblanquer fasse le nécessaire pour y mettre bon ordre.	800
5 (negative)	BREAKING: le ministère de l'Education nationale précise que les manuels de pédophilie à l'usage des écoles maternelles seront rédigés en écriture inclusive et en arabe.	284
6 (negative)	L'écrivain Arturo Perez-Reverte menace de démissionner de l'Académie espagnole si elle fait inscrire l'écriture inclusive dans la Constitution. [*link to story in Spanish press*]	236

Position (attitude)	Tweet text	Number of favourites
7 (negative)	Pour faire grève il faut d'abord être travailleur, un étudiant ne peut donc pas être en grève, il eût mieux fallu écrire sur la copie 'étudiant qui n'a rien révisé et se réjouit que ca ne se voit pas' ... sinon désolée l'écriture inclusive c'est au delà de mes forces [*link to another tweet about a student strike*]	175
8 (negative)	Pauvre @user! L'écriture inclusive ne doit pas servir de cache-sexe à une syntaxe bancale. Dans cette phrase, ce sont les droits qui sont bafoués. Aucune raison d'inclure une option féminine « bafoué.e.s ». Comble du ridicule et de l'ignorance. [*link to another tweet which features inclusive writing*]	132
9 (negative)	@user @user Pourquoi vous mettez l'écriture inclusive là où il n'y en a pas besoin ? Je savais pas que les mecs avaient besoin de tampons ou de serviettes hygiéniques ... [*link to image of a poster about period products with inclusive writing*]	124
10 (negative)	Étonnée d'entendre qu'on a utilisé l'entrée de Simone #Veil au Panthéon pour défendre l'introduction de l'écriture inclusive dans la #Constitution. Elle qui était attachée à l'Académie française et se disait « premier président » du Parlement européen. #PJLConstit #DirectAN	115

about the government's position on the matter. In the others, familiar themes can be identified:

- the damage to the language inclusive writing will cause; e.g. tweet 3, which talks about *la lourdeur graphique*; *aberration nominale*;
- the fact that it is ridiculous and unnecessary; e.g. tweet 2, invoking 'la littérature contre les précieuses ridicules', referencing Molière; tweet 8, 'comble du ridicule et de l'ignorance'; and tweet 9, mocking a sign in which inclusive writing is used;
- that it will result in disorder and chaos; e.g. tweet 4, which calls on the Education Minister to restore order;
- that people who use inclusive writing fail to master French orthography; e.g. tweet 1, which is the only favourited tweet to also feature in the retweet top ten (Table 15.5, tweet 5); and tweet 8, which criticizes another tweeter's syntax and mishandling of agreement rules.

15.6 Discussion

The aim of this exploratory study was to investigate attitudes to inclusive writing on Twitter. The first research question asked, 'What kinds of arguments are used for and against French inclusive writing in the corpus of tweets?' Arguments against inclusive writing have been particularly prominent; proponents of *écriture inclusive* are much less visible. In the top ten retweets, for example, there was only one tweet which was clearly pro-inclusive writing; in the favourites, there were none. This is not to say that there are no positive tweets, but they are not to be found amongst the top-rated tweets. Arguments against inclusive writing centred around its potential to threaten the vitality, or damage the beauty, of the French language; such arguments were uncovered by the corpus linguistic analysis (Section 15.5.1) and were found amongst the retweets and favourites (Section 15.5.2). In contrast, amongst the hashtags, the most common theme was that inclusive writing represented a distraction from real feminist issues, such as wage equality and sexual harassment. There was also frequent reference to (ability with) French orthography in the retweets and favourites, and in the corpus linguistic analysis. Tweeters implied, or stated explicitly, that anyone who uses inclusive writing is likely to make mistakes with French orthography. Inclusive writing was argued to be unnecessary, since the masculine can successfully fulfil a neutral or unmarked function; also that it is confusing and exclusionary, given the complexity of French orthography.

The second research question asked, 'What kinds of attitudes and ideologies do these arguments reveal?' Following Ryan, Giles, and Sebastian's (1982) definition of language attitudes (see Section 15.3), we must consider evidence of feelings and beliefs that the arguments around inclusive writing reveal, as well as behaviour. The arguments centred around the threat that inclusive writing poses to the language can be split into two strands: those that see it as a mortal threat (cf. Académie 2017), where feelings such as fear and indignation are expressed, and those that see it as an aesthetic issue, i.e. damage to the beauty of the language, where we see feelings of disgust, revulsion, and annoyance. Standard language ideology, prescriptivism, and purism are at play in both strands. As noted earlier, standard language ideology is 'a bias toward an abstract, idealized homogeneous language, which is imposed and maintained by dominant institutions and which has as its model the written language' (Lippi-Green 1997: 64, emphasis added). Since inclusive writing is a bottom-up initiative, unsanctioned—indeed, banned—by the dominant institutions charged with protecting and maintaining the French language, it is to be rejected by those subscribing (consciously or unconsciously) to this ideology. And since France is argued to be an example of a 'standard language culture', i.e. one where (all?) speakers believe their language exists in a standardized form, that means 'virtually everyone' (Milroy 2001: 535).[20] As Lodge (1993: 12) argues (see also Humphries 2016), standard language ideology leads to other

---

[20] That a publisher was inclined to use inclusive writing in a school publication, however, raises the interesting question of where such organizations (non-governmental but still relatively official) fit on the ideological divide—this question may yet be addressed explicitly by the new law proposed by Masson (2021); see Section 15.2.2.

ideologies, such as links between the standard and nationhood, education, and upward social mobility; hence, to threaten the standard language is to threaten the nation. This link is made explicit in a tweet sent in November 2017 by Jean-Michel Blanquer, then Minister for Education, at the height of the controversy (Figure 15.12), which exemplifies some of the more hyperbolic sentiments seen in the corpus.

Figure 15.12 Tweet sent by J.-M. Blanquer, 15 November 2017

Arguments centred around aesthetics are nothing new, harking back to a golden age when French was deemed to be perfect, usually understood as the seventeenth and eighteenth centuries. Indeed, the playwright Molière is referenced in the top favourited tweets (and in others in the corpus, not discussed), as Humphries (2019) also found in her corpus of tweets about spelling reform. Humphries (2019: 318) notes that nostalgia about a time when the language was perfect is common in both prescriptivism (Watts 2000: 35) and purism (Thomas 1991: 76; both cited by Humphries (2019: 318); see also Walsh (2016b) on this 'golden age' of perfect language). Comments on the beauty of French abound in Humphries's corpus, and are argued to be characteristic of purism (Paveau and Rosier 2008: 57). As Humphries notes (2019: 318), '[b]eauty is presented as reason enough to protect a language; whether this makes an efficient or usable language is insignificant'.

There are other parallels with Humphries's corpus of tweets: many tweets ridicule inclusive writing, and those using it, by likening it to an orthographic error, and saying that those who use it are likely to make orthographic errors. While this may seem a flimsy insult, in a standard language culture, like that which is argued to obtain in France, it is a serious slur which has implications for social mobility. As Humphries (2019: 306) notes:

> Mastery of the spelling system is strived for in France; the popularity of dictation [exemplifies] this societal celebration of orthographic prowess. At the other end of the spectrum, making spelling errors in France is a cultural faux pas which carries societal consequences, such as reduced potential for social mobility (Paveau and Rosier 2008: 141).

The most prominent argument amongst the top hashtags of the corpus was that inclusive writing is a distraction from real feminist issues. Abbou et al. (2018)

discuss the 'hierarchisation' of feminist problems, noting that it is wearyingly familiar. Abbou et al. (2018: 144) further observe that this argument has been much used to downplay the importance of the linguistic aspects of equality, and to imply that, since 'la dimension langagière [est] symbolique et donc abstraite, idéelle, peut-être virtuelle?', it is therefore less worthy of attention than material issues, such as wage inequality. By advancing such arguments, language users are thus able to dismiss inclusive writing as *une bagatelle*, and consequently, to defuse the threat it poses.

The third research question asked, 'To what extent do these [attitudes] correspond to those at the official level?' It is clear from Section 15.2.2.1 that there is a large degree of overlap. Discourse from the Académie focuses on the threat to the language posed by inclusive writing, the aesthetic reasons for rejecting it, and the justifications for its superfluity. Attitudes in the tweets are more extreme—likely due to the disinhibiting effect of online debate (cf. Casale, Fiovaranti, and Caplan 2015, cited in Humphries (2019); Rosier 2019). In fact, the Académie's tweet about its *déclaration* of October 2017 was still being widely favourited and retweeted at the time of the corpus collection (though it did not make it into the top ten), showing the extent to which individuals were propagating the official view of inclusive writing.

The fourth research question asked, 'How does this debate fit into the larger context of the feminization of the French language/*langage non sexiste*?' It is clear from the tweets that there is a lack of understanding among the general public about exactly what inclusive writing is, and how it relates to other changes proposed under the banner of non-sexist language. Nonetheless, when it erupted into public consciousness in late 2017, it seems to have provided a useful outlet for feelings about feminization of the language—and even other language changes (cf. comments linking it to reforms in orthography)—as well as wider feminist issues, such as #*metoo*/#*balancetonporc*. However, the exponential growth in the use of the term *écriture inclusive* seems to have engendered a (misleading) impression that the issue can be reduced to one specific technique, i.e. the use of the *point médian*. Klinkenberg (2019: 15) argues that such high profile polemical debates may be unhelpful for the drive towards linguistic equality, since 'certains progrès en termes d'équité [peuvent] être payés de reculs'.

15.7 Conclusion

This study has used techniques from corpus linguistics and discourse analysis to examine the expression of language attitudes on social media from two angles: both lexicosemantic and domain-specific features. Together, these angles allowed for an exploration of the expression of attitudes as well as the extent to which they are shared amongst Twitter users. As with any study, there are limitations imposed by the resources available for its execution, and the space available for its reporting. I make no claims here that the attitudes uncovered by my analysis are representative of the French-speaking population in general, or even of all Twitter users, and emphasize the exploratory nature of the investigation, which is intended as a starting point for further investigations, and as a complement to some of the recent research which has considered this topic from other points of view (see e.g. Rabatel and Rosier 2019). Future work building upon these findings, with analyses of larger, more representative corpora, complemented by data from different sources (e.g. comments under online news stories, surveys, interviews), could establish how widely the views found here are held. These limitations notwithstanding, the analysis presented gives meaningful insights into attitudes of individuals towards inclusive writing on Twitter and contributes to the growing body of work which considers attitudes towards language features (as opposed to language varieties or dialects; see Kutlu and Kircher (2021: 3, n.1), and discussion in Section 15.3).

The analysis demonstrates that arguments against inclusive writing featured much more prominently in the corpus than arguments for it. The attitudes show a large degree of overlap between individuals and the official level, providing support for the view that French is surrounded by a standard language ideology, and that prescriptive and purist ideas about language permeate society (Lodge 1991, 1993). Nevertheless, the platform on which the discourse was produced, Twitter, which is part of a landscape of online social media which have dominated public discourse for the last ten to fifteen years, is noted for encouraging disinhibition and for amplifying certain viewpoints in polemical debates (cf. Rosier 2019). Though the venue for discussion may be new, it is a case of old wine in new bottles: arguments about protecting the beauty, clarity, and purity of French, which have been around since the seventeenth century, were amongst the most prominent. If the Académie française seems to have lowered the drawbridge a fraction, to permit feminized forms (which have in fact been widely used since the late 1980s and 1990s), its position against inclusive writing in the narrow sense—the various graphical and syntactical ways of making both genders visible in writing—remains steadfast; nor is there as yet consensus among academic linguists and language professionals.

16
Breton dictionaries and contemporary corpus planning
Vocabulary and purism in the minoritized languages of France

Merryn Davies-Deacon

16.1 Introduction

This chapter focuses on Breton as an example of a minoritized[1] language of France. Breton is a Celtic language traditionally spoken in the western part of Brittany, with around 200,000 speakers.[2] As a minoritized language, Breton has been undergoing a decline in speaker numbers that has escalated since the mid-twentieth century (Broudic 2013: 14–16), linked to factors including population shift, industrialization, and the declining influence of the Church, which traditionally made use of Breton. In tandem with this language obsolescence, however, a revitalization movement has also emerged, and has made one of its aims the standardization of Breton, including the expansion of its lexicon to include terms not present in the language as traditionally spoken, a common feature of language standardization processes (Haugen 1966: 931). This chapter examines the evolution of the standard lexicon of Breton, as prescribed and listed in dictionaries and terminology databases, drawing from a corpus of such resources spanning from the late fifteenth century to the present. It focuses in more detail on recent sources and contemporary terminological prescription, particularly on the part of official language planning bodies, given their significance in the officialization and institutionalization of Breton as a minoritized language. By investigating which languages provide the sources for neologisms and borrowings used in contemporary Breton, we can probe claims about purism, i.e. 'the manifestation of a desire to preserve

---

[1] The term 'minoritized' will be used throughout. While a number of terms exist and have been applied in similar contexts (autochthonous, regional, indigenous, or minority languages), minoritized has been deliberately chosen here in order to emphasize that the lesser status of such languages is due to complex historical factors and subjugation by speakers of a more powerful dominant language, rather than any innate property of the minoritized language itself.
[2] See https://brezhoneg.bzh/56-sifrou-pennan.htm (accessed 1 September 2021).

Merryn Davies-Deacon, *Breton dictionaries and contemporary corpus planning*. In: *Historical and Sociolinguistic Approaches to French*. Edited by: Janice Carruthers, Mairi McLaughlin, and Olivia Walsh, Oxford University Press. © Merryn Davies-Deacon (2024). DOI: 10.1093/oso/9780192894366.003.0016

a language from, or rid it of, putative foreign elements held to be undesirable' (Thomas 1991: 12), and determine whether the standard Breton of today should be considered more or less purist than earlier iterations of this standard variety.

Minoritized languages, lacking the status of national languages and hence often perceived as less significant in contexts related to written production, tend to have a less substantial written tradition than their dominant counterparts. However, the minoritized languages of Europe form part of a wider historical culture of writing, and many do possess a written tradition of their own. In the French context, for example, the poetry of the troubadours provides us with a rich resource for comprehending the literary language of medieval Occitania. Breton, too, offers evidence of a modest written tradition including a body of secular medieval literature (Abalain 2000: 98), as well as popular literature in the post-Revolutionary period, which, while underdeveloped (Le Berre 2001: 51), offers insights into the development of the language and its dialects into the modern era.

From a lexicographic perspective, and considering Breton in terms not only of its own linguistic history but also in terms of the linguistic history of French, a particularly important text is *Le Catholicon*,[3] a trilingual dictionary compiled during the mid-fifteenth century and printed in 1499, which presents Breton headwords glossed with their French and Latin equivalents. As the first published dictionary of Breton (Jean 1979: 154) and one of the earliest dictionaries of French, this work marks the beginning of the Breton lexicographic tradition, a tradition that gained particular momentum and impact when Breton began experiencing a steep decline in usage in the twentieth century and became the target of language revitalization initiatives. The most well-known early efforts towards the revitalization of Breton were carried out by the literary group *Gwalarn*, which began publishing its magazine in 1925 with the release of a manifesto announcing its intention to make Breton a literary language, with a standardized form and orthography (Abalain 2000: 60). Their intention to use Breton in hitherto underexplored domains such as literature and academic writing necessitated the expansion of the lexicon, a process that is still ongoing.

In Breton, the choice of sources for new vocabulary intersects with the issue of lexical purism. The question of what constitutes the 'foreign influence' (Thomas 1991: 12) that must be purged from the language is pertinent here, as it relates to issues around Breton identity. For speakers for whom the importance of Breton's position as a Celtic language is predominant, the 'foreign' element is interpreted as French, the language of the state that is understood as the oppressor, and so new vocabulary will consist of neologisms coined on the basis of Celtic roots. For those for whom Celtic identity is felt to be irrelevant, this perceived foreignness of French words may not be an issue: indeed, for these speakers, it is Celtic

---

[3] See Chauveau (1992) for remarks on the significance of this text for the study of Middle French.

neologisms that may be construed as foreign. For speakers in this second group, borrowings from French are to be preferred over neologisms.

This choice between borrowings and neologisms plays into a wider issue, identified by researchers (early examples include McDonald 1989; Timm 1989; Jones 1995) as being at the heart of the Breton revitalization movement: the rapid decline of the traditional speaker population in the mid-twentieth century[4] and its slow replacement with newer generations of Breton speakers who are more likely to have acquired the language in formal settings, i.e. new speakers, who have acquired Breton through means other than intergenerational transmission.[5] Jones (1995: 428) refers to new speakers of Breton as *néo-bretonnants* and notes that they rose in prominence after the establishment of immersion education in Breton in the 1970s; she names their linguistic variety *néo-breton*. These terms have since recurred in the literature (e.g. Timm 2003; Le Nevez 2013), sometimes with pejorative associations.[6] It should be noted, however, that even at the time of *Gwalarn* from the 1920s onwards, a number of the writers and activists involved in these early revitalization efforts were already new speakers, in that they had not acquired Breton in a community setting:[7] the *néo-bretonnant* community is not a particularly new one, even if it has only gained the attention of researchers more recently.

Much has been made of the differences between traditional and new speakers of Breton, in terms of both the form of Breton that they use and their demographic characteristics. One particularly salient difference relates to their use of either dialectal or standard Breton. Like all languages, Breton exhibits diatopic variation, and different dialectal varieties remain in existence, particularly in the language of traditional speakers, i.e. those who acquired the language through intergenerational transmission. Breton is typically divided into four dialects,[8] with some scholars suggesting that the differences between them are so great as to render the different dialects mutually unintelligible (e.g. Ternes 1992: 378).[9] These dialect areas are a result of the historical influence of the Church, being clustered around the four bishoprics that make up the traditionally Breton-speaking area. While

---

[4] Broudic (2013: 14) dubs the 1950s 'les années décisives'. In relation to dates and terminology, see also the discussion of Irish in Chapter 18 (this volume).

[5] Hornsby (2015: 108) defines new speakers according to 'transmission, attitude, and origin': they acquire the language in settings other than traditional intergenerational transmission, are positively disposed towards it, and need not originate from the traditional speaker community. However, the definition is loose, and different researchers have made use of different criteria according to the context of study.

[6] For example, Jones (1995: 428) claims that *néo-bretonnants*' 'standardized pronunciation is arbitrarily "clipped" for authenticity and crammed full of regionalisms, randomly selected from all four corners of the province'.

[7] 'Certains d'entre eux ont même dû apprendre la langue bretonne, et n'ont pas vécu l'expérience de leurs aînés' (Abalain 2000: 60).

[8] See Chapter 1 (this volume), footnote 54.

[9] However, see German (2007: 153) for an alternative view that highlights the importance of local identity in this context.

some scholars (Jackson 1967:18; Wmffre 1998: 2) have suggested that basing the dialectal division on bishoprics may have become less valid as a result of the move towards a more secular society, most traditional speakers of Breton nonetheless speak a variety of the language that clearly indexes their local origin.

In contrast, the revitalization movement that began in the early twentieth century has typically sought to minimize or even suppress these dialectal differences, working instead towards the creation of a standard supradialectal variety. The Office public de la langue bretonne (OPLB), the language planning body for Breton funded by regional and departmental government, appears from the way it is presented on its own website to follow this same inclination, as it emphasizes the advantages of the standard variety, noting that 'une langue standardisée commune s'est développée afin de pouvoir faire face à toutes les situations de communication et être mieux à même de répondre aux enjeux technologiques du monde d'aujourd'hui'.[10] This standardized variety of Breton may also be seen to strengthen the position of the language by presenting a united front in the face of the hegemony of French.

Standard Breton is typically assumed to be the preserve of the *néo-bretonnants*, who are considered more active in revitalization efforts than their traditional speaker counterparts. As noted above, *néo-bretonnants* and *néo-breton* have been characterized in various ways, and it is worth noting some of their stereotypical attributes in order to understand the relevance of the choice between borrowings and neologisms in a corpus planning context. Broadly, *néo-breton* is claimed to resemble French on a deep structural level, given that it is typically acquired as a second language by native speakers of French. As a result, *néo-breton* is said to be unavoidably close to French in terms of features such as its intonation (Timm 2003: 42; German 2007: 186) and its syntax (Jones 1995: 429), following the SVO word order of French rather than the more flexible but typologically verb-first syntax (Timm 1989: 376) of traditional Breton and other Celtic languages. On the other hand, more surface-level features of language that can more easily be altered, most notably the lexicon, are said to be subject to conscious manipulation in order to render them less similar to French, and closer to a more Celticized linguistic variety that fits with the pro-Celtic, potentially anti-French type of purism noted earlier. Thus, stereotypically, the lexicon of standard *néo-breton* is suffused with neologisms that are based on obsolete Breton or sometimes Welsh words in order to avoid having to borrow such terms from French (German 2007: 153; Adkins 2013: 58), just as French in turn is subject to the publication of official vocabulary in an effort on the part of language authorities to discourage its speakers from using English-derived loanwords (Walsh 2016b). For Breton, Timm (2001: 456) gives examples including *abeg* instead of traditional Breton *rezen* for French *raison*, *prof*

---

[10] http://www.fr.brezhoneg.bzh/4-histoire.htm (accessed 6 April 2021).

instead of *prezen* for French *présent*, and *baraerezh* instead of *boulangerezh* for French *boulangerie*.

Faced with these linguistic differences between *néo-* and traditional Breton, some researchers (e.g. McDonald 1989: 279) have claimed that it would almost be more appropriate to speak of two separate languages, used for different purposes by two contrasting communities of speakers: the motivations of *néo-bretonnants* are also depicted as highly divergent from those of traditional speakers, with the former being characterized as 'militants and scholars' (German 2007: 187) with a strong sense of pan-Breton identity that it is claimed traditional speakers do not feel (Jones 1995: 428; Le Nevez 2013: 92; Rottet 2014: 213).[11] However, the conception of *néo-breton* in particular is perhaps based too firmly on the standard literary Breton of the early twentieth century. At that time, the Breton revitalization movement was connected to a strong sense of ethnic nationalism; however, later in the century the political context shifted, and perspectives based more on regionalism and civic nationalism gained ground in the Breton movement (Wmffre 2007: 176–7). This shift created the potential for an ideology that took a more positive view of the role of traditional Breton and its speakers, instead of denigrating them as peasants unable to play a part in the future of Breton as a modern language; and, furthermore, it created the potential for a perspective on lexical expansion not predicated on the view that French is a foreign influence that must be purged. Moreover, the recent growth of the Breton new speaker community, and the increased variety of ways to acquire the language in settings ranging in formality, suggest that it would be inaccurate to assume that all new speakers have identical views on the language and the linguistic features it should have. Speakers' motives for acquiring and learning Breton will undoubtedly have changed and diversified, as will the fora in which they use it; this may have had an effect on which version of Breton is used and promoted.

This chapter will examine the lexicon as an aspect of that potential evolution and diversification, based on two methods of enquiry. After a discussion in Section 16.2 of the methodology and corpora used, Section 16.3 looks at a range of dictionaries from before and during the revitalization of Breton, as an attempt at measuring how attitudes towards borrowing and neologism have evolved in the standard Breton lexicon. One of the sources used for this investigation is the OPLB's online database of terminology, which, as an official and freely accessible source of specialist Breton vocabulary, merits more investigation. Section 16.4 therefore looks into the practices surrounding this database in more detail, presenting findings from an interview with a representative of TermBret, the division within the OPLB responsible for corpus planning and the maintenance of this online tool. The interviewee gives information on the process used

---

[11] See the related discussion around legitimacy and authenticity in Chapter 18, this volume.

to determine which words should be included in this database, illustrating how concern for both international and community norms is taken into consideration in an attempt to render the procedure more objective than earlier attempts at corpus planning.

16.2 Methodology

This section gives an overview of the methodology employed for the quantitative part of this research, which consisted of a comparison between two corpora: one corpus of dictionaries and terminology databases, and a second corpus of lexemes. The corpus of lexemes, taken from a range of contemporary media sources in Breton (described in Section 16.2.2), provided a list of specific lexical items that can be considered to index either pro-Celtic or pro-French attitudes; the dictionaries and terminology databases chosen were then checked for attestations of these words. By grouping the lexemes in question according to their language of origin (i.e. whether they can be classed as borrowings or neologisms), we can investigate how attitudes to these different sources of the Breton lexical stock have changed over time.

16.2.1 The corpus of dictionaries

This study takes a small sample of dictionaries and online terminology databases, selected based on their popularity or historical significance, in order to represent the mainstream current in Breton lexicography and corpus planning over time: it does not claim to identify different concurrent ideological approaches to Breton as evidenced in dictionary publication, but instead to investigate whether any clear pattern of change in attitudes towards borrowings and neologisms emerges. Other studies on similar topics include that carried out by Rottet (2014), who investigated ten dictionaries offering various ideological perspectives with respect to fifty neologistic terms, and by Le Pipec (2018), who examined twenty-four terms in the field of mathematics in forty-four dictionaries. The current study offers a less in-depth but broader comparison, using a sample of 1,344 terms gathered from a corpus of Breton taken from media sources, described in more detail in Section 16.2.2.

The oldest two dictionaries used for this study date from before the twentieth century and hence from before the revitalization of Breton is considered to have begun. The first of these dictionaries is the previously mentioned *Catholicon* (1499), and the second is the Breton–French dictionary of Jean-François Le Gonidec, in the edition augmented by Théodore Hersart de la Villemarqué and published in 1850 (Le Gonidec 1850). While these are not the only dictionaries of Breton that predate revitalization, they are two of the most well known and span the period between the publication of the first Breton dictionary, the *Catholicon* itself, and the beginning of the Breton revitalization movement in the early twentieth century. Le Gonidec's dictionary was also the first to take an approach to describing the lexicon of Breton that can be related to a specific ideological purpose: to emphasize Breton's status as a Celtic language. In a typology of Breton dictionaries and corpus planning initiatives, Le Pipec (2018: 52) names Le Gonidec and Villemarqué's dictionary as part of the first current that aimed to do more than merely describe the language: unlike *Le Catholicon*, this later dictionary forms part of 'le projet romantique', during which 'on croit se souvenir que le breton est aussi la langue des guerriers celtes du fond des âges'. Hence, for ideological reasons, this dictionary includes certain words based on Welsh and unattested in the language of ordinary Breton speakers at the time (Trépos 1960: 394; Morvannou 2004). Le Gonidec and Villemarqué's inclusion of vocabulary of this type highlights the major role that external factors can play in these language-internal decisions: in this case, a new interest in the status of Breton as a Celtic language among the educated classes in France at the time motivated this presentation of the language, and indeed, the dictionary's very publication (Guiomar 1992: 63). This can be seen as an early example of the type of lexical purism that seeks to preserve Breton from French influence. Nonetheless, the 1850 dictionary does not go as far in this purism as some later dictionaries, as it also continues to include certain French-derived terms that do not appear in some later publications.

As Le Pipec (2018: 52) points out, the tendency towards neologism was heightened when the current of Breton lexicography turned more towards the formation of 'une langue nationale' in the early part of the twentieth century. This early period in the revitalization of Breton was at times overtly nationalistic; during the Occupation, several Breton nationalists, including language activists, were involved in collaborationist activities 'to the point of participating in armed engagements against the Resistance' (Wmffre 2007: 175), with the hope of ensuring autonomy for Brittany and protection for the Breton language. During this period, the trend for Celtic-based neologisms continued, based in some cases on an overt 'rejet de la francité' (Le Pipec 2018: 53) as part of the construction of a national Breton identity. Once the war was over, however, the concept of a Breton national or regional identity necessarily became more nuanced and plural, and Le Pipec (2018: 53–8) identifies a further six currents in Breton lexicography that took hold, sometimes concurrently, in the later part of the twentieth century, each motivated by different political and cultural beliefs, and beliefs about the role and the utility of Breton. Supporters of these different currents were motivated to take different attitudes towards the question of whether to favour neologisms or borrowings as a result. It is not simply the case that newer dictionaries are more receptive to French borrowings, or indeed that newer dictionaries always take a less overtly Breton nationalist position: Rottet (2014: 227) notes that the ten twentieth- and twenty-first-century dictionaries in his study 'are fairly evenly split in terms of alignment with "traditionalist" or "purist" ideologies', while the *Geriadur An Here*, a monolingual Breton dictionary published in 2001 (Menard and Kadored 2001), was condemned in the French press for anti-French political views,[12] indicating the persistence in some quarters of a nationalist ideology.

As well as the two older dictionaries, the current study considers five sources dating from the second half of the twentieth century onwards, comprising two printed dictionaries, two online databases, and the glossary section of a beginners' textbook. The older of the two dictionaries is the third edition of the *Dictionnaire breton-français* compiled by Roparz Hemon (Hemon 1964), one of the most prolific grammarians of Breton and editor of the literary journal *Gwalarn*, which played a major role in the Breton revitalization movement during the early twentieth century. Hemon's dictionary went through several editions, later versions of which were named the *Nouveau dictionnaire breton-français* to mark their significant expansion from their predecessors. While Hemon's political views align him with the earlier nationalist trend of Breton language activism, Le Pipec (2018: 54) notes that he is 'assez difficilement "classable"' with respect to the different currents of Breton lexicography he identifies, showing enthusiasm for both neologisms and certain foreign words, i.e. borrowings from languages other than French in particular.

The newest paper dictionary used in this study is a 1994 publication produced by the specialist Breton-language publishing house Mouladurioù Hor Yezh (Kadored, Desbordes, and Kervella 1994). This is the second edition of a pocket-sized dictionary that has become one of the most popular Breton–French/French–Breton dictionaries in use today; editions using English and German in place of French are also available. This dictionary is in effect the successor to earlier works such as Hemon's publications, having been produced by scholars from the same tradition. Using this dictionary as a source reflects the fact that the intent of this research is not to compare dictionaries with large ideological differences,[13] but instead to track any changes in the mainstream *néo-breton* current over time.

Given the small size of the Mouladurioù Hor Yezh dictionary, and its age, it is unsurprising that it does not contain some more complex items of vocabulary or words for more recently invented concepts (for example, 'broadband'). Two more recent online terminology databases were also consulted to make up for this gap. The first, TermOfis,[14] a database of mostly technical terms, is maintained by the OPLB, and is therefore accorded the legitimacy of being produced by the body

---

[12] 'Cet outil linguistique dissimule, sous couvert de citations pédagogiques, des slogans militants. Ainsi, le verbe "être" est illustré par "La Bretagne n'existera vraiment que lorsque le français sera détruit en Bretagne"; la préposition "entre" par "Il faut choisir entre la Bretagne et la France", etc.' http://www.lexpress.fr/informations/le-coup-de-balai_642102.html (accessed 26 October 2017).
[13] Rottet (2014) and Le Pipec (2018) go into more detail on this topic.
[14] https://www.brezhoneg.bzh/72-termenadurezh.htm (accessed 15 July 2022).

officially responsible for Breton language planning. The second, Brezhoneg21,[15] was chosen for its comprehensive coverage of scientific terminology. This database was created by Kreizenn ar geriaouiñ, a body set up in 1985 in order to provide normative terminology for use in Breton-language education (Le Pipec 2018: 55) as a more moderate alternative to bodies such as Preder, a terminology commission notorious for its overuse of Celtic-derived vocabulary (Rottet 2014: 223).[16] Brezhoneg21's recommendations can be expected to be in wide currency, as they are officially advised for use in educational contexts, i.e. those contexts in which the majority of *néo-bretonnants* acquire the language, according to the academic research that has sought to characterize them.[17] These sources are clearly not directly comparable with general dictionaries, as they focus on more specialist terms, but they allow greater insight into a domain that is particularly relevant in the context of corpus expansion, as many terms in this category would not have existed in Breton prior to its revitalization. Moreover, both of these sources can be considered officially sanctioned to a degree not experienced by other online databases or by contemporary printed specialist dictionaries, and they thus merit inclusion here.

While the two online databases contain a larger amount of rarer and more specialist vocabulary, the final source used for this study is the beginners' textbook *Brezhoneg... buan hag aes* (Denez 1977; henceforth *BBHA*). As an introductory textbook, this text contains only the most basic Breton vocabulary, much of which is unsurprisingly of Celtic origin, of long standing in Breton, and hence entirely uncontroversial, not suggesting alignment with either traditional Breton or *néo-breton*. However, there remain certain items of vocabulary in its glossary, including terms for more recently invented concepts such as radio and television, where the choice of whether to use a neologism or a borrowing can be made and hence an ideological position can potentially be indexed. As in the case of the 1994 dictionary, the existence of translations of *BBHA* into several other languages, including English, Welsh, German, and Esperanto, indicates its popularity.

The printed publications selected thus offer a broad overview of mainstream Breton lexicography from the late fifteenth to late twentieth centuries, and supplementing these dictionaries with the two online terminology databases allows us to identify the extent to which more recent terminological advice follows the

---

[15] https://www.brezhoneg21.com/geriadurGB.php (accessed 15 July 2022).

[16] Indeed, Brezhoneg21 cites Preder as having taken the tendency towards neo-Celtic coinages too far, asserting that by them, 'the instinct for "purification" was thus taken further ... in this way, a new Breton microlect became established, scarcely comprehensible to the ordinary Breton speaker' (my translation; http://brezhoneg21.com/pivomp.php (accessed 13 November 2017)).

[17] See Jones (1995: 428); Adkins (2013: 59); Le Dû and Le Berre (2013: 53); Rottet (2014: 213).

same trends as earlier dictionaries with respect to the origins of the vocabulary it advises.

16.2.2 The corpus of lexemes

Lexemes that would serve as a means of comparing the sources were identified based on a second corpus.[18] A sample of around 35,000 words of Breton was collected, from printed, radio, and online sources: news articles and features from magazines and a newspaper, news and cultural programmes from the radio, and posts from a group of Breton speakers on social media. The sample was transcribed as an XML file according to the conventions of the Text Encoding Initiative.[19] Taking a maximally inclusive approach, tokens were then tagged for analysis if their use was potentially relevant in determining whether the sample of Breton in question (e.g. the magazine article, conversational turn in a radio interview, or social media post) could be characterized as either *néo-breton* or traditional Breton. Working on the basis of claims in the academic literature that the Breton of traditional speakers is assumed to be dialectally fragmented (Jones 1995: 427) and more receptive towards French borrowings (German 2007: 184), as described above, and that conversely *néo-breton* is supposedly more reliant on neologisms based on Celtic lexical roots, the following three categories of words were tagged:

(i) transparent borrowings from French (as opposed to long-standing, well-assimilated borrowings,[20] the use of which would not be contentious among speakers);
(ii) words specific to particular dialects and not considered part of standard Breton;
(iii) words borrowed from other Celtic languages or older forms of Breton, and neologisms formed from Breton morphemes of Celtic origin.

Words in categories (i) and (ii) may be considered emblematic of traditional Breton, and words in category (iii) are an expected feature of *néo-breton* or standard Breton. A workflow was devised in order to enable the systematic identification of these tokens (see Davies-Deacon 2020: 57–63 for details), which resulted in the annotation of 3,904 tokens, i.e. 11.9% of the total sample. These tokens consisted of 1,344 individual lexemes, and it is these lexemes that formed the basis of the investigation of the dictionaries in this study, allowing, as noted, for a less in-depth but far broader investigation than those carried out by Rottet (2014) and Le Pipec (2018). Each of the 1,344 lexemes was tagged to note whether or not it appeared in

---

[18] For more details on methodology, see Davies-Deacon (2020: 55–68).
[19] See https://tei-c.org (accessed 15 July 2022).
[20] For example, *mous* ('boy'), from French *mousse* ('cabin boy').

the seven sources listed above with a definition matching its use in the corpus; lexemes were given an additional tag if they were found to be attested in Breton prior to 1900, going by their appearance in Devri,[21] an online corpus compiling texts in Breton from a wide range of sources dating from the ninth to twenty-first centuries. Checking items in Devri allowed a distinction to be made between words that appeared in Breton prior to the period of language revitalization and those that entered the language during the revitalization period.

16.3 Dictionary attestations

The tokens in this study were tagged to note various additional details, including part of speech and inflection information as well as whether words borrowed from French deviated from the source lexeme with respect to their phonology, orthography, or both. However, this chapter will focus on one criterion specifically, the language of origin for the lexemes in question. This allows us to investigate claims about lexical purism, based on the correlation stated in the literature between stereotypical *néo-breton* and a lower prevalence of words borrowed from French: German (2007: 153) notes that 'many critics claim that the new norm is ... lexically "neo-Celtic"'. Comparing the occurrence of words of different origin allows us to determine whether there has been any change in this supposed feature of *néo-breton* over time.

Before presenting the data, it is necessary to clarify how the origin of a word is understood in this context. Of course, tracing the etymology of a word that appears to have been borrowed into Breton from English, for example, may, in many cases, lead back to French. However, the important factor in this context is not the word's ultimate provenance but instead the language from which it was adopted into Breton most recently. As the focus here is on lexicographers', language planners', and speakers' attitudes and ideologies, the language from which a word is perceived to come will be of much greater importance than its ultimate provenance, which will often be unknown to users of the language. Mills (2015) makes a similar point about revived Cornish, showing that purist lexicography for this language tends to advise against the use of words borrowed from Middle English when those words have counterparts in Modern English; but in cases where the English word has fallen out of use, its use in Cornish is considered acceptable. This attention to surface forms shows why it is more revealing to interpret the origin of a word as relating to the language it was borrowed from directly. Terms such as 'French-derived' are hence used here not to suggest that the word is not used in languages other than French or that it was originally coined in French, but to show that it would have been borrowed into Breton via French and would in most cases be recognized by speakers of modern Breton as a word that is also used in French.

---

[21] http://devri.bzh (accessed 15 July 2022).

The categories used are as follows:

- **Breton:** words with Celtic roots, either attested in traditional Breton sources or coined as part of the language revitalization process (e.g. *emgav* 'meeting')
- **French:** words consisting of roots borrowed into Breton from French (e.g. *salud* 'hi', from French *salut*)
- **French/international:** a subcategory of 'French'—words used in French, but also used in other languages (e.g. *festival*); often scientific or technical terms, as these tend to be coined based on Greek/Latin roots and shared across languages
- **Welsh:** words borrowed directly from Welsh; of Celtic roots, but not found in traditional Breton (e.g. *delwenn* 'statue')
- **Older Breton:** words found in older attestations of traditional Breton (before the early modern period, using a cut-off date of 1700), but not found in later texts and therefore apparently reintroduced during the revitalization period (e.g. *dazont* 'future')
- **English:** words borrowed directly from English and not used in French (e.g. *manx* 'Manx language')
- **Other:** words from languages other than those listed (e.g. *Euskadi* 'the Basque country')

The appearances of the 1,344 unique tagged lexemes in these sources were tabulated, comparing their origins with their attestation in the dictionaries and databases investigated as well as in Breton sources prior to 1900.

Table 16.1 allows us to see how words of different origins are generally distributed among the sources, using the lexemes tagged in the corpus as a sample. In pre-1900 Breton, the split between Breton- and French-derived words is extremely

Table 16.1 Occurrence of lexemes in sources consulted[a]

	Total	Breton	French	French/international	Welsh	Older Breton	English	Other
Breton before 1900	256	128	126	1	0	2	0	0
Le Catholicon (1499)	52	19	32	0	0	1	0	0
Le Gonidec/ Villemarqué (1850)	73	59	14	0	0	0	0	0
Hemon (1964)	415	322	85	15	6	1	0	1

Continued

Table 16.1 Continued

	Total	Breton	French	French/international	Welsh	Older Breton	English	Other
BBHA (1977)	25	19	6	1	0	0	0	0
Mouladurioù Hor Yezh (Kadored et al. 1994)	488	336	144	28	5	1	0	2
Brezhoneg21 (online)	305	191	112	31	1	0	1	0
TermOfis (online)	634	394	228	65	7	0	3	2
Not given in TermOfis	*328*	*131*	*193*	*32*	*0*	*0*	*4*	*0*
Total	**1344**	**733**	**580**	**132**	**10**	**3**	**14**	**4**

[a] The column headed 'French' includes internationally used terms; the column headed 'French/International' refers to a subset of 'French'. Note also that the 'total' figures do not refer to the totals of each row and column, but to the total number of lexemes in each category, some of which appear in multiple sources and/or contain elements of different origins. As a result, the 'total' given in each row or column is different from the sum of each of that row or column's values.

even. As befits the fact that processes of globalization were less advanced during this period, none of the words derived from other languages is attested in pre-1900 texts, and only one of the 126 French-derived words counts as an internationally-used term (*gitar*).

The individual pre-1900 dictionaries each evidently contain a smaller number of words than the entire pre-1900 corpus, and the way in which the sampled words are distributed within them varies noticeably. In *Le Catholicon*, the proportion of French-derived words is noticeably higher than both the overall average (43.2% of all tagged lexemes) and the average for pre-1900 Breton (49.2%), at 61.5%. In the 1850 dictionary, however, the proportion is far lower, at only 19.2%. This indicates that *Le Catholicon* shows a particularly accepting attitude towards French-derived words, having been compiled before ideological considerations began to hold sway, but equally that Le Gonidec and Villemarqué invert this, greatly preferring words of Celtic origin. This confirms the earlier observation that Le Gonidec and Villemarqué's dictionary is already a source of pro-Celtic purism. It is worth bearing in mind, however, that the sample size is small here: only seventy-three of the lexemes investigated appear in this dictionary at all, as many of them refer to concepts invented more recently than 1850. The practice of adapting Welsh vocabulary can also be seen not to have been widespread enough to affect the corpus under investigation here.

The post-1900 sources contain the lexemes under investigation in greater number, other than *BBHA*, which includes only a short vocabulary list. Among them,

Hemon's dictionary contains the lowest proportion of French-derived words, with 20.5%, but interestingly, this rate is still not quite as low as in Le Gonidec and Villemarqué's dictionary, suggesting that Hemon's attitude was less purist in this respect than that of these earlier lexicographers. However, while none of the French-derived words in Le Gonidec and Villemarqué's dictionary are used internationally, 17.6% of those in Hemon's dictionary are. Removing these words from the count, as they may be seen as more acceptable from a pro-Celtic standpoint, results in a proportion of French-derived words in Hemon's dictionary that is lower than in its predecessor. Both these details substantiate Le Pipec's (2018: 54) contention that Hemon's aim was 'de faire du breton une langue moderne ... sortie de sa sujétion au français ... mais pas expurgée de toute influence étrangère'. Hemon's dictionary also includes Welsh-derived words and words with elements found only in older Breton; one word from another language (*euskarad* 'Basque'); and no words derived from English. Overall, this points to Hemon's favouring sources from Celtic and other minoritized languages, not only fitting with the suggestion that *néo-breton* of this time was less tolerant of words derived from French, but also showing the importance of expressing solidarity with other minoritized peoples that characterizes the Breton revitalization movement.[22]

BBHA is difficult to measure against the other sources, given that it contains only a limited wordlist. In terms of how many of the words in the sample of tagged lexemes are included therein, it contains 2.6% of the Breton-derived words and 1.0% of the French-derived words—i.e. it seems from the sample that Breton-derived words are over twice as likely to appear in it. Hemon's dictionary contains 43.9% of the Breton-derived words and 14.7% of the French-derived words, so here, Breton-derived words are nearly three times as likely to occur. This suggests that *BBHA* has a slightly lower tendency towards the use of Breton-derived words than Hemon's dictionary. As internationally used words tend to be used mostly for more complex concepts, it is unsurprising that only one of the French-derived words found in *BBHA* is internationally used (*sport*). Overall, it appears that *BBHA* continues Hemon's tradition of favouring Breton-derived words over French-derived ones.

The later sources show a slightly different attitude towards word origins. The Mouladurioù Hor Yezh dictionary is the best direct comparator to Hemon's dictionary, as both are general-purpose dictionaries published in the twentieth century, emerging from the same lexicographic tradition. The proportion of the tagged lexemes in this dictionary that are derived from French is 29.5%, noticeably higher than Hemon's 20.5%. However, 19.4% of these are internationally used, a slight increase on Hemon's 17.6%; this higher use of international terms may reflect the

---

[22] In an interview conducted for this research with an employee of a Breton-language magazine, the participant noted that 'depuis le début [of the magazine's publication, in the 1980s] ... les peuples sans état en quelque sorte auront une place importante dans les articles ... c'est quelque chose que presque tous les rédacteurs ont en tête'.

growth of globalization and a corresponding increase in words for new technology, the French terms for which are often borrowed from English, being coined on the basis of Greek or Latin roots and used across a number of languages. There are still no words directly from English used in the 1994 dictionary. The higher proportion of French-derived words, though, indicates a progression towards a greater tolerance of them, even in publications that continue in the same tradition as Hemon's work.

Brezhoneg21 and the TermOfis database are different from the other sources in that they contain vocabulary only from specific lexical fields, although TermOfis has the wider remit of the two. As online databases, they are also the newest of the sources. It can be noted that they are the only two to contain any of the words in the sample that derive from English and are not used in French; again, a possible sign of increased globalization, but also of greater tolerance of such words on the understanding that English has a perhaps less ideologically charged role in its function as a neutral international language.

These two sources also continue the progression from a smaller to a larger proportion of French-derived words: in Brezhoneg21, 36.7% of the words in the sample derive from French, and in TermOfis, it is 36.0%. Both also contain a noticeably higher proportion of internationally used words among these French-derived words, at 27.7% and 28.5% respectively; again, this is likely to be affected by the fact that many newer French terms will have come from English, as these terms will be more likely to appear in these sources.

Words for which an alternative term was given in TermOfis were also noted, as 'not given in TermOfis'. This means that the French translation of each word was checked in TermOfis, and if there was an entry that advised a different Breton term instead of the lexeme found in the corpus, that lexeme was assigned to this category: for example, the term *depute* (for French *député*) appeared in the corpus, but TermOfis advises *kannad*, so *depute* was assigned to the 'not given in TermOfis' category. Some tokens were assigned to both the TermOfis and 'not given in TermOfis' categories, as multiple definitions for slightly different terms in the database occasionally gave conflicting advice. For example, the word *stirad* appeared in the corpus with the meaning '[television] series'. TermOfis instead advises the word *heuliad* as a translation for *série* in its section on audiovisual terminology, but also includes *stirad* in the phrase *stirad skinwel*, the translation it provides for *série télévisée*; due to this, *stirad* was assigned to both these categories. This is not the only example of recommendations in TermOfis that appear to contradict each other, suggesting a potentially more tolerant attitude towards lexical variation than may be displayed in some older sources. However, the lack of a clear explanation for such alternations may be confusing to speakers.

In the 'not given by TermOfis' category, French-derived words are greater in number, making up 58.8% of the sample. This suggests that those who regulate Breton today continue to prioritize Celtic- over French-derived words in the majority of cases. This promotion of Celtic neologisms may be at odds with speaker practices involving the creation of new vocabulary: 78.3% of the words in the sample with French-derived elements are not found in Breton prior to 1900, showing that borrowing remains a productive practice even in the age of *néo-breton*. Even in the media context, which we might expect to be mostly populated by *néo-bretonnants*, the corpus shows that both Breton and French appear to have been extensively used as sources for coining new vocabulary since the beginning of the revitalization period, despite attempts to prioritize those of Breton origin.

As noted earlier, TermOfis merits further investigation as the closest Breton has to an official source of vocabulary, regulated by the state-supported language planning body for Breton. The findings of this section show that while certain *néo-breton* principles continue to be followed in the rejection of French-derived words, the tolerance of internationally used words in particular may be increasing. The presentation of TermOfis on the OPLB website, however, does not go into detail about how terms are researched and approved, minimizing the insight we can gain into this evolution based on the examination of the database alone. Examining TermOfis from this quantitative perspective gives us information about the types of words prescribed and the sort of policy that can be assumed to be followed by the OPLB in this regard, but does not explain the interaction between this top-down language planning body and the speaker community. In order to probe this in more detail, an interview was conducted with an OPLB representative.

16.4 The work of TermBret

This section of the chapter draws on a 50-minute interview conducted in August 2018 with a representative of the OPLB on the subject of TermBret, the division within the OPLB responsible for maintaining TermOfis. This interview aimed to explore the decisions made in the compilation of TermOfis more thoroughly and examine how corpus planning for Breton has evolved now that the language is in this more official position.

The interviewee began by stressing that TermBret's primary concern is for Breton speakers, rather than for the language itself: in his view, prioritizing speakers distances the organization from any preference for either neologisms or borrowings. As an illustration of this avoidance of bias, he pointed out that TermBret works from an established set of criteria based on ISO standards for terminology, and that it also consults panels of Breton speakers working in professions related to the terminology being developed. This means that it differs from some longer-established terminology commissions:

il y a d'autres gens qui travaillent sur la terminologie en Bretagne, et il y a des visions différentes sur les façons d'appréhender les choses. Certaines personnes essayent de développer une langue moderne uniquement à partir de racines celtiques, donc ils vont aller chercher dans le vieux-breton, et ils vont aller chercher dans le gallois, dans l'irlandais, et cetera … et d'autres personnes à l'opposé, ils vont dire 'non non, la langue bretonne est une langue européenne, les mots que l'on peut retrouver en français, en anglais, en allemand, et en russe sont aussi des mots bretons'. Donc voilà, pour nous ces deux approches-là sont des approches encore idéologiques et non pragmatiques. Donc nous n'avons adopté aucune de ces deux approches-là; on se base plutôt sur ce qui sont des normes internationales ISO qui concernent la terminologie, qui utilisent un certain nombre de critères, d'ordre linguistique, terminologique, et aussi des critères sociologiques … il n'y a pas de présupposés ou de prédécisions, c'est vraiment au cas par cas.[23]

The recommendation of new terms by TermBret comes about as a result of two separate processes. The first, undertaken periodically, begins with the decision to work on a specific lexical field: this entails in-depth research and collaboration with panels of speakers in order to produce a list of terms relating to a particular domain. The OPLB has published a number of booklets containing lists of terms decided on in this way, which may be distributed to relevant organizations in the form of professionally produced hard copies ranging from one-page leaflets to small paperback books, as well as being viewable online. Subjects covered include names of animals and birds, education, and vocabulary for public administration.

The second circumstance in which new terms are recommended is as a result of specific requests, either from external organizations or individuals, or from the translators employed by the OPLB itself. Responses to these requests tend to be required on an urgent basis: the OPLB representative gave the example of schoolteachers developing learning resources for upcoming lessons. This means that the decision on which term is to be recommended in these circumstances must be made more quickly, without as much time for research.

The description of the second process in particular implies that TermOfis is regularly consulted by speakers of Breton who are not otherwise connected with the OPLB. Indeed, the interviewee stressed the volume of such external requests, and the OPLB's website states that in 2019, 341 requests for new terms were made to TermBret.[24] However, employees of Breton-language media organizations interviewed for the same research project often saw TermOfis as a secondary resource, to be used only for ascertaining terms related to certain official contexts such as public administration. It is possible that members of particular professions, such

---

[23] All unattributed quotations in this chapter are taken from the interview.
[24] See http://www.brezhoneg.bzh/170-termbret.htm (accessed 4 May 2021). It is not specified whether this figure includes internal requests from the translators working at the OPLB.

as teaching, may feel a greater need to use a more institutional form of Breton and hence rely more closely on the OPLB. Nonetheless, the media were perceived by most participants as a more important vector for spreading new vocabulary, which will not necessarily come from TermOfis.

The interviewee explained how recommended terms are classified once they are added to TermOfis. Terms are assigned to one of three categories, *proposé*, *étudié*, or *recommandé*. These categories denote the level of study that has been undertaken on the individual term: words that are merely *proposé* have been created in response to urgent queries, with little opportunity to spend time on researching historical and contemporary usage or testing with focus groups; these terms may have been approved by an individual person who has been unable to take the time to consult colleagues. Words that are *étudié* have undergone more in-depth investigation by a team of researchers, while those with *recommandé* status have been subject to the most rigorous degree of analysis, including approval from the OPLB's scientific board, made up of academic linguists specializing in Breton and other highly respected members of the language community. When a word is *recommandé*, the OPLB's own translators 'doivent obligatoirement utiliser ce terme-là', according to the interviewee.

Terms are listed in TermOfis with an indication of their category, so users are able to evaluate the level of rigour behind each word before adopting it. The descriptions of the three categories in the French version of TermOfis are as follows:

> **Proposé:** un terme qu'il a été jugé utile de rentrer dans la base TermBret car susceptible de répondre à un besoin précis
> **Etudié:** un terme qui a fait l'objet de recherches par TermBret afin de répondre à un besoin précis
> **Recommandé:** un terme qui a été adopté par le Conseil scientifique de l'Office public de la langue bretonne[25]

While the explanations of each category are similar to those given by the OPLB representative interviewed, they do not indicate the hierarchy that was described in the interview in as clear a manner. It is not necessarily clear to external users, for example, whether the adoption of a term by the OPLB's scientific board bestows on it more or less legitimacy than its having been the subject of research by TermBret. Moreover, these terms are not displayed in a list for comparison, but only appear individually attached to the particular words they designate. This feature of how TermOfis is presented contributes to a lack of transparency in comparison with some other sources: little information is given in the database about how or by whom it is compiled, and there

---

[25] Definitions taken from http://www.fr.brezhoneg.bzh/36-termofis.htm (accessed 27 April 2021).

is no option to download the database in any form, unlike Brezhoneg21 or the French government's database of officially recommended French terminology, FranceTerme.

The interviewee gave two examples of new terms that had been proposed by TermBret and seen some success within the Breton-speaking population, both relating to technology. The first was *postel*, meaning 'email', a compound of *post* ('post') and the first syllable of *elektronek* ('electronic'). Both these words clearly have cognates in French,[26] and the way in which they are combined mirrors the officially recommended French term *courriel*; as a result, *postel* cannot be considered an entirely purist, stereotypically *néo-breton* term. The second example given, however, was *poellgomzer* ('smartphone'), formed on the basis of *pellgomzer*, meaning 'telephone', from *pell* ('far'), *komz* ('speak'), and *-er*, an agentive suffix. The choice of *pellgomzer* is already interesting, as it has been cited in the literature as an unnecessarily purist neologism, given that most languages make do with a form of the learned word *telephone* (Lossec 2013: 184; Le Dû and Le Berre 2013: 49). In *poellgomzer*, the first element of the compound, *pell*, is replaced by *poell*, meaning 'logic' or 'reason'.

In the French of metropolitan France, the most commonly used words for these two concepts are *mail* and *smartphone*, clearly derived from, and in the latter case visually indistinguishable from, the English terms.[27] The interviewee was keen to point out that in contrast, Breton had found ways of creating new words, noting that 'parfois le français reste bloqué sur le mot anglais, et le breton a plus facilement un autre mot'. While only one of the two words can be considered purist in the sense of using exclusively Celtic roots, this attitude, favouring the creation of a specific Breton term even though French uses English borrowings, can again be identified as connected to purist attitudes that may in the case of these particular lexemes go beyond those displayed in modern dictionaries; as we have seen, these international words tend to be more tolerated than borrowings that are otherwise specific to French.

While the terms *postel* and *poellgomzer* have been generally accepted as part of the modern lexicon of Breton, the OPLB representative noted that the use of newly recommended words tends to be less widespread among older people, even in fields other than new technologies. This suggests that an element of the stereotypical new/traditional speaker divide is evident within the community: older traditional speakers may be reluctant to adopt neologisms.[28] He related the greater willingness of younger speakers to accept new terms to the fact that these speakers

---

[26] *Post* is a lexeme of long standing in Breton, however.

[27] The officially recommended terms in French, on the other hand, are *courriel* and *mobile multifonction* (see http://www.culture.fr/franceterme (accessed 27 April 2021)).

[28] It should be noted, however, that at this point it would certainly be inaccurate to claim that all new speakers of Breton are young—perhaps older new speakers are equally reluctant to change the way they speak Breton after many years.

are more likely to be literate in Breton, and, like other interviewees, emphasized the role of the media in spreading new words, suggesting that a stronger presence of Breton-language media would help a greater number of words spread more quickly through the speaker community:

> ce qui nous manque pour faciliter encore l'adoption des termes, ce sont des médias beaucoup plus forts, beaucoup plus présents. Si l'on avait une véritable chaîne de télévision, par exemple, qui proposait des émissions sur tous les thèmes, il est évident qu'il y aurait beaucoup plus de vocabulaire, beaucoup plus de mots à passer beaucoup plus rapidement dans le langage courant. Mais ça n'existe pas, donc les termes, ils passent par la presse, par les quelques émissions de radio qu'il peut y avoir.

The interviewee also stressed that TermBret's recommendations are not binding, and that they have been known to revise earlier suggestions. He emphasized that they did not want to be seen as an equivalent to the Académie française: 'ça serait dommage de reproduire'. As an example of a term that had not met the same acceptance as *postel* and *poellgomzer*, he gave *armerzh*, a formerly recommended word meaning 'economy', and explained that this word was not a neologism as such, as it had come from the Vannetais dialect. However, the attestations listed in Devri suggest that it was used to mean 'economy' in the sense of 'being economical' or saving money, and it was perhaps the semantic expansion involved in adopting it to the more technical sense of 'the economy', as well as the recommendation of a word that would have been previously known only to Vannetais speakers, that inhibited its spread within the community. In this case, when it turned out that the French-derived *ekonomiezh* maintained currency, TermBret decided to stop recommending *armerzh*: 'on n'est pas restés sur une position dogmatique'. However, *armerzh* and its derivatives are still listed in several entries in TermOfis, often as alternatives to terms involving *ekonomiezh*, which gives a slightly contradictory message to that conveyed during the interview. Similar inconsistencies can be observed in French terminology commissions, as different commissions are operated by different ministries and can vary in the number of terms they recommend as well as their decision to promote a particular term (Walsh 2016b: 55).

Lastly, the interviewee gave some information on TermBret's terminology forum, a feature of the OPLB's website that offers a few French terms each month for which members of the public are invited to propose their own Breton translations and vote on the suggestions. The interviewee noted that very few people tend to participate in this activity: he estimated that there are under thirty regular users, of whom fewer than ten tend to vote on any given term. TermBret makes an effort to share each set of new terms under consideration on social media, as well as maintaining a mailing list, but this does not appear to have gained a great deal of traction. The small number of participants means it would be ill-advised to assume that their views reflect those of the entire Breton-speaking community, particularly when stereotypical *néo-bretonnants* are portrayed as more involved in language activism; it is perhaps unsurprising to note that most of the terms that gain the most votes are Celtic-derived neologisms. The interviewee nonetheless believed there to be value in the exercise, as it encourages the staff of the OPLB to be on the lookout for appropriate terms that could be translated in this way: the forum tends to concentrate on words that are prevalent in current news. He noted that these terms often arise from casual discussions among colleagues:

> on prend un café ou un thé, on discute des infos, et puis on se trouve bloqués pour dire telle ou telle chose. Donc on peut le plus souvent faire une périphrase, on peut s'en sortir comme ça, mais [on se dit], 'si je voulais être plus précis, comment j'aurais pu dire ça?

While the OPLB thus makes efforts to include the general public in its corpus planning activities, many of them may be reluctant to become involved; the interviewee observed that 'comme dans d'autres domaines, ils sont consommateurs finalement, ils demandent des solutions'. Members of the population appear either to be happy to be dictated to by the experts, or to ignore their recommendations altogether, rather than wishing to work with them to bring about a consensus that may be more appropriate for the community: there is perhaps a sense that speakers unaffiliated with decision-making institutions such as the OPLB would not be listened to by the authorities. Nonetheless, as the interviewee pointed out, TermBret does attempt to engage with them in ways that are perhaps more difficult to implement for more widely spoken languages such as French. While there is a limited use of crowdsourcing for FranceTerme, the database of recommended terminology for French in France, the process is less transparent and does not make use of the voting function, perhaps hindered by the lack of a group of activist new speakers.

16.5 Conclusion

This chapter has shed light on some of the problems facing corpus planning in the revitalization of minoritized languages, showing how tensions surrounding lexical purism in Breton have affected lexicography and corpus planning over the history of the language and its revitalization, often motivated by ideological considerations. In sources from earlier in the revitalization of Breton, the stereotypically *néo-breton* trend is followed more closely, but over time, dictionaries and terminological prescription appear to have become slightly more receptive to the use of French borrowings, and particularly to the use of words that appear in multiple languages including English, showing the increased effect of globalization as well as the recognition that vocabulary denoting new concepts is often in this 'international' category. Indeed, the wider research undertaken for this project (Davies-Deacon 2020), examining the lexicon of Breton in a range of media sources, found that newer publications less tightly linked to the history of the Breton revitalization movement also seem to be more receptive to these international terms.

The approach taken by the OPLB, as explained by its representative, also indicates an attempt to move towards methods of corpus planning that are seen as more objective and inclusive, involving the use of ISO standards and the disavowal of approaches that are 'idéologiques et non pragmatiques', as well as the involvement of speakers who use Breton in their everyday working lives instead of only those deemed to be experts. While the explicit corpus planning undertaken by the OPLB is influenced by the fact that such language planning also occurs in the familiar context of French, and to a certain extent replicates the goals and strategies of French language planning, there is nonetheless an acceptance of the fact that the community does not always take up the vocabulary that is proposed, and the OPLB seeks to maintain engagement with the speaker community using crowdsourcing through its online forum.

The results presented in this chapter have shown that while the lexicographic tradition of mainstream *néo-breton* still tends to favour neologisms over French borrowings, later sources show potential signs of increased tolerance towards international vocabulary in particular, and on an official level, language planners show concern for the needs of the speakers they serve. To suggest that *néo-breton* and its speakers are totally intolerant of French borrowings would be overly reductive, particularly as the community of new speakers continues to expand and diversify: such criticism is in danger of invalidating the efforts of the Breton revitalization movement in the eyes of the academic community, ignoring more pressing issues such as Breton speakers' continued marginalization by the French state. Instead of relying on generalizations that may be inaccurate or outdated, we should seek to reflect the multiplicity of ideologies and practices seen in these communities and the inherent variation within their linguistic varieties, just as with any of the world's languages.

17
France and its difficult relationship with foreign languages

Philippe Caron

17.1 Introduction

As a member state of the European Union, the attitude maintained in France towards French and the other languages spoken there is often criticized for being excessively protectionist. Indeed, France has still not ratified the 1992 European Charter for Regional or Minority Languages.[1] Moreover, France could perform more strongly in the area of foreign language education despite the fact that considerable funds and teaching hours are dedicated to this.

In 2016, an important research project was launched in the UK: 'Multilingualism: Empowering Individuals, Transforming Societies' (MEITS),[2] with the underlying aim of better understanding, theoretically and practically, 'how the insights gained from stepping outside of a single language, culture, and mode of thought are vital to individuals and societies' (AHRC 2021). The objectives of the MEITS project are set out as follows on the Arts and Humanities Research Council website (AHRC 2021):

- Create new knowledge about the opportunities and challenges of multilingualism for individuals, communities, and nations
- Change attitudes towards multilingualism in the general public and among key stakeholders and policymakers
- Develop new interdisciplinary research paradigms and methodologies
- Demonstrate how an innovative interdisciplinary project can integrate language-led research with literary–cultural studies, thereby addressing key issues of our times.

---

[1] Council of Europe, European Charter for Regional or Minority Languages: https://rm.coe.int/1680695175 (accessed 22 December 2021).

[2] See https://www.meits.org/ (accessed 4 December 2021). MEITS was one of four projects funded by the Arts and Humanities Research Council (AHRC) in their Open World Research Initiative (AHRC 2021). The Principal Investigator was Wendy Ayres-Bennett (University of Cambridge). MEITS involved a large team from the University of Cambridge, University of Edinburgh, University of Nottingham, and Queen's University, Belfast.

Philippe Caron, *France and its difficult relationship with foreign languages*. In: *Historical and Sociolinguistic Approaches to French*. Edited by: Janice Carruthers, Mairi McLaughlin, and Olivia Walsh, Oxford University Press.
© Philippe Caron (2024). DOI: 10.1093/oso/9780192894366.003.0017

Amongst many other areas, the MEITS project examined, at an opportune moment, the UK education system, which tends towards monolingualism (Albert 2018).[3] Since 2004, British children have been able to opt out of language study at the age of fourteen, with no obligation to take a language at GCSE level (McLelland 2018: 12–13). Of those who do take a language to GCSE level, a large majority of students do not continue any further (Tinsley 2019). A 2016 British Council study noted that 'only 34 per cent of pupils obtain a good GCSE in a language, and less than 5 per cent do so in more than one language' (Campbell-Cree 2017).[4]

At first glance, the situation in France seems to stand in stark contrast to that of the UK. As we will see, foreign language teaching (which currently involves the teaching of at least two languages for most students from the age of twelve) continues until the final year of secondary school and the time invested in language teaching is not insignificant. However, compared with the rest of Europe, the two countries, for different reasons, find themselves at the bottom of the barrel when it comes to students' linguistic capabilities. How is it that a country like France, which supports foreign language teaching from primary school at both a financial and institutional level, ends up with such bad results in European studies (see Section 17.3)? A partial response to this question comes from the complexity of France's attitude to foreign languages, in a European and broader global context. This chapter will, first, trace the historical background of this attitude through to the present day. It will then provide a discussion of the current language teaching landscape in France, examining both the investment made and the end results. This will then be compared with a second area of French language policy: attitudes towards loanwords and the official neologisms intended to prevent the integration of such loanwords into French. Finally, the link between these two attitudes will be explored.

17.2 Reticence towards foreign languages in France

France's reticence towards foreign languages is nothing new; evidence of it can be seen, for instance, in eighteenth-century reactions to neologisms coming into French from English (see Section 17.4.1). This reticence also indicates an early

---

[3] This is despite notable efforts in recent years: 'the English Baccalaureate—which requires pupils to enter GCSEs in English, maths, a science, either history or geography, and a foreign language; the Scottish "1+2" language education policy—which aims to introduce every child to two new languages in addition to English by the end of primary school; and the Welsh "Global Futures" strategy—which aims to make Wales "bilingual plus one" and introduces foreign language teaching in primary schools' (Campbell-Cree 2017).

[4] The most recent reports are not included because the Covid-19 pandemic, as the British Council mentions in their latest report, affected the results. Analysis from the 2021 report is nevertheless alarming: 'Thirty-one per cent of state schools and 48% of independent schools in our survey state that the number of pupils taking post-16 courses in languages has decreased over the past three years'. The same decline has been observed for all foreign languages except Spanish which is increasing slightly (Collen 2021: 20).

form of nationalism which manifests as soon as a foreign power starts to encroach and to enter into competition with what is felt to be the legitimate hegemony. Today, this nationalism has even greater justification, given the radical changes to lives and habits that have come about since the 1990s, almost always due to technological innovations from the US. First came the spread of personal computing, then the internet, and finally the mobile phone, which enables easy telephone communication and provides access not only to information, decision making tools, applications, and storage, but also entertainment. France's attempts to compete with these products were not always successful; its Bull computers and Minitel[5] were soon pushed aside by their American and Asian competitors, and no French firm managed to profit from the lucrative mobile phone market. We could say, then, that like many other middle powers, France freely embraced trends from abroad; the only area in which it managed to impose a cultural exception policy was that of the arts, which are protected from free competition (Buchsbaum 2017), i.e. from the force of major players such as Hollywood. These technological innovations have generated countless uses for telecommunication devices: email, shopping and online banking, GPS, but also the large-scale surveillance of our lives and of our choices, and the subtle (and sometimes less subtle) influencing of users towards certain purchases and corporate giants.

France has reacted to this change with a certain reticence, but it has been unable to escape the fact that it is part of a European Union whose culture is largely dominated by neoliberalism, notably free trade and deregulation which remove all practical barriers to the circulation of people, money, and goods (Gordon and Meunier 2001). France's economic culture, which gives the state sector a significant place in industries including telecommunications, energy, banking, transport, and space, is at odds with this ideology which, every so often, precipitates crises, such as the 2008 subprime mortgage crisis. In the 1980s, François Mitterrand maintained that the optimal economic status for France was a mixed-economy society in which two strong sectors coexisted: the public and the private.[6] We must now examine the effects that this partial cooperation with a dominant economic model may have on language use,[7] and this is the backdrop for this chapter's discussion of, first, language teaching in France and, second, attitudes to loanwords in France.

---

[5] Minitel was an online service launched in 1982 that used videotext (similar to teletext) and was accessible through a telephone line. It was made up of a screen and a keyboard and is considered a precursor to the internet. It provided access to the phone directory, mail-order retail companies, air and rail ticket purchases, and message boards, amongst other things. It was decommissioned in 2012 (Minitel no date).

[6] See, for example, Mitterrand's 1984 interview for *Libération* (Mitterrand 1984).

[7] Indeed, this period of increasing globalization is exactly when French groups operating internationally grew in number and stature (e.g. Renault, Vivendi, Danone, Vinci, Bolloré, Accor, Total, PSA, Alsthom, Sanofi).

17.3 Modern foreign languages: Investment and end results

A country like France, which is part of an economic and political coalition, must constantly communicate with and make itself understood by its neighbouring countries. Languages are both an essential vehicle for, and a serious challenge to this, in particular the English language, which has emerged as the *lingua franca* of science and business. The challenges for France are twofold. First, it must strengthen the position of its own language on the world stage and, second, it must promote language learning amongst its citizens and at an institutional level. Regarding the first challenge, France has a network of colleges, Alliances françaises, and cultural centres, which aim to defend the status of French globally; other Francophone countries, with their own similar networks, are equally important in this context.[8] French cinema (or cinema financed by France) also plays a leading role in maintaining the global presence of French culture, as does the development of French-speaking TV channels such as TV5 Monde, which reaches some 300 million French-speakers worldwide.[9] But this is not enough. French-speakers, particularly in France, must also learn and use foreign languages. The geopolitical influence of the French-speaking world transcends borders, but it is not global. The creation, in 2005, of France 24, a TV channel which broadcasts in French, English, Arabic and, more recently, Spanish, suggests an awareness of this fact. The greatest show of awareness, however, comes in the form of language teaching in schools and this is the focus of this chapter.

17.3.1 The first foreign language in France

Following official guidelines published in 1890, secondary education in France has included the teaching of at least one modern foreign language. Primary education, on the other hand, contained almost no language teaching, despite having been a part of early years teaching elsewhere for some time, notably in Scandinavia. Furthermore, language teaching focused almost exclusively on the written language, with little attention paid to spoken language skills (Puren 1988: 39, 58). This changed following greater European integration, particularly following the introduction of the Common European Framework of Reference for Languages

---

[8] According to the Agence pour l'enseignement français à l'étranger (2021), 138 different countries share 540 institutions for French as a foreign language, which teach 365,000 students. See the map of these institutions according to their status here: https://www.aefe.fr/rechercher-une-ressource-documentaire/carte-du-reseau-des-etablissements-denseignement-francais (accessed 4 December 2021).

[9] This number comes from the latest report from L'Observatoire de la langue française, using data from 2018 (Organisation internationale de la francophonie no date).

in 2001,[10] which standardized language proficiency levels and foregrounded a communicative and a practical approach to language teaching. Two initiatives have been favoured at an institutional level: (i) familiarization with a foreign language in primary education, already fairly widespread in Northern Europe, and (ii) introduction of a second foreign language in secondary education.

The first initiative is based on the widely accepted understanding of the benefits of introducing additional languages from an early age. The widespread teaching of a foreign language in primary education was introduced in France in 2002 and implementing this somewhat belated change required additional means. For instance, many primary school teachers did not have sufficient training in, or experience of, a foreign language to be able to teach a language to their young pupils (CEDRE 2016). It was, therefore, necessary to hire qualified staff (native speakers of the language being taught where possible). The main challenges, then, concerned finances and recruitment. For the initiative to succeed, very generous support policies and budgets for training and recruitment would be necessary. The reality was, however, that recruitment was difficult and, in the beginning, language teaching was only introduced from the ages of eight/nine.[11] The well-meaning—but clumsily implemented—reform had an additional unwanted effect.

The diversity of possible language choices available for a European Union country should have led to great variety, but, in reality, it resulted largely in the teaching of one language: English.[12] The dominance of English at primary level subsequently influenced the choice of first foreign language at *collège* (ages eleven to fifteen) and then at *lycée* (equivalent to sixth form in the UK system). Once established, the law of least effort, alongside the economic lure of English, naturally led an overwhelming majority of students to make the same choice. Benefits and other subsidies would have been needed to avoid this almost automatic siphoning towards English. The situation was further affected by the *Loi Haby* (11 July 1975)[13] which led to what are known as *classes indifférenciées,* classes comprising children of mixed abilities, in comprehensive schools. In the years preceding this reform, German was still a popular choice of first foreign language; classes taking this language tended to be classes with high intellectual ability given that German had the reputation of being a difficult language to learn (at the beginning at least). It may be that the introduction of mixed-ability classes discouraged students from selecting German. According to figures from 2017, only 3.4% of school pupils study German as their first foreign language (Table 17.1).

---

[10] The Common European Framework of Reference for Languages (CEFR: Council of Europe 2001) outlines syllabuses and proficiency levels in foreign language learning, for use in a wide range of contexts.

[11] This changed to age six/seven in 2013, either during *Cours préparatoire* (CP, age six) or *Cours élémentaire 1* (CE1, age seven).

[12] See, for example, the French Senate's 2021 critical report about foreign language teaching in France (Sénat 2021).

[13] *Loi n° 75-620 du 11 juillet 1975 relative à l'éducation *Loi Haby**: https://www.legifrance.gouv.fr/loda/id/JORFTEXT000000334174/2000-06-21/ (accessed 14 July 2022).

Table 17.1 Choice of first foreign language in France

	Total number of students	Students studying a first foreign language No.	%	German	English	Spanish	Italian	Other
Sixième (11–12 years old)	809,803	808,732	99.9%	37,524	763,573	4,585	1,257	1,793
Cinquième (12–13 years old)	799,272	798,736	99.9%	31,708	758,919	5,540	1,136	1,433
Quatrième (13–14 years old)	787,544	787,069	99.9%	29,991	749,296	5,345	1,019	1,418
Troisième (14–15 years old)	799,697	799,121	99.9%	29,563	761,384	5,801	958	1,415
DIMA, dispo-relais[a]	885	396	44.7%	29	342	25	0	0
ULIS at collège level[b]	31,492	25,873	82.2%	833	24,848	145	42	5
Segpa[c]	86,314	86,212	99.9%	2,551	83,124	537	0	0
Total number of students at collège level (including Segpa)	3,315,007	3,306,139	99.7%	132,199	3,141,486	21,978	4,412	6,064
Seconde (15–16 years old)	562,870	562,175	99.9%	17,284	538,835	4,329	678	1,049
Première (16–17 years old)	531,596	531,269	99.9%	15,294	509,644	4,651	679	1,001
Terminale (17–18 years old)	504,519	504,186	99.9%	14,116	480,104	8,056	790	1,120
ULIS (lycée général et technologique)	172	132	76.7%	1	129	0	1	1
Total number of students (at lycées généraux et technologiques)	1,599,157	1,597,762	99.9%	46,695	1,528,712	17,036	2,148	3,171
Total number of students (lycée professionnel only)	665,190	654,060	98.3%	9,762	634,131	9,470	389	308
Total	5,579,354	5,557,961	99.6%	188,656	5,304,329	48,484	6,949	9,543
%				3.4%	95.4%	0.9%	0.1%	0.2%
Public school system	4,398,836	4,384,535	99.7%	154,856	4,177,112	38,081	6,658	7,828
Private school system	1,180,518	1,173,426	99.4%	33,800	1,127,217	10,403	291	1,715

[a] DIMA are scholarly programmes which allow pupils aged 15 to start a professional apprenticeship of their choosing alongside their studies.
[b] ULIS are classes which are designed to accommodate the specific needs of children with disabilities.
[c] Segpa are collège level classes for children with learning difficulties who would benefit from an alternative pedagogy.

The most relevant statistics from the Ministry of National Education in France (Ministère de l'Éducation nationale 2017: §4.15) presented in Table 17.1 can be summarized as follows. In 2017, there were:

- 5,579,354 students in secondary education
- 5,557,961 (99.6%) studying one modern language
- 5,304,329 (95.4%) studying English
- 188,656 (3.4%) studying German
- 48,484 (0.9%) studying Spanish
- 9,543 (0.2%) studying other languages
- 6,949 (0.1%) studying Italian

The monopoly of English has only increased over the last few years. Moreover, experimental classes which teach core subjects in a foreign language are scarce and are even under threat in some institutions. In 2016, so-called European classes, which reinforced language teaching with the teaching of a subject in a foreign language, were removed for pupils aged thirteen to eighteen, except in international schools, which are rare and highly selective. In these schools, students work towards either a special qualification in a foreign language at the end of secondary education, or the double baccalaureate (Onisep 2020). The reform was criticized and was subject to some minor amendments.

17.3.2 Performance

This section focuses on the quantitative results of secondary school language teaching which receives a not insignificant amount of classroom time (four hours a week for eleven to twelve year old pupils, then three hours a week until the age of fourteen/fifteen, upon introduction of the second foreign language). The 2011 European survey on language competences (Étude européenne sur les compétences en langues, ESLC) analysed the language skills of pupils aged fourteen to sixteen from sixteen European Union countries in both their first and second foreign language in oral comprehension, written comprehension, and written expression (Ministère de l'Éducation nationale 2011: 1–2). The results showed that, compared to many other countries in the study, a particularly high level of pupils in France did not achieve or just managed to achieve A1 level proficiency.[14] For example, whereas in six countries, the majority of students achieved B1 or B2

---

[14] A1 is the lowest level of proficiency (C2 is the highest). Learners at A1 level have minimal ability in comprehension and conversation. They can use simple vocabulary and make simple speech acts, e.g. asking for directions, telling someone where they come from, writing a postcard, reading a text which uses common vocabulary from everyday life.

level[15] in all three activities in the English language,[16] in two countries, including France, the majority of students were below A2 standard. In fact, in France, only 26% of students reached at least A2 level proficiency in oral comprehension in English, compared to 46% on average across all countries in the study (Ministère de l'Éducation nationale 2011: 2–3). Similar results were found, using different criteria, by a French study commissioned by Ministère de l'Éducation nationale (CEDRE 2016). These studies show that young people in France are considerably behind many other countries in the European Union in terms of foreign language proficiency. The likely causes of this are discussed in Section 17.4.

17.3.3 The introduction of a second foreign language

The teaching of a second foreign language was first introduced in 1995. Since 2016, 2.5 hours per week have been allocated to teaching a second foreign language, starting from *cinquième* (twelve to thirteen years old), for all pupils in non-professional education routes.[17] In a multilingual Europe, the aim was to move away from the monopoly of English, so that speakers would not have to use a language that, in most cases, was not the first language of either participant. From this angle, France does not seem like a closed-off country, or as reluctant to learn foreign languages.[18] The second foreign language also seems to be an attempt at linguistic multilateralism; in an ideal world, French pupils would move towards this, and towards widespread trilingualism. The question, then, was how students would (or would not) diversify their choice of language. Given the geographic position of France, in the middle of western Europe, one might hope that a variety of language candidates would be poised to seize this opportunity. That has not been the case, however, and one language, Spanish, firmly imposed itself as the second language, except in the *départements* which border Germany and Italy. Below are the results of a 2017 study from the Ministry of National Education in France (Ministère de l'Éducation nationale 2017: §4.15).

The most relevant statistics presented in Table 17.2 can be summarized as follows. In 2017, 5,492,155 pupils were in secondary education. Amongst these:

---

[15] At B1 level, a learner should be able to understand the key points of a discussion comprising clear and standard language, to recount a memory, to conduct their daily life autonomously in a country where the language is spoken. At B2 level, learners can conduct their daily life and can present and discuss topics of their choosing—in both cases, with ease.
[16] That is, in oral comprehension, written comprehension, and written expression.
[17] In France, *sixième* is the first year of secondary education (eleven to twelve years old). This is followed by *cinquième* (twelve to thirteen years old), *quatrième* (thirteen to fourteen years old), and *troisième* (fourteen to fifteen years old), the last year of *collège*.
[18] An optional third language from *seconde* (fifteen to sixteen years old) has even been proposed. The teaching offer is not, therefore, insignificant, which raises the delicate question of why performance does not correspond to the effort being made at institutional level. See Section 17.4.

Table 17.2 Choice of second foreign language in France

	Total number of students	Students studying a second foreign language No.	%	German	English	Spanish	Italian	Other (all other)	Other (regional languages only)
Sixième (11–12 years old)	809,803	93,181	11.5%	35,348	38,256	12,612	3,549	3,416	360
Cinquième (12–13 years old)	799,272	798,038	99.8%	123,737	39,272	579,181	44,616	11,232	130
Quatrième (13–14 years old)	787,544	786,982	99.9%	112,309	37,250	585,225	42,250	9,948	91
Troisième (14–15 years old)	799,697	798,746	99.9%	112,767	37,528	596,401	42,186	9,864	139
ULIS at collège level	31,492	12,160	38.6%	569	418	10,102	910	161	53
Total number of students at collège level	3,227,808	2,489,107	77.1%	384,730	152,724	1,783,521	133,511	34,621	773
Seconde (15–16 years old)	562,870	561,331	99.7%	97,180	23,023	405,165	27,691	8,272	366
Première (16–17 years old)	531,596	530,332	99.8%	94,786	21,603	379,687	26,126	8,130	362
Terminale (17–18 years old)	504,519	503,017	99.7%	90,704	23,812	355,408	25,023	8,070	574
ULIS (lycée général et technologique)	172	119	69.2%	7	1	98	9	4	1
Total number of students (at lycées généraux et technologiques)	1,599,157	1,594,799	99.7%	282,677	68,439	1,140,358	78,849	24,476	1,303
Total number of students (lycée professionnel only)	665,190	232,045	34.9%	19,357	6,652	192,504	11,132	2,400	143
Total	5,492,155	4,315,951	78.6%	686,764	227,815	3,116,383	223,492	61,497	2,219
%				15.9%	5.3%	72.2%	5.2%	1.4%	0.1%
Public school system	4,316,252	3,392,740	78.6%	531,484	186,911	2,438,101	191,050	45,194	1,702
Private school system	1,175,903	923,211	78.5%	155,280	40,904	678,228	32,442	16,357	460

- 4,315,951 (78.6%) were learning a second foreign language
- 3,116,383 (72.2%) were learning Spanish
- 686,764 (15.9%) were learning German
- 223,492 (5.3%) were learning Italian
- 227,815 (5.2%) were learning English
- 61,497 (1.4%) were learning other languages, 2,219 of whom were learning regional languages.

17.3.4 A failure to diversify

In what follows, I explore the question of why France has not managed to achieve diversity in its pupils' choice of second foreign language, despite its privileged geographic positioning in Europe. As a starting point, we must consider the status of English as a generally 'useful language' which, as we have seen, gives it an almost total monopoly on the first foreign language. What is a pupil in *cinquième* (aged twelve to thirteen) to do? German, in France, as in French-speaking Switzerland, has the reputation of being a difficult language, which is off-putting. Essentially, that leaves Spanish and Italian to fight it out—two Romance languages which are the languages of France's neighbours and which are linguistically close to French. This is where an additional criterion comes into play: whereas Italian is spoken almost exclusively in Italy, Spanish enjoys majority-language status across many countries in Central and South America. Numbers studying Portuguese, Russian, and Dutch are negligible, attracting more or less as many learners as regional languages (Basque, Creole, Occitan, Alsatian, Breton, and Catalan). The argument surrounding the usefulness of German in the EU, convincing in and of itself given that Germany is France's largest trading partner, does not seem to carry the weight that it might be expected to.

17.4 From mediocre performance towards an explanation

Moving beyond the question of which languages are taught, this section turns to why young people in France are underperforming in languages. A French study which analysed the 2004–2010 results even reported an 11% drop in oral comprehension abilities between these years (Inspection générale de l'Éducation nationale 2013). The reasons are multiple. On the one hand, immersion in, or exposure to, foreign languages is impeded in France by the fact that films are often dubbed, rather than subtitled (Ministère de l'Éducation nationale 2011: 5).[19] This

---

[19] However, the situation is changing: 'En 2016, 34% des élèves de 3ᵉ déclarent regarder, au moins une fois par semaine, des émissions, des films, des vidéos, ou des séries en anglais avec des sous-titres en français (contre seulement 10% en 2004). Ils sont même 17% à regarder chaque semaine des versions originales sans sous-titres, soit trois fois plus qu'en 2004 (5%)' (CNESCO 2019: 19).

is changing with the use of platforms such as Netflix, but this unfortunate habit is indicative of two implicit attitudes: that language is of little importance in audio-visual productions; and that the audience is neither capable of understanding nor interested in exposure to languages. Beginning to emerge here are signs of a disinterest in or a reticence towards the languages of others, since dubbing is, to some extent, a means of adapting which assimilates foreign productions.

In addition, in France, a belief in the usefulness of foreign languages is far from universal, unlike in other countries, where foreign languages are more likely to be seen as useful.[20] However, judging by the 2016 CEDRE report, the situation is changing: 'en 2016, les élèves de 3ᵉ ne sont plus que 18% à déclarer ne pas du tout ou ne pas beaucoup aimer l'anglais, contre 29% en 2010. 59% des élèves considèrent même qu'il est très important de connaitre l'anglais, contre 42% en 2010' (CNESCO 2019: 16). Yet, it seems unlikely that this is the main reason; it is more likely to be linked to the retraining of teachers. A 2019 report from the Conseil national d'évaluation du système scolaire (CNESCO 2019: 31) states that 'les enseignants de langues se considèrent tout à fait préparés aux contenus disciplinaires qu'ils ont à enseigner (à 91%). Cependant, plus d'un tiers d'entre eux déclarent ne pas être préparés aux pratiques de classe dans leur matière (39%) et à la pédagogie appliquée aux contenus enseignés (37%)'. Worse still, 'seul un enseignant de langues sur deux (54%) déclare avoir participé à des stages de formation continue lors des 12 derniers mois'. In addition, three bad habits hinder satisfactory language-learning performance in France. The first is more general and is not limited to the study of foreign languages: the status of errors in the French education system. In the study of languages, as much if not more than in other areas, progression can only be achieved by diving in, even if that means making mistakes (Rojas 2016: § le droit à l'erreur):

> la peur de se tromper commence très tôt chez les élèves français et se manifeste à tous les niveaux de l'enseignement. Souvent l'absence de participation orale est due à la peur du mépris que produit l'erreur, non à l'absence réelle de connaissances. C'est qu'il y a, d'une part, une association entre l'erreur et le ridicule public, nourrie par un discours de recherche de l'excellence très présent dans l'interaction quotidienne, et d'autre part, très peu d'intérêt pour encourager la prise de risques et valoriser positivement les erreurs.

Teachers must, therefore, highlight the pupil's effort and correct errors without stigmatizing them, since making errors is an integral part of learning. It is the process of perfecting that counts, not perfection. Yet, this is not always achieved in classrooms. Peer pressure is an additional factor: pupils are always being closely

---

[20] For example: 'Globalement, les élèves trouvent l'anglais "assez utile". Mais ils sont beaucoup moins nombreux à juger l'anglais utile dans leur vie ou pour leur satisfaction personnelle. En revanche, 77% des Suédois jugent qu'il est utile dans les loisirs et 74% des Grecs qu'il leur sera utile pour l'avenir, contre 37% des Français dans les deux situations' (Ministère de l'Éducation nationale 2011: 5).

observed by their peers and often end up in a lose/lose situation: too good and they will be seen as the teacher's pet; not good enough and they may also face ridicule. As a result, students often avoid speaking in class. This is already an issue in the classroom, stemming from the pedagogical tendency in France to load pupils with large amounts of information. Pupils often passively receive the curriculum and, consequently, do not imagine that knowledge can be co-constructed in several ways: 'dans la relation enseignant-élève, le premier est vu comme le dépositaire d'une vérité qui doit être transmise au second. Le premier informe, montre et fait répéter; le deuxième écoute, mémorise et répète [...] la voix de l'enseignant devient le point de départ de chaque situation d'apprentissage'(Rojas 2016).[21] In conclusion, it is not that France has not institutionally supported language teaching. The reasons, as has been shown, lie elsewhere, partly in the broader landscape, partly in the classroom, and, partly, finally, in popular thought.

17.5 Lexical borrowings

A useful comparison can be made between language teaching in France and a second aspect of language policy in France: the state's attitude to lexical borrowings. Much has already been said on this topic, notably on the measures to combat borrowings through the creation of French neologisms (Depecker 2001). Since the 1970s, under the government of Pierre Messmer, terminology commissions have been set up in every governmental department, tasked not only with creating specialist neologisms for technical sectors but also with replacing English borrowings which might be integrated into the language. The 1994 *Loi Toubon*[22] and its related decrees gave even more weight to linguistic protectionism, leading to the creation of a *Dictionnaire des termes officiels de la langue française* (DGLF 1994), first published by what was then known as the Délégation générale à la langue française (DGLF) in 1994 and then online (Ministère de la Culture 2022). This protectionist attitude is all the more surprising given the fact that the supposedly invasive English language itself has a lexis which includes a very large number of borrowings from French (McLaughlin 2018). Indeed, the *Dictionnaire des anglicismes* of 1990 records only 3,000 English borrowings in 60,000 commonly used words in French, a maximum of 5%.[23]

---

[21] Rojas (2016) adds that there is a further preconceived idea, not restricted to classrooms, that the French are bad at languages. We know, from teaching psychology, that such beliefs can negatively affect the effort made and motivation, and, above all, are a distraction for a child, focusing their effort on this and away from the class.
[22] *Loi n° 94-665 du 4 août 1994 relative à l'emploi de la langue française*: https://www.legifrance.gouv.fr/loda/id/LEGITEXT000005616341/ (accessed 14 July 2022).
[23] According to the Académie française (no date): 'un *Dictionnaire des anglicismes* de 1990 en enregistre moins de 3,000, dont près de la moitié sont d'ores et déjà vieillis. Les anglicismes d'usage,

The wider public in France is more welcoming to Anglicisms than those in power. But it has been the case for a long time now that borrowings have been perceived negatively, as a symptom of invasion, or even of degeneration. Yet, it is quite rare that borrowings are anything more than lexical. As such, they do not threaten the language system at all and they are frequently integrated phonetically, indeed sometimes even graphically, into the target language. This tension has been well studied (see McLaughlin 2018) and can be usefully compared with the observations made in previous sections on foreign language teaching in the French school system. What do the *Loi Toubon* (4 August 1994) and its associated decree of 3 July 1996 have in common with foreign language skills in France? Both cases involve France's relationship to the other through language. In the study of languages, it is about investing time and energy to be able to join the other on their linguistic territory, i.e. by speaking their language. In the case of borrowings, it is about accepting (or not) that the other can penetrate the language to a greater or lesser extent. Notable in both cases, however, is a large degree of reticence. Whether the French move towards the language of the other, or, conversely, whether they allow the other into the core of their identity, their attitude is fundamentally ambiguous or even obstinate. The regulatory framework introduced by the *Loi Toubon* is impressive when considering France's relationship to otherness. It is clear, upon consultation of the *Dictionnaire des néologismes officiels de la Documentation française* (Ministère de la Culture 2022), that the aim is not so much to adapt French to accommodate new concepts or new objects but, rather, to resist the intrusion of foreign words. The idea of a state creating terminology commissions, particularly to deal with the specialist jargon that accompanies new technologies, is not so shocking. The fact that most neologisms were created as alternatives to borrowings is much more surprising. However, this is a reticence which has a long history in France.

17.5.1 An historical fear

During the first three centuries of its push to gain prestige (roughly from the fourteenth to the sixteenth centuries), French borrowed heavily from other languages. It needed a sufficiently broad lexicon to enable its use in a variety of functions (including the popularization of Latin works, legal and administrative functions, as well as in science and theology). Latin was borrowed from heavily. Reactions

donc, représenteraient environ 2.5% du vocabulaire courant qui comprend 60,000 mots. Un *Dictionnaire des mots anglais* du français de 1998, plus vaste, évalue les emprunts de l'anglais à 4 ou 5% du lexique français courant. Si l'on considère les fréquences d'emploi de ces anglicismes, on constate que beaucoup appartiennent à des domaines spécialisés ou semi-spécialisés et sont donc assez peu fréquents dans la langue courante. Quant aux termes purement techniques d'origine anglaise en usage en France, leur pourcentage est du même ordre'. See https://www.academie-francaise.fr/questions-de-langue#12_strong-em-anglicismes-et-autres-emprunts-em-strong (accessed 15 January 2024).

to neologisms, of all forms, really started to appear from the seventeenth century onwards.[24] English did not feature at this time, but the fear of Anglicisms is part of this much older and broader attitude of reticence towards the adoption of new words, be they borrowings or new lexical items formed by, for example, derivation or compounding. The first significant signs of this fear are found in the work of the *remarqueurs*, writers who discussed the acceptability of words and expressions (Ayres-Bennett and Seijido 2011). Reticence towards neologisms, be that their form or their meaning, is not limited to borrowings, but extends to prefixal and suffixal derivation, and within the domain of borrowings, is concerned as much with dialectalisms as with Latinisms or Italianisms. Even the word itself, *néologisme*, suggests reticence, pejorative as it is, and as it was from the outset. The word first appeared in a dictionary in 1762, in the fourth edition of the *Dictionnaire de l'Académie*:

(1) NÉOLOGISME. s.m. Mot tiré du Grec. On s'en sert pour signifier l'habitude de se servir de termes nouveaux, ou d'employer les mots reçus dans des significations détournées. Ce mot se prend presque toujours en mauvaise part, & désigne une affectation vicieuse & fréquente en ce genre. *La Néologie est un Art, le Néologisme est un abus. La manie du Néologisme.*

The related lexical field *néologie, néologisme, néologique* was recorded much earlier in Desfontaines' (1726) *Dictionnaire néologique*.

English was not really seen as a threat until the eighteenth century, with the word *anglicisme* first being mentioned, it seems, in Féraud's (1787–8, vol.1, s.v.) *Dictionaire critique de la langue française*:

(2) ANGLICISME, s. m. Façon de parler et d'écrire propre de la langue Anglaise, et qui n'est pas reçue dans notre langue. Les Traductions des Livres Anglais sont pleines d'*anglicismes*, que les Auteurs auraient pu aisément éviter, en consultant seulement les Dictionaires. Nous en avons relevé une foule dans celui-ci.

In fact, Féraud's dictionary mentions the word *anglicisme* 131 times, in comparison to just three mentions of *italianisme*, and sixty-seven of *latinisme*, indicating a clear change in predominance. Féraud, whose observations of usage are likely the most up-to-date of the time, displays a sensitivity which shows similarities to our own—this resistance is nothing new. The following examples show some of the critical discourse surrounding Anglicisms. For instance, under the entry *astérisque* (Féraud 1787–8, vol.1, s.v.):

---

[24] The work of Henri Estienne (1578) shows hostility towards Italianisms which, according to him, were prospering in the *Cour des derniers Valois*. However, this was a passing fad, a code-switching phenomenon specific to a context where, temporarily, the dominant influence of Catherine de Médici had created a sort of passing dandyism which does not seem to have lasted to the end of her regency. It is difficult to speak here about neologism(s) as the phenomenon left only a few small traces in the French lexicon.

(3) ASTÉRISQUE, s. m. Terme d'Imprimerie. Petite marque en forme d'étoile, qui se met ordinairement dans les Livres, pour marquer un renvoi, une addition, ou une chôse digne de remarque. Ici nous l'employons devant les mots suranés, ou forgés, devant les barbarismes, les Anglicismes, etc.

Three further examples make similarly critical remarks (Féraud 1787–8, vol.1, s.v.):

(4) *COMPÉTITION, concurrence, est un anglicisme. 'Les mécontens répandoient le bruit, qu'il se servoit de son crédit pour nuire au commerce d'Angleterre, afin que celui de son propre pays (la Hollande) pût fleurir sans *compétition*'. Targe, *Traduction de Smollet*.—On a remarqué que la plupart des Auteurs font leur traduction à *coups de Dictionaires*: il serait à souhaiter qu'ils le fissent plus souvent. (s.v. COMPÉTITEUR).

(5) *CONCILIATOIRE, adj. est un anglicisme. Des bills *conciliatoires*. Linguet. C'est le mot Anglois *conciliatory*. Ce mot peut être bon au Palais et dans des Gazettes.

(6) *DÉRESPECTUEUX, EûSE, adj. On dit dans le *Dict. Gram.* que c'est un mot peu heureûsement inventé. Il n'a pas paru tel à M. l'*Ab. Grosier*. La conduite du Général Arnold a été trouvée *dérespectueuse* pour la suprême autorité exécutive de cet Etat.—C'est un anglicisme: *disrespectful*.

These examples show the process by which Anglicisms are brought into French, by translators of English texts who sometimes adapt the English word into French without checking whether it exists in French or, indeed, whether it has the same meaning. The entry for *calculer* is perhaps the most explicit example of the lexicographical discourse (Féraud 1787–8, vol.1, s.v.):

(7) 'Dans un siècle où les moeurs se sont dépravées jusqu'au point de *calculer le degré de* tendresse que l'on doit à ses parens.' *Id.*[25]—Les Traducteurs des Livres Anglais emploient souvent ce verbe, parce que les Anglais font un grand usage de leur verbe *to calculate*. 'Henri VIII *calcula* (pensa) que sa faveur étant l'unique bâse du crédit de *Wolsey*, les atentions de Charles-Quint pour ce Ministre n'étoient qu'un hommage de plus pour le Maître.—C'est un vrai anglicisme'.

17.5.2 The situation today

It is significant that the *Loi Toubon* legislation is still in place in France. Every year, the terminology commissions keep working towards the official removal of

---

[25] Extract from the author Palissot, previously mentioned by Féraud (1787–8: vol.1, s.v.).

borrowings through the creation of neologisms. The word *voyagiste* conveniently replaces *tour operator*, but many words created by these commissions fail to counteract fleeting borrowings which would be easy to Gallicize. Moreover, using the official neologisms is only obligatory in institutional situations (and even then it is rarely respected) and the Commission générale only controls usage within the limits of statutory obligations. In the event of an appeal, the Conseil constitutionnel's position is that the prescription of terminology for use on TV and radio or by individuals in their daily activities contravenes the principle of free speech and thought (Article 11 of the *Déclaration des droits de l'homme et du citoyen*).[26] The legislator, it states, can only regulate the vocabulary of public legal entities and private individuals working in public service functions (Article 5). Its coercive measures are, therefore, narrowly contained; nonetheless, it reflects an almost obsessive concern about borrowings at state level. The Délégation générale à la langue française et aux langues de France (DGLFLF) is charged with verifying that the legislation is applied, a role which sees, for example, one of its delegates sent to every Olympic Games to ensure that French is being used alongside English in official campaigns. In sum, however, the extent to which these measures, which do not carry any criminal or financial sanctions, are effective in practice is questionable.

17.6 Discussion

On the surface, these two areas, language learning and attitudes to borrowings, seem quite separate, but their similarities are surprising. The question of otherness is prevalent in both cases. When we speak the language of the other, we take a step towards them. We agree to meet them on their own linguistic territory. On the other hand, accepting a neologism from abroad means allowing for such flexibility in our own language that we can welcome in elements of other civilizations. In either case, it is a question of making room for the other in our day-to-day language use. What sort of identity-related insecurities are at play when a country institutionally braces itself against civilizations with which it has, for centuries, been in constant interaction, exchanging words, commerce, thought, aesthetics, philosophy, ideologies, politics, and religion? Languages, it is true, are a crucial part of our identity (Oakes 2001) and, consequently, are a vital part of the nation state and its cohesion. Yet, the process of borrowing is almost universal. It is a constant in the development of languages; there are, after all, very few places which exist in perfect isolation on this planet, particularly in the modern day where civilizations are so intertwined. This does not necessarily have to be a bad thing. A reader

---

[26] *Déclaration des droits de l'homme et du citoyen de 1789*: https://www.legifrance.gouv.fr/contenu/menu/droit-national-en-vigueur/constitution/declaration-des-droits-de-l-homme-et-du-citoyen-de-1789 (accessed 14 July 2022).

of English books may possibly note the heavy influence of French on the English lexicon. The more scholarly or formal the text, the greater the presence of French on the page. But the same linguistic ostracism is not present amongst our British neighbours, who, if they shared the same negative attitude as France, would have serious cause to be alarmed. So what is the right attitude?

Can comparing these two cases shed light on common French ideologies? Regardless of the answer, the French state's position is somewhat contradictory: trying to help its nationals to better communicate in foreign languages, whilst also displaying a distrust of English that borders on obsession. This is not particularly difficult to explain. In France, there remains—undoubtedly—nostalgia for a glorious past which saw French as a sort of lingua franca in European courts during the eighteenth century. This nostalgia positions the language as a *totem identitaire* according to a CNESCO (2019: 3) report. The report also highlights a link between the rejection of regional languages in France and its reluctance to embrace foreign languages (CNESCO 2019: 3):

> Unifiée par la langue (française) comme beaucoup d'États-nations, mais déniant longtemps toute reconnaissance aux langues régionales, les combattant farouchement dans son école, la France s'est frontalement opposée dans sa construction nationale au développement d'une identité plurilingue, là où d'autres pays accueillaient favorablement leur multilinguisme originel comme la Suisse ou encore la Belgique.

The result was, undoubtedly, a more assured contempt for the civilization which followed, a civilization which, from 1815, saw France replaced as the leading colonial, political, military, and even artistic power in a European and global context.

17.7 Conclusion

From the two cases discussed in this chapter, it is clear that the same feelings of reticence can lead, in education, to mediocre foreign language skills, and, from a linguistic point of view, to an almost outright refusal to accept borrowings from a dominant language. Losing the top spot on the podium is always difficult to come to terms with, but, on the international stage, France would be much better off sharing, not only the debt of gratitude resulting from the Second World War, but also mutual concerns—rather than putting up the barricades. In recent years, encouraging signs are appearing in the motivation of pupils and their abilities to use foreign languages. Moreover, the state's prejudices against English are far from shared by young people in France (see, for example, Walsh 2016b). In time, we will see the extent to which the country is better able to adapt to the presence of the other in its linguistic practices, for instance, through more active campaigning in favour of a relaxed attitude to plurilingualism which is open and extended to regional languages, immigrant languages, and the languages spoken by its closest neighbours. Paradoxically, perhaps in the eyes of the most conservative commentators, it is ultimately a question of influence, and therefore of prestige.

18

Minoritized languages in France and Ireland

Policy, practice, vitality

Janice Carruthers and Mícheál B. Ó Mainnín

18.1 Introduction

This chapter[1] discusses language policy and practice in relation to minoritized languages in France and Ireland,[2] with a focus on the period from the end of the nineteenth century to the present day. France and Ireland have been selected because they demonstrate contrasting language-policy contexts; in the case of Ireland, this is complicated further by the partition of the island into two jurisdictions in 1921 and the varying status of, and attitudes to, minoritized languages in the Republic of Ireland and Northern Ireland since that point (Mac Síthigh 2018). Despite historical narratives that share certain common experiences, practices, and tropes (Section 18.2.1), France and, since independence, the Republic of Ireland have travelled in very different language policy directions. Legislation, education policy, and economic support are all areas where they have diverged significantly. Whereas France has multiple regional minoritized languages[3] and a powerful official language (French), the Republic of Ireland has a minoritized

---

[1] The research for this chapter was funded by the Arts and Humanities Research Council through the Open World Research Initiative project 'Multilingualism: Empowering Individuals, Transforming Societies' (MEITS): AH/N004671/1. The authors are grateful to the AHRC, the Principal Investigator (Wendy Ayres-Bennett), and the members of the wider research team for their support. For more information on the project, see www.meits.org (accessed 1 May 2023). Thanks also to the two anonymous readers for their comments. See also Caron (Chapter 17, this volume).

[2] Throughout the chapter, the term 'Ireland' will refer to the island of Ireland, including both the Republic of Ireland and Northern Ireland. Where reference is made to one of the two contemporary jurisdictions, the term 'Republic of Ireland' or 'Northern Ireland' will be used.

[3] In France, government policy in relation to the *langues de France* distinguishes between *langues régionales*, *langues des outre-mer*, and *langues non-territoriales*: https://www.culture.gouv.fr/Thematiques/Langue-francaise-et-langues-de-France/Nos-missions/Promouvoir-les-langues-de-France (accessed 2 July 2022). Our focus here is on the *langues régionales*, since this lends itself most readily to a comparison between France and Ireland.

Janice Carruthers and Mícheál B. Ó Mainnín, *Minoritized languages in France and Ireland*. In: *Historical and Sociolinguistic Approaches to French*. Edited by: Janice Carruthers, Mairi McLaughlin, and Olivia Walsh, Oxford University Press.
© Janice Carruthers and Mícheál B. Ó Mainnín (2024). DOI: 10.1093/oso/9780192894366.003.0018

language (Irish) which is also the national language and the first in status of two official languages (the second being English). In the case of Northern Ireland, two minoritized languages (Irish and Ulster Scots) were recognized in the political context for the first time in the *Good Friday Agreement* (Northern Ireland Office 1998). The question of their current status, which is complicated, is considered further below (see Section 18.3.2).

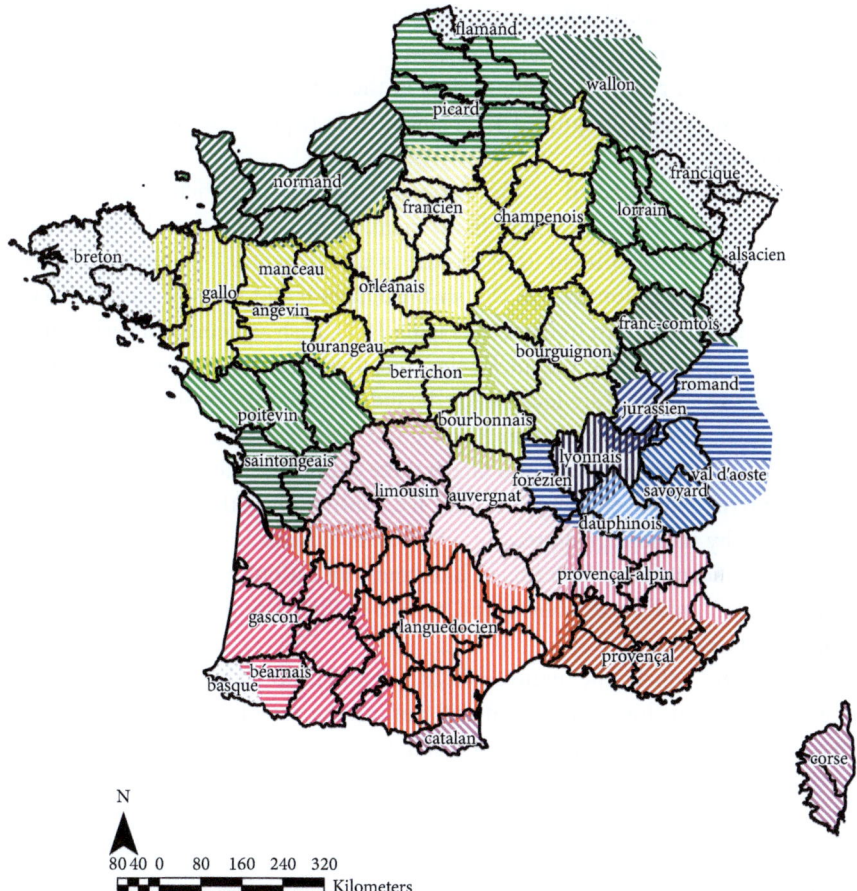

Figure 18.1 Linguistic map of France

In France, the majority of the regional languages are Romance and include multiple varieties and dialects within the three major zones of the *langues d'oïl* (broadly the areas to the north in shades of green and yellow in Figure 18.1),[4] the *langues*

---

[4] Our thanks to Rebecca Milligan for drawing the maps in Figures 18.1 and 18.2. Note that precise boundaries around varieties can vary in different sources. Indeed, in the case of France, there is a continuum and areas of overlap rather than clear lines between varieties, and names for different

d'oc (broadly the areas to the south in shades of red/pink), and *francoprovençal* (to the east in blue).[5] In very generalized terms, we can say that the *langues d'oc*, and to a large extent the varieties of *francoprovençal*, were slower to decline than most of the *langues d'oïl* which were both geographically and linguistically closer to the variety from which French emerged.[6] In addition to Romance varieties, we also find Germanic languages (e.g. *flamand* and *alsacien*), *breton* (a Celtic language with several dialects), and *basque*. The linguistic context in France is thus multilingual, with different zones and a mix of language families at play; this diversity is one of the major contrasts with the Irish context and an issue to which we will return at several points in the chapter. However, French is the sole official language, designated as 'la langue de la République' in Article 2 of the Constitution.[7]

While Irish is described as the 'national language' in Article 8 of the *Constitution of Ireland* (1937),[8] there is no mention of Ulster Scots; its status as a language was not established until the late twentieth century. In the present day, it is spoken in east Donegal (in the Irish Republic), and parts of Derry, Down, and Antrim (in Northern Ireland: see Figure 18.2). Irish as a community language is largely confined to the *Gaeltacht*, the collective term for Irish-speaking areas (see Figure 18.2); these are located for the most part on the west coast (in counties Donegal, Mayo, Galway, and Kerry), and also in parts of Cork, Waterford, and Meath. Most varieties fall into one of three dialects, i.e. Ulster, Connacht, and Munster Irish. However, they do not form a continuum as they are divided from each other by monolingual areas in which only English is spoken and this had been a significant factor in terms of intercommunication (and for some, mutual intelligibility) until the establishment in 1972 of the Irish-medium radio station, Raidió na Gaeltachta.

Section 18.2 will set the theoretical (18.2.1) and historical (18.2.2) contexts for the discussion in this chapter and will outline the research questions (18.2.3). Section 18.3 will explore these questions in relation to policy and practice in the

---

varieties can also vary. A number of sources are publicly available for both Ireland and France. For Ireland, see https://www.gov.ie/en/collection/aacde-list-of-the-26-language-planning-areas-and-maps/ and https://en.wikipedia.org/wiki/Ulster_Scots_dialect#/media/File:English_dialects_in_Ulster_contrast.png (accessed 2 July 2022). For France, see https://www.archives-nationales.culture.gouv.fr/documents/10157/84911/carte_linguistique-france-2019.pdf/4b4c2b3a-8478-41b0-91b7-f11ff0fd8374 and https://lingvo.info/en/linvopedia/french (accessed 5 April 2023).

[5] Application of terms such as 'language' and 'dialect' can be controversial, particularly in a twentieth- or twenty-first century context: see the comment in Chapter 1 (this volume), footnote 54. In the case of Irish, Breton, and Occitan, the term 'dialect' in this chapter will refer to a regional variety of the language; in many instances in the case of France, we will use the more neutral term 'variety'. See also the discussion in Chapters 10 and 12 (this volume).

[6] See Lodge (1993).

[7] https://www.conseil-constitutionnel.fr/le-bloc-de-constitutionnalite/texte-integral-de-la-constitution-du-4-octobre-1958-en-vigueur (accessed 2 July 2022).

[8] https://www.irishstatutebook.ie/eli/cons/en/html#part1 (accessed 2 July 2022).

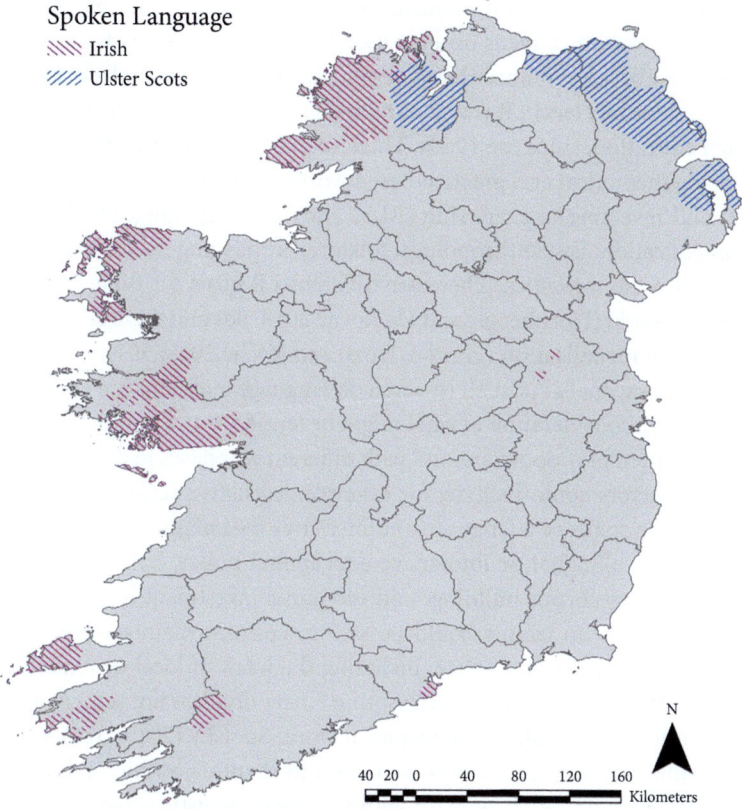

Figure 18.2 The official *Gaeltacht* and an estimation of the areas of Ulster Scots speech

twentieth and twenty-first centuries in both settings, before drawing together perspectives on the future vitality of minoritized languages in France and Ireland in Section 18.4.

18.2 Context and questions

18.2.1 Theoretical context: Language revitalization research

There is a vast literature on language revitalization (LR), including cross-linguistic theoretical work in very different language policy situations around the world.[9] Hinton, Huss, and Roche (2018: xxiii) note that contemporary LR research was

---

[9] See for example Jones and Ogilvie (2013); Jones (2015a, b); Hinton, Huss, and Roche (2018).

preceded by years of work on language loss, death, and shift; they pinpoint a 'turn' in the 1990s towards a focus on language maintenance and revitalization which has gathered pace ever since. However, this turn in the research focus was well behind community level LR which, they argue, had been taking place, particularly through education, since the 1960s. The research field is highly interdisciplinary, embracing theoretical and practice-based work on 'language policy and planning (LPP)' and 'reversing language shift (RLS)', and involving a range of scholarly fields such as education, law, anthropology, folklore, corpus linguistics, linguistic landscape, and sociolinguistics. There are different LR goals for different languages around the world (Hornberger and De Korne 2018: 96) and there is no one model for successful revitalization (Hinton, Huss, and Roche 2018: 501).

It is fair to say that almost all research on language maintenance and revitalization involves a consideration of what might be termed 'top-down' and 'bottom-up' factors, in different proportions and with different emphases in different contexts. Top-down factors could include, for example, legislative action (or inaction) in relation to the status of a language and measures that might flow from that such as support for bilingual or immersive educational policy, language visibility in the public space, corpus building, and economic investment in particular communities. Bottom-up factors could be said to concern mainly community and family-level policies and practice, including the work of local or regional grassroots organizations. However, this tempting binary divide is not sufficiently robust to account for the complexity of factors at work. Spolsky (2019: 326) labels it an oversimplification in the face of 'a complex and chaotic non-hierarchical system' where 'each level and each domain within a sociolinguistic ecology can have its own variety of language policy, and each can influence and be influenced by all the other domains'. For example, as McCarty (2018: 23) points out, highly localized instances of community practice can evolve into proactive organizations that become involved in status-, corpus-, and acquisition-planning on both a local and regional level. This was the case for the Shaw's Road *Gaeltacht* in Belfast, where a small group of families built homes together to form an Irish-speaking community whose members came to influence immersive education policy and planning for Irish (Mac Póilín 2018: 240–64). Similarly, as we shall see in our discussion of France in Section 18.3.2, national-level policy can support regional-level policy in cases where funds are devolved to allow regional organizations to engage in LPP.

Overall, then, LPP in the context of language revitalization involves a wide range of interlinked components from national level legislation to policy and practice by communities and speakers. There is widespread agreement in the literature that community-based language planning (CBLP) is particularly important (McCarty 2018). Lo Bianco (2018: 36) argues that successful revitalization requires LPP to go well beyond legal issues and education, important as these are, and notes the 'weak traction of law- and education-based RLS'. He supports a model for language planning which reflects the complexity of the dynamic between its different components, proposing the formulation 'A3 x P4 x G6', i.e. three 'authorisations' (through which laws are made, enacted, and facilitated), four modes of 'participation' (authorizations are activated by legal and policy texts, public discourse, performative action by powerful institutions or individuals, or technological innovation), and six 'goals' (participation aims to elevate the status of a language, modernize its corpus, promote its acquisition, expand its usage domains, elevate its prestige, and generate discourse that challenges negative attitudes and/or supports desired attitudes).

Lo Bianco (2018: 38) also discusses the need for 'discourse planning', i.e. 'how language ideologies, values, and attitudes are constructed, negotiated, and circulated in the rhetorical space of a particular polity and among RLS activists'. This involves complex multifaceted issues that raise questions about, and generate commentary on, which varieties and their speakers are considered to be legitimate or authentic. The negotiation of legitimacy and authenticity in turn can be related to debates around standardization, and/or ethnolinguistic, political, or cultural identity. Moreover, such debates intersect with discussion of the concept of 'new speakers', defined by O'Rourke, Pujolar, and Ramallo (2015) as speakers who have learnt a language outside the home, normally acquiring it through the education system or as adult learners. Hinton, Huss, and Roche (2018: 496–8) further note that there are a number of 'negatives to watch out for' in the process of LR, including strong potential for contestation within the speech community itself as well as tension in relations with wider society as regards political, cultural, or ethnolinguistic issues.

18.2.2 Historical context: The long nineteenth century

Developments in both France and Ireland in the long nineteenth century are critical in setting the historical context for policy and practice in the twentieth and twenty-first centuries. In terms of the legislative position at the end of the eighteenth century, French and English were already the languages officially designated for use in legal and administrative contexts. In the case of France, the variety spoken in the *Île de France* area (*francien*) had gradually gained prestige from the late Middle Ages onwards. Affirmed as the official language of administration in the *Ordonnance de Villers-Cotterêts* in 1539, it became in due course what we know as modern standard French.[10] English was introduced into Ireland following the Anglo-Norman conquest in 1169 but it was the more thorough conquests in the late sixteenth and seventeenth centuries that led to enduring

---

[10] For the archive copy, see https://archive.org/details/OrdonnanceVillersCotterets/mode/2up (accessed 6 September 2022) and for the legal text, see *Ordonnance de Villers-Cotterêts* (1539). It is important to note that regional languages continued to be found in many legal documents (such as wills) long after 1539.

English hegemony. By the beginning of the nineteenth century, while there were many more Irish speakers than in preceding centuries because of major growth in the population, the percentage that was Irish speaking may have been as little as 40%, and only 15%, perhaps, may have been Irish-speaking monoglots (Fitzgerald 2005: 19; Ó Tuathaigh 2015: 10; cf. Fitzgerald 1984, 2003). In France, by contrast, the vast majority of the population were still monolingual speakers of one of the regional languages: the Abbé Grégoire's (1794) *Rapport sur la nécessité et les moyens d'anéantir les patois et d'universaliser la langue française* famously put the figure for the number of fluent French speakers at just three million out of a population of twenty-five million (Chervel 2010: 14).[11] Nonetheless, as we shall see, there were many similarities across the two settings in the nature of the language–power dynamic, the tropes found in language ideologies, and in education policy.

In France, the promotion of French was a central tenet of post-revolutionary policy and strongly tied to Jacobin republican values. This is articulated particularly clearly in the Abbé Grégoire's report (Grégoire 1794) which associates the regional languages of France with the tropes of war, disease, superstition, obscurantism, and backwardness, contrasting them with French and its supposed associations with diplomacy, clarity, sophistication, and enlightenment. Crucially, alongside the centralization of government, French is promoted as a unifying force at every level of society: 'une république une et indivisible' requires 'l'usage unique et invariable de la langue de la liberté' (Grégoire 1794: 5–6). Language rights, in the revolutionaries' eyes, concerned first and foremost the right to speak the unifying, national language and to have access to all the perceived benefits this could bring. This status at home was matched, particularly in the second half of the nineteenth century, by opportunities for linguistic expansion abroad provided by France's colonial development. By the early twentieth century, French was established as the language of colonial power in significant parts of Africa, French Indo-China, the Caribbean, and the South Pacific, often with education systems for the more elite layers of society which were modelled on the French system and promoted the French language.

The nineteenth century was also marked by significant political instability and constitutional change in Ireland. The rebellion in 1798 by the United Irishmen, who had been inspired by the principles of the French revolution of 1789 (and had enlisted French military support) was quashed and the decision taken in its aftermath to centralize power in London, resulting in the Union of Great Britain and Ireland under one parliament in 1801. The devastation wrought on the Irish-speaking community by the famine of 1845–52 was severe and accelerated the

---

[11] https://archive.org/details/rapportsurlanece00greg/mode/2up (accessed 2 July 2022). Regarding the term *patois*, see Section 18.3.2, and Chapters 10 and 12 (this volume).

shift to English.[12] Irish had come to be seen as the language of poverty and backwardness and English as the language of progress and modernity (Denvir 1997: 45; Nic Craith 2012: 582). The eminent parliamentarian and leading nationalist, Daniel O'Connell, who was educated in France for a time during the Revolution,[13] is quoted as having described himself as being 'sufficiently utilitarian' not to regret the abandonment of Irish. The 'superior utility' of English, as the 'medium of modern communication', was more important and 'it would be of vast advantage to mankind if all . . . spoke the same language' (Daunt 1848: I, 14–15). We have seen that the role of a national unifying language, French, was crucial in the construction of post-revolutionary France; to this end, the language of the old elite became the language promoted by the new elite. For supporters of the union between Great Britain and Ireland, unity in language was also necessary and, as power resided in London, this language could only be English. In addition, while it would be difficult to conceive of English as a national language in Ireland in the nineteenth century, most prominent Irish nationalists came to accept its utility and power as an international language. The tropes of universality, modernity, superiority, utility, and civility articulated in relation to French were thus echoed not just in Britain but in the acceptance of English as the language of the political establishment in Ireland.

In terms of language policy impact, the most significant domain in both France and Ireland in the nineteenth century concerned education.[14] In France, this meant a plan to spread French to all sections of the population through the primary school system and the connected desire to eliminate the regional languages (Talleyrand-Périgord report of 1791; see Talleyrand-Périgord 1791; Chervel 2010: 30; Kibbee in preparation). Practices such as the *symbole* (Blanchet 2020), where pupils were punished for speaking *breton* by wearing a symbol around the neck, reinforced stigmatization, and indeed this practice was also found in the form of the tally stick in Ireland and in other forms elsewhere. In many regions, the task of teaching and spreading French was fraught with difficulties, given the high proportion of the population with no French and the consequential difficulty of finding appropriate teachers. For example, Duruy's survey in 1863 records that only 52% of school pupils could read and write French (Chervel 2010: 14). Nonetheless, the *Lois Jules Ferry* (1881–6),[15] which introduced compulsory free schooling through the medium of French for all children aged six to thirteen, marked an important

---

[12] Famine could be considered to fall into Spolsky's (2019) category of 'non-linguistic forces' (e.g. genocide, drought, war) that can have a dramatic impact on language vitality.
[13] See https://www.dib.ie/biography/oconnell-daniel-a6555 (accessed 2 July 2022) which alludes to his education in the English Colleges at Douai and St Omer.
[14] Space limits the discussion to the educational domain here. For detail on other domains such as the law and the church, see Lagrée, Roudeau, and Brunel (1995); Lagrée (1995); Doyle (2015); Phelan (2019); Kibbee (in preparation).
[15] For example, the 1881 legislation can be viewed here: https://www.legifrance.gouv.fr/download/securePrint?token=BcXoQ$fr7Qm$VKKbD6iC (accessed 8 September 2022).

point in the increasing consolidation of French as the national language. In Ireland, 1831 saw the establishment of a new school system (Akenson 2011 [1970]; Ó Ceallaigh and Ní Dhonnabháin 2015: 182), the national schools, and these were intended to advance English as the means to assimilation and enlightenment. They were endorsed (undoubtedly with some regret) by Irish-speaking parents keen to equip their children, particularly in the aftermath of the Great Famine, for the emigrant ship to Britain, America, and other parts of the Anglophone world. A report by a school inspector in 1856 describes the 'strong passion for education' possessed by a people 'who are themselves utterly illiterate' and ascribes the source of that passion to 'the desire to speak English' (Crowley 2000: 165). Literacy in English was a significant achievement of the national-school system. While in 1851, 53% of people aged five years and older could read in English, it was close to 90% by 1911 (Ó Gráda 1994: 240; Ó Tuathaigh 2015: 28). The teaching of Irish was prohibited at the outset and continued to be excluded from the curriculum during school hours until 1900 (Ó Huallacháin 1994: 55).

The nineteenth century ended with the Irish language in danger of extinction. An estimate of three million (largely monoglot) Irish speakers at the beginning of the century declined to 38,121 monoglot speakers recorded in the census of 1891 (Denvir 1997: 45). In France, despite significant cultural movements such as the Félibrige[16] in the case of *occitan*, French was established increasingly as the national language, particularly after the introduction of free and compulsory schooling. The language is firmly intertwined with French identity, with colonial expansion, and with the values of the Jacobin Republic. What distinguishes the situation in Ireland is the complexity of the nexus between language, religion, and identity as well as questions of political unity and separation. Whereas O'Connell was utilitarian in his acceptance of English, there were some in the Young Ireland movement, founded in 1842 and associated with a new national weekly paper called *The Nation* (inspired by the French daily *Le National*), who viewed the Irish language more positively. This was particularly true of Thomas Davis, a Protestant, who differed from O'Connell in favouring language over religion as a primary marker of Irish identity; in an article published in *The Nation* in 1843 entitled 'Our National Language', he argued for the restoration of Irish throughout society and the teaching of the language in the education system (Crowley 2000: 161–3). However, his support for Irish cannot be claimed to have had any immediate impact. Davis was before his time; the link between language, the nation, and political separatism was to be crucial later, as we shall see in Section 18.3.

---

[16] Founded by Frédéric Mistral in 1854. See http://www.felibrige.org (accessed 6 September 2022).

18.2.3 Research questions

In the light of the theoretical and historical contexts outlined in Sections 18.2.1 and 18.2.2, this chapter will ask: what are the key policy differences in France and Ireland in the twentieth and twenty-first centuries and what has been the impact of these for minoritized languages? To what extent do conflicting attitudes within the language community or negative reactions from wider society (Hinton, Huss, and Roche 2018) pose similar challenges for language revitalization in both settings? How do the complexities of debates relating to legitimacy, authenticity, and identity (Lo Bianco 2018) play out in the two cases? What roles might new speakers play (O'Rourke, Pujolar, and Ramallo 2015)? To what extent does the evidence in France and Ireland underscore Lo Bianco's (2018) point that law and education are not enough on their own and McCarty's (2018) emphasis on the importance of community practice? In the case of France, there will be more detailed discussion, by way of example, of *occitan* and *breton*,[17] but other regional languages will be mentioned. In the case of Ireland, the emphasis will be on Irish.

18.3 Minoritized languages in Ireland and France: The twentieth and twenty-first centuries

18.3.1 Overview

In France, the full impact of the education policy outlined in Section 18.2.2 on minoritized languages was to be dramatic and was complemented by national conscription during the two World Wars. The direction of travel has been consistently one of French becoming increasingly widespread and regional languages losing out, with intergenerational transmission dropping substantially. Although the French census does not ask specifically about language use, the Enquête famille (1999),[18] undertaken by the Institut national de la statistique et des études économiques and the Institut national d'études démographiques, shows a clear trajectory of decline in the course of the twentieth century, albeit at different paces for different languages. The survey focuses on intergenerational transmission between adults to whom their parents regularly spoke a regional language, and the children of these adults, showing substantial decline across the board. For example, regular use of *breton* between parent and child fell from around 70% in the early twentieth century to less than 5% in the later part of the century (Héran, Filhon, and Deprez 2002).

---

[17] See Chapter 16 (this volume) for a detailed discussion of *breton*.
[18] https://ehf.web.ined.fr/Publications/INSEE/C_Stat_93_fr.pdf (accessed 2 July 2022).

The situation in Ireland was more complex. We have noted that Thomas Davis believed in the revival of the Irish language and the Gaelic League was established in Dublin in 1893 expressly with that purpose.[19] Its philosophy, initially articulated most strongly by Douglas Hyde, its first President, was grounded in romanticism, particularly the belief that a nation must honour and maintain its national language. However, the cultural nationalism which had been the cornerstone of the Gaelic League at its foundation had morphed into political and militant nationalism by the outbreak of World War I. Patrick Pearse and the majority of the leaders of the 1916 uprising against British rule were members of the Gaelic League. The *Anglo-Irish Treaty* (1921)[20] provided for the foundation of the Irish Free State and confirmed the partition of Ireland and creation of Northern Ireland. Despite support for Irish in the *Constitution of the Irish Free State Act* (1922)[21] and, particularly, in the *Constitution of Ireland* (1937), the Irish language has continued to decline in the *Gaeltacht* and is now in an extremely precarious position (Ó Giollagáin and Mac Donnacha 2008; Mac Donnacha 2014).[22] However, the foundations set down by the Gaelic League have ensured that there are large numbers of L2 speakers: in the most recent census which dates from 2022 (Central Statistics Office 2023), 40.4% of respondents claim the ability to speak Irish (a similar figure to 39.8% in the 2016 census), although only 1.45% use it daily outside the education system.[23] In the most recent Northern Ireland census of 2021 (NISRA 2023), at least 6.48% claim to be able to speak the language to some degree, while 12.45% claim to have 'some ability' in Irish,[24] an increase from 10.65% in 2011[25] (NISRA 2014).

In this section, we will approach both contexts from a national policy perspective, including legislation (in Section 18.3.2), and from a perspective that focuses on practice by communities and speakers, including discussion of questions relating to identity, authenticity, and legitimacy (in Section 18.3.3). In certain key respects, particularly in the policy domain, France and the Republic of Ireland stand in sharp contrast, while at the same time, common challenges can be identified.

---

[19] https://cnag.ie/en/ (accessed 17 September 2022).
[20] https://cain.ulster.ac.uk/issues/politics/docs/ait1921.htm (accessed 10 September 2022).
[21] https://www.irishstatutebook.ie/eli/1922/act/1/enacted/en/print (accessed 10 September 2022).
[22] For a differing interpretation of the sociolinguistic evidence, see Ó Laighin (2022: 11, 196).
[23] For the 2016 census figures for Irish, see Central Statistics Office (2017: 66–7) and for 2022, see https://www.cso.ie/en/releasesandpublications/ep/p-cpsr/censusofpopulation2022-summaryresults/educationandirishlanguage/ (accessed 9 June 2023).
[24] https://www.nisra.gov.uk/publications/census-2021-main-statistics-language-tables (accessed 25 May 2023).
[25] https://www.nisra.gov.uk/publications/2011-census-key-statistics-tables-ethnicity-identity-language-and-religion (accessed 29 June 2020).

18.3.2 The legal and policy context

There has been relatively little by way of positive intervention in terms of legislation and/or policy in relation to regional languages in the course of the twentieth and twenty-first centuries at national level in France. The *Loi Deixonne* (1951)[26] permitted the teaching of certain regional languages at primary level (*langues d'oc, breton, basque, catalan*, later extended to include *alsacien* and *corse*) for one hour per week (later extended to three elective hours), with the *Loi Haby* (1975)[27] introducing provision at secondary level.[28] However, not only were there obvious exclusions, notably all the *langues d'oïl*, but also, the *Loi Deixonne* is widely regarded as having been of limited value in terms of revitalization or even language maintenance (Jacob and Gordon 1985: 121). French was reaffirmed in 1992 as the language of the Republic in an amendment to the Constitution (Article 2: 'La langue de la République est le français') and France refused to ratify the European Charter for Regional and Minority Languages in 1999,[29] considering it to be anti-constitutional, despite a report commissioned for the Prime Minister (written by Bernard Poignant) which was largely favourable to ratification (Roger 2019).[30] As noted in Section 18.1, the choice of terminology is not without controversy: while the term *langues régionales* is now used widely, both politically and by bodies such as the Délégation générale à la langue française et aux langues de France, many speakers and some dialectologists use the term *patois*, especially for the Romance varieties, a term which suggests a lack of prestige and linguistic capital, or even a value judgement on the speaker's French.[31] The issue is particularly controversial in relation to the *langues d'oïl* (McCrea 2019), many of which are in an advanced state of decline.

In the twenty-first century, there have been glimpses of a more benign approach, including a 2008 amendment to the Constitution (Article 75.1 which states: 'les langues régionales appartiennent au patrimoine de la France').[32] There is publicly funded support at regional level through the Offices publics which take a leading role in promoting *breton, occitan, basque*, and *catalan*, for example, and

---

[26] https://www.legifrance.gouv.fr/jorf/id/JORFTEXT000000886638 (accessed 17 September 2022).
[27] https://www.legifrance.gouv.fr/jorf/id/JORFTEXT000000334174/ (accessed 17 September 2022).
[28] See Mooney (2015: 155); Harrison (2019); McCrea (2019); Kibbee (in preparation).
[29] https://coe.int/en/web/european-charter-regional-or-minority-languages/text-of-the-charter (accessed 10 September 2022).
[30] https://www.vie-publique.fr/rapport/24310-langues-et-cultures-regionales-rapport-au-premier-ministre (accessed 7 September 2022).
[31] For discussion of terminology, see Chapters 10 and 12, this volume; see also Joubert (2015); Costa (2017); Dourdet (2019); Harrison and Joubert (2019).
[32] This was created after a failed attempt to have a clause about regional languages inserted into Article 1 (Nolan 2018).

there is some, if limited, use of regional languages by television and radio stations.[33] In the educational sphere, the picture is highly variable across France, with tangible progress for *breton, corse, alsacien, basque*, and *occitan*, although immersion/bilingual schools (e.g. the *Diwan* and *Calandreta* schools) are not funded in the same way as French-language schools in the public system and are therefore under considerable financial pressure.[34] A vote in the Assemblée nationale in 2014 could have facilitated a constitutional amendment which in turn would have permitted ratification of the European Charter for Regional and Minority Languages (1999). However, despite a comprehensive report to the Minister for Culture by the Comité consultatif pour la promotion des langues régionales et de la pluralité linguistique interne in 2013,[35] public protests, and an IFOP[36] poll that suggested that 75% of the French population would support greater recognition of regional languages (Nolan 2018), the Charter has never been ratified in France.[37] The arguments working against ratification have included the perceived adequacy of current legislation, the costs of support for regional languages, 'the spectre of migrants' languages', the threat of ethnic separatism, and, above all, the 'attack' on French sovereignty and its constitutional principles (Roger 2019: 316–27). Most recently (in May 2021), a significant development has been the passing of the *Loi relative à la protection patrimoniale des langues régionales et à leur promotion* (proposed by Deputy Paul Molac), giving regional languages the status of *trésor national* (which recalls the description of the Māori language in Aotearoa–New Zealand as a *taonga*) and offering significantly improved support for their use in public services, education, and heritage. The *patrimoine linguistique* is formally redefined as 'la langue française et les langues régionales', greater support will be provided for bilingual and immersive education, bilingual signage will be possible without restriction (including spelling features that do not exist in French), and regional languages can, in theory, be offered to all pupils at all levels of the education system.[38]

---

[33] See Woehrling (2013) for an excellent account of regional policies. See also Ó hIfearnáin (2013) for discussion of policies in Brittany; Coyos (2019) for *basque*; and Costa and Gasquet-Cyrus (2013) for *occitan*.

[34] See, for example, Lieutard and Verny (2007); Moal (2009); Beacco and Cherkaoui Messin (2010); Broudic (2010, 2011, 2013); Goalabré (2015); Martel (2016).

[35] https://www.culture.gouv.fr/Thematiques/Langue-francaise-et-langues-de-France/Nos-missions/Promouvoir-les-langues-de-France/Langues-regionales/Rapport-du-Comite-consultatif-pour-la-promotion-des-langues-regionales-et-de-la-pluralite-linguistique-interne-2013 (accessed 7 September 2022).

[36] IFOP is l'Institut d'études opinion et marketing en France et à l'international.

[37] It has not been ratified in the Republic of Ireland either because of the Irish language's status there as 'national' and 'first official' language (rather than 'minority' or 'regional').

[38] https://www.legifrance.gouv.fr/loda/id/JORFTEXT000043524722?init=true&page=1&query=Loi+Molac&searchField=ALL&tab_selection=all (accessed 2 June 2023).

In contrast to the French situation, legislative support for Irish in the Irish Republic is well-established.[39] For reasons of identity, there is strong support for the maintenance of Irish; 64% of the population in the Irish Republic agreed in 2013 that 'without Irish, the Republic of Ireland would lose its identity as a separate culture' while 33% of respondents in Northern Ireland agreed that Irish was 'a fundamental part of the identity of Northern Ireland' (Darmody and Daly 2015; Walsh 2020).[40] Support in the Irish Republic has been underpinned by the *Gaeltacht Act* (2012),[41] and by the *Official Languages (Amendment) Act* (2021), which amends the *Official Languages Act* (2003).[42] The 20-Year Strategy for the Irish Language aims to increase the number of daily speakers of Irish from 83,000 to 250,000 by 2030.[43] The language is visible in official signage and is a compulsory element of primary and second level education.[44] In addition, there is a vibrant Irish-medium immersion sector at both levels although the figures for those enrolled in this sector are small.[45] Irish is a requirement to matriculate for entry into the colleges of the National University (O'Rourke and Walsh 2020: 60). It is also supported in the media; the creation in 1996 of the Irish-medium television station, TG4, has raised the profile of Irish across the island. In terms of linking use of Irish to economic development, *Gaeltacht* communities are supported by the state agency Údarás na Gaeltachta, whose objective is 'to ensure that Irish remains the main communal language of the Gaeltacht' by fostering enterprise and job creation.[46]

However, there is widespread criticism in recent research of both policy and its implementation. There is clear evidence that, in linguistic terms, Ireland has been marketed internationally as an English-speaking country since the 1950s (Walsh 2021: 327). Indeed, this period has been noted as heralding the end of the policy of regaelicization (i.e. the revitalization of Irish as *'the* national language'), and the publication in 1965 of a White Paper (i.e. a policy document produced by government) on the restoration of the Irish language has been stressed as a

---

[39] See Walsh (2016: 452) who has identified 197 sections or schedules in which clear reference is made to the promotion or use of Irish in enactments of the Irish government in the period 1922–2016. Note that all references to Walsh in this chapter are to John Walsh (not Olivia Walsh as elsewhere in the volume).

[40] Note that there is a problem with the wording of the question in relation to Northern Ireland (which is a contested term). Respondents may have responded differently if the context was 'the island of Ireland'.

[41] https://www.gov.ie/en/publication/cc6a9-gaeltacht-act-2012/ (accessed 2 July 2022). Note also the *Gaeltacht* Education Policy which was formulated in 2016: https://assets.gov.ie/24606/a526faa89eb64675ab685c074f93b0af.pdf (accessed 2 July 2022).

[42] https://www.gov.ie/en/press-release/77070-official-languages-act-amendment-2021-signed-by-the-president-of-ireland/# (accessed 2 July 2022).

[43] See https://www.gov.ie/en/publication/f67134-20-year-strategy-for-the-irish-language-2010-2030/ p. 3 (accessed 2 July 2022).

[44] There is concern, however, that the conditions which allow exemptions from studying Irish are being exploited and that this is bringing the policy into disrepute (Walsh 2022: 193).

[45] See further O'Rourke and Walsh (2020: 61).

[46] https://udaras.ie/ (accessed 15 August 2022).

'critical juncture' (Walsh 2021: 326).[47] While restating the primacy of Irish as the national language, the White Paper emphasized the importance of English (Government of Ireland 1965: 12), and the senior civil servant responsible for it, T.K. Whitaker, commented later (in 1983) on the 'unattainability' of the 'extreme aim' of replacing English with Irish which would 'sharpen the antagonism of those who see no point in preserving Irish' and 'alienate the sympathy of those who cherish Irish but value the possession of English' (Chambers 2008: 341). The covert language policy in the Irish Republic, therefore, is viewed by many as an acceptance of the primacy of English and the public service has been described in the past as 'less than enthusiastic' about policy implementation when it comes to Irish (Walsh 2015: 74).[48] Moreover, support for Irish is vulnerable to 'non-linguistic forces' (Spolsky 2019): the financial crisis of 2008 resulted in draconian cuts on spending on the *Gaeltacht* and Údarás na Gaeltachta suffered a 73% reduction in funding in the period 2008–15 (Ó Ceallaigh 2019: 96; Walsh 2021: 317).

The wider legislative picture for minoritized languages in Ireland is also complicated by the existence of the two jurisdictions.[49] None of the traditional *Gaeltacht* regions extends into Northern Ireland and support for the language is polarized to a considerable degree on the basis of political allegiance. The *Good Friday Agreement*, in acknowledging for the first time the importance of linguistic diversity in Northern Ireland (Northern Ireland Office 1998: 19), led to the establishment of the cross-border Language Body comprised of Foras na Gaeilge (the Irish Language Agency) and the Boord o Ulstèr–Scotch (the Ulster–Scots Agency). In the same year, the *Education (Northern Ireland) Order* (1998) placed a duty on the Department of Education to encourage and facilitate the development of Irish-medium education.[50] The *St Andrews Agreement* (2006)[51] included an undertaking by the UK government to introduce Irish language legislation; this was never legally binding and has led in recent years to political mobilization by activists, particularly An Dream Dearg. The lack of consensus over Irish language legislation was catapulted to the top of the political agenda with the fall of the Northern Ireland Assembly in 2017 and played a major role in the failure to restore the Assembly for three years until the British and Irish governments brokered the *New*

---

[47] Walsh (2021: 324–6) has identified two periods: 'revival and gaelicisation' (1922–65) and 'bilingualism' (1965 to the present). Ó Riagáin (1997: 19, 23) distinguishes between 'stagnation and retreat' (1948–70) and 'benign neglect' (since 1970). Ó Giollagáin (2014b: 25) identifies four periods: 'traditional revivalism' (1920s–1971), 'aspirational bilingualism' (1971–90s), 'minority survivalism' (1990s–2009), and 'rhetorical bilingualism' (since 2009). For further discussion of the discourse of retreat, see also Ó Giollagáin (2014a) and Ó Murchú (2002).

[48] The *Official Languages (Amendment) Act* (2021) has been described as 'a key turning point' which has the potential to increase the provision of public services in Irish (Walsh 2022: 2) and we await the impact of this.

[49] For an explanation of the two jurisdictions, see Section 18.1. For more on the political and legislative context in Northern Ireland, see Ó Mainnín (2021).

[50] https://www.legislation.gov.uk/nisi/1998/1759/article/89/made (accessed 10 September 2022).

[51] https://www.legislation.gov.uk/ukpga/2006/53/contents (accessed 10 September 2022).

Decade New Approach agreement (Northern Ireland Office 2020). This formed the basis of the legislation enacted at Westminster in 2022, the *Identity and Language (Northern Ireland) Act,* which specifies its purpose in Part 7B (78J) to be the provision of 'official recognition of the status of the Irish language'.[52] However, it does not make similar provision for Ulster Scots or specify what the status of the Irish language is.[53] Together, the 2020 agreement and 2022 Act have provided for the creation of an Office of Identity and Cultural Expression, two language commissioners, a central translation service, the use of both languages in the Assembly, the employment of Ulster Scots in the education system, and a requirement that the Northern Ireland Executive produces strategies for both Irish and Ulster Scots (Northern Ireland Office 2020: 15–16).[54]

18.3.3 Practice: Communities, speakers, identity, authenticity, legitimacy

In Section 18.2.1 we noted that Hinton, Huss, and Roche (2018: 496–8) mention a number of negative factors in the context of language revitalization, one of which concerns conflicting attitudes inside the language community. In the French context, there can be a lack of consensus about names, legitimacy, political alignment, and ethnolinguistic groupness; this is all the more complex given the multiplicity of languages and contexts.[55] One particularly clear example concerns *occitan,* where linguistic, ethnolinguistic, historical, political, and territorial factors come into play. Some speakers identify more closely with particular varieties (e.g. *béarnais, provençal, auvergnat, limousin*), while revivalists are split into different groupings such as *occitanistes* and the *provençal* movement, the former identifying with a broader linguistic entity that embraces different varieties and the latter with *provençal* as originally promoted by the Félibrige movement in the nineteenth century (Mooney 2015; Joubert 2019). In 2000, a third group of revivalists entered the scene, i.e. the Collectif Prouvènço, claiming strong alignment with the people (as opposed to perceived middle class movements), overlaid with territorial discourse which 'rejects any Occitanist claim to legitimacy in Provence' (Costa and Gasquet-Cyrus 2013: 219). As Costa and Gasquet-Cyrus (2013) show, factions can also map onto political positions: for example, the *provençal* movement is centre-right

---

[52] https://www.legislation.gov.uk/ukpga/2022/45/contents/enacted (accessed 6 January 2024).
[53] For Ulster Scots, see Part 7C.
[54] The Department of Culture, Arts, and Leisure had formulated strategies for both Irish and Ulster Scots for the period 2015–35. This department has since been replaced by the Department for Communities which established expert advisory panels in 2021 to advise on updated strategies for both languages. The panels' reports were published in 2022 and a public call for views on these was conducted in March and April 2022. No further publications have appeared at the time of writing (which is just a month after the restoration of the NI government in February 2024, following a two-year haitus). See https://www.communities-ni.gov.uk/publications (accessed 2 June 2023).
[55] See Costa and Gasquet-Cyrus (2013) and Costa (2017) for a discussion of 'groupness'.

in political orientation whereas the *occitan* movement is firmly left of centre. The wider *anti-occitaniste* movement includes both scholarly and grassroots members, and embraces a strong contingent of *gascon* (including *béarnais*) speakers. The challenges of conflicting perspectives on legitimacy and divergent political allegiances are considerable and can impact on the choice of varieties/dialects used and examined in the education system where there can also be inconsistencies; while children in the *Calandreta* learn *occitan*, which is openly identified as potentially different from what they hear at home (Mooney 2015: 161), they are asked to specify a dialect at *baccalauréat* level.[56]

These diverse and multilevel groupings within the community of language speakers are further interwoven with questions of standardization and new speakers.[57] Although the latter term is not used as much in the context of *occitan* as *breton*, the Collectif Prouvènço advocates for the standard (the *graphie classique*) and this differs from the form advocated by the *Félibres* and from the orthography used by speakers of localized varieties such as *béarnais* (Joubert 2015). Joubert (2015: 178) maintains that the 'selection' and 'acceptance' stages of a standardized form are important for the '(re)discovery of a sense of legitimacy with speakers who have hitherto been deprived of frames of reference'; she argues that these stages have not occurred for *occitan*. Indeed, speakers can sometimes take contradictory positions: Costa (2017: 129 ff.) discusses a case where an *occitan* teacher defines legitimacy broadly while simultaneously disapproving of new-speaker features that may be due to French influence. Costa's (2017) discussion of attitudes relating to, and the attitudes of, traditional speakers also points up serious contradictions: on the one hand, traditional speakers are viewed as totemic, given their status as those who pass on the language through intergenerational transmission; on the other hand, activists and/or dialectologists can hold, at times, very different views from traditional speakers on specific linguistic features. Joubert goes so far as to argue that the *occitan* revitalization effort in the first half of the twentieth century largely ignored the needs of speakers, where one size clearly does not fit all: the needs of the young activists are not the same as those of particular scholarly groups which in turn are different from those of self-defined *patois* speakers (Joubert 2015: 178–82).

In the case of *breton*, in addition to dialectal differences across four regions in Brittany, many scholars have focused on the issue of new speakers who have often learnt *breton* through the *Diwan* school system (Hornsby and Le Quentel 2013; Hornsby 2017). Hornsby and Le Quentel (2013) add 'native authenticists' to these categories: an ideologically entrenched counter-elite who revere native speakers and are highly critical of new speakers (Hornsby 2017; Moal, Ó Murchadha, and

---

[56] See Harrison (2019) for a discussion of the lack of clarity amongst teachers in Alsace in relation to the varieties they are permitted to use in class.
[57] See Section 18.2.1. See also Costa (2015) and O'Rourke (2018).

Walsh 2018). At the same time, research with traditional native speakers who have different levels of *breton* shows evidence that they consistently denigrate their own speech, even in the case of fluent speakers who were brought up speaking *breton*. Adkins (2013: 66) argues, in relation to one informant, that the lack of an educational dimension to her *breton* and an assimilation of metalinguistic attitudes from her French education have both contributed to her low opinion of her ability to speak *breton* while at the same time she evaluates *néo-breton* as not 'real'. Hornsby (2017: 99) also cites the case of a native speaker telling a new-speaker neighbour that the latter's *breton* is 'good' but 'not the same'. In recent years, the existence of divides—such as new vs. traditional speakers—has been strongly challenged. Amongst *breton* users in media contexts, Davies-Deacon (2020: 301) observes 'a multiplicity of practices [. . .], affected by context, medium, register, personal attitudes and ideologies, and individual speakers' trajectories regarding the acquisition and use of Breton'. For Hornsby (2017), it is more positive and productive to view these different categories as a continuum of speech that includes a range of different ways of speaking in a postvernacular context, whereby *breton* is now used in many domains where it was not previously found. Indeed Le Nevez (2013: 100) argues for the need to focus on the community of speakers using *breton* as 'situated social practice' rather than a 'fixed and normative code': 'for initiatives to be truly effective they must be inclusive of people who speak *breton* in diverse and different ways and also take into account the complex relationships between diverse and different language communities in Brittany'.[58]

Finally, but importantly in the case of France, levels of ethnolinguistic mobilization also vary significantly across the different regional languages. For example, Cole and Hardindéguy (2013) demonstrate the strength of ethnolinguistic mobilization (albeit taking different forms) in the case of both *corse* and *breton*; as community-level activism is extremely strong, this has worked in favour of the vitality of both languages, despite differing views on questions such as legitimacy and authenticity. The authors contrast this with the much weaker situation in the case of *picard* (one of the *langues d'oïl*), where it is not possible to speak of significant levels of ethnolinguistic mobilization. When combined with what Cole and Hardindéguy (2013) term 'assymetric endogenous institutionalisation' (i.e. differential institutionalized support for different languages within France: see Section 18.3.1), the position of some regional languages such as *picard* can become extremely weak, and this is further underscored by linguistic proximity to French in the case of most *langues d'oïl*.

As regards Ireland, questions relating to legitimacy, authenticity, identity, and new speakers differ in some respects across the two minoritized languages, Irish and Ulster Scots. Politico-cultural alignments are much more salient than in

---

[58] For discussions of similar issues in other regional languages, see Kasstan (2019) on *francoprovençal/arpitan*; Harrison (2019) on *alsacien*; Dourdet (2019) on *poitevin-saintongeais*.

France. Historically, Irish was viewed as having a high degree of association with Irish identity throughout the island. However, recent research has highlighted that there is no longer a simple binary relationship between language and identity in the Irish Republic. While cultural nationalism may be a factor for some, there is a wide range of 'identity constellations' to which younger speakers now adhere (O'Rourke and Walsh 2020: 172; Walsh 2020: 40-1). In the course of the conflict in Northern Ireland between 1969 and 1998, Irish was seen as a 'language of resistance' by some in the nationalist community,[59] and continuing hostility towards the promotion of the language from sections of the unionist community certainly constitutes a 'negative reaction from the surrounding society', one of the potential obstacles to revitalization identified by Hinton, Huss, and Roche (2018: 496-8). Nonetheless, recent years have seen renewed engagement with the language as a shared heritage, and some breaking down of binary oppositions, particularly in the context of the *Turas* project in east Belfast.[60]

It would also be over-simplistic to assume that the question of the status of Ulster Scots (see Crowley 2006) dovetails neatly with divisions around identity; it has its detractors in the unionist community despite the fact that it was the unionist community's political representatives who argued the case for it in the negotiations leading to the *Good Friday Agreement* of 1998 (Northern Ireland Office 1998; Mac Póilín 2018: 49-51). For some in urban areas it is a marked rural variety (see Wolf 2020: 132). For others, while Ulster Scots is respected as part of a broader Scottish cultural inheritance, it is an oral variety with which they may be less comfortable when it is committed to writing.[61] This is despite an earlier written tradition and—in the case of its antecedent, Scots—power and prestige in late medieval Scotland. Ulster Scots cannot be said to have a prominent community of new speakers and there have been major debates about its authenticity as a language. Its greatest obstacle is its close kinship with English, which has made it (and Scots in Scotland) very vulnerable to Anglicization,[62] and there are some, therefore, who see it as a regional variety of English.

As in the case of *breton*, scholars emphasize the complexity of the dynamic between new and traditional speakers, and agree that the social conditions of late modernity and globalization have impacted strongly on the perception and practice of speaking minoritized languages (Ó hIfearnáin 2018; Hornsby and Ó

---

[59] On the use of Irish by republican prisoners, see Mac Giolla Chríost (2012) and Mac Ionnrachtaigh (2013).

[60] https://www.ebm.org.uk/turas/ (accessed 2 July 2022). See also Mac Coinnigh, Ervine, and Deeds (2019) and Dunlevy (2020).

[61] For an instance of antagonism towards Ulster Scots from within the unionist community in the aftermath of its elevation in status by the *Good Friday Agreement*, see the letter from a 'Concerned Taxpayer' published in the *Belfast Telegraph*, 27 November 1999.

[62] On concern about Anglicization as witnessed in the Ulster Scots Language Society's journal, *Ullans*, see Gardner (2015: 18). As noted in Section 18.1 and earlier in the current section, a similar issue arises for several of the *langues d'oïl* in France due to their proximity with French.

Murchadha 2021). In terms of authenticity and legitimacy in relation to Irish, the traditional dialects have been seen historically as the only authentic spoken varieties and the teaching of the language in universities has validated these as the target varieties for learners (Ó Murchadha and Ó hIfearnáin 2018: 461; Ó Murchadha 2020: 44–5). The status of Irish as first national language in the Republic naturally required the development of a written 'standard' (*An Caighdeán Oifigiúil*) which was first published in 1958 (and revised in 2012 and 2017).[63] The process has always been accompanied by controversy (Ó Háinle 1994: 754–64, 781–5, 791–3); the standard remains primarily a written variety and attempts to encourage a spoken standard (Ó Baoill 1986) have not met with success. Recently, however, arguments have been made for reviving the idea of a spoken standard for those who 'do not feel linguistic affiliation with the Gaeltacht' and for the option of 'becoming an Irish speaker without necessarily adopting a traditional variety' (O'Rourke and Walsh 2020: 175). Those researching the Irish of new speakers have highlighted the evidence for emerging speech practices which are not modelled primarily on that of the *Gaeltacht* but on varieties that have arisen from the use of the written standard in education and, notably, in Irish-medium schools outside the *Gaeltacht* (Ó Murchadha 2021: 749, 752). This has been described as 'post-Gaeltacht speech' (Ó Murchadha and Ó hIfearnáin 2018: 460, 467) and it has been suggested that younger generations of *Gaeltacht* speakers (discussed in the next paragraph) and new speakers alike are coming to see this as a legitimate variety through a process of value-levelling which has been termed 'democratization' (Ó Murchadha 2021: 750; see also Ó Murchadha 2013, 2018a, b, 2019, 2020). The legitimization of new speaker supralocal levelled forms has also recently been noted in relation to France, with Hall, Kasstan, and Hornsby (2019: 163) commenting that 'the social advantages enjoyed by many new-speaker activists lend prestige to the levelled forms that they tend to prefer'.[64]

As Irish continues to decline in its traditional heartlands, it is clear that the language revival has failed to ensure the survival of the *Gaeltacht* as a distinct and vibrant linguistic community. The increasing prevalence of English in the *Gaeltacht* has led to subtractive bilingualism (Lenoach, Ó Giollagáin, and Ó Curnáin 2012; Ó Giollagáin and Ó Curnáin 2016) and, consequently, concern has been expressed about incomplete language acquisition and the relative competence of native speakers of Irish.[65] The year 1960 has been identified as a milestone in the transformation of traditional life and the Irish language in Ireland (Ó Riagáin 1997: 141) and dialectologists working on the linguistic characteristics of native-speaker Irish distinguish between 'traditional' and 'post-traditional'

---

[63] Note that the Republic and Northern Ireland use the same standardized form.
[64] Note that this reference is to David Hornsby and not to Michael Hornsby, as in the other references in the chapter.
[65] The controversial question of competence and the ideologies which play a role in this are discussed in Ó Murchadha (2020).

speakers, the former born before 1960. They further distinguish two sub-categories of post-traditional Irish: 'untraditional' Irish spoken by those born between 1960 and 1990, and 'reduced' Irish spoken by those born since 1990 who are further down the continuum of language acquisition and language shift (Ó Curnáin 2009: 117, 2012: 287; Lenoach 2012: 21–5). Indeed, we have referred above to the possible convergence in speech practices between the reduced Irish of young speakers (born post 1990) from the *Gaeltacht* and the Irish of post-*Gaeltacht* new speakers. The *Comprehensive Linguistic Study of the Use of Irish in the Gaeltacht* (Ó Giollagáin et al. 2007; see also Ó Giollagáin and Charlton 2015) has illustrated that opportunities for the social use of Irish by young people are now so limited that speaking Irish is associated by them with two institutional settings, the home and classroom, and is not in accordance with norms which their own cohort has established (Ó Giollagáin and Mac Donnacha 2008: 116).[66]

The insufficient response by government and institutions to the continuing decline in the vitality of the *Gaeltacht* has led to calls for a whole new regeneration strategy which would include the prioritization of the needs of L1 over L2 speakers (Ó Giollagáin and Ó Curnáin 2016: 107–12). The government for its part responded to the 2007 report by dividing the *Gaeltacht* into twenty-six language-planning districts under the terms of the *Gaeltacht Act* of 2012. It also created two new territorial categories: 'Gaeltacht Service Towns' and 'Irish Language Networks' (Walsh 2021: 313). The commendable strides in attempts to form new *Gaeltacht* communities in Northern Ireland, notably the *Gaeltacht* Quarter in west Belfast and An Carn (Carntogher) in County Derry, have also received recognition under these plans. However, while all of this appears to empower communities, the approach has been criticized, as LPP now takes place 'at arm's length from the state' which outsources it (without sufficient funding) to voluntary committees (see Ó Giollagáin 2014b; Walsh 2021: 317, 336). It has been argued that if the LPP process is to have a chance of national success, a more comprehensive spread of adequately resourced Irish Language Networks is required (O'Rourke and Walsh 2020: 175) in the light of the growth in numbers of new speakers.

18.3.4 The impact of the policy–practice dynamic

As we have seen, France and the Republic of Ireland in the twentieth and twenty-first centuries contrast sharply in terms of national policy and legislation. Only in 2021 has France shown evidence of more concrete legislative support but it remains to be seen how this operates in practice. While the Irish Republic, on

---

[66] In the 2007 survey, only 24% of young people in the strongest of the Irish-speaking districts spoke Irish within their peer group and this figure dropped to 9% in the *Gaeltacht* as a whole (Ó Giollagáin et al. 2020: 137).

the other hand, has a variety of legislation which supports the Irish language, there have been major criticisms of the practical effect of that support. The language planning regime is inconsistent, and it has been alleged that no government since independence has adopted a programmatic approach to implementing policy aims. On the contrary, significant policy initiatives have been achieved due to 'vigorous campaigns by civil society and are not a result of the magnanimity of government' (Walsh 2015: 62).

Political and cultural affiliations vary greatly in strength for different languages in France and there is evidence, at least in some cases, of substantial conflicting views within language communities. Ethnolinguistic mobilization has been more salient in the case of Ireland, although there are important nuances here, too, in the case of both Irish and Ulster Scots, and there is certainly tension in Northern Ireland in wider societal conversation in relation to language. In both France and Ireland there is a complex debate around issues concerning authenticity, legitimacy, and different categories of speakers and their varieties, with many similar issues emerging in both settings. Moreover, in both contexts, the dynamic between falling numbers of native speakers and the increasing prominence of new speakers is very important, although that dynamic is extremely variable in France given the multiplicity of languages involved. There are also some emerging parallels in the apparent breakdown of a putative sharp divide between new and traditional speakers (in particular as regards *breton* and Irish), although the factors and terminology involved can vary in different contexts, both within France and between France and Ireland. This is a live issue in the two contexts, both for the evolution of the languages in question and for communities of speakers in the future.

18.4 Perspectives on the future

Having noted a number of common challenges between France and Ireland in Section 18.3, we assess, in this final section, the extent to which, in the light of the literature on LPP and RLS, the contrasting policy contexts in France and Ireland may result in different levels of vitality for minoritized languages in the future.

In France, it is to be hoped that the *Loi Molac* may indeed herald enhanced status and esteem for regional languages, although political support is not universal (see Section 18.3.2). Moreover, President Macron has made a number of statements suggesting support for regional languages, and ratification of the European Charter was in En Marche's founding manifesto.[67] One of the conundrums of the French context is that many citizens who are advocates for regional languages are also supporters of core values attached to the French Republic, one of which has

---

[67] https://storage.googleapis.com/en-marche-fr/COMMUNICATION/Programme-Emmanuel-Macron.pdf (accessed 7 September 2022).

been the elevation and promotion of French above all other languages. However, identities such as *occitan* or *breton* do not necessarily attenuate, let alone cancel out, a strong sense of French identity and the republican values that accompany it. More recent commentary on the question of language rights has focused not on the opposition between republican values and the group rights associated with advocating for regional languages, but rather on the modernization of Jacobin republicanism: 'the key to successful minority language revitalisation in France lies within, specifically in the modernisation of French republicanism, not in measures that seek to undermine its core ideals. Indeed, most linguists and activists in France concerned with the plight of regional languages themselves subscribe to republican values in some form' (Oakes 2019: v). Oakes (2017, 2019) argues that the modernization of French republicanism would have the added advantage of not relegating regional languages to the domain of cultural artefacts rather than living forms of communication, a possible danger with the terminology of article 75–1 (see Section 18.3.2) which defines them as an important part of the heritage of France and perhaps also with the framing of the *Loi Molac*, where regional languages have the status of *trésor national*.

This tension between modern French republicanism and the position of regional languages is evident in the then-Prime Minister Jean Castex's comments on finding a solution to the question of immersive education (following President Macron's intervention in support of the *Loi Molac* in May 2021): Castex cites 'la volonté politique du gouvernement de préserver la richesse que constituent, dans le cadre de l'unité de la République, les langues régionales'.[68] That said, as pointed out by multiple scholars of language revitalization (see Section 18.2.1), any favourable legislative moves would need to be matched by stronger and more strategic practice in terms of CBLP, since all the evidence suggests that 'the real language policy of a community is much more likely to be found in its practices than its management' (Spolsky 2004: 222). The current reality, given the multiplicity of languages in the case of France, is that there is great variability in relation to how well positioned and supported the different regional languages are to build strong CBLP in the future. The internet could potentially have a positive part to play in revitalization and regeneration, both in Ireland and in France, in the formation of online communities of practice,[69] as could the facilitation of digital corpus-building to reinforce and strengthen the domains in which minoritized languages may be utilized.[70]

---

[68] https://www.lemonde.fr/politique/article/2021/05/26/langues-regionales-emmanuel-macron-defend-leur-enseignement_6081548_823448.html (accessed 2 July 2022).

[69] See Scott Warren and Jennings (2015); Éloy, Martin, and Mathiru (2019).

[70] See for example the *Restaure* corpus of *occitan*: https://zenodo.org/record/1182949# (accessed 2 July 2022) and Davies-Deacon (Chapter 16, this volume). Bel and Gasquet-Cyrus (2015) warn, however, that there is a need to build productive collaborations between research-based corpus building and local organizations/language advocates in order to maximize possible benefits across society.

In the Republic of Ireland, broad support for Irish continues to exist across the political spectrum,[71] with underpinning legislation relating to education, the public space, and the media, as well as a certain level of economic investment (including in CBLP), all of which contrasts with the French context. Legislation was strengthened at the end of 2021 and Irish was upgraded to full official and working status in the EU from 1 January 2022.[72] As mentioned in Section 18.3.2, levels of knowledge of Irish as a second language are very high in the population and official language policy has ensured that competence in Irish has a 'market value' for speakers (not least new speakers) in some settings (O'Rourke and Walsh 2020: 172–3). Indeed, considering the weakness of other minoritized languages globally, Ireland's attempts at revitalization (sometimes deemed an 'archetypal failure' (May 2012: 147)), and the considerable extent of institutional support, may even be the envy of speakers of other endangered languages (Romaine 2008: 24; Walsh 2022: 316, 319).

However, a number of factors are mitigating against the future vitality of Irish. The language regime in the Irish Republic has been beset by a basic contradiction between an overt policy of support for Irish as the national language and a covert policy which accepts the primacy of English, and markets Ireland's Anglophone credentials as a strength in a globalized economy. Moreover, although the numbers of L2 speakers are high as a result of education policy (unlike the French context), only a subset of these L2 speakers might be described as 'new speakers' in that they proactively opt to use Irish in their daily lives. Lo Bianco (2018: 42) points to the gap between declared competency in Irish and daily usage (which is low, even in *Gaeltacht* areas), arguing that 'the sobering conclusion is that the status planning "corner" is very small and cannot itself increase users or expand uses of threatened languages'. Ó hIfearnáin (2013), drawing on Spolsky, makes a similar distinction between revitalization (where education is the central plank) and regeneration (where the expansion of domains and media is crucial). There is considerable variation in the extent to which Irish is—or is not—associated with economic growth in the *Gaeltacht*: this is strongest in parts of south Connemara where the headquarters of Irish-language media are located (Walsh 2012) but in more peripheral areas of the *Gaeltacht* (both within and beyond Connemara) regeneration is a major challenge, and Irish remains associated with economic disadvantage (see also Depau's (2019) discussion of *francoprovençal*).

---

[71] See, however, Walsh's (2021: 314 ff.) discussion of the past role of two political parties, Fine Gael and Labour, in the watering down of Irish qualification requirements.

[72] For optimism in relation to the potential impact of this on the language in terms of legitimization and cultural capital, see Ó Laighin (2022: 10, 245); Walsh (2022: 320).

The next twenty-five to fifty years will be critical for minoritized languages in both France and Ireland. In France, a key question is whether Jacobin republicanism can find a way of embracing minoritized languages within its political ethos, rather than relegating them to the margins, and whether such an improvement in status (e.g. through implementation of the *Loi Molac*) could lead to more robust support for praxis within communities. In Northern Ireland, the linguistic context continues to be conditioned by the shadow of conflict and considerable opposition to the Irish language persists in some sections of the community. On the other hand, the previous view of Irish as a language of resistance shows some potential for morphing into a language of reconciliation and shared heritage, although there is a long way to go in terms of broad cross-community acceptance.

Hinton, Huss, and Roche (2018: 495) observe that 'a "healthy" language is one that is supported at home, at school, in the community, on the job, and in the media. [. . .] attention to only one of these venues is never enough'. In the early twenty-first century, Ireland is much closer to achieving this for Irish than France is for any of its regional languages, not least in terms of the high number of L2 speakers of Irish created through education policy. However, the future vitality of Irish cannot be assumed; there is considerable anxiety over the erosion of the *Gaeltacht* and the fear that the language may ultimately be confined to symbolic rather than instrumental use. For the Republic of Ireland, the question is whether language planning can be re-evaluated and resourced to the extent that what has been described as 'the retreat of the state' on the ground can be overturned, the remaining *Gaeltacht* nourished and strengthened, and the growth in new speakers galvanized in a way that increases everyday usage and strengthens language networks. In short, while there is little doubt that the opposing policy positions with respect to regional languages in France and Irish in the Republic of Ireland have resulted in major differences in relation to status and L2 language acquisition, the two settings share many common challenges, including some which are familiar from other settings around the world (Hinton, Huss, and Roche 2018), most obviously in terms of ensuring long-term support, survival, and growth at community level.

References

Abalain, Hervé (2000). *Histoire de la langue bretonne*, 2nd edn. Paris: Gisserot.
Abbou, Julie, Aron Arnold, Maria Candea, and Noémie Marignier (2018). 'Qui a peur de l'écriture inclusive? Entre délire eschatologique et peur d'émasculation: entretien', *Semen–Revue de sémio-linguistique des textes et discours* 44: 133–51.
Abouda, Lotfi and Marie Skrovec (2017). 'Alternance futur simple/futur périphrastique: variation et changement en français oral hexagonal', *Revue de sémantique et pragmatique* 41-2: 155–79.
Académie française (1635). 'Statuts et règlements de l'Académie françoise'. https://www.academie-francaise.fr/linstitution/statuts-et-reglements accessed 14 April 2021.
Académie française (1694). *Dictionnaire de l'Académie françoise*. Paris: J. B. Coignard.
Académie française (1740). *Dictionnaire de Académie françoise*, 3rd edn. Paris: J. B. Coignard.
Académie française (1762). *Dictionnaire de l'Académie françoise*, 4th edn. Paris: La Veuve de Bernard Brunet.
Académie française (1984). 'Déclaration du 14 June 1984: Féminisation des noms de métiers, fonctions, grades et titres'.
Académie française (2002). 'Déclaration du 21 mars 2002: Féminisation des noms de métiers, fonctions, grades et titres'.
Académie française (2011–present). 'Courrier des internautes'. http://academie-francaise.fr/dire-ne-pas-dire/courrier-des-internautes accessed 14 April 2021.
Académie française (2014). 'La Féminisation des noms de métiers, fonctions, grades ou titres. Mise au point de l'Académie française', 10 October 2014. https://www.academie-francaise.fr/actualites/la-feminisation-des-noms-de-metiers-fonctions-grades-ou-titres-mise-au-point-de-lacademie accessed 30 April 2021.
Académie française (2017). 'Déclaration de l'Académie française sur l'écriture dite "inclusive"', 26 October 2017. https://www.academie-francaise.fr/actualites/declaration-de-lacademie-francaise-sur-lecriture-dite-inclusive accessed 30 April 2021.
Académie française (2019). 'La Féminisation des noms de métiers et de fonctions. Rapport'. https://www.academie-francaise.fr/sites/academie-francaise.fr/files/rapport_feminisation_noms_de_metier_et_de_fonction.pdf accessed 30 April 2021.
Académie française (no date). 'Les Immortels, Abel Hermant'. http://www.academie-francaise.fr/les-immortels/abel-hermant accessed 22 July 2022.
Académie française (no date). 'Questions de langue: Anglicismes et autres emprunts'. https://www.dictionnaire-academie.fr/article/QDL012 accessed 4 December 2021.
Académie française (no date). 'Terminologie & néologie'. https://www.dictionnaire-academie.fr/article/QDL012 accessed 31 July 2022.
Adami, Hervé (2012). 'La Formation linguistique des migrants adultes', *Savoirs* 29(2): 9–44.
Adams, Marianne (1987). *Old French, Null Subjects and Verb Second Phenomena*, doctoral thesis, University of California, Los Angeles.
Adamson, Robin (2007). *The Defence of French: A Language in Crisis?*. Clevedon: Multilingual Matters.

Adamson, Silvia and Wendy Ayres-Bennett (2011). 'Linguistics and Philology in the 21st Century: Introduction', *Transactions of the Philological Society* 109(3): 201–6.

Adelung, Johann Christoph (1774–86). *Versuch eines vollständigen grammatisch-kritischen Wörterbuches Der Hochdeutschen Mundart [...]*. Leipzig: Breitkopf.

Adelung, Johann Christoph (1793–1801). *Grammatisch-kritisches Wörterbuch der hochdeutschen Mundart: mit beständiger Vergleichung der übrigen Mundarten, besonders aber der oberdeutschen*. 4 vols. Leipzig: Johann Gottlob Immanuel Breitkopf und Comp.

Adkins, Madeleine (2013). 'Will the Real Breton please Stand up? Language Revitalization and the Problem of Authentic Language', *International Journal of the Sociology of Language* 223: 55–70.

Agard, Frederick (1971). 'Language and Dialect: Some Tentative Postulates', *Linguistics* 65: 5–24.

Agence pour l'enseignement français à l'étranger (2021). 'Carte du réseau des établissements d'enseignement français à l'étranger'. https://www.aefe.fr/rechercher-une-ressource-documentaire/carte-du-reseau-des-etablissements-denseignement-francais accessed 4 December 2021.

Ager, Dennis (1999). *Identity, Insecurity and Image: France and Language*. Clevedon: Multilingual Matters.

AHRC (Arts and Humanities Research Council) (2021). 'Learn about our projects'. https://www.ukri.org/what-we-offer/browse-our-areas-of-investment-and-support/open-world-research-initiative/ accessed 4 December 2021.

Aikhenvald, Alexandra Y. (2012). 'Round Women and Long Men: Shape, Size, and the Meanings of Gender in New Guinea and Beyond', *Anthropological Linguistics* 54(1): 33–86.

Akenson, D. H. (2011 [1970]). *The Irish Education Experiment: The National System of Education in Ireland in the Nineteenth Century*. London: Routledge.

Albert, Eric (2018). 'Le Royaume-Uni, mauvais élève en langues étrangères'. *Le Monde*, September 2018. https://www.lemonde.fr/m-actu/article/2018/09/11/le-royaume-uni-mauvais-eleve-en-langues-etrangeres_5353287_4497186.html accessed 4 December 2021.

Alberti di Villanova, Francesco (1772). *Nuovo dizionario italiano-francese, estratto da' dizionari dell'Accademia di Francia e della Crusca, ed arricchito di più di trenta mila articoli sovra tutti gli altri dizionari finor pubblicati*. Marseilles: Giovanni Mossy.

Alessandri, Giovan Mario (1560). *Il paragone della lingua toscana et castigliana*. Naples: Mattia Cancer.

Alim, H. Samy, Angela Reyes, and Paul V. Kroskrity (eds) (2020). *The Oxford Handbook of Language and Race*. Oxford: Oxford University Press.

Alim, H. Samy, John R. Rickford, and Arnetha F. Ball (2016). *Raciolinguistics: How Language Shapes our Ideas about Race*. Oxford: Oxford University Press.

Alliance française (no date). 'L 'Alliance française Paris Ile-de-France'. https://www.alliancefr.org/fr/qui-sommes-nous/alliance-francaise-paris-ile-de-france accessed 14 April 2021.

Andersen, Henning (2001). 'Actualization and the (Uni)directionality of Change', in Henning Andersen (ed.), *Actualization: Linguistic Change in Progress*. Amsterdam/Philadelphia: John Benjamins, 225–48.

Anon. (1699(?)). *Impartial Animadversions Upon Monsieur Boyer's Royal Dictionary: Exposing plainly the Injustice of his Attempt, and Weakness of his Performance*, Harley 5927/404.

Anon. (1721). *Dictionnaire universel françois et latin*. Paris: F. Delaulne.

Aquino-Weber, Dorothée, Sara Cotelli, and Andres Kristol (eds) (2009). *Sociolinguistique historique du domaine gallo-roman: enjeux et méthodologies.* Bern: Peter Lang.

Ardinghelli, Maria Angela (1756). 'A chi legge', in Stephen Hales, *Statica de' vegetabili ed analisi dell'aria. Opera del signor Stefano Hales della società regale delle scienze. Tradotta dall'inglese con varie annotazioni,* trans. Maria Angela Ardinghelli. Naples: Giuseppe Raimondi, unpaginated.

Ariel, Mira (1988). 'Referring and Accessibility', *Journal of Linguistics* 24: 65–87.

Armstrong, Nigel and Jennifer Low (2008). 'C'est encoeur plus jeuli, le Mareuc: Some Evidence for the Spread of /o/-fronting in French', *Transactions of the Philological Society* 106(3): 432–55.

Armstrong, Nigel and Tim Pooley (2010). *Social and Linguistic Change in European French.* Basingstoke: Palsgrave.

Armstrong, Nigel and Tim Pooley (2013). 'Levelling, Resistance and Divergence in the Pronunciation of English and French', *Language Sciences* 39: 141–50.

Arnauld, Antoine and Claude Lancelot (1968 [1660]). *Grammaire générale et raisonnée de Port Royal.* Paris: Chez Perlet. Facsimile edition Menston: The Scolar Press Limited.

Arnold, Theodor (1736). *Grammatica anglicana concentrata.* Leipzig: Jn der Großischen Handlung.

Arnold, Theodor and Nathan Bailey (1752). *A Compleat English Dictionary: oder Vollständiges englisch-deutsches Wörter-buch.* Leipzig: In der Großischen Handlung.

Ashby, William J. (1976). 'The Loss of the Negative Morpheme, *ne* in Parisian French', *Lingua* 39: 119–37.

Ashby, William J. (1981). 'The Loss of the Negative Particle *ne* in French: A Syntactic Change in Progress', *Language* 57(3): 674–87.

Ashby, William J. (1982). 'The Drift of French Syntax', *Lingua* 57: 29–46.

Ashby, William J. (1984). 'The Elision of /l/ in French Clitic Pronouns and Articles', in Ernst Pulgram (ed.), *Romanitas: Studies in Romance Linguistics.* Ann Arbor: Michigan University Press, 1–16.

Ashby, William J. (1988). 'The Syntax, Pragmatics and Sociolinguistics of Left- and Right Dislocations in French', *Lingua* 75: 203–29.

Ashby, William J. (1991). 'When does Variation Indicate Linguistic Change in Progress?', *Journal of French Language Studies* 1: 1–19.

Ashby, William J. (2001). 'Un nouveau regard sur la chute du *ne* en français parlé tourangeau: s'agit-il d'un changement en cours?', *Journal of French Language Studies* 11: 1–22.

ATILF (Analyse et traitement informatique de la langue française) (no date). *Trésor de la langue française informatisé.* https://www.atilf.fr/ressources/tlfi/ accessed 31 July 2022.

Auer, Anita (2009). *The Subjunctive in the Age of Prescriptivism. English and German Developments during the Eighteenth Century.* London: Palgrave Macmillan.

Auer, Anita (2015). 'Stylistic Variation', in Anita Auer, Daniel Schreier, and Richard J. Watts (eds), *Letter Writing and Language Change.* Cambridge: Cambridge University Press, 133–55.

Auer, Anita, Catharina Peersman, Simon Pickl, Gijsbert Rutten, and Rik Vosters (2015). 'Historical Sociolinguistics: The Field and its Future', *Journal of Historical Sociolinguistics* 1(1): 1–12.

Aurembou, Marie-Rose (1973). 'Aspects phonétiques de l'*Atlas de l'Île de France et de l'Orléanais*: unité ou diversité?', in Georges Straka (ed.), *Les Dialectes romans de France à la lumière des atlas régionaux.* Paris: Éditions du Centre National de la Recherche Scientifique, 379–400.

Aurrekoetxea, Gotzon, Esteve Clua, Aitor Iglesias, Iker Usobiaga, and Miquel Salicrú (2020). 'Characterizing Dialect Groups: Distance and Informativeness Associated with Linguistic Features', *Zeitschrift für Dialektologie und Linguistik* 87(2): 307–26.

Auzzas, Ginetta (1985). 'Gallomania e anglomania', in Girolamo Arnaldi and Manlio Pastore Stocchi (eds), *Storia della cultura veneta*. Vol. V/1: *Il Settecento*. Vicenza: Neri Pozza, 579–606.

Avanzi, Mathieu, Alain Rey, and Aurore Vicenti (2020). *Comme on dit chez nous. Le Grand Livre du français de nos régions*. Paris: le Robert.

Ayres-Bennett, Wendy (1987). *Vaugelas and the Development of the French Language*. London: Modern Humanities Research Association.

Ayres-Bennett, Wendy (1990). 'Variation and Change in the Pronunciation of French in the Seventeenth Century', in John N. Green and Wendy Ayres-Bennett (eds), *Variation and Change in French: Essays Presented to Rebecca Posner on the Occasion of her Sixtieth Birthday*, 151–79.

Ayres-Bennett, Wendy (1993). 'The Authority of Grammarians in 17th-century France and their Legacy to the French Language', in Rodney Sampson (ed.), *Authority of the French Language*. Münster: Nodus Publikationen, 33–45.

Ayres-Bennett, Wendy (ed.) (1994a). *Grammaire pour les Dames*, special issue of *Histoire épistémologie langage*: 16(2).

Ayres-Bennett, Wendy (1994b). 'Le Rôle des femmes dans l'élaboration des idées linguistiques au XVIIe siècle en France', *Histoire épistémologie langage* 16(2): 35–53.

Ayres-Bennett, Wendy (1994c). 'Negative evidence: Or Another Look at the Non-use of Negative *ne* in Seventeenth-century French', *French Studies* 48(1): 63–85.

Ayres-Bennett, Wendy (1996). *A History of the French Language through Texts*. London: Routledge.

Ayres-Bennett, Wendy (2001). 'Socio-historical Linguistics and the History of French', *Journal of French Language Studies* 11(2): 159–77.

Ayres-Bennett, Wendy (2004). *Sociolinguistic Variation in Seventeenth-century France: Methodology and Case Studies*. Cambridge: Cambridge University Press.

Ayres-Bennett, Wendy (2006). 'Reading the Remarqueurs: Changing Perceptions of 'Classic' Texts', *Historiographia Linguistica* 33(3): 263–302.

Ayres-Bennett, Wendy (2009) 'Presenting Grammar to a Non-specialist Audience: Vaugelas's Use of Metaphors in his *Remarques sur la langue françoise* (1647)', *Seventeenth-Century French Studies* 31(1): 36–45.

Ayres-Bennett, Wendy (ed.) (2011a). *Corpus des remarques sur la langue française (XVIIe siècle)*. Paris: Classiques Garnier Numérique.

Ayres-Bennett, Wendy (2011b). 'Metaphors in Metalinguistic Texts: The Case of Observations and Remarks on the French Language', in Gerda Haßler (ed.), *History of Linguistics 2008: Selected Papers from the Eleventh International Conference on the History of the Language Sciences (ICHoLS XI), 28 August– 2 September 2008*. Amsterdam: John Benjamins, 239–49.

Ayres-Bennett, Wendy (2015) 'La Persistance de l'idéologie linguistique des remarqueurs dans les chroniques de langage de 1925 à nos jours', *Circula* 1: 44–68.

Ayres-Bennett, Wendy (2016) 'Codification and Prescription in Linguistic Standardisation: Myths and Models', in Francesc Feliu and Josep Maria Nadal (eds), *Constructing Language: Norms, Myths and Emotions*. Amsterdam: John Benjamins, 99–130.

Ayres-Bennett, Wendy (2018a). *Claude Favre de Vaugelas, Remarques sur la langue française. Édition critique*. Paris: Classiques Garnier.

Ayres-Bennett, Wendy (2018b). 'Historical Sociolinguistics and Tracking Language Change: Sources, Text Types and Genres', in Wendy Ayres-Bennett and Janice Carruthers (eds), *Manual of Romance Sociolinguistics*. Berlin/Boston: de Gruyter, 253–79.

Ayres-Bennett, Wendy (2020a) 'From Haugen's Codification to Thomas's Purism: Assessing the Role of Description and Prescription, Prescriptivism and Purism in Linguistic Standardisation', *Language Policy* 19: 183–213.

Ayres-Bennett, Wendy (2020b). 'Women as Authors, Audience, and Authorities in the French Tradition', in Wendy Ayres-Bennett and Helena Sanson (eds), *Women in the History of Linguistics*. Oxford: Oxford University Press, 91–119.

Ayres-Bennett, Wendy and John Bellamy (eds) (2021). *The Cambridge Handbook of Language Standardization*. Cambridge: Cambridge University Press.

Ayres-Bennett, Wendy, Anne Carlier, Julie Glikman, Thomas M. Rainsford, Gilles Souffi, and Carine Skupien Dekens (eds) (2018a). *Nouvelles voies d'accès au changement linguistique*. Paris: Classiques Garnier.

Ayres-Bennett, Wendy, Anne Carlier, Julie Glikman, Thomas M. Rainsford, Gilles Siouffi, and Carine Skupien Dekens (2018b). 'Introduction', in Wendy Ayres-Bennett, Anne Carlier, Julie Glikman, Thomas M. Rainsford, Gilles Souffi, and Carine Skupien Dekens (eds), *Nouvelles voies d'accès au changement linguistique*. Paris: Classiques Garnier, 7–19.

Ayres-Bennett, Wendy and Philippe Caron (2016). 'Periodization, Translation, Prescription and the Emergence of Classical French', *Transactions of the Philological Society* 114(3): 339–90.

Ayres-Bennett, Wendy and Janice Carruthers (eds) (2018). *Manual of Romance Sociolinguistics*. Berlin/Boston: de Gruyter.

Ayres-Bennett, Wendy, Janice Carruthers, with Rosalind Temple (2001). *Studies in the Modern French Language: Problems and Perspectives*. Harlow: Longman.

Ayres-Bennett, Wendy and Bernard Colombat (2016). 'L'Extension du *Grand corpus des grammaires françaises, des remarques et des traités sur la langue*: questions théoriques et méthodologiques', *Histoire épistémologie langage* 38(2): 55–71.

Ayres-Bennett, Wendy and Mairi McLaughlin (eds) (2024). *The Oxford Handbook of the French Language*. Oxford: Oxford University Press.

Ayres-Bennett, Wendy and Thomas Rainsford (eds) (2014). *L'Histoire du français. État des lieux et perspectives*. Paris: Classiques Garnier.

Ayres-Bennett, Wendy and Helena Sanson (2020). 'Women in the History of Linguistics: Distant and Neglected Voices', in Wendy Ayres-Bennett and Helena Sanson (eds), *Women in the History of Linguistics*. Oxford: Oxford University Press, 1–29.

Ayres-Bennett, Wendy and Magali Seijido (2011). *Remarques et observations sur la langue française. Histoire et évolution d'un genre*. Paris: Classiques Garnier.

Ayres-Bennett, Wendy and Magali Seijido (eds) (2013a). *Bon usage et variation sociolinguistique. Perspectives diachroniques et traditions nationales*. Lyon: ENS Éditions.

Ayres-Bennett, Wendy and Magali Seijido (2013b). 'Introduction', in Wendy Ayres-Bennett and Magali Seijido (eds), *Bon usage et variation sociolinguistique. Perspectives diachroniques et traditions nationales*. Lyon: ENS Éditions, 7–19.

Ayres-Bennett, Wendy and Ingrid Tieken-Boon van Ostade (2016). 'Prescriptivism in a Comparative Perspective: The Case of France and England', in Ingrid Tieken-Boon van Ostade and Carol Percy (eds), *Prescription and Tradition in Language: Establishing Standards Across Time and Space*. Bristol: Multilingual Matters, 105–20.

Baggioni, Daniel and Philippe Martel (eds) (1997). *De François Raynouard à Auguste Brun. La Contribution des Méridionaux aux premières études de linguistique romane*, special issue of *Lengas: Revue de Sociolinguistique*: 42.

Bailey, Nathaniel (1721). *An Universal Etymological English Dictionary* [...] London: Printed for E. Bell, etc.

Baker, Paul (2010). *Sociolinguistics and Corpus Linguistics*. Edinburgh: Edinburgh University Press.

Baker, Paul, Costas Gabrielatos, Majid KhosraviNik, Michał Krzyżanowski, Tony McEnery, and Ruth Wodak (2008). 'A Useful Methodological Synergy? Combining Critical Discourse Analysis and Corpus Linguistics to Examine Discourses of Refugees and Asylum Seekers in the UK Press', *Discourse & Society* 19(3): 273–306. https://doi.org/10.1177/0957926508088962

Ballerini, Roberto (1985). 'Alla ricerca di un nuovo metodo: il corso grammaticale nel secolo dei Lumi', in Gian Paolo Brizzi (ed.), *Il catechismo e la grammatica*. Vol. I: *Istruzione e controllo sociale nell'area emiliana e romagnola nel '700*. Bologna: Il Mulino, 225–85.

Balon, Laurent and Pierre Larrivée (2016). 'L'ancien français n'est déjà plus une langue à sujet nul–nouveau témoignage des textes légaux', *Journal of French Language Studies* 26(2): 221–37.

Bandiera, Giovanni Niccolò (1740). *Trattato degli studj delle donne, in due parti diviso, opera d'un Accademico Intronato*. 2 vols. Venice: Francesco Pitteri.

Barba, Giovanni (1734). *Dell'arte e del metodo delle lingue*. Rome: Giovanni Zempel.

Barbapiccola, Giuseppa Eleonora (1722). 'La traduttrice a' lettori', in René Descartes, *I principj della filosofia di Renato Des-cartes. Tradotti dal francese col confronto del latino in cui l'autore gli scrisse da Giuseppa Eleonora Barbapiccola tra gli Arcadi Mirista*. Turin: Giovanni Francesco Mairesse, fols †3r–†††4v.

Barthélemy, Louis (1788). *La Cantatrice grammairienne, ou l'art d'apprendre l'orthographe françoise seul, sans le secours d'un maître, par le moyen des chansons érotiques, pastorales, villageoises, anacréoniques, &c.* [...] *Ouvrage dédié aux Dames, & dédié à Madame la Comtesse de Beauharnais*. Geneva: Joseph-Sulpice Grabit.

Bartlett, Jamie, Richard Norrie, Sofia Patel, Rebekka Rumpel, and Simon Wibberley (2014). 'Misogyny on Twitter'. London: Demos. https://www.demos.co.uk/files/MISOGYNY_ON_TWITTER.pdf accessed 5 August 2022.

Bauer, Brigitte L. M. (1996). 'The Verb in Indirect Speech in Old French: System in Change', in Theo A. J. M. Janssen and Wim Van der Wurff (eds), *Reported Speech: Forms and Functions of the Verb*. Amsterdam/Philadelphia: John Benjamins, 75–96.

Bayley, Robert, Richard Cameron, and Ceil Lucas (2013). 'The Study of Language and Society', in Robert Bayley, Richard Cameron, and Ceil Lucas (eds), *The Oxford Handbook of Sociolinguistics*. Oxford: Oxford University Press, 1–8.

Beacco, Jean-Claude and Kenza Cherkaoui Messin (2010). 'Les Politiques linguistiques européennes et la gestion de la diversité des langues de France', *Langue française* 167: 95–111.

Beal, Joan (2008). 'Pronouncing Dictionaries – I. Eighteenth and Early Nineteenth Centuries', in A. P. Cowie (ed.), *Oxford History of English Lexicography*. Oxford: Oxford University Press, 149–75.

Beal, Joan, Camela Nocera, and Massimo Sturiale (eds) (2008). *Perspectives on Prescriptivism*. Frankfurt: Peter Lang.

Beck-Busse, Gabriele (1994). 'Les "Femmes" et les "illiterati"; ou: la question du latin et de la langue vulgaire', *Histoire épistémologie langage* 16(2): 77–94.

Beck-Busse, Gabriele (2014). *Grammaires des Dames – Grammatiche per le Dame: Grammatik im Spannungsfeld von Sprache, Kultur und Gesellschaft*. Frankfurt: Peter Lang.

Becquer, Anne-Marie, Nicole Cholewka, Martine Coutier, and Marie-Josèphe Mathieu (1999). *Femme, j'écris ton nom. Guide d'aide à la Féminisation des noms de métiers, titres, grades, fonctions*. Paris: La Documentation française. https://www.vie-publique.fr/sites/default/files/rapport/pdf/994001174.pdf accessed 30 May 2021.

Bédarida, Henri (1928). *Parme et la France de 1748 à 1789*. Paris: Champion.

Bédarida, Henri and Paul Hazard (1934). *L'Influence française en Italie au dix-huitième siècle*. Paris: Les Belles Lettres.

Begley, Conor and Hugh McCurtin (1732). *The English–Irish Dictionary: An Foclóir Béarla Gaoidheilge*. Paris: Guerin.

Bel, Bernard and Médéric Gasquet-Cyrus (2015). 'Digital Curation and Event-driven Methods at the Service of Endangered Languages', in Mari C. Jones (ed.), *Endangered Languages and New Technologies*. Cambridge: Cambridge University Press, 113–26.

Bell, Allan (1984). 'Language Style as Audience Design', *Language in Society* 13(2): 145–204.

Bell, Allan (2001). 'Back in Style: Reworking Audience Design', in Penelope Eckert and John R. Rickford (eds), *Style and Sociolinguistic Variation*. Cambridge: Cambridge University Press, 139–69.

Bell, Allan, David Britain, and Devyani Sharma (eds) (2016). *Labov and Sociolinguistics. Fifty Years of Language in Social Context*, special issue of *Journal of Sociolinguistics*: 20(4).

Benincà, Paola (1995). 'Complement Clitics in Medieval Romance: The Tobler-Mussafia Law', in Adrian Battye and Ian Roberts (eds) *Clause Structure and Language Change*. Oxford: Oxford University Press, 325–44.

Berengo, Marino (ed.) (1962). *Giornali veneziani del Settecento*. Milan: Feltrinelli.

Bergs, Alexander T. (2004). 'Letters: A New Approach to Text Typology', *Journal of Historical Pragmatics* 5(2): 207–27.

Bermel, Neil (2007). *Linguistic Authority, Language Ideology, and Metaphor: The Czech Orthography Wars*. Berlin: de Gruyter.

Berti, Michele (1692). *L'arte d'insegnare la lingua francese per mezzo dell'italiana o' vero la lingua italiana per mezzo della francese*. Venice: Stefano Curti.

Bertucci, Paola (2013). 'The In/visible Woman: Mariangela Ardinghelli and the Circulation of Knowledge between Paris and Naples in the Eighteenth Century', *Isis* 104(2): 226–49.

Betri, Maria Luisa and Elena Brambilla (eds) (2004). *Salotti e ruolo femminile in Italia: tra fine Seicento e primo Novecento*. Venice: Marsilio.

BFM (Base de français médiéval) (2012–present). Lyon, UMR ICAR (CNRS & ENS de Lyon). http://bfm.ens-lyon.fr accessed 1 November 2020.

BVH (Bibliothèques virtuelles humanistes) (2009). http://www.bvh.univ-tours.fr accessed 5 August 2022.

Bichurina, Natalia (2016). *Transborder Communities in Europe and the Emergence of 'New' Languages. From 'Francoprovençal patois' to 'Arpitan' and 'Arpitania'*, doctoral thesis, University of Perpignan via Domitia.

Blackledge, Adrian and Angela Creese (2019). *Voices of a City Market: An Ethnography*. Bristol: Multilingual Matters.

Blainey, Darcie (2015). 'Same Process, Different Meaning: /ɛ/ Lowering over Time in Louisiana Regional French', *Journal of French Language Studies* 27: 121–42.

Blanc, Étienne (2022). *Proposition de loi no. 385*. https://www.senat.fr/dossier-legislatif/ppl21-385.html accessed 28 February 2022.

Blanche-Benveniste, Claire (1997). *Approches de la langue parlée en français*. Paris: Ophrys.

Blanche-Benveniste, Claire, Mireille Bilger, Christine Rouget, and Karel van den Eynde (1990). *Le Français parlé. Études grammaticales*. Paris: CNRS.

Blanche-Benveniste, Claire and Colette Jeanjean (1987). *Le Français parlé: transcription et édition*. Paris: Didier Erudition.

Blanchet, Philippe (ed.) (2020). *Lou coulas de la vergougno (Le Collier de la honte). Études sur le signal ou symbole employé à l'école française pour dénoncer et punir les enfants qui parlaient une langue 'locale'*, special issue of *Revue d'études d'Oc*: 171.

Blanchet, Philippe and Nigel Armstrong (2006). 'The Sociolinguistic Situation of "Contemporary Dialects of French" in France Today: An Overview of Recent Contributions on the Dialectalisation of Standard French', *Journal of French Language Studies* 16: 251–75.

Blanquer, Jean-Michel (2021). *Circulaire du 5 mai 2021 Règles de féminisation dans les actes administratifs du ministère de l'Éducation nationale, de la Jeunesse et des Sports et les Pratiques d'enseignement, Bulletin officiel de l'Éducation nationale, de la jeunesse et des sports*, NOR: MENB2114203C. https://www.education.gouv.fr/bo/21/Hebdo18/MENB2114203C.htm accessed 28 February 2022.

Blommaert, Jan (2007). 'Sociolinguistics and Discourse Analysis: Orders of Indexicality and Polycentricity', *Journal of Multicultural Discourses* 2(2): 115–30.

Blommaert, Jan (2011). 'The Long Language-ideological Debate in Belgium', *Journal of Multicultural Discourses* 6(3): 241–56.

Blommaert, Jan (2015). 'Meaning as a Nonlinear Effect: The Birth of Cool', in Theresa Lillis (ed.), *Theory in Applied Linguistics Research: Critical Approaches to Production, Performance and Participation*. Amsterdam/Philadelphia: John Benjamins, 7–27.

Blum-Kulka, Shoshana, Juliane House, and Gabriele Kasper (1989). 'Investigating Cross-cultural Pragmatics: An Introductory Overview', in Shoshana Blum-Kulka, Juliane House, and Gabriele Kasper (eds), *Cross-Cultural Pragmatics: Requests and Apologies*. Norwood, N.J: Ablex, 1–26.

Boaistuau, Pierre (1977 [1559]). *Histoires tragiques*, ed. Richard A. Carr. Paris: Champion.

Bochnakowa, Anna (2005). *Le Bon Français de la fin du XXe siècle. Chroniques du 'Figaro' 1996–2000*. Krakow: Wydawnictwo Uniwersytetu Jagiellońskiego.

Bochnakowa, Anna (2013). 'Chroniques de langage dans *Le Figaro* (1996–2000)', in Wendy Ayres-Bennett and Magali Seijido (eds), *Bon usage et variation sociolinguistique. Perspectives diachroniques et traditions nationales*. Lyon: ENS Éditions, 171–7.

Bödiker, Johann (1690). *Grund-Sätze der Deutschen Sprache*. Cölln an der Spree: no publisher.

Bodin, Jean (1583). *Les Six livres de la République. Ensemble une Apologie de René Herpin*. Paris: Jacques Du Puys.

Boersma, Paul and David Weenink (1992–2021). 'Praat: Doing Phonetics by Computer'. https://www.fon.hum.uva.nl/praat/ accessed 5 July 2022.

Boileau, Nicolas (1961 [1674]). *L'Art poétique*, ed. G. Montgrédien. Paris: Classiques Garnier, 159–88.

Boisson, Claude, Pablo Kirtchuk, and Henri Béjoint (1991). 'Aux origines de la lexicographie: les premiers dictionnaires monolingues et bilingues', *International Journal of Lexicography* 4(4): 261–315.

Booij, Geert (1999). 'The Role of the Prosodic Word in Phonotactic Generalizations', in Tracy Alan Hall and Ursula Kleinhenz (eds), *Studies on the Phonological Word*. Amsterdam: John Benjamins, 47–72.

Borsa, Matteo (1785). *Del gusto presente in letteratura italiana. Dissertazione*. Venice: Antonio Zatta e figli.

Bosworth, Yulia (2021). 'Gender Inclusivity in the Linguistic Landscape of Parisian Universities', *The French Review* 93(2): 175–96.

Bouchard, Chantal (2002). *La Langue et le nombril: une histoire sociolinguistique du Québec*. Saint-Laurent: Fides.

Boughton, Zoe (2005). 'Investigating Puristic Attitudes in France: Folk Perceptions of Variation in Standard French', in Nils Langer and Winifred Davies (eds), *Linguistic Purism in the Germanic Languages*. Berlin: de Gruyter, 282–99.

Boughton, Zoe (2011). 'La Standardisation continue de la langue française: l'apport des perceptions et attitudes langagières', *La Bretagne linguistique* 16: 37–57.

Boughton, Zoe and Katherine Pipe (2020). 'Phonological Variation and Change in the Regional French of Alsace: Supralocalization, Age, Gender and the Urban-Rural Dichotomy', *Journal of French Language Studies* 30: 327–53.

Bouhours, Dominique (1671). *Les Entretiens d'Ariste et d'Eugene*. Paris: Sebastien Mabre-Cramoisy.

Bouhours, Dominique (1674). *Doutes sur la langue françaíse proposés aux Messieurs de l'Académie française*. Paris: Sébastien Mabre-Cramoisy.

Bouhours, Dominique (1675). *Doutes sur la langue françaíse proposés aux Messieurs de l'Académie française*, corrected 2nd edn. Paris: Sébastien Mabre-Cramoisy.

Bouhours, Dominique (1692). *Remarques nouvelles sur la langue françoise*, 13th edn. Paris: George & Louis Josse.

Boula de Mareuil, Philippe, Frédéric Vernier, and Albert Rillard (2017). 'Enregistrements et transcriptions pour un atlas sonore des langues régionales de France', *Géolinguistique* 17: 23–48.

Bourciez, Édouard (1895). *Recueil des idiomes de la région gasconne*. https://1886.u-bordeaux-montaigne.fr/s/1886/item/390705#?c=&m=&s=&cv=9&xywh=2062%2C-308%2C2763%2C4006 accessed 5 August 2022.

Bourdieu, Pierre (1991). *Language and Symbolic Power*, edited and introduced by John B. Thompson, trans. Gino Raymond and Matthew Adamson. Cambridge: Polity Press.

Bourdoncle, Stéphane (2009). *La Langue occitane du Tarn-et-Garonne au début du XIXe siècle*. Toulouse: Presses de l'Université de Toulouse 1 Capitole.

Bourgeade, Pierre (1991). *Chroniques du français quotidien*. Paris: Belfond.

Bourhis, Richard Y. and Fred H. Genesee (1980). 'Evaluative Reactions to Code Switching Strategies in Montreal', in Howard Giles, W. Peter Robinson, and Philip M. Smith (eds), *Language: Social Psychological Perspectives*. Oxford: Pergamon Press, 335–43.

Boutan, Pierre (2003). 'Apprendre le français par le provençal: l'échec du Frère Savinian', *Tréma* 22: 6–28. http://journals.openedition.org/trema/1519 accessed 16 May 2021.

Bovelles, Charles (1973 [1533]). *Sur les langues vulgaires et la variété de la langue française*, ed. Colette Dumont-Demazière. Paris: Klincksieck.

Boyer, Abel (1699). *The Royal Dictionary. In Two Parts, First French and English. Secondly, English and French. The French Taken out of the Dictionaries of Richelet, Furetiere, Tachart, the Great Dictionary of the French-Academy, and the Remarks of Vaugelas, Menage, and Bouhours. And The English Collected Chiefly of the Best Dictionaries, and the Work of the Greatest Masters of the English Tongue; Such as Archbishop Tillotson, Bishop Sprat, Sir Roger l'Estrange, Mr Dryden, Sir William Temple &c. For the Use of His Highness the Duke of Gloucester*. London: Printed for R. Clavel, H. Mortlock […].

Boyer, Abel (1700). *The Royal Dictionary Abridged. In Two Parts. I. French and English. II. English and French. […] Containing Near Five Thousand Words More than Any French and English Dictionary yet Extant, besides the Royal. To Which Is Added, The Accenting of All English Words, to Facilitate the Pronunciation of the English Tongue for Foreigners*. London: Printed for R. Clavel, H. Mortlock […].

Boyer, Abel (1753). *The Royal Dictionary, French and English, and English and French: Extracted from the Writings of the Best Authors, in Both Languages*. London: J. Brotherton, W. Innys, etc.

Boyer, Abel (1756). *Dictionnaire royal, françois-anglois et anglois-françois, tiré des meilleurs auteurs qui ont ecrit dans ces deux langues; par Mr. A. Boyer. The New Edition Revised, Corrected, and Most Richly Amplifyed*. Lyon: J. Marie Bruyset, Libraire, grande rue Merciere, au Soleil.

Branca-Rosoff, Sonia, and Nathalie Schneider (1994). *L'Écriture des citoyens: une analyse linguistique de l'écriture des peu-lettrés pendant la période révolutionnaire*. Paris: Klincksieck.

Bray, Laurent (2000). *Matthias Kramer et la lexicographie du français en Allemagne au XVIIe siècle: avec une édition des textes métalexicographiques de Kramer*. Tübingen: Max Niemeyer.

Breeze, Ruth and Inés Olza (eds) (2017). *Evaluation in Media Discourse: European Perspectives*. Bern: Peter Lang.

Bretel, Jacques (1932 [1285]). *Le Tournoi de Chauvency*. Ed. Maurice Delbouille. Paris: Les Belles Lettres.

Brezina, Vaclav, Pierre Weill-Tessier, and Anthony McEnery (2020). '#LancsBox (software)'. http://corpora.lancs.ac.uk/lancsbox/ accessed 5 August 2022.

Britain, David (2018). 'Paris: A Sociolinguistic Comparative Perspective', *Journal of French Language Studies* 28: 291–300.

Broudic, Fañch (2010). *L'Enseignement du et en breton*. Brest: Emgleo Breiz.

Broudic, Fañch (2011). 'Quels médias pour la langue bretonne?', in Annie Lenoble-Bart and Michel Mathien (eds), *Les Médias de la diversité culturelle dans les pays latins d'Europe*. Brussels: Bruylant, 85–97.

Broudic, Fañch (2013). 'Langue bretonne. Un siècle de mutations', *International Journal of the Sociology of Language* 223: 7–21.

Brown, Penelope and Stephen C. Levinson (1987). *Politeness: Some Universals in Language Usage*. Cambridge: Cambridge University Press.

Bruña-Cuevas, Manuel (1988). 'Le Style indirect libre chez Marie de France', *Revue de linguistique romane* 52: 421–46.

Bruña-Cuevas, Manuel (1989). 'Changer l'appelation "Style Indirect Libre"?', *Romania* 110: 1–39.

Bruneau, Charles (1931). *Manuel de phonétique pratique*, 2nd edn. Paris: Berger–Levrault.

Brunot, Ferdinand (1905–53). *Histoire de la langue française des origines à 1900 (à nos jours)*. 13 vols. Paris: Armand Colin.

Brunot, Ferdinand (1911). 'Discours', in *Inauguration des Archives de la Parole, 3 juin 1911*. Paris: Université de Paris/Imprimerie Albert Manier, 7–26.

Brun-Trigaud, Guylaine (1992). 'Les Enquêtes dialectologiques sur les parlers du Croissant: corpus et témoins', *Langue française* 93: 23–52.

Bucholtz, Mary and Kira Hall (2005). 'Identity and Interaction: A Sociocultural Linguistic Approach', *Discourse Studies* 7(4–5): 585–614.

Buchsbaum, Jonathan (2017). *Exception Taken: How France Has Defied Hollywood's New World Order*. New York: Columbia University Press.

Buffet, Marguerite (1668). *Nouvelles observations sur la langue françoise...* Paris: Jean Cusson.

Bulletin de la Société des Parlers de France (1893–9). Paris: H. Welter.

Bulot, Thierry (1999). *Langue urbaine et identité*. Paris: L'Harmattan.

Buridant, Claude (2019). *Grammaire du français médiéval*. Strasbourg: ELiPhi.

Burnett, Ashley Layna (2011). *Enclisis in Early Old French*, doctoral thesis, University of Calgary.

Burnett, Heather (2019). 'Sentential Negation in North-eastern Gallo-Romance Dialects: Some Insights from the *Atlas linguistique de la France*', *Journal of French Language Studies* 29: 189–207.

Burnett, Heather and Oliver Bonami (2019). 'Linguistic Prescription, Ideological Structure, and the Actuation of Linguistic Changes: Grammatical Gender in French Parliamentary Debates', *Language in Society* 48(1): 65–93. https://doi.org/10.1017/S0047404518001161

Burnett, Heather and Céline Pozniak (2021). 'Political Dimensions of Gender Inclusive Writing in Parisian Universities', *Journal of Sociolinguistics* 25: 808–31.

Burr, Elisabeth (2003). 'Gender and Language Politics in France', in Marlis Hellinger and Hadumod Bussman (eds), *Gender across Languages*. Vol. 3. Amsterdam/Philadelphia: John Benjamins, 119–39.

Busse, Winfried and Françoise Dougnac (1992). *François-Urbain Domergue: le grammairien patriote (1745–1810)*. Tübingen: Gunter Narr Verlag.

Callières, François de (1692). *Des mots à la mode, et des nouvelles façons de parler: avec des observations sur diverses matières d'agir & de s'exprimer: et un discours en vers sur les mêmes matières*. Paris: Claude Barbin.

Callières, François de (1698). *Du bon et du mauvais usage dans les manieres de s'exprimer. Des façons de parler bourgeoises, et en quoy elles sont differentes de celles de la cour. Suitte des Mots à la mode*, Paris: Michel Brunet.

Calvet, Louis-Jean (1979). *Linguistique et colonialisme. Petit traité de glottophagie*, 2nd edn. Paris: Payot.

Calvet, Louis-Jean (1994). *Les Voix de la ville. Introduction à la sociolinguistique urbaine*. Paris: Payot.

Calvet, Louis-Jean (1999). *Pour une écologie des langues du monde*. Paris: Plon.

Cameron, Deborah (2012). *Verbal Hygiene*. Oxford: Routledge.

Caminer Turra, Elisabetta (trans.) (1772). *Composizioni teatrali moderne*. 4 vols. Venice: Pietro Savioni.

Caminer Turra, Elisabetta (trans.) (1774–6). *Nuova raccolta di composizioni teatrali*. 6 vols. Venice: Pietro Savioni.

Caminer Turra, Elisabetta (trans.) (1794). *Drammi trasportati dal francese idioma ad uso del teatro*. 2 vols. Venice: Angelo Albrizzi.

Campbell-Cree, Alice (2017). 'Which Foreign Languages will be most Important for the UK Post-Brexit?'. https://www.britishcouncil.org/research-policy-insight/insight-articles/which-foreign-language accessed 4 December 2021.

Cantarutti, Giulia and Stefano Ferrari (eds) (2013). *Traduzione e* transfert *nel XVIII secolo tra Francia, Italia e Germania*. Milan: Franco Angeli.

Cappeau, Paul (ed.) (2021). *Une grammaire à l'aune de l'oral?*. Rennes: Presses universitaires de Rennes.

Cardinal, Linda (2008) 'Linguistic Peace: A Time to Take Stock', *Inroads* 23: 62–70.

Cardinaletti, Anna and Michael Starke (1999). 'The Typology of Structural Deficiency: A Case Study of the Three Classes of Pronoun', in Henk van Riemsdijk (ed.), *Clitics in the Languages of Europe*. Berlin: Mouton de Gruyter, 145–233.

Cargile, Aaron C. and Howard Giles (1997). 'Understanding Language Attitudes: Exploring Listener Affect and Identity', *Language and Communication* 17(3): 195–217.

Cargile, Aaron C., Howard Giles, Ellen B. Ryan, and James J. Bradac (1994). 'Language Attitudes as a Social Process: A Conceptual Model and New Directions', *Language and Communication* 14(3): 211–36.

Carles, Hélène and Martin Glessgen (eds) (2020). *Les Écrits des poilus: miroir du français au début du XXe siècle*. Strasbourg: Éditions de linguistique et de philologie.

Caron, Philippe (ed.) (2004). *Les Remarqueurs sur la langue française du XVIe siècle à nos jours*. Rennes: Presses universitaires de Rennes.

Caron, Philippe and Wendy Ayres-Bennett (2019). La Prescription linguistique en France de 1647 à 1720: l'exemple des remarqueurs', *Histoire épistémologie langage* 41(2): 41–66.

Carruthers, Janice (2006). 'The Syntax of Oral French', *French Studies* 60(2): 251–60.

Carruthers, Janice (2018). 'Postposition of the Subject in Contemporary French. An Exploration of Medium, Register and Genre', *Modern Languages Open* 1(12): 1–20. http://doi.org/10.3828/mlo.v0i0.189

Carruthers, Janice and Sophie Marnette (2007). 'Tense, Voices and Point of View in Medieval and Modern "Oral" Narration', in Emmanuelle Labeau, Carl Vetters, and Patrick Caudal (eds), *Sémantique et diachronie du système verbal français*. Amsterdam/New York: Rodopi, 177–202.

Carruthers, Janice and Daniel McAuley (2022). 'Indexicalities in the Multilingual City: Listeners' Perceptions of Urban Vernacular French', in Wendy Ayres-Bennett and Linda Fisher (eds), *Multilingualism and Identity. Interdisciplinary Perspectives*. Cambridge: Cambridge University Press, 109–30.

Cartago, Gabriella (1990). *Ricordi d'italiano: osservazioni intorno alla lingua e italianismi nelle relazioni di viaggio degli inglesi in Italia*. Bassano del Grappa: Ghedina & Tassotti.

Carton, Fernand (2001). 'Quelques évolutions récentes dans la prononciation du français', in Marie-Anne Hintze, Tim Pooley, and Anne Judge (eds), *French Accents: Phonological and Sociolinguistic Perspectives*. London: CILT–AFLS, 7–23.

Casad, Eugene H. (1974). *Dialect Intelligibility Testing*. Dallas: Summer Institute of Linguistics.

Casale, Silvia, Guilia Fiovaranti, and Scott Caplan (2015). 'Online Disinhibition: Precursors and Outcomes', *Journal of Media Pyschology* 27: 170–7.

Casali, Roderic F. (1997). 'Vowel Elision in Hiatus Contexts: Which Vowel Goes?', *Language* 73: 493–533.

Castelvecchi, Stefano (2013). *Sentimental Opera: Questions of Genre in the Age of Bourgeois Drama*. Cambridge: Cambridge University Press.

Castiglione, Baldassar (2003 [1528]). *Il libro del Cortegiano*, introduction by Amedeo Quondam and notes by Nicola Longo. Milan: Garzanti.

CEDRE (Cycle d'évaluations disciplinaires réalisées sur échantillons) (2016). 'Anglais en fin de collège'. *Les Dossiers de la DEPP* 212. https://www.education.gouv.fr/media/47945/download accessed July 2022.

Cellard, Jacques (1979). *La Vie du langage, chroniques 1971–1975, Le Monde*. Paris: Le Robert.

Cellard, Jacques (1983). 'Les Chroniques de langage', in Édith Bédard and Jacques Maurais (eds), *La Norme linguistique*. Quebec: Gouvernement du Québec, Conseil de la langue française, 651–66.

Central Statistics Office (2017). 'Census 2016 Summary Results – Part I'. https://www.cso.ie/en/media/csoie/releasespublications/documents/population/2017/7._The_Irish_language.pdf accessed 1 September 2022.

Central Statistics Office (2023). 'Census of Population 2022'. https://www.cso.ie/en/statistics/population/censusofpopulation2022 accessed 9 July 2023.

Cerquiglini, Bernard (1981). *La Parole médiévale*. Paris: Éditions du Seuil.

Cerquiglini, Bernard (1984). 'Le Style indirect libre et la modernité', *Langages* 73: 7–16.

Cerquiglini, Bernard (2003). *Les Langues de la France.* Paris: Presses universitaires de France.

Cerquiglini, Bernard (2019). 'La Parité dans la langue. Réflexions sur une exception française', *Le Discours et la langue* 11(1): 27–39.

Cesarotti, Melchiorre (1785). *Saggio sopra la lingua italiana.* Padua: Stamperia Penada.

Chambaud, Lewis (1750a). *A Grammar of the French Tongue. With a Prefatory Discourse, Containing an Essay on the Proper Method for Teaching and Learning that Language.* London: printed for A. Millar, at Buchanan's-Head over against Catharine-Street in the Strand.

Chambaud, Lewis (1750b). *The Treasure of the French and English Languages. Part I. Containing, I. A Vocabulary, French and English. II Familiar Forms of Speech upon the Most Common and Useful Subjects.* London: A. Millar.

Chambaud, Lewis (1761). *A Dictionary French and English: Containing the Signification of Words, with Their Different Uses, the Terms of Arts, Sciences and Trades; the Constructions, Forms of Speech, Idioms, and Proverbs Used in Other Languages: The Whole Extracted from the Best Writers.* London: A Millar.

Chambers, Anne (2008). *T.K. Whitaker. Portrait of a Patriot.* Dublin: Transworld Publishers.

Chambers, J. K. and Natalie Schilling (2013). *The Handbook of Language Variation and Change*, 2nd edn. Chichester: Wiley-Blackwell.

Champollion-Figeac, Jacques-Joseph (1809). *Nouvelles recherches sur les patois ou idiomes vulgaires de la France....* Paris: Goujon.

Charaudeau, Patrick (2019). 'Retour sur l'écriture inclusive au défi de la neutralisation en français', *Le Discours et la langue* 11(1): 97–124.

Chasle, Natalie (2008). 'Manifestation de la latence en ancien français aux Xème et XIème siècles: liaison et redoublement syntaxique', in Jacques Durand, Benoît Habert, and Bernard Laks (eds), *Congrès mondial de linguistique française 2008.* Paris: EDP Sciences, 1645–56. https://doi.org/10.1051/cmlf08175.

Châtenet, Véronique (2000). 'Le Processus de mort d'un patois: l'exemple de Saint-Gervais-sur-Couches (Saône-et-Loire)', in Gérard Taverdet (ed.), *Adieu les patois.* Dijon, L'Association Bourguignonne d'Études Linguistiques et Littéraires, 31–64.

Chauveau, Jean-Paul (1992). 'Sur le français du *Catholicon* de Jehan Lagadeuc', *Études celtiques* 29: 121–36.

Chenu, Sébastien, Ludovic Pajot, Nicolas Meizonnet, Marine Le Pen, Bruno Bilde, Agnès Thill, Joachim Son-Forget, Emmanuelle Ménard, and Marie-France Lorho (2020). *Proposition de loi no. 3273.* https://www.assemblee-nationale.fr/dyn/15/textes/l15b3273_proposition-loi# accessed 28 February 2022.

Chervel, André (1992). *L'Enseignement du français à l'école primaire.* Paris: Institut national de recherche pédagogique.

Chervel, André (2010). *Histoire de l'enseignement du français du XVIIe au XXe siècle.* Paris: Retz.

Cheshire, Jenny (1982). *Variation in an English Dialect. A Sociolinguistic Study.* Cambridge: Cambridge University Press.

Cheshire, Jenny and Penelope Gardner-Chloros (eds) (2018). *Multicultural Youth Vernaculars in Paris and Urban France*, special issue of *Journal of French Language Studies*: 28(2).

Chiari, Pietro (1751–65). *Lettere scelte di varie materie piacevoli, critiche, ed erudite, scritte ad una dama di qualità.* 3 vols. Venice: Angelo Pasinelli.

Chiflet, Laurent (1659). *Essay d'une parfaite Grammaire de la langue françoise*. Anvers: Van Meurs.

Choi, E-Jung (2006). *Grammaticalité de l'accord du participe passé conjugué avec avoir dans le 'Journal de la langue française' d'Urbain Domergue*, doctoral thesis, University of Illinois, Urbana-Champaign.

Choi, E-Jung (2007). 'Quels facteurs (linguistiques ou historiques) considérer dans l'accord en français? Étude de certains cas dans le *Journal de la langue française* (1784–1792) d'Urbain Domergue', in Douglas A. Kibbee (ed.), *History of Linguistics 2005: Selected Papers from the 10th International Conference on the History of the Language Sciences (ICHOLS X), 1–5 September 2005, Urbana-Champaign, Illinois*. Amsterdam: John Benjamins, 183–96.

Choi, E-Jung (2008). 'À la recherche de la vérité linguistique dans le *Journal de la langue française* (1784–1792): le cas de l'accord du participe passé conjugué avec "avoir"', in Yves Bourassa, Alexandre Landry, Marie-Lise Laquerre, and Stéphanie Massé (eds), *Critique des savoirs sous l'ancien régime: érosion des certitudes et émergence de la libre pensée*. Quebec: Presses de l'Université Laval, 207–16.

Christofides, Sarah (2019). 'Inclusive Writing *avant la lettre*: Linguistic Feminization in the Nineteenth-century French Press', *Women & Language* 42(2): 227–62.

'Circulaire 76–123 Prise en compte dans l'enseignement des patrimoines culturels et linguistiques français', *Bulletin officiel de l'Éducation nationale* 14, 8 April 1976.

Clifton, Jonathan and Dorien Van De Mieroop (2010). '"Doing" Ethos – A Discursive Approach to the Strategic Deployment and Negotiation of Identities in Meetings', *Journal of Pragmatics* 42(9): 2449–61.

CNESCO (Conseil national d'évaluation des systèmes scolaires) (2019). 'De la découverte à l'appropriation des langues vivantes étrangères: comment l'école peut-elle mieux accompagner les élèves?'. https://www.cnesco.fr/wp-content/uploads/2019/04/190410_Dossier_synthese_Langues_.pdf accessed 4 December 2021.

Cohen, Marcel (1950). *Regards sur la langue française*. Paris: Sedes.

Cole, Alistair and Jean-Baptiste Paul Harguindéguy (2013). 'The Jacobin Republic and Language Rights: Ethnolinguistic Mobilisations in France', *Regional and Federal Studies* 23(1): 27–46.

Collen, Ian (2021). 'Language Trends 2021: Language Teaching in Primary and Secondary Schools in England'. https://www.britishcouncil.org/sites/default/files/language_trends_2021_report.pdf accessed 4 December 2021.

Colombini Mantovani, Adriana (2000). 'Il Collegio Reale delle Fanciulle di Milano e i suoi primi maestri di francese', in Nadia Minerva (ed.) [in collaboration with Brigitte Soubeyran], *Dames, demoiselles, honnêtes femmes: studi di lingua e letteratura francese offerti a Carla Pellandra*. Bologna: CLUEB, 107–21.

Colombo Timelli, Maria (2000). 'Grammaires italiennes pour l'enseignement du français (1625–1700)', in Jan De Clercq, Nico Lioce, and Pierre Swiggers (eds), *Grammaire et enseignement du français*. Leuven/Paris/Sterling: Peeters, 565–87.

Colombo Timelli, Maria (ed.) (2001). 'L'insegnamento della lingua francese a Milano nei secoli XVIII-XIX', *Acme, Annali della Facoltà di lettere e filosofia dell'Università degli studi di Milano* 54(2), 211–98.

Combettes, Bernard (1988). *Recherche sur l'ordre des éléments de la phrase en moyen français*, doctoral thesis, Université de Nancy.

Combettes, Bernard (1993). 'Les Marques linguistiques de l'opposition des plans: valeurs aspectuelles et progression thématique', *Mélanges C. Conter. Études romanes* 6: 103–12.

Combettes, Bernard (2011). 'Subordination inverse et opposition des plans à l'époque classique', in Gilles Corminboeuf and Marie-José Béguelin (eds), *Du système linguistique aux actions langagières*. Brussels: De Boeck-Duculot, 83–94.

Comman, Henri-Joseph (1806). *Abrégé de la grammaire française propre à préparer les enfans du second âge à l'étude de l'orthographe et à faciliter à ceux qui n'ont appris qu'à lire ou à parler patois le moyen de participer aux avantages inappréciables de l'instruction publique*. Courgenay: publisher unnamed.

Commynes, Philippe de (2007 [1479]). *Mémoires*, ed. Joël Blanchard. Geneva: Droz.

Conrick, Maeve and Vera Regan (2007). *French in Canada. Language Issues*. Bern: Peter Lang.

Considine, John (2008). *Dictionaries in Early Modern Europe. Lexicography and the Making of Heritage*. Cambridge: Cambridge University Press.

Considine, John (2014). *Academy Dictionaries 1600–1800*. Cambridge: Cambridge University Press.

Conti, Antonella (2001). 'Le grammatiche per l'insegnamento del francese pubblicate a Milano nel periodo napoleonico (1796–1814)', in Colombo Timelli 2001: 228–44.

Cook, Peter (2015). 'Onontio Gives Birth: How the French in Canada became Fathers to their Indigenous Allies, 1645–73', *Canadian Historical Review* 96(2): 165–93.

Copland, Fiona and Angela Creese (2015). *Linguistic Ethnography: Collecting, Analysing and Presenting Data*. London: Sage.

Coquebert de Montbret, Eugène and Jean de Labouderie (1831). *Mélanges sur les langues, dialectes et patois, renfermant, entre autres, une collection de versions de la parabole de l'Enfant prodigue en cent idiomes ou patois différens, presque tous de France; précédés d'un essai d'un travail sur une géographie linguistique de la langue française*. Paris: Delaunay.

Cormier, Monique C. (2003) 'From the Dictionnaire de l'Académie Française dediée au roi (1694) to the Royal Dictionary (1699) of Abel Boyer: Tracing Inspiration', *International Journal of Lexicography* 16: 19–41.

Cormier, Monique C. (2005). 'The Reception of Abel Boyer's Royal Dictionary in the 18th Century', *Journal of the Dictionary Society of North America* 26: 174–93.

Cormier, Monique C. (2008). 'Usage Labels in the Royal Dictionary (1699) by Abel Boyer', *International Journal of Lexicography* 21(2): 153–71.

Cormier, Monique C. (2010). 'Fragments of History Prior to two Editions of the Dictionary by Lewis Chambaud, a Rival of Abel Boyer', *International Journal of Lexicography* 23(2): 173–87.

Cormier, Monique C. and Heberto Fernandez (2004). 'Influence in Lexicography: A Case Study. Abel Boyer's *Royal Dictionary* (1699) and Captain John Stevens' *Dictionary English and Spanish* (1705)', *International Journal of Lexicography* 17(3): 291–308.

Coşeriu, Eugenio (1981). 'Los conceptos de *dialecto, nivel* y *estilo de lengua* y el sentido propio de la dialectología', *Lingüística española actual* 3: 1–32.

Costa, James (2012). 'De l'hygiène verbale dans le sud de la France ou Occitanie', *Lengas* 72: 83–112.

Costa, James (2015). 'New Speakers, New Language: On Being a Legitimate Speaker of a Minority Language in Provence', *International Journal of the Sociology of Language* 231: 127–45.

Costa, James (2017). *Revitalising Language in Provence. A Critical Approach*. Oxford: Wiley-Blackwell.

Costa, James and Médéric Gasquet-Cyrus (2013). 'What is Language Revitalisation Really about? Competing Language Revitalisation Movements in Provence', in Mari C. Jones and Sarah Ogilvie (eds), *Keeping Languages Alive*. Cambridge: Cambridge University Press, 212–24.

Costa-Carreras, Joan (2018). 'Variation and Prescriptivism', in Wendy Ayres-Bennett and Janice Carruthers (eds), *Manual of Romance Sociolinguistics*. Berlin/Boston: de Gruyter, 307–31.

Cotelli Kureth, Sara (2014). 'Sur les traces de William Pierrehumbert ou de Philippe Godet? Les Chroniques de langage neuchâteloises des années 1950 à 1970', in Federica Diémoz and Dorothée Acquino-Weber (eds), *'Toujours langue varie...': mélanges de linguistique historique du français et de dialectologie galloromane offerts à M. le Professeur Andres Kristol par ses collègues et anciens élèves*. Geneva: Droz, 329–48.

Cotelli Kureth, Sara (2021). 'The Authority of *Usage*: Columns on Language, from the Purist- to the "Scientific"', in Carmen Marimón Llorca and Sabine Schwarze (eds), *Authoritative Discourse in Language Columns: Linguistic, Ideological and Social Issues*. Berlin: Peter Lang, 141–62.

Council of Europe (2001). 'Common European Framework of Reference for Languages: Learning, Teaching, Assessment (CEFR)'. https://www.coe.int/en/web/language-policy/cefr accessed 4 December 2021.

Courdès-Murphy, Léa and Julien Eychenne (2021). 'Dynamiques à l'œuvre dans le nivellement des voyelles nasales à Marseille', *Journal of French Language Studies* 31(3): 245–69.

Courouau, Jean-François (2005). 'L'Invention du *patois* ou la progressive émergence d'un marqueur sociolinguistique français XIIIe-XVIIe siècles', *Revue de linguistique romane* 69: 185–225.

Coutonnier, Guillaume (1734). *Metode pour apprendre aisément le françois, tirèe des meilleurs grammaires. [...] Ouvrage rèduit à un moindre volume pour plus grande facilitè des amateurs du françois*. Milan: Beniamino Sirtori.

Coveney, Aidan (1996). *Variability in Spoken French. A Sociolinguistic Study of Interrogation and Negation*. Exeter: Elm Bank Publications.

Cowie, A. P. (ed.) (2009). *The Oxford History of English Lexicography*. Oxford: Oxford University Press.

Cowling, David (2007). 'Henri Estienne and the Problem of French–Italian Code-switching in Sixteenth-century France', in Wendy Ayres-Bennett and Mari C. Jones (eds), *The French Language and Questions of Identity*. Oxford: Legenda, 162–70.

Coyos, Jean-Baptiste (2019). 'Public Language Policy and the Revitalisation of Basque', in Michelle Harrison and Aurélie Joubert (eds), *French Language Policies and the Revitalisation of Regional Languages in the 21st Century*. London: Palgrave Macmillan, 245–64.

Cremona, Joseph (2002). 'Italian-Based Lingua Francas around the Mediterranean', in Anna Laura Lepschy and Arturo Tosi (eds), *Multilingualism in Italy Past and Present*. Oxford: Legenda, 24–30.

Cristiani, Andrea (2003). '*Colpo d'occhio su lo stato presente della letteratura italiana*, di Giovanni Ristori', *Lettere italiane* 55(2): 267–92.

Crowley, Tony (1990). 'That Obscure Object of Desire. A Science of Language', in John E. Joseph and Talbot J. Taylor (eds), *Ideologies of Language*. London: Routledge, 27–50.

Crowley, Tony (2000). *The Politics of Language in Ireland 1366–1922: A Sourcebook*. London: Routledge.

Crowley, Tony (2006). 'The Political Production of a Language', *Journal of Linguistic Anthropology* 16(1): 23–35.

Culpeper, Jonathan and Merja Kytö (2010). *Early Modern English Dialogues: Spoken Interaction as Writing*. Cambridge: Cambridge University Press.

D'Anglejan, Alison and G. Richard Tucker (1973). 'Sociolinguistic Correlates of Speech Style in Quebec', in Roger W. Shuy and Ralph W. Fasold (eds), *Language Attitudes: Current Trends and Prospects*. Washington: Georgetown University Press, 1–27.

D'Anjou, René (1980). *Le Livre du cuer d'amours espris*, ed. Susan Wharton. Paris: UGE.

D'Urfé, Honoré (1966). *L'Astrée*. Geneva: Slatkine.

Dangeau, Abbé Louis de (1754). 'Essais de grammaire', in Abbé Pierre-Joseph Thoulier D'Olivet (ed.), *Opuscules sur la langue françoise. Par divers académiciens*. Paris: Brunet, 5–242.

Dardel, Robert de and Ans C. de Kok (1996). *La Position des pronoms régimes atones—personnels et adverbiaux—en protoroman: avec une considération spéciale de ses prolongements en français*. Geneva: Droz.

Dardi, Andrea (1984). 'Uso e diffusione del francese', in Lia Formigari (ed.), *Teorie e pratiche nell'Italia del Settecento*. Bologna: Il Mulino, 347–72.

Dardi, Andrea (1992). *Dalla provincia all'Europa: l'influsso francese sull'italiano tra il 1650 e il 1715*. Florence: Le Lettere.

Darmody, Merike and Tania Daly (2015). *Attitudes towards the Irish Language on the Island of Ireland*. Dublin: Foras na Gaeilge and ESRI.

Daunt, William J. Neill (1848). *Personal Recollections of the Late Daniel O'Connell. M.P.* London: Chapman and Hall.

Dauzat, Albert (1927). *Les Patois. Évolution. Classification. Étude*. Paris: Delagrave.

Dauzat, Albert (1939). 'Un nouvel Atlas linguistique de la France', *Le Français moderne* 7: 97–101.

Dauzat, Albert (1950). *Phonétique et grammaire historiques de la langue française*. Paris: Larousse.

Davidson, Justin and Mairi McLaughlin (2021a). '(Semi-)spontaneous Translation as Sociolinguistic Production: The Social Underpinnings of Variation in News Translation from English to French', presented at *New Ways of Analyzing Variation 49*, University of Texas, Austin, Texas, United States (virtual).

Davidson, Justin and Mairi McLaughlin (2021b). 'Translator Style as a Sociolinguistic Variable: Variation in News Translation from English to Romance', presented at *Linguistic Symposium on Romance Languages 51*, University of Illinois, Urbana-Champaign, Illinois, United States (virtual).

Davies, J. D. (2009). 'Temple, Sir William, Baronet (1628–1699)', in David Cannadine (ed.), *Oxford Dictionary of National Biography*. Oxford: Oxford University Press. https://doi.org/10.1093/ref:odnb/27122

Davies-Deacon, Merryn (2020). *New Speaker Language and Identity: Practices and Perceptions around Breton as a Regional Language of France*, doctoral thesis, Queen's University Belfast.

De Béthune, Conon (1921 [c.1180]). *Les Chansons de Conon de Béthune*, ed. Axel Wallensköld. Paris: Honoré Champion.

De Bèze, Theodore (1584). *De francicae linguae recta pronuntiatione tractatus*. Geneva: Vignon.

De Brosses, Charles (1931). *Lettres familières sur l'Italie, publiées d'après les manuscrits avec une introduction et des notes par Yvonne Bezard*. 2 vols. Paris: Firmin-Didot.

De Choisy, Abbé François Timoléon (1754). 'Journal de l'Académie françoise', in Abbé Pierre-Joseph Thoulier D'Olivet, (ed.), *Opuscules sur la langue françoise. Par divers académiciens*. Paris: Brunet, 243–340.

De Clercq, Jan, Nico Lioce, and Pierre Swiggers (eds) (2000). *Grammaire et enseignement du français, 1500–1700*. Leuven/Paris/Sterling: Peeters.

De Coincy, Gautier (1966 [1218]). *Miracles de Notre Dame*, ed. Frederic Koenig. Geneva: Droz.

De Fontenay, l'Abbé (1785–90). *Journal général de France*.

De Gaulle, Charles (2001 [1870]). *Pétition pour les langues provinciales*. Genève: Arbre d'Or.

De Gouges, Olympe (1791). *Déclaration des droits de la femme et de la citoyenne*. Paris: no pub.

De Houwer, Annick (1999). 'Environmental Factors in Early Bilingual Development: The Role of Parental Beliefs and Attitudes', in Guus Extra and Ludo Verhoeven (eds), *Bilingualism and Migration*. Berlin/New York: Mouton de Gruyter, 75–95. https://abp.bzh/pdfs/c/chdegpetitionentiere2001.pdf accessed 16 May 2021.

De la Sale, Antoine (1965 [1456]). *Le Roman de Jehan de Saintré*, ed. Jean Misrahi and Charles A. Knudson. Geneva: Droz.

De Lafayette, Mme (2006 [1671]). *Zayde*, ed. Camille Esmein-Sarrazin. Paris: Garnier.

De Mauro, Tullio (1963). *Storia linguistica dell'Italia unita*. Bari: Laterza.

De Navarre, Marguerite (1960 [c.1545]). *L'Heptaméron*, ed. Michel François. Paris: Garnier.

De Paolis, Alessandra (2006). 'Una letterata veneta tra giornalismo e traduzioni: Elisabetta Caminer Turra', in Giuseppe Coluccia and Beatrice Stasi (eds), *Traduzioni letterarie e rinnovamento del gusto: dal Neoclassicismo al primo Romanticismo. Atti del Convegno internazionale, Lecce-Castro, 15–18 giugno 2005*. Vol I. Galatina: Congedo, 137–48.

De Rosset, François (1997). 'Histoires tragiques', in Raymond Picard (ed.), *Nouvelles du XVIIe siècle*. Paris: Gallimard, 11–66.

De Schryver, Gilles-Maurice (2002). 'Web for/as Corpus: A Perspective for the African Languages', *Nordic Journal of African Studies* 11(2): 266–82.

De Visé, Donneau (1672–1710). *Mercure galant*.

De Wailly, Noël-François (1782). *L'Orthographe des dames, ou L'Orthographe fondée sur la bonne prononciation, démontrée la seule raisonnable*. Paris: Mérigot le jeune.

Dees, Anthonij, with contributions by Marcel Dekker, Onno Huber, and Karin van Reenen-Stein (1987). *Atlas des formes linguistiques des textes littéraires de l'ancien français*. Tübingen: Max Niemeyer.

Dees, Anthonij, Pieter van Reenen, and Johan de Vries (1980). *Atlas des formes et des constructions des chartes françaises du 13e siècle*. Tübingen: Max Niemeyer.

Del Lungo Camiciotti, Gabriella (2006a). '"Conduct yourself towards all persons on every occasion with civility and in a wise and prudent manner; this will render you esteemed": Stance Features in Nineteenth-century Business Letters', in Marina Dossena and Susan M. Fitzmaurice (eds), *Business and Official Correspondence: Historical Investigations*. Bern: Peter Lang, 153–74.

Del Lungo Camiciotti, Gabriella (2006b). 'From *Your obedient humble servants* to *Yours faithfully*: The Negotiation of Professional Roles in Commercial Correspondence of the Second Half of the Nineteenth Century', in Marina Dossena and Irma Taavitsainen (eds), *Diachronic Perspectives on Domain-specific English*. Bern: Peter Lang, 153–72.

Del Lungo Camiciotti, Gabriella (2010). 'Introduction', in Nicholas Brownlees, Gabriella Del Lungo Camiciotti, and John Denton (eds), *The Language of Public and Private Communication in a Historical Perspective*. Newcastle upon Tyne: Cambridge Scholars Publishing, 1–23.

Delattre, Pierre (1966). *Studies in French and Comparative Phonetics*. The Hague: Mouton.

Deletanville, Thomas (1771). *A New French Dictionary, in Two Parts: The First, French and English; the Second, English and French: ... To Which Is Prefixed, a French Grammar* [...] London: printed for J. Nourse and P. Vaillant.

Denez, Per (1977). *Brezhoneg... buan hag aes: A Beginner's Course in Breton*. English edn, translated and adapted by Raymond Delaporte. Cork: Cork University Press.

Denoyelle, Corinne (2013). *De l'oral à l'écrit. Le Dialogue à travers les genres romanesque et théâtral*. Orléans: Paradigme.

Denoyelle, Corinne (2016). *Poétique du dialogue médiéval*. Rennes: Presses universitaires de Rennes.

Denvir, Gearóid (1997). 'Decolonizing the Mind: Language and Literature in Ireland', *New Hibernia Review/Iris Éireannach Nua* 1(1): 44–68.

Depau, Giovanni (2019). 'Diffusion and Transmission of Franco-Provençal: A Study of Speakers' Linguistic Conscience', in Michelle Harrison and Aurélie Joubert (eds), *French Language Policies and the Revitalisation of Regional Languages in the 21st Century*. London: Palgrave Macmillan, 129–48.

Depecker, Loïc (2001). *L'Invention de la langue. Le Choix des mots nouveaux*. Paris: Armand Colin.

des Périers, Bonaventure (1980 [1558]). *Récréations et joyeux devis*. ed. Krystyna Kasprzyk. Paris: Champion.

Descartes, René (1644). *Renati Des-Cartes Principia philosophiae*. Amsterdam: apud Ludovicum Elzevirium.

Descartes, René (1722). *I principj della filosofia di Renato Des-cartes. Tradotti dal francese col confronto del latino in cui l'autore gli scrisse da Giuseppa Eleonora Barbapiccola tra gli Arcadi Mirista*. Turin: Giovanni Francesco Mairesse.

Desfontaines, Pierre-François Guyot, dit abbé (1726). *Dictionnaire néologique à l'usage des beaux esprits du siècle*. Paris: Lottin.

Desgrouais, Jean (1766). *Les Gasconismes corrigés*. Toulouse: J-J. Robert.

Detey, Sylvain, Jacques Durand, Bernard Laks, and Chantal Lyche (eds) (2010). *Les Variétés du français parlé dans l'espace francophone. Ressources pour l'enseignement*. Paris: Ophrys.

Detey, Sylvain, Jacques Durand, Bernard Laks, and Chantal Lyche (eds) (2016). *Varieties of Spoken French*. Oxford: Oxford University Press.

Detey, Sylvain, Chantal Lyche, Isabelle Racine, Sandra Schwab, and David Le Gac (2016). 'The Notion of Norm in Spoken French: Production and Perception', in Sylvain Detey, Jacques Durand, Bernard Laks, and Chantal Lyche (eds), *Varieties of Spoken French*. Oxford: Oxford University Press, 55–67.

Detges, Ulrich (2003). 'Du sujet parlant au sujet grammatical. L'Obligatorisation des pronoms sujets en ancien français dans une perspective pragmatique et comparative', *Verbum* 25(3): 307–33.

Devoto, Giacomo (1953). *Profilo di storia linguistica italiana*. Florence: La Nuova Italia.

Dewaele, Jean-Marc and James McCloskey (2015). 'Attitudes towards Foreign Accents among Adult Multilingual Language Users', *Journal of Multilingual and Multicultural Development* 26(3): 221–38.

DGLF (Délégation générale à la langue française) (1994). *Dictionnaire des termes officiels de la langue française*. Paris: Direction des journaux officiels.

Diderot, Denis and Jean le Rond d'Alembert (eds) (1751–72). *Encyclopédie, dictionnaire raisonnée des sciences, des arts et des métiers par une société de gens de lettres*. 28 vols. Paris: Briasson/ David/ Le Breton/ Durand.

Din, Gilbert C. (2014). *Populating the Barrera: Spanish Immigration Efforts in Colonial Louisiana*. Lafayette: University of Louisiana at Lafayette Press.

Dister, Anne (2023). 'De la féminisation des titres à la féminisation des textes: les politiques linguistiques en Belgique et en France', *Le Français moderne* 91(1).

Dister, Anne and Marie-Louise Moreau (2006). '"Dis-moi comment tu féminises, je te dirai pour qui tu votes". Les Dénominations des candidates dans les élections européennes de 1989 et de 2004 en Belgique et en France', *Langage et société* 115(1): 5–45.

Dister, Anne and Hubert Naets (2020). 'Les Rectifications de l'orthographe en Belgique francophone: de la politique linguistique aux pratiques des écoliers et de la presse', *Cahiers de praxématique* 74: 65–9.

Domergue, François Urbain (ed.) (1784–95). *Journal de la langue françoise, soit exacte soit ornée*.

Donaldson, Bryan (2014). 'Socio-stylistic Reflexes of Syntactic Change in Old French', *Journal of French Language Studies* 24(3): 319–45.

Donaldson, Bryan (2018). 'Diachronie de la négation phrastique en français: apports d'une approche sociolinguistique', *The Canadian Journal of Linguistics* 63(2): 221–41.

Dossena, Marina (2006). 'Stance and Authority in Nineteenth-century Bank Correspondence – A Case Study', in Marina Dossena and Susan M. Fitzmaurice (eds), *Business and Official Correspondence: Historical Investigations*. Bern: Peter Lang, 175–92.

Douglas, Allen (2002). *War, Memory and the Politics of Humor: The Canard Enchaîné and World War I*. Berkeley/London: University of California Press.

Dougnac, Françoise (1981). *François-Urbain Domergue. Le Journal de la langue françoise et la néologie lexicale (1784–1795)*, doctoral thesis, Université Sorbonne Nouvelle Paris III.

Dougnac, Françoise (1982). 'Aspects de la néologie lexicale dans le *Journal de la langue françoise* (1784–1795) de F.-U. Domergue', *Linx* 7: 7–53.

Dougnac, Françoise (1989). 'Questions d'actualité: vouvoiement et titre de personnes dans le *Journal de la langue française* (1er janvier 1791–24 mars 1792)', *Archives et documents de la Société d'histoire et d'épistémologie des sciences du langage* 1: 53–62.

Dougnac, Françoise (1991). 'Le Journal de la langue française (1784–1795)', in Jean Sgard (ed.), *Dictionnaire des journaux 1600–1789*. 2 vols. Oxford/Paris: Voltaire Foundation/Universitas, 591–96.

Dougnac, Françoise, Tristan Hordé, and Sylvain Auroux (1982). 'Les Premiers Périodiques linguistiques français', *Histoire épistémologie langage* 4(1): 117–32.

Dourdet, Jean-Christophe (2019). 'Opposition to the Process of Language Identification and Standardisation in "Limousin Occitan" and "Poitevin-Saintongeais"', in Michelle Harrison and Aurélie Joubert (eds), *French Language Policies and the Revitalisation of Regional Languages in the 21st Century*. London: Palgrave Macmillan, 63–82.

Dourdy Laura-Maï and Michela Spacagno (2020). 'Donner la parole aux interrogés: une étude de l'oral représenté dans les comptes rendus de procès médiévaux aux XIVe et XVe siècles', *Langages* 217(1): 119–32.

Dourdy, Laura-Maï, Michela Spacagno, and Laetitia Sauwala (2019). 'Observer les marqueurs discursifs à travers le prisme du genre textuel en moyen français', *Studia linguistica romanica* 2: 7–33.

Dousset-Seiden, Christine (2005). 'La Nation française et l'Antiquité à l'époque napoléonienne', *Anabases* 1: 59–74.

Doyle, Aidan (2015). *A History of the Irish Language*. Oxford: Oxford University Press.
Droixhe, Daniel (2007). *Souvenirs de Babel. La Reconstruction de l'histoire des langues de la Renaissance aux Lumières*. Brussels: Académie royale de langue et de littérature françaises de Belgique.
Du Bellay, Joachim. (2001 [1549]) *La Deffence, et illustration de la langue françoyse*, Geneva: Librairie Droz.
Dubois, Sylvie, Emilie Gagnet Leumas, and Malcolm Richardson (2018). *Speaking French in Louisiana, 1720–1955: Linguistic Practices of the Catholic Church*. Baton Rouge: Louisiana State University Press.
Dunlevy, Deirdre A. (2020). 'Learning Irish amid Controversy: How the Irish Language Act Debate has Impacted Learners of Irish in Belfast', *Journal of Multilingual and Multicultural Development*. https://doi.org/10.1080/01434632.2020.1854272
Dupleix, Scipion (1651). *Liberté de la langue françoise dans sa pureté*. Paris: D. Bechet.
Durand, Jacques, Bernard Laks, and Chantal Lyche (2014). 'French Phonology from a Corpus Perspective: The PFC Programme', in Jacques Durand, Ulrike Gut, and Gjert Kristoffersen (eds), *The Oxford Handbook of Corpus Phonology*. Oxford: Oxford University Press, 486–97.
Durand, Pierre (1625). *Grammatica italiana per imparare la lingua francese*. Rome: Francesco Corbelletti a istanza di Maurizio Bona.
Duret, Claude (1613). *Thrésor de l'histoire des langues de cest univers*. Cologny: Berjon.
Dyche, Thomas and William Pardon (1735). *A New General English Dictionary; Peculiarly Calculated for the Use and Improvement of Such as Are Unacquainted with the Learned Languages. Wherein the Difficult Words, and Technical Terms [...]*. Dublin: printed for Peter Wilson, at Gay's-Head, in Dame-Street, Bookseller.
Dyche, Thomas and William Pardon (1744). *A New General English Dictionary; Peculiarly Calculated for the Use and Improvement of Such as Are Unacquainted with the Learned Languages. Wherein the Difficult Words, and Technical Terms [...]*, 2nd edn. Dublin: printed for Peter Wilson, at Gay's-Head, in Dame-Street, Bookseller.
Eckert, Penelope (1989). *Jocks and Burnouts: Social Categories and Identity in the High School*. New York: Teachers College Press.
Eckert, Penelope (2012). 'Three Waves of Variation Study. The Emergence of Meaning in the Study of Sociolinguistic Variation', *Annual Review of Anthropology* 41(1): 87–100.
Eckert, Penelope (2016). 'Variation, Meaning and Social Change', in Nikolas Coupland (ed.), *Sociolinguistics: Theoretical Debates*. Cambridge: Cambridge University Press, 68–85.
Edwards, John (1994). *Multilingualism*. London: Routledge.
Edwards, John (2012). 'Preface: Language, Prescriptivism, Nationalism and Identity', in Carol Percy and Mary Catherine Davidson (eds), *The Language of Nation: Attitudes and Norms*. Bristol: Multilngual Matters, 11–36.
Egger, Émile (1843). 'Des dialectes et des patois', *Revue de l'instruction publique* 2(16): 248–50.
Éloy, Jean-Michel (1997). 'Français, langue française, et autres langues. Le Travail de dénomination des langues chez les parlementaires français en 1994', in Andrée Tabouret-Keller (ed.), *Le Nom des langues I. Les Enjeux de la nomination des langues*. Louvain-la-Neuve: Peeters, 81–97.
Éloy, Jean-Michel (ed.) (2004). *Les Langues collatérales. Problèmes linguistiques, sociolinguistiques et glottopolitiques de la proximité linguistique*. Paris: L'Harmattan.

Éloy, Jean-Michel (2004). 'Les Langues collatérales: problèmes et propositions, in Jean-Michel Éloy (ed.), *Les Langues collatérales. Problèmes linguistiques, sociolinguistiques et glottopolitiques de la proximité linguistique*. Paris: L'Harmattan, 6–25.

Éloy, Jean-Michel, Fanny Martin, and Cécile Mathiru (2019). 'Picard in the Digital World: A Language that Is Seen', in Michelle Harrison and Aurélie Joubert (eds), *French Language Policies and the Revitalisation of Regional Languages in the 21st Century*. London: Palgrave Macmillan, 203–20.

Encrevé, Pierre (1988). *La Liaison avec et sans enchaînement*. Paris: Seuil.

Engelaere, Olivier (1994). 'Le Mouvement picard en France du début des années 1970 à la fin des années 1980', *De Franse Nederlanden/Les Pays-Bas Français* 19: 90–113.

Ernout, Alfred and François Thomas (1951). *Syntaxe latine*. Paris: Klincksieck.

Escafré-Dublet, Angéline (2014). 'Mainstreaming Immigrant Integration Policy in France'. Brussels: Migration Policy Institute Report.

Ess, Charles (2019). *Digital Media Ethics*, 3rd edn. Cambridge: Polity.

Estienne, Henri (1578). *Deux dialogues du nouueau langage françois italianizé ou autrement deguizé*. Anvers: Guillaume Niergue.

Estienne, Robert (1538). *Dictionarium latinogallicum*. Paris: Ex Office Roberti Stephani.

Estienne, Robert (1972 [1549]). *Dictionnaire françois-latin [...] corrigé et augmenté*. Paris: de l'imprimerie de Robert Estienne. Facsimile reprint Geneva: Slatkine.

Estienne, Robert (1972 [1557]). *Traicté de la grammaire françoise*. Geneva: Estienne. Facsimile reprint Geneva: Slatkine.

Estival, Dominique and Alastair Pennycook (2011). 'L'Académie française and Anglophone Language Ideologies', *Language Policy* 10: 325–41.

Fabius, Laurent (1986). 'Circulaire du 11 mars 1986 relative à la féminisation des noms de métier, fonction, grade ou titre', *Journal officiel de la République française* 64(16 Marc): 04267. https://www.legifrance.gouv.fr/jorf/id/JORFTEXT000000866501 accessed 30 April 2021.

Fabre, Antoine (1626). *Grammatica per imparare le lingue italiana, francese e spagnola [...] Arricchita di osservazioni, e precetti necessari, [...] Aggiontovi al fine alcuni Dialoghi dove contengono motti acuti e maniere di dire per chi desidera far viaggio*. Rome: Francesco Corbelletti.

Fagyal, Zsuzsanna (2010). *Accents de banlieue: aspects prosodiques du français populaire en contact avec les langues de l'immigration*. Paris: L'Harmattan.

Fairclough, Norman (2013). *Critical Discourse Analysis: The Critical Study of Language*. Abingdon: Routledge.

Fasoli, Fabio and Peter Hegarty (2020). 'A Leader doesn't Sound Lesbian! The Impact of Sexual Orientation Vocal Cues on Heterosexual Persons' First Impression and Hiring Decision', *Psychology of Women Quarterly* 44(2): 234–55.

Faure, Christian (1989). *Le Projet culturel de Vichy. Folklore et révolution nationale 1940–1944*. Lyon: Presses universitaires de Lyon.

Fénelon, François (1699). *Les Aventures de Télémaque, fils d'Ulysse*. Paris: chez Gueffier.

Féraud, Jean-François (1787–8). *Dictionaire critique de la langue française*. 2 vols. Marseille: Jean Mossy Père et Fils.

Feri de la Salle, Michel (1697). *La lingua franzese spiegata co' più celebri autori moderni*. Florence: da Cesare, e Francesco Bindi, all'insegna di S. Bernardo.

Ferrari, Luigi (1925). *Le traduzioni italiane del teatro tragico francese nei secoli 17 e 18: saggio bibliografico*. Paris: Librairie ancienne Édouard Champion.

Firbas, Jan (1992). *Functional Sentence Perspective in Written and Spoken Communication*. Cambridge: Cambridge University Press.

Fishman, Joshua A. (1968). 'Sociolinguistics and the Language Problems of the Developing Countries', in Joshua Fishman, Charles Ferguson, and Jyotirindra Das Gupta (eds), *Language Problems of Developing Nations*. New York: Wiley, 491–8.

Fishman, Joshua A. (1991). *Reversing Language Shift: Theoretical and Empirical Foundations of Assistance to Threatened Languages*. Clevedon: Multilingual Matters.

Fitzgerald, Garret (1984). 'Estimates for Baronies of Minimum Level of Irish-speaking amongst Successive Decennial Cohorts: 1771–1781 to 1861–1871', *Proceedings of the Royal Irish Academy: Archaeology, Culture, History, Literature* 84C: 117–55.

Fitzgerald, Garret (2003). 'Irish Speaking in the Pre-famine Period: A Study based on the 1911 Census Data for People Born before 1851 and still Alive in 1911', *Proceedings of the Royal Irish Academy: Archaeology, Culture, History, Literature* 103C(5): 5–283.

Fitzgerald, Garret (2005). *Ireland in the World: Further Reflections*. Dublin: Liberties Press.

Flaitz, Jeffra (2007). 'French Attitudes toward the Ideology of English as an International Language', *World Englishes* 12(2): 179–91.

Fleischman, Suzanne (1990). *Tense and Narrativity. From Medieval Performance to Modern Fiction*. London/Austin: Routledge/University of Texas Press.

Flutre, Louis Ferdinand (1954). 'Du rôle des femmes dans l'élaboration des Remarques de Vaugelas', *Neophilologus* 38(4): 241–48.

Flydal, Leiv (1951). 'Remarques sur certains rapports entre le style et l'état de langue', *Norsk Tidsskrift for Sprogvidenskap* 16: 240–57.

Fontenelle, Thierry (2015). 'Bilingual Dictionaries: History and Development; Current Issues', in Philip Durkin (ed.), *The Oxford Handbook of Lexicography*. Oxford: Oxford University Press, 44–61.

Forestier, G. and E. Bury (2007). 'Libertés du classicisme français', in Jean-Yves Tadié (ed.), *La Littérature française: dynamique et histoire*. Vol. 1. Paris: Gallimard, 616–70.

Fouché, Pierre (1959). *Traité de prononciation française*. Paris: Klincksieck. 2nd revised edn.

Foulet, Lucien (1924). 'Accent tonique et l'ordre des mots: formes faibles du pronom personnel après le verbe', *Romania* 50: 54–93.

Foulet, Lucien (1930 [1919]). *Petite syntaxe de l'ancien français*. Paris: Champion.

Foulet, Lucien (1935). 'L'Extension de la forme oblique du pronom personnel en ancien français', *Romania* 61 (243/244): 257–315/401–63.

Fournet, Arnaud (2012). 'La Linguistique du XIXe entre description et norme: *Le Patois boulonnais* de Daniel Haigneré', *Dialectologia* 8: 65–83.

Franciosini, Lorenzo (1624). *Gramatica spagnola e italiana, hora nuovamente uscita in luce, mediante la quale può il Castigliano con facilità, e fondamento impadronirsi della lingua toscana, & il Toscano, della castigliana; con la dichiarazione, & esempi di molte voci, e maniere di parlare dell'una, e dell'altra nazione [...] E con una chiarissima, e breve regola per leggere, e scrivere con vero accento*. Venice: Giacomo Sarzina.

Franciosini, Lorenzo (2018 [1624]). *Gramatica spagnola e italiana (1624)*, ed. Felix San Vicente. Padua: Cleup.

FRANTEXT (*Base textuelle Frantext*) (no date). ATILF (CNRS & Université de Lorraine). http://www.frantext.fr accessed 1 November 2020.

Franzén, Torsten (1939). *Étude sur la syntaxe des pronoms personnels sujets en ancien français*. Upsal: Almqvist et Wiksells.

Frugoni, Francesco Fulvio (1689). *Del cane di Diogene*. 7 vols. Venice: Antonio Bosio.

Furet, François and Jacques Ozouf (1977). *Lire et écrire: l'alphabétisation des Français de Calvin à Jules Ferry*. Paris: Éditions de Minuit.

Furetière, Antoine (1690). *Dictionaire universel Contenant generalement tous les mots françois tant vieux que modernes, & les termes de toutes les sciences et des arts [...]*. The Hague/Rotterdam: Arnout and Reinier Leers.

Gadet, Françoise (1997). 'La Variation, plus qu'une écume', *Langue française* 115: 5–18.

Gadet, Françoise (2003a). 'Is there a French Theory of Variation?', *International Journal of the Sociology of Language* 160: 17–40.

Gadet, Françoise (2003b). *La Variation sociale en français*. Paris: Ophrys.

Gadet, Françoise (2004). 'Mais que font les sociolinguistes?', *Langage et société* 107: 85–94.

Gadet, Francoise (ed.) (2017a). *Les Parlers jeunes dans l'Île de France multiculturelle*. Paris: Ophrys.

Gadet, Françoise (2017b). '*Variatio delectat*. Variation et dialinguistique', *Langage et société* 160(1): 75–91.

Gaiffe, Félix, Ernest Maille, Ernest Breuil, Simone Jahan, Léon Wagner, and Madeleine Marijon (1936). *Grammaire Larousse du XXe siècle. Traité complet de la langue française*. Paris: Larousse.

Gal, Susan (1989). 'Language and Political Economy', *Annual Review of Anthropology* 18: 345–67.

Gal, Susan (2006). 'Contradictions of Standard Language in Europe: Implications for the Study of Practices and Publics', *Social Anthropology* 14: 163–81.

Galeani Napione, Gian Francesco (1791). *Dell'uso, e dei pregj della lingua italiana libri tre con un discorso intorno alla storia del Piemonte*. 2 vols. Turin: Gaetano Balbino and Francesco Prato.

Garcia, Nuria (2015). 'Tensions between Cultural and Utilitarian Dimensions of Language: A Comparative Analysis of 'Multilingual' Education Policies in France and Germany', *Current Issues in Language Planning* 16(1–2): 43–59.

Gardelle, Laure (2019). 'Écriture inclusive et genre: quelles contraintes systématiques et cognitives à l'intervention sur une catégorie grammaticale et lexicale? Étude comparée anglais-français', *Le Discours et la langue* 11(1): 151–87.

Gardin, Bernard (1975). 'Loi Deixonne et langues régionales: représentation de la nature et de la fonction de leur enseignement', *Langue française* 25: 29–36.

Gardner, Peter (2015). 'Unionism, Loyalism, and the Ulster-Scots Ethnolinguistic "Revival"', *Studies in Ethnicity and Nationalism* 15(1): 4–25.

Gardner, Robert C. (1982). 'Language Attitudes and Language Learning', in Ellen Bouchard Ryan and Howard Giles (eds), *Attitudes towards Language Variation: Social and Applied Contexts*. London: Edward Arnold, 132–47.

Gardner, Robert C. and P. D. MacIntyre (1993). 'On the Measurement of Affective Variables in Second Language Learning', *Language Learning* 43: 157–94.

Garrapa, Luigia (2012). 'Hiatus Resolution between Function and Lexical Words in French and Italian: Phonology or Morphology', in Sascha Gaglia and Marc-Olivier Hinzelin (eds), *Inflection and Word Formation in Romance Languages*. Amsterdam: Benjamins, 141–78.

Garrett, Peter (2010). *Attitudes to Language*. Cambridge: Cambridge University Press.

Garrett, Peter, Nikolas Coupland, and Angie Williams (2003). *Investigating Language Attitudes: Social Meanings of Dialect, Ethnicity and Performance*. Cardiff: University of Wales Press.

Gauchat, Louis (1905). 'L'Unité phonétique dans le patois d'une commune', in Ernst Burger Bovet et al. (eds), *Aus romanischen Sprachen und Literaturen: Festschrift Heinrich Morf*. Halle: Max Niemeyer, 175–232.

Géa, Jean-Michel and Médéric Gasquet-Cyrus (eds) (2017). *Marseille. Entre gentrification et ségrégation langagière*, special issue of *Langage et société*: 162.
Geisler, Hans (1982). *Studien zur typologischen Entwicklung: Lateinisch, Altfranzösisch, Neufranzösisch*. Munich: Fink.
Genesee, Fred and Naomi E. Holobow (1989). 'Change and Stability in Intergroup Perceptions', *Journal of Language and Social Psychology* 8(1): 17–39.
German, Gary (2007). 'Language Shift, Diglossia and Dialectal Variation in Western Brittany: The Case of Southern Cornouaille', in Hildegard L. C. Tristram (ed.), *The Celtic Languages in Contact: Papers from the Workshop within the Framework of the XIII International Congress of Celtic Studies*. Bonn: Universitätsverlag Potsdam, 146–92.
Gerson, Stéphane (2003). *The Pride of Place: Local Memories and Political Culture in Modern France*. Ithaca: Cornell University Press.
Gessner, Conrad (1555). *Mithridates. De differentiis lingvarvm tvm vetervm tum quae hodie apud diuersas nationes in toto orbe terrarum in usu sunt*. Zurich: Froscoverus.
Gibbs, Graham C. (2004). 'Boyer, Abel (1667?–1729), Lexicographer and Journalist', in David Cannadine (ed.), *Oxford Dictionary of National Biography*. Oxford: Oxford University Press. https://doi.org/10.1093/ref:odnb/3122
Giles, Howard (1970). 'Evaluative Reactions to Accents', *Educational Review* 22(3): 211–27.
Giles, Howard (2022). 'Foreword', in Ruth Kircher and Lena Zipp (eds), *Research Methods in Language Attitudes*. Cambridge: Cambridge University Press, xiii–xviii.
Giles, Howard and Richard Y. Bourhis (1976). 'Methodological Issues in Dialect Perception: Some Social Psychological Perspectives', *Anthropological Linguistics* 18(7): 294–304.
Giles, Howard and Patricia Johnson (1981). 'The Role of Language in Ethnic Group Formation', in John C. Turner and Howard Giles (eds), *Intergroup Behavior*. Oxford: Basil Blackwell, 199–243.
Gilliéron, Jules (1880). *Patois de la commune de Vionnaz (Bas-Valais)*. Paris: École pratique des Hautes études/H. Vieweg.
Gilliéron, Jules and Pierre-Jean Rousselot (eds) (1887–92). *Revue des patois gallo-romans*.
Gilliéron, Jules and Edmond Edmont (1902). *Notice servant à l'intelligence des cartes*. Paris: H. Champion.
Gilliéron, Jules and Edmond Edmont (1902–10). *Atlas linguistique de la France*. Paris: H. Champion.
Ging, Debbie and Eugenia Siapera (2018). 'Special Issue on Online Misogyny', *Feminist Media Studies* 18(4): 515–24. https://doi.org/10.1080/14680777.2018.1447345
Giornale enciclopedico (1774–82). Venice: nella Stamperia Fenziana a spese del giornalista.
Girard, Gabriel (1982 [1747]). *Les Vrais Principes de la langue françoise*, Édition de Paris, with an introduction by Pierre Swiggers. Genève: Droz.
Giuliano, Mariella (2019). 'Esperienze di scritture al femminile nell'Italia del Settecento: sondaggi linguistici e stilistici su Elisabetta Caminer Turra e Gioseffa Cornoldi Caminer', *Italiano LinguaDue* 2: 697–714.
Givón, Talmy (1979). *On Understanding Grammar*. New York: Academic Press.
Glatigny, Michel (2001). 'Les Jugements d'acceptabilité dans le *Courrier de Vaugelas* (1868–1881)', *Le français moderne* 69(2): 129–60.
Glatigny, Michel (2004). 'Les Méthodes d'un "Remarqueur" du XIXe siècle', in Philippe Caron (ed.), *Les Remarqueurs: sur la langue française du XVIe siècle à nos jours*. Rennes: Presse Universitaire de Rennes, 185–200.
Glikman, Julie and Nicolas Mazziotta (2013). 'Représentation de l'oral et syntaxe dans la prose de la Queste del saint Graal (1225–1230)', in Dominique Lagorgette and Pierre

Larrivée (eds), *Représentations du sens linguistique 5*. Chambéry: Presses de l'Université de Savoie, 43–64.

Glikman, Julie and Stefan Schneider (2018). 'Constructions parenthétiques, marques d'oralité et type de textes en diachronie du français', in Wendy Ayres-Bennett, Anne Carlier, Julie Glikman, Thomas M. Rainsford, Gilles Siouffi, and Carine Skupien-Dekens (eds), *Nouvelles voies d'accès au changement linguistique*. Paris: Classiques Garnier, 317–34.

Glück, Helmut (2019). 'Matthias Kramer als Grammatiker und Lexicograph', in Mark Häberlein and Helmut Glück (eds), *Matthias Kramer. Ein Nürnberger Sprachmeister der Barockzeit mit gesamteuropäischer Wirkung*. Bamberg: University of Bamberg Press, 17–32.

Goalabré, Fabienne (2015). 'Immersion Education and the Revitalisation of Breton and Gaelic as Community Languages', in Mari C. Jones (ed.), *Policy and Planning for Endangered Languages*. Cambridge: Cambridge University Press, 48–66.

Godard, Thomas (2020). *John Priestley and the French Connection. A Study in Eighteenth-century Grammaticography*, doctoral thesis, University of Cambridge.

Goebl, Hans (2004). 'Bref aperçu sur les problems et méthodes de la dialectométrie (avec application à l'ALF)', in Jean-Michel Éloy (ed.), *Les Langues collatérales. Problèmes linguistiques, sociolinguistiques et glottopolitiques de la proximité linguistique*. Paris: L'Harmattan, 39–60.

Goebl, Hans (2008). 'Sur le changement macrolinguistique survenu entre 1300 et 1600 dans le domaine d'oïl. Une étude diachronique d'inspiration dialectométrique', *Dialectologia* 1: 3–43.

Goebl, Hans (2018). 'Dialectometry', in Charles Boberg, John Nerbonne, and Dominic Watt (eds), *The Handbook of Dialectology*. Hoboken NJ: John Wiley & Sons, 123–42.

Goffman, Erving (1963). *Behavior in Public Places. Notes on the Social Organization of Gatherings*. New York: The Free Press.

Gondret, Pierre (1989). 'L'Utilisation du patois parisien comme niveau de langue dans la littérature française au XVIIe siècle', *Cahiers de l'Association Internationale des Études Françaises* 41: 7–24.

Goodman, Dena (2002). 'L'Ortografe des dames: Gender and Language in the Old Regime', *French Historical Studies* 25(2): 191–223.

Gooskens, Charlotte, Vincent J. van Heuven, Jelena Golubović, Anja Schüppert, Femke Swarte, and Stefanie Voigt (2018). 'Mutual Intelligibility between Closely Related Languages in Europe', *International Journal of Multilingualism* 15(2): 169–93.

Gordon, David C. (1978). *The French Language and National Identity, 1930–1975*. The Hague: Mouton.

Gordon, Philip and Sophie Meunier (2001). *The French Challenge: Adapting to Globalization*. Washington DC: Brookings Institution Press.

Goudar, Lodovico (1744). *Nuova grammatica italiana e francese*. Milan: Agnelli.

Government of Ireland (1965). *Athbheochan na Gaeilge: The Restoration of the Irish Language*. Dublin: The Stationery Office.

Graf, Arturo (1911). *L'anglomania e l'influsso inglese in Italia nel secolo XVIII*. Turin: Loescher.

Greco, Luca (2020). 'Analyser la complexité sociale et sémiotique des pratiques à partir des notions d'agencement, de dispositif et d'assemblage', *Langage et société* 170: 221–8.

Green, John N. and Marie-Anne Hintze (2001). 'The Maintenance of Liaison in a Family Network', in Marie-Anne Hintze, Tim Pooley, and Anne Judge (eds), *French Accents: Phonological and Sociolinguistic Perspectives*. London: CILT–AFLS, 24–44.
Green, John N. and Marie-Anne Hintze (2004). 'Le *h* aspiré en français contemporain: stabilité, variation ou déclin?', in Aidan Coveney, Marie-Anne Hintze, and Carol Sanders (eds), *Variation et francophonie*. Paris: L'Harmattan, 241–80.
Green, John N. and Marie-Anne Hintze (2021). 'L'élision en français: une catégorie qui n'est plus catégorique', *Studii de Lingvistică* 11: 123–46.
Grégoire, Henri, dit abbé (1790). 'Le Questionnaire de l'abbé Grégoire'. https://www.axl.cefan.ulaval.ca/francophonie/gregoire-questionnaire.htm accessed 1 September 2022.
Grégoire, Henri, dit abbé (1794). 'Rapport sur la nécessité et les moyens d'anéantir les patois et d'universaliser la langue française', *Archives parlementaires* 91: 318–26.
Grevisse, Maurice (1980). *Le Bon Usage*, 11th revised edn. Paris/Gembloux: Duculot.
Grevisse, Maurice and André Goosse (1986). *Le Bon Usage. Grammaire francaise*, 12th revised edn. Gembloux: Duculot.
Grosjean, François (1982). *Life with Two Languages: An Introduction to Bilingualism*. London: Harvard University Press.
Grund, Peter J. and Terry Walker (2021). *Speech Representation in the History of English. Topics and Approaches*. Oxford: Oxford University Press.
Gruny, Pascale et al. (2022). *Proposition de loi no. 404*. https://www.senat.fr/leg/ppl21-404.pdf accessed 28 February 2022.
Guarnieri, Elisabetta (2001). 'Louis Guillaume Coutonnier e il suo *Metodo per imparare facilmente il francese* (Milano 1734, 1739, 1747)', in Colombo Timelli 2001: 245–63.
Guerci, Luciano (1987). *La discussione sulla donna nell'Italia del Settecento*. Turin: Tirrenia.
Guilbert, Louis, René Lagane, and Georges Niobey (1972). 'L'Hiatus', in Louis Guilbert, René Lagane, and Georges Niobey (eds), *Grand Larousse de la langue française*. Vol. 3. Paris: Larousse, 2424–6.
Guillot, Céline, Serge Heiden, Alexei Lavrentiev, and Bénédicte Pincemin (2015). 'L'Oral représenté dans un corpus de français médiéval (9e–15e): approche contrastive et outillée de la variation diasystémique', in Kirsten Jeppesen Kragh and Jan Lindschouw (eds), *Les Variations diasystémiques et leurs interdépendances dans les langues romanes. Actes du Colloque DIA II à Copenhague (19–21 nov. 2012)*. Strasbourg: Éditions de linguistique et de philologie, 15–28.
Guillot, Céline, Alexei Lavrentiev, Bénédicte Pincemin, and Serge Heiden (2013). 'Le Discours direct au Moyen Âge: vers une définition et une méthodologie d'analyse', in Dominique Lagorgette and Pierre Larrivée (eds), *Représentations du sens linguistique 5*. Chambéry: Presses de l'Université de Savoie, 17–41.
Guillot Céline, Sophie Prévost, and Alexei Lavrentiev (2014). 'Oral représenté et diachronie: étude des incises en français médiéval', in Franck Neveu, Peter Blumenthal, Linda Hriba, Annette Gerstenberg, Judith Meinschaefer, and Sophie Prévost (eds), *4e Congrès Mondial de Linguistique Française*. Les Ulis: EDP Sciences, 259–76.
Guillot-Barbance, Céline, Bénédicte Pincemin, and Alexei Lavrentiev (2017). 'Représentation de l'oral en français médiéval et genres textuels', *Langages* 208: 53–68.
Guillot-Barbance, Céline, Serge Heiden, Alexei Lavrentev, and Bénédicte Pincemin (2018). 'Diachronie de l'oral représenté. Délimitation et segmentation interne du dialogue (ixe–xve siècle)', in Wendy Ayres-Bennett, Anne Carlier, Julie Glikman, Thomas M. Rainsford, Gilles Siouffi, and Carine Skupien-Dekens (eds), *Nouvelles voies d'accès au changement linguistique*. Paris: Classiques Garnier, 279–96.

Guiomar, Jean-Yves (1992). 'La Révolution française et les origines celtiques de la France', *Annales historiques de la révolution française* 287: 63–85.
Gumperz, John (1982). *Discourse Strategies*. Cambridge: Cambridge University Press.
Gumperz, John (2003). 'Interactional Sociolinguistics: A Personal Perspective', in Deborah Schiffrin, Deborah Tannen, and Heidi Hamilton (eds), *The Handbook of Discourse Analysis*. Malden: Wiley Blackwell, 215–28.
Haddad, Raphaël (2017). *Manuel d'écriture inclusive: faites progresser l'égalité femmes.hommes par votre manière d'écrire*. Paris: Mots Clés.
Hafid-Martin, Nicole (1995). *Voyage et connaissance au tournant des Lumières (1780–1820)*. Oxford: Voltaire Foundation.
Hagège, Claude (1987). *Le Français et les siècles*. Paris: Éditions Odile Jacob.
Hales, Stephen (1727). *Vegetable staticks: or, An Account of Some Statical Experiments on the Sap in Vegetables: Being an Essay towards a Natural History of Vegetation. Also, a Specimen of an Attempt to Analyse the Air*. London: printed for W. and J. Innys, and T. Woodward.
Hales, Stephen (1735). *La Statique des végétaux, et l'analyse de l'air. Expériences nouvelles lûes à la Societé royale de Londres. Par M. Hales […] Ouvrage traduit de l'anglois, par M. de Buffon*. Paris: Chez Jacques Vincent.
Hales, Stephen (1750–2). *Emastatica, o sia Statica degli animali: esperienze idrauliche fatte sugli animali viventi dal signor Hales, […] tradotta dall'inglese nel franzese, e commentata dal signor De Sauvages, […] e dal franzese nuovamente trasportata nell'italiano idioma*, trans. Maria Angela Ardinghelli. 2 vols. Naples: Giuseppe Raimondi.
Hales, Stephen (1756). *Statica de' vegetabili ed analisi dell'aria. Opera del signor Stefano Hales della società regale delle scienze. Tradotta dall'inglese con varie annotazionii*, trans. Maria Angela Ardinghelli. Naples: Giuseppe Raimondi.
Hales, Stephen (1776a). *Emastatica o sia Statica degli animali esperienze idrauliche fatte sugli animali viventi dal signor Stefano Hales […]. Tradotta dall'inglese nel franzese, e commentata dal signor Francesco Boissier de Sauvages […]. E dal franzese nell'italiano idioma trasportata, e parimente comentata dalla Sig. M.A.A. [Maria Angela Ardinghelli]. Edizione terza accresciuta, e corretta*. Naples: Gaetano Castellano.
Hales, Stephen (1776b). *Statica de' vegetabili, ed analisi dell'aria, opera del Signor Stefano Hales […] tradotta dall'inglese in italiano, confrontata con la traduzione franzese, e comentata dalla Signora D.M.A. Ardinghelli. Edizione terza accresciuta, e corretta*. Naples: Gaetano Castellano.
Hall, Damien (2013). 'The Linguistic Geography of the French of Northern France: Do We Have the Basic Data?', *Language and Linguistics Compass* 7: 477–99.
Hall, Damien (2019). '(e) in Normandy: The Sociolinguistics, Phonetics and Phonology of the *Loi de position*', *Journal of French Language Studies* 29: 1–33.
Hall, Damien and David Hornsby (2015). 'Top-down or Bottom-up? Understanding the Diffusion of Supra-local Norms in France', in Winfred V. Davies and E. Ziegler (eds), *Language Planning and Microlinguistics: From Policy to Interaction and Vice-versa*. Basingstoke: Palgrave, 105–27.
Hall, Damien, Jonathan R. Kasstan, and David Hornsby (2019). 'Beyond Obsolescence: A Twenty-first Century Research Agenda for the *langues régionales*', *Journal of French Language Studies* 29: 155–68.
Hall, David J. (2004). 'Sewel, Willem (1653–1720)', in David Cannadine (ed.), *Oxford Dictionary of National Biography*. Oxford: Oxford University Press.
Hambye, Philippe and Michel Francard (2008). 'Normes endogènes et processus identitaires. Le Cas de la Wallonie romane', in Claudine Bavoux, Lambert-Felix Prudent,

and Sylvie Wharton (eds), *Normes endogènes et plurilinguisme. Aires francophones, aires créoles*. Lyon: ENS, 45–60.

Hamon, Maurice (2010). *Madame Geoffrin: femme d'influence, femme d'affaires au temps des Lumières*. Paris: Fayard.

Hanse, Joseph (1987). *Nouveau dictionnaire des difficultés du français moderne, 2e éd. mise à jour et enrichie*. Paris: Duculot.

Härmä, Juhani (1993). 'Regards sur les constructions disloquées en moyen francais', in Liliane Dulac, Jean-Claude Aubailly, Emmanuèle Baumgartner, Francis Dubost, and Marcel Faure (eds), *Et c'est la fin pour quoy sommes ensemble. Hommage à Jean Dufournet. Littérature, histoire et langue du Moyen Age*. Paris: Champion, 717–25.

Harrison, Michelle (2019). 'The Influence of Teachers' Language Attitudes on Classroom Practices in Alsace', in Michelle Harrison and Aurélie Joubert (eds), *French Language Policies and the Revitalisation of Regional Languages in the 21st Century*. London: Palgrave Macmillan, 287–308.

Harrison, Michelle and Aurélie Joubert (eds) (2019). *French Language Policies and the Revitalisation of Regional Languages in the 21st Century*. London: Palgrave Macmillan.

Haugen, Einar (1966). 'Dialect, Language, Nation', *American Anthropologist* New Series 68(4): 922–35.

Hausmann, Franz Josef (1988). 'Grundprobleme des zweisprachigen Wörterbuchs', in Karl Hyldgaard-Jensen (ed.), *Symposium on Lexicography III. Proceedings of the Third International Symposium on Lexicography May 14–16, 1986 at the University of Copenhagen*. Tübingen: Max Niemeyer, 137–54.

Hausmann, Franz Josef (1991). 'La Lexicographie bilingue anglais-francais, francais-anglais', in Franz Josef Hausmann, Oskar Reichmann, Herbert Eernst Wiegand, and Ladislav Zgusta (eds), *Wörterbücher, Dictionaries, Dictionnaires: ein internationales Handbuch zur Lexikographie*. Berlin: de Gruyter, 2956–61.

Hausmann, Franz Josef and Margaret Cop (1985). 'Short History of English–German Lexicography', in K. Hyldgaard-Jensen and A. Zettersten (eds), *Symposium on Lexicography II. Proceedings of the Second International Symposium on Lexicography, May 16–17, 1984 at the University of Copenhagen*. Tubingen: Max Niemeyer, 183–97.

Hausmann, Franz Josef, Oskar Reichmann, Herbert Eernst Wiegand, and Ladislav Zgusta (eds) (1991). *Wörterbücher, Dictionaries, Dictionnaires: ein internationales Handbuch zur Lexikographie*. Berlin: de Gruyter.

Havinga, Anna (2018). *Invisibilising Austrian German: On the Effect of Linguistic Prescriptions and Educational Reforms on Writing Practices in 18th-century Austria*. Berlin: de Gruyter.

Hawkey, James and Jonathan R. Kasstan (2015). 'Regional and Minority Languages in France: Policies of Homogenization or a Move towards Heterogeneity? A Case Study on Francoprovençal', *The French Review* 89(2): 110–35.

Hawkey, James (2018). *Language Attitudes and Minority Rights: The Case of Catalan in France*. Cham: Palgrave Macmillan.

Hawkey, James (2020). 'Language Attitudes as Predictors of Morphosyntactic Variation: Evidence from Catalan Speakers in Southern France', *Journal of Sociolinguistics* 24(1): 16–34.

Hawkey, James and Kristine Horner (2022). 'Officiality and Strategic Ambiguity in Language Policy: Exploring Migrant Experiences in Andorra and Luxembourg', *Language Policy* 21: 195–215.

Hawkey, James and Damien Mooney (2021). 'The Ideological Construction of Legitimacy for Pluricentric Standards: Occitan and Catalan in France', *Journal of Multilingual and Multicultural Development* 42(9): 854–68.

Hazard, Paul (1910). *La Révolution française et les lettres italiennes 1789–1815*. Paris: Hachette.

Hazard, Paul (1921). *La Crise de la conscience européenne (1680–1715)*. 3 vols. Paris: Boivin.

Heiden, Serge (2010). 'The TXM Platform: Building Open-source Textual Analysis Software Compatible with the TEI Encoding Scheme', in Ryo Otoguro, Kiyoshi Ishikawa, Hiroshi Umemoto, Kei Yoshimoto, and Yasunari Harada (eds), *24th Pacific Asia Conference on Language, Information and Computation, Nov. 2010, Sendai, Japan*. Institute for Digital Enhancement of Cognitive Development, Waseda University, 389–98.

Heitz, Raymond, York-Gothart Mix, Jean Mondot, and Nina Birkner (eds) (2011). *Gallophilie und Gallophobie in der Literatur und den Medien in Deutschland und in Italien im 18. Jahrhundert/Gallophilie et gallophobie dans la littérature et les médias en Allemagne et en Italie au XVIIIe siècle*. Heidelberg: Universitätsverlag Winter.

Heller, Monica (2008). 'Language and the Nation-state: Challenges to Sociolinguistic Theory and Practice', *Journal of Sociolinguistics* 12(4): 504–24.

Heller, Monica (2010). 'Media, the State and Linguistic Authority', in Sally Johnson and Tommaso M. Milani (eds), *Language Ideologies and Media Discourse: Texts, Practices, Politics*. London: Continuum, 277–82.

Hemon, Roparz (1964). *Dictionnaire breton-français*, 3rd edn. Brest: Al Liamm.

Henne, Helmut (ed.) (2001). *Deutsche Wörterbücher des 17. und 18. Jahrhunderts. Einführung und Bibliographie*, 2nd extended edn. Hildesheim: Olms.

Héran, François, Alexandra Filhon, and Christine Deprez (2002). 'La Dynamique des langues en France au fil du XXe siècle', *Population & sociétés* 376: 1–4.

Hermant, Abel (1923). *Xavier ou Les Entretiens sur la grammaire française*. Paris: Le Livre.

Hermant, Abel (1925). *Lettres à Xavier sur l'art d'écrire*. Paris: Librairie Hachette.

Hermant, Abel (1936). *Savoir parler*. Paris: Éditions Albin Michel.

Hernández-Campoy, Juan Manuel and Juan Camilo Conde-Silvestre (eds) (2012a). *The Handbook of Historical Sociolinguistics*. Malden/Oxford: Blackwell.

Hernández-Campoy, Juan Manuel and Juan Camilo Conde-Silvestre (2012b). 'Introduction', in Juan Manuel Hernández-Campoy and Juan Camilo Conde-Silvestre (eds), *The Handbook of Historical Sociolinguistics*. Malden/Oxford: Blackwell, 1–8.

Hernández-Campoy, Juan Manuel and Tamara García-Vidal (2018). 'Persona Management and Identity Projection in English Medieval Society: Evidence from John Paston II', *Journal of Historical Sociolinguistics* 4(1): 33–63.

Herslund, Michael (1976). *Structure phonologique de l'ancien français: morphologie et phonologie du francien classique*. Copenhagen: Akademisk Forlag.

Heyd, Theresa (2014). 'Folk-linguistic Landscapes: The Visual Semiotics of Digital Enregisterment', *Language in Society* 43: 489–514.

Highfield, Tim (2015). 'Tweeted Joke Life Spans and Appropriated Punch Lines: Practices Around Topical Humor on Social Media', *International Journal of Communication* 9: 2713–34.

Hill, Archibald (1962). *Third Texas Conference on Problems of Linguistic Analysis in English, 9–12 May 1958*. Austin: University of Texas Press.

Hinton, Leanne, Leona Huss, and Gerald Roche (eds) (2018). *The Routledge Handbook of Language Revitalisation*. New York/London: Routledge.

Hirschbühler, Paul (1989). 'On the Existence of Null Subjects in Embedded Clauses in Old and Middle French', in Carl Kirschner and Janet Ann DeCesaris (eds), *Studies in Romance Linguistics*. Amsterdam: John Benjamins, 155–76.
Hirschbühler, Paul (1990). 'La Légitimation de la construction V1 en subordonnée dans la prose et le vers en ancien français', *Revue québécoise de linguistique* 19(1): 33–55.
Hodson, Jane (2006). 'The Problem of Joseph Priestley's (1733–1804) Descriptivism', *Historiographia Linguistica* 33: 57–84.
Hoenigswald, Henry (1966). 'A Proposal for the Study of Folk-linguistics', *Sociolinguistics* 16: 26.
Hohenhaus, Peter (2002). 'Standardization, Language Change, Resistance and the Question of Linguistic Threat: 18th-century English and Present-day German', in Andrew R. Linn and Nicola McLelland (eds), *Standardization: Studies from the Germanic Languages*. Amsterdam: John Benjamins, 153–78.
Hopper, Paul (1979). 'Aspect and Foregrounding in Discourse', in Talmy Givón (ed.), *Discourse and Syntax*. New York: Academic Press, 213–41.
Hornberger, Nancy and Haley De Korne (2018). 'Is Revitalisation through Education Possible?', in Leanne Hinton, Leona Huss, and Gerald Roche (eds), *The Routledge Handbook of Language Revitalisation*. New York/London: Routledge, 94–103.
Horne, Merle (1990). 'The Clitic Group as a Prosodic Category in Old French', *Lingua* 82(1): 1–14.
Horner, Kristine (2009). 'Language Policy Mechanisms and Social Practices in Multilingual Luxembourg', *Language Problems and Language Planning* 33(2): 101–11.
Horner, Kristine and Jean Jacques Weber (2008). 'The Language Situation in Luxembourg', *Current Issues in Language Planning* 9(1): 69–128.
Hornsby, David (2006). *Redefining Regional French: Koineization and Dialect Levelling in Northern France*. Oxford: Legenda.
Hornsby, David and Mari C. Jones (2013). '"Exception française?" Levelling, Exclusion, and Urban Social Structure in France', in Mari C. Jones and David Hornsby (eds), *Language and Social Structure in Urban France*. Oxford: Legenda, 94–109.
Hornsby, David and Tim Pooley (2001). 'La Sociolinguistique et les accents français d'Europe', in Marie-Anne Hintze, Tim Pooley, and Anne Judge (eds), *French Accents: Phonological and Sociolinguistic Perspectives*. London: AFLS/CILT, 305–43.
Hornsby, Michael (2015). 'The "New" and "Traditional" Speaker Dichotomy: Bridging the Gap', *International Journal of the Sociology of Language* 231: 107–25.
Hornsby, Michael (2017). 'Finding an Ideological Niche for New Speakers in a Minoritized Language Community', *Language, Culture and Curriculum* 30(1): 91–104.
Hornsby, Michael and Gilles Le Quentel (2013). 'Contested Varieties and Competing Authenticities: Neologisms in Revitalised Breton', *International Journal of the Sociology of Language* 223: 71–86.
Hornsby, Michael and Noel Ó Murchadha (2021). 'Standardization, New Speakers, and the Acceptance of (New) Standards', in Wendy Ayres-Bennett and John Bellamy (eds), *The Cambridge Handbook of Language Standardization*. Cambridge: Cambridge University Press, 347–70.
Hornsby, Michael and Dick Vigers (eds) (2013). *Breton: The Postvernacular Challenge*, special issue of *International Journal of the Sociology of Language*: 223.
Hosington, Brenda M. (2017). 'Collaboration, Authorship, and Gender in the Paratexts Accompanying Translations by Susan Du Verger and Judith Man', in Patricia Pender (ed.), *Gender, Authorship, and Early Modern Women's Collaboration*. Basingstoke: Palgrave Macmillan, 95–121.

Hotman, François (1573). *Franco-Gallia*. Cologne: Stoerius.

Houdebine, Anne-Marie (1987). 'Le Français au féminin', *La Linguistique* 23: 13–34.

Humphries, Emma (2014). *The Feminisation of Job Titles in France and Quebec*, undergraduate dissertation, University of Nottingham.

Humphries, Emma (2016). *Defending the French Language: An Online Battle?*, Masters by Research dissertation, University of Nottingham.

Humphries, Emma (2019). '#JeSuisCirconflexe: The French Spelling Reform of 1990 and 2016 Reactions', *Journal of French Language Studies* 29(3): 305–21. https://doi.org/10.1017/S0959269518000285

Humphries, Emma (2021). *Judging French. Lay and Expert Language Commentary in Nineteenth- and Twenty-first-century France*, doctoral thesis, University of Nottingham.

Hundt, Marianne, Lena Zipp, and André Huber (2015). 'Attitudes in Fiji towards Varieties of English', *World Englishes* 34(4): 688–707.

Hüning, Matthias, Ulrike Vogl, and Oliver Moliner (eds) (2012). *Standard Languages and Multilingualism in European History*. Amsterdam/Philadelphia: John Benjamins.

Huot, Sylvia (1987). *From Song to Book: The Poetics of Writing in Old French Lyric and Lyrical Narrative Poetry*. Ithaca: Cornell University Press.

Hydrator app (no date). https://github.com/DocNow/hydrator accessed 31 January 2021.

Hyland, Ken (2009). 'Corpus Informed Discourse Analysis: The Case of Academic Engagement', in Maggie Charles, Diane Pecorari, and Susan Hunston (eds), *Academic Writing: At the Interface of Corpus and Discourse*. London: Continuum, 110–28.

Hymes, Dell (1974). *Foundations in Sociolinguistics: An Ethnographic Approach*. Philadelphia: University of Pennsylvania Press.

IFTTT (If This Then That) (no date). https://ifttt.com/ accessed 31 December 2020.

Il Genio delle lingue: le traduzioni nel Settecento in area franco-italiana (1989). Rome: Istituto della Enciclopedia Italiana.

Ingham, Richard (2016). 'Investigating Language Change Using Anglo-Norman Spoken and Written Register Data', *Linguistics* 54(2): 381–409.

Ingham, Richard (2018). 'Topic, Focus and Null Subjects in Old French', *Canadian Journal of Linguistics* 63(2): 242–63.

Inspection générale de l'Éducation nationale (2013). 'Les Enseignements à tirer des résultats des élèves de troisième lors de l'étude européenne réalisée en 2011 sur les compétences en langues étrangères. Rapport 2013-086'. http://langues.ac-dijon.fr/IMG/pdf/2013-086_rapport_eleves_troisieme_competences_langues_284730.pdf accessed 31 July 2022.

Irvine, Judith T. (1989). 'When Talk isn't Cheap: Language and Political Economy', *American Ethnologist* 16(2): 248–67. https://doi.org/10.1525/ae.1989.16.2.02a00040

Irvine, Judith T. and Susan Gal (2000). 'Language Ideology and Linguistic Differentiation', in Paul V. Kroskrity (ed.), *Regimes of Language: Ideologies, Polities and Identities*. Oxford: James Currey, 35–84.

Jackson, Kenneth Hurlstone (1967). *A Historical Phonology of Breton*. Dublin: Institute for Advanced Studies.

Jacob, James and David Gordon (1985). 'Language Policy in France', in William Beer and James Jacob (eds), *Language Policy and National Unity*. Totowa: Rowman and Allanheld, 106–31.

Jacobs, Haike (1991). 'Old French Proclisis and Enclisis: The Clitic Group or the Prosodic Word?', in Frank Drijkoningen and Ans van Kemenade (eds), *Linguistics in the Netherlands*. Amsterdam: John Benjamins, 91–100.

Jacobs, Haike (1992). 'The Interaction between the Evolution of Syllable Structure and Foot Structure in the Evolution from Classical Latin to Old French', in Christiane Laeufer and Terrell A. Morgan (eds), *Theoretical Analyses in Romance Linguistics*. Amsterdam: John Benjamins, 55–79.

Jacobs, Haike (1993). 'The Phonology of Enclisis and Proclisis in Gallo-Romance and Old French', in William J. Ashby, Marianne Mithun, Giorgio Perissinotto, and Eduardo Raposo (eds), *Linguistic Perspectives on the Romance Languages: Selected Papers from the 21st Linguistic Symposium on Romance Languages (LSRL XXI), Santa Barbara, 21–24 February 1991*. Amsterdam: John Benjamins, 149–64.

Jacobs, Haike (1994). 'Catalexis and Stress in Romance', in Michael L. Mazzola (ed.), *Issues and Theory in Romance Linguistics: Selected Papers from the Linguistic Symposium on Romance Languages XXIII, April 1–4, 1993*. Washington: Georgetown University Press, 49–67.

Jakobson, Roman (1963). *Essais de linguistique générale*. Vol. 1. Paris: Éditions de Minuit.

Jane, Emma A. (2017). *Misogyny Online. A Short (and Brutish) History*. London: Sage Swifts.

Jean, Loicq (1979). '*Catholicon*. Dictionnaire breton-latin-français, publié avec une introduction par Chr.-J. Guyonvarc'h. Vol. 2. réproduction de l'éd. J. Calvez, Tréguier 1499', *Revue belge de philologie et d'histoire* 57(1): 154–6.

Jochnowitz, George (1973). *Dialect Boundaries and the Question of Franco-Provençal*. The Hague: Mouton.

Johnson, Samuel (1755). *A Dictionary of the English Language: In Which the Words are Deduced from their Originals, and Illustrated in their Different Significations by Examples from the Best Writers. To which are Prefixed, a History of the Language, and an English Grammar. By Samuel Johnson, A.M. In Two Volumes*. London: printed by W. Strahan, for J. and P. Knapton; T. and T. Longman; C. Hitch and L. Hawes; A. Millar; and R. and J. Dodsley.

Jones, Mari C. (1995). 'At what Price Language Maintenance? Standardization in Modern Breton', *French Studies* 49(4): 424–38.

Jones, Mari C. (ed.) (2015a). *Endangered Languages and New Technologies*. Cambridge: Cambridge University Press.

Jones, Mari C. (ed.) (2015b). *Policy and Planning for Endangered Languages*. Cambridge: Cambridge University Press.

Jones, Mari C. and David Hornsby (eds) (2013). *Language and Social Structure in Urban France*. London: Legenda.

Jones, Mari C. and Sarah Ogilvie (eds) (2013). *Keeping Languages Alive*. Cambridge: Cambridge University Press.

Jones, William J. (1999). *Images of Language: Six Essays on German Attitudes to European Languages from 1500 to 1800*. Amsterdam/Philadelphia: John Benjamins.

Jones, William J. (2000). *German Lexicography in the European Context: A Descriptive Bibliography of Printed Dictionaries and Word Lists Containing German Language (1600–1700)*. Berlin: de Gruyter.

Jørgensen, Marianne and Louise Phillips (2002). *Discourse Analysis as Theory and Method*. London: SAGE.

Joseph, John E. (1987). *Eloquence and Power: The Rise of Language Standards and Standard Languages*. London: Frances Pinter.

Joseph, John E. (2020). 'Is/Ought: Hume's Guillotine, Linguistics and Standards of Language', in Don Chapman and Jacob D. Rawlins (eds), *Language Prescription: Values, Ideologies, and Identities*. Bristol: Multilingual Matters, 15–31.

Jospin, Lionel (1998). 'Circulaire du 6 mars 1998 relative à la féminisation des noms de métier, fonction, grade ou titre', *Journal officiel de la République française*, 8 March 1998, 3565. https://www.legifrance.gouv.fr/jorf/id/JORFTEXT000000556183 accessed 30 April 2021.

Joubert, Aurélie (2015). 'Occitan. A Language that cannot Stop Dying', in Mari C. Jones (ed.), *Policy and Planning for Endangered Languages*. Cambridge: Cambridge University Press, 171–87.

Joubert, Aurélie (2019). 'Evolution of Linguistic Identity in a Super-region. The Case of Catalans and Occitans in Occitanie', in Michelle Harrison and Aurélie Joubert (eds), *French Language Policies and the Revitalisation of Regional Languages in the 21st Century*. London: Palgrave Macmillan, 107–28.

Jucker, Andreas H., Gerd Fritz, and Franz Lebsanft (1999). *Historical Dialogue Analysis*. Amsterdam/Philadelphia: John Benjamins.

Kamblé-Bagal, Nikita and Anaïs Tatossian (2022). 'Étude comparative sur l'usage de l'écriture inclusive dans deux médias écrits français et québécois', *SHS Web of Conferences* 138, 12003. https://doi.org/10.1051/shsconf/202213812003

Kasstan, Jonathan R. (2018). 'Exploring Contested Authenticity among Speakers of a Contested Language: The Case of 'Francoprovençal', *Journal of Multilingual and Multicultural Development* 39(5): 382–93.

Kasstan, Jonathan R. (2019). 'New Speakers and Language Revitalisation', in Michelle Harrison and Aurélie Joubert (eds), *French Language Policies and the Revitalisation of Regional Languages in the 21st Century*. London: Palgrave Macmillan, 149–70.

Kadored, Iwan, Yann Desbordes, and Divi Kerwella (1994). *Geriadur bihan brezhoneg-galleg, galleg-brezhoneg/Dictionnaire élémentaire breton-français, français-breton*, 2nd edn. Saint-Thonan: Mouladurioù Hor Yezh.

Kearney, Michael W. (2019). 'rtweet: Collecting and Analyzing Twitter Data', *Journal of Open Source Software* 4(42): 1829. https://doi.org/10.21105/joss.01829

Kersey, John (1969 [1702]). *A New English Dictionary. […] By J. K.* London: Printed for Henry Bonwicke, at the Red Lion, and Robert Knaplock, at the Angel in St. Paul's Church-Yard (London). Menston: Scolar Press.

Kerswill, Paul (2003). 'Dialect Levelling and Geographical Diffusion in British English', in Dave Britain and Jenny Cheshire (eds), *Social Dialectology. In Honour of Peter Trudgill*. Amsterdam: John Benjamins, 223–43.

Kibbee, Douglas A. (in preparation). *French Language Policy Timeline*.

Kibbee, Douglas A. (1991). *For to Speke Frenche Trewely. The French Language in England, 1000–1600: Its Status, Description, and Instruction*. Amsterdam/Philadelphia: John Benjamins.

Kibbee, Douglas A. (2021). 'Standard Languages in the Context of Language Policy and Planning and Language Rights', in Wendy Ayres-Bennett and John Bellamy (eds), *The Cambridge Handbook of Language Standardization*. Cambridge: Cambridge University Press, 201–33.

Kibbee, Douglas A. and Alan Craig (2019). 'Understanding Prescription in Action. A Corpus-based Approach', *Histoire épistémologie langage* 41(2): 67–81.

King, Jeremy (2011). 'Power and Indirectness in Business Correspondence: Petitions in Colonial Louisiana Spanish', *Journal of Politeness Research. Language, Behaviour, Culture* 7(2): 259–83.

King, Ruth, France Martineau, and Raymond Mougeon (2011). 'The Interplay of Internal and External Factors in Grammatical Change: First-person Plural Pronouns in French', *Language* 87(3): 470–509.

Kinnaird, Lawrence (1946). *Spain in the Mississippi Valley, 1765–1794*. Washington: U.S. Government Printing Office.

Kircher, Ruth (2012). 'How Pluricentric is the French Language? An Investigation of Attitudes towards Quebec French Compared to European French', *Journal of French Language Studies* 22(3): 345–70.

Kircher, Ruth (2014). 'Thirty Years after Bill 101: A Contemporary Perspective on Attitudes towards English and French in Montreal', *The Canadian Journal of Applied Linguistics* 17(1): 20–50.

Kircher, Ruth (2015). 'Quebec's Shift from Ethnic to Civic National Identity: Implications for Language Attitudes amongst Immigrants in Montreal', in David Evans (ed.), *Language and Identity: Discourse in the World*. New York: Bloomsbury, 55–80.

Kircher, Ruth (2016). 'Montreal's Multilingual Migrants: Social Identities and Language Attitudes after the Proposition of the Quebec Charter of Values', in Vera Regan, Chloe Diskin, and Jennifer Martyn (eds), *Language, Identity and Migration: Voices from Transnational Speakers and Communities*. Bern: Peter Lang, 217–47.

Kircher, Ruth (2022). 'Intergenerational Language Transmission in Quebec: Patterns and Predictors in the Light of Provincial Language Planning', *International Journal of Bilingual Education and Bilingualism* 25(2): 418–35.

Kircher, Ruth and Sue Fox (2019). 'Multicultural London English and its Speakers: A Corpus-informed Discourse Study of Standard Language Ideology and Social Stereotypes', *Journal of Multilingual and Multicultural Development* 42(9): 1–19. https://doi.org/10.1080/01434632.2019.1666856

Kircher, Ruth and Lena Zipp (eds) (2022a). *Research Methods in Language Attitudes*. Cambridge: Cambridge University Press.

Kircher, Ruth and Lena Zipp (2022b). 'An Introduction to Language Attitudes Research', in Ruth Kircher and Lena Zipp (eds), *Research Methods in Language Attitudes*. Cambridge: Cambridge University Press, 1–17.

Klausenburger, Jürgen (1994). 'How Abstract is/was French Phonology? A Twenty-five Year Retrospective', in Chantal Lyche (ed.), *French Generative Phonology: Retrospective and Perspectives*. London: AFLS/ESRI – Middlesex University Press, 151–65.

Klausenburger, Jürgen (2014). *Ockham's Razor in Linguistics: An Application to Studies in French Phonology over the Last Half Century*. Munich: LINCOM Europa.

Klavans, Judith L. (1985). 'The Independence of Syntax and Phonology in Cliticization', *Language* 61(1): 95–120.

Klingler, Thomas (2003). *If I could Turn my Tongue like that: The Creole Language of Pointe Coupée Parish, Louisiana*. Baton Rouge: Louisiana State University Press.

Klinkenberg, Jean-Marie (2019). 'Quelle écriture pour quelle justice? "Écriture inclusive" et politique linguistique', *Le Discours et la langue* 11(1): 15–26.

Klippel, Friederike (1994). *Englischlernen im 18. und 19. Jahrhunderts. Die Geschichte der Lehrbücher und Unterrichtsmethoden*. Münster: Nodus.

Kloss, Heinz (1967). '*Abstand* languages and *ausbau* languages', *Anthropological Linguistics* 9: 29–41.

Knisely, Kris A. (2020). '*Le Français non-binaire*: Linguistic Forms Used by Non-binary Speakers of French', *Foreign Language Annals* 53: 850–76.

Koch, Peter and Wulf Oesterreicher (2001). 'Langage parlé et langage écrit', in Günter Holtus, Michael Metzeltin, and Christian Schmitt (eds), *Lexikon der Romanistischen Linguistik*. Berlin: Max Niemeyer, 584–627.

Kok, Ans C. de (1985). *La Place du pronom personnel régime conjoint en français: une étude diachronique*. Amsterdam: Rodopi.

Krause, Thomas and Amir Zeldes (2016). 'ANNIS3: A New Architecture for Generic Corpus Query and Visualization', *Digital Scholarship in the Humanities* 31: 118–39. https://doi.org/10.1093/llc/fqu057

Kremnitz, Georg (ed.) (2013). *Histoire sociale des langues de France*. Rennes: Presses universitaires de Rennes.

Kremnitz, Georg (2016). 'Les Langues de la migration, parents pauvres de l'éducation bilingue', in Christine Hélot and Jürgen Erfurt (eds), *L'Éducation bilingue en France. Politiques linguistiques, modèles et pratiques*. Strasbourg: Lambert-Lucas, 433–41.

Kroch, Anthony (1989). 'Reflexes of Grammar in Patterns of Language Change', *Language Variation and Change* 1(3): 199–244.

Kroskrity, Paul V. (2000). 'Regimenting Languages: Language Ideological Perspectives', in Paul V. Kroskrity (ed.), *Regimes of Language: Ideologies, Polities and Identities*. Oxford: James Currey, 1–34.

Kroskrity, Paul V. (2004). 'Language Ideologies', in Alessandro Duranti (ed.), *A Companion to Linguistic Anthropology*. Chichester: Wiley-Blackwell, 496–517.

Kroskrity, Paul V. (2010). 'Language Ideologies – Evolving Perspectives', in Jürgen Jaspers, Jan-Ola Östman, and Jef Verschueren (eds), *Society and Language Use*. Amsterdam: John Benjamins, 192–211.

Kroskrity, Paul V. (2016). 'Language Ideologies: Emergence, Elaboration, and Application', in Nancy Bonvillain (ed.), *The Routledge Handbook of Linguistic Anthropology*. London: Routledge, 95–108.

Kroskrity, Paul V. (2020). 'Theorizing Linguistic Racisms from a Language Ideological Perspective', in H. Sami Alim, Angela Reyes, and Paul V. Kroskrity (eds), *The Oxford Handbook of Language and Race*. Oxford: Oxford University Press, 69–89.

Kutlu, Ethan and Ruth Kircher (2021). 'A Corpus-assisted Discourse Study of Attitudes toward Spanish as a Heritage Language in Florida', *Languages* 6(1): 1–18. https://doi.org/10.3390/languages6010038

Kytö, Merja and Terry Walker (2006). *Guide to* A Corpus of English Dialogues 1560–1760, Uppsala: Acta Universitatis Upsaliensis.

Kytö, Merja and Terry Walker (2020). 'L'Interaction orale du passé: A Corpus of English Dialogues 1560–1760', *Langages* 217(1): 55–69.

L'Europa letteraria: giornale (1768–73). Venice: Tip. Palese

La Queste del Saint Graal (1949 [c.1225]). Ed. By Albert Pauphilet. Paris: Champion.

La Bruyère, Jean de (1688). *Les Caractères*. Paris: Estienne Michallet.

La Suite du Roman de Merlin (2006 [1218]). Ed. by Gilles Roussineau. Geneva: Droz.

Labov, William (1966). *The Social Stratification of English in New York City*. Washington: Center for Applied Linguistics.

Labov, William (1972a). *Sociolinguistic Patterns*. Philadelphia: University of Pennsylvania Press.

Labov, William (1972b). 'Some Principles of Linguistic Methodology', *Language in Society* 1(1): 97–120.

Labov, William (1994). *Principles of Linguistic Change*. Vol. I: *Internal Factors*. Oxford: Blackwell.

Lady Morgan, Sydney (1821). *Italy*. 2 vols. London: Henry Colburn and Co.

Lafitte, Jean and Henri Féraud (2006). *Langues d'oc, langues de France*. Pau: Pyrémonde-Princi-Negue.

Lagrée, Michel (1995). 'La Littérature religieuse dans la production bretonne imprimée: aspects quantitatifs', in Michel Lagrée (ed.), *Les Parlers de la foi*. Rennes: Presses universitaires de Rennes, 85–94.

Lagrée, Michel, Fañch Roudeau, and Christian Brunel (1995). 'Avant-propos', in Michel Lagrée (ed.), *Les Parlers de la foi*. Rennes: Presses universitaires de Rennes, 11–18.

Lalande, Jérome de (1769–70). *Voyage d'un françois en Italie, fait dans les années 1765 & 1766*. 8 vols. Yverdon: no pub.

Lambert, Wallace E., Robert C. Hodgson, Robert C. Gardner, and Samuel Fillenbaum (1960). 'Evaluational Reactions to Spoken Language', *Journal of Abnormal and Social Psychology* 60(1): 44–51.

Lambrecht, Knud (1987). 'On the Status of SVO Sentences in French Discourse', in Russell Tomlin (ed.), *Coherence and Grounding in Discourse*. Amsterdam: John Benjamins, 217–61.

Lambrecht, Knud (1994). *Information Structure and Sentence Form. Topic, Focus and the Mental Representations of Discourse Referents*. Cambridge: Cambridge University Press.

Landeweerd, Rita and Co Vet (1996). 'Tense in (Free) Indirect Discourse in French', in Theo Janssen and Wim Van der Wurff (eds), *Reported Speech: Forms and Functions of the Verb*. Amsterdam/Philadelphia: John Benjamins, 141–64.

Langer, Nils and Winifred V. Davies (2006). *The Making of Bad Language. Lay Linguistic Stigmatisations in German: Past and Present*. Oxford: Peter Lang.

Langer, Nils and Agnete Nesse (2012). 'Linguistic Purism', in Juan Manuel Hernández-Campoy and Juan Camilo Conde-Silvestre (eds), *The Handbook of Historical Sociolinguistics*. Chichester: Wiley-Blackwell, 607–25.

Lantto, Hanna (2018). 'New Basques and Code-switching: Purist Tendencies, Social Pressures', in Cassie Smith-Christmas, Noel Ó Murchadha, Michael Hornsby, and Máiréad Moriarty (eds), *New Speakers of Minority Languages: Linguistic Ideologies and Practices*. London: Palgrave Macmillan, 165–88.

Larousse (2002). *Dictionnaire mondial des littératures*. Paris: Larousse.

Le Berre, Yves (2001). 'La Littérature moderne en langue bretonne: ou Les Fruits oubliés d'un amour de truchement', *Bibliothèque de l'École des chartes* 159: 29–51.

Le Couronnement de Louis (1920 [1130]). Ed by Ernest Langlois. Paris: Champion.

Le Draoulec, Anne (2014). '*Avant que, avant de*, suspens, coups de théâtre, et autres effets de mise en relief', *4e Congrès mondial de linguistique française, SHS Web of Conferences* 8: 3149–64.

Le Dû, Jean and Yves Le Berre (2013). 'La Langue bretonne dans la société régionale contemporaine', *International Journal of the Sociology of Language* 223: 43–54.

Le Gonidec, Jean-François (1850). *Dictionnaire breton-français*, revised and edited by Théodore Hersart de la Villemarqué. Saint-Brieuc: Éditions L. Prudhomme.

Le Nevez, Adam (2013). 'The Social Practice of Breton: An Epistemological Challenge', *International Journal of the Sociology of Language* 223: 87–102.

Le Pipec, Erwan (2018). 'Le Lexique mathématique breton: bilan et perspectives', *La Bretagne linguistique* 22: 41–75.

Le Roman du comte d'Artois (1966 [1453]). Ed. by Jean-Charles Seigneuret. Geneva: Droz.

Lebsanft, Franz (1999). 'A Late Medieval French Bargain Dialogue (Pathelin II) or: Further Remarks on the History of Dialogue Forms', in Andreas H. Jucker, Gerd Fritz, and Franz Lebsanft (eds), *Historical Dialogue Analysis*. Amsterdam/Philadelphia: John Benjamins, 269–92.

Ledgeway, Adam (2021). 'V2 Beyond Borders: *The Histoire Ancienne Jusqu'a César*', *Journal of Historical Syntax* 5(29): 1–65.

Lefeuvre, Florence and Gabriella Parussa (eds) (2020). *L'Oral représenté en diachronie et en synchronie: une voie d'accès à l'oral spontané?*, special issue of *Langages*: 217.

Lenoach, Ciarán (2012). 'An Ghaeilge Iarthraidisiúnta agus a Dioscúrsa', in Ciarán Lenoach, Conchúr Ó Giollagáin, and Brian Ó Curnáin (eds), *An Chonair Chaoch: an Mionteangachas sa Dátheangachas*. Indreabhán: Leabhar Breac, 19–109.

Lenoach, Ciarán, Conchúr Ó Giollagáin, and Brian Ó Curnáin (eds) (2012). *An Chonair Chaoch: an Mionteangachas sa Dátheangachas*. Indreabhán: Leabhar Breac.

Léonard, Jean Léoand Lilianne Jagueneau (2013). 'Disparition, apparition et réapparition des langues d'oïl: de l'invisibilisation au nouveau regard', *Bulletin de la société linguistique de Paris* 108(1): 283–343.

Les cent nouvelles nouvelles (1966 [c.1465]). Ed. by Franklin P. Sweetser, Franklin. Geneva: Droz.

Les Invités de Médiapart, Mediapart.fr (2020). 'Au delà de l'écriture inclusive: un programme de travail pour la linguistique d'aujourd'hui', 25 September. https://blogs.mediapart.fr/les-invites-de-mediapart/blog/250920/au-dela-de-l-e-criture-inclusive-un-programme-de-travail-pour-la-linguistique-d-aujour accessed 31 December 2020.

Leslau, Wolf (1988). *Fifty years of Research: Selection of Articles on Semitic, Ethiopian Semitic, and Cushitic*. Wiesbaden: Harrassowitz.

Lieutard, Hervé and Marie-Jeanne Verny (eds) (2007). *L'École française et les langues régionales. XIXe–XXe siècles*. Montpellier: Presses universitaires de la Méditerranée.

Lillo, Jacqueline (1990). *Les Grammaires de Ludovico Goudar 1744–1925*. Palermo: Università di Palermo, Facoltà di Lettere, Istituto di lingue e letterature straniere.

Lillo, Jacqueline (2000). 'La Bibliothèque du pensionnat Marie-Adélaïde de Palerme. Miroir et mémoire d'un établissement d'éducation pour jeunes filles', in Nadia Minerva (ed.) [in collaboration with Brigitte Soubeyran], *Dames, demoiselles, honnêtes femmes: studi di lingua e letteratura francese offerti a Carla Pellandra*. Bologna: CLUEB, 123–41.

Lillo, Jacqueline (2004). *L'Enseignement du français à Palerme au XIXe siècle*. Bologna: CLUEB.

Lillo, Jacqueline (2016). 'Maîtres et professeurs, manuels, dictionnaires (XIXe siècle)', *Documents pour l'histoire du français langue étrangère ou seconde* 56: 1–15.

Lindemann, Stephanie (2003). 'Koreans, Chinese or Indians? Attitudes and Ideologies about Non-native English Speakers in the United States', *Journal of Sociolinguistics* 7: 348–64.

Linn, Andrew R. (2013). 'Vernaculars and the Idea of a Standard Language', in Keith Allan (ed.), *The Oxford Handbook of the History of Linguistics*. Oxford: Oxford University Press, 359–74.

Linn, Andrew R. and Nicola McLelland (eds) (2002). *Standardization: Studies from the Germanic Languages*. Amsterdam: John Benjamins.

Lippi-Green, Rosina (1997). *English with an Accent: Language, Ideology, and Discrimination in the United States*. London: Routledge.

Lippi-Green, Rosina (2012). *English with an Accent: Language, Ideology, and Discrimination in the United States*, 2nd edn. Abingdon: Routledge.

Littré, Émile (1863–78). *Dictionnaire de la langue française*. Paris: Hachette.

Lo Bianco, Joseph (2018). 'Re-invigorating Language Policy and Planning for Intergenerational Language Revitalisation', in Leanne Hinton, Leona Huss, and Gerald Roche (eds), *The Routledge Handbook of Language Revitalisation*. New York/London: Routledge, 36–48.

Lodge, R. Anthony (1991). 'Authority, Prescriptivism and the French Standard Language', *Journal of French Language Studies* 1(1): 93–111.

Lodge, R. Anthony (1993). *French, from Dialect to Standard*. London/New York: Routledge.

Lodge, R. Anthony (1996). 'Stereotypes of Vernacular Pronunciation in 17th–18th-century Paris', *Zeitschrift für romanische Philologie* 112: 205–31.

Lodge, R. Anthony (2004). *A Sociolinguistic History of Parisian French.* Cambridge: Cambridge University Press.

Loi Bas-Lauriol (*Loi 75–1349 du 31 décembre 1975 relative à l'emploi de la langue française*) (1975). https://www.legifrance.gouv.fr/loda/id/JORFTEXT000000521788/ accessed 8 September 2022.

Loi Deixonne (*Loi 51–46 du 11 janvier 1951 relative à l'enseignement des langues et dialectes locaux*) (1951). *Journal officiel de la République française*, 13 January 1951: 483. https://www.legifrance.gouv.fr/loda/id/JORFTEXT000000886638 accessed 8 September 2022.

Loi Molac (*Loi 2021–641 du 21 mai 2021 relative à la protection patrimoniale des langues régionales et à leur promotion*) (2021). https://www.legifrance.gouv.fr/dossierlegislatif/JORFDOLE000041575354/ accessed 8 September 2022.

Loi Toubon *(Loi 94-665 du 4 août 1994 relative à l'emploi de la langue française)* (1994). https://www.legifrance.gouv.fr/loda/id/LEGITEXT000005616341/ accessed 21 July 2022.

López-Muñoz, Juan Manuel (1994–5). 'Pour une typologie des verbes introducteurs du discours indirect', *Estudios de Lengua y Literatura francesas* 8–9: 149–67.

López-Muñoz, Juan Manuel (1997). *El estilo indirecto en la narrativa francesa del siglo XII y principios del XIII*, doctoral thesis, Universidad de Cádiz.

López-Muñoz, Juan Manuel (1999). 'Fórmulas señalizadoras de estilo indirecto en la Mort Artu', *Las voces del texto. Estudios de lengua y literatura francesas* 12: 131–49.

López-Muñoz, Juan Manuel (2002). 'Discours rapporté et subordonnée relative en ancien français', *Faits de Langues* 19: 51–60.

Loporcaro, Michele (1997). *L'origine del raddoppiamento fonosintattico: saggio di fonologia diacronica romanza*. Basel: Francke.

Lossec, Hervé (2013). *Ma Doue benniget! Histoires drôles en brezhoneg et en français*. Rennes: Ouest-France.

Louisiana Papers (1767–1816). BANC MSS M-M 508. UC Berkeley Bancroft Library.

Love, Harold (2007). 'L'Estrange, Sir Roger (1616–1704)', in David Cannadine (ed.), *Oxford Dictionary of National Biography*. Oxford: Oxford University Press. https://doi.org/10.1093/ref:odnb/16514.

Ludwig, Christian (1706). *A Dictionary English, German, and French: Containing not Only the English Words in their Alphabethical Order, Together with their Several Significations, but Also their Proper Accent, Phrases, Figurative Speeches, Idioms & Proverbs, Composed from the Best New English Dictionaries = Englisch–Teutsch–Französisch Lexicon: worinnen nicht allein die englischen Worte in ihrer gehörigen Ordnung, samt ihrer verschiedewnen Bedeutung, sondern auch der Worte eigentlicher accent, und die figürlichen Redens-Arten, idiotismi und Sprichwörter enthalten sind: aus den besten und neuesten englischen Dictionariis.* Leipzig: bey Thomas Fritschen.

Ludwig, Christian (1716). *Teutsch–Englisches Lexicon: worinnen nicht allein die Wörter, samt den Nenn-, Bey- und Sprich-Wörtern, sondern auch sowol die eigentliche als verblümte Redens-Arten verzeichnet sind. Aus den besten Scribenten und vorhandenen Dictionariis mit grossem Fleiss zusammen getragen.* Leipzig: Bey Thomas Fritschen.

Ludwig, Christian (1717). *Gründliche Anleitung zur englischen Sprache*. Leipzig: Fritsch.

Lynch Piozzi, Hesther (1789). *Observations and Reflections Made in the Course of a Journey, through France, Italy, and Germany*. Dublin: H. Chamberlaine, L. White, etc.

Mac Coinnigh, Marcas (2012). 'Tracing Inspiration in Proverbial Material: From the *Royal Dictionary* (1699 & 1729) of Abel Boyer to the *English–Irish Dictionary* (1732) of Begley and McCurtin', *International Journal of Lexicography* 26(1): 23–57.

Mac Coinnigh, Marcas, Linda Ervine, and Pól Deeds (2019). 'The Irish Language in Belfast. The Role of a Language in Post-conflict Resolution', in Matthew Evans (ed.), *The Routledge Handbook of Language in Conflict*. London/New York, 556–73.

Mac Donnacha, Joe (2014). 'The Death of a Language', *Dublin Review of Books*, February 2014. https://drb.ie/tag/joe-mac-donnacha/ accessed 2 September 2022.

Mac Giolla Chríost, Diarmait (2012). *Jailtacht: The Irish Language, Symbolic Power, and Political Violence in Northern Ireland, 1972–2008*. Cardiff: University of Wales Press.

Mac Ionnrachtaigh, Feargal (2013). *Language, Resistance, and Revival. Republican Prisoners and the Irish Language in the North of Ireland*. London: Pluto Press.

Mac Póilín, Aodán (2018). *Our Tangled Speech. Essays on Language and Culture*, ed. Róise Ní Bhaoill. Belfast: Ulster Historical Foundation and Ultach Trust.

Mac Síthigh, Dáithí (2018). 'Official Status of Languages in the UK and Ireland', *Common Law World Review* 47(1): 77–102.

Macé, Jean (1651?). *Méthode universelle pour apprandre facilemant les langues, pour parler puremant et escrire nettemant en françois*. Paris: Jean Jost.

Madonia, Francesco Paolo Alexandre (2006). 'Aspect négligé de la conscience esthétique révolutionnaire: la laideur des patois', *Nottingham French Studies* 45(1): 42–51.

Malécot, André (1975). 'The Glottal Stop in French', *Phonetica* 31: 51–63.

Manesse, Danièle and Gilles Siouffi (2019). *Le Féminin et le masculin dans la langue: l'écriture inclusive en questions*. Paris: ESF Sciences humaines.

Marazzini, Claudio (1992). 'Il Piemonte e la Valle d'Aosta', in Francesco Bruni (ed.), *L'italiano nelle regioni: lingua nazionale e identità regionali*. Turin: UTET, 1–44.

Marchello-Nizia, Christiane (1995). *L'Évolution du français. Ordre des mots, démonstratifs, accent tonique*. Paris: Armand Colin.

Marchello-Nizia, Christiane (1997 [1979]). *La Langue française aux XIVe et XVe siècles*. Paris: Nathan.

Marchello-Nizia, Christiane (1998). 'Dislocations en diachronie: archéologie d'un phénomène de "français oral"', in Mireille Bilger, Karel van den Eynde, and Françoise Gadet (eds), *Analyse linguistique et approches de l'oral. Recueil d'études offert en hommage à Claire Blanche-Benveniste*. Paris/Louvain: Peeters, 327–37.

Marchello-Nizia, Christiane (2012). '"L'Oral représenté" en français médiéval, un accès construit à une face cachée des langues mortes', in Céline Guillot, Bernard Combettes, Alexei Lavrentiev, Evelyne Oppermann-Marsaux, and Sophie Prévost (eds), *Le Changement en français. Études de linguistique diachronique*. Bern: Peter Lang, 247–64.

Marchello-Nizia, Christiane (2014a). 'Le Français en mouvement, tendances et évolution', *Neuphilologische Mitteilungen* 115(4): 471–90.

Marchello-Nizia, Christiane (2014b). 'L'Importance spécifique de l'"oral représenté" pour la linguistique diachronique', in Wendy Ayres-Bennett and Thomas Rainsford (eds), *L'Histoire du français. État des lieux et perspectives*. Paris: Classiques Garnier, 161–74.

Marchello-Nizia, Christiane (2017). 'Les Débuts de l'"oral représenté" en français: marquage du discours direct dans les plus anciens textes', in Claire Badiou-Monferran, Samir Bajrić, and Philippe Monneret (eds), *Penser la langue. Sens, texte, histoire. Hommages à Olivier Soutet*. Paris: Champion, 117–28.

Marchello-Nizia, Christiane (2020). 'L'Objet', in Christiane Marchello-Nizia, Bernard Combettes, Sophie Prévost, and Tobias Scheer (eds), *Grande grammaire historique du français*. Berlin/Boston: de Gruyter, 1126–56.

Marchello-Nizia, Christiane, Bernard Combettes, Sophie Prévost, and Tobias Scheer (2020). *Grande grammaire historique du français*. Berlin/Boston: de Gruyter.
Marnette, Sophie (1996). 'Réflexions sur le discours indirect libre en français médiéval', *Romania* 114: 1–49.
Marnette, Sophie (1998). *Narrateur et point de vue dans la littérature française médiévale: une approche linguistique*. Bern: Peter Lang.
Marnette, Sophie (1999a). '*Il le vos mande, ge sui qui le vos di*: les stratégies du dire dans les chansons de geste', *La Revue de linguistique romane* 63(251–2): 387–417.
Marnette, Sophie (1999b). 'Narrateur et points de vue dans les chroniques médiévales: une approche linguistique', in Eric Kooper (ed.), *The Medieval Chronicle, Proceedings of the 1st International Conference on the Medieval Chronicle, Utrecht 13–16 July 1996*. Amsterdam/Atlanta: Rodopi, 174–90.
Marnette, Sophie (2001). 'Du discours insolite: le discours indirect sans *que*', *French Studies* 55(3): 297–313.
Marnette, Sophie (2005). *Speech and Thought Presentation in French*. Amsterdam/Philadelphia: John Benjamins.
Marnette, Sophie (2006a). 'La Ponctuation du discours rapporté dans quelques manuscrits de romans en prose médiévaux', *Verbum* 28(1): 29–46.
Marnette, Sophie (2006b). 'La Signalisation du discours rapporté en français médiéval', *Langue française* 149(1): 31–47.
Marnette, Sophie (2011). 'Voix de femmes et voix d'hommes dans les fabliaux', *Cahiers de recherches médiévales* 22: 104–22.
Marnette, Sophie (2013a). 'Forms and Functions of Reported Discourse in Medieval French', in Deborah Arteaga (ed.), *Research on Old French: The State of the Art*. Dordrecht/Heidelberg/New York/London: Springer, 299–326.
Marnette, Sophie (2013b). 'Oralité et locuteurs dans les lais médiévaux', *Diachroniques* 3: 21–48.
Marnette, Sophie (2016). 'L'Énonciation féminine dans les lais médiévaux', *Le Discours et la langue* 8(1): 97–120.
Marnette, Sophie (2018). 'Énonciation et locuteurs dans les lais de Marie de France', *Op. cit., revue des littératures et des arts [online]* 19. https://revues.univ-pau.fr/opcit/index.php?id=427 accessed 4 July 2022.
Marnette, Sophie (2022). 'Ignaure: Gender and Genre', *Medium Aevum* 91(1): 100–123.
Martel, Philippe (2016). *L'École française et l'occitan: le sourd et le bègue*, 2nd edn. Montpellier: Presses universitaires de la Méditerranée.
Martin, Éman (1868–81). *Le Courrier de Vaugelas: journal bi-mensuel consacré à la propagation de la langue française*.
Martin, Fanny, Christophe Rey, and Philippe Reynès (2020). 'Enseigner le picard au XXIe siècle: pour qui, comment?', in Gilles Forlot and Louise Ouvrard (eds), *Variation linguistique et enseignement des langues*. Paris: Presses de Inalco, 191–201.
Martineau, France (2005). 'Perspectives sur le changement linguistique: aux sources du français canadien', *The Canadian Journal of Linguistics/La revue canadienne de linguistique* 50: 173–213.
Martineau, France (2007). 'Variation in Canadian French Usage from the 18th to the 19th Century', *Multingua* 26: 203–27.
Martineau, France (2008). 'Un corpus pour l'analyse de la variation et du changement linguistique', *Corpus* 7: 135–55.
Martineau, France (2009). 'A Distance de Paris: usages linguistiques en France et en Nouvelle France à l'époque classique', in Dorothée Aquino-Weber, Sara Cotelli, and

Andres Kristol (eds), *Sociolinguistique historique du domaine gallo-roman: enjeux et méthodologies*. Bern: Peter Lang, 221–42.

Martinon, Philippe (1913). *Comment on prononce le français*, 2nd edn. Paris: Larousse.

Masson, Jean Louis (2021). *Proposition de loi no. 546*. https://www.senat.fr/leg/ppl20-546.html accessed 31 July 2021.

Matarrese, Tina (1993). *Il Settecento*. Bologna: Il Mulino.

Mathieu, Abel (1559). *Devis de la langue françoise*. Paris: Breton.

Matoré, Georges (1968). *Histoire des dictionnaires francais*. Paris: Larousse.

Mattarucco, Giada (2003). *Prime grammatiche d'italiano per francesi: secoli XVI–XVII*. Florence: Accademia della Crusca.

Mattarucco, Giada (2018). 'Grammatiche per stranieri', in Giuseppe Antonelli, Matteo Motolese, and Lorenzo Tomasin (eds), *Storia dell'italiano scritto*. Vol IV: *Grammatiche*. Rome: Carocci, 141–68.

Maurel, Jean-Pierre (1992). 'Subordination inverse et neutralisation du relatif', *Travaux linguistiques du Cerlico* 5: 72–88.

May, Stephen (2011). 'Language Rights: The "Cinderella" Human Right', *Journal of Human Rights* 10(3): 265–89.

May, Stephen (2012). *Language and Minority Rights. Ethnicity, Nationalism, and the Politics of Language*. 2nd edn. New York: Routledge.

Mazière, Francine (2010). 'Du dictionnaire bilingue de Nicot (1606) au dictionnaire monolingue de l'Académie (1694): l'émergence du "mot français"', in Michaela Heinz (ed.), *Cultures et lexikographies*. Berlin: Frank & Timme, 79–102.

Mazziotta, Nicolas and Julie Glikman (2019). 'Oral représenté et narration en ancien français. Spécificités syntaxiques dans trois textes de genres distincts', *Linx* 78: 6.

Mazzuchelli, Giammaria (1753). *Gli scrittori d'Italia cioè Notizie storiche, e critiche intorno alle vite, e agli scritti dei letterati italiani*. Vol. I. Brescia: Giambatista Bossini.

McAuley, Daniel (2017). 'L'Innovation lexicale chez les jeunes des quartiers urbains pluriethniques: "c'est banal, ouèche"', in Mireille Bilger, Laurie Buscail, and Françoise Mignon (eds), *Langue française mise en relief: aspects grammaticaux et discursifs*. Perpignan: Presses universitaires de Perpignan, 175–86.

McCain, Stewart (2018). *The Language Question under Napoleon*. Cham: Palgrave Macmillan.

McCarty, Teresa (2018). 'Community-based Language Planning: Perspectives from Indigenous Language Revitalisation', in Leanne Hinton, Leona Huss, and Gerald Roche (eds), *The Routledge Handbook of Language Revitalisation*. New York/London: Routledge, 22–35.

McCrea, Patrick Sean (2019). 'Linguistic Classification: The Persistent Challenge of the Langues d'oïl', in Michelle Harrison and Aurélie Joubert (eds), *French Language Policies and the Revitalisation of Regional Languages in the 21 st Century*. London: Palgrave Macmillan, 37–62.

McDonald, Maryon (1989). *'We are not French!': Language, Culture, and Identity in Brittany*. London: Routledge.

McIlvanney, Siobhán (2019). *Figurations of the Feminine in the Early French Women's Press, 1758–1848*. Liverpool: Liverpool University Press.

McLaughlin, Mairi (2011). 'When Written is Spoken: Dislocation and the Oral Code', *Journal of French Language Studies* 21(2): 209–29.

McLaughlin, Mairi (2015). 'Prolégomènes à l'étude des idéologies et attitudes linguistiques dans la presse périodique sous l'Ancien Régime', *Circula: revue d'idéologies linguistiques* 1: 4–25.

McLaughlin, Mairi (2018). 'When Romance Meets English', in Wendy Ayres-Bennett and Janice Carruthers (eds), *Manual of Romance Sociolinguistics*. Berlin: de Gruyter, 644–73.
McLaughlin, Mairi (2021). *La Presse française historique: histoire d'un genre et histoire de la langue*. Paris: Classiques Garnier.
McLelland, Nicola (2011). *J.G. Schottelius's Ausführliche Arbeit von der Teutschen Haubtsprache (1663) and its Place in Early Modern European Vernacular Language Study*. Oxford: Blackwell.
McLelland, Nicola (2013). 'Des guten Gebrauchs Wegzeigere: du bon usage dans la tradition allemande 1200–2000', in Wendy Ayres-Bennett and Magali Seijido (eds), *Bon usage et variation sociolinguistique: perspectives diachroniques et traditions nationales*. Lyon: ENS Éditions, 207–20.
McLelland, Nicola (2014). 'Language Description, Prescription and Usage in Seventeenth-century German', in Gijsbert Rutten, Rik Vosters, and Wim Vandenbussche (eds), *Norms and Usage in Language History, 1600–1900. A Sociolinguistic and Comparative Perspective*. Amsterdam: John Benjamins, 251–76.
McLelland, Nicola (2015). *German through English Eyes. A History of Language Teaching and Learning in Britain, 1500–2000*. Wiesbaden: Harrassowitz.
McLelland, Nicola (2017). *Teaching and Learning Foreign Languages: A History of Language Education, Assessment and Policy in Britain*. London: Routledge.
McLelland, Nicola (2018). 'The History of Language Learning and Teaching in Britain', *The Language Learning Journal* 46(1): 6–16.
McLelland, Nicola (ed.) (2021a). *Multilingual Perspectives on Language Standards, Variation and Ideologies*, special issue of *Journal of Multicultural and Multilingual Development*: 42(2).
McLelland, Nicola (2021b). 'Grammars, Dictionaries, and other Metalinguistic Texts in the Context of Language Standardization', in Wendy Ayres-Bennett and John Bellamy (eds), *The Cambridge Handbook of Language Standardization*. Cambridge: Cambridge University Press, 263–93.
McLelland, Nicola (2021c). 'Introduction. Language Standards, Standardisation and Standard Ideologies in Multilingual Contexts', *Journal of Multicultural and Multilingual Development* 42(2): 109–24.
McLelland, Nicola and Hui Zhao (eds) (2021). *Language Standards and Variation in Multilingual Contexts: Asian Perspectives*. Bristol: Multilingual Matters.
Megiser, Hieronymus (1593). *Specimen quadraginta diversarum et inter se differentium linguarum et dialectorum*. Frankfurt: Spiess.
Meier, Franz (2019). 'Diatopismes et degrés de normativité dans le discours sur le français en Belgique au tournant du 21e siècle. Analyse d'une chronique de langage de Cléante', in Anne Dister and Sophie Piron (eds), *Les Discours de référence sur la langue française*. Brussels: Presses de l'Université Saint-Louis, 253–82.
Meillet, Antoine (1916). 'Compte-rendu du *Cours de linguistique générale* de F. de Saussure', *Bulletin de la société linguistique de Paris* 64: 32–6.
Meillet, Antoine (1928). *Les Langues dans l'Europe nouvelle*, 2nd edn. Paris: Payot.
Melander, Johann (1928). *Étude sur l'ancienne abréviation des pronoms personnels régimes dans les langues romanes*. Uppsala: Almqvist & Wiksells.
Ménage, Gilles (1672). *Observations sur la langue française*. Paris: Claude Barbin.
Ménage, Gilles (1675). *Observations de Monsieur Ménage sur la langue françoise*. Paris: Claude Barbin.
Ménage, Gilles (1676). *Observations sur la langue française*, 2nd edn. Paris: Claude Barbin.

Menard, Martial and Iwan Kadored (2001). *Geriadur brezhoneg An Here*. Plougastel-Daoulas: An Here.

Merle, René (2010). *Visions de l'"idiome natal" à travers l'enquête impériale sur les patois (1807–1812)*. Canet: Trabucaire.

Mesmes, Jean-Claude de (1549). *La Grammaire italienne, composée en françoys*. Paris: par Estienne Groulleau, demourant en la rue Neuve nostre Dame, à l'enseigne Saint Jan Baptiste.

Mesmes, Jean-Claude de (2002 [1549]). *La Grammaire italienne*, ed. Giada Mattarucco. Pescara: Libreria dell'Università Editrice.

Meune, Manuel (2018). 'Du patois à l'"harpetan", entre (petite) patrie et nation imaginée: le discours sur le francoprovençal dans le *Journal de Genève* (1826–1998)', *International Journal of the Sociology of Language* 249: 199–216.

Mills, Jon (2015). 'Etymology and the Relexification of Cornish in the Twentieth Century', presented at *Etymological Thinking in the Nineteenth and Twentieth Centuries*, Taylor Institution, Oxford, 7 November. https://youtube.com/watch?v=p0iwUqQHeWE accessed 5 May 2021.

Milroy, James (2001). 'Language Ideologies and the Consequences of Standardization', *Journal of Sociolinguistics* 5(4): 530–55. https://doi.org/10.1111/1467-9481.00163

Milroy, James and Lesley Milroy (2012). *Authority in Language: Investigating Standard English*, 4th edn. London: Routledge.

Milroy, Lesley (1980). *Language and Social Networks*. Oxford: Blackwell.

Minerva, Nadia (1996). *Manuels, maîtres, méthodes: repères pour l'histoire de l'enseignement du français en Italie*. Bologna: CLUEB.

Minerva, Nadia (2002). *La Règle et l'exemple: à propos de quelques manuels du passé (XVIIe–XXe siècles)*. Bologna: CLUEB.

Minerva, Nadia and Carla Pellandra (eds) (1997). *Insegnare il francese in Italia. Repertorio analitico di manuali pubblicati dal 1625 al 1860*. Bologna: CLUEB.

Ministère de l'Éducation nationale (2011). 'Les Compétences en langues étrangères des élèves en fin de scolarité obligatoire. Premiers résultats de l'étude européenne sur les compétences en langues 2011'. http://cache.media.education.gouv.fr/file/2012/40/5/DEPP-NI-2012-11-competences-eleves-langues-etrangeres-survey-lang-2011_218405.pdf accessed 15 May 2023.

Ministère de l'Éducation nationale (2016). 'CEDRE 2004-2010-2016—Compétences en anglais en fin de collège'. https://www.education.gouv.fr/cedre-2004-2010-2016-competences-en-anglais-en-fin-de-college-en-2016-les-eleves-sont-plus-2675 accessed 15 May 2023.

Ministère de l'Éducation nationale (2017). 'Repères et références statistiques. Enseignements. Formation. Recherche'. https://www.enseignementsup-recherche.gouv.fr/sites/default/files/content_migration/document/depp-RERS-2017-maj-janv-2018_877976%281%29%281%29%281%29_894573.pdf accessed 15 May 2023.

Ministère de la Culture (2022). 'France Terme'. http://www.culture.fr/Ressources/FranceTerme accessed 4 December 2021.

Minitel (no date). https://www.minitel.fr/histoire-minitel accessed 22 December 2021.

Miranda, Juan de (1566). *Osservationi della lingua castigliana divise in quatro libri, ne' quali s'insegna con gran facilità la perfetta lingua spagnola*. Venice: Gabriel Giolito de' Ferrari.

Mitterrand, François (1984). 'Interview de M. François Mitterrand, Président de la République, accordée au journal "Libération", Paris, jeudi 10 mai 1984'. https://www.elysee.fr/front/pdf/elysee-module-5910-fr.pdf accessed 4 December 2021.

Moal, Stefan (2009). 'La Langue bretonne dans l'enseignement en 2009: Quelques éléments', *Tréma* 31: 27–37.

Moal, Stefan, Noel Ó Murchadha, and John Walsh (2018). 'New Speakers and Language in the Media: Audience Design in Breton and Irish Broadcast Media', in Cassie Smith-Christmas, Noel Ó Murchadha, Michael Hornsby, and Mairéad Moriarty (eds), *New Speakers of Minority Languages: Linguistic Ideologies and Practices*. London: Palgrave Macmillan, 189–212.

Molière (Jean-Baptiste Poquelin) (1673). *Le Malade imaginaire*. http://clicnet.swarthmore.edu/litterature/classique/moliere/mi/mi.introduction.html accessed 30 August 2022.

Montreuil, Jean-Pierre (1987). 'Asyllabism and stray adjunction in Romance', in Carol Neidle and Rafael A. Núñez Cedeño (eds), *Studies in Romance Languages*. Dordrecht: Foris, 203–13.

Mooney, Damien (2015). 'Confrontation and Language Policy: Non-militant Perspectives on Conflicting Revitalisation Strategies in Béarn, France', in Mari C. Jones (ed.), *Policy and Planning for Endangered Languages*. Cambridge: Cambridge University Press, 153–79.

Mooney, Damien (2016a). 'Transmission and Diffusion: Linguistic Change in the Regional French of Béarn', *Journal of French Language Studies* 26: 327–52.

Mooney, Damien (2016b). *Southern Regional French: A Linguistic Analysis of Language and Dialect Contact*. Oxford: Legenda.

Morcos, Hannah (2019). 'Digital Edition and Linguistic Database: A fully Lemmatised and Searchable Model', poster presented at *Digital Humanities Conference 2019*, Utrecht, Netherlands. https://dev.clariah.nl/files/dh2019/boa/1218.html accessed 24 September 2021.

Morcos, Hannah, Geoffroy Noël, and Marcus Husar (2021). 'Lemmatization in the Collaborative Editorial Workflow of a Medieval French Text: The Digital Edition of the *Histoire ancienne jusqu'à César*', *Digital Scholarship in the Humanities* 36/(supplement 2): ii203–ii209. https://doi.org/10.1093/llc/fqaa060

Morgan, John (2008). 'Sprat, Thomas (Bap. 1635, d. 1713)', in David Cannadine (ed.), *Oxford Dictionary of National Biography*. Oxford: Oxford University Press. https://doi.org/10.1093/ref:odnb/26173

Morgana, Silvia (1994). 'L'influsso francese', in Luca Serianni and Pietro Trifone (eds), *Storia della lingua italiana*. Vol. III: *L'italiano e le altre lingue moderne*. Turin: Einaudi, 671–719.

Morin, Yves Charles (1986). 'On the Morphologization of Word-final Consonant Deletion in French', in Henning Andersen (ed.), *Sandhi Phenomena in the Languages of Europe*. Berlin: Mouton de Gruyter, 167–210.

Mormile, Mario (1989). *L'italiano in Francia, il francese in Italia: storia critica delle opere grammaticali francesi in Italia ed italiane in Francia dal Rinascimento al primo Ottocento. In appendice: repertorio cronologico delle opere grammaticali e lessicali italo-francesi dalle origini al primo Ottocento*. Turin: Albert Meynier.

Mormile, Mario (1993). *Storia dei dizionari bilingui italo-francesi: la lessicografia italo-francese dalle origini al 1900: con un repertorio bibliografico cronologico di tutte le opere lessicografiche italiano-francese e francese-italiano pubblicate*. Fasano: Schena.

Morvannou, Fañch (2004). 'Regards sur 700 ans de breton écrit', in Louis Lemoine and Bernard Merdrignac (eds), *Corona monastica. Moines bretons de Landévennec: histoire et mémoire celtiques. Mélanges offerts au Père Marc Simon*. Rennes: Presses universitaires de Rennes, 365–79.

Mousset, Sophie (2003). *Olympe de Gouges et les droits de la femme*. Paris: Félin.

Müller, Andreas [Pseudonym Thomas Ludekenius] (1680). *Oratio orationum.* Berlin: Rungiana.

Muller, Charles (1994). 'Du féminisme lexical', *Cahiers de lexicologie* 65: 103–9.

Munier, Charles (1720). *Nuovo metodo per insegnare il francese agl'italiani, il quale contiene il modo di ben pronunziare, scrivere, e parlare, secondo l'uso moderno della corte, e de' buoni autori.* Naples: Felice Mosca.

Munro-Hill, Mary (2017). *Aristide of* Le Figaro. Newcastle upon Tyne: Cambridge Scholars Publishing.

Munro-Hill, Mary (2018). *Claude Duneton,* Chroniqueur *at* Le Figaro. Newcastle upon Tyne: Cambridge Scholars Publishing.

Muratori, Lodovico Antonio (1706). *Della perfetta poesia italiana spiegata, e dimostrata con varie osservazioni.* 2 vols. Modena: Bartolomeo Soliani.

Musiani, Elena (2003). *Circoli e salotti femminili nell'Ottocento: le donne bolognesi tra politica e sociabilità.* Bologna: CLUEB.

Nevalainen, Terttu (2015). 'What are Historical Sociolinguistics?', *Journal of Historical Sociolinguistics* 1(2): 243–69.

Nic Craith, Máiréad (2012). 'Legacy and Loss: The Great Silence and its Aftermath', in John Crowley, William J. Smyth, and Michael Murphy (eds), *Atlas of the Great Irish Famine, 1845–1852.* Cork: Cork University Press, 580–8.

Nicot, Jean (1606). *Thresor de la language françoyse.* Paris: David Douceur.

Nodier, Charles (1834). *Notions élémentaires de linguistique, ou Histoire abrégée de la parole et de l'écriture, pour servir d'introduction à l'alphabet, à la grammaire et au dictionnaire.* Paris: Librairie d'Eugène Renduel.

Nolan, J. Shaun (2018). 'Maintenance and Revitalisation of Gallo', in Leanne Hinton, Leona Huss, and Gerald Roche (eds), *The Routledge Handbook of Language Revitalisation.* New York/London: Routledge, 289–96.

Northern Ireland Office (1998). *The Belfast Agreement, also Known as the Good Friday Agreement.* https://www.gov.uk/government/publications/the-belfast-agreement accessed 2 September 2022.

Northern Ireland Office (2020). *New Decade, New Approach. January 2020.* https://assets.publishing.service.gov.uk/government/uploads/system/uploads/attachment_data/file/856998/2020-01-08_a_new_decade__a_new_approach.pdf accessed 2 September 2022.

NISRA (Northern Ireland Statistics and Research Agency) (2014). 'Northern Ireland Census 2011'. https://www.nisra.gov.uk/statistics/census/2011-census accessed 29 June 2020.

NISRA (Northern Ireland Statistics and Research Agency) (2023). 'Northern Ireland Census 2021'. https://www.nisra.gov.uk/statistics/census/2021-census accessed 2 June 2023.

Ó Baoill, Dónall P. (1986). *Lárchanúint don Ghaeilge.* Dublin: Institiúid Teangeolaíochta Éireann.

Ó Ceallaigh, Ben (2019). *Neoliberalism and Language Shift: The Great Recession and the Sociolinguistic Vitality of Ireland's Gaeltacht, 2008–2018,* doctoral thesis, University of Edinburgh.

Ó Ceallaigh, T. J. and Áine Ní Dhonnabháin (2015). 'Reawakening the Irish Language through the Irish Education System: Challenges and Priorities', *International Electronic Journal of Elementary Education* 8(2): 179–98.

Ó Curnáin, Brian (2009). 'Mionteangú na Gaeilge', in Brian Ó Catháin (ed.), *Sochtheangeolaíocht na Gaeilge.* Maigh Nuad: An Sagart, 90–153.

Ó Curnáin, Brian (2012). 'An Ghaeilge Iarthraidisiúnta agus an Phragmataic Chódmheasctha Thiar agus Theas', in Ciarán Lenoach, Conchúr Ó Giollagáin, and Brian Ó Curnáin (eds), *An Chonair Chaoch: An Mionteangachas sa Dátheangachas.* Indreabhán: Leabhar Breac, 284–364.

Ó Giollagáin, Conchúr (2014a). 'From Revivalist to Undertaker: New Developments in Official Policies and Attitudes to Ireland's "First Language"', *Language Problems and Language Planning* 38(2): 101–27.

Ó Giollagáin, Conchúr (2014b). 'Unfirm Ground: A Re-assessment of Language Planning in Ireland since Independence', *Language Problems and Language Planning* 38(1): 19–41.

Ó Giollagáin, Conchúr, Gòrdan Camshron, Pàdruig Moireach, Brian Ó Curnáin, Iain Caimbeul, Brian MacDonald, and Tamás Pétervary (2020). *The Gaelic Crisis in the Vernacular Community. A Comprehensive Sociolinguistic Survey of Scottish Gaelic.* Aberdeen: Aberdeen University Press.

Ó Giollagáin, Conchúr and Martin Charlton (2015). *Nuashonrú ar an Staidéar Cuimsitheach Teangeolaíoch ar Úsáid na Gaeilge sa Ghaeltacht.* Na Forbacha: Údarás na Gaeltachta.

Ó Giollagáin, Conchúr and Seosamh Mac Donnacha (2008). 'The Gaeltacht Today', in Caoilfhinn Nic Pháidín and Seán Ó Cearnaigh (eds), *A New View of the Irish Language.* Dublin: Cois Life, 108–20.

Ó Giollagáin, Conchúr, Seosamh Mac Donnacha, Fiona Ní Chualáin, Aoife Ní Shéaghdha, and Mary O'Brien (2007). *Comprehensive Linguistic Study of the Use of Irish in the Gaeltacht: Principal Findings and Recommendations.* Dublin: The Stationery Office.

Ó Giollagáin, Conchúr and Brian Ó Curnáin (2016). *Beartas Úr na nGael: Dálaí na Gaeilge san Iar-Nua-Aoiseachas.* Indreabhán: Leabhar Breac.

Ó Gráda, Cormac (1994). *Ireland: A New Economic History, 1780–1939.* Oxford: Oxford University Press.

Ó Háinle, Cathal (1994). 'Ó Chaint na nDaoine go dtí an Caighdeán Oifigiúil', in Kim McCone, Damian McManus, Cathal Ó Háinle, Nicholas Williams, and Liam Breatnach (eds), *Stair na Gaeilge. In Ómós do Pádraig Ó Fiannachta.* Maigh Nuad: Roinn na Sean-Ghaeilge, Coláiste Phádraig, 745–93.

Ó hIfearnáin, Tadhg (2013). 'Institutional Breton Language Policy after Language Shift', *International Journal of the Sociology of Language* 223: 117–35.

Ó hIfearnáin, Tadhg (2018). 'The Ideological Construction of Boundaries between Speakers, and their Varieties', in Cassie Smith-Christmas, Noel Ó Murchadha, Michael Hornsby, and Mairéad Moriarty (eds), *New Speakers of Minority Languages: Linguistic Ideologies and Practices.* London: Palgrave Macmillan, 151–64.

Ó Huallacháin, Colmán (1994). *The Irish and Irish – A Sociolinguistic Analysis of the Relationship between a People and their Language.* Dublin: Assisi Press.

Ó Laighin, Pádraig Breandán (2022). *Pobal na Gaeilge. Daonra, Institiúidí, Stádas agus Cumhacht.* Baile Átha Cliath: Cló na nGael.

Ó Mainnín, Mícheál B. (2021). 'Empowering Multilingualism? Provisions for Place-names in Northern Ireland and the Political and Legislative Context', in Robert Blackwood and Deirdre Dunlevy (eds), *Multilingualism in Public Spaces.* London: Bloomsbury, 59–87.

Ó Murchadha, Noel (2013). 'Authority and Innovation in Language Variation: Teenagers' Perceptions of Variation in Spoken Irish', in Tore Kristiansen and Stefan Grondelaers (eds), *Language (De)standardisation in Late Modern Europe: Experimental Studies.* Osló: Novus, 71–96.

Ó Murchadha, Noel (2018a). *An Ghaeilge sa Nua-Aoiseacht Dhéanach*. An Spidéal: An Clóchomhar.
Ó Murchadha, Noel (2018b). 'Iniúchadh ar Dhearcadh Cainteoirí Gaeltachta ar Éagsúlacht na Gaeilge Comhaimseartha', in Tadhg Ó hIfearnáin and John Walsh (eds), *An Meon Folaithe. Idé-eolaíochtaí agus Iompar Lucht Labhartha na Gaeilge in Éirinn agus in Albain*. Baile Átha Cliath: Cois Life, 74–102.
Ó Murchadha, Noel (2019). 'An Aird ar an Éagsúlacht Teanga, an Daonteangeolaíocht agus Canúintí na Gaeilge', in Tadhg Ó hIfearnáin (ed.), *An tSochtheangeolaíocht: Taighde agus Gníomh*. Dublin: Cois Life, 79–101.
Ó Murchadha, Noel (2020). 'Múnlaí Teanga na Gaeilge agus an Idé-eolaíocht Teanga: Language Models and Language Ideologies in Relation to Irish', *TEANGA, the Journal of the Irish Association for Applied Linguistics* 27: 44–64.
Ó Murchadha, Noel (2021). 'Renegotiating Language Norms in Minority Contexts', in Wendy Ayres-Bennett and John Bellamy (eds), *The Cambridge Handbook of Language Standardization*. Cambridge: Cambridge University Press, 741–64.
Ó Murchadha, Noel and Tadhg Ó hIfearnáin (2018). 'Converging and Diverging Stances on Target Revival Varieties in Collateral Languages: The Ideologies of Linguistic Variation in Irish and Manx Gaelic', *Journal of Multilingual and Multicultural Development* 39(5): 458–69.
Ó Murchú, Máirtín (2002). *Ag Dul ó Chion? Cás na Gaeilge 1952–2002*. Dublin: Coiscéim.
Ó Riagáin, Pádraig (1997). *Language Policy and Social Reproduction, Ireland 1893–1993*. Oxford: Oxford University Press.
Ó Tuathaigh, Gearóid (2015). *I mBéal an Bháis: The Great Famine and the Language Shift in Nineteenth-century Ireland*. Hamden: Quinnipiac University Press.
O'Rourke, Bernadette (2018). 'New Speakers of Minority Languages', in Leanne Hinton, Leona Huss, and Gerald Roche (eds), *The Routledge Handbook of Language Revitalisation*. New York/London: Routledge, 265–73.
O'Rourke, Bernadette, Joan Pujolar, and Fernando Ramallo (2015). 'New Speakers of Minority Languages. The Challenging Opportunity', *International Journal of the Sociology of Language* 231: 1–20.
O'Rourke, Bernadette and John Walsh (2020). *New Speakers of Irish in the Global Context. New Revival?* London: Routledge.
Oakes, Leigh (2001). *Language and National Identity: Comparing France and Sweden*. Amsterdam/Philadelphia: John Benjamins.
Oakes, Leigh (2017). 'Normative Language Policy and Minority Language Rights. Rethinking the Case of Regional Languages in France', *Language Policy* 16: 365–84.
Oakes, Leigh (2019). 'Foreward', in Michelle Harrison and Aurélie Joubert (eds), *French Language Policies and the Revitalisation of Regional Languages in the 21st Century*. London: Palgrave Macmillan, v–x.
Oakes, Leigh and Yael Peled (2018). *Normative Language Policy: Ethics, Politics, Principles*. Cambridge: Cambridge University Press.
Oaks, Dallin D. (2021). 'Linguistic Encounters in Real World Prescriptivism: Acknowledging its Place and Role', *Lingua* 264. https://doi.org/10.1016/j.lingua.2021.103159
Oesterreicher, Wulf (1997). 'Types of Orality in Text', in Egbert Bakker and Ahuvia Kahane (eds), *Written Voices, Spoken Signs: Tradition, Performance, and the Epic Text*. Cambridge: Harvard University Press, 190–214.
Office national d'information sur les enseignements et les professions (2020). 'Les Sections linguistiques au lycée. Les Sections binationales: AbiBac, BachiBac, EsaBac'. https://www.onisep.fr/Choisir-mes-etudes/Au-lycee-au-CFA/Dispositifs-specifiques/Les-

sections-linguistiques-au-lycee/Les-sections-binationales-AbiBac-Bachibac-Esabac accessed 4 December 2021.

Omer, Danielle (2020). 'La Fin du masculin générique? Expériences et débats autour de l'écriture inclusive', in Alexandra Cuniță and Coman Lupu (eds), *Normă și uz în limbile romanice actuale*. Bucharest: Bucharest University Press, 1–19.

Oppermann-Marsaux, Evelyne (2012). 'L'Évolution des marqueurs discursifs *tiens* et *tenez* du français médiéval jusqu'au français classique (1450–1800)', *Zeitschrift für französische Sprache und Literatur* 122: 1–16.

Oppermann-Marsaux, Evelyne (2014). 'Les Emplois du marqueur discursif *dea* du moyen français jusqu'au français classique', in Jean-Claude Anscombre, Evelyne Oppermann-Marsaux, and Amalia Rodríguez Somolinos (eds), *Médiativité, polyphonie et modalité en français: études synchroniques et diachroniques*. Paris: Presses de la Sorbonne Nouvelle, 179–96.

Oppermann-Marsaux, Evelyne (2018). 'Quelques observations sur l'oral représenté en moyen français, à partir de la comparaison de discours directs et de dialogues de théâtre', in Wendy Ayres-Bennett, Anne Carlier, Julie Glikman, Thomas M. Rainsford, Gilles Siouffi, and Carine Skupien-Dekens (eds), *Nouvelles voies d'accès au changement linguistique*. Paris: Classiques Garnier, 221–37.

Ordonnance de Villers-Cotterêts (*L'Ordonnance d'août 1539 sur le fait de la justice*) (1539). https://www.legifrance.gouv.fr/loda/id/LEGITEXT000006070939/ accessed 8 September 2022.

Organisation internationale de la francophonie (no date). 'La Langue française dans le monde'. https://www.francophonie.org/la-langue-francaise-dans-le-monde-305 accessed 4 December 2021.

Osthus, Dietmar (2003). 'Le Bon Usage d'Internet: discours et conscience normatifs dans des débats virtuels', in Dietmar Osthus and Claudia Polzin-Haumann (eds), *La Norme linguistique: théorie—pratique—médias—enseignement; actes du colloque tenu à Bonn le 6 et le 7 décembre 2002*. Bonn: Romanistischer Verlang, 139–52.

Osthus, Dietmar (2006). 'Laienlinguistik und Sprachchroniken. Französisch/Okzitanisch', in Gerhard Ernst, Martin-Dietrich Gleßgen, Christian Schmitt, and Wolfgang Schweickard (eds), *Romanische Sprachgeschichte. Ein internationales Handbuch zur Geschichte des romanischen Sprachen/Manuel international d'histoire linguistique de la Romania*. Vol. 2. Berlin/New York: de Gruyter, 1533–46.

Osthus, Dietmar (2015). 'Linguistique populaire et chroniques de langage: France', in Claudia Polzin-Haumann and Wolfgang Schweickard (eds), *Manuel de linguistique française*. Berlin: de Gruyter, 160–70.

Osthus, Dietmar (2016). 'The French *chroniques de langage* between Prescriptivism, Normative Discourse and Anti-prescriptivism', *Journal of Multilingual and Multicultural Development* 37(3): 334–42.

Oudin, Antoine (1640). *Grammaire françoise rapportée au langage du temps*. Paris: Sommaville.

Paffey, Darren (2012). *Language Ideologies and the Globalization of 'Standard' Spanish*. London: Bloomsbury.

Pagani-Naudet, Cendrine (2014). 'La Langue des grammairiens est-elle une langue exemplaire?', in Wendy Ayres-Bennett and Thomas M. Rainsford (eds), *L'Histoire du français: état des lieux et perspectives*. Paris: Classiques Garnier, 187–98.

Palsgrave, John (1530). *Lesclarcissement de la langue francoyse*. London: J. Haukyns.

Paris, Gaston (1888). *Les Parlers de France. Lecture faite à la réunion des Sociétés savantes, le 26 mai*. Paris: Imprimerie Nationale.

Parussa, Gabriella (2018). 'La Représentation de l'oral à l'écrit et la diachronie du français. Un nouveau projet de recherche', in Wendy Ayres-Bennett, Anne Carlier, Julie Glikman, Thomas M. Rainsford, Gilles Siouffi, and Carine Skupien-Dekens (eds), *Nouvelles voies d'accès au changement linguistique*. Paris: Classiques Garnier, 181–99.

Parussa, Gabriella (2020). '*Dea, dia, da*: un marqueur discursif en diachronie dans un corpus de dialogues en français', *Langages* 217(1): 87–102.

Pasquier, Estienne (1607). *Les Recherches de la France*. Paris: Laurent Sonnius.

Passy, Paul (1917). *Les Sons du français. Leur formation, leur combinaison, leur représentation*, 8th revised edn. Paris: Didier.

Pasta, Renato (2014). 'Mediazioni e trasformazioni: operatori del libro in Italia nel Settecento', *Archivio Storico Italiano* 172(2/640): 311–54.

Patin, Guy (1907 [1643]). *Lettres de Guy Patin 1630–1672*. Paris: Champion.

Paveau, Marie-Anne and Laurence Rosier (2008). *La Langue française: passions et polémiques*. Paris: Vuibert.

Pazzi, Valeria (2001). 'Manuali per l'insegnamento del francese pubblicati in Italia (1625–1860). I fondi della Biblioteca Ambrosiana', in Colombo Timelli 2001: 213–26.

Pellandra, Carla (ed.) (1989). *Grammatiche, grammatici, grammatisti: per una storia dell'insegnamento delle lingue in Italia dal Cinquecento al Settecento*. Pisa: Libreria Goliardica.

Pellandra, Carla (2003). 'Lingue classiche e lingue moderne nella cultura femminile fra Sette ed Ottocento', in Susana Bonaldi and Patrizia Garelli (eds), *L'educazione della donna in età romantica: Atti della Giornata svoltasi il 20 novembre 2001. Centro Interdisciplinare di Studi Romantici. Dipartimento di Lingue e Letterature Straniere Moderne*. Florence: Aletheia, 31–59.

Peperkamp, Sharon (1997). *Prosodic Words*. The Hague: Holland Academic Graphics.

Pescarini, Diego (2011). 'The Evolution of Lat. ILLUM in Old Veronese: Apocope and Related Phenomena', *Vox Romanica* 70: 63–78.

Pescarini, Diego (2016). 'Clitic Pronominal Systems: Morphophonology', in Adam Ledgeway and Martin Maiden (eds), *The Oxford Guide to the Romance Languages*. Oxford: Oxford University Press, 742–60.

Pétin, L. M. (abbé) (1842). *Dictionnaire patois-français à l'usage des écoles rurales et des habitants de la campagne, ouvrage qui, par le moyen du patois usité dans la Lorraine, conduit à la connaissance de la langue française*. Nancy: Thomas.

Phelan, Mary (2019). *Irish Speakers, Interpreters, and the Courts, 1754–1921*. Dublin: Four Courts Press.

Philippe, Édouard (2017). 'Circulaire du 21 novembre 2017 relative aux règles de féminisation et de rédaction des textes publiés au Journal officiel de la République française', *Journal officiel de la République française*, 22 November 2017, PRMX1732742C. https://www.legifrance.gouv.fr/jorf/id/JORFTEXT000036068906 accessed 30 April 2021.

Picoche, Jacqueline and Marchello-Nizia, Christiane (1991 [1989]). *Histoire de la langue française*. Paris: Nathan-Université.

Pierquin de Gembloux, Claude Charles (1841). *Histoire littéraire, philologique, et bibliographique des patois*. Paris: Brockhaus.

Pingeot, Mazarine (2022). 'Les Contresens de l'écriture inclusive', *Études* 10: 57–68. https://doi.org/10.3917/etu.4297.0057

Pinkster, Harm (1987). 'The Strategy and Chronology of the Development of Future and Perfect Tense Auxiliaries in Latin', in Martin Harris and Paolo Ramat (eds), *Historical Development of Auxiliaries*. Berlin: Mouton de Gruyter, 193–223.

Piva, Franco (1973). *Cultura francese e censura a Venezia nel secondo Settecento*. Venice: Istituto veneto di scienze lettere ed arti.

Polo, Anna (2017). *La tradición gramatical del español en Italia: 'Il paragone della lingua toscana et castigliana' di Giovanni Mario Alessandri d'Urbino. Estudio y edición crítica*. Padua: CLEUP.

Pooley, Tim (1994). 'Word-final Consonant Devoicing in a Variety of Working-class French – A Case of Language Contact?', *Journal of French Language Studies* 4(2): 215–33.

Pooley, Tim (2006). 'On the Geographical Spread of Oïl French in France', *Journal of French Language Studies* 16(3): 357–90.

Pooley, Tim and Dominique Lagorgette (eds) (2011). *On Linguistic Change in French: Socio-historical Approaches. Studies in Honour of R. Anthony Lodge/Le Changement linguistique en français: aspects socio-historiques. Études en hommage au Professeur R. Anthony Lodge*. Chambéry: Université de Savoie.

Poplack, Shana, Rena Torres Cacoullos, Nathalie Dion, Rosane de Andrade Berlinck, Salvatore Digesto, Dora Lacasse, and Johnathan Steuck (2018). 'Trajectories of Change in Romance Linguistics', in Wendy Ayres-Bennett and Janice Carruthers (eds), *Manual of Romance Sociolinguistics*. Berlin: de Gruyter, 217–52.

Posner, Rebecca (1997). *Linguistic Change in French*. Oxford: Oxford University Press.

Pouliquen, Yves (2013). '"Dire, Ne pas dire" un an après'. http://www.academie-francaise.fr/dire-ne-pas-dire-un-apres accessed 14 April 2021.

Prager, Johann Christian (1757 [1760]). *Neueingerichtetes englisches Wörterbuch*. 2 vols. Coburg/Leipzig: Georg Otto.

Prager, Johann Christian (1768). *The English Cellarius or a Dictionary English and German*. Hildburghausen: Hanisch.

Preston, Malcolm S. (1963). *Evaluational Reactions to English, Canadian French and European French Voices*, Masters dissertation, McGill University.

Prévost, Sophie (2018). 'Increase of Pronominal Subjects in Old French: Evidence for a Starting-point in Late Latin', in Anne Carlier and Céline Guillot (eds), *Latin tardif - français ancien: continuités et ruptures*. Berlin: de Gruyter, 171–200.

Prévost, Sophie and Christiane Marchello-Nizia (2020). 'Le Sujet', in Christiane Marchello-Nizia, Bernard Combettes, Sophie Prévost, and Tobias Scheer (eds), *Grande grammaire historique du français*. Berlin/Boston: de Gruyter, 1055–126.

Prévost, Sophie and Monique Dufresne (2020). 'L'Approche du changement linguistique dans la GGHF', in Christiane Marchello-Nizia, Bernard Combettes, Sophie Prévost, and Tobias Scheer (eds), *Grande grammaire historique du français*. Berlin/Boston: de Gruyter, 15–36.

Price, Glanville (1971). *The French Language: Present and Past*. London: Edward Arnold.

Prodhomme, Jean-Baptiste (ed.) (1867–69). *Revue grammaticale et littéraire*.

Puren, Christian (1988). *Histoire des méthodologies de l'enseignement des langues*, Paris: Nathan-CLE International. https://www.aplv-languesmodernes.org/docrestreint.api/1849/b1a776bacb5d6ccbb0a692b19bd88566e4b5a707/pdf/puren_histoire_methodologies.pdf accessed 4 December 2021.

Pustka, Elissa (2011). 'Le Conditionnement lexical de l'élision des liquides en contexte postconsonantique final', *Langue française* 169: 19–38.

Quemada, Bernard (1967). *Les Dictionnaires du français moderne, 1539–1863: étude sur leur histoire, leurs types et leurs méthodes*. Paris: Didier.

R Core Team (2013). *R: A Language and Environment for Statistical Computing. R Foundation for Statistical Computing, Vienna, Austria*. http://www.R-project.org/ accessed 28 February 2021.

Rabatel, Alain and Laurence Rosier (eds) (2019). *Les Défis de l'écriture inclusive*, special issue of *Le Discours et la langue*: 11(1).
Rainsford, Thomas M. (2011a). 'Dividing Lines: The Changing Syntax and Prosody of the Mid-line Break in Medieval French Octosyllabic Verse', *Transactions of the Philological Society* 109(3): 265–83.
Rainsford, Thomas M. (2011b). *The Emergence of Group Stress in Medieval French*, doctoral thesis, University of Cambridge. https://doi.org/10.17863/CAM.16503
Rainsford, Thomas M. (2014). 'Sur la disparition de l'enclise en ancien français', in Wendy Ayres-Bennett and Thomas Rainsford (eds), *L'Histoire du français. État des lieux et perspectives*. Paris: Classiques Garnier, 21–44.
Rainsford, Thomas M. (2020). 'Syllable Structure and Prosodic Words in Early Old French', *Papers in Historical Phonology* 5: 63–89. https://doi.org/10.2218/pihph.5.2020.4433
Rainsford, Thomas M. (2021). *Old Gallo-Romance Corpus*, preview version 0.2. Stuttgart: Institut für Linguistik/Romanistik. http://www.ogr-corpus.org accessed 31 August 2022.
Ratouis, Alix (2018). 'Internet au secours du français', *Le Point*, 14 April 2021. https://www.lepoint.fr/education/internet-au-secours-du-francais-14-10-2018-2262896_3584.php accessed 14 April 2021.
Reddick, Allen (2009). 'Johnson and Richardson', in A. P. Cowie (ed.), *The Oxford History of English Lexicography*. Oxford: Oxford University Press, 155–81.
Reinhart, Tania (1984). 'Principles of Gestalt Perception in the Temporal Organization of Narrative Texts', *Linguistics* 22: 779–809.
Remysen, Wim (2005). 'La Chronique de langage à la lumière de l'expérience canadienne-française: un essai de définition', in Julie Bérubé, Karine Gauvin, and Wim Remysen (eds), *Les Journées de linguistique: actes du 18e colloque 11–12 mars 2004*. Quebec: Centre interdisciplinaire de recherches sur les activités langagières, 267–81.
Remysen, Wim (2010). *Description et évaluation de l'usage canadien dans les chroniques de langage: contribution à l'étude de l'imaginaire linguistique des chroniqueurs canadiens-français*, doctoral thesis, Université Laval.
Remysen, Wim (2011). 'L'Application du modèle de l'imaginaire linguistique à des corpus écrits: le cas des chroniques de langage dans la presse québécoise', *Langage et société* 135: 47–65.
Remysen, Wim (2012). 'Les Représentations identitaires dans le discours normatif des chroniqueurs de langage canadiens-français depuis le milieu du XIXe siècle', *Journal of French Language Studies* 22(3): 419–44.
Remysen, Wim (2013a). 'Comment définir le bon usage au Canada français? Le Point de vue des chroniqueurs de langage', in Wendy Ayres-Bennett and Magali Seijido (eds), *Bon usage et variation sociolinguistique. Perspectives diachroniques et traditions nationales*. Lyon: ENS, 179–93.
Remysen, Wim (2013b). 'Le Rôle des dictionnaires français dans le discours normatif d'Étienne Blanchard, chroniqueur de langue', *Revue de linguistique romane* 77(307–8): 517–40.
Remysen, Wim (2016). 'Langue et espace au Québec: les Québécois perçoivent-ils des accents régionaux?', *Lingue, culture, mediazioni* 37: 31–57.
Remysen, Wim (ed.) (2016–17a). *Les Idéologies linguistiques dans la presse francophone canadienne: approches critiques*, special issue of *Francophonies d'Amérique*: 42–3.
Remysen, Wim (2016–17b). 'Introduction', *Francophonies d'Amérique* 42–3: 13–21.

Remysen, Wim, Ada Luna Salita, and Mélanie Barrière (2020). 'Les Accents régionaux au Québec: représentations et perceptions linguistiques dans la région de Beauce', *Cahiers de l'Association d'études en langue française* 23(1): 21–54.
Remysen, Wim, and Sandrine Tailleur (eds) (2020). *L'Individu et sa langue: hommages à France Martineau*. Québec: Presses de l'Université Laval.
Rettig, Wolfgang (1991). 'Die Zweisprachige Lexikographie Französisch-Deutsch, Deutsch-Französisch', in Franz Josef Hausmann, Oskar Reichmann, Herbert Eernst Wiegand, and Ladislav Zgusta (eds), *Wörterbücher, Dictionaries, Dictionnaires: ein internationales Handbuch zur Lexikographie*. Berlin: de Gruyter, 2997–3007.
Revithiadou, Anthi (2011). 'The Phonological Word', in Marc van Oostendorp, Colin J. Ewen, Elizabeth Hume, and Keren Rice (eds), *The Blackwell Companion to Phonology*. Vol. 2: *Suprasegmental and Prosodic Phonology*. Malden: Wiley-Blackwell, 1204–27.
Revue des patois gallo-romans (1887–8). Continued as the *Revue de philologie française et provençale* (1889–1896).
Ricento, Thomas (ed.) (2006). *An Introduction to Language Policy. Theory and Method*. Malden: Blackwell.
Richardson, Brian (2002). 'The Italian of Renaissance Elites in Italy and Europe', in Anna Laura Lepschy and Arturo Tosi (eds), *Multilingualism in Italy Past and Present*. Oxford: Legenda, 5–23.
Richelet, César-Pierre (1680). *Dictionnaire françois contenant les mots et les choses, plusieurs nouvelles remarques sur la langue françoise. [...]*. Geneva: Jean Herman Wiederhold.
Rickard, Peter (1989). *A History of the French Language*. London: Unwin Hyman.
Rickard, Peter (1992). *The French Language in the Seventeenth Century: Contemporary Opinion in France*. Cambridge: D. S. Brewer.
Rivarol, Antoine de (1784). *De l'universalité de la langue française; discours qui a emporté le prix à l'Académie de Berlin*. Berlin/Paris: Chez Bailly [...] Chez Dessenne.
Rivers, Isabel (2004). 'Tillotson, John (1630–1694)', in David Cannadine (ed.), *Oxford Dictionary of National Biography*. Oxford: Oxford University Press. https://doi.org/10.1093/ref:odnb/27449
Rjéoutski, Vladislav, Gesine Argent, and Derek Offord (eds) (2014). *European Francophonie: The Social, Political, and Cultural History of an International Prestige Language*. Oxford: Peter Lang.
Roberts, Ian (2014). 'Taraldsen's Generalisation and Diachronic Syntax: Two Ways to Lose Null Subjects', in Peter Svenonius (ed.), *Functional Structure from Top to Toe: The Cartography of Syntactic Structures*. Oxford: Oxford University Press, 115–48.
Robitaille, Louis-Bernard (2002). *Le Salon des immortels: une académie très française*. Paris: Editions Denoël.
Rodriguez, Jose I., Aaron C. Cargile, and Mark D. Rich (2004). 'Reactions to African-American Vernacular English: Do More Phonological Features Matter?', *The Western Journal of Black Studies* 28(3): 407–14.
Rodríguez Somolinos, Amalia (ed.) (2013). *Les Marques de l'oralité en français médiéval*, special issue of *Diachroniques*: 3.
Rodríguez Somolinos, Amalia (ed.) (2016). *Énonciation et marques d'oralité dans l'évolution du français*, special issue of *Linx*: 73.
Rodríguez Somolinos, Amalia (2018). 'Paroles rituelles et marqueurs de véridiction en français médiéval. "Si vraiement com c'est voirs que je di"', in Wendy Ayres-Bennett, Anne Carlier, Julie Glikman, Thomas M. Rainsford, Gilles Siouffi, and Carine Skupien-Dekens (eds), *Nouvelles voies d'accès au changement linguistique*. Paris: Classiques Garnier, 335–54.

Roger, Geoffrey (2019). 'The *langues de France* and the European Charter for Regional or Minority Languages: Keeping Ratification at Bay through Disinformation 2014–2015', in Michelle Harrison and Aurélie Joubert (eds), *French Language Policies and the Revitalisation of Regional Languages in the 21st Century*. London: Palgrave Macmillan, 309–34.

Rogler, John Bartholomew (1763). *A Dictionary English, German and French, Containing Not Only the English Words in their Alphabetical Order, Together with their Several Significations, but Also their Proper Accent, Phrases, Figurative Speeches, Idioms and Proverbs, by Mr Christian Ludwig. Now Carefully Revised, Corrected and throughout Augmented with More Than 12,000 Words, Taken out of Samuel Johnson's English Dictionary and Others, by John Bartholomew Rogler*, 3rd edn. Leipzig: Gleditsch.

Rojas, Daniel-Emilio (2016). 'Les Français et les langues étrangères'. https://www.larevuedesressources.org/les-francais-et-les-langues-etrangeres,2920.html#nb9 accessed 04 December 2021.

Rolland, Jean-Michel (1810). *Dictionnaire des expressions vicieuses et des fautes de prononciation les plus communes dans les Hautes et les Basses-Alpes, accompagnées de leurs corrections, d'après la V.e Édition du Dictionnaire de l'Académie. Ouvrage nécessaire aux jeunes personnes de l'un et de l'autre sexe, aux instituteurs et institutrices, et utile à toutes les classes de la Société*. Gap: Allier.

Rollin, Charles (1730). *De la manière d'enseigner et d'étudier les belles-lettres, par rapport à l'esprit et au cœur*. Paris: J. Estienne.

Romaine, Suzanne (1982). *Socio-historical Linguistics: Its Status and Methodology*. Cambridge: Cambridge University Press.

Romaine, Suzanne (1988). 'Historical Sociolinguistics: Problems and Methodology', in Ulrich Ammon, Norbert Dittmar, and Klaus J. Mattheier (eds), *Sociolinguistics: An International Handbook of the Sciences of Language and Society*. Vol. 2. Berlin/New York: de Gruyter, 1452–69.

Romaine, Suzanne (2008). 'Irish in the Global Context', in Caoilfhionn Nic Pháidín and Seán Ó Cearnaigh (eds), *A New View of the Irish Language*. Dublin: Cois Life, 11–25.

Ronsard, Pierre (1550). 'Suravertissement au lecteur', *Les quatre premiers livres des odes de P. de Ronsard*. Paris: Guillaume Cavellart.

Ronsard, Pierre (1585). *Art poétique françoys*. Paris: Guillaume Linoncier.

Rosa, Jonathan (2019). *Looking like a Language, Sounding like a Race: Raciolinguistic Ideologies and the Learning of Latinidad*. Oxford: Oxford University Press.

Rosier, Laurence (2008). *Le Discours rapporté en français*. Paris: Ophrys.

Rosier, Laurence (2019). '"Touche pas à ma langue": réformes, polémiques et violence verbale sur fond d'enjeux idéologiques', *Le Discours et la langue* 11(1): 41–52.

Rossebastiano Bart, Alda (1984). *Antichi vocabolari plurilingui d'uso popolare: la tradizione del «Solenissimo Vochabuolista»*. Alessandria: Edizioni dell'Orso.

Rottet, Kevin J. (2014). 'Neology, Competing Authenticities, and the Lexicography of Regional Languages: The Case of Breton', *Journal of the Dictionary Society of North America* 35: 208–47.

Rouquier, Magali and Christiane Marchello-Nizia (2012). 'De (S)OV à SVO en français: où et quand? L'Ordre des constituants propositionnels dans la *Passion de Clermont* et la *Vie de saint Alexis*', in Monique Dufresne (ed.) *Constructions en changement. Hommage à Paul Hirschbühler*. Laval: Presses de l'Université de Laval, 111–55.

Rousseau, Jean-Jacques (1781 [1755]). 'Essai sur l'origine des langues', in *Œuvres posthumes de Jean-Jacques Rousseau*. Vol 3. Genève: Du Peyrou, 211–327.

Rousselot, Pierre-Jean (1887). 'Introduction', *Revue des patois gallo-romans* 1: 1–22.
Roussineau, Gilles (ed.) (2006 [1218]). *La Suite du Roman de Merlin*. (2006 [1218]). Ed. by Gilles Roussineau. Geneva: Droz.
Rowe, Nicholas (1723). *The Works of Monsieur de La Bruyere [...] Written after the Method of M. Bruyere, by N. Rowe, Esq*. London: printed, and sold by A. Bettesworth [et al.].
Rubin, Donald L. (1992). 'Nonlanguage Factors Affecting Undergraduates' Judgments of Nonnative English-speaking Teaching Assistants', *Research in Higher Education* 33(4): 511–31.
Russell, Matthew A. (2013). *Mining the Social Web*. California: O'Reilly.
Russi, Cinzia (2016). 'Introduction', in Cinzia Russi (ed.) *Current Trends in Historical Sociolinguistics*. Warsaw/Berlin: de Gruyter Open, 1–18.
Russo, Michela (2011). 'Liaison, assimilation et redoublement syntaxique. Le Sandhi consonantique du latin à l'italo-roman', in Anja Overbeck and Günter Holtus (eds), *Lexikon, Varietät, Philologie: Romanistische Studien. Günter Holtus zum 65. Geburtstag*. Berlin: de Gruyter, 227–42.
Russo, Michela (2013a). 'Il raddoppiamento fonosintattico dell'italiano. Tratti prosodici e struttura fonologica', in Fernando Sánchez Miret and Daniel Recasens Vives (eds), *Studies in Phonetics, Phonology, and Sound Change in Romance*. Munich: LINCOM Europa, 145–78.
Russo, Michela (2013b). 'La Lénition romane et le redoublement syntaxique entre oralité et écriture (IXe–XIIe siècles): évolution non linéaire du latin classique au latin parlé tardif et médiéval au roman', in Marie-Guy Boutier, Pascale Hadermann, and Marieke Van Acker (eds), *La Variation et le changement en langue (langues romanes)*. Helsinki: Société néophilologique, 435–60.
Russo, Michela (2014). 'L'Italia dell'anno 1000: le origini del raddoppiamento sintattico nell'italiano meridionale antico e non solo. Un'analisi scrittologica', in Paul Danler and Christine Konecny (eds), *Dall'architettura della lingua italiana all'architettura linguistica dell'Italia: saggi in omaggio a Heidi Siller-Runggaldier*. Frankfurt am Main: Peter Lang, 145–63.
Rutten, Gijsbert and Rik Vosters (2021). 'Language Standardization "from above"', in Wendy Ayres-Bennett and John Bellamy (eds), *The Cambridge Handbook of Language Standardization*. Cambridge: Cambridge University Press, 65–92.
Ryan, Ellen Bouchard and Howard Giles (eds) (1982). *Attitudes towards Language Variation: Social and Applied Contexts*. London: Edward Arnold.
Ryan, Ellen Bouchard, Howard Giles, and Richard J. Sebastian (1982). 'An Integrative Perspective for the Study of Attitudes toward Language Variation', in Ellen Bouchard Ryan and Howard Giles (eds), *Attitudes towards Language Variation: Social and Applied Contexts*. London: Edward Arnold, 1–19.
Rychner, Jean (1987). 'Description subjective et DIL: observations sur leurs formes au XIIe siècle', in Georges Lüdi, Hans Stricker, and Jakob Th. Wüest (eds), *Romania ingeniosa*. Frankfurt: Peter Lang, 221–36.
Rychner, Jean (1989). 'Le Discours subjectif dans les Lais de Marie de France. A propos d'une étude récente', *Revue de linguistique romane* 53: 57–83.
Rychner, Jean (1990). *La Narration des sentiments, des pensées et des discours dans quelques oeuvres des douxième et treizième siècles*. Geneva: Droz.
Säily, Tanja, Anja Nurmi, Minna Palander-Collin, and Anita Auer (2017). *Exploring Future Paths for Historical Sociolinguistics*. Amsterdam/Philadelphia: John Benjamins.
Salhi, Kamal (ed.) (2002). *French in and out of France. Language Policies, Intercultural Antagonisms and Dialogue*. Oxford: Peter Lang.

Sampson, Rodney (2016). 'Sandhi Phenomena', in Adam Ledgeway and Martin Maiden (eds), *The Oxford Guide to the Romance Languages*. Oxford: Oxford University Press, 669–80.

Sankoff, Gillian and Hélène Blondeau (2007). 'Language Change across the Lifespan: /r/ in Montreal French', *Language* 83: 560–88.

Sanson, Helena (2011). *Women, Language and Grammar: Italy 1500–1900*. Oxford and London: Oxford University Press for the British Academy.

Sanson, Helena (2014). '"Simplicité, clarté et précision": Grammars of Italian "pour les Dames" and other Learners in Eighteenth- and Early Nineteenth-century France', *Modern Language Review* 109(3): 593–616.

Sanson, Helena (2015). '"Ma e in latino nulla? Qualcosa sì, ma tanto poco, che paja un nulla": donne e latino in Italia fra Sette e Ottocento', *Romanische Forschungen* 127(4): 449–81.

Sanson, Helena (2016). 'Grammatiche dell'italiano "pour les dames" nel Settecento: Antonio Curioni fra Parigi e Londra', *The Italianist* 36(3): 447–71.

Sanson, Helena (2020). 'Women and Language Codification in Italy: Marginalized Voices, Forgotten Contribution', in Wendy Ayres-Bennett and Helena Sanson (eds), *Women in the History of Linguistics*. Oxford: Oxford University Press, 59–90.

Sanson, Helena (ed.) (2022a). *Women and Translation in the Italian Tradition*. Paris: Classiques Garnier.

Sanson, Helena (2022b). 'Introduction: Women and Translation in Italy: From the Renaissance to the Present', in Helena Sanson (ed.), *Women and Translation in the Italian Tradition*. Paris: Classiques Garnier, 9–51.

Sanson, Helena (forthcoming). *Knowledge across Boundaries: Women, Language and Translation in Italy's Long Eighteenth Century*. Paris: Classiques Garnier.

Santangelo, Giovanni Saverio and Claudio Vinti (1981). *Le traduzioni italiane del teatro comico francese dei secoli XVII e XVIII*. Rome: Edizioni di Storia e Letteratura.

Saulière, Jérôme (2014). 'Corporate Language: The Blind Spot of Language Policy? Reflections on France's Loi Toubon', *Current Issues in Language Planning* 15(2): 220–35.

Saussure, Ferdinand de (1916). *Cours de linguistique générale, publié par Charles Bally et Albert Sechehaye; avec la collaboration de Albert Reidlinger*. Paris: Payot.

Sauwala, Laetitia (2018). 'Les Marques linguistiques de l'oral représenté dans le théâtre médiéval. L'Exemple du *Mystère des Trois Doms* (1509)', in Wendy Ayres-Bennett, Anne Carlier, Julie Glikman, Thomas M. Rainsford, Gilles Siouffi, and Carine Skupien-Dekens (eds), *Nouvelles voies d'accès au changement linguistique*. Paris: Classiques Garnier, 201–20.

Scheer, Tobias, Philippe Ségéral, Randall S. Gess, Haike Jacobs, and Bernard Laks (2020). 'Partie 3: phonétique historique', in Christiane Marchello-Nizia, Bernard Combettes, Sophie Prévost, and Tobias Scheer (eds), *Grande grammaire historique du français (GGHF)*. Berlin/Boston: de Gruyter, 151–490.

Schlieben-Lange, Brigitte (1996). *Idéologie, révolution et uniformité de la langue*. Brussels: Éditions Mardaga.

Schmid, Stephan (2016). 'Segmental Phonology', in Adam Ledgeway and Martin Maiden (eds), *The Oxford Guide to the Romance Languages*. Oxford: Oxford University Press, 471–83.

Schnakenberg, J. F. (1840). *Tableau synoptique et comparatif des idiomes populaires ou patois de la France*. Berlin: Albert Foerstner.

Schneider, Edgar W. (2013). 'Investigating Variation and Change in Written Documents', in J. K. Chambers and Natalie Schilling-Estes (eds), *The Handbook of Language Variation and Change*, 2nd edn. Hoboken: Wiley-Blackwell, 67–96.

Schøsler, Lene (1984). *La Déclinaison bicasuelle de l'ancien français, son rôle dans la syntaxe de la phrase, les causes de sa disparition*. Odense: Odense University Press.

Schøsler, Lene (2001). 'From Latin to Modern French: Actualization and Markedness', in Henning Andersen (ed.), *Actualization: Linguistic Change in Progress*. Amsterdam/Philadelphia: John Benjamins, 169–85.

Schøsler, Lene (2002). 'La Variation linguistique: le cas de l'expression du sujet', in Rodney Sampson and Wendy Ayres-Bennett (eds), *Interpreting the History of French. A Festschrift for Peter Rickard on the Occasion of his Eightieth Birthday*. Amsterdam/New York: Rodopi, 187–208.

Schøsler, Lene (2013). 'The Development of the Declension System', in Deborah Arteaga (ed.) *Research on Old French: The State of the Art*. Dordrecht/Heidelberg/New York/London: Springer, 167–86.

Schottelius, Justus Georg (1663). *Ausführliche Arbeit von der teutschen Haubtsprache*. Braunschweig: Zilliger.

Schrader, Norbert (2012). 'Adelung: Grammatisch-kritisches Wörterbuch der hochdeutschen Mundart', in Ulrike Haß (ed.), *Große Lexika und Wörterbücher Europas: Europäische Enzyklopädien und Wörterbücher in historischen Porträts*. Berlin: de Gruyter, 163–77.

Schröder, Konrad (1975). *Lehrwerke für den Englischunterricht im deutschsprachigen Raum 1665-1900. Einführung und Versuch einer Bibliographie*. Darmstadt: Wissenschaftliche Buchgesellschaft.

Schrott, Angela (1999). '*Que fais, Adam?* Questions and Seduction in the *Jeu d'Adam*', in Andreas H. Jucker, Gerd Fritz, and Franz Lebsanft (eds), *Historical Dialogue Analysis*. Amsterdam/Philadelphia: John Benjamins, 331–70.

Scott Warren, Anthony and Geraint Jennings (2015). '"Allant contre vent et mathée": Jèrriais in the Twenty-first Century', in Mari C. Jones (ed.), *Endangered Languages and New Technologies*. Cambridge: Cambridge University Press, 127–40.

Seguin, Jean-Pierre (1999). 'La Langue française aux XVIIe et XVIIIe siècles', in Jacques Chaurand (ed.) *Nouvelle histoire de la langue française*. Paris: Éditions du Seuil, 227–344.

Séguy, Jean (1973). 'La Fonction minimale du dialecte', in Georges Straka (ed.), *Les Dialectes romans de France à la lumière des atlas régionaux*. Paris: Éditions du Centre National de la Recherche Scientifique, 21–42.

Selkirk, Elisabeth (1996). 'The Prosodic Structure of Function Words', in James L. Morgan and Katherine Demuth (eds), *Signal to Syntax: Bootstrapping from Speech to Grammar in Early Acquisition*. Mahwah: Erlbaum, 187–214.

Sénat (2021). 'Les Principales Propositions'. https://www.senat.fr/rap/r03-063/r03-0631.html#toc38 accessed 4 December 2021.

Senn, Harry (1981). 'Folklore Beginnings in France, the *Académie Celtique*: 1804–1813', *Journal of the Folklore Institute* 18(1): 23–33.

Serianni, Luca (1999). 'Lingue e dialetti d'Italia nella percezione dei viaggiatori sette-ottocenteschi', in Mariasilvia Tatti (ed.), *Italia e Italie: immagini tra Rivoluzione e Restaurazione. Atti del Convegno di studi, Roma 7-8-9 novembre 1996*. Rome: Bulzoni, 25–51.

Serianni, Luca (2002). *Viaggiatori, musicisti, poeti: saggi di storia della lingua italiana*. Milan: Garzanti.

Sériot, Patrick (2019 [1997]). 'Faut-il que les langues aient un nom? Le Cas du macédonien', in Andrée Tabouret-Keller (ed.), *Le Nom des langues I. Les Enjeux de la nomination des langues*. Louvain-la-Neuve: Peeters, 167–90. (Revised and updated version consulted 26 April 2021 at https://www.academia.edu/38846968/Faut_il_que_les_langues_aient_un_nom_Le_cas_du_macédonien.)

Sewel, William (1691). *A New Dictionary of English–Dutch*. Amsterdam: de Weduwe van Steven Swart.

Sewel, William (1766). *A Compleat Dictionary English and Dutch [...] Originally Compiled by William Sewel; but Now, Not Only Reviewed, and More Than the Half Part Augmented, Yet According to the Modern Spelling, Entirely Improved; by Egbert Buys, Counsellor of their Poliss and Prussian Majesties, &c. [...]*. Amsterdam: Kornelis de Veer.

Shifman, Limor (2011). 'An Anatomy of a Youtube Meme', *New Media and Society* 14(2): 187–203. https://doi.org/10.1177/1461444811412160

Silverstein, Michael (1979). 'Language Structure and Linguistic Ideology', in Paul R. Clyne, William F. Hanks, and Carol L. Hofbauer (eds), *The Elements: A Parasession on Linguistic Units and Levels*. Chicago: Chicago Linguistic Society, 193–247.

Simon, Anne Catherine and Clémence Vanhal (2022). 'Renforcement de la féminisation et écriture inclusive: étude sur un corpus de presse et de textes politiques', *Langue francaise* 215(3): 81–102. https://doi.org/10.3917/lf.215.0081

Simonenko, Alexandra, Benoît Crabbé, and Sophie Prévost (2019). 'Agreement Syncretisation and the Loss of Null Subjects: Quantificational Models for Medieval French', *Language Variation and Change* 31(3): 275–301.

Siouffi, Gilles (2007a). 'De la Renaissance à la Révolution', in Alain Rey, Frédéric Duval, and Gilles Siouffi (eds), *Mille ans de langue française: histoire d'une passion*. Paris: Éditions France Loisirs, 457–957.

Siouffi, Gilles (2007b). 'Langue française et questions d'identité: quelques propositions sur le XVIIe siecle', in Wendy Ayres-Bennett and Mari C. Jones (eds), *The French Language and Questions of Identity*. London: Legenda, 14–22.

Skårup, Povl (1975). *Les Premières Zones de la proposition en ancien français. Essai de syntaxe de position*. Copenhague: Akademisk Forlag.

Skupien Dekens, Carine (2018). 'Un genre sous-exploité en histoire du français préclassique et classique, le sermon', in Wendy Ayres-Bennett, Anne Carlier, Julie Glikman, Thomas M. Rainsford, Gilles Souffi, and Carine Skupien Dekens (eds), *Nouvelles voies d'accès au changement linguistique*. Paris: Classiques Garnier, 69–84.

Sloan, Luke and Anabel Quan-Haase (eds) (2017). *SAGE Handbook of Social Media Research Methods*. London: SAGE.

Smith, Maya Angela (2019). *Senegal Abroad: Linguistic Borders, Racial Formations, and Diasporic Imaginaries*. Madison: The University of Wisconsin Press.

Sorel, Charles (1972). *Le Berger extravagant*. Geneva: Slatkine.

Spaëth, Valérie (ed.) (2010). *Le Français au contact des langues: histoire, sociolinguistique, didactique*, special edition of *Langue française*: 167.

Spini, Mathilde and Cyril Trimaille (2017). 'Les Significations sociales de la palatalisation/affrication à Marseille: processus ségrégatifs et changement linguistique', *Langage et societé* 162: 53–78.

Spolsky, Bernard (2004). *Language Policy*. Cambridge: Cambridge University Press.

Spolsky, Bernard (2018). 'Language Policy in French Colonies and after Independence', *Current Issues in Language Planning* 19(3): 231–315.

Spolsky, Bernard (2019). 'A Modified and Enriched Theory of Language Policy (and Management)', *Language Policy* 18: 323–38.

Stammerjohann, Harro (2013). *La lingua degli angeli: italiano, italianismi e giudizi sulla lingua italiana.* Florence: Accademia della Crusca.

Statista (no date). 'Social media usage in France—Statistics & Facts'. https://www.statista.com/topics/6278/social-media-usage-in-france/ accessed 28 February 2021.

Steele, Richard (1724–7). *Bibliothèque des dames contenant des règles générales pour leur conduite, dans toutes les circonstances de la vie. Ecrite par une Dame, & publiée par Mr le Chevalier R. Steele. Traduite de l'anglois.* 3 vols. Amsterdam: François Changuion.

Stein, Gabriele (1985). 'Englisch–German/German–English Lexicography: Its Early Beginnings', *Lexicographica. International Annual for Lexicography* 1985: 134–64. https://doi.org/10.1515/9783110244052.134

Steiner, B. Devan (2014). *The Evolution of Information Structure and Verb Second in the History of French,* doctoral thesis, Indiana University, Bloomington.

Sten, Holger (1952). 'Élision ou non-élision? Les Causes de l'hésitation entre un tampon de ouate et un tampon d'ouate', *Le Français moderne* 20: 123–6.

Stendhal [Marie-Henri Beyle] (1817). *Rome, Naples et Florence, en 1817.* Paris: Delauney.

Stevens, Captain John (1705–6). *A New Spanish and English Dictionary. Part II A Dictionary English and Spanish.* London: George Sawbridge.

Stieler, Kaspar (1691). *Der Teutschen Sprache Stammbaum und Fortwachs [...].* Nuremberg: Johann Hoffmann.

Swadesh, Morris (1950). 'Salish Internal Relationships', *International Journal of American Linguistics* 16(4): 157–64.

Tachard, Guy (1692). *Dictionnaire nouveau françois-latin: plus ample et plus exact, que ceux qui ont paru jusques à present.* Paris: Chez André Pralard.

Tagliamonte, Sali (2012). *Variationist Sociolinguistics. Change, Observation, Interpretation.* Maldon: Wiley-Blackwell.

Tajfel, Henri (1974). 'Social Identity and Intergroup Behavior', *Social Science Information* 13: 65–93.

Tajfel, Henri and John C. Turner (1986). 'The Social Identity Theory of Intergroup Behavior', in Stephen Worchel and William G. Austin (eds), *Psychology of Intergroup Relations.* Chicago: Nelson-Hall, 7–24.

Talleyrand-Périgord, Charles-Maurice de (1791). *Rapport sur l'instruction publique, fait au nom du Comité de constitution, à l'Assemblée nationale, les 10, 11, et 19 septembre 1791.* Paris: Imprimerie nationale.

Tarnarutckaia, Elizaveta, and Astrid Ensslin (2020). 'The Myth of the "clarté française": Language Ideologies and Metalinguistic Discourse of Videogame Speech Accents on Reddit', *Discourse, Context, & Media* 33: 1–9.

Taverdet, Gérard (1975–88). *Atlas linguistique et ethnographique de Bourgogne.* Paris: CNRS.

Taverdet, Gérard (2012). *Le Parler de Bourgogne.* Clermont-Ferrand: Christine Bonneton.

Teissier, Guy, et al. (2021). *Proposition de loi no. 4003.* https://www.assemblee-nationale.fr/dyn/15/textes/l15b4003_proposition-loi# accessed 28 February 2022.

Temple, Rosalind A. M. (2000). 'Old Wine into New Wineskins: A Variationist Investigation into Patterns of Voicing in Plosives in the *Atlas linguistique de la France*', *Transactions of the Philological Society* 98: 353–94.

Ternes, Elmar (1992). 'The Breton Language', in Donald McAulay (ed.), *The Celtic Languages.* Cambridge: Cambridge University Press, 371–452.

Terracher, Adolfe (1942). 'Le Secrétaire d'état à l'Éducation nationale et à la Jeunesse à Messieurs les Inspecteurs d'académie (en communication à MM. les recteurs, à MM. les préfets)', *Calendau* 10(93): 221–222.

The Histoire ancienne jusqu'à César: *A Digital Edition*, ed. Hannah Morcos, Simon Gaunt, Simone Ventura, Maria Teresa Rachetta, Henry Ravenhall, Natasha Romanova, and Luca Barbieri, technical ed. Geoffroy Noël, Paul Caton, Ginestra Ferraro, and Marcus Husar. http://www.tvof.ac.uk/textviewer/ accessed 17 May 2021.

Thiesse, Anne-Marie (1992). 'L'Invention du régionalisme à la Belle époque', *Le Mouvement social* 160: 11–32.

Thomas, George (1991). *Linguistic Purism*. London: Longman.

Thomas, Jenelle (2020). 'L'Espagnol, une langue administrative?: le multilinguisme et le français écrit des gouverneurs hispanophones de la Louisiane coloniale', in Davy Bigot, Denis Liakin, Robert Papen, Adel Jebali, and Mireille Tremblay (eds), *Les Français d'ici en perspective*. Quebec: Presses de l'Université de Laval, 35–50.

Thompson, Sandra (1987). '"Subordination" and Narrative Event Structure', in Russell Tomlin (ed.), *Coherence and Grounding in Discourse*. Amsterdam: John Benjamins, 435–54.

Tibblin, Julia (2020) 'Les Attitudes envers le langage inclusif des francophones et leur effet sur l'évaluation d'un texte', *SHS Web of Conferences* 78: 13006. https://doi.org/10.1051/shsconf/20207813006

Tieken Boon van Ostade, Ingrid (2019). 'Usage Guides and the Age of Prescriptivism', in Birte Bös and Claudia Claridge (eds), *Norms and Conventions in the History of English*. Amsterdam: John Benjamins, 7–28.

Tillinger, Gábor (2013). 'Langues, dialectes et patois – problèmes de terminologie dialectologique. Réflexions sur la situation géolinguistique en France et la terminologie française', *Argumentum* 9: 1–18.

Timm, Leonora A. (1989). 'Word Order in 20th-century Breton', *Natural Language and Linguistic Theory* 7(3): 361–78.

Timm, Leonora A. (2001). 'Transforming Breton: A Case Study in Multiply Conflicting Language Ideologies', *Texas Linguistic Forum* 44(2): 447–61.

Timm, Leonora A. (2003). 'Breton at a Crossroads: Looking back, Moving forward', *e-Keltoi* 2: 25–61.

Tinsley, Teresa (2019). 'Language Trends 2019: Language Teaching in Primary and Secondary Schools in England, Survey Report'. London: The British Council.

Tomlin, Russell (1985). 'Foreground-background Information and the Syntax of Subordination', *Text* 5: 85–122.

Torreira, Francisco and Mirjam Ernestus (2011). 'Vowel Elision in Casual French: The Case of Vowel /e/ in the Word *c'était*', *Journal of Phonetics* 39: 50–8.

Torres-Tamarit, Francesc and Clàudia Pons-Moll (2019). 'Enclitic-induced Stress Shift in Catalan', *Journal of Linguistics* 55(2): 407–44.

Tosi, Arturo (2020). *Language and the Grand Tour: Linguistic Experiences of Travelling in Early Modern Europe*. Cambridge: Cambridge University Press.

Touratier, Christian (1994). *Syntaxe latine*. Louvain-la-Neuve: Peeters.

Tourtoulon, Charles de and Octavien Bringuier (1876). *Étude sur la limite géographique de la langue d'oc et de la langue d'oïl*. Paris: Imprimerie Nationale.

Tranel, Bernard (1996). 'French Liaison and Elision Revisited: A Unified Account within Optimality Theory', in Claudia Parodi, Carlos Quicoli, Mario Saltarelli, and Maria Luisa Zubizarreta (eds), *Aspects of Romance Linguistics*. Washington: Georgetown University Press, 433–55.

Trask, Robert L. (1999). *Key Concepts in Language and Linguistics*. London/New York: Routledge.

Trépos, Pierre (1960). 'Francis Gourvil. *Théodore-Claude-Henri Hersart de la Villemarqué (1815–1895) et le Barzaz-Breiz (1839–1845–1867). Origines. Editions. Sources. Critiques. Influence*. I–VI, 609 p. Rennes, Imprimeries Oberthur, 1960', *Annales de Bretagne* 67(4): 389–97.

Tribune Collective, Marianne.net (18 September 2020) 'Une "écriture excluante" qui "s'impose par la propagande": 32 linguistes listent les défauts de l'écriture inclusive'. https://www.marianne.net/agora/tribunes-libres/une-ecriture-excluante-qui-s-impose-par-la-propagande-32-linguistes-listent-les accessed 31 December 2020.

Trifone, Pietro (2006). *Rinascimento dal basso: il nuovo spazio del volgare tra Quattro e Cinquecento*. Rome: Bulzoni.

Trifone, Pietro (2008). *Storia linguistica di Roma*. Rome: Carocci.

Trudeau, Danielle (1992). *Les Inventeurs du bon usage (1529–1647)*. Paris: Les Éditions de Minuit.

Trudgill, Peter (1974). 'Linguistic Change and Diffusion: Description and Explanation in Sociolinguistic Dialect Geography', *Language in Society* 3: 215–46.

Tuomarla, Ulla (1999). *La Citation mode d'emploi: sur le fonctionnement discursif du discours rapporté direct*. Helsinki: Academia Scientiarum Fennica.

Turner, Dale Antony (2006). *This is not a Peace Pipe: Towards a Critical Indigenous Philosophy*. Toronto: University of Toronto Press.

Tuten, Donald N. and Fernando Tejedo-Herrero (2011). 'The Relationship between Historical Linguistics and Sociolinguistics', in Manuel Díaz-Campos (ed.) *The Handbook of Hispanic Sociolinguistics*. Chichester: Wiley-Blackwell, 283–302.

Unfer Lukoschik, Rita (2000). 'L'educatrice delle donne. Elisabetta Caminer Turra (1751–1796) e la *Querelle des femmes*', *Memorie dell'Accademia delle scienze di Torino. Classe di Scienze morali, storiche e filologiche* V. 24(3): 249–63.

Väänänen, Veikko (1981). *Introduction au latin vulgaire*. Paris: Klincksieck.

Valdman, Albert (1993). *Bien entendu! Introduction à la prononciation française*. Englewood Cliffs, NJ: Prentice Hall.

Vallisnieri, Antonio (1733). 'Che ogni italiano debba scrivere in lingua purgata italiana, o Toscana, per debito, per giustizia, e per decoro della nostra Italia', in Antonio Vallisnieri, *Opere fisico-mediche [...] corredate d'una prefazione in genere sopra tutte, e d'una in particolare sopra il Vocabolario della Storia Naturale*. Vol. 3. Venice: Sebastiano Coleti, 254–68.

Van Compernolle, Rémi A. (2009). 'What Do Women Want? Linguistic Equality and the Feminization of Job Titles in Contemporary France', *Gender and Language* 3: 33–52.

Van der Wal, Marijke J. and Gijsbert Johan Rutten (2013). 'Ego-documents in a Historical-sociolinguistic Perspective', in Marijke J. van der Wal and Gijsbert Johan Rutten (eds), *Touching the Past: Studies in the Historical Sociolinguistics of Ego-documents*. Amsterdam: John Benjamins, 1–17.

Van Dijk, Suzanna (1988). *Traces de femmes: présence féminine dans le journalisme français du XVIIIe siècle*. Amsterdam/Maarssen: APA-Holland University Press.

Van Rooy, Raf (2016). 'The Diversity of Ancient Greek through the Eyes of a Forgotten Grammarian. Petrus Antesignanus (ca. 1524/1525–1561) on the Notion of "Dialect"', *Histoire épistémologie langage* 38(1): 123–40.

Van Rooy, Raf (2020). *Language or Dialect? The History of a Conceptual Pair*. Oxford: Oxford University Press.

Vance, Barbara (1981). *A Syntactic and Semantic Study of Subject Personal Pronoun Usage in Old French*, Masters dissertation, Cornell University.

Vance, Barbara (1997). *Syntactic Change in Medieval French. Verb-second and Null Subjects.* Dordrecht/Boston/London: Kluwer Academic Publishers.

Vanelli, Laura (1998 [1992]). 'Da "lo" a "il": storia dell'articolo definito maschile singolare in italiano e nei dialetti settentrionali', reprinted in Laura Vanelli, *I dialetti italiani settentrionali nel panorama romanza. Studi di sintassi e morfologia.* Rome: Bulzoni, 169–214.

Vaugelas, Claude Favre de (1647). *Remarques sur la langue françoise utiles à ceux qui veulent bien parler & bien escrire.* Paris: Veuve Jean Camusat et Pierre Le Petit.

Vaugelas, Claude Favre de (1984 [1647]). *La Préface des "Remarques sur la langue française", éditée avec introduction et notes de Z. Marzys.* Geneva: Droz.

Vennemann, Théo (1975). 'An Explanation of Drift', in Charles N. Li (ed.), *Word Order and Word Order Change.* Austin: University of Texas Press, 267–305.

Vennemann, Theo (1974). 'Topics, Subjects and Word-order: From SXV to SVX via TVX', in John. M. Anderson and Charles Jones (eds), *Historical Linguistics: Proceedings of the First International Congress of Historical Linguistics.* Amsterdam: John Benjamins, 339–76.

Ventura, Simone (2019). 'Digital Editing and Linguistic Analysis: The First Redaction of the *Histoire ancienne jusqu'à César*', *Textual Cultures* 12(2): 33–56.

Vermander, Pierre (2019). 'L'Apport des textes de la pratique pour l'étude des marques d'oralité en moyen français', *Studia Linguistica Romanica* 2: 34–68.

Vermander, Pierre (2020). 'Analyse de conversation et documents littéraires médiévaux', *Langages* 217(1): 71–86.

Vessey, Rachelle (2016). 'Language Ideologies in Social Media: The Case of Pastagate', *Journal of Language and Politics* 15(1): 1–24. https://doi.org/10.1075/jlp.15.1.01ves

Vessey, Rachelle (2017). 'Corpus Approaches to Language Ideology', *Applied Linguistics* 38(3): 277–96. https://doi.org/10.1093/applin/amv023

Viaut, Alain (2020). 'De "langue régionale" à "langue de France" ou les ombres du territoire', *Glottopol* 34: 46–56.

Viaut, Alain and Antoine Pascaud (2017). 'Pour une définition de "langue régionale"', *Lengas* 82. https://doi.org/10.4000/lengas.1380

Viennot, Éliane (2017). *Non, le masculin ne l'emporte pas sur le féminin! Petite histoire des résistances de la langue française.* 2nd edn. Donnemarie-Dontilly: Éditions iXe.

Viennot, Éliane, Maria Candea, Yannick Chevalier, Sylvia Duverger, and Anne-Marie Houdebine (2016). *L'Académie contre la langue française: le dossier 'féminisation'.* Paris: Éditions iXe.

Vigário, Marina (2003). *The Prosodic Word in European Portuguese.* Berlin: Mouton de Gruyter.

Vigilante, Marianna (1789). 'La traduttrice a chi legge', in Isaac Watts, *Elementi di geografia, ed astronomia del signore Isacco Watts tradotti dalla settima, ed ultima edizione inglese nell'idioma italiano da Maria Vigilante con alcune picciole osservazioni, ed aggiunzioni della medesima.* Naples: Gaetano Raimondi, VII–X.

Voegelin, Carl and Zellig Harris (1951). 'Methods for Determining Intelligibility among Dialects of Natural Languages', *Proceedings of the American Philosophical Society* 95(3): 322–9.

Vogl, Ulrike (2012). 'Multilingualism in a Standard Language Culture', in Matthias Hüning, Ulrike Vogl, and Olivier Moliner (eds), *Standard Languages and Multilingualism in European History.* Amsterdam: John Benjamins, 1–42.

Vogl, Ulrike, Olivier Moliner, and Matthias Hüning (2013). 'Europe's Multilingualism in the Context of a European Culture of Standard Languages', in Anne-Claude Berthoud,

François Grin, and Georges Lüdi (eds), *DYLAN. Exploring the Dynamics of Multilingualism*. Amsterdam: John Benjamins, 417–38.

Volney, Constantin-François (1826 [1795]). *Leçons d'histoire prononcées à l'École normale*. Paris: Baudouin Frères.

Wagner, Suzanne and Gillian Sankoff (2011). 'Age Grading in the Montréal French Inflected Future', *Language Variation and Change* 23(3): 275–313.

Walker, Douglas C. (1981). *An Introduction to Old French Morphophonology*. Ottawa: Didier.

Walker, Terry (2007). *Thou and You in Early Modern English Dialogues: Trials, Depositions, and Drama Comedy*. Amsterdam: John Benjamins.

Walsh, John (2012). *Contests and Contexts: The Irish Language and Ireland's Socio-Economic Development*. Oxford/Bern: Peter Lang.

Walsh, John (2015). 'The Irish Language Regime and Language Ideology in Ireland', in Linda Cardinal and Selma K. Sonntag (eds), *State Traditions and Language Regimes*. Montréal: McGill-Queen's University Press, 62–78.

Walsh, John (2016). 'Enactments Concerning the Irish Language, 1922–2016', *Dublin University Law Journal* 39(2): 449–66.

Walsh, John (2020). 'The Irish Language and Contemporary Irish Identity', in Raymond Hickey and Carolina P. Amador-Moreno (eds), *Irish Identities: Sociolinguistic Perspectives*. Berlin/Boston: de Gruyter Mouton, 21–44.

Walsh, John (2021). 'The Governance of Irish in the Neoliberal Age: The Retreat of the State under the Guise of Partnership', in Huw Lewis and Wilson McLeod (eds), *Language Revitalisation and Social Transformation*. Cham: Springer Nature, 311–42.

Walsh, John (2022). *One Hundred Years of Irish Language Policy, 1922–2022*. Oxford: Peter Lang.

Walsh, Olivia (2014). '"Les Anglicismes polluent la langue française". Purist Attitudes in France and Quebec', *Journal of French Language Studies* 24(3): 423–49. https://doi.org/10.1017/S0959269513000227

Walsh, Olivia (2015). 'Attitudes towards English in France', in Andrew Linn, Neil Bermel, and Gibson Ferguson (eds), *Attitudes towards English in Europe*. Berlin: de Gruyter, 27–54.

Walsh, Olivia (2016a). '*Les Chroniques de langage* and the Development of Linguistic Purism in Québec', *Nottingham French Studies* 55(2): 132–57.

Walsh, Olivia (2016b). *Linguistic Purism: Language Attitudes in France and Quebec*. Amsterdam: John Benjamins.

Walsh, Olivia (ed.) (2021a). *In the Shadow of the Standard: Standard Language Ideology and Attitudes towards Non-standard Varieties and Usages*, special issue of *Journal of Multilingual and Multicultural Development*: 42(9).

Walsh, Olivia (2021b) 'Introduction: In the Shadow of the Standard: Standard Language Ideology and Attitudes towards "Non-standard" Varieties and Usages', *Journal of Multilingual and Multicultural Development* 42(9): 773–82.

Walsh, Olivia (2021c). 'The Construction of Authority in 20th-century Language Columns in France', in Carmen Marimón-Llorca and Sabine Schwarze (eds), *Authoritative Discourse in Language Columns: Linguistic, Ideological, and Social Issues*. Berlin: Peter Lang, 65–91.

Walsh, Olivia (2021d). 'The French Language: Monocentric or Pluricentric? Standard Language Ideology and Attitudes towards the French Language in Twentieth-century

Language Columns in Quebec', *Journal of Multilingual and Multicultural Development* 42(9): 869–81.
Walsh, Olivia (2022). 'Discourse Analysis of Print Media', in Ruth Kircher and Lena Zipp (eds), *Research Methods in Language Attitudes*. Cambridge: Cambridge University Press, 19–33.
Walsh, Olivia and Sara Cotelli Kureth (2021). 'Les Métaphores dans les chroniques de langage en France et en Suisse', in Carmen Marimón Llorca, Wim Remysen, and Fabio Rossi (eds), *Les Idéologies linguistiques: débats, purismes et stratégies discursives*. Berlin: Peter Lang, 495–519.
Walsh, Olivia and Douglas A. Kibbee (2024). 'Metalinguistic Texts', in Wendy Ayres-Bennett and Mairi McLaughlin (eds), *The Oxford Handbook of the French Language*. Oxford: Oxford University Press.
Walter, Henriette (1982). *Enquête phonologique et variétés régionales du français*. Paris: Presses universitaires de France.
Waquet, Françoise (2002). *Latin or the Empire of a Sign: From the Sixteenth to the Twentieth Centuries*. London/New York: Verso.
Watts, Isaac (1726). *The Knowledge of the Heavens and the Earth Made Easy, or, The First Principles of Astronomy and Geography Explain'd by the Use of Globes and Maps*. London: Printed for J. Clark and R. Hett; E. Matthews, etc.
Watts, Isaac (1789). *Elementi di geografia, ed astronomia del signore Isacco Watts tradotti dalla settima, ed ultima edizione inglese nell'idioma italiano da Maria Vigilante con alcune picciole osservazioni, ed aggiunzioni della medesima*. Naples: Gaetano Raimondi.
Watts, Richard J. (2000). 'Mythical Strands in the Ideology of Prescriptivism', in Laura Wright (ed.), *The Development of Standard English 1300–1800: Theories, Descriptions, Conflicts*. Cambridge: Cambridge University Press, 29–48.
Weinreich, Uriel (1954). 'Is a Structural Dialectology Possible?', *Word* 10: 388–400.
Wichmann, Søren (2019). 'How to Distinguish Languages and Dialects', *Computational Linguistics* 45(4): 823–31.
Wild, Kate (2009). 'Johnson's Prescriptive Labels - A Reassessment', *Dictionaries: Journal of the Dictionary Society of North America* 30: 108–18.
Wise, Hilary (1997). *The Vocabulary of Modern French: Origins, Structure and Function*, London: Routledge.
Wmffre, Iwan (1998). *Central Breton*. Munich: LINCOM Europa.
Wmffre, Iwan (2007). *Breton Orthographies and Dialects: The Twentieth-century Orthography War in Brittany*. 2 vols. Oxford: Peter Lang.
Woehrling, Jean-Marie (2013). 'Histoire du droit des langues de France', in Georg Kremnitz (ed.), *Histoire sociale des langues de France*. Rennes: Presses universitaires de Rennes, 71–88.
Wolf, Göran (2020). 'Ulster Scots Identity in Contemporary Northern Ireland', in Raymond Hickey and Carolina P. Amador-Moreno (eds), *Irish Identities: Sociolinguistic Perspectives*. Berlin/Boston: de Gruyter Mouton, 131–50.
Wolf, Lothar (1983). 'La Normalisation du langage en France: de Malherbe à Grevisse', in Édith Bédard and Jacques Maurais (eds), *La Norme linguistique*. Paris: Le Robert, 105–37.
Wolff, Hans (1959). 'Intelligibility and Inter-ethnic Attitudes', *Anthropological Linguistics* 1(3): 34–41.
Woolard, Kathryn A. (1998). 'Introduction: Language Ideology as a Field of Inquiry', in Bambi B. Shieffelin, Kathryn A. Woolard, and Paul V. Kroskrity (eds), *Language Ideologies: Practice and Theory*. Oxford: Oxford University Press, 1–47.

Woolard, Kathryn A. (2020). 'Language Ideology', in James Stanlaw (ed.), *The International Encyclopedia of Linguistic Anthropology*. Hoboken: Wiley Blackwell. https://doi.org/10.1002/9781118786093.iela0217

Wooldridge, Terence Russell (1977). *Les Débuts de la lexicographie française: Estienne, Nicot et le Thresor de la langue françoyse (1606)*. Toronto: University of Toronto.

Zappavigna, Michele (2011). 'Ambient Affiliation: A Linguistic Perspective on Twitter', *New Media and Society* 13(5): 788–806. https://doi.org/10.1177/1461444810385097

Zappavigna, Michele (2015). 'Searchable Talk: The Linguistic Functions of Hashtags', *Social Semiotics*, 25(3): 274–91. https://doi.org/10.1080/10350330.2014.996948

Zgusta, Ladislav (2006). *Lexicography then and now: Selected Essays*, ed. Frederic F. M. Dolezal and Thomas B. I. Creamer. Berlin: de Gruyter.

Zhao, Hui and Hong Liu (2021). '(Standard) Language Ideology and Regional Putonghua in Chinese Social Media: A View from Weibo', *Journal of Multilingual and Multicultural Development* 42(9): 882–96.

Zink, Gaston (1997). *Morphosyntaxe du pronom personnel (non réfléchi) en moyen français (14e–15e siècles)*. Genève: Droz.

Zolli, Paolo (1971). *L'influsso francese sul veneziano del XVIII secolo*. Venice: Istituto Veneto di Scienze, Lettere ed Arti.

Zufferey, François (2020). *La Chanson de saint Alexis: essai d'édition critique de la version primitive, avec apparat synoptique de tous les témoins*. Paris: Société des anciens textes français.

Index

Académie celtique, 209
Académie française, 181*n*1, 188, 276–7, 281, 285, 293–4, 298, 300–2
affectation, 144–5, 151–5, 160
Altas linguistique de la France, 200–1, 240–53
analogy, 47, 188–9
aphaeresis, 30, 217
argot, 293–4
   see also register
argument structure, 86–7
article, 38–43, 43*n*26, 247, 250
   see also enclitic asyllabic article and pronoun
attenuation, 175, 383
authenticity, 53*n*11, 208, 215, 377–82
   see also legitimacy; new speaker

Base de français médiéval, 13, 59*n*23, 61*n*31, 63
bilingualism, 145, 149, 181–97, 345*n*3, 373–4, 376*n*47, 381
   see also multilingualism
blog, 252, 283
   see also Internet; metalinguistic text; social media
bon usage, 18, 123–4, 129–30, 186, 188, 191, 204–6, 261–5, 269–70, 281–2, 278–80, 282, 289
   see also language usage; prescriptivism; standard language ideology
borrowing, 10, 295, 323–6, 328–9, 331–3, 340, 342–3, 355–6, 359
   see also Loi Bas-Lauriol; Loi Toubon
Breton, 212*n*25, 322–43, 363*f*, 378–9
   dialect of, 324–5
   dictionary, 322–43
   see also néo-breton
Burgundian, 240, 244–5, 247

Canada (French in), *see* Quebec
Catholicon, Le, 323, 327–8, 334
Celtic language, 209, 323–5, 328
   see also Breton; Cornish; Irish; *néo-breton*
centralization, 202–4, 211, 215, 368
chronicle (medieval), 53–4

chronique de langage, *see* language column
clause, 83*t*, 86–94, 90*t*, 97–8, 120
   main declarative, 66, 78–9, 86, 89–93
   subordinate, 51–2, 78–9, 81, 86–94, 97–102, 113–17, 237
   see also hypotaxis; inverse subordination; parataxis; subordinate; word order
clitic, 25–48
   see also article; enclisis; enclitic asyllabic article and pronoun; pronoun
CoDiF, 61, 63, 67
codification, 143, 183, 196, 257–8
   see also standardization
colonial period, 9, 161–80, 368
Common European Framework of Reference for Languages, 348*n*10, 350*n*14, 351*n*15
   see also proficiency level
community-based language planning, 366, 384
conjunction, 51, 63, 99–118, 178, 227, 245*t*
consonant
   articulation, 246, 249
   geminate, 35–7
   nasal place assimilation, 34–5
   word-final, 29–30, 39, 246, 249
conversation manual, 146
conversational turn, 64, 118, 220, 230*n*15
Cornish, 332
corpus, 1, 13–14, 48, 49, 58–62, 70, 179–80, 286, 321, 327–32
   see also source
corpus planning, 322–43
correctness, 188–9, 207, 262–8, 280, 288–92, 354–5
correlation, 99, 105–9, 113
Côte d'Or, 240, 244, 250
Courrier de Vaugelas, 124, 208, 276–96
Courrier des internautes, 276–96

Délégation générale à la langue française et aux langues de France, 359, 373
descriptivism, 258–61, 266, 274–5
   see also language ideology; prescriptivism; prescriptivist-descriptivist continuum
diachrony, 13, 42, 59*n*26, 62, 70, 72–3, 80, 98, 117, 252, 276–7
dialect levelling, 3–4, 238–40, 250–1, 381

dialect, 22n54, 85–6, 144–5, 148, 155n30, 198–215, 239, 242–4, 250–3, 324–5, 331, 363f, 364n4–5, 377
  see also Breton (dialect of); dialect levelling; dialectalization; dialectology; Irish (dialect of); Italian (dialect of Italy); Occitan (dialect of); regional language; *patois*
dialectalization, 239–40, 242
dialectology, 3, 200–2, 208–12, 215, 239, 242n13, 244, 253, 278, 381
dialogue, 15n42, 57, 61–2, 67, 282
dictionary, 59n23, 140, 150–1, 181–97, 198, 207–8, 211–12, 281, 322–43, 355–8
  bi/multilingual, 181n1, 181–97, 323, 327–30
  monolingual, 181n1, 185–6
  see also Breton; corpus planning; lexicography
discourse, 139–43, 219, 237, 255–6, 282, 305, 367
  gendered, 55–6
  see also metalinguistic text; text type; reported discourse
discourse marker, 64, 68–70, 97–8, 220, 237, 311
discourse relation, 98, 103–5, 112–16, 118–20

écriture inclusive, see inclusive language
education, 11–12, 147–8, 152, 154, 156, 208, 276, 283, 302, 330, 344–5, 347–55, 365–7, 369–76, 385
  see also language education; language teaching; language tutor
effacement, 217, 228, 236
elidable vowel, 32, 223–4, 230–1
  see also elision; schwa deletion
elision, 31–3, 37–8, 44–6, 63–4, 216–37, 249
  see also elidable vowel; schwa deletion
enchaînement, 217, 221, 230, 236n19
  see also linking phenomenon
enclisis, 25–48
enclitic asyllabic article and pronoun, 26, 38–43, 47
  see also clitic; enclisis; pronoun
enunciation theory, 59
  see also reported discourse; speech and thought presentation
equality, 122, 137, 203–4, 207, 300–2, 313, 320
  linguistic, 122, 300–2, 313, 320
  of varieties, 203–4, 207
  see also gender; inclusive language; language ideology; *point médian*
ethnolinguistic mobilization, 379, 382
etymology, see word origin
European Charter for Regional or Minority Languages, 10, 213, 344, 373, 383
  see also minoritized language

feminization, see gender
filler, 64, 219–21, 225, 236
  see also pause sonore
formality, see register
formula, 131, 137–8, 142, 162, 168–74, 178–9, 268–9
  epistolary, 131, 137–8, 142, 162, 178–9
  see also letter writing; reporting; requesting; text type
français régional, 213, 239–40, 242–4, 250–3
francoprovençal, 211, 213–14, 239, 363f, 363–4, 379n58
  see also regional language
FranceTerme, 239, 342
FranCHRO, 255, 259
Frantext, 13, 98n1
French Academy, see *Académie française*

Gallo-Romance, 16, 25–48, 198–215, 240, 242
  northern, 25–48, 239
  regional variety of, 201–3, 209–11, 213
  southern, 28, 31, 37, 40, 213
  see also *langues d'oc*; *langues d'oïl*; Old Gallo-Romance Corpus; regional language
Gaeltacht, 365f, 381–2
gender
  feminized form/feminization, 8n15, 122, 136–42, 300–2, 320
  generic masculine, 122, 298–301, 301n5, 311–12
  grammatical, 122, 131, 136, 297, 301
  and orthography, 130, 132, 136, 308, 317–18
  see also language ideology; inclusive language; misogyny; *point médian*; *remarqueur*; translation; women
genre, see text type
glottal onset, 233, 236
grammar (linguistic), 42, 49–70, 191–2, 197, 226–7, 269
  see also language teaching; speech and thought presentation
grammar (metalinguistic), 146, 150–3, 192, 195–7, 207, 211–12, 255, 274–5
Gwalarn, 323–4, 329

h aspiré, 216, 222, 236
hiatus, 31–3, 217, 217n3, 236–7
hierarchy
  gender, 132–3
  language, 269, 289, 339
  social, 137, 162, 164–5, 167–70, 175
  see also power relationship
hypotaxis, 97, 100, 103, 107–9, 111, 119
  see also subordinate

identity
    language and, 7, 209n20, 211–14, 252, 293, 323–4, 326, 328, 359–60, 370, 374, 377–82
    negotiation of, 162, 170, 177–9
idiom, 190, 195, 198–9, 203, 205–6, 209, 214
imagery, 292–5
    see also analogy; metaphor
imperfect, *see* tense
inclusive language, 8n16, 122, 138n28, 141, 297–321
    see also gender; language ideology; *point médian*
indexicality, 5, 172, 273–4, 302–3, 325, 327, 330
informality, *see* register
information-sharing, *see* reporting
innovation
    linguistic, 50, 58, 64–71, 73, 76, 86, 94–5, 133, 142, 145
    methodological, 4, 14, 19–20
    technological, 346
    see also language change; neologism
intelligibility, 199–200, 301–2, 324, 364
Internet, 276–8, 283, 292, 295–6, 346n5, 384
    see also blog; metalinguistic text; social media
intertextual variation, 39, 50, 53, 56–8, 58n20, 62–4, 70–1
intratextual variation, 50, 56–8, 66, 70–71
intrusive hesitation, 221, 221n9, 231
inverse subordination, 98, 106–7, 109, 117–20
    see also subordinate
Irish, 184, 364, 371–2, 374–5, 384–5
    dialect of, 364, 380–1
Italian, 36, 144–60, 349–50, 352–3, 357
    dialect of Italy, 144–5n3, 155n30

Journal de la langue françoise, soit exacte soit ornée, 121–43, 208, 282

language advice, 132, 254–5, 259, 261–2, 268–72, 276–96, 330, 336
language attitude, 6–9, 121–3, 130, 140, 202–7, 252, 254–75, 295, 297–321, 324n5, 327, 334–6, 340, 344–61, 366–7, 377–9
    see also authenticity; borrowing; language ideology; language legitimacy; neologism; new speaker
language authority, 181–97, 123, 125–30, 132–5, 257–8, 264n13, 270, 276–96, 342–3
    see also Académie française; dictionary; language advice; language column; language commentary; metalinguistic text; prescriptivism; purism; remark; *remarqueur*; standard language ideology; text type

language change, 2–5, 13–15, 17, 42, 47, 58, 60n29, 64–5, 72–96, 97–119, 141–3, 234, 239–40, 258, 263, 295, 302, 320
    see also innovation; language spread
language choice, 9–10, 128–9, 141, 162, 163–5, 168, 179–80, 217, 225, 323–5, 330, 340, 348–53, 377
language column, 9, 16–17, 122–4, 254–75, 277, 280n5, 282
    see also Courrier de Vaugelas; *Journal de la langue françoise, soit exacte soit ornée*; metalinguistic text
language commentary, 276–7, 281–3, 295
    see also metalinguistic text
language decline, 66, 93, 145, 160, 220, 239, 251–2, 257, 322–4, 342, 364, 370–3, 381
language education, 11–12, 150, 152, 154–6, 208, 324, 330, 344–5, 347–55, 369–77, 384–5
    see also education; language revitalization; language teaching; language tutor; standardization; women
language ideology, 6, 8–9, 16–17, 18n52, 122–3, 132, 138–40, 181–97, 255, 258–9, 261, 273, 278–80, 300–1, 303, 318–19, 326–9, 342–3, 346, 360, 367, 378–9
    gender-related, 54–5, 132–3, 145, 153–5, 300–2
    see also bon usage; descriptivism; gender; inclusive language; prescriptivism; prescriptivist-descriptivist continuum; purism; standard language ideology
language legislation, 10–12, 213, 239, 359, 369n15, 372–76, 382, 384
    see also Loi Bas-Lauriol; Loi Deixonne; Loi Molac; Loi Toubon
language policy and planning, 9–12, 301, 322–3, 325, 337, 343, 345n3, 355–6, 366, 382
language revitalization, 11, 214, 322–6, 328–9, 335, 342–3, 365–7, 377–9, 384–6
language right, 9, 211–14, 368, 383
language spread, 8, 47, 72–3, 75–6, 141–2, 146–51, 153–4, 190–1, 235, 237, 239, 258, 282, 284, 340–1, 347, 368–9
language survey, 201, 207–10, 235, 303–4, 345n4, 350, 369, 370–2, 382n66
language teaching, 145, 152, 189–92, 207–8, 210–13, 249–51, 338, 345, 345n3, 347n8, 347–53, 355, 369–70, 372–5, 380–1
    grammar-based, 154–5, 191–2, 196–7
language tutor, 150, 152, 155n30, 182n4, 185, 192–3, 195, 197, 207, 210, 212, 283–4, 338, 348, 354–5, 369, 378

language usage, 4, 6, 75–6, 118–19, 123–4, 131, 133, 139, 161, 183, 186, 193–4, 196, 206, 220n7, 234t, 235–6, 254, 257–8, 263, 265–6, 268, 271–4, 289, 294, 323, 355n23, 359, 371, 385
    see also bon usage
langues d'oc, 196n15, 211–14, 239, 363f, 363–4, 377–8
langues d'oïl, 211, 213–14, 239–40, 244, 247–8, 250–3, 363–4, 363f, 373, 379
Latin, 14, 28–9, 33–5, 42–3, 60n29, 79–80, 82, 86, 88–9, 94–5, 123, 134–6, 145, 148–9, 160, 181n1, 197, 202–3, 357
legitimacy, 132, 186–90, 206, 258, 273–4, 329, 367, 377–82
    see also authenticity; borrowing; new speaker; neologism; standard language ideology
letter (text type), 130–6, 138, 142–3, 158, 161–80, 280n6
    official, 161–80
    reader, 130–6, 138, 142–3, 280n6
    see also formulae
liaison, 220–1, 237
linking phenomenon, 216, 220–1, 236
    linking [ð], 32–4, 38
    see also enchaînement; sandhi process
Loi Bas-Lauriol, 10, 214
Loi Deixonne, 10, 212–13, 372–3
Loi Haby, 348, 372
Loi Molac, 10, 213, 374, 383–5
Loi Toubon, 10, 214, 355–6, 359

metalanguage, 182, 254–75, 276–8, 287–92
metalinguistic labelling, 183–4, 193–5, 197
metalinguistic text, 121–4, 125, 128n16, 142, 150, 275, 277–8, 280–3, 289, 292–3
    see also blog; dictionary; grammar; language advice; language column; language commentary; periodical; remark; *remarqueur*
metaphor, 260–1, 292–3, 295
    see also analogy; imagery
Middle French, 38, 60n29, 64, 67, 99–107
minoritized language, 8–11, 211, 213, 322–43, 344, 362–86
    see also European Charter for Regional and Minority Languages
minority treaty, 211, 213
misogyny, 145, 153–4, 304
multilingualism, 1, 6, 8, 12, 18–19, 164–5, 185, 344, 351, 360–1, 364
    see also bilingualism

narrative, *see* text type
narrator, 53–8
nation, 149–50, 154, 163–4, 175, 177–9, 190, 199, 202–3, 206–15, 360, 370–1
national language, 10–11, 155n30, 160, 202–3, 207–8, 212–14, 293, 328, 364, 368–70, 375, 380
    see also language education; language policy and planning; protectionism; standardization; standard language ideology
nationalism, 293, 319, 326, 328–9, 345–6, 371, 379
negation
    grammatical, 4, 58, 66, 107–9, 117, 119, 223, 245t, 248
    lexical, 263–7, 271–4, 315–17
    marker, 223
néo-breton, 324–6, 330–7, 340–3, 378
    see also Breton; new speaker
neologism, 124, 141, 186–7, 323–9, 324–5, 327–31, 336–7, 340–3, 345, 355–9
new speaker, 214, 324–6, 324n5, 340–3, 367, 372, 377–83, 385–6
Normandy, 251–2

Occitan, 212–13, 353, 370, 373, 377–8
    dialect of, 212–13, 377–8
    see also langues d'oc; regional language
Occitan, Old, 14, 28, 323
    see also Gallo-Romance; *langues d'oc*
Office public de la langue bretonne, 325–6, 337–43
Old French, 13–15, 28, 41n24, 43n29, 47, 51, 60n29, 66, 79–81, 99–100, 117–18
    see also Gallo-Romance
Old Gallo-Romance corpus, 14, 28, 48
oral représenté, 49–50, 59n26, 60–70
orality, *see* spoken language
orthography, 7–8, 35–6, 116–17, 130, 132, 136, 203–4, 213–14, 223, 308, 310, 317–19, 374
    of tweets, 309n15, 316
    variation, 203–4, 213–14, 215, 374
    see also consonant; correctness; gender; standardization

parataxis, 102–5, 110–12, 113–16
    see also clause; conjunction; hypotaxis; subordinate
paratext, 156, 159, 190–2
parler, 198–9, 210, 212, 242–3, 250, 252–3
    see also dialect; *patois*; regional language
passé antérieur, *see* tense
passé simple, *see* tense

patois, 22n55, 198–215, 242–3, 250–2, 373
   see also dialect; *parler*; regional language
pause sonore, 221, 230n15
   see also filler; transcription
periodical, 124, 129, 132, 136–8, 142–3, 208, 254–75, 276–96
   see also *Courrier de Vaugelas*; *Journal de la langue françoise, soit exacte soit ornée*; language column
personal title, 124–5, 131, 136–40
   see also gender; pronoun
phonological phrase, 26, 32, 38, 44–7
Piedmont, 19, 149, 151
pluperfect, *see* tense
plurilingualism, *see* multilingualism
point médian, 297, 299f, 302
   see also inclusive language
power relationship, 162, 164, 167–8, 170–5, 178–9, 198, 202–5, 214–15, 257–8, 322n1, 346, 368–9
   see also hierarchy
pragmaticalization, 68–9, 117
Pre-Classical French, 112–16
prescriptivism, 182–3, 257–61, 268, 273–5, 276–96, 303, 318–19, 321
   see also language ideology; prescriptivist-descriptivist continuum; purism; standard language ideology
prescriptivist-descriptivist continuum, 259–60
   see also language ideology; descriptivism; prescriptivism
proclisis, 25–48
proficiency level, 347–8, 350–1
   see also Common European Framework of Reference for Languages
pronoun, 25–48, 51, 66, 79, 81–3, 86–9, 92, 122n7, 124, 137, 223, 226, 234, 245, 250–1, 290–1, 309
   clitic, 25–6, 33, 38t, 39–47
   enclitic, 26n4, 33, 38–43
   object, 25, 46, 223, 245
   personal, 79, 81–3, 86–9, 122n7, 226, 234, 250–1, 290–1, 309
   relative, 26
   strong, 38t, 39, 43–7, 245
   subject, 26, 46, 66, 79, 81–3, 86–9, 245, 250–1
   tu vs. *vous*, 124, 137, 171n10
   see also enclitic asyllabic article and pronoun
pronunciation, 63, 80n9, 128n18, 188, 192–3, 195–7, 207, 217n1, 244–9, 324n6
   see also spoken language
prosodic word, 26, 29–30, 32–7, 39–48

protectionism, 10, 281, 292–4, 318–19, 321, 344, 355
   see also Loi Bas-Lauriol; Loi Toubon
purism, 280, 292–4, 303, 319, 321–3, 328, 330n16, 334–5, 340
   see also language ideology; prescriptivism; standard language ideology

que (and compounds), 33, 50n4, 68, 99, 101, 108–10, 113, 115, 117, 228–34, 236–7, 245, 248
   see also subordinate
Quebec (French in), 7, 16, 122, 255, 282, 303

regional language, 10–11, 33n54, 195–6, 198–215, 238–58, 322–43, 344, 352t, 353, 360–1, 362n3, 363f, 363–4, 368–9, 371–4, 379, 383–6
   see also Breton; Burgundian; European Charter for Regional or Minority Languages; *francoprovençal*; *langues d'oc*; *langues d'oïl*; Loi Deixonne; Loi Molac; Occitan; *patois*
regional variation, 3, 85–6, 192, 195, 197, 198–215, 238–40, 250–3, 324
register, 76, 148, 161, 171n10, 193–5, 223–7, 232, 235, 237, 293–4
   see also pronoun
remark (genre), 16–17, 121–4, 191n11, 254, 280–1
remarqueur, 17, 204–5, 216, 259, 277, 280–1, 357
   woman *remarqueur*, 123
reported discourse, 49–71
   direct discourse, 49, 76, 87–9, 95, 50n4, 51, 51n5–6, 53, 61n31
   free indirect discourse, 51–3
   indirect discourse, 50n4, 51–2, 51n5–6
   see also speech and thought presentation
reporting (pragmatics), 51, 162, 167–8, 172–4
requesting (pragmatics), 162, 168–72, 179, 338
resyllabification, 31, 34, 216, 221, 237
   see also syllable
Revolution of 1789, 124–5, 130, 133–4, 136–7, 139, 205–7, 368
rhythm group, 219, 230–1, 236

sandhi process, 26, 30–8, 41–2
schwa deletion, 223, 235–6
   see also elidable vowel; elision
situation (enunciative), 51, 72, 75, 87–9
slang, *see* register

social change, 122, 137–8, 141, 163, 184, 300–2, 346, 368
social media, 252*n*27, 297–321, 331
　see also Internet
source
　of linguistic data, 1, 13–14, 64, 98*n*1, 156, 179–80, 255–7, 277–8, 282, 304, 321, 327–31, 363*n*4
　lexicographic, 184–90
　see also corpus
Spanish rule, 147, 163–5, 174–80
speaker, 4–7, 15, 17, 51, 64, 75, 162, 200–2, 213–14, 218–34, 243, 247–53, 257–8, 270, 273–4, 279, 302–3, 322–6, 337–8, 340–3, 367–8, 377–83
　see also new speaker; *oral représenté*; reported speech; speech and thought presentation; speech community; spoken language
speech and thought presentation, 49–71
　macro-grammar of, 49–50, 53–58
　micro-grammar of, 49–50, 58–70
　see also reported discourse
speech community, 6, 200–2, 201*n*5, 324, 326, 340–3, 364, 366–7, 377–83, 385–6
　see also authenticity; community-based language planning; Gaeltacht; identity; legitimacy; new speaker; speaker
spelling, *see* orthography
spoken language, 58–61, 64, 75–6, 161, 282
　see also oral représenté; pronunciation; reported discourse; speaker; speech and thought presentation
standard language, 8, 11, 197, 199, 210, 212–15, 218, 247, 276, 281, 283, 294, 325–6, 367, 380
　see also codification; dialect levelling; protectionism; standard language ideology; standardization; prescriptivism
standard language ideology, 8, 182–4, 195–7, 257–8, 260–1, 264*n*13, 273–4, 280, 303, 318–19
　see also language ideology; prescriptivism; purism; standard language; standardization
standardization, 6, 8, 15–16, 183, 203–4, 207–8, 212*n*24, 215, 257, 278, 280, 322–6, 377–8, 380–1
　see also standard language; standard language ideology
stress, 26*n*4, 29–30, 43, 45–8, 249
　see also prosodic word
subordinate, 86, 97–9, 100–1, 113, 115, 117, 119, 230, 248
　circumstantial, 99, 101, 117

hypothetical, 119
　relative, 97–8, 100–1, 113, 115, 117, 119, 230, 248
　see also clause; hypotaxis; inverse subordination; parataxis; *que*
subordination, *see* subordinate
syllable, 29–31, 40, 43*n*29, 220, 236, 246–7, 249
　structure, 28–30, 34, 38
　see also prosodic word; resyllabification; stress
syntax, *see* word order

tense, 51–2, 60, 61*n*31, 97, 99–100, 104–5, 107–9, 111, 113, 117–18, 168, 235
　imperfect, 100, 104–5, 107–9, 111, 235
　passé antérieur, 107, 113, 117–18
　passé simple, 99–100, 107–9, 111, 117–18
TermBret, 337–42
terminology databases, 327–30
text domain, 72, 75–7, 82–5, 93, 95, 307
text type, 1, 13–17, 53–8, 58*n*20, 60–1, 63*n*36, 70–1, 75–6, 77, 82–5, 98, 121, 161, 178, 181, 254–5, 258, 262, 277, 280–2, 296
　descriptive, 98, 114–16, 172, 258
　dialogic, 61, 64, 276–7, 280, 282, 296
　literary, 13, 49–50, 53–8, 58*n*20, 60, 70–1, 77, 93, 95, 129, 189–90, 205, 260–1, 323
　narrative, 9, 49, 53*n*10–11, 55–6, 60–4, 69–71, 87–9, 97–9, 120
　see also conversation manual; dictionary; Frantext; grammar; *Gwalarn*; language advice; language column; language commentary; letter; metalinguistic text; paratext; periodical; translation; remark; reporting; requesting
transcription, 28, 48, 125, 219, 221, 253
　see also filler; *pause sonore*
translation, 14, 82, 145, 155–60, 201, 208, 336, 376
　woman translator, 156–9
Trésor de la langue française (informatisé), 13, 198

unification (political), 155*n*30, 202–3, 368–9
uniformity (linguistic), 206–7, 215, 238, 244, 250
　see also dialect levelling; standard language; standardization
United States of America (French in), 161–80
usage, *see bon usage*; language usage

Vannetais, 341
verbal aspect, *see* tense
Vichy (régime), 212–13

women, 17–18, 55, 121–143, 144–60
   and language learning, 130, 144–5, 151–6
   see also gender; *remarqueur*; translation
word order, 60*n*29, 67, 72–96, 97, 245, 248, 325
   dislocation, 67–8
   subject position, 78–81, 89–93
   subject-verb, 66, 78–9, 94, 325
word origin, 26, 33, 43, 243, 323–4, 330–7, 333*t*, 356–8
   see also borrowing; corpus planning; neologism

Author Index

Abbé Grégoire, 201, 205n15, 207, 283, 368
Ardinghelli, Maria Angela, 158–9
Armstrong, Nigel, 3n4, 328
Arnold, Theodor, 182n4, 184–5
Ashby, William J., 4
Ayres-Bennett, Wendy, 14, 16–18, 21, 59n26, 62, 73n2, 122–3, 161, 183, 258–9, 263n10, 277n2, 279, 281, 292n33, 344n2, 262n1

Barbapiccola, Giuseppa Eleonora, 157–8
Beck-Busse, Gabriele, 134n23
Blackledge, Adrian, 4
Blanche-Benveniste, Claire, 58
Blanchet, Philippe, 238
Blondeau, Hélène, 3n4, 246
Bouchard, Chantal, 16, 18n53
Boughton, Zoe, 3n4
Bouhours, Dominique, 153, 204
Boyer, Abel, 181–97
Brunot, Ferdinand, 13, 16n48, 146, 148n12, 149n14–n17, 155, 160, 249–50, 253
Busse, Winfried, 124, 282

Caminer Turra, Elisabetta, 156–7
Cellard, Jacques, 256–74
Cerquiglini, Bernard, 12n31, 52n8, 56–7, 59n24, 213
Chambaud Lewis (Louis), 181–97
Chomsky, Noam, 200
Conde-Silvestre, Juan-Camilo, 15
Coquebert de Montbret, Charles-Étienne, 201, 208
Cotelli Kureth, Sara, 16, 260–2, 282
Creese, Angela, 4

Dauzat, Albert, 212, 227, 235
Deletanville, Thomas, 185
Domergue, François Urbain, 121–43, 282
Donaldson, Bryan, 60, 66
Dougnac, Françoise, 124–6, 137–8, 140, 282
Dyche, Thomas, 188

Eckert, Penelope, 2, 4–5
Edmont, Edmond, 200–1, 242n13
Estienne, Henri, 284, 357n24
Estienne, Robert, 181n1, 217

Féraud, Jean-François, 127, 130, 206n16, 357–8

Gadet, Françoise, 3–5, 74–5, 238
Garcia, Nuria, 11
Gauchat, Louis, 252
Gilliéron, Jules, 200–1, 201n8, 242–3, 242n13, 253
Goebl, Hans, 200–1
Grevisse, Maurice, 220, 227

Hales, Stephen, 158–9
Hall, Damien, 184, 239, 251, 381
Hemon, Roparz, 329, 334–6
Hérnandez-Campoy, Juan Manuel, 15
Hornsby, David, 3, 238–9, 241
Hornsby, Michael, 324n5, 378–80

Jacobs, Haike, 42n28
Johnson, Samuel, 181, 188
Jones, Mari C., 3, 324, 324n6
Joseph, John E., 274–5
Joubert, Aurélie, 377–8

Kircher, Ruth, 6–7, 302
Klausenburger, Jürgen, 216, 236n19
Kroskrity, Paul, 278–9

Labov, William, 2–3, 3n2, 74, 78, 201n5
Lagorgette, Dominique, 16
Lambert, Wallace E., 6–7
Lefeuvre, Florence, 15n42, 61
Lillo, Jacqueline, 185
Lo Bianco, Joseph, 366–7, 385
Lodge, R. Anthony, 16, 318–19
López-Muñoz, Juan Manuel, 59
Ludwig, Christian, 181–97

Marchello-Nizia, Christiane, 13, 49, 56, 59n23–4, 60, 61n31, 62, 64–8
Martineau, France, 16, 18
Milroy, James, 257–8, 280
Milroy, Lesley, 257–8, 280
Mooney, Damien, 239

Nicot, Jean, 181n1, 186n7

Ó Giollagáin, Conchúr, 375n47, 381–2
Ó Murchadha, Noel, 380–1

Pardon, William, 188
Parussa, Gabriella, 15n42, 61, 63–4, 67, 69
Paveau, Marie-Anne, 278, 293
Philippe, Edouard, 301–2
Pooley, Tim, 16, 238
Pope, Alexander, 187

Rabatel, Alain, 298
Remysen, Wim, 122, 282
Ricento, Thomas, 9
Roberts, Ian, 80
Rogler, John Bartholomew, 187–8, 192, 196–7
Rojas, Daniel-Emilio, 355n21
Romaine, Suzanne, 15, 78
Ronsard, Pierre, 203, 217, 217n3, 235
Rosier, Laurence, 59, 278, 293, 298, 304
Russo, Michaela, 35–6

Sankoff, Gillian, 3n4, 246
Schøsler, Lene, 80, 86
Schottelius, Justus Georg, 191, 196–7
Seijido, Magali, 18, 124, 263n10
Silverstein, Michael, 278
Spolsky, Bernard, 9–10, 10n24, 12, 366, 368n12, 385
Sprat, Thomas, 187
Staël-Holstein, Germaine de, 129
Swift, Jonathan, 187

Thomas, George, 292, 294
Tillotson, John, 187

Valdman, Albert, 228, 236
Vaugelas, Claude Favre de, 16, 123, 186, 188, 204, 206, 217n3, 254, 259, 280–1, 283n9
Vigilante, Marianna, 158

Walsh, John, 374n39, 375n47
Walter, Henriette, 238–9